·95

# MR. SEC

*The Life of Sir*

*By the same author*

POLITICS IN THE AGE OF PEEL
REACTION AND RECONSTRUCTION IN ENGLISH POLITICS
    1832–1852
SIR ROBERT PEEL
ARISTOCRACY AND PEOPLE: BRITAIN 1815–1865
LORD LIVERPOOL

# MR. SECRETARY PEEL

*The Life of Sir Robert Peel to 1830*

Second Edition

NORMAN GASH

'How miserable is all worldly business, take it for a course of time, that is not carried on by men who make a conscience of what they do in it.'

SPEAKER ONSLOW

LONGMAN
London and New York

Longman Group Limited
Longman House, Burnt Mill, Harlow
Essex CM20 2JE, England
Associated companies throughout the world

Published in the United States of America
by Longman Inc., New York

© Norman Gash 1961
This edition © Longman Group Limited 1985
First published 1961
Second impression 1961
Third impression 1964
New edition in paperback, with revisions, 1985

British Library Cataloguing in Publication Data

Gash, Norman
  Mr. Secretary Peel: the life of Sir Robert
  Peel to 1830.
  1. Peel, Sir Robert, bart.  2. Prime ministers—
  Great Britain—Biography
  I. Title
  941.081′092′4   DA536.P3
  ISBN 0-582-49723-X

Library of Congress Cataloguing in Publication Data

Gash, Norman
  Mr. Secretary Peel.

  Bibliography: p.
  Includes index.
  1. Peel, Robert, Sir, 1788–1850. 2. Prime ministers
  —Great Britain—Biography. I. Title.
DA536.P3G3   1985   941.081′092′4 [B]   85-7751
ISBN 0-582-49723-X (pbk.)

Produced by Longman Group (FE) Limited
Printed in Hong Kong

# CONTENTS

# ACKNOWLEDGEMENTS

I am grateful to the Leverhulme Trust whose research grant first made this book possible and to the Court of St. Andrews University for additional financial aid.

Much of the work was done in Ireland and it is a singular pleasure to record the wide and hospitable assistance given to me by the officials of the Public Record Office of Ireland, the State Paper Office, the National Library, and the Royal Irish Academy; and of the Public Record Office of Northern Ireland, the Linenhall Library of Belfast, and the County Museum, Armagh. My debt to similar institutions on this side of the water is too long to be recapitulated; but I must thank the staffs of the National Register of Archives, the Public Library at Tamworth, and not least St. Andrews University Library for services that went beyond official duties.

My indebtedness to individuals is even deeper. Some are mentioned elsewhere; to others this is the only place where I can express my obligation. The Rt. Hon. the Earl Peel and Countess Peel, the late Hon. George Peel and Lady Agnes Peel, and G. F. Peel, Esq., allowed me access to family papers, portraits and other relics in their possession and gave constant assistance and encouragement. I am particularly grateful to Earl Peel for permission to use reproductions of the paintings at Hyning Hall as illustrations for this volume. My acknowledgments are also due to the governing body of Christ Church, Oxford, to their sometime librarian Mr. G. Bill, and to Mr. Steven Watson, for providing facilities for consulting the college archives. Dr. Edith Johnston gave me not only the benefit of her expert knowledge of eighteenth-century Irish administration but assistance on many other points; Mr. J. L. J. Hughes of the Public Record Office of Ireland allowed me to read his unpublished work on the Chief Secretaries of Ireland; Mr. C. Collyer kindly put at my disposal transcripts from the Canning Papers at Harewood; the Professors of Humanity and Greek in this college in various classical matters helped their less learned colleague; the Rev. Cyril Bishop sent information from the parish registers of Drayton

Bassett; Professor T. W. Moody of Trinity College, Dublin, and my old friend Mr. A. J. Taylor aided in a number of enquiries.

Another friend, Dr. G. Kitson Clark, read the first draft of this book and discussed with me many of its problems. My obligation to him cannot easily be measured.

*St. Salvator's College*  NORMAN GASH
*St. Andrews*
*February 1960*

# FOREWORD

In the quarter of a century since this book was written no new facts have been uncovered, as far as I know, which would necessitate any rewriting of the original text. The opportunity has, however, been taken to correct a few minor errors which survived the first reprint and to supplement the *Bibliographical Note* with a short list of publications containing material bearing on Peel's career which have appeared since 1960. The late Professor A. Aspinall, from his incomparable knowledge of the sources for early nineteenth-century British political history, provided a few further items of information in his review of *Mr Secretary Peel* in *Parliamentary Affairs* (1961). It might be useful to record these here. In September 1811 Perceval suggested to Peel that he should stand for Weymouth at the next general election; Peel declined on the grounds of uncertainty and expense. In June 1824 Peel told the Duke of Wellington that he was so conscious of the evils of a divided Irish administration that he was sorry he had taken the Home Office; it would have been better for all four men chiefly concerned to be 'Catholic' in sympathy. In 1826 Peel was invited to stand for Westminster as a 'Protestant' candidate but the electors were put off when told he was unlikely to abandon his Oxford University seat.

That there seems so little of further significance to discover about the facts of Peel's career is not surprising. A great mass of information has been accessible for a very long time. No prime minister before Peel had made such minute provision for the transmission to posterity of the records of his political life. Not long before his death he prepared for publication carefully documented accounts of the two great controversial episodes of his career, Catholic Emancipation and the Repeal of the Corn Laws. These, with the rest of his political papers, were bequeathed to two trustees, Viscount Mahon and Edward

Cardwell, with full powers to publish any part of them. He also left the sum of £1,000 to be invested and used for the expenses of administration as well as a personal payment to each of them of £500. For the permanent custody of the papers he authorised their ultimate deposit in the State Paper Office, the British Museum, or any similar institution. In 1856–57 the trustees published the *Memoirs*, including a third, written at an earlier date, on the formation of his 1834 ministry, which they found among the papers. Their intention was to publish next a selection of Peel's political correspondence. This plan was abandoned, in the event unhappily, in favour of a formal biography to be written by Goldwin Smith, Regius Professor of Modern History at Oxford University. His removal to the new American university of Cornell in 1868 put an end to this project when only the notes for the first chapter had been written. Smith was an adherent of the mid-Victorian Manchester School and the kind of biography he would have written can be inferred from the article on Peel he contributed to the *Encyclopaedia Britannica* in 1858 and the long discussion of Peel in his *Reminiscenses* (New York 1910) in the chapter entitled somewhat misleadingly 'Bright and Cobden'.

Mahon, who succeeded as 5th Earl Stanhope in 1855, died in 1875. Cardwell, in failing health, became anxious that the task of editing the Peel Papers should be taken over by a younger man. After his death in 1886 the succeeding trustees made an eminently suitable appointment for this purpose in the person of C. S. Parker, Cardwell's former private secretary and subsequently M.P. for Perthshire and Perth. The result was the massive three-volume *Sir Robert Peel From His Private Papers* which appeared between 1891 and 1899. These, together with four (admittedly vilely printed) volumes of parliamentary speeches published in 1853, and such later historical works as *The Croker Papers* and the *Wellington Despatches*, provided ample material for critical judgement. 'The historical monument to Sir Robert Peel,' pronounced Lord Rosebery in 1899, 'is now almost complete.'[1]

The remark was justified. When the Peel Papers, eventually

[1] *Sir Robert Peel* (reproduced from the *Anglo-Saxon Review* 1899) p. 7.

deposited in the British Museum, became accessible to scholars after the First World War, there were no political secrets to be revealed, no dark corners of private life, as with Palmerston and Disraeli, to be exposed. The masterly portrait which Lord Rosebery was able to paint in 1899 can stand today without any retouching. All that the Peel papers offered was immense corroborative detail. All that was lacking was a rounded literary biography of a kind which Parker's three volumes, for all their information, did not pretend to offer. Even so, the materials for a just assessment not only of Peel's career but of his personality were available long before Miss A. A. Ramsay and Dr George Kitson Clark began their researches in the Manuscript Department of the British Museum in the 1920s. Lord Rosebery, for example, had been as perceptive on Peel's private character as he had been on his public life. He noted the continuity and steadfastness of his nature. 'So far back as we can discern him at all,' he wrote, 'we find him from the outset the same able, conscientious, laborious, sensitive being that we leave him at his death.' Elsewhere he mentions Peel's 'fun, sometimes broad, his ready stories, his robust fits of laughter', his 'highly-strung, nervous temperament, and a prompt pugnacity which we can scarcely realise in these days'.

Rosebery, an infant of three when Peel died, could draw both on the rich documentary evidence available to him, and on the oral traditions of contemporaries who had known Peel. He was among other things a nephew of the Earl Stanhope who was Peel's literary executor. The fact that before the end of Victoria's reign he could give so sympathetic and revealing an account of Peel's more human side leaves little excuse for error in those who came after him. Yet it is remarkable how slow to die in this century has been the legend of the formal, cold statesman. Literary allusions have something to answer for. One of the best-known and most frequently-quoted witticisms about Peel is Daniel O'Connell's remark about 'a smile like the silver plate on a coffin'. One would have thought that even on general grounds the verbal sally of a bitter opponent ought not to be treated as conclusive evidence. There is also the curious circumstance that nowhere, as far as I am aware, has it been

shown that O'Connell ever used those words in relation to Peel.
What, on the other hand, is incontrovertible is that O'Connell
was not the author of that arresting simile and that on the
known occasion when he borrowed it, he applied it to another
future leader of the Conservative Party, namely Edward
Stanley, later 14th earl of Derby. It happened in a debate on the
address in February 1835 in the course of which O'Connell
launched an attack on Lord Stanley, the Whig Chief Secretary
for Ireland in 1830–33. 'How delightful would it be . . .'
observed the orator satirically, 'to see the noble Lord strutting
proudly with his sequents behind him, and with a smile passing
over his countenance—something like, as Curran[1] said, "a
silver plate on a coffin".'[2] To repeat a familiar quotation
without verifying its authenticity is something we all do; and it
is dull work destroying a good story. Yet that, after all, is part of
a historian's trade; and in a biographer may be even accounted a
duty.

The important issues, however, concern not Peel's private
manners but his public conduct. With figures of the past, as with
contemporaries, so much of the mind and temper of the critic
enters into such judgements that complete agreement is not easy
to come by. When the case is a controversial one, disagreement
is certain. Men differ sharply about Peel and will continue to do
so. There is, moreover, a special reason why his career still
arouses hard feelings. His career was bound up with a great
political party which not only lives on with undiminished
strength but nourishes a strong if sometimes less than well-
informed interest in its own past. To those who put party above
everything else, particularly if they are Conservatives, Peel's
conduct still rankles. To those who accept that what he did was
in the national interest, particularly if they belong to other
parties, his offence is forgivable. Yet the issue is not a simple one
between 'party' and 'country'. The preservation of a healthy
party system, it may be argued, is itself a national interest. As the

---

[1] Irish politician and lawyer 1750–1817.
[2] *Hansard Parl. Deb.* 3rd series, vol. 26, coln 397. It is regrettable that the editors of
the *Oxford Dictionary of Quotations* (3rd edn. 1979) have lent their authority to the
legend; but they have promised to make amends in any future edition.

British representative system has developed, party is an indispensable basis of stable government. For party to operate efficiently requires discipline; and discipline is only acceptable when there is a felt loyalty. In the last analysis, no doubt, few would deny that the needs of the country should come before the claims of party. The difficulty always is to determine when that final, ineluctable choice has to be made. It can only be done by individuals and their decision will depend on time and circumstance. There are no rules.

The business of history, however, is not so much to judge as to understand. The longer I have reflected on Peel's career after 1841, the more I have come to appreciate the importance of two underlying influences, both having their origins in the period before 1830. The first is his basic view of the economy and its needs. He approached the economic problems of his last great ministry with certain concepts which had been formed fifteen or twenty years earlier. He acted as one would expect a close colleague of Lord Liverpool to act who had similar ideas but more resolution and greater power. The concentration of historical interest on the Reform Act of 1832 has made it easy to forget this continuity. In the 1830s the preoccupation of the Whigs with constitutional, religious and Irish reform, and the nature of the parliamentary support on which they depended, put a halt to the unfinished revolution in financial and fiscal policy started by Liverpool's administration between 1819 and 1826. Yet the problems which that administration had tried to solve had not gone away; in some respects they had worsened in the interval through Whig neglect. When Peel became prime minister in 1841 his economic policy was virtually determined for him by the pressing needs of government and his own fundamental convictions.

His financial and free-trade views had been shaped by study and reflection, by his chairmanship of the Bullion Committee in 1819, and by his association in cabinet with Liverpool, Huskisson and Robinson. His Home Office duties explain why he rarely spoke on economic affairs in the 1820s, apart from the government's currency policy. Even so, his views were never in doubt. A brief speech he made on the silk trade in March 1824 when he described free trade as the establishment of sound principles of commerce; his positive declaration to the House of Commons in March 1827 that the Corn Laws must be revised, and that he took his full share of responsibility for the governmental changes in commercial policy and the corn tariff; and his strong support for a return to an income tax in Wellington's cabinet of 1830—all this makes his economic outlook clear long before the start of his last administration. It was obvious to all competent observers in 1841 that the new cabinet was saturated with the economic ideas of Lord Liverpool's ministry twenty years earlier. Indeed, it is one of the lost felicities of Peel's career that he did not in February 1827 introduce the first important change in the Corn Laws since 1815, as he did the second and third. Had not Canning recovered from illness in time, Peel as acting leader of the House of Commons had been designated for that task.

The other formative influence that needs to be brought out is an even wider one. It is Peel's primary conception of the duties and responsibilities of a prime minister. By 1830, the point at which the present volume ends, he was forty-two, an age when a man's outlook and character are commonly settled. He had spent half his life in politics, most of the time under Lord Liverpool. In that administration the concept of party in the modern or even late-Victorian sense hardly existed. The cabinet was not the creation of a parliamentary majority; it acted almost as an independent link between the Crown and legislature. The political realities on which the strength and stability of government depended were the confidence of the monarch, the prestige of the ministers, the traditional support of the House of Lords, and a general ability to procure majorities in the House of Commons for necessary finance and legislation. These indispensable majorities were not of a permanent, disciplined character, though they contained an element of regular support. While on such matters as law and order, subversion, and radical agitation, the executive could count on the backing of the more conservative country gentlemen, on other issues like taxation, currency and agriculture these same M.P.s provided some of the most damaging opposition. On delicate subjects—the Royal family, pensions and retrenchment—ministers in fact were not infrequently defeated, or at least successfully opposed, by men who in other respects were conventionally described as their natural supporters. What sustained ministers in these difficult situations was a professional sense of their responsibilities as servants of the Crown pursuing a national policy in the best interests of the country at large.

To men reared in this political and parliamentary school, now vanished beyond the horizon of most people's imagination, the post-1832 development of the party-system came as a novel, useful, occasionally embarrassing extension of political techniques. Yet the claims of party as a focus of loyalty could not immediately compete on equal terms with the older habits and traditions of statesmen. In the period between the first and second reform Acts parties and politicians were only gradually coming to terms with each other over their reciprocal rights and obligations. The history of the time is littered with incidents which reveal the fragility of the new relationships. The disruption of the Conservative Party in 1846 was only an extreme, not an isolated, example. It is not difficult to understand therefore, why Peel in 1845, at the greatest crisis of his career, did not regard his responsibilities to his party with the same respect as a subsequent party leader would have done. He looked on party in a utilitarian light, as a necessary and natural instrument of government, but not one which ought to be allowed to decide or unduly constrain executive policy.

To condemn Peel for what he did in 1846 is to judge him by criteria he never in his life accepted and which he made plain he did not accept. His most telling utterances on this subject are not those he made during the Corn Law debates nor his remark to Prince Albert afterwards that he had made too many concessions to party, not too few. These expressions could have been coloured by contemporary passions. The significant statement is the twice-repeated warning in 1840 and 1841, before he took office, that if he ever came to power, he would exercise it according to his own conception of public duty and would give up office as soon as he found he could not do so. Whether Peel was the right leader for the Conservative Party can be argued either way; though it is probable that without him that party would not have won the general election of 1841. What is hardly in doubt is that it would have required a great and unlikely change in Peel himself to have behaved any differently in 1845–46 than he did. The seeds of his achievement, success, crisis and fall were sown before 1830. It is this which makes his early political life an integral part of his career. To say, as Gladstone did, that there were two Peels, one before and one after the Reform Act, is to make a judgement which takes into account only the externals. It would be truer to say that the second part of Peel's life can never be properly understood without studying the first.

*February 1985*                                         NORMAN GASH

# CHRONOLOGICAL TABLE

| | | |
|---|---|---|
| 1788 | Robert Peel born | |
| | | 1789 *French Revolution* |
| | | 1793 *War with Revolutionary France* |
| 1796 | Drayton Manor purchased | |
| 1800-4 | at Harrow School | |
| | | 1805 *Trafalgar* |
| 1805-9 | at Oxford University | |
| 1809 | enters Parliament | *Perceval Prime Minister* |
| 1810 | Under-Secretary for War and Colonies | |
| | | 1811 *Regency begins* |
| 1812 | Chief Secretary for Ireland | *Liverpool Prime Minister* |
| 1813 | Lord Whitworth appointed Lord Lieutenant | |
| 1814 | Dissolution of Catholic Board; Insurrection and Peace Preservation Acts | |
| 1815 | O'Connell affair | *Waterloo* |
| 1817 | Catholic debate; M.P. for Oxford University; Irish famine | |
| 1818 | resigns Irish Secretaryship | |
| 1819 | Bullion Committee; Currency Act | *Peterloo; Six Acts* |
| 1820 | marriage with Julia Floyd | *accession George IV; Queen's trial* |
| 1822 | Home Secretary | *death of Castlereagh* |
| 1823 | Gaols Act; legal reforms | *Catholic Association* |
| 1825 | Jury Act | *Burdett's Catholic bill; financial crisis* |
| 1826 | Industrial disorders | *general election* |
| 1827 | consolidation of criminal law; resignation from government | *Canning Prime Minister* |
| 1828 | Home Secretary; Police Committee; repeal of Test and Corporation Acts | *Wellington Prime Minister; Clare election* |
| 1829 | Catholic Emancipation; resigns seat for Oxford University; Metropolitan Police Act | |
| 1830 | Forgery Act; death of his father; M.P. for Tamworth; resignation of ministry | *accession of William IV; general election* |

Robert Peele purchased Oldham's Cross (Peel Fold) in 1731
d. 1734

William Peele (1682–1757) of Peel Fold

Robert (Parsley) Peel (1723–95) m. Elizabeth Haworth of Darwen

William

Edmund

Jonathan — m. — (i) Ellen Yates
b. 1766
d. 1803

Robert Peel
1st Bt.
b. 1750
d. 1830

Lawrence

Joseph

John — (ii) Susanna Clerke
d. 1824, o.s.p.

Anne m. Rev. B. Willock

Mary
b. 1785
m. Geo.
Dawson,
M.P.

Elizabeth
b. 1786
m. Rev. Wm.
Cockburn,
later Dean of
York

William Yates
b. 1789
m. Jane d. of
E. of Mount-
cashel

Robert Peel
2nd Bt.
b. 5 Feb. 1788
m.
Julia
d. of Gen. Sir John Floyd
b. 1795

Edmund
b. 1791
m. Emily
Swinfen

John
b. 1798
m. Augusta
Swinfen

Jonathan
b. 1799
m. Alice
Jane,
d. of
M. of
Ailsa

Lawrence
b. 1801
m. Jane
d. of
D. of
Richmond

Harriet
b. 1803
m. Robert
Henley Eden
Lord Henley

Eleonora d. 1803

Anne d. 1799

Julia
b. 1821

Robert
b. 1822

Frederick
b. 1823

William
b. 1824

John Floyd
b. 1827

Arthur Wellesley
b. 1829

Eliza
b. 1832

# INTRODUCTION

English history has been at once adorned and domesticated by great families—Cecils, Churchills, Howards, Percys, Russells, the Pitts, Greys, Pelhams, and Foxes—whose services to state and society bridge the centuries and link one era with another. The Peels were late-comers on the national stage; yet their secular achievement in the century that followed the great war against Napoleon can stand the rivalry of any others. To have produced in four successive generations an industrial millionaire, a Prime Minister, the owner of a Derby winner, a Speaker of the House of Commons, a V.C., and a Secretary of State for India, is a varied and remarkable record. The achievement was the more striking because of the rapid rise of the family from obscurity to fame by their own efforts and talents, unaided by royal and aristocratic patronage or the chance favours of military fortune. English society has always been kept healthy by its social fluidity. The rise and fall of families and classes has acted as a kind of political metabolism; fresh energies have been released, exhausted elements reabsorbed, which unassimilated or retained might have endangered the body politic. The Peels are a notable example of this perpetual process of social readjustment. The third Robert Peel, who became not only Prime Minister but the greatest statesman of his time, was the grandson of a man who started life as a small Lancashire yeoman farmer. Between them lay the cotton revolution of the late eighteenth century which made his father's fortune. But so close in time was the Prime Minister to his social origins that his life in politics was largely conditioned by the forces which produced his family's wealth. The same historical process created both the economic revolution and the man who did more than any other single figure in politics to lessen its impact on society and to reconcile the new industrial elements with the older frame-work of aristocratic government.

But between the first and third Robert Peel came the second; and in the history of the Peel family he was the decisive figure. It was he

I

that broke through the respectable anonymity of the prosperous middle classes into the real ruling class of the country. From working with his own hands at cotton-mills, bleaching-grounds and clerk's ledgers, he became (alone of his father's family) an M.P. and a baronet, and he ended his life as a wealthy landowner and fund-holder. His father had put his sons to industry, trade, and finance; he placed his own children in the traditional occupations of the aristocracy—politics, the army, the law, the church, the land. Yet this social transformation was accomplished with no marked change of intellectual outlook; and the other significant aspect of the first Sir Robert Peel was the social conservatism which preceded as well as accompanied his upward progress. The Protestant, Anglican, conservative middle-class Peels were merely transmuted by his wealth into the Protestant, Anglican, conservative upper-class Peels of the third generation. English politics were enriched, in the person of his eldest son, by a family tradition which was originally nurtured in the rural isolation of pre-industrial Lancashire. The activities of Sir Robert himself, both in his pioneer work for the reform of factory conditions and in his brushes with the radicalism of a young and disorderly industrial society, form a kind of rough sketch for the large political canvas of his son's career.

Yet with the continuity there were also differences. The opinions of the first Sir Robert were those of a prosperous industrialist, firmly rooted in his experience of life. A largely self-made man, he drew his ideas from his own environment and from his practical observation of men and affairs. If the environment and observation were alike limited, they were nevertheless directly related to life as he lived it. His economic theories were derived not from books but from business. His charitable but restricted legislation for factory apprentices and cotton-mill children, his desire for greater freedom of trade from tariff restrictions, his consistent support for an inflationary paper-money system, were all the empirical fruits of his own career. To the end of his life he preferred to find things out for himself, and to pick up information from persons rather than paper. 'His great object,' wrote one of his Staffordshire neighbours, 'appeared to me on all occasions to be the procuring information, by collecting in his intercourse with mankind all he could. His manner was to appear as *knowing nothing* and trying to make you believe he enquired from ignorance and flattered you from that motive to tell *all you could*.'[1] In his temperament and views the first Sir Robert Peel was essentially a creature of nature.

His eldest son, by contrast, was severed from the practical framework of his father's life. He never had to earn his own living; he never entered trade or industry. His only direct contact with economic life was something he shared with most of the aristocracy of his day, the management of his own estate; but even in his own county of Staffordshire he was always an unfamiliar and isolated figure. A conventional education from private tutor, public school, and university led on without a break and without an effort into politics. He obtained a parliamentary seat as soon as he came of age and sat in the House of Commons for the rest of his life. He never fought a popular election and the five constituencies which he represented during his career were four pocket boroughs and a university. His first ministerial appointment came when he was twenty-two; he was Home Secretary at the age of thirty-four, Prime Minister at the age of forty-six. The first forty years of his life exhibited an almost monotonous record of success—a scholar at school, a double first at Oxford, and a distinguished politician and administrator thereafter. He had a strong body and good health; his marriage was singularly happy; and on his father's death he succeeded to a fortune and a baronetcy. It was a text-book example of a model career. Compared with his father and grandfather, Peel was an artifact set beside the natural product. Qualities natural and instinctive in the older men were, by a not uncommon trick of family evolution, intellectualised and self-conscious in the grandson. He possessed the family attributes but they were refined and intensified, as though the careful product of breeding and training rather than the sturdy accident of nature. The Lancashire middle-class Peels had in fact produced a thoroughbred, with all the intelligence, high potentiality, and nervous temperament of its type. The difference is seen even in the physical appearance of the three Robert Peels. The grandfather was a round-faced, cheerful yeoman whose appropriate background seemed more the farmstead and byre than the cotton-mill; the father, a burly, determined man with a more elongated but still rugged and plebeian countenance; the son, tall

[1] *Dyott*, II, 75.

and elegant, with the long handsome face depicted by Lawrence in the first phase of his manhood. The first Robert Peel of Peel Fold was a simple and hard-working countryman, caught up almost by chance in the pioneer era of the cotton-industry; the second a shrewd, strong-willed and successful manufacturer; the third an intellectual set in the environment of the English governing class.

It is not surprising, therefore, that when other influences did not intervene, Peel's opinions constantly tended to be those of the advanced and intelligent experts in all fields of public life. Those expert and intellectual views were not always, perhaps not often, those of public opinion. That, in Peel's day as at any other time, was emotional, partisan, changeable; sometimes wrong and short-sighted, sometimes displaying an instinctive percipience on issues where the experts were perplexed by their own intellectual refine-ments; and always endowed with the rough vigour that comes from life itself. The fools, as Melbourne cynically noted, are often right in politics, and the wise men wrong. But political activity cannot safely dispense with the intellectual process; and for Peel public opinion was something to scrutinise rather than to follow. Even when he was himself most prejudiced, he viewed issues with the detachment of a rational intellect, seeing far but sometimes hampered by an inability to see simply, and not always able to distinguish between the facts and the theories through which the facts were approached. Yet Peel was not a pure intellectual; no successful statesman is. Before he was halfway through his career, he had gathered experi-ence of a depth and variety unmatched by any other contemporary politician; but it was experience of a special kind. As a parliamentary leader he had to deal with an assembly swayed by interests, allegiances, and ambitions; and much of his working life was devoted to countering the kind of argument brought forward in debate, and elaborating the kind of argument likely to be effective in a division, neither of which were necessarily the considerations that intellectually were the most fundamental. In the end, perhaps, this debating technique, of which he became a master, itself obtained a form of mastery in his own mind. As an administrator he saw life through the medium of official correspondence and official callers, life in fact as it appeared from a desk—a detached and elevated window of observation which shaped and coloured, sometimes stained, his observant mind. It was rarely a pleasant side of life that presented itself to him in his working hours. He saw a great deal of folly, cupidity, corruption, selfishness, and brutality, though these raw aspects of his trade were compensated by the order, efficiency, and integrity which it was his task to create and maintain. It was an experience of life of a kind not dissimilar to that of a doctor, a priest, a lawyer, or a policeman: life at one remove, not as he lived it, but as it came to him for attention, repair, and regulation. It did not destroy his belief in his task; but it created a certain cynicism and a not very elevated notion of human nature.

To this task, however, he brought a fine apparatus of personal qualities: complete integrity, a high standard of duty, a lucid and powerful intellect, an immense capacity for hard work. Behind those frontal characteristics lay his own essential temperament, usually held in check and not always visible to the casual observer, but exercising a profound influence on his actions. He had a pleasure in achievement, an instinct for leadership, a quick pride and a hot temper, a stubbornness of purpose, an intense mental and physical sensitivity which was both a strength and a weakness in the rough school of politics; and, finally, concealed in the recesses of his nature, a curious self-consciousness and lack of assurance which formed the one great flaw in his emotional equipment. It was a flaw that betrayed itself in time of strain and injury, and it had disagreeable secondary effects which won him many enemies. In Peel's complex personality jarring forces were at work; and though his strong mind and character dominated his life, it was at the cost of internal conflicts and bitterness that left scars on his soul and made him to many people a cold and unattractive figure. These were basic elements, however, which only revealed themselves fully when time and events had eroded the surface of his youthful energy and spirits. But from the start, family background, his training, and his own cast of mind stamped on him qualities which remained with him to the end. He had an intellectual caution and an ingrained instinct for historic continuity which made him a conservative before the epithet passed into political vocabulary. He had a strong Protestant outlook in religious matters which made him a church politician almost before he was anything else. At the moment of entering public life he was already an ideal recruit for the small knot of men who controlled the country's policy.

The political world into which he made his entry in 1809 was as though designed to confirm these early attitudes. Contemporaneously with the Industrial Revolution which bore the Peels to affluence and station was the other great Revolution in France; and the intellectual debate to which that gave rise furnished a kind of philosophic accompaniment to the main domestic theme of the 'Condition of England'. The connection in fact was tenuous and accidental, and a native strain of radical liberalism was already in existence before 1789. Yet it was a natural if misleading development that the ideas of the two revolutions should be to a certain extent interfused. The revolution taking place within English society was straggling, disorderly, and incomprehensible, its effects and significance difficult to diagnose. By comparison the revolution on the continent was superficially easy to understand, more swift and dramatic in its action. To an English governing class fed on classical literature, the remorseless transition from democratic revolution to military tyranny was not so much self-evident as inevitable; and the moral they drew for their own country was a commonplace. But that commonplace was borne home to them by the most costly and dangerous war the country had ever had to face; and its effects on Britain were profound and far-reaching. Peel grew up under the shadow of the Revolutionary and Napoleonic Wars. He was a child of five when the struggle began; sixteen years later, when he entered parliament, the British effort against Napoleon was entering its last heroic and decisive stage. When the crowning news of Waterloo reached an expectant London, he had already five years experience of office. The events and recollections of the Napoleonic Wars, slowly diminishing into nostalgic perspective, captured the imagination of many people in the peaceful, sunny decades of the later Victorian era. For Peel, however, it was the first great formative experience of his career; and when peace came at last, the country was swept on, unprepared and untutored by any historical precedent, to grapple with problems which were the direct social and economic consequences of the great war.

But this was only the overture to the nineteenth century. The real body of the drama was the development that had been going on before and during the war—the unparalleled growth of industry, mechanical power, population, transport, and urban communities, which form what later historians were to call the Industrial Revolution, and the social changes, political struggles, the war of classes, institutions, and ideas, to which it gave rise. Peel, born in 1788 in the world of Gibbon and Joshua Reynolds, of stage-coaches, highwaymen, and the judicial burning of women, died in 1850 in the age of Faraday and Darwin, of *Punch*, railway excursions, trade unions, and income tax. Between those two terminal dates lay a period of revolutionary change and quasi-revolutionary violence. In the first half of the nineteenth century British society was remodelled into recognisably modern shape; but the process, logical and successful as it seems in retrospect, was for the men of the time a confused and painful experience. The crashing of ancient landmarks was more obvious and perhaps seemed more significant than the tentative approaches to a new society, more united, more contented, more prosperous, and more orderly, which in the latter part of the century was able to work out its problems of democratic government, industrial regulation, public health, and popular education, at greater leisure and with greater stability. It is true, no doubt, that the Industrial Revolution has in one sense never finished, or more accurately that it was the first of a series of industrial revolutions. But what gave unique importance to the initial wave of industrialisation was that it struck what was essentially a decentralised rural community, governed by a parliamentary aristocracy under the narrow Anglican constitution laid down at the Revolution of 1688. Not until fundamental alterations had been made in that historic fabric was the way clear for later Victorian developments.

The problem of government within the traditional constitution provided the first of the two special problems that lay within the wider framework of an emerging industrial society. For a century the landed aristocracy had governed England through the medium of parliament and the local magistracy. It was a system that functioned partly because the authority and patronage of the crown supplied a measure of cohesion and direction; partly because the issues of domestic politics were restricted to a context in which defeats and victories did not particularly disturb the system itself.

The executive confined itself to the basic functions of war, diplomacy, justice, order, and taxation. Parliament was a legislative, not a governing machine; it criticised and sometimes secured the dismissal of royal ministers, but it did not claim the right to choose those ministers; and its preferred mode of dealing with administrative problems was by way of piecemeal and *ad hoc* delegation to local and sometimes private administrative bodies. The needs of executive government had extended political patronage to wide areas of public life, and it was natural for both politicians and their constituents to believe that the expenditure of public money necessarily involved corruption, jobbery, and inefficiency. Long before *laisser-faire* became the catchword of the economists, an administrative and parliamentary tradition of minimum control and intervention in social and economic affairs had entrenched itself in English life. Only so, perhaps, could the amateur oligarchic government of the eighteenth century have worked; but so long as its political contests issued in a relatively non-controversial policy, the limited crown executive and the independent country gentry of England which had been yoked together in 1688 pulled along the lumbering state-coach without disaster.

After 1815 the partnership rapidly deteriorated. The decline of patronage under the steady pressure of public opinion removed one tangible means of ensuring proper harnessing of executive and legislature; and the stresses to which agriculture was subjected in the post-war period supplied a perennial source of discontent to one member of the alliance. High prices, marginal cultivation, over-capitalisation during the war years were followed by economic slump and a sharp deflationary policy on the part of the government. The country gentry secured a high corn tariff in 1815 and threw off the burden of Pitt's wartime property tax in 1816. But within half a dozen years the ministers had forced a return to the gold standard and followed that up by a modification of the Corn Laws in 1828. The sharp economic medicine of deflation was succeeded by an agricultural depression in the 1820s; and if farmers defaulted on rent, three-quarters of the House of Commons felt the pinch. When to the economic grievances of the 'Church and King' gentry was added the shock of Catholic emancipation in 1829, the breach between the professional administrators in the cabinet and their conventional supporters in the Commons opened wide enough to let in the whigs and produce in 1831 a majority of English county members in favour of parliamentary reform. Only with time and trouble were the bulk of the country gentry slowly reassembled behind the new conservative party of the thirties and, even so, the form of the alliance was both novel and uneasy. The economic dominance of the agriculturalists had gone for ever before the steam-engine and the textile-loom. Though they remained a powerful in-terest, their parliamentary leaders had other equally powerful interests to confront and were trained in a wider sense of responsibility than their followers were prepared to envisage. With a rapidly mounting population, a discontented proletariat, and a ruthlessly thrusting industrial society looking for new channels of expansion, it was only a matter of years before not only the degree but the very existence of high agricultural protection was called in question.

How in all these circumstances to keep the governmental and parliamentary alliance in working order was a task of constant difficulty. It was a task that fell on an extraordinarily small and isolated group of men. The crown had ceased to govern; and though there was a parliamentary tradition of general support for the executive, parliament itself had not yet evolved a party system capable of producing alternative sets of ministers. The existence of a formed whig opposition was an exception, not a contradiction, to this characteristic shapelessness of politics. They had excluded themselves, and by some were regarded as rightly excluded, from participation in government; but that was historical accident rather than constitutional principle. The whigs in fact were in the anomal-ous position of forming a party in a non-party political system. In the first twenty years of Peel's political career, they were never able to offer an alternative to the existing government and on occasion came near to absorption in it. When in 1830 they at last obtained power, it was as the preponderant element in a coalition rather than as a party in their own right. Real political power was in the hands not of party but of the cabinet. Between the crown which had the legal appointment of ministers and the Commons who had a practical veto on them, a cabinet system, in the sense of a succession of professional politicians bound by loyalty to a chief and able to work the machinery of state, had emerged as a kind of third political force. Their strength was their indispensability. The constant limitation on the power of both crown and Commons was the difficulty of finding substitutes for the men in office. In fact, at no time between 1807 and November 1830 did the king dismiss or the Commons overthrow the cabinet of the day. But the ministers themselves worked within narrow limits. George IV as regent and king gave only grudging support and at times offered malicious obstruction to the men whom he dared not try to replace; and the cabinet itself, though it could invoke, could never compel the allegiance of the Commons. With the confined, corrupt, and inert electoral system of the day, an appeal to the electorate was an appeal to an authority only fractionally different from parliament itself. Management, compromise, concession, an unsteady equilibrium, were therefore the features of early nineteenth-century government. It was not a very solid basis for executive action. With a discontented public and an unreliable legislature, there were times indeed after Waterloo when the ministers of the crown appeared almost like the garrison of a beleaguered citadel.

Yet to follow an executive policy that merely took into account the interests and feelings of the squirearchy was impossible in the face of the fresh tides sweeping over English society after the war. The need for administrative reform, freer outlets for trade, a more efficient financial system; the problem of the poor and the aspirations of the industrial workers; the demands for political equality by Protestant dissenters and Roman Catholics, for more direct and less arbitrary parliamentary representation: all these forces were steadily undermining the classic eighteenth-century forms of government and society. Though the disgruntled gentry could on occasion take tactical advantage of the government's embarrassments, and indeed themselves possessed a liberal wing, implicated or ready to compromise with industrialism, fundamentally the world into which they were moving was not a world they wanted. Nevertheless the structure of parliamentary representation, even after the Reform Act of 1832, made their co-operation indispensable for strong government and their hostility could bring major administrative activity almost to a standstill. Much therefore depended on their traditional virtues—their loyalty, discipline, and sense of national duty—and on the chances of finding leaders who could carry them along unfamiliar and unpleasant paths.

These were difficulties enough; but outside and menacing was the problem of Ireland. If the task of securing parliamentary co-operation was arduous, the complex of ills represented by the sister-island was harsh and alien to the point of despair. Ireland had been conquered many times in British history, but never permanently subdued and never reconciled. All that conquest had done was to impose a governing class of different origin and religion on the mass of the Celtic peasantry. But the long tale of conquest, rebellion, confiscation, and penal laws had left the Irish people brutalised, vindictive, and impoverished; and when the sudden rise in population took place at the close of the eighteenth century, the Irish peasants were pressed to the edge of famine. The result was a bitter social struggle for survival in which all the old racial and religious animosities came horribly to the surface. For the task of governing Ireland the English executive had the imperfect instrument of the Anglo-Irish aristocracy, itself corrupt, demoralised, dependent, and often absentee, together with the island of Protestantism—more Presbyterian and republican than monarchical and Anglican—formed by the historic plantation of Ulster. The incipient movement of united Irish nationalism in the late eighteenth century foundered on the rock of religious disunity, and the rebellion of 1798 ended the brief experiment of an independent Irish parliament, freed from the close English supervision which had been imposed on it since the early Tudors.

The Union with Ireland in 1800 was an attempt to meet the problem of governing Ireland in another fashion. The Dublin parliament disappeared; a hundred Irish members were admitted to the House of Commons at Westminster; and with them came direct legislative responsibility for Irish destinies. To the Anglo-Irish aristocracy, bribed and cajoled into unwilling surrender of their parliament, was held out the prospect of permanent security within the fortress of the British constitution. To the Catholic Irish was given the virtual assurance of admittance to political equality once union had been effected. Pitt's inability to carry out the second half of his Irish programme presented Catholic Ireland with a grievance and British politicians with the first immediate consequence of the Union, a struggle within the parliament of the United Kingdom for Catholic emancipation. In itself emancipation was an issue of great constitutional significance; but what made it a dominating controversy in early nineteenth-century British politics was that it became the explicit national demand of a community which for social and economic reasons provided an almost insoluble problem of administration for the British government. Liberal minds in England, already inclining to a renunciation of the historic privileges of the Anglican state, were prepared to believe that the administrative deadlock in Ireland might be solved by this gesture of conciliation. Public opinion in the larger island, therefore, was divided on the expediency of emancipation; and under the shelter of English liberalism and English party politics the Irish emancipation movement began to make headway even before the end of the Napoleonic Wars. The executive government, crippled by internal disagreement on the issue, was further hampered by the restraints of a legal constitution and the need for parliamentary sanction in any repressive policy. The emancipation campaign, on the other hand, not only formed the opening attack of what was essentially an Irish nationalist movement, but drew on forces that were not engendered by purely political, let alone religious, causes. O'Connell canalised all Irish discontents into his specialised political struggle; but it followed from that feat of propaganda that emancipation when achieved neither allayed those discontents nor ended the Irish problem. In one sense, indeed, the passage of emancipation had greater immediate effects on English rather than on Irish politics and, when it was all over, the Irish question remained as brutal and intractable as ever. The solution to Ireland's basic troubles —the problem of poverty and the problem of disorder—still had to be found; and as long as those evils continued to fester, Irish nationalism and Irish separatism possessed an ever-welling source of popular support. Solutions even when devised, moreover, had to be worked out in a political context that made the acceptance of any solution a difficult and complicated matter. The historic intermingling of the government, religion, and people of England and Ireland had as its legacy powerful interests and profound emotions that spanned the narrow waters between the two countries and made it impossible for influential elements in English society not to identify themselves with classes and institutions of the other island. Ireland was not only a problem for, but a problem in, English politics.

It was in this divided and unhappy world that the younger Peel's political career was cast; and it was to these problems that his mind was turned for the forty years in which he was engaged in public affairs. That by the end of this life he dominated the British political scene as no one since Pitt had done, was a measure of the impress which his character and statesmanship finally made on the national consciousness. But that position was only secured through a succession of achievements, crises, and bitter controversies; and the two great 'betrayals' of his followers, over Catholic emancipation in 1829 and over the Corn Laws in 1846, marked the abnormal strain to which his sense of administrative duty and national necessity was subjected. His career therefore was controversial, both in his own lifetime and afterwards. To succeeding Victorian generations, whose outlook was conditioned by the ordered warfare of a more modern parliamentary system, it seemed a natural conclusion that Peel had 'chosen the wrong party'. But by the late nineteenth century the age of Peel had already passed into the twilight that falls on the period dividing the remembered present from the historical past; and most of the late-Victorian verdicts on Peel were intrinsically unsound because they projected back into his time the conventions and images of their own. To judge Peel by subsequent standards of parties and programmes is a patent anachronism. His lifework was to fashion a viable compromise between the system he inherited and the pressing necessities of the changing world in which he found himself. Too often posterity judged him as though that compromise were already in existence; or, at least, as though the machinery for contriving that compromise lay already to hand.

The political tradition to which Peel was heir, however, though not without its virtues, did not include a balanced rivalry of parties and policies through which all necessary political and social adjustments could be made; and Peel was in a fundamental sense never a party politician. Son of a cotton-spinner though he was, he carried on the aristocratic tradition of 'the king's ministers' and 'the king's government'. He looked first, not to party, but to the state; not to programmes, but to national expediency. His conservatism was not a party label, still less a class interest, but an instinct for continuity and the preservation of order and good government in a society which was confronted with the choice between adaptation or upheaval. If he 'broke' the conservative party, that was of secondary importance compared with the fact that by insisting on changes in the national interests, and on concessions to national demands, he helped to preserve —as no other statesman of his time—the flexibility of the parliamentary constitution and the survival of aristocratic influence in a period of distress and challenge. To the next generation, entering the political vineyard after the heat and burden of the day, that was not always obvious. Rarely can such a clever character sketch by such an intelligent man have been based on such false premisses as, for example, the famous essay on Peel by Walter Bagehot. But this misunderstanding, common enough in the generation that succeeds any great historical career, is doubly comprehensible in this case. The later Victorian liberals could feel with some impatience that, however liberal in his policy, Peel was never one of them. Later Victorian conservatives, looking to the disruptions of 1829 and 1846, and influenced perhaps more than they realised by the brilliant political pamphlet which Disraeli wrote under the title of *Lord George Bentinck*, found it equally hard to recognise in Peel one of the principal architects of the modern conservative tradition. Romantic tory historians, following the pseudo-historical inspiration of those two great men of literature, Bolingbroke and Disraeli, could pass him over almost without mention in the genealogy of titled families and broad acres that constitutes for them the history of the 'Tory Party'. But though the myth of conservatism has been more often Disraelian, its practice has been almost uniformly Peelite. With that Peel would have been content; he preferred facts to phrases.

# THE PEELS OF TAMWORTH

At the time of the outbreak of the French Revolution there still stood a few miles south of Tamworth, on the borders of Stafford-shire and Warwickshire, the old manor house of Drayton Bassett. In the sixteenth century it had been in the possession of the famous Earl of Leicester, Elizabeth's favourite. At his death he had left it to his wife, Lettice Knollys, who resided there with her third husband, Sir Christopher Blount. From the Blounts it passed into the hands of the Earl of Essex and later to the family of Thynne. The house, sur-rounded by some six hundred acres of deer park, was a rambling half-timbered structure, with a tall detached banqueting hall in the walled gardens near by. Its low, gabled buildings were arranged in rough quadrangular shape not unlike an old-fashioned decayed college, with small rooms and separate staircases, and a hall hung with portraits and stagsheads. To the contemporaries of George III it appeared a rude and antique dwelling-place, 'a curious specimen of the occa-sional simplicity of our antient nobility'.[1] Little remained of its Tudor glories, and latterly the house was inhabited only by a steward.

Not only the manor house but its proprietor also had fallen on lean times. Thomas Thynne, who succeeded his father as Viscount Weymouth in 1751 and was created Marquess of Bath in 1789, like many other great landowners before and after had wasted his substance on ephemeral pleasures. It was unkindly written of him that his chief amusement was burgundy; and not only drink but love of gaming had absorbed his time and faculties, and ultimately his estate.[2] In 1790 he sold a large block of his Staffordshire estates, including the manor and house of Drayton. The purchasers were

[1] Stebbing Shaw, *History . . . of Tamworth and Drayton Bassett* (Birmingham, 1812); *History . . . of Staffordshire* (1798), II, 8-9, description and plates.
[2] *Complete Peerage*, G.E.C., etc., new. edn. Vicary Gibbs (1912-59), II, 25 n.

two north-country industrialists, Joseph Wilkes of Measham, Leicestershire,[1] and Robert Peel of Bury in Lancashire. The price paid was £123,000 (very much, it was said, under its real value), and the property which changed hands included besides Drayton Bassett, the hamlets and villages of Sherrold and Fazeley, Bonehill with its rectory, and corn and paper-mills at Comberford and Wigginton. The total extent was an estimated 4,755 acres, all but six lying within the county of Staffordshire, of an annual value reckoned at £3,217. To finance the purchase Wilkes and Peel raised a mortgage on part of the estate for £50,000 and it was originally intended that the property should be divided equally between them. Peel, however, paid separately a sum of £19,000 for lands at Comberford and Wigginton, and certain pieces at Drayton and Fazeley, which were taken out of the main estate and freed from the mortgage. The partners then each put up £27,000 to pay off the balance of the purchase price. Once the property was in their hands the new owners sold off part of the unmortgaged estates and divided the remainder. Wilkes took Drayton Manor and Bonehill, and since this was the most valuable part of the property remaining in their possession, he agreed to pay his partner £40,000 in compensation and in addition to discharge himself the £50,000 mortgage. Whether for lack of capital or because he regarded the purchase solely as a speculation, Wilkes in turn sold Drayton Manor to his son-in-law, Mr. Thomas Fisher, for £74,880, a figure which included the unpaid residue of the original mortgage, amounting to £20,000. Fisher seemed to have thoughts of settling down at Drayton, for he pulled down the banqueting hall, demolished the old quadrangle as far as the hall, and repaired the remaining buildings for his own residence. Nevertheless, within a short time he too abandoned the enterprise and sold house and manor at the reduced price of £66,952, the sum of £20,172[2] still outstanding on the mortgage to be paid out of the purchase money.

The date of this final transfer of Drayton was 1796 and the purchaser was the same Robert Peel who had partnered Joseph Wilkes in the negotiations for the main Thynne estates in 1790. His share

---

[1] He started as partner in the Tamworth cotton-mills, later became cotton-manufacturer and banker at Measham.

[2] £20,000 taken over from Wilkes together with unpaid interest.

in the complicated transactions which had taken place since that date offered a singular example of the good fortune in money matters for which he was proverbial in his family circle. Of the three principals he had emerged in the end with the lion's share of the property. Wilkes in direct purchase, mortgage, and compensation, had paid out a total of £117,000 and received £74,880 from Fisher and an additional unknown amount for other parts of the property. Fisher had bought Drayton Manor less mortgage for £54,880 and sold it for £46,780. Peel, on the other hand, had paid out a total of £46,000 for his half-share and separate purchases, but had received both a share (presumably) of the minor sales and a sum of £40,000 which together must virtually have covered his original expenditure. He then bought Drayton Manor for only £66,952, unencumbered and with certain modest improvements in the way of new farms and other buildings erected by Fisher. By 1796, therefore, he was the owner of his separate purchases of property at Comberford, Wigginton, Drayton and Fazeley, certain lands, tenements, and mills from his share in the principal estate, and the Manor of Drayton by purchase from Fisher, the first and last items alone amounting to over 2,600 acres.[1]

Even this was not the total of his Staffordshire purchases, however, for by another separate transaction in 1790 he had acquired from the Thynnes lands and property in the borough of Tamworth, including 120 houses, for the sum of £15,500.[2] It is probable, indeed, that from the start Robert Peel was bent on securing a permanent position in the county. His Tamworth purchase enabled him to succeed to the half-share in the representation of the borough formerly enjoyed by the Thynnes, and the year of the sale saw the new proprietor returned as M.P. for the constituency. From the north he brought his industrial interests. Cotton- and bleaching-mills were started at Fazeley and Bonehill, springs at Drayton harnessed to provide a source of pure water, and for a time Tamworth Castle and the Castle mill were used for calico printing.[3] The final step was

[1] Close Rolls, C 54/7308, indenture of sale of Drayton Bassett dated 5 April 1796.
[2] I am indebted for the details of this transaction to Mr. D. G. Stuart, who quotes from the Thynne family papers in his unpublished thesis on the parliamentary history of Tamworth.
[3] *Mitchell*, I, 75; H. Wood, *Borough by Prescription* (Tamworth, 1958), p. 30.

the removal of his family from Bury and the establishment of a new home for the Peels at Drayton Bassett. What was left of the ancient manor house after Fisher's improvements was completely pulled down and before the end of the century there rose in its place a large modern building—Old Drayton Hall[1]—solid, rectangular, three-storeyed, large enough for a prosperous manufacturer with a numerous family, even though Croker was to complain thirty years later that it would only hold three or four guests at a time. But though the house was undistinguished, the combination of the Drayton estate, industrial wealth, and a parliamentary seat at Tamworth, was more than enough to secure for Robert Peel a position of influence in the county and make him the object of respectful if curious attention among the Wolseleys, Bagots, Wrottesleys, Chetwynds, Littletons, and other old-established Staffordshire families among whom he had chosen to settle.

## II

The new owner of Drayton Manor was the second generation of a Lancashire family that had risen to wealth in the cotton revolution of the eighteenth century. The constant reinforcement of the land-owning and aristocratic classes by successful members of the great mercantile, banking, and brewing families was not a novel pheno-menon in English social history; but Robert Peel was an early repre-sentative of a new class, the industrial magnate. He was not, however, entirely a self-made man, for it was his father who had laid the foundations of the family's industrial fortune. Originally the Peels were small yeoman farmers and traced their ancestry back no further than a certain William Peele who in 1600 migrated from the Craven district of Yorkshire to a farm called Hole or Hoyle House near Blackburn in Lancashire. Even that derivation is uncertain for there were many Peeles in the neighbourhood of Bolton from at least the middle of the sixteenth century, and a later family historian, Jona-than Peel of Knowlmere,[2] argued strongly for a descent from this

---

[1] A vignette of the house is on the title-page of *Peel*, II.
[2] Peel, *Family Sketch*, pp. 20-9. The more conventional account is in Miss Jane Haworth's MS. Memoir of the Peel Family (40610) and in Peel, *Life*, pp. 6-8.

more numerous Lancastrian branch. The first Peele that can clearly be identified is a Robert Peele who in 1731 bought a small farm called The Crosse or Oldham's Cross at Oswaldtwistle and renamed it Peele Fold. His son and heir William was a man of indifferent health who lived a retired life on his farm and died in 1757, leaving four sons and two daughters. It was his eldest son Robert—'Parsley' Peel —who lifted the Peels out of their narrow rural environment into the small but rapidly expanding industrial society that was taking shape north of the Trent. The event owed almost everything to the accident of time and place. The same revolutionary process that transformed the barren uplands and lonely hamlets of Lancashire and Yorkshire carried to early fortune and reputation the obscure yeomen Peels.

At the start of the eighteenth century the development of a native British cotton industry was hindered by various statutory prohibitions and restrictions passed by parliament to protect the great staple woollen trade that had been the backbone of English industry since the Middle Ages. But in 1736 a limited relaxation of this protective barrier was made, legalising for domestic use the printing of a mixed linen and cotton cloth. As a result a small weaving trade grew up round Blackburn, though in the primitive condition of the northern industry the cloth produced—Blackburn 'greys' as these fustians were known—had until the middle of the century to be sent down to the craftsmen in London to be printed. Then in 1774 the full domestic use of ordinary cotton cloth, or calico, was permitted, subject to a small duty on printing, and the way was open for the expansion of the industry. The problems now were technical: the devising of efficient machinery for the various processes involved—carding, spinning, weaving, and printing—that would enable cottons to compete with woollens in quality and price. By the late 1760s Hargreaves' spinning-jenny was in use, especially in the Blackburn area, and greatly increased the output of the domestic spinners, even though the yarn was of an inferior quality. But it was Arkwright with his roller-spinning that prepared the way for the cotton-factory system. By the 1780s new carding machinery was in operation, together with Arkwright's improved spinning machines, and in the decade 1780-90 the import of raw cotton into England increased nearly fivefold. Simultaneously the technique of printing, formerly done by hand-blocks of wood or copper, was improved and mechanical cylinder-printing began in Lancashire about 1785.

The Peels, like many farmers and cottagers had intermittently combined wool-weaving with agriculture, and it was natural that Robert Peel of Peel Fold should be interested in the little pocket of gradually expanding manufacture and piecemeal mechanical invention that was beginning to take shape in his neighbourhood. During his father's lifetime he had farmed first at Hole House and then at Fish Lane, Blackburn; and it was at the latter place that he is reputed to have begun his experiments in pattern-printing. After his father's death, when he removed to Peel Fold, came the first serious venture. His brother-in-law, Jonathan Haworth (the son of a 'chapman' or dealer in woven fabrics), had been sent to London to learn the mysteries of calico-printing with a Dutch firm in Spitalfields. On his return he proposed to Peel that they should jointly set up a print-works at Blackburn. Peel raised a mortgage on his small freehold estate; further capital was provided by William Yates, a young Blackburn man whose father kept the Black Bull Inn; and about 1760 a factory (one of the first of its kind in Lancashire) was established at Brookside in the parish of Church, not far from Peel Fold. In this they were aided by their neighbour James Hargreaves, the intelligent and inventive weaver of Stanhill, who worked with Peel on improvements to a new form of carding-cylinder and between 1764 and 1767 supplied the Brookside factory with a number of the spinning-jennies that made his fame as an inventor.[1] Peel himself evidently possessed much inventive and mechanical skill. He was one of the first Lancashire manufacturers to try the new devices which the practical mechanics of the day were evolving; and he was said to have made at least one important

[1] Abram, *Blackburn*, pp. 204-6, 212-24, gives much information on the rise of the early Peels. I am also indebted to Major W. A. Hunter of Stanhill, Accrington, for the following additional details on the origin of the firm of Haworth, Peel, and Yates. The Spitalfields firm that trained Haworth and also sold him equipment with which to begin printing in Lancashire were Messrs. Voortmann. Haworth was introduced to them by an excise officer who had lodged at the Black Bull while on a tour of duty in the north. There seems good evidence for dating the Brookside factory from 1760 rather than the more commonly quoted date of 1764.

improvement in cotton-spinning machinery which was never patented. At Peel Fold he continued his pattern-making experiments and according to tradition it was his small daughter Anne who suggested the parsley-leaf design that was known in the family as 'Nancy's pattern' and later, when it became popular in the trade, earned her father his nickname. Though the original intention of the partners at Brookside may only have been to print Blackburn 'greys', the enterprise soon developed into a more ambitious organisation, embracing all the processes of carding, spinning, weaving, and printing; and along with the Claytons of Bamber Bridge, Preston, the firm of Haworth, Peel, and Yates could claim the honour of being the founders of the great Lancashire calico-printing industry. As profits increased, Peel became master, either alone or in partnership, of print-works at Church, spinning-mills at Altham, warehouses at Manchester, and other factories at Burnley and Foxhill Bank. After some years the partners disbanded and Haworth and Yates moved to Bury; but though Peel remained at Brookside, he had his own difficulties to face. In 1779 there occurred at Blackburn one of the many sporadic outbreaks of rioting against the new spinning-jennies. Peel had his machinery at Altham thrown into the river and was in some danger himself from the mob. His response, like that of many other master-manufacturers, was to migrate southward to a more peaceable district. He transferred his home to Burton in Staffordshire and built new cotton-mills on the banks of the Trent. There he continued a flourishing business until, about 1792, he relinquished direct control, leaving his extensive interests in Lancashire and Staffordshire in charge of some of his sons.

Outside his commercial circles Parsley Peel did not achieve and perhaps cared little for distinctions and honours. 'My father,' wrote the first baronet, 'moved in a confined sphere and employed his talents in improving the cotton-trade. He had neither wish nor opportunity of making himself acquainted with his native country, or society far removed from his native county of Lancaster. . . . The only record of my father is to be found in the memory of his surviving friends.'[1] Yet he was not an unlearned man. He had been

[1] T. Briggs, *Pedigree of . . . Sir Robert Peel* (Blackburn, 1885); cf. *Peel*, I, 5. Quoted but wrongly attributed in *Sir Robert Peel and his Era* (anon. 1844), p. 7.

educated at the grammar school at Blackburn and the signatures that were preserved in the family in the nineteenth century showed a trained literate hand. It is also clear that he was marked by a single-minded application to his work, an independence of spirit, and a business acumen that made him by the end of his life an outstanding figure in the Lancashire cotton-trade. Beneath the outward reserve that characterised him, as so many other members of his family, was a strong and tenacious individualism. Barring accidents, he liked to say, a man could be what he chose. Certainly he had come far himself and at Burton-on-Trent he was something of a celebrity. The inhabitants nicknamed him the philosopher; and the stooping, silent old man in bushy wig and dark ample garm nts was one of the sights of the town as he paced slowly through t he streets with his gold-headed stick on its leathern thong, gazing abstractedly at the cobbles. It was a great change in worldly circumstances since the days when he had gone about his farm-work at Fish Lane burly and erect in woollen apron, calf-skin waistcoat and wooden-soled clogs, his head uncovered except by his own grizzled reddish hair. Yet to the end of his life he retained a countryman's fresh complexion, with big nose, fleshy chin, brown eyes, and round blunt features.[1] A silhouette taken late in life exhibited the profile—the prominent Peel nose, thin firm lips, strong jaw and double chin, surmounted by a full wig and low, broad-brimmed hat.[2] On his retirement he moved from Burton to Ardwick near Manchester and in his will dated 1792 described himself as a merchant of Ardwick. He died at the age of seventy-two and was buried in St. John's Church, Manchester.

In many respects—in his commercial ability, his strong utilitarian outlook, his personal and private generosity—he seems to have been closely akin to his third and most successful son Robert, the future purchaser of Drayton Bassett. It was a natural touch that led him to drop the final 'e' from his name as obsolete and unnecessary; and the disposal of his fortune directed by his will showed an impartial

---

[1] Jonathan Peel stated that there was no portrait of Parsley Peel in existence, but there is no reason to doubt the authenticity of the painting (? by Philip Reinagle) formerly at Drayton Manor and now in the possession of Earl Peel.

[2] The silhouette is now in the possession of G. F. Peel, Esq. For verbal descriptions of Parsley Peel at different dates see Abram, *Blackburn*, p. 218; Peel, *Life*, p. 24; Peel, *Family Sketch*, p. 93.

desire to benefit every member of his family. He had married in 1744 Elizabeth Haworth of Darwen and by her had seven sons and one daughter. His eldest son William predeceased him but the family estate of Peel Fold was left to William's son. A life interest on £10,000 was left to his widow and small legacies to his brothers and sisters. The rest of the estate was divided into eight equal parts and distributed among his children or their immediate heirs. Jonathan Peel, the family historian, stated that the value of these portions was over £17,000.[1] If true, this would make the total fortune left by Parsley Peel not far short of £140,000, a substantial sum by the standards of the eighteenth century. It was in any case a remarkable achievement for a man who had started life as an obscure yeoman farmer with an estate of about £100 a year and whose business career ended before the great phase of cotton expansion made possible by the power-loom. One other legacy he left his family, less lucrative but more enduring. In March 1792, the same year as that in which he made his will, he obtained the grant of a coat of arms. His motive in procuring this mark of gentility was perhaps family rather than personal pride, since the grant was not merely for himself but for the other descendants of his father William Peele.[2] Yet if the instinct was that of the yeoman of Peel Fold, the arms were those of the cotton-spinner of Blackburn: *argent*, three sheaves of as many arrows proper, banded *gules*, on a chief *azure* a bee volant *or*; crest, a demi-lion rampant *argent* collared *azure* holding a shuttle *or*. According to Croker, who looked into the matter with his customary inquisitiveness many years later,[3] the arms were completely original and had been contrived by the family. The bundles of arrows were adopted as an emblem of family unity, the bee and the shuttle as symbols of industry and manufacture. The motto *Industria*, with its double sense of work and trade, repeated the dominant theme not only of the arms themselves but of the man to whom they were granted. Arms and motto were equally appropriate for the family that inherited them. Neither then nor for some time after did the Peels show much interest in their forebears and they were

---

[1] £13,000 according to Miss Haworth.
[2] Information on date of grant and limitation of arms from the College of Arms.
[3] 40321 f. 1 (Jan. 1834). Croker based his interpretation on information from the College of Arms and conversations with the first Sir Robert Peel.

not disposed either to conceal or parade their plebeian origin. 'The only ancestry we care about,' said Lady Henley, a great grand-daughter of Parsley Peel, on one occasion, 'is the shuttle.'[1] But if the shuttle was the true ancestor of the Peels, it was Parsley Peel that placed it like the golden spoon of the proverb in the hands of his children.

In the simple and sagacious belief that happiness as well as pros-perity was best promoted by 'brotherly intercourse, fenced round by family connections',[2] he had trained his sons in all branches of the industry and when they reached manhood he placed them in situations where they could assist each other in the great industrial and mercantile expansion of the late eighteenth century. Of his seven surviving sons, William (until his early death in 1791) and a younger son Jonathan took over the main printing-works at Church Bank; and three others became merchants: Lawrence in Manchester, Joseph (who stood surety for his brother in the purchase of the Thynne estate) in London, and John at Burton-on-Trent. But it was his third son Robert, born in 1750, who most closely followed his father. Educated like him at Blackburn Grammar School, he was sent for a while to London to enlarge his experience before returning to the family business at Brookside. Ambitious, self-confident, and hard-working, he could not easily reconcile himself to the sub-ordinate place of a younger son. Even at the age of eighteen he told his father that they were 'too thick on the ground' and offered to go elsewhere if he were given £500 with which to start himself. The offer was not accepted but about 1773 it was arranged that he should leave the family concern and become a partner with his father's old associates, Messrs. Haworth and Yates at Bury. The two firms, linked by marriage and kinship, both flourished and were for a time the acknowledged leaders of the Lancashire cotton-industry. In the Bury firm the younger Peel by his energy and assiduity soon became the dominant personality. Haworth retired and Yates increasingly deferred to his younger partner. In the early days when capital was short and the competition of the London calico printers still formid-able, Robert Peel worked unceasingly. In bad weather he would rise in the night to visit the bleaching-grounds and once a week he would

---

[1] E. Peel, *Recollections of Lady Georgiana Peel*, (1920), p. 201.
[2] Davies, *Memoirs*, p. 4.

stay up with his pattern-drawer to receive the latest patterns that came down at midnight on the London coach. Though the firm was steadily enlarging its profits, much of the money went back into schemes of expansion and his own life was frugal and temperate. For many years he lived as a lodger with his partner and when at the age of thirty-three he relaxed his concentration of energy and emotion to allow himself the luxury of marriage, it was the eldest daughter of the house, Ellen Yates, a pretty affectionate girl of eighteen, on whom his choice fell.

At the time of his marriage in 1783 Robert Peel was already a wealthy man and the virtual head of a flourishing concern. Ten years of unremitting effort had put him abreast if not ahead of his father and when in 1795 the body of British merchants and manufacturers petitioned against Pitt's Irish trade resolutions, Robert Peel of Bury was one of those to be examined at the bar of the House.[1] By the start of the nineteenth century he was one of the richest cotton-manufacturers in the kingdom, employing some 15,000 workpeople and paying over £40,000 annually to the government in duties on his printed goods.[2] The extent and complexity of his industrial activities in themselves demonstrated not only his business skill but his practical judgement of men; for as his interests multiplied, he had increasingly to rely on his right choice of managers and agents to conduct the daily supervision of the work. When asked once why Peels of Bury prospered so much more than any of the other firms with which his family was concerned, his brother Joseph said reflectively, 'I think they had more brains.' Certainly initiative and judgement as well as energy went into the building up of Robert Peel's economic enterprises. His firm seems to have invented a method of printing by means of wooden rollers which was an early version of cylinder printing;[3] and it was he apparently that began the practice of bringing pauper children from the London workhouses to serve in the mills. Dependent on water for their source of power the cotton manufacturers in the early years of the industry frequently built their factories in the open countryside away from the large centres of population. The apprentice children, fed, clothed and housed by their masters, furnished an

[1] *Parl. Hist.*, XXXIV, 478ff.    [2] Davies, *Memoirs*, pp. 31 n., 33.
[3] *Victoria County History of Lancaster* (1908), II, 396.

invaluable labour-force and at one time Peel's firm was employing nearly a thousand of them. There was, perhaps inevitably, a dark side to this impressive upward progress. Factory buildings were then designed for machines and not for persons; and the contemporary view of what constituted a fitting day's labour was not a lenient one. Though Peel's earlier personal supervision had diminished, he did not fail to observe the external appearances of ill-health, malnutrition and stunted growth among the children in his mills. 'Ill health was visible,' as he admitted to a parliamentary committee in 1816, 'which pained me very much.' Though fed and clothed as adequately as they would have been in the homes of the poor, they were peculiarly exposed to exploitation by managers and foremen whose own earnings were dependent on the output of the factories in their charge. The regulations of the firm prescribed a twelve-hour day, but often—induced by threats or petty bribes—the children worked as much as fourteen or fifteen hours. The overseers ignored Peel's instructions, and a practical reluctance to interfere with the men in charge, combined with the knowledge that his competitors were imposing equally long hours, inhibited him from making any immediate improvements in conditions which he realised were indefensible. As a result some at least of Peel's mills were for a time as bad as any. One of them, at Radcliffe Bridge near Manchester, where the day and night shifts used the same beds, was involved in an epidemic of fever in 1784 which provoked one of the first public enquiries into factory conditions.[1]

Peel was by now engrossed in a widening sphere of activity from which the children of Radcliffe Bridge were becoming increasingly remote. Yet he was not without a sense of public responsibility. Indeed, it was an ingrained element of his belief, as it had been of his father's, that the progress of commerce and mechanical industry was as beneficent to the country at large as to the individual capitalists. If wealthy, he was also an outstandingly generous man and his later career was marked by an association with various benevolent bodies that was more than merely formal. He became vice-president of the Society for Benefiting the Condition of the Poor and in 1801 contributed £1,000 to its funds. He was president of the House of

---

[1] P.P. 1816, III, (*Children in Manufactories*), 132ff.; Ramsay, *Peel*, pp. 5-6; S. J. Chapman, *Lancashire Cotton Industry* (Manchester, 1904), pp. 85-90.

Recovery in Manchester; a governor of Christ's Hospital; and vice-president of the Literary Fund founded by David Williams in 1788. He was not the only mill-owner with reason to be ashamed of some of the conditions that produced his wealth; but at least he was the first to move in parliament for intervention by the legislature on behalf of the factory children. In 1802 he carried through the Health and Morals of Apprentices Act which limited the hours of labour to twelve, forbade in principle night employment, and made provision for clothing, education, and conditions of work. Over a decade later he acted as parliamentary spokesman for Robert Owen and other reformers in securing the 1816 committee which finally resulted in an Act of 1819 laying down similar provisions for all cotton-mill children. Neither act, it is true, was very effective. There were no factory inspectors to watch for infringements; it was difficult to get local people to lay information before magistrates; and not only owners but also adult operatives for their own profit connived at breaking the law. But at least the law was on the statute book. Public attention was in some measure drawn to the evil; and in Peel's factories at any rate there was reasonable observance of the regulations. After 1802 he was able to pride himself with some justice on the state of his little mill-hands. Certainly in his later years his mills had no cause to shrink from publicity. William Ward, first Earl of Dudley, who visited Peel's Staffordshire cotton-works in 1822, noted that there were fewer children employed there than in similar mills he had seen in Glasgow and that their appearance was healthier. The manager, who impressed his visitors as an intelligent and sensible man, told them that profits were less than in Sir Robert's earlier days but the sale of the products greater than ever.[1]

## III

In 1790 Robert Peel reached his fortieth birthday, wealthy, married, and with a rising family. It is a time of life when most men's careers settle into a mould that remains unbroken for the rest of their course. For Peel it was a point at which to reorganise his resources for a fresh phase of activity. Though the able and opportunistic way in

[1] *Dudley Letters*, p. 344.

which he had carried through the purchase of Drayton Manor bore the characteristic imprint of his commercial skill, his extensive acquisitions of property around Tamworth between 1790 and 1796 and his election to the House of Commons as member for the borough in 1790 marked a deliberate entry into a sphere to which neither his father nor any of his brothers ever aspired. Yet it was no sudden impulse that led him to that decision. From his early years he had been conspicuous in his family for his determination, his dislike of being surpassed, and his ambition to raise himself and his descendants to 'rank and consequence' in society.[1] The change in his worldly position which he achieved in the last decade of the century was the long matured success of a youthful resolve.

At the date when Peel first went into parliament, six years had elapsed since public opinion and royal influence had confirmed Pitt's choice as minister of the Crown against the efforts of the politicians under Fox and North to impose their will on the sovereign. During that time the Prime Minister's stature and authority had grown until he now seemed as firmly entrenched at the head of the government as the Pelhams and Walpoles of an earlier generation. George III himself, with the old days of Bute's unpopularity and the temporary depression of the American War far behind him, had established himself as a patriotic and constitutional monarch; and the popular rejoicings which marked the recovery from his first fit of insanity in 1789 gave evidence of a deep-seated loyalty and affection which continued for the rest of his long life. Across the Channel there was a deep and darkening contrast. The same year in France the Estates General had met and by 1790 a Constituent Assembly, with the monarchy politically captive in Paris, was at work on a radical reconstruction of the political framework of the *ancien régime*. Two more years of peace remained before Europe was to go to war with the French Revolution, and three before Britain began the long and exhausting struggle with the republic and empire which with one short and uneasy intermission in 1802-3 was to last till 1815.

Among all these events it was natural that the new member for Tamworth should take his place as a supporter of the government and of the minister. In his first peaceful decade of office Pitt showed

[1] Davies, *Memoirs*, pp. 2-3.

himself the friend and patron of the great commercial and manufacturing interests of the day. His financial reforms, the reduction of
customs and excise duty, the diversion of surplus revenue into a
sinking fund to reduce the national debt, his encouragement of
British commercial enterprise abroad, all displayed his appreciation
of that powerful current in the national life which men like Peel
represented in parliament. 'No minister', said Peel in 1802, when
defending Pitt from a motion of censure put forward during
Addington's administration, 'ever understood so well the commercial interests of the country. He knew that the true sources of its
greatness lay in its productive industry and he therefore encouraged
that industry. . . . The late minister had been the benefactor of his
country and had neglected no one's interest but his own.' Nor did
Pitt ignore the political value of the support given to him by the
great cotton-manufacturer. He took note of his opinions and consulted him on financial and commercial matters.[1]

Peel was no orator and not much of a debater. He spoke infrequently and almost always on subjects of commercial, financial,
or local interest. But for all his blunt manners and provincial
accents he was something more than a plain unlettered calico-printer
from distant Lancashire. Even in the busiest days of his manufacturing career he had continued to read books and enlarge his own
education. Though not a trained economist, he formed views, usually
strong and sometimes shrewd, on the controversial issues of the day.
In 1780, when the increase in the national debt as a result of the
American War was causing alarm, he published a pamphlet, *The
National Debt productive of National Prosperity*, to expound his view
that debts owed by the state to members of society could not
possibly impair the sum of national wealth and that the interest paid
to creditors accelerated the circulation of money and assisted the
economy. Paper currency, he argued, was an admirable adjunct to
commercial credit and need not be backed in full by hard cash.
Coming at the time and having a certain novelty in its views, the
pamphlet attracted some interest. But it was only rarely that he
spoke on more extended topics and though it is unlikely that all his
parliamentary utterances were recorded in *Cobbett* or *Hansard*, he
was never a fluent or frequent speaker. His first speech of any

[1] *Parl. Hist.*, XXXVI, 622 (7 May 1802).

length that is preserved was one of February 1799, later published in Dublin, supporting Pitt's plan for a Union with Ireland; and he spoke again on the same topic in May 1800.[1] But it was a period when parliamentary speaking was almost monopolised by a narrow ring of front-rank politicians, and the value of Peel's support did not consist merely in his eloquence or even his vote. If he appeared almost entirely as a representative, as he more than once reminded the House, of the commercial interest, he at least knew as well as anyone on the benches around him what that interest was; and to practical knowledge and experience the House of Commons has always been disposed to pay attention. Even after Pitt's death in 1806, when Peel transferred his allegiance first to Perceval and then to Liverpool, his position as a commercial authority was unshaken. It is clear, for example, from the correspondence of Lord Bathurst when President of the Board of Trade (1807-12), that Peel's views, whether in agreement or conflict with government policy, had to be respected in matters affecting the cotton industry.[2]

Yet there was another and perhaps deeper strain in Peel's nature that made him a Pittite in politics. Like his father he was by temperament and upbringing a Church-and-King tory of the instinctive and unreflecting school. In this he was characteristic of many of the middle and lower classes in Lancashire both then and, despite the meteoric and perhaps misleading episode of the Anti-Corn Law League in the 1840s, for much of the nineteenth century. Unimaginative and undoctrinaire, he shared that innate feeling for order, piety, and authority which George III and Pitt were able to rally to the side of the government when the long struggle not only against the power but also against the ideas of revolutionary France began in 1793. Robert Peel came into early prominence in the ranks of those who organised in defence, as they believed, of liberty, order, and property against Jacobin agitation. On 11 December 1792 he was present at the foundation meeting in Manchester of an *Association for Preserving Constitutional Order* and made a speech in which he was reported by the newspapers as having said that there was need for the country to awake from its lethargy as incendiaries were abroad. The same evening riots broke out in the town, directed against certain Manchester radicals, and several houses were destroyed.

[1] *Parl. Hist.*, XXXIV, 478; XXXV, 123.    [2] *Bathurst*, pp. 143-8.

Coming after the anti-dissenter riots in Birmingham of 1791 and the government proclamation of May 1792 against the publication of seditious writings, the Manchester riots received some attention and Peel had subsequently to defend himself against whig criticism in the House of Commons.[1]

When the long-awaited war broke out a few months later, Peel steadfastly supported the government. As a commercial man he could not but prefer peace, but as a subject he had no doubt where his duty lay. The war opened badly and continued worse. For year after year the British public had to endure a succession of military failures by their own forces. Their allies one after the other retired defeated from the struggle or joined the camp of the enemy. Sea-power alone, the patiently cruising squadrons in the Channel and Biscay, stood between Britain and the French armies. At the end of 1796 British Funds sank to their lowest point since the American war. The following year saw the suspension of cash payments by the Bank of England, the withdrawal of the fleet from the Mediterranean, and the mutiny at the Nore. It was the crisis of the war and two budgets in 1797 marked the effort that Pitt was making to grapple with the danger. In his 'war budget' of November Pitt proposed a general augmentation of assessed taxes[2] amounting to nearly treble the previous vote. A clause was added in committee allowing 'persons of affluent fortunes' to make such a contribution above the amount of their legal assessment as would be commensurate with their real property. Two million pounds of voluntary contributions were received in this way during the succeeding year and among the contributors the firm of Yates and Peel put themselves down for £10,000.[3] A year earlier, in 1796, Pitt had brought forward his plan to create a supplementary militia in readiness for invasion. In the next twelve months Peel took an active part in raising volunteer forces in the localities with which he was connected. He assisted in the formation of the Lancashire Fencibles and the Tamworth Armed Association; and in 1798 he raised and commanded six companies of men under the title of the Bury Loyal

[1] *Parl. Hist.*, XXX, 105, 128-31.
[2] i.e. on houses, windows, carriages, servants, etc.
[3] The system was discontinued when the income tax was introduced the following year.

Volunteers, mainly recruited from his own employees.[1] All this patriotic effort did not pass unnoticed by the Prime Minister and a little later the offer was made of a baronetcy. Peel accepted and the patent appeared in November 1800.[2]

## IV

It was as Sir Robert Peel therefore that the owner of Drayton Bassett settled down with his family in the new manor house.[3] The children of his marriage with Ellen Yates were already beginning to grow tall around him. Mary, the eldest, had been born in 1785 and was followed by another girl, Elizabeth, in 1786. Then, on 5 February 1788, came the first son, blue-eyed and reddish-haired like many of his family, who was christened Robert after his father and grandfather. He was born at Chamber Hall, Bury, into which the Peels had moved soon after their marriage, 'in the old ivied room at the back, overlooking the court'.[4] A second son William, who was given the additional patronymic of Yates, after his maternal grandfather, was born in 1789; and a third, Edmund, in 1791. Two more girls followed, Eleonora and Anne, both of whom died in childhood. Then came John (1798), Jonathan (1799), and Lawrence (1801). The last two were almost certainly born after the final transfer of the Peel home to Staffordshire, for in August 1799 their small sister Anne was buried at Drayton, the first of her family to be recorded in the church registers there. The quiverful was completed by Harriet Eleonora, born in April 1803 at 16 Upper Grosvenor Street, the house which her father had taken for his London residence. Before the end of that year the family of nine children was left motherless. According to the few surviving

---

[1] C. F. Palmer, *History of . . . Tamworth* (Tamworth 1845), p. 437n.; Davies, *Memoirs*, p. 16.

[2] According to family tradition a similar offer was made to Yates but declined.

[3] The final move from Bury seems to have been made in 1798 or the first half of 1799. William Peel spoke of his brother's education at Bury continuing until his tenth year, i.e. 1798.

[4] *G.M.* (no. 5 N.S.) 1 May 1866, letter from W. M. Brookes of Accrington whose grandparents were neighbours of the Peels at the time. The story that Robert was born in a cottage in the grounds, later the porter's lodge, while the Hall was being repaired seems to have been due to a confusion with his brother William.

accounts, Ellen Yates was a lively, energetic woman, graced with a happy temperament and high spirits. Until the last years of her life she had enjoyed good health, and it was from her perhaps that the children inherited their love of sport and strong active physique, qualities not inappropriate in a daughter of William Yates, once of the Black Bull. But she had borne eleven children in the space of eighteen years and not long after Harriet's birth she caused concern to her family by taking her eldest daughters to a ball at Lord Derby's. To that premature recommencement of social activity her relatives attributed the illness which followed. Towards the end of the year she went to Buxton for the benefit of the waters and there on 28 December she died.[1]

Two years later, in October 1805, the month and year of Trafalgar, Sir Robert married again. His second wife was Susanna Clerke, a sister of the Rev. Sir William Clerke, Bt., the rector of Bury, and her husband's junior by three years. According to gossip in London, which may have had a foundation of truth, Peel had made an offer to Miss Clerke many years earlier, before his marriage to Ellen Yates; but she had turned him down as not being of equal rank to herself. Now at the age of fifty-two she accepted the wealthy and widowed baronet of Tamworth. The marriage was not a success. She did not get on well with the two elder daughters of the house, Mary who was now twenty years old, and Elizabeth, who in December 1805 married the Rev. William Cockburn; and it was rumoured that Sir Robert took the side of his children. In the end there was a separation and Lady Peel retired to Warwickshire where she died at the house of her nephew, Edward Willis, at Newbold Conyers in 1824. At the time of her death, Sir Robert Peel was gravely ill and his children concealed the news from him until after his recovery. Instead they travelled themselves the thirty miles from Drayton to attend the funeral. Though the outward courtesies were preserved, however, Lady Peel had no influence on the careers and fortunes of her step-children and there is a notable absence in their letters of references to her.[2] For all practical purposes the younger Peel children grew up without the warmth and care that a mother or even, in happier circumstances, a stepmother might have bestowed

[1] *Ann. Reg.*, 1803, p. 531. She was buried at Drayton on 3 January 1804.
[2] Peel MSS.; *The Farington Diary*, ed. J. Greig (1922), VIII, 191.

on them. Of the affection their father had for them, and of his absorption in their welfare, there could be no doubt. Coarse-mannered and blunt in his speech as he appeared to outsiders, he had a strong vein of personal kindliness and good humour. But, except perhaps in his old age, he was by nature a man who could not easily express his more tender emotions and his love for his family issued as often as not in rough, half-joking, exhortation and admonition. Certainly he placed high standards before them and the Peel boys grew up in the gospel of work and achievement as the proper duty of man. It was perhaps fortunate for the children, however, that there were so many of them and that a large family circle could after 1803 compensate in some measure for the loss of their mother.

The transfer from Bury to Drayton was the first decisive break in the close Peel family connection which had grown up in Lancashire and Staffordshire; but even so the separation was neither sudden nor complete. The Peels of Sir Robert's generation, wealthy, prolific, and socially rising, tended naturally to form an intimate network of kinship in an age which in any case held family relationship in high esteem. Besides the two households of the grandparents at Bury and Manchester, Sir Robert Peel had four surviving brothers, all married, who founded flourishing Peel families in Manchester, Burton-on-Trent, and London. There was also a younger sister, Anne, who married a clergyman, the Rev. B. Willock, and produced at least two nephews to add to the circle of relatives. Finally there were the children of his elder brothers, William and Edmund. With four uncles and an aunt, and seven different sets of cousins, it must have been difficult for the children of Drayton Hall to be quite sure at any time how many relatives of their own generation they really had.

But for the family at Drayton at the beginning of the century, the ever-widening growth of the Peels was still in its early stages. At Manchester, London, and in Staffordshire their uncles and cousins were neither strangers nor remote. Even so, with the indifferent roads and heavy vehicles of the period, it took two days and part of a third to travel from Drayton to their grandfather Yates's house in Bury, though the journey probably seemed more tedious to the adults than to the children. In London there was the family of their uncle, Joseph Peel, which with six boys and five girls was even larger than their own; though the intercourse between the cousins was perhaps less than it might have been in the provinces. When the Drayton children visited London they lived at their own house in Grosvenor Street and for the older ones among them there were all the other interests and distractions of the capital. It was at Bury and Manchester that they were brought most vividly into contact with the world of their father and mother, a simpler and more old-fashioned society than that to which manor-house and public school were rapidly accustoming them. Old William Yates still lived near the mills at Bury, modest, kindly, and paternally interested in his dead Ellen's children. The other grandfather Parsley Peel died in 1795, and his wife the following year at her daughter's house at Great Harwood. Even Mary, the oldest of the Peel children, could scarcely have known them in their active days at Burton-on-Trent. But the old couple survived to see their son Robert's success in life and were present at the christening of his sixth child, Eleonora.

As small children the young Peels used to visit their grandparents at Ardwick, then a pleasant and fashionable suburb of Manchester; and Robert, though he could not have been more than seven at the time, carried away for later life the impression of his grandfather as a venerable, fine-looking old man. Even in the new house that Parsley Peel had built for his retirement, much of their old provincial simplicity clung to them. Old Mrs. Peel, still addressing her husband in rustic fashion as 'thee' and 'thou', and smoking her pipe against the asthma in the privacy of her kitchen, was already a whole world away from her little grandchildren. But though half-severed, the link was still there and Robert in later life spoke of them with affection and respect. After Parsley Peel's death the gold-headed cane with the worn leather thong, on which he had leaned as he went about the streets of Burton, passed as a treasured relic to one of his younger sons, Jonathan Peel of Accrington. When he died in 1834 the cane was presented to Robert as the most worthy of the old man's descendants and preserved by him as a reminder of those distant childhood days.[1]

[1] Peel, *Life*, pp. 26-30. A pierced walking-stick with a metal head (still showing traces of gilt) bearing the inscription 'Robert Peel 1765' is still in the possession of G. F. Peel, Esq.

Robert the eldest son had received most of his early education from his father and his own reading. When he was a small boy his father would make him repeat on Sunday morning and evening after church the substance of the sermon he had heard; and with his brothers and sisters he was taught to recite from Goldsmith, Pope, and other poets and encouraged not merely to repeat but to give the sense in his own words and ask for explanations of difficult passages. It was a system that his father had used in his own education and it was not without profit for his children. 'His eldest son, a youth of the most promising talents, who is little more than fifteen years of age,' wrote an admirer of Sir Robert in 1804, 'has been so much in the habit of exercising the retentiveness of his memory, conformably to this method, that very few indeed of his age can carry with them more of the sentiments of an author than himself.'[1] The four elder children were also instructed by the local curate, Mr. James Hargreaves, who came daily to Chamber Hall for a couple of hours. From this first tutor Robert secured the rudiments of formal English, Latin grammar, and some miscellaneous general knowledge. In these early years he was a quiet, well-mannered and disciplined boy, praised by his elders and not over-popular with the young, and already endowed with a certain fastidiousness that kept him aloof from much of the coarseness and ribaldry of boys' society. At Bury the Peel family was in a position of local eminence which probably exposed the children to some ridicule and jealousy on the part of the young urchins of the neighbourhood. Lawrence Peel records that Robert 'would walk a mile round rather than encounter the rude jests of the Bury lads'.[2] This evasiveness was due to self-consciousness rather than cowardice, for from other childhood incidents it is clear that Robert had all the quick temper, activity, and fearlessness of his family. Sir Robert's eldest son had in fact a more complex nature than gratified adults always realised: a determined character and a keen mind accompanied by abnormal personal sensitivity and perhaps a certain repressiveness of emotion.

After the move to Drayton he was sent to a small school for the sons of neighbouring gentry kept by the Rev. Francis Blick, vicar of Tamworth, who lived nearby at Bonehill in a house belong-

[1] Davies, *Memoirs*, p. 9.    [2] Peel, *Life*, p. 49.

ing to Sir Robert. There he extended his classical studies and was soon distinguished as the best scholar of his years among his school companions. But Drayton had other advantages; with its broad park and surrounding countryside it furnished every opportunity to develop the love of outdoor life and country pursuits that marked many of the family in later life. Robert early took up shooting, an enthusiasm that was shared by his second brother William, though Jonathan, their junior by ten years, was later to be better known as a racehorse owner. It does not appear that their sober father did much to preserve the game on his estate, but there was plenty of rough shooting in the flat water-logged meadows and spinneys round Drayton, wild duck on the park lake, partridges, hares, and an occasional bittern. The first recorded trophies of Robert's gun were a couple of pigeons, duly consumed by an admiring family at an early meal one day before setting off for Bury in the heavy old family coach; he was then about fourteen. As was a matter of course for young men of his class, he rode both for exercise and utility, and later on in Ireland tried his hand at driving. But he seems never to have cared for hunting, and his favourite exercise, for the rest of his life, was on foot with a gun. A good eye and constant practice from boyhood made him an excellent shot, and at more than one country-house party in later life wagers were made and won on his unusual skill in the field. Partly, perhaps, as a result of his early passion for sport, he grew up strong and active, a good walker and capable of great physical endurance.

Years afterwards, when his career was made, legends began to circulate about his boyhood for which various proud but embarrassing parental utterances seemed to furnish some basis. There was a story, for example, that at his birth the elder Peel fell on his knees and dedicated his first-born son to the service of his country; and that at the christening he publicly expressed the hope that he would walk in the footsteps of the immortal Pitt. Even apart from the circumstance that Pitt in 1788 was scarcely as yet enshrined in the political pantheon, there is no real evidence for the incident and the origin of the tale seems to have been words uttered much later by his father in the House of Commons. In a debate in May 1819 on the restriction of cash payments, in which Sir Robert had to acknowledge that he took a view opposed to that of his son, or as he put it, of 'a very near and dear relation', the old baronet went on to speak of his political hero Pitt.

> He always thought him the first man in the country. . . . He well remembered, when that near and dear relation was only a child, he observed to some friends who were standing near him, that the man who discharged his duty to the country in the manner in which Mr. Pitt had, did most to be admired, and was most to be imitated; and he thought at that moment, if his own life and that of his dear relation should be spared, he would one day present him to his country, to follow in the same path.

It might have shown more consideration for his son, if this silent thought had never been communicated, even twenty years afterwards, to an audience such as the House of Commons. But in itself it was a modest enough spasm of parental ambition and the reference to it in the debate was elicited not by pride in his son but by a desire to show his veneration for the memory of Pitt.[1]

It was true, however, that Sir Robert was ambitious for his children. For himself, he had achieved by 1810 all that was possible and more than he could have hoped for; and at sixty years of age the active part of his career was coming to an end. But as he had been helped to a successful commercial career by his own father, so he in turn placed his children in positions from which nothing was beyond their reach. What money, education, influence, and admonition could achieve was theirs if they chose to use it; and if they used it, they could rise as far above him as he had above old Parsley Peel. If his thoughts centred on his eldest son and heir, it would only have been natural; and since that son won fame, and the others did not, it was remembered what his father had said and done on his behalf. But there can be no question that he was ambitious for them all; and all the sons in their different ways were assisted to a start in life that needed only talent, industry, and good judgement to ripen into success. Even when Robert was fairly launched on his political career, his father on more than one occasion solicited the Prime Minister for some equally promising opening for the second son

[1] For a discussion of the 'dedication to country' legend see A. F. Robbins in N & Q, 7 S., XII, 61.

William. Nor was it clear in the early years that Robert was the ablest of the family. His two nearest brothers, William and Edmund, showed externally at least far greater liveliness and initiative and their uncle Joseph for one thought that William had by nature the quicker parts. It was of his second and not of his first son that Sir Robert was speaking when he asked one of their clerical tutors whether he would be a William Pitt. 'I hope so,' the answer is reported to have been, 'but Robert will be Robert Peel.'

Whether authentic or not, the phrase showed insight as well as neatness. Many of the characteristics of his father, and indeed of his grandfather, were repeated in the Robert of the third generation; and perhaps for that reason there always appeared a bond between father and son. Formal, according to the habits of their age and class, as their outward relations were, a steady affection united them and there is no record, even when they disagreed on matters political, of any quarrel or estrangement. If Robert was ever restive under the clumsily expressed feelings of his father's hopes, there is no evidence that he ever showed it. Fond as he was of his parent and accustomed to his ways from early childhood, he was not of a disposition to rebel against paternal authority. The sedateness of the eldest Peel son which observers noted in contrast to the exuberance of the younger boys, sprang from a strong nature held normally in good control rather than from a warped or timid temperament. Certainly in after-life when in communicative mood he would good-humour-edly relate to friends some of the remarks made by his father when he was a boy. He told Samuel Rogers, for instance, that Sir Robert was accustomed to say to him, 'Bob, you dog, if you are not prime minister some day, I'll disinherit you.'[1] Sir Robert Peel is not the only male parent to have addressed his young in those terms and the effect of such repeated admonitions depends largely on the character of the children to whom they are made. But as the younger Robert's life fell more and more into the pattern which his father had hoped to see, it is possible that the high aims which were con-stantly held before him were not without effect in stimulating his own youthful ambitions.

Prime Ministers in the early nineteenth century, however, were not likely to be produced in very great number by the schools of

[1] *Recollections . . . of Samuel Rogers*, ed. A.D. (1856), p. 250.

Tamworth or any other small north-country industrial town. Sir Robert early determined to send his sons to public schools. He was too shrewd to overlook the advantages of coming into contact at an impressionable age and on equal terms with the future governing classes of England. So Robert and William were in due course despatched to Harrow, and later John, Jonathan, and Lawrence to Rugby. For Robert, who in February 1800[1] at the age of twelve was the first to leave home, boarding-school meant the first real separation from his home, his parents, and his flock of younger brothers and sisters and the first upward step from his father's own environment.

[1] Parker (*Peel*, I), quoting William Peel, gives the date as January 1801 but see *Harrow Register*.

# HARROW AND OXFORD

At the beginning of the nineteenth century, and for many generations after, Harrow was an isolated village separated from the brick
and mortar tide of the metropolis by some ten miles of meadow and
hedgerow. The school stood on the wooded hill looking across the
flat Middlesex fields towards Windsor much as John Lyon had
designed it at the end of the sixteenth century. But though the
appearance of the old Jacobean grammar school had changed little
in Peel's time, its character had been transformed in the intervening
centuries and it was already established as one of the leading public
schools in the country. The reforming days of Dr. Vaughan were
still to come but under another eminent headmaster, Dr. Joseph
Drury, its numbers were flourishing as never before and no fewer
than four future Prime Ministers sat on its benches during his twenty
years of office from 1785 to 1805.[1] Drury's influence pervaded the
place in more senses than one; for his son, grandson, brother, and
nephew all served on the staff and it was to the house of Mark
Drury, his brother, that Robert Peel was assigned when he came up at
the beginning of 1800. Drury's house was in the High Street on a
site later occupied by the school bookshop and other buildings, but
the boys assembled for lessons in the ancient mellowed brick schoolhouse built by John Lyon's governors in 1608-15. Until several
years after Peel had left this was the only real school building, and
all the forms, numbering in Drury's time over three hundred boys,
did their work together in the one room. Below was a basement for
wood and coals; above, the private rooms of the headmaster and
ushers. On the middle floor, in the long room made familiar by
Ackermann's print, the boys sat on benches facing the square
mullioned windows under the eye of the masters aloft at their high

[1] Goderich, Peel, Aberdeen, and Palmerston.

desks. Around them rose the wainscotted walls covered with initials of past and present inhabitants, to which in due course Robert Peel added his own.

The organisation of the school was of a kind that later became familiar in most public schools. At the top were the monitors, the privileged aristocrats. Then came the sixth form, fifth form, Shell, and the two fourth forms, comprising the upper school, with the various divisions of the third form in the lower school. Peel was placed in the lower fourth form and found himself with fifteen other companions of similar age, one of them another Staffordshire boy, George Chetwynd, who was later to become M.P. for Stafford and succeed his father as second baronet. Among the others were Murray, son of the Bishop of St. Davids, who left in 1803 to enter the Bengal civil service and was dead within five years; William Williams of Glamorgan who went on to Cambridge and became an expert in Bardic literature; and Dawkins who joined the Guards in 1804, served in the Peninsula and at Waterloo, and survived to become a member for Boroughbridge in the last ten years of its existence as a parliamentary constituency. In the upper third were William Lowther, the future second Earl of Lonsdale, and George Pechell, a future M.P. for Brighton and equerry to Queen Adelaide, on whose account Peel was to have some difficulties thirty-five years later. In the Shell was another Murray, later Bishop of Rochester, and George Granville, later second Duke of Sutherland. George Dawson, who was to become Peel's private secretary, brother-in-law, and political supporter, did not arrive at Harrow until a year later; but Sir Thomas Acland, the great west-country member who sat for Devonshire almost continuously from 1812 to 1857, was already at school and became one of Peel's friends. With Palmerston, who left the year Peel arrived and was both older and in a different house, he could scarcely have become acquainted; but a year later a new boy called Byron joined the school.[1]

In 1800 the great war had still many years to run before the final decision on the plains of Belgium. The fifteen months truce of Amiens came during Peel's Harrow days; but before he left, the war had entered on its last, and for England, its most costly phase.

[1] For Peel's contemporaries see *Harrow Register*, 1571-1800 and 1800-1911. For a general description see J. Fischer Williams, *Harrow* (1901), pp. 73ff.

In almost every form at Harrow were boys waiting for the day when they could leave school and put on the king's uniform. Fremantle in the lower third was to serve as Wellington's aide-de-camp at Waterloo. Elphinstone in the upper fourth left at the same time as Peel to enter the 41st, fought at Waterloo, and went on to a professional military career that ended with the ill-fated British army at Cabul in 1842. Others had a briefer course to run, like his form-mate Henry Powys, who died of wounds at Badajoz in 1812, or Long and Morant who entered the school a year after Peel, the one to be drowned on his way to join the army in the Peninsula, the other to die off Walcheren in 1809. When it was over, with Wellington his country's hero and Napoleon an exile on St. Helena, the gaps in the generation of Englishmen to which Peel belonged were not comparable to those of a century later. Nevertheless, it was the greatest and most expensive war the country had ever fought, and for those who had grown up under its shadow and waited for the news of Waterloo, the memory of these years could hardly ever have been completely effaced.

But while the outer world was marked by war and rumours of invasion, life at Harrow proceeded on its even course. If the future was obscure, the present was a not altogether useless preparation for what lay ahead. Like other schools of the time, it was a hard and unruly society. Swearing and getting drunk were fashionable, even if there were aristocrats like young Palmerston who thought the first ungentlemanly and the second unpleasant.[1] The monitors were autocratic and sometimes tyrannical, and there were various rough customs and rougher sports, including nocturnal paper-chases and fights behind the schoolhouse. There were also the innumerable small pursuits to which schoolboys are perennially addicted. Little Althorp, who went to Harrow in 1790 at the age of eight, and busied himself with silkworms, making cork-boats, and rearing greenfinches, probably had his counterparts in Peel's time. Organised compulsory games after the pattern of the later nineteenth century hardly existed, though cricket and football were played, and there were cross-country runs and in the summer swimming in the school pool known as Duck Puddle. If the boys lived together without much supervision, there were also more opportunities to wander over the countryside and

---

[1] Bulwer, *Palmerston*, I, 8.

also perhaps time to indulge in wider if more sporadic reading than a stricter educational establishment would have afforded. A system which allowed the young Palmerston to learn Spanish and begin *Don Quixote* in the original, and Aberdeen to get acquainted with the Italian poets and modern European history, was not without its merits. Enjoyment of liberty, individual initiative, and respect for courage and physical pluck, or, in the language of the time, 'bottom', if not the only virtues, were virtues all the same; and boys made their own interests and chose their own level of company as their tastes inclined.

Peel's most unpleasant recorded experience at Harrow came, as often happens, early on. The formal education of the school was mainly confined to a study of the classical languages of Greek and Latin, and the fourth form in which Peel was placed on arrival required a rudimentary knowledge of versification which he had not been taught at his Tamworth school. He was accordingly kept back for a time for special instruction in Latin verse composition, and in the view of some of the senior boys he consequently could not claim the exemption from fagging which was the privilege of the upper school. Having been told, however, by his tutor that he might expect to be placed in a form which would free him from that obligation, he was bold enough to refuse when ordered to carry out some fagging duty and was chastised in the usual schoolboy style in consequence. The story, told by Moore on third-hand evidence many years later,[1] that the young Byron came forward with an offer to take half the punishment, is clearly apocryphal since the incident almost certainly took place within a short time of Peel's arrival and Byron did not come to Harrow until over a year later.

Nevertheless Byron (whose name at Harrow was always pronounced Birron, a form which Peel retained for the rest of his life),[2] was on good terms with Robert though it was William Peel, the next brother, who became his intimate friend. Byron's subsequent judgement on the elder of the two Peels is well known.

[1] Moore, *Byron*, p. 23.
[2] Sir Algernon West, *Recollections* (1899), I, 2; J. A. Froude, *Carlyle . . . in London* (1885), II, 45.

There were always great hopes of Peel amongst us all, masters and scholars, and he has not disappointed them. As a scholar he was greatly my superior, as a declaimer and actor I was reckoned at least his equal. As a schoolboy out of school I was always in scrapes, and he never; in school he always knew his lesson and I rarely; but when I knew it, I knew it nearly as well. In general information, history, etc., I think I was his superior, as well as of most boys of my standing.

After he had mastered his deficiency in verse, Peel soon achieved the reputation as a scholar to which Byron refers. Though not the school prodigy of the time (this according to Byron was George Sinclair, the son of the famous Sir John), he maintained to the end an easy and apparently effortless superiority in his school work. For years afterwards his tutor, Mark Drury, kept many of his exercises, and occasionally showed them to his pupils as models of terseness and clarity in both Latin and English.[1] A fellow Harrovian recalled in later days the picture of a smiling good-natured boy, 'surrounded, while the school-bell was yet ringing, with boys who had neglected their exercises, calling upon him to supply them, which he did, writing now Latin, now Greek, with as much facility as though it were his mother tongue and upon everyday topics'. Though not so gregarious in his habits as some, his generosity and good nature, together with his physical strength and courage, made him popular with his fellows; and his intellectual powers so far impressed his seniors as to evoke from Mark Drury a prophecy which Sir Robert Peel would have rejoiced to hear, that 'you boys will one day see Peel Prime Minister'. The steadiness of his character, and what the same Harrovian contemporary called his physical indolence, though it is more likely to have been a psychological quality, kept him from the more impulsive escapades of his companions, and he was hardly ever in trouble with authority.

Yet he was not without private interests of his own of which the school fortunately remained in ignorance. It was noticed in his early days at Harrow that he rarely joined in the conventional sports of cricket, football, and hare-and-hounds, but went off into the countryside, occasionally returning with a bird or two which his

---

[1] Lord Dalling, *Sir Robert Peel* (1874), p. 7.

more ingenuous fellows thought he had knocked down with a stone. In fact, with a degree of organisation and secrecy which Stalky & Co. would have respected, he was carrying on at Harrow the same field pursuits which were already his passion at Drayton. Together with his inseparable companion, Robert Anstruther, he arranged for his guns to be kept for him during term in the home of a cottager. When the two boys were thought to be peacefully rambling abroad, communing with nature like Byron beneath the immemorial elms, they were actually beating the distant hedgerows and coverts for small game, returning their weapons to sanctuary before walking back with their trophies to school. In his last year at Harrow, however, he took a greater part in school football, and since physique and pluck were more necessary in the rudimentary form of the game then prevalent than any technical skill, he was considered according to William Peel 'one of the best players in the school'.

Certainly Peel's Harrow days were far from being absorbed in bookish studies. Perhaps the very ease with which his excellent memory and clear mind enabled him to accomplish the work of the school, together with the absence of any external incentive, prevented him from extending his faculties to their limits. In after-life, when advising a friend on the choice of a school for a son, he wrote that 'I was at Harrow myself, but I would not send my boys there unless I believed what I have reason to believe, that it is better conducted now than it was when I misspent my time there.' Such regrets for missed opportunities are not uncommon among sensitive adults; but they indicate perhaps the high standards afterwards achieved rather than any real backsliding when young. Yet if there was any perceptible relaxation or dissipation of energy during Peel's time at Harrow, it may not have been without some positive advantages. The years between 1800 and 1804 were the first when Peel had for any length of time been taken out of his family environment. If he had been influenced, however subconsciously, by the stringency of his father's supervision and by his position as eldest son, Harrow provided a different and in some respects a freer atmosphere. But more important than any subsequent self-depreciation is the fact, which it would be difficult to doubt, that his life at school was happy and successful. It lasted, however, only five years. In 1803 he reached the upper fifth; in 1804 he was monitor; and the speech-day of that year on 5 July when Peel declaimed as Turnus with Byron, sitting to hide his lameness, as Latinus, crowned his Harrow career. He went back for one more term but at Christmas came the final departure.[1]

Oxford was the next step, but he had some nine months at his disposal before going into residence in October 1805. The winter season of 1804-5 he spent at the Peels' town house in Grosvenor Street, attending lectures on Natural Science at the Royal Institution but more often to be found under the gallery of the House of Commons listening to debates. It may not have been his first sight of the interior of the old chapel of St. Stephen's, the same room that had heard the harsh vehement speeches of Cromwell and St. John's eloquent invective. A little incident of which he was reminded many years afterwards might have referred to this, or an even earlier period. One day, while still a schoolboy, he was standing at the entrance to the House of Commons with his father and Samuel Oldknow, another great cotton manufacturer, when Pitt came up to them. He asked who the boy was, and when told he was Sir Robert's son, took him by the hand and led him into the House.[2] Yet it was probably only now that the scene made any clear impact on his mind. The parliamentary session opened in January 1805 and for the tall schoolboy on the visitors' bench there could hardly have been a better introduction to the parliamentary personalities and issues of the day. The course of the war, the breach with Spain, Indian affairs, disaffection in Ireland, the Catholic question, the defence of the country, the enquiry into naval administration that led to the dismissal and impeachment of Lord Melville, made up with the routine business of the House a full and momentous session. Pitt, who had resigned in 1801 because of his inability to carry Catholic emancipation, was now back in office and the period from January to July saw the final bout in the classic duel between Pitt and Fox which had lasted since 1783. One encounter, in particular, left Peel with an ineffaceable memory which he was to recall in the

---

[1] I am indebted to Mr. L. J. Verney for additional details of Peel's career at Harrow. There is also a brief and valueless essay on Peel's early schooldays in *The Harrovian* (1828) by an anonymous writer.

[2] H.O. 44/16, Oldknow to Peel, 22 July 1826.

same place twenty-three years later. It was the debate of 13-14 May on the petition of the Roman Catholics of Ireland, an occasion 'which he should never forget. . . . He never heard a speech which made a greater impression on his mind, than that delivered by Mr. Fox during that debate.'[1] It was the last time any of the younger generation had the opportunity to see the two great eighteenth-century parliamentarians in combat. Eight months later Pitt was dying at Putney and the following autumn the brilliant but un-successful and sometimes irresponsible Fox followed him to the grave.

Returning to Drayton at the end of the session, Robert settled down in earnest to fill the gaps in his Harrow education and prepare for Oxford. Two Latin tags[2] he wrote on his desk,

'nocturna versate manu, versate diurna'

and,

'quid ferre recusent,
quid valeant humeri'

indicated the self-conscious mood in which (sharpened perhaps by his experience of the great political world) he turned once more to his books. When William came back from Harrow at the end of the summer term, he found his brother immersed in a solid course of reading from which he would only allow himself two hours a day to accompany William out shooting. But Oxford required a know-ledge of both the classics and mathematics; and in the latter his Harrow training had been completely deficient. Not until Butler succeeded Drury as Headmaster was Euclid first introduced into the school curriculum. Peel told his father that he would like to have some coaching in mathematics before going to the university, and Sir Robert, with a businessman's instinct for getting the best his money could buy, took counsel with his friends and engaged the services of a Cambridge senior wrangler, the Rev. R. Bridge. During the summer months of 1805, while the *grande armée* stood at

[1] *Speeches*, I, 663 (3 July 1828).
[2] Both from Horace, *Ars Poetica*. The first is advice to budding poets to study their Greek models: 'ply your book diligently by night, ply it by day'. The second refers to the need to choose a subject within one's powers: 'what burdens your shoulders must refuse and what they have strength to carry'.

Boulogne and the British ships of the line cruised off Brest and Cadiz, waiting for Villeneuve, Bridge coached his young pupil in the rural tranquillity of Drayton park. Summer gave way to autumn and on 21 October, the day when Peel in his gentleman commoner's cap and gown was being inducted as a matriculated member of the university of Oxford, a thousand miles away the last great fleet action of the war was being fought off Cape Trafalgar.

## II

Oxford, in Peel's as in Gladstone's time, was in essentials the same city that had welcomed Elizabeth and resisted the troopers of the New Model Army half a century later. The fortifications of the Civil War had been levelled, gates and ditches had disappeared, but the town itself still stood small and compact around its five halls and twenty colleges. Another generation was to pass before the steam-engines pounding away in the northern cotton-mills were to be mounted on wheels and start a revolutionary age of railway building. In the remaining interval came the golden age of the fast coach. Oxford, on the great highway from London to the west, saw a bustle of horses and vehicles in High Street and Cornmarket from dawn to dusk; and at the beginning of every term some eight hundred undergraduates arrived in coaches and drags from all over the kingdom.[1] The dome of the Radcliffe Camera, the great tower of Magdalen, the fretted pinnacles and spires of churches and colleges rose into the soft damp skies of the Thames valley above busy, clattering, dung-soiled streets.

The Jacobite toryism of the early years of the eighteenth century had passed away even before the accession of George II and Oxford had sunk into a period of academic as well as political lethargy. Even in its worst years there were to be found scholarly fellows and hard-reading undergraduates. But the Laudian statutes under which the university still granted its degrees had degenerated into a hollow and rather irreverent ritual, and for several decades there was for its junior members little incentive to work and little academic substance in the degree they secured. As a training ground for the

---

[1] The average number of students matriculating annually in the first thirteen years of the century was about 267 (*O.U.C. Rep.*, 1852, pp. 17-18).

Established Church, and as a pleasant haunt where youths of fashion and eccentric bibliophiles could spend a few not unprofitable years, Oxford still attracted each term its store of young men; but its scholarship was largely a matter of isolated and individual effort. From about 1780, however, a new spirit began to make headway in the university. Eveleigh of Oriel, Parsons of Balliol, and Jackson of Christ Church, led the movement for a reform of the degree system, and the same year that Peel first went to Harrow the new examination regulations finally received the assent of Congregation.[1]

The statutes of 1800 allowed candidates to present themselves either at the ordinary degree examination held each term or at a more stringent examination in the Easter term for those who aimed at distinction. Six public examiners were to be appointed, of which a minimum of three were to be present at each examination. The examination was to last at least three hours and could not be sat until the thirteenth term from matriculation.[2] The number of those aiming at distinction was limited to twelve, but in the first years of the new system even this modest total was never reached. In 1802, the year of its inception, there were only two applicants for distinction; in 1803 four; and in 1805 only one. The subjects for the degree included all the traditional disciplines—grammar, logic, rhetoric, and the formal sciences—though the groundwork was still provided by the classical Greek and Roman writers. In addition there was required from all candidates a knowledge of the rudiments of religion. The syllabus proved in fact too wide to permit the ordinary student to study very deeply in any one subject, and even the pass men did not come forward in the expected numbers. As traditionally they had always been, the examinations were oral and this circumstance in itself was an additional deterrent to the more nervous or ignorant undergraduates. They were in the literal sense public examinations, and it was expected that as many members of the university as possible, senior and junior, should attend them.

Nevertheless, the reforms of 1800 were a sign of different temper

[1] C. E. Mallet, *History of . . . Oxford* (1924-7), III, ch. xxiii; H. L. Thompson, *Christ Church* (1900), ch. viii.
[2] The summer term (Paschal and Trinity) counted as two terms and there were for statutory purposes four terms therefore in the calendar year.

in the colleges, and if the standards of examination were pitched too high at the outset, the quality of college tutors was steadily improving. Of the nature of the education they imparted there were even then severe critics. The queen of the classroom and lecture-hall was still the literature of Greece and Rome. Mathematics was mainly taught only in so far as it admitted geometrical treatment. Of philosophy and history there was very little. The conservative character of the resident fellows, celibate but expectant clergy engaged in the instruction of wealthy and titled youth, seemed in itself a positive intellectual limitation. The Earl of Dudley writing a few years later remarked that Oxford was a place where the mind lost its plastic quality; that though it abounded in good sense, learning, and worth, the power of giving consideration to anything that was, or even seemed to be new, was something that it lacked.[1] Yet he was himself a witness to the change which had come over Oxford's academic habits since his own time as an undergraduate. Returning in 1812 he was astonished to find it a hard-working university, a place of real education. Idleness, he discovered, was no longer fashionable and it was now more the thing to read than otherwise.[2] Moreover, under the autocratic rule of Cyril Jackson, who became Dean of Christ Church in 1783, that college had reached a peak of intellectual reputation unsurpassed by any other; and it was to Christ Church that Peel went.

Not only was it the largest and academically the most eminent of the Oxford foundations, but in some respects it had a weight and influence which balanced all the others put together. That this was so was due to a compound of elements. Some were permanent features: its unique status as college and cathedral; its size and wealth; the visible magnificence of its buildings. But in addition under Dean Jackson the college had attracted a succession of able and influential young men who in after-life strengthened the prestige of the college far beyond the confines of the university. If there were scholars like Gaisford, Conybeare, and Hallam, there were also wits, politicians, and noblemen. In the period just before Peel's arrival, there had passed through Jackson's hands Canning, Jenkinson (later Lord Liverpool), Sturges Bourne, Granville Leveson

[1] *Dudley Letters*, pp. 7-8.
[2] *Letters to Ivy from ... Earl of Dudley*, ed. S. H. Romilly (1905), p. 182.

Gower (later first Earl Granville), Morpeth (later Earl of Carlisle), Henry Fox (the third and famous Lord Holland), Charles Ellis, and Nicholas Vansittart. To external observers, indeed, the secular grandeur of the Christ Church undergraduates overshadowed their academic performance; and Dudley noted with disapproval in 1818 that the college had secured an 'almost exclusive connection with Oxford-going nobility and great gentry'.[1] It was a company such as the Dean delighted in. A scholar and a disciplinarian, he loved his young men, entertained them hospitably, stimulated their exertions, followed up their careers, and kept in touch with them when they went down. With a touch of pomposity and perhaps a little snobbishness, he was one of the great university characters of his time. When he passed through Tom Quad in full wig and flowing gown, with cap pulled down over his nose, tutors and noblemen as well as humbler undergraduates bared their heads. It was this formidable figure who remarked with satisfaction a short time afterwards that 'Harrow has sent us up at least one good scholar in Mr. Peel'.

As it had been in Colman's time a decade earlier,[2] Christ Church at the beginning of the century was full to overflowing, and wealthy young men were glad to secure garrets and basements which in their own homes would have been thought scarcely respectable for the servants. There were 132 junior members of the college when Peel took up residence in 1805, including nine noblemen, thirty-seven gentlemen commoners, and fifty-eight commoners. Michaelmas Term 1805 opened on Thursday 10 October, and the first entry for battels[3] under the name *Robertus Peele* appeared in the college accounts for 11 October. His rooms for the first year were No. 6 on staircase 7, on the east side of Peckwater Quad.[4] Acland, his friend and fellow Harrovian, was on an adjoining stair. They were not a particularly large or expensive set of chambers, and the following year he moved out of Peckwater entirely; where to, the college

---

[1] *Dudley Letters*, p. 193.

[2] *Reminiscences of Oxford*, ed. Quiller-Couch (Oxford Hist. Soc., 1892, XXII), pp. 173-4.

[3] College board and lodging dues.

[4] The present (1956) no. 7 staircase is the centre one on the east side and room no. 6 is on the second floor. It is quite possible that the numbering has not been altered since Peel's day.

accounts have not recorded. Of the more domestic details of his life at Christ Church little in fact is known. Long afterwards a venerable scout, rejoicing in the name of Cicero Cook, would relate to subsequent generations of undergraduates sundry anecdotes of Peel's life in college from which it appeared that the pleasures of the chase and the bottle were not entirely absent.[1] But recollections by aged domestics of famous men in the period of their youth are apt to grow more vivid with the passage of time. Peel's battels, which have been preserved for the whole of his time at Christ Church, show no special extravagance. His ordinary weekly kitchen and buttery accounts were never more than £1 and sometimes half that amount. In general, if a little above the average, they were not among the highest on the college books. But these in any case would cover only a small part of an undergraduate's expenses. Such items as laundry, fuel, tea, wine, and dessert, would all be additional to the ordinary college battels and subscriptions; and it was here that extravagance would show.[2]

It is probable indeed that Peel continued to expand the personal habits and tastes he had already developed at Drayton and Harrow; and for young gentlemen who wanted amusement and recreation there were no lack of opportunities at Oxford even if the university statutes suffered thereby some infraction. Cock-fighting, hunting, shooting, riding hacks from the livery stables, driving tandems, and for the bucks and corinthians a turn with the leathers on one of the public coaches, were all among the recognised Oxford dissipations of Peel's time. There were other more modest games and sports, though as yet not on any organised or competitive basis. Cricket and tennis were played, and though the day of the eight-oared skiff and inter-college race was still to come, boating in a variety of costumes and craft was a feature of the Oxford summer scene. Peel acquired a moderate taste for sport; it is hard to believe that he always left his guns behind in Staffordshire; and Lawrence Peel has recorded that he was a boater and a cricketer. 'The hen,' his cousin went so far as to say, 'was a good deal off the nest.' One of Peel's

[1] W. Harvey, *Sir Robert Peel* (1850), p. 28.
[2] Christ Church muniments, esp. the Collections Book and Battels Books. See also details of undergraduate expense at Christ Church in 1850 (*O.U.C. Rep.*, 1852, evidence of C. R. Conybeare, p. 339), which show no great change since Peel's time.

own college contemporaries endorsed this description. Peel, he said, 'was fond of athletic exercises. He took great delight in cricket and in boat-racing and exercise on the river.'[1] Handsome, tall, with his strong physique masked by his height, so that he gave a slender and elegant appearance, Peel moved in the congenial atmosphere of Oxford as something of a dandy. Despite the splendour of a nobleman's or the flowing grace of a gentleman commoner's gown, it was increasingly the rule to discard academic dress on ordinary occasions for more fashionable attire. Young men of position were expected to dress for dinner, and though wigs were now the mark of the older generation, it was still customary to powder the hair. Peel's good sense saved him from extremes but he dressed well and expensively, and it is unlikely that his father grudged him the means to do so. For friendship and company there were plenty of fellow-Harrovians around him at Christ Church, like George Granville, Henry Drummond, Charles Chaplin, John Mills, and Lord Plymouth,[2] or lesser known individuals such as Thornhill and James who went down from the elegance of Oxford to the quiet obscurity of country rectories. One of his close college friends, however, was not a Harrovian. This was Henry Vane, the son and heir of Lord Darlington, and later Duke of Cleveland, who came up to Christ Church in April 1806. Never having been to a public school, he had few acquaintances at the university, and as he later expressed it, Peel took him by the hand and they lived together on terms of closest intimacy for three years. At the time of Melville's impeachment in 1806 Peel and Vane posted together in a hack chaise from Oxford to be present at the trial. With these and others he passed his lighter moments; and an anecdote of a practical joke played on an Irish and reputedly unclassical freshman, in which Peel, dressed up as the Vice-Chancellor, conducted an impromptu examination in the Greek Testament, showed a characteristic turn

[1] Henry Vane, 2nd Duke of Cleveland, speaking in the House of Lords, 4 July 1850 (*Hansard*, 3 S., 112, 865-6).
[2] George Granville Leveson Gower, and 2nd Duke of Sutherland, matric. 1803; Henry Drummond, matric. 1803, of Albury Park, Surrey, M.P. for Plympton 1810-12; Charles Chaplin, matric. 1805, of Blankney, Lincs., M.P. for Stamford 1809-12, Lincs. 1812-31; John Mills of Bisterne, Hants, matric. 1807, served with the Coldstream Guards in the Peninsular War, M.P. Rochester 1831-4; Other Archer Windsor Hickman, Earl of Plymouth, matric. 1807; all of Christ Church.

for the ludicrous which was never far from the surface in these youthful days.

In the Christ Church of Cyril Jackson, however, there was work to be done; and a careful watch was kept on the studies and progress of his fashionable young men. Peel's first tutor was Gaisford, later Professor of Greek, the best scholar, though probably not the best teacher, in the college. But from Gaisford he soon passed to Charles Lloyd, later Regius Professor of Divinity and Bishop of Oxford, an excellent tutor though inclined to be timid and irresolute in his handling of mundane affairs. Peel also went to Webber, the senior tutor, who generously gave much time to one who was not his own pupil. But his main work was with Lloyd and a close friendship developed between the two which lasted until the latter's premature death in 1829. Lloyd lectured in mathematics and theology, but his greatest gifts were displayed in his private tutoring. Like the Dean, though less formidable, he was something of a college character. His eccentric dress, his constant snuff-taking, his habit of kicking the shins and pulling the ears of his students, were oddities which apparently did nothing to detract from the affection which he inspired; and in Peel he found his most brilliant pupil.

Peel's formal reading list gives a typical picture of the Oxford education of his time. In his first year he read in Greek most of the plays of Euripides and all Herodotus; in Latin part of Livy, Horace's *Satires*, Persius, and Juvenal; and in mathematics Rowe's *Fluxions* and Robertson's *Conic Sections*. In the next (1806-7) Thucydides, Xenophon's *Hellenica*, all the tragedies of Aeschylus, and Pindar's odes; Virgil's *Georgics* and Velleius Paterculus; in mathematics Wood's *Mechanics* and some of Newton's works; and he also attended in all three terms college lectures in logic and rhetoric. Finally, in the Michaelmas and Hilary terms of 1807-8, he read Demosthenes' *Orations*, Aeschines (in connection with *De Corona*), Aristotle's *Ethics*, Aristophanes' *Acharnians*, Longinus, and four tragedies of Sophocles; in Latin Sallust and Lucretius. Noticeable in this record is the preponderance of Greek (though Plato and Homer are surprising omissions), and the relatively small number of books on mathematics and science. Nevertheless, it was a by no means contemptible syllabus and by the summer of 1808 the time was rapidly approaching when all this reading was to be tested in the examination schools. Since Peel had come to Oxford, a further change had been made in the degree statutes which went some way both to answer the critics of the 1800 regulations and to establish the degree on a recognisably modern basis. By the revised statutes of 1807 the unwieldy list of subjects was divided into two separate schools: *Literae Humaniores*, which included Greek, Latin, Logic, Rhetoric, and Moral Philosophy; and Mathematics and Physics. Two stated times for examination were appointed, the Michaelmas and Easter terms; and the successful candidates in each school were divided into first and second classes and a pass list, arranged in alphabetical order within each division. Though split into separate schools, however, the examinations took place all at one time and it was clear that a candidate who offered himself for both was in fact submitting himself to two degree examinations almost simultaneously. Not until many years after Peel had left Oxford was an interval of a fortnight mercifully interposed between the *Lit. Hum.* and Mathematical examinations. Peel made up his mind all the same to try for the double achievement.

The effort involved was a prodigious one. Most candidates, both then and later, who sat the joint examination offset its severity by concentrating, as one examiner expressed it, on winning 'classical glory' at the expense of the academically less reputable 'black arts'.[1] But Peel, as tenacious as his father and grandfather, determined to make a bid for the highest honours in both schools. The task was the greater since his mathematical knowledge was of more recent acquirement and the subject itself was not the most congenial to him. Writing to Lloyd after he had left Oxford, to assure him of his eagerness to continue their friendly intercourse, he added with some feeling, 'except as regards conic sections and matters of that kind'. In his final year he began intensive preparations for the ordeal ahead. Formal work with his tutors concluded in the Hilary term 1808. All the ensuing summer term and for five weeks after the rest of the undergraduates had gone down for the long vacation, he remained in college among his books. At the end of September he

[1] There is an interesting letter to Peel on this point written in 1826 by Cooke, who had been one of Peel's examiners in 1808, in which he refers to the mental strain on candidates attempting the double school under the old system (40342 f. 358).

was back in Christ Church again for the last term before schools. 'I doubt,' wrote his brother afterwards, 'whether anyone ever read harder than Robert for two or three terms before he passed his examination. He assured me that he had read eighteen hours in the day and night.' But he miscalculated both his physical strength and powers of mental endurance, and in consequence, for one of the few recorded occasions in his life, he momentarily lost his nerve. Before the date of the examination arrived, from lack of sleep and exercise he had brought himself to such a nervous condition that he wrote to his father to suggest that he should not go up before the examiners, as he was convinced he would achieve nothing. The old baronet, cooler and more experienced than his highly-strung son, returned him sound advice mixed with timely encouragement. Robert recovered his self-control and with it his usual sound judgement. On the day before he was due to present himself in the schools, a friend was astonished to find him nonchalantly engaged in a vigorous game of tennis.

In the event he gained a spectacular success which is recorded in a letter from George Dawson to their old Harrow tutor, Mark Drury.

*Christ Church, Oxford*                              *19 November 1808*
I hasten to have the pleasure of acquainting you with the result of our friend Peel's examination. Previous to it he could not but have been aware that the knowledge of his great abilities had excited considerable expectation not only in his own college, but through-out the whole university, and his conduct on that account was characterised with a pleasing modesty which (as it was more amiable in a man of his extraordinary talents) interested everyone more in his favour. This morning he went into the schools, and then indeed was the time in which it was to be proved whether the reputation he had acquired was exaggerated or not. Expectation was not disappointed, but rather he exceeded what even the expectation of his friends had conceived of him. The crowd that went to hear him resembled more the assembly of a public Theatre than that attend-ing a scholastic examination, and it was hard to decide which seemed the more diffident of entering upon the business, the examiners or the examined.

After having questioned him in Divinity, which is a kind of qualifier to the rest of the examination, the Masters proceeded to Aristotle. One answer was sufficient to render any further

57

disquisition unnecessary, for it embraced and anticipated whatever could afterwards follow. His flow of language and strength of reasoning clearly showed that he comprehended what he had undertaken, and Mr. Hodson, one of the examining masters, testified the same opinion by saying to him that the comprehensive and enlightened manner in which he had replied rendered but few questions from him necessary. In every other branch his excellence was the same, and what is very rare, the Examining Masters separately thanked him for the pleasure they had received. In his construing of Sophocles, Aeschylus, Pindar, and Lucretius, it seemed as if the whole assembly was actuated with one sentiment of applause.[1]

Dawson says little in his letter of the mathematical side of Peel's examination, but another and greater judge of academic performance, Dr. Gaisford, used to relate that when Peel was questioned on Robertson's *Conic Sections*, the way in which he answered called forth the admiration of all that heard him. In *Literae Humaniores* he was placed in the first class, and it was a mark of his college's predominance in those days that of the other four men in the highest class, three were also from Christ Church. In Mathematics and Physics too he was given a first class, and so became not only the one candidate in 1808 to achieve that honour but the first to be awarded the double distinction since the two schools were divided in 1807. Cleaver and Conybeare, two other Christ Church men who sat the double degree, had to be content with a second in Mathematics to accompany their first in Classics. Moreover, if we may judge from the private entry put by the Christ Church censors in their Collections book—*examinationibus publicis, in utraque serie primum sibi locum vindicavit*—Peel was the best candidate in both schools.

By contemporary standards Peel's achievement was one of unusual distinction. To compare it, however, with the later Oxford first-class degree, gained in different circumstances and under different conditions, is not easy. The mathematical school in its early days was

---

[1] 40605 f. 5, printed with minor discrepancies in *Peel*, I, 22. It long remained an Oxford tradition that in the famous passage from Lucretius beginning 'suave mari magno turbantibus aequora ventis', Peel construed 'suave' as 'it is a source of gratification'.

less developed and less formidably contested; and in the classical school it is clear that translation and construing of difficult passages played a larger, Philosophy and Ancient History a smaller part than they did later on. It is not unlikely that the early nineteenth-century degree requirements would have struck the students of Jowett's day as being wider but more superficial than their own well-regulated curriculum. There is, too, the important difference between an examination conducted orally and one, as later became the mode, principally on paper. Both had their merits but the qualities leading to distinction in each were not altogether the same. Oral examination needed a quick mind, an instantaneous memory, and a power of verbal expression. A good man would probably have got a first class under both systems, but he would have been trained in different ways.

For Peel, perhaps, the type of examination in force at that date was of more direct service for his later career than a series of purely literary exercises would have been. Even from the academic point of view the subsequent change from a single wide-ranging oral examination to a set of formal written papers was not an unmixed improvement. Long afterwards, the same Conybeare that took his degree examination with Peel, but now risen to be Dean of Llandaff, gave some interesting evidence to the University Commission of 1850 on this point. He agreed that since his day the examination system at Oxford had acquired a greater stringency from the raising of standards and the more intense competition, but he maintained that 'the earlier and more lax administration of our amended Examination Statutes' possessed virtues which had since diminished. It had provided, he thought, stimulus to general exertions without requiring men to devote their powers exclusively to 'one narrow line of academical study' and he told the commissioners that 'the student of that period . . . could in no other place have found a concentration of advantages calculated so efficiently to aid in the development of his powers as in Oxford'.[1]

For Peel in 1808, however, it was enough that he had satisfied and indeed surpassed the expectations of his friends and tutors. Pleased as he must have been with his success, he was as modest the day after his triumph in the schools as he had been before. He took his

[1] *O.U.C. Rep.*, 1852, Evidence 221.

bachelor's degree before the end of the same term and after Christmas returned to Christ Church from January to March 1809 for a final term's residence. It is conceivable that he took this opportunity to begin reading law, for later in the year he entered Lincoln's Inn. But of greater importance was the circumstance that on 5 February 1809 he came of age. For Sir Robert, to whom his son's Oxford career must have come as a crowning joy, it was a significant date, and the following month negotiations were in train to bring Robert into the House of Commons. There was a vacancy at Cashel, a corrupt Irish borough with a couple of dozen voters, where money was the best persuader. Sir Robert had no scruples on the score of expense where his brilliant son was concerned, but he did not omit to engage the additional influence of the government on his behalf. As he was a back-bencher of some importance on the ministerial side of the House, his wishes were attended to in London. Sir Arthur Wellesley, not long back from Portugal after the victory of Vimeiro and the less satisfactory Convention of Cintra, dealt with this among other tedious items of business in the Irish Office before going off to Spain the following month. The new writ for Cashel was ordered to be issued on 23 March. Two days later Wellesley wrote to Ireland conveying a brief request that Mr. Peel ('I will let you know his Christian name by express tomorrow') should be elected. 'We wish to have him returned by the meeting of Parlt. after the Recess.'[1] The transference of the Oxford double-first from the quadrangles of Christ Church to the halls of Westminster was quickly and smoothly effected. Though the Irish electors characteristically failed to obey the time-table laid down by Lt.-Gen. Wellesley, they were not far behind it. The House of Commons reassembled after Easter on 11 April. Three days later Robert Peele, as he was still spelt on the parliamentary roll, was returned for Cashel City in the county of Tipperary.

The session of 1809, in the middle of which he inconspicuously took his seat, was scarcely an edifying introduction to the political stage. The first half of it had been largely engrossed in the enquiry into the alleged sale of army patronage at the hands of Mrs. Clarke while installed as mistress of the Commander-in-Chief, the Duke of York; the last half in a consideration of charges of illegal traffic

[1] Chart, *Ireland*, p. 12; cf. *W.S.D.*, V, 619, 627.

in East India patronage which led on to a wider inquest on the use of government influence at elections. At one point a direct charge was brought against Perceval, then Chancellor of the Exchequer, and Lord Castlereagh, of corruptly employing the power of the Treasury to influence the return of members of parliament. There was much discussion of the perennial question of parliamentary reform, and Curwen brought forward a number of proposals which, though modified by the government, issued in a well-known Act against the sale of seats. Peel's own constituency of Cashel provided some of the material for the charges against the ministry, for it was alleged that the previous member, Quintin Dick, having secured his seat by government influence, had been obliged to resign in consequence of his vote against the Duke of York in the proceedings of the earlier part of the year. It was more than ordinarily prudent, therefore, in the new member to hold his peace for a season. There is no record in *Hansard* of his having spoken during the 1809 session; and though parliamentary reporting at this period is defective, it seems clear that if he opened his mouth at all, it was not to deliver a speech and anything he might have said attracted no attention. His brother in fact has recorded that he took no part in the debates of this year.

The session ended in June and the same month Peel put his name on the books of Lincoln's Inn. It was probably during this summer[1] also that he took that first holiday in the Highlands to which he referred in a speech at Glasgow many years later. Though unconnected with Scotland, and a stranger to it, he told a receptive audience in 1837, he burned with anxiety to see it. He went to Glasgow, hired a horse, and partly in the saddle and partly on foot, traversed the greater part of the wild countryside south of Inverness. His chief desire no doubt was to see an unfamiliar part of the British Isles and to relax in solitude after a singularly strenuous eighteen

---

[1] Parker (*Peel*, I, 24), taking literally a casual phrase by Peel that he went to Scotland the moment his education was completed, infers that the trip was made immediately after he took his degree in November 1808. But it is clear from the Christ Church battels that he was at Oxford up to 15 December 1808 and again after Christmas from 23 January to 25 March. The interval between the two terms seems an improbable season of the year for a ramble on foot in the Highlands; and even the early part of April when he was again free would scarcely be a suitable time for the journey Peel undertook.

months. The form of holiday was, however, characteristic. Through-out his life he showed an affection for natural scenes, exercise in the open air, and the peace of the countryside, which must have an-swered some essential need in his temperament. The magnificent scenery of the Scottish Highlands and the patriarchal courtesy of its inhabitants impressed him deeply and this was to be the first of many journeys across the border. In 1809, however, there must have been an irrecoverable quality in his Scottish travels. It was a halcyon period in his life; twenty-one, personable and vigorous, heir to a baronetcy and a fortune, he had achieved all his boyhood and student objectives. He had few ties, and fewer responsibilities; and the future stretched before him, clear, pleasant, and empty.

Returning to London in November he took chambers in Lincoln's Inn, and there with his own servant in attendance, settled down to read some law. The first letter from his father that has been pre-served, written at Drayton on 13 November 1809, reached him shortly after his arrival.

> It will afford me much pleasure to hear from you that you have been introduced to your new society, and that you have a prospect of having rooms to your satisfaction. You are engaging in a pro-fession that will render your attainments at school and college of much use, and if I mistake not, the study of the law will not be found very difficult. You have hitherto afforded me unspeakable pleasure in the manner you have conducted yourself, and I have no fears for the future. Your good sense will convince you of the importance of being distinguished amongst those with whom you live and study, and that by reading men and books you will not fail to rise to eminence in the profession of the law.... believe me,
>
> Yours affectionately,
> ROBERT PEEL[1]

The letter clearly indicated an assumption on the father's part that he was going to make a profession of the law; but whether at this date Peel was still hesitating between politics and the bar is not known. The combination of the two professions has never been an uncommon one in parliamentary history. Training in the one leads

---

[1] 40605 f. 7, printed with minor omissions *Peel*, I, 24.

to a certain dexterity in the other; and political patronage is often a shorter ladder to legal success than forensic specialisation. It is less common, however, for a politician to turn to law after he has secured his seat in parliament. At this period, moreover, a term or two in chambers at one of the Inns of Court was regarded as a useful, almost a conventional part of a young man's education. Yet the precise phrasing of the letter cannot be overlooked and the calmness with which Sir Robert discussed the prospect of a legal career discounts the legend of the single-minded and undeviating training of his eldest son from earliest years for high political office. What is equally significant perhaps is that there was never any sign in Sir Robert of a desire that his sons should carry on the family tradition of industry and trade. Robert's choice of career in 1809 was merely setting the pattern for the rest of the family. Of the five other brothers William in due course was to try his hand at law and politics; John entered the Church; Jonathan was unpropitiously gazetted as a 2nd lieutenant three days before Waterloo. Three of them married into the aristocracy; the other two into the old Staffordshire family of Swinfen. Lawrence, the least distinguished of them, made the grandest matrimonial alliance of all by his marriage with a daughter of the Duke of Richmond. Edmund, the only one of Sir Robert's sons who showed any taste for a business career, came to his ownership of mills at Fazeley and chairmanship of the Trent Valley railway company after holding a junior commission in the navy, marriage with Emily Swinfen, and the establishment of his home at Bonehill. For all six the paternal fortune was munificent enough to set them up as independent gentlemen on their own property even if they had little inclination or found few openings for advancement in professional life. The girls, too, reflected the changed social status which their father had given his family. One married a clergyman, another a politician and landowner, and a third, the eldest son of a peer. For the family as a whole the decisive move to a Staffordshire manor house at the end of the eighteenth century had brought an entry into a new circle of English society. Robert, poised at the start of his career between politics and the bar, symbolised in his own person the family revolution which his father had achieved.

How much legal knowledge he acquired at this time is doubtful.

In later life he was always prompt to disclaim any special acquaintance with the law, and was careful to consult and give credit to his legal advisers on all technical matters. Yet some law books at any rate he probably read through, and his brief contact with life in chambers perhaps made it easy for him subsequently to understand legal problems and the legal point of view. That same summer and autumn, however, even possibly while he was traversing the mountains and glens of Badenoch with his hired horse, events were taking place in the higher circles of parliamentary life which in their final repercussions were to launch him irretrievably into a political career.

# POLITICAL OVERTURE

The death of Pitt in 1806 had left the country leaderless at the height of the war against the most redoubtable opponent in its history; and there was no obvious successor. Apart from the small rump of the historic whig clan—Fox, Grey, Tierney, Sheridan, and their few supporters—nearly all the leading politicians had been at one time or another followers or associates of the dead statesman, and his departure from the scene left a group of rival claimants to supreme office. Meanwhile the war had to be fought and all responsible sections of British society concurred in thinking that it must be fought to a finish. Yet for fifteen years their military leaders had been unable to devise any successful strategy against the Napoleonic empire. It was true that the Spanish revolt in 1808 had opened for the first time a breach in the European fortress. But the Convention of Cintra in the summer of 1808 and the evacuation of Moore's army from Corunna the following December gave no encouragement for a major effort in the peninsula. Even though Wellesley again beat the French at Talavera the next year, his subsequent retreat to the shelter of Portugal appeared to conform to a pattern with which the British public was dishearteningly familiar. It was natural that many people, from feelings that did not solely spring from a desire to embarrass the government, saw in the Spanish expedition a wasteful and useless dissipation of resources. The ministry itself, by parallel efforts against Naples and Walcheren, showed an apparent inability to frame any master-plan; and the ignominious failure of the Walcheren expeditionary force, thrown on the Belgian coast to die of malaria after the Austrian campaign was already decided at Wagram, left little confidence in the military conduct of the war among the public at large.

At home the war of faction continued. The Grenville ministry which took office after Pitt's death was mainly composed of a coalition of Grenville and Foxite groups. As such it represented the closest approximation to a purely whig ministry that the country had seen since 1783 or was to see again until 1830. It fell in March 1807, having quarrelled with the king on a question of Catholic disabilities. The Portland administration which followed effected a complete cabinet reconstruction. With Perceval (Chancellor of the Exchequer and leader of the House of Commons), Canning (Foreign Office), Hawkesbury (Home Department), Castlereagh (War), and in addition Eldon, Camden, Westmorland, Mulgrave, Bathurst, and Dundas, it exhibited a combination of Pittites of all shades and origins which was ultimately to secure a domination in British politics for the next twenty years. The opposition to it was negligible. Fox was dead; Grenville was aloof; Grey had gone to the House of Lords; and Sidmouth was reluctant to lend himself to any systematic hostility. The issue on which the government had taken office was a popular one, and a premature dissolution (something of a novelty at that period), followed by a general election in which the old *No Popery* cry was raised, returned a sympathetic House of Commons. In a full House the government enjoyed a majority of nearly two hundred over their opponents. As it appeared at the beginning of the session in which Peel entered Parliament, it was the strongest ministry since 1800; but there were weaknesses within. It lacked effective leadership; it was seriously divided by recent animosities; and the strain of war was soon to foment new rivalries and criticisms within the cabinet as well as without. The Duke of Portland, over seventy and suffering from the painful malady of the stone, was unlikely to hold his office long; and the more ambitious politicians were already aiming in private at the reversionary interest.

Continued lack of success in the war, and the embarrassments to which the government was exposed by the domestic events of the 1809 session, put an intolerable strain on the ill-knit ministry. The discontent started with Canning. The last and most brilliant pupil of Pitt, spoiled perhaps by the partiality of his mentor and regarding himself as the peculiar heir to the Pitt tradition, he had already served his apprenticeship in subordinate office and would probably have attained cabinet rank in 1806 had Pitt survived. His oratory was outstanding in an age still familiar with the formal eloquence of eighteenth-century debate; his talents were respected; and his wit feared. There was no office of state to which he might not in time aspire, but time was an element of which he was impatient. As early as the spring of 1809 Canning had made up his mind that there must be changes in the direction of the war and had taken steps to secure Castlereagh's removal. In the course of the summer Portland's illness and the failure of the Walcheren expedition brought the ministry to the ground. Castlereagh and Canning both resigned and the two Secretaries fought a duel on Putney Heath. Canning's conduct in the Castlereagh affair, savouring as much of intrigue as of public principle, laid on him an odium beyond anything perhaps which he had justly incurred. His immediate hope of gaining the premiership vanished; and for the rest of his career a cloud of distrust surrounded his name. The old king, now over seventy and almost blind, chose Perceval as his new chief minister and though the weakened cabinet failed to secure the services of Grenville and Grey, and were unwilling to admit Sidmouth, sufficient reinforcements were obtained elsewhere to ensure the continuance of the king's government. The Marquess Wellesley, an errant and incalculable figure since his return from India, was brought back from his diplomatic post in Spain to take the Foreign Office. Young Palmerston came in as Secretary at War, a junior administrative post. Hawkesbury, now Lord Liverpool, transferred from the Home Department to War and Colonies in succession to Castlereagh. Ryder took the Home Department, and Dundas, the son of Lord Melville, became president of the Board of Control. The Prime Minister himself, for want of a suitable substitute, retained his former post of Chancellor of the Exchequer. It was not an impressive array of talent, but as he told Ward in November, being abandoned by so many of the old connection, the government was obliged to obtain assistance in new quarters and by bringing forward young men who from their character and respectability had created expectations.[1]

[1] *Ward Memoirs*, I, 291.

## II

The 1810 session of parliament opened on 23 January, when the king's speech was read. To move and second the reply in the House of Commons the Prime Minister selected two younger members, Viscount Bernard and Robert Peel, aged twenty-four and twenty-two respectively. For backbenchers such an invitation was in the nature of a mild compliment, and some thought was bestowed by the minister and his Chief Whip on a suitable choice. It was custom-ary to divide the honours between a county and a borough member, and if possible to find representatives of different interests on the government side of the House. They were not expected to say much, and the main lines of their speeches were usually indicated to them. Acceptance of the invitation, however, was a clear token of political allegiance; and this, at the start of a session which no one could be sure that the ministry would survive, argued that the younger Peel had made up his mind. His father was paternally pleased and wrote in gratified terms to thank Perceval for the distinction bestowed on his family. 'If,' he concluded, 'he has the good fortune to be hon-oured with your confidence, I flatter myself he will be found deserv-ing of the trust reposed in him. He possesses capacity, industry, and virtuous habits; and under the guidance of a judicious and well-informed friend, he may become a useful member of society.'[1] If flattering, the choice was not surprising. Perceval himself was a Harrovian, and his greatest ally in the cabinet, Lord Liverpool, had been at Christ Church. In debating talent the ministry was lament-ably weak in the House of Commons. Besides Perceval, the only cabinet members in the lower House were Ryder and Dundas, later joined by Yorke, none of them outstanding speakers. The party, as Palmerston observed, was ill off for second-rates, and it was only prudent leadership to draw out any political talent among the new members.

Bernard, also making his maiden speech, made no impression on his audience. Peel, by contrast, had an undoubted success. Speaking with youthful fire and eloquence, and some occasional neat if latinised antitheses, he defended the government's conduct of the

[1] Walpole, *Perceval*, II, 58 n.

war, justified the purpose if not the outcome of the expedition to the Scheldt, and looked hopefully to the future of Lord Wellesley's army in Spain. Then, turning to the difficulties with America, he referred (a touch of his father perhaps) to the buoyancy of British commerce in finding new markets when old ones were blocked by war, and urged a unanimous and effectual resistance to the tyranny of Bonaparte. He was on his feet for forty minutes without showing any sign of nerves, and when he sat down he received a general acclamation. Up in the crowded galleries were his father, his brother William, and his old Bury tutor, the Rev. J. Hargreaves. Sir Robert Peel had taken a place facing his son across the packed house, and as the cheers rang out, tears rolled down his cheeks. Afterwards he wrote to friends with pride to say that the Speaker and the leading men on both sides had assured him that Robert's was the best first speech since Pitt's.

> I have been congratulated by members alike entertaining different political opinions, as he said nothing which could give offence. He has already raised himself a character which in future may be highly useful to him, if his health is preserved, and he should feel attached to the study of politics.

Old Cyril Jackson, now retired from his Christ Church deanery, wrote benignly to say that he was very pleased, more than he thought he could have been with anything of that sort,—'and if I had you here I would feed you with ling and cranberry tart'. In default of that delicacy he urged Peel to give a last high polish to his mind by a continual study of Homer.

Other more detached critics were only a degree less encomiastic. William Lamb (the future Lord Melbourne), who himself made what he characteristically dismissed as a 'bothering bungling speech at a bad moment' in the course of the debate, told his Caroline that 'Lord Bandon[1] moved the Address in the House of Commons, miserably; Mr. Peele seconded it fluently and in a good manner, but with poor argument'.[2] Creevey, another opposition whig, recorded that Peel 'made a capital figure for a first speech. I think it

---

[1] This was really his father's title.
[2] *Lady Bessborough and Her . . . Circle*, ed. Earl of Bessborough (1940), p. 202.

was a *prepared* speech, but it was a most produceable *Pittish* performance, both in matter and manner.'[1] Creevey's surmise was correct,
though it would have been very remarkable in such circumstances
had it not been a prepared speech. Robert told his brother some years
later that he had written down every word he meant to say; and
William Peel retained in later life the copy of the speech in his
brother's writing.

But despite the flutter of pride in the Peels' circle, the ministry
still had most of its difficulties in front of it. As it moved out into
the full tide of the parliamentary session, it encountered the mounting weight of the opposition gale. An amendment to the address,
censuring the general conduct of military operations the previous
year, was defeated with ease. But on more detailed issues not
directly affecting the fate of the government, it was increasingly
hard to find a majority. A motion of enquiry into the Walcheren
expedition was carried against the ministers by nine votes; and the
independent temper of the House which had been so noticeable
the preceding session was again exhibited in the refusal to accept
ministerial nominations to the Finance Committee. The Walcheren
enquiry itself added fresh inflammatory matter to debate. In the
course of the investigations a letter was produced which had been
sent by Lord Chatham to the king without passing through ministerial hands, giving a narrative of the campaign and largely placing
the blame for its failure on the naval commander, Sir Richard
Strachan. The opposition speakers severely condemned this letter;
a motion of censure was successfully moved in the House of Commons; and Chatham consequently resigned his place as Master-
General of the Ordnance. The speculation now was when rather
than whether Perceval would resign, and the opposition moved in
for the *coup de grâce*. At the close of the enquiry Lord Porchester
brought forward a series of detailed resolutions, ending with one of
severe censure on the ministers. A long debate followed, which
beginning on 26 March, and successively adjourned, lasted until the
31st. Castlereagh, Canning, and Perceval all spoke; and though
there could have been little certainty on either side until the very
end, the government triumphed in the division. Porchester's
resolutions were negatived by a majority of forty-eight, a result

[1] *Creevey Papers*, p. 122.

attributed as much to the cogency of the arguments against them as to the strength of actual ministerial influence; though the fact that a defeat could scarcely have failed to bring down the government was probably an additional motive.

On the fourth night of the debate, Friday 30 March, Peel spoke on the government side. His speech was brief and inevitably lacked the interest of a maiden effort. Indeed, a second speech, following an opening success, is not an easy undertaking. But with less conscious oratory his arguments were more incisive. He said he was persuaded by the evidence before the House that the expedition had been undertaken with a fair prospect of success. It had been not merely proper but almost obligatory for the ministry to make some endeavour to assist Austria in her renewed bid for independence; and no better target for our operations could have been found than the great naval port and arsenals of the Scheldt. All this was good sense, and he wisely refrained from entering on any discussion of the military reasons for the failure of the expedition. The speech was well received, and one of Cyril Jackson's many correspondents was kind enough to tell him that Peel had even surpassed his previous performance. The old Dean concluded therefore that Peel had been reading Homer and wrote to offer another instalment of practical advice.

> Work very hard and unremittingly. Work, as I used to say sometimes, like a tiger, or like a dragon, if dragons work more and harder than tigers. Don't be afraid of killing yourself. Only retain, which is essential, your former temperance and exercise, and your aversion to mere lounge, and then you will have abundant time both for hard work and company, which last is as necessary to your future situation as even the hard work I speak of, and as much is to be got from it. . . . I trust and hope you will not be tempted to take employment too early, nor any, at any time, but what is really efficient and of high consideration. Therefore wait till the time for that is come.

The time in fact was drawing closer than either of them could have realised; but Jackson clearly assumed that Peel would be ready to take office under Perceval if he were asked.

The assumption was perhaps self-evident. It is true that in his first year in Parliament Peel displayed certain manifestations of independent thought which were noted by older members on the watch for coming young men. But it is questionable whether he ever went beyond the normal freedom exercised by a private member. Creevey, for example, noted with satisfaction that in the selection of the Finance Committee in January 1810 he cast a vote against one of the government candidates.[1] A few weeks later in the Burdett case occurred another small incident which showed that he was far from being a government hack. Burdett had been committed to the Tower for his part in a public controversy over the action of the House in enforcing the standing order against strangers during the enquiry into the Scheldt expedition. The Prime Minister had taken the lead in insisting on summary action against Burdett, but it was probable that not all his supporters shared his views. Canning, though he had spoken in defence of the government on the Scheldt enquiry, was equally critical. Writing to his wife a few days later he told her that

> I found many of those who were voting, decidedly of the same opinion, and wishing that I had taken a line against Govt. which they could have followed. Peele, whom I told you I hoped to seduce, was one—who told me that he would have gone with me, and would *not* have voted *with* Govt., if *I* had not.[2]

But the mere fact that Canning could talk in terms of seduction showed that Peel was counted already on the government side; and if without Canning's authority to shield him he refused to vote against the ministers, it was a clear indication that he did not want to be identified with the whigs of the Sheridan, Folkestone, and Romilly school. At the same time it would be dangerous to read too much in Canning's casual words to his wife. There is no version on Peel's side of what was said and he made no recorded intervention in the debate. But in May the Lord Mayor and Aldermen of London delivered a petition in which they protested in strong and indeed half-insolent language against the committal of

[1] *Creevey Papers*, p. 126.
[2] I am indebted for this reference (from the Canning Papers, dated 7 April 1810) to Professor Aspinall.

Burdett, and seized the opportunity to descant on the question of parliamentary reform, the charges of electoral corruption against Perceval and Castlereagh, and the Walcheren expedition. In the ensuing debate Peel made a brief but spirited speech, in which he asked pertinently whether the parliamentary supporters of the petition who condoned its phraseology thought there were any terms strong enough to justify the House in rejecting a petition. He thought that such papers should at least have the merit of decency; the worst way to avoid insult was to acquiesce in it.[1] There was little disposition evinced here to compromise, and Perceval must have approved of every word he uttered.

It is not easy to imagine in fact that Peel could have entertained any sympathy for the small and isolated group of Foxite whigs. One of the distinguishing features of their conduct in the 1809 and 1810 sessions was their opposition to the war policy of the government, including even the choice of Commander-in-Chief for Spain. It would be facile, in the light of its ultimate success, to condemn the opposition whigs out of hand for their criticism of the Peninsular campaign. But the personal attacks on the soldier in charge of that campaign were spiteful and ungrounded; and while they blackened his professional reputation, they offered no constructive alternative to what the government were trying to accomplish. So bitter and indecent indeed were their criticisms of Wellington that their own supporters sometimes shrank from giving them parliamentary approval; and with the ineffectual Ponsonby in charge of the squad in the House of Commons, they lacked any wise or even temperate control. Opposition in wartime is never an easy business, but at the period when Peel entered parliament, the whigs were in one of their least inviting attitudes, factious in their public utterances, divided and quarrelsome within. For Peel on the other hand, as for most of the British public, the paramount political object was the war; and it can scarcely be a coincidence that the refrain in both of his first two speeches was the need for national unity in a vigorous prosecution of the struggle against Napoleon.

From the start, therefore, Peel was a government man. His training and family life had given his mind a colour and bias even

[1] Cobbett's *Debates*, XVI, 935 (9 May 1810).

before he entered politics. The tradition of his father and grand-father was that of middle-class Pittite toryism: not an inflexible and doctrinaire resistance to change but a desire for legality and order, for evolutionary and peaceful progression, combined with a respect for established institutions and an old-fashioned evangelical Protestantism not far removed from that of Wilberforce or Perceval. It is unlikely that Harrow or Christ Church had done anything to weaken this emotional and intellectual framework. When as a young M.P. Peel visited the more liberal-minded household of his uncle Joseph in London, this fact was recognised and deplored. After one conversa-tion with his nephew in which Peel, with a detachment rare among Englishmen at that date, had praised Napoleon's military and administrative genius, Joseph Peel observed with a sigh that he wished 'Robert were as liberal in his home as in his foreign politics'.[1] To the whig satirists he seemed for many years no more than a new chip off the old block.

> What is young Peel made of, made of,
> What is young Peel made of?
> Ginger hair,
> And Sir Robert's stare,
> Such is young Peel made of.

What he would be in future depended on time, events, and his own character; but in 1810 there was little doubt where his allegiance lay.

### III

In the cabinet reconstruction of 1809 Lord Liverpool had taken over the Department of War and Colonies vacated by Castlereagh. As one of his Under-Secretaries he brought with him from the Home Department his brother Cecil Jenkinson. After less than a year in the new office, however, Jenkinson resigned. Lord Liverpool thereupon offered the post to the young member from his own college who had made so promising a debut in the House of Com-mons at the beginning of the year; and Peel accepted.

[1] Peel, *Life*, pp. 61-2.

Whether the post came up to Dean Jackson's notion of what was efficient and of high consideration, there was no doubt that Sir Robert was delighted. He hastened to convey the sentiments appropriate to the occasion in his best copy-book style.

> *16 Upper Grosvenor Street*             *1 June 1810*
> MY LORD,
>
> Permit me to express my high satisfaction and warm acknowledgements for the honour you have conferred on my son by placing him in a situation in your Lordship's own department in the government. From a knowledge of his virtues and prudence I may be allowed to indulge a hope that he will be found to merit your confidence and patronage and that he will have the good fortune to secure your friendship. I have the honour to be with sentiments of high respect,
>
>                        Your Lordship's faithful servant,
>                                  ROBERT PEEL[1]

When he heard the news of his grandson's entry to office, old William Yates marked the event with the thrifty present of a brace of 'moor-game' and a congratulatory letter. Robert's reply on 18 August from Downing Street, the earliest surviving letter of a career that was to be full of letters, still showed something of the round, unhurried, and unpractised hand of a schoolboy. He spoke regretfully of not being able to accompany Colonel Yates to shoot on Church Moor, promised sport for them both at Drayton in September, and told his grandfather that 'your simple assurance that anything I have done gives you pleasure and satisfaction is the dearest and proudest reward I can receive'.[2] Meanwhile, on 14 June, exactly a week before the end of the session, he had signed his first official letter. He was then a few months past his twenty-second birthday and it was just fourteen months since he had been returned as member for Cashel.

As an introduction to administration the post in which he found

[1] 38571 f. 146.
[2] Original in Peel MSS., printed Peel, *Letters*, p. 14.
Colonel Jonathan Yates was Peel's uncle. His promotion to Lt.-Col. had just taken place (19 July 1810) and in 1813 he received command of the 49th (Princess Charlotte of Wales's) Foot with whom he saw service in Canada during the American War.

himself was not without its salutary aspects. It involved much writing and even more reading of formal correspondence. Most of the work was routine and detailed, requiring neither urgency in its performance nor responsibility for its policy. It had little in the way of heroics and it was of a highly miscellaneous nature. Nevertheless, it placed him, however junior and unimportant, in the centre of things. He was working under the eye of a cabinet minister; and occasionally he came into momentary touch with the great happenings in Europe. Liverpool himself, as was proper, devoted himself almost entirely to the military side of his department and himself conducted the major correspondence between the office and the Commander-in-Chief in Spain. The other Under-Secretary, Colonel Bunbury, handled the routine military matters, while to Peel was delegated the colonial side of the business,—'an ample field . . .,' as he later wrote, 'extending from Botany Bay to Prince Edward Island'[1]—together with the administration of the secret service money. Most of his work was unexciting, though Liverpool noted the manner in which his fledgling junior dealt with it and made his own estimate of his ability. Indeed an even more authoritative eye may occasionally have perused some of Peel's early official compositions. There was a family story that one of his letters was laid before the old king, who was pleased to pass a commendation on its businesslike style: a compliment which his secretary, Sir Herbert Taylor, goodnaturedly took the trouble to pass on to Sir Robert. But not much of his correspondence would have ascended to this august level. Pay, establishments, disbursements on civil and military accounts; correspondence with the Home Department on convict transportations or with the Treasury on certification of financial requisitions made by colonial authorities; questions of sea transport; provision of wine, medical, and other stores; pensions for colonial civil servants; recruitment of native regiments in the West Indies—these made up his daily diet. Occasionally an exotic item momentarily relieved the formality of statement and returns. In October 1810 he was writing about a feathered cloak sent to George III by the king of the Sandwich Islands and in the summer of the following year was engaged in making up a reciprocal presentation composed of flag bunting, hatchets, saws, nails, a new red coat and uniform

[1] Goulburn, II/13 (12 August 1812).

complete, a gold-laced cocked hat and feathers, and '2 speaking trumpets handsomely ornamented'. There was much correspondence about a certain Captain Bligh and the recent mutiny against him when Governor of New South Wales; and there was an awkward business of a British naval officer who had eloped with a girl from Heligoland; while all through the despatches and letter-books recurred the names of those far-flung places he had never seen, and never would see—Simonstown, Goree, Sierra Leone, Cape of Good Hope, Van Diemen's Land, Mauritius, Newfoundland, and Senegal.

As the junior of the two Under-Secretaries, he was left in charge of the office over Christmas 1810 but the following summer he enjoyed a generous leave, some six weeks from the end of August to mid-October. When his colleague Bunbury was similarly away on holiday, Peel took over his work and was able to imbibe a few draughts of a more military atmosphere than that which surrounded his normal correspondence. In the late autumn of 1810 he was dealing with transports for Gibraltar, equipment of Portuguese troops, and captured French artillery. During Bunbury's leave the succeeding summer, Peel was called upon to handle the details of transport for general officers, the supply of horses from America for the army of the Peninsula, a charger for General Picton, and the assignment of a Captain Johnson to run a cargo of swords, pistols, and muskets to the insurgents in Galicia.[1] Even apart from these periodic forays into military administration, however, the atmosphere of the department could scarcely have been other than warlike. Peel had access to the correspondence between Lord Liverpool and Wellington; and much of the conversation between the minister and his juniors must have revolved round the progress of the war over which their department was presiding. Moreover, the war at long last was going well. Masséna, pushing slowly into Portugal with an army treble that of Wellington's small expeditionary force, was sharply checked at Busaco in September 1810 and brought to a halt before the lines of Torres Vedras at the beginning of winter. Next summer Portugal was almost cleared of the enemy, and though Fuentes d'Onoro and Albuera were not among the more

[1] For Peel's work at War and Colonies see C.O. 324/132, 324/134; W.O. 6/29-30, 6/50, 6/122-3.

classic British victories of the war, Masséna was recalled and the French could do no more than cling to their last defences along the frontier. When the 1811 campaign ended, the British army not only was still in being but had thrown back the first major effort that Napoleon had organised against it. It was the first pale and uncertain dawn of success.

Part at least of the credit for the defence of Portugal was due to Wellington's skill in mobilising, arming, and disciplining the Portuguese troops into an effective force equal in size to his own expeditionary army. It was a policy that despite parliamentary obstruction at home had the support of the government, and on 18 March 1811 Perceval proposed an additional grant of two million pounds to meet the cost of these invaluable auxiliaries. The opposition, headed by Ponsonby, professed to see no end to these experiments and extravagancies on the part of the government; and in the debate which ensued Fremantle, an inveterate and violent opponent of the war in the Peninsula, delivered a powerful speech to prove the impossibility of making any headway in Spain where Napoleon would always be able to bring superior forces to bear against the British army. Peel, the only representative of his department in the Commons, answered him in a speech that compelled the admiration even of his adversaries. He pointed to the success already achieved by the Portuguese in British pay; criticised the inconsistency of the opposition in denouncing the government first for dispersing and then for concentrating their military resources; and argued the peculiar advantages of the Peninsula where one-sixth of the total British forces could hold in check one-half of Napoleon's disposable strength. Then, turning to the personal critics of Wellington, he offered a warm defence of his cautious and defensive tactics, and of the talents he had already demonstrated in his conduct of the campaign.

> Perhaps at this very hour, while they were deliberating on the vote which they should give, Lord Wellington might be preparing for action tomorrow; and when he reflected on the venal abuse which had been disseminated against that illustrious character, he felt a hope that if a momentary irritation should ruffle his temper on seeing those malicious effusions, he would console himself by the general feeling which existed in his favour. . . . He cherished the

sanguine expectation that the day would soon arrive, when another transcendent victory would silence the tongue of envy, and the cavils of party animosity.

The motion was carried by an overwhelming majority, and the government supporters were delighted—not least by the showing of their young official man. Plumer Ward, after describing Fremantle's speech, added happily that

> he was answered and pulled to pieces in one of the most beautiful as well as argumentive speeches ever delivered in the House, by young Peel; who gave another proof that there was ability on our side of the House. He was applauded almost as much by opposition as by us at the end of his speech, and by Whitbread not least. As to argument, he put the whole matter at rest.[1]

Peel in fact was already achieving the distinction, not always an easy one to live up to, of being a coming man; and Plumer Ward was not the only one to think so. Dining a few days later in whig company at Lord Tankerville's, he recorded that 'they talked of the rising generation, and seemed disposed to allow, what Tierney once allowed to me before, that we had the best in Peel, and they the second best in J. Ward, of all the young men'.[2] It was probably not altogether in his disfavour that Peel was sometimes to be found elsewhere than in his office in Downing Street or on the benches of the House. He was completely independent now, and he was taking Jackson's advice to find time for company as well as work. Not only did he have an official post under government, but even an address of his own. When he entered the Department of War and Colonies, Lord Liverpool gave him a small house for his own use. Though serving as a detached dwelling, it was part of Fife House, Liverpool's town residence, which stood near the river, north of Whitehall Stairs. Peel's house had its own entrance in Little Scotland Yard.[3] He furnished it himself at considerable expense, according to his brother, and frequently entertained there. Sometimes his visitors were old college friends such as John Mills, now in the Coldstream

---

[1] *Ward Memoirs*, I, 406-7.     [2] *ibid.*, p. 408.
[3] 11 Little Scotland Yard according to *A Biographical List of the House of Commons* (1812). The site is now covered by the War Office.

Guards; more often little coteries of other young politicians on the government side—Croker, Goulburn, Vesey Fitzgerald, Lord Desart, Manners Sutton, and Palmerston, whose conversation was exclusively professional; while William Peel used the house almost as his own whenever he was in town during these years.

It was at this period rather than at school or university that Peel's closest friendships were formed; and his two greatest intimates— Goulburn and Croker—were neither of them Oxonians. They formed a curiously contrasting pair. Henry Goulburn, the descendant of a Jamaica family, was a Cambridge man who had settled at Betchworth in Surrey and entered parliament as member for Horsham in 1808. Though four years senior to Peel he soon became his devoted friend and their careers and opinions were thereafter almost inseparable. Quiet, solid, completely honest, and unswervingly loyal, he was the perfect foil to his more nervous and brilliant companion. John Wilson Croker, on the other hand, came of an Anglo-Irish family long settled in Co. Waterford. His father had made a successful career in the Irish Customs service and after taking his degree at Trinity College, Dublin, Croker launched first into literature and the law, and then into politics. In a second attempt he was returned for Downpatrick in 1807, and at the age of twenty-seven took his seat on the government side under Perceval. His talents were perhaps literary rather than political; he could write well, and had a wide knowledge of many things and even wider curiosity. In politics he tended to prefer the confidences and friendships of the great to the personal responsibilities of high office; though there was a hard polemical side to his nature that made him on occasion a pertinacious and formidable debater. He was a supporter of Catholic emancipation, something of a Canningite, and that circumstance—together with his own restless, pushing temperament—made some members of the government regard him with a degree of distrust. For Peel he early conceived a demonstrative affection; for many years they lived on terms of close friendship and when in 1817 the Crokers had their first and eagerly desired child, Peel became his godfather.

Besides these early personal acquaintanceships, Peel was also beginning to be known in a wider society. Plumer Ward met him on several occasions between 1810 and 1812, usually in company with other junior politicians and sometimes with his father.[1] In February 1811 he was at a dinner party at the Prime Minister's where the company, which included the Perceval ladies, told ghost stories till midnight. He also joined his first London club, the Alfred in Albemarle Street, which had been founded only a year or two previously. It was sober and literary rather than fashionable, with perhaps more than the usual complement of club bores, but he was able to meet Byron, Ward, and other agreeable acquaintances there; and even the fastidious Byron admitted that it was 'upon the whole, a decent resource in a rainy day, in a dearth of parties, or parliament, or in an empty season'.[2] In these early London days the younger Peel presented to the outward observer an enviable combination of good looks, good clothes, wealth, and talent. According to his cousin Lawrence, who saw perhaps more of him at this time than ever before or after, he was still very much the Oxonian in society, attentive to dress and following the fashion. It was still modish to wear powder at dinner or in the evening, and this custom, which concealed the reddish colour of his hair and suited his complexion, became him very well. With good features, a pleasant smile, a well-formed head, and a countenance which when animated took on a certain fire and expressiveness, he was an extremely presentable person, even though overshadowed in point of looks by his brother William, a tall and at this date unusually handsome man. To these physical graces were added a lively conversation, a sense of fun, a keen eye for absurdities and a quiet, slightly malicious, relish in exposing them, though the last was a propensity which he reserved for his more intimate acquaintances. In society where he felt at home, he was an amusing and intelligent companion, and to his relatives in Joseph Peel's house he appeared uniformly frank, unreserved, and kind.[3] The formidable Miss Berry, who in her sixtieth year was past the impressionable age, allowed him a line of approval in her journal. 'Sunday, 3 May 1812. Dined at Mr. Montague's with Lord and Lady Hardwicke, and Lady Elizabeth, Lord and Lady Elliott, etc., and Mr. Peel. The latter, he who spoke so well in the House of Commons, has a very agreeable countenance.'[4] This,

---

[1] Ward Memoirs, I, 340, 392, 429, 439, 476.
[2] Moore, Byron, p. 303.     [3] Peel, Life, pp. 60-1.
[4] Journals . . . of Miss Berry, ed. Lady Theresa Lewis (1865), II, 497.

from one who had been an intimate of Horace Walpole and a friend of Mme. de Staël, was an undoubted compliment.

But while Peel, socially and officially, was making an auspicious beginning to a career, the ministry which he served was encountering difficulties which threatened to bring it to an early close. Perceval could have been excused for thinking it a peculiar malevolence of fate that, at the moment when the war for the first time was going well, disaster struck the government in another quarter. Towards the end of October 1810, as a result of the illness and subsequent death of Princess Amelia, his youngest and favourite daughter, the king's mind again gave way. After several adjournments of parliament, it became clear that legislation would be necessary and at the end of December Perceval brought in proposals for a Regency based on provisions made in similar circumstances during Pitt's ministry in 1788-9. The proposals were unpopular with the royal princes and with the opposition, since they denied to the Prince of Wales any automatic right of Regency and enabled restrictions to be imposed on him which temporarily at least would make it difficult to effect a major change of government. Perceval, however, showed his usual pluck and tenacity in pushing the measure through; and though the government majorities wavered at times, the Regency Act was finally passed according to the Pittite formula in February 1811. Nevertheless, the real Regency crisis was only thereby postponed. The restrictions on the Regent's use of the royal prerogative expired in February 1812. If the king had not by that time recovered, it was obvious that a new political situation would have to be faced in which the place of George III in the constitution would be filled by another and very different man. All that the Regency Act had secured for Perceval's ministry was a respite for twelve months; only the king's recovery could grant a reprieve. As the session of 1811 wore on, it seemed increasingly certain that this was not going to happen; and various forces in the fluid political field began to shift their direction accordingly.

In the complicated story of negotiations and intrigue which filled cabinet politics for the next two years, there were two simple issues. One was political, the other religious; and it was almost unavoidable that they should emerge at this time. Old and infirm as George III had been at the date of his final insanity, he had done two things.

He had given his confidence and support to a particular set of ministers, and he had secured a policy of uncompromising Protestantism. With his withdrawal from the political world, both these questions were in doubt once more; and men turned their faces to the newly risen luminary for guidance. The Prince Regent, however, was in no haste to expose his intentions; but it was generally assumed that once the period of restrictions expired, changes in the ministry would take place. In his youth, after the fashion of Hanoverian princes, he had put himself at the head of an opposition party; and though his boon-companion Fox was no more, it was not unreasonable that the band of Foxite whigs entertained hopes of entering the promised land after their long sojourn in the wilderness. That in itself was enough to shake the position of the ministry. Unable to reinforce itself to any notable extent after the disruption of 1809, it now had the prospect of reconstruction if not dismissal in 1812; and the more prudential politicians might well be tempted during the interval to make timely provision for that event. But there was also a principle in the Regency crisis which touched profounder depths. The end, for political purposes, of the reign of George III, and the coming to power of a successor identified with Foxite liberalism, put the question of Catholic emancipation on a new and hopeful footing. The agitation in Ireland took on a sudden and alarming activity, and it seemed clear that the cabinet would have to formulate some definite policy on the issue. There were discussions between Dublin and London in the winter of 1811-12, and in an important memorandum drawn up by Pole, the Chief Secretary, in December 1811 it was laid down as an axiom that the Prince Regent ought to come to a settled and personal decision over emancipation and convey it to the public in some suitable form.[1] The question whether the prince would in fact undertake a fundamental reconstruction of the ministry was thus bound up with the question of Catholic policy. Some expected that the Regency would mean new men in power; others that it would mean new measures. It did not need much perspicacity to see that there might be a close connection between the two.

As with Portland's ministry in 1809, the rot began from within; this time it was Wellesley who played the role of Canning. His

[1] Walpole, *Perceval*, II, 248 ff.

resignation in January 1812, timed to coincide with the expiry of the Regency restrictions the following month, was designed to advertise his claims to the premiership. The Regent had other notions, however, and when his half-hearted demonstration of ancient loyalties towards Grey and Grenville failed to persuade the two whig magnates to join the ministry, he confirmed Perceval in his office and authorised him to take steps to strengthen the ministry. Castlereagh now consented to return and took over the Foreign Department vacated by Wellesley; and through Castlereagh a reconciliation between the Pittites and the Sidmouth group was at last effected. Sidmouth entered the cabinet as prospective Lord President of the Council, bringing with him an alarming number of followers for whom provision had to be made. Equilibrium thus seemed once more restored when a second disaster overtook the government. On 11 May a discharged bankrupt named Bellingham, with a grievance against the government and a history of family insanity, shot Perceval dead in the lobby of the House of Commons.

Perceval's relatively short political career, his uncompromising tory and Protestant views, the popular discontents at the time which issued in some unseemly rejoicing at his death, all subsequently conspired to detract from the position he had won by 1812. In fact his popularity with the country gentlemen, his courage and good humour, had in a short space of time given him a remarkable influence in the political world and his death crippled the ministry in the place where they could least afford a diminution of strength—the House of Commons. With their leader gone, with Canning, Wellesley, Grey, and Grenville all potentially in opposition, the remainder of the cabinet once more addressed itself to what seemed the perennial task of finding fresh sources of power. Peel's chief, Lord Liverpool, who had served in all three secretaryships (Foreign, War, and Home Departments), and was the most experienced of all Perceval's colleagues, took over the temporary leadership of the government and was authorised by the Prince Regent to open negotiations with persons who might be thought to agree most nearly with the general policy of the cabinet. Overtures were accordingly made to Canning and Wellesley. But since it was made clear to both that in the reconstruction envisaged Liverpool would become Prime Minister, Castlereagh would remain leader of the House of Commons, Sidmouth and his friends stay in office, and there would be no immediate change in the Catholic question, both politicians found ample reasons for rejecting the advances. It seemed in any case that the government in its existing form could not go on; and ten days after Perceval's death a motion was carried in the Commons for an address to the Prince Regent, praying him to take measures for the formation of an efficient administration.

The prince, who in other circumstances might have been content to continue with Liverpool and the rest of the cabinet, as he had been content to continue with Perceval, now embarked on the most serious attempt of his career to form a government. Wellesley was commissioned to draw up a plan for a new ministry and Canning participated in the negotiations. They encountered on the part of the other leading politicians a complete and mortifying determination not to co-operate. Liverpool and his colleagues, when approached by Canning, refused to take any part in a government led by Wellesley; Grenville and Grey distrusted the prince too much after his previous conduct to take office in any ministry which they did not themselves control. In the end there was nothing to be done but patch up the old Perceval cabinet and set it going once more under Liverpool's leadership. If that cabinet was not strong, it had at least shown the virtues of loyalty and discipline; and there was nothing at that moment which could be substituted for it. All that remained to be done was to redistribute the attenuated forces of the government. This was done in June 1812. Liverpool became Prime Minister and First Lord of the Treasury; Vansittart took Perceval's other post of Chancellor of the Exchequer; Sidmouth went to the Home Department; Lord Harrowby to the Presidency of the Council; and Bathurst moved from the Board of Trade to fill the vacancy left by Liverpool at War and Colonies. It was a prosaic and unhopeful beginning for a ministry which was to last substantially for the next fifteen years, and much was going to depend on what Wellington and his little professional army were able to do in Spain.

## IV

Through all the cabinet negotiations of 1812 the question of Catholic disabilities ran like a refrain. Grey, Grenville, Wellesley, and Canning, had all adduced it as part or principal reason for declining to join the Perceval-Liverpool ministry; and the reconstruction of that ministry in the summer did nothing to remove the question from the political scene. Indeed, the continuance in opposition of those politicians made it certain that the government would have to face a trial of strength on the issue. Not only was the movement still active and unsatisfied, but a double attack, in the Commons by Canning and in the Lords by Wellesley, was launched at the end of June and beginning of July. If the absence of those two political figures from Liverpool's cabinet was a proof that the Pittites were still deeply divided on personalities, the Catholic issue was a reminder that they were also deeply divided on policy; and the two lines of cleavage were not identical. The debate in the Commons was remarkable for a liberal speech by Castlereagh, the Foreign Secretary, urging an enquiry into Catholic claims; and Canning's motion to take the laws affecting Roman Catholics into consideration the following session was carried by a decisive majority. The similar motion brought forward by Wellesley in the upper House was rejected by only one vote. The arena was thus staked out for a pitched battle in 1813.

With these difficulties looming ahead, Liverpool was more than ever conscious of the weakness of his ministry in the House of Commons and before the end of the session he made one more effort to bring in Canning. To make this possible Castlereagh agreed to resign the Foreign Department and become Chancellor of the Exchequer, retaining the lead in the House of Commons. A variety of other posts, mainly in the Irish government, were also made available for the men whom Canning wished to bring in with him. There seemed every prospect of a junction being effected on these terms and some hard bargaining ensued, mainly centred on the respective positions of Canning and Castlereagh in the Commons. Castlereagh was prepared to concede to Canning the lead on matters of war as well as diplomacy, but would go no further.

Canning, however, in the end would not accept any degree of superiority in Castlereagh's status and on 28 July, two days before parliament was prorogued, the negotiations finally ended.[1] It was Canning's last chance of recovering the position he had thrown away three years earlier and he had over-reached himself once more. It was to be another decade before he held the seals of the Foreign Office again. There was now nothing for the government to do but go forward as best they could; and Liverpool faced the task in much the same spirit as Perceval in 1809. As he wrote at this time to Wellington,

> I have had therefore no resource but to bring forward the most promising of the young men, and the fate of the government in the House of Commons in another session will depend very much on their exertions. I should be most happy if I could see a second Pitt arise amongst them, and would most willingly resign the government into his hands, for I am fully aware of the importance of the minister being, if possible, in the House of Commons.[2]

Even the fact that the Prime Minister was a peer might not have mattered so much, had the ministry been otherwise well represented in the lower House. But of the twelve members of Liverpool's cabinet, only three were in the Commons: Castlereagh, Vansittart, and the insignificant Bragge Bathurst. Of the two leading men, the first was a poor debater and the second one of the weakest Chancellors of the Exchequer in modern British history. The prospects of young men of talent on the government side of the House were certainly not obscured by a phalanx of experienced and able senators on the benches in front of them.

As part of the abortive bargain with Canning, it had been agreed that Wellesley should go to Ireland as Lord Lieutenant. Knowledge of these projected arrangements soon spread, and it was rumoured that Huskisson would accompany him as Chief Secretary.[3] Though that possibility had now vanished, Liverpool was still faced with the task of reconstructing the Irish executive. Richmond, the Lord

[1] Richmond, 1300 (Bathurst to Richmond, 29 July 1812).
[2] *W.S.D.* VII, 402 (19 August 1812).
[3] cf. *Dublin Correspondent*, 1, 5 August 1812.

Lieutenant, was anxious to be relieved and had watched the negotiations during the summer with considerable anxiety. A Pittite and a 'Protestant', in the sense in which politicians were already beginning to be labelled, he resented strongly the behaviour of Wellesley and made it clear to his government that he would not stay in Ireland if there was any change in official policy on the Catholic question, or even if Wellesley came into the cabinet.[1] Both contingencies were now unlikely, but in the interval his Chief Secretary, Wellesley Pole, had compromised himself irredeemably in the eyes of the cabinet. A younger brother of Lord Wellesley, he allowed himself to be associated with Wellesley's political manœuvring in a way which his other brother in Spain had sagaciously avoided. His abilities as an administrator were recognised, and he had been under consideration for a cabinet post even before Perceval's death. But he had refused an offer of the War Department in May and had told Liverpool that he could not continue in office because of his connection with his elder brother and a feeling that Perceval's death had altered the whole complexion of the Catholic question. Finally he had voted with Canning on the Catholic motion in June, thereby not only reversing all the opinions he had professed in Ireland but openly differing from the policy of the Irish executive of which he was a member. Though personally on good terms with his Secretary, Richmond acknowledged privately to his brother-in-law, Bathurst, that Pole's hot temper and favouritism had made him unpopular in Ireland; and in any case he had stated to Bathurst in June that he would not stay in office under Liverpool.[2]

In the spring, when it seemed as if Pole might be promoted elsewhere, Richmond had viewed with some disquiet the prospect of fighting the unending battle against Irish jobbery with an inexperienced Secretary. Now that it was certain that Pole was going (a victim, Richmond thought, to the folly and vanity of his brother), the Lord Lieutenant grew even more apprehensive about the choice of his successor. In a sense, indeed, two successors might have to be chosen, since Pole had combined the offices of Chief Secretary and Chancellor of the Irish Exchequer, and it was doubtful whether that experiment would be repeated. For the Exchequer Richmond

[1] Richmond, 1578 (24 May 1812).
[2] ibid., 337, 1058-9, 1064, 1069, 1120, 1140, 1770, 1897; Bathurst, p. 155.

suggested two possible candidates, Fitzgerald and Barry; though he admitted that the first was too young and the second too heavy. 'As for a Secretary,' he wrote to Bathurst on 12 June 1812, 'I know not who will take it or who is most proper for it. Pray don't let them send me a Catholic or a timid Man.'[1] Normally such an appointment would be the subject of previous discussions between the Lord Lieutenant, the Prime Minister, and the Secretary for the Home Department under whose general jurisdiction Irish affairs were included. But Sidmouth's transfer to the Home Office had not yet been gazetted and Liverpool was immersed in the details of cabinet reconstruction. For the time being, therefore, Richmond confined the expression of his anxieties to his brother-in-law. In the event everything depended on the outcome of the negotiations with Canning and only towards the end of the following month did Liverpool make up his mind that if they broke down, he would offer the Irish Secretaryship to his former Under-Secretary in the Colonial Department, Robert Peel. It was not a post that was easy to fill or attractive to many politicians; and since the cabinet were anxious that Richmond should stay on until at least the following year, someone would have to be found who would be acceptable to him. Of Peel's ability to take the office Liverpool was better placed than anyone to judge; and of his sound Protestant opinions there was no doubt. Though he apparently took no part in the debate on Canning's motion which came on at precisely this juncture, he had intervened in an earlier discussion on Ireland brought on by Lord Morpeth in February. On that occasion he had expressed sentiments of which Richmond himself could not fail to approve. He had strongly defended the actions of the Irish government in their handling of Catholic agitation and though refusing to pledge himself against the principle of emancipation, he argued against any relaxation at the moment in the securities provided by law for Protestant interests. It was not a very notable speech but it had clearly put him on the Protestant side in a debate which was remembered for a glowing, if noncommittal, speech by Canning on the ultimate political wisdom of giving Catholics access to all the offices of state from which they were still debarred. Nevertheless, to accept the Irish Secretaryship at such a time was a serious step and

[1] Richmond, 1580 (printed *Bathurst*, p. 180).

Peel took time to consider his answer. On one point, however, he had already made up his mind. He told his new chief Bathurst that in any event it must be understood that should the negotiations with Canning come on again, and Lord Wellesley go as Lord Lieutenant to Ireland, he would not be able to remain there himself.

Writing to Richmond on 29 July, Lord Bathurst added a few lines to prepare him for the impending development.

> I think Peel, the Under-Secretary of State belonging to this Office, will be Secretary to Ireland. I had not much acquaintance with him, until I came here. I have found him a very laborious and clever young man and what is of full as great importance, a man of strict honour, and proper feelings, one on whom while you continue in Ireland you can place securely great confidence. You will not like him the less for his having voted against the Catholic Question last division.[1]

To this unconventional announcement of his prospective secretary Richmond briefly replied at the end of a long letter mainly concerned with Canning.

> I am not personally acquainted with Mr. Peele but from all I have heard, I should think he would be a very proper Secretary. I don't know that he would be a proper person to be Chancellor of the Exchequer. If not, and if one is to be taken from our Treasury, I believe W. Fitzgerald would be the best. I should certainly approve of Mr. Peele the more for his vote against Canning's motion.[2]

Before this letter left Dublin, Peel had resolved his doubts and accepted the appointment. Two letters written in London on the same day apprised the Lord Lieutenant of the decision. The first was from the Prime Minister; and, as Bathurst had done a few days earlier, he gave Richmond his own impression of the man he had selected.

> I can speak with more confidence of Mr. Peel than I could of most persons to whom such an office might be offered. He has been under me in the Secretary of State's office for two years and has

---

[1] Richmond, 1300.    [2] *ibid.*, 1590.

acquired all the necessary habits of official business. He has a particularly good temper, and great frankness and openness of manners, which I know are particularly desirable on your side of the water. He acquired great reputation, as you must have heard, as a scholar at Oxford, and he has distinguished himself in the House of Commons on every occasion on which he has had an opportunity of speaking. I have the greatest hopes, therefore, that this appointment will prove acceptable to you and advantageous to the Government.

The second letter, written (to judge from the heavily scored and amended draft preserved by Peel among his papers) with some degree of nervousness, was from the young Secretary-Designate himself. Its tone was modest.

I can assure your Grace that I am by no means unconscious of the many disqualifications under which I labour in undertaking the duties of this situation. All that I can oppose to them is a most anxious desire to acquit myself to the satisfaction of those under whom I am to be employed and to prove myself not unworthy of their confidence.

But he ended courteously with an expression of regret at learning that Richmond's period of office would shortly be coming to an end; and a hope that the principles of his administration would be continued under his successor.[1]

Richmond, a kindly and sociable man of the world, returned a friendly reply; though in reality he was piqued at the failure of the government to consult him on the appointment and further annoyed by Liverpool's other suggestion of giving the Irish Exchequer to Leslie Foster. Indeed, writing privately to Bathurst, he relented sufficiently to say that there was no reason why Peel should not combine both positions. 'The task is not too arduous for him.' But while highly approving of the selection, he complained strongly of the informality of the transaction.[2] Though it was a post in which the Prime Minister was bound to have the final decision in filling, the Chief Secretaryship was still technically in the gift of the Lord Lieutenant and Liverpool had shown less than his usual tact in

[1] Richmond, 1881, partly printed *Peel*, I 33; cf. 40185 fos. 1-3.
[2] Richmond, 1593.

failing to observe this punctilio. Of this Peel was duly warned a few days later by one of Bathurst's sons, and though the message was sweetened by an assurance of Richmond's personal satisfaction at his appointment, it was not an encouraging start to a post of such known difficulty. However, the die was cast and the next few weeks were full of correspondence, congratulations, and preparation. Richmond was anxious that he should come over as soon as possible and Liverpool promised to expedite his departure, at the same time concurring in the view that Fitzgerald would be the best man to take over the Exchequer.[1] It was arranged that Goulburn, who was then Under-Secretary in the Home Department, should fill his place at War and Colonies and in the intervals of reading the recent files of Irish correspondence in the Home Office Peel cleared up the business in his own department and prepared to hand over to his successor.

A long letter to Goulburn, started on 12 August and finished on the 15th in a mood of haste and exhilaration, conveyed a lively if irreverent picture of the duties he was relinquishing.

> I will attempt to give you a sort of general outline of the business in which I have been concerned and which has been executed, as you will find, I fear, very imperfectly. In the first place I had the charge of the Secret Service which gave me very little trouble as I am no great advocate of sending people to the Continent to collect information which generally reaches us in the papers before it arrives from the spy. Jenkinson sent a man to Holland for this purpose, he staid there a long time waiting for events and arrived in this country, with the greatest possible expedition to inform him of Louis' abdication of the throne which appeared even in the *Morning Post* just a week before he landed in England.
>
> However, if a man upon whom you can place dependence can be found with access to the Department at Paris and who has the means of getting some better information than that which news-papers supply, there can be no doubt that it would be sound policy to incur a very considerable expence in employing him in doing the thing effectively. I am sure it is the only way in which the secret service money can be usefully employed. A great part of that which I have received (for the amount as you are aware is unlimited) has been expended in annual allowances to French Royalists and others.

[1] 38328 f. 35.

The office is divided into two branches, war and colonial and more strictly perhaps the war under-secretary has charge of *all Europe* with the exception of Heligoland and Anhalt, which come with the colonial who superintends those valuable possessions and every part of the world excepting the north coast of Africa, which he consigns to his colleague in exchange I suppose for Anhalt and Heligoland.

*15 August.* I have been so much engaged that I have had no time to resume my pen before. You will of course have the superintendance of the correspondence with all the British colonies on the face of the globe on all subjects military and civil but when you are master of the routine which I am sure *you* will be in a month you will find it go on very smoothly. There is no occasion in most cases for an immediate decision and in many it does not much signify if it is deferred for some time. Perhaps the most important and difficult points are those which arise out of the collisions of the governor and assemblies. The usual remedy is a dissolution and the usual consequence, the election of the same members or others more violently disposed.

Questions of trade and commercial intercourse of all descriptions and which are generally the most intricate are of course referred to the Board of Trade and will afford a pleasing recreation to Robinson. But I really do not know what to send you. If I send you one of the 1200 folios it will be only a brick of the edifice. The correspondence from Ceylon including everything, minutes of council, etc., etc., amounts to not less than twenty volumes for the last four or five years. I say *from* Ceylon for the letters addressed to it are comprised in about the same number of papers.

The quantity of writing which you have bears no proportion whatever to the quantity of reading. You will immortalize yourself if you will frame a constitution for Trinidad. It has baffled all your predecessors who have uniformly left it as they found it, governed by Spanish laws and petitioning for English. Trinidad is a subject in an anatomy school or rather a poor patient in a county hospital on whom all sorts of surgical experiments are tried to be given up if they fail and to be practised on others if they succeed. Stephen is the operator and there are occasional consultations with Drs. Wilberforce and Z. Macaulay on the state of the patient's health and the progress of the Experiments. The poor patient has to go through some very severe operations. She is now actually bound down for a most painful one—a registration of slaves with penalties upon penalties on those who fail to observe the regulations of an order in Council prescribed by Dr. Stephen. The operation is so severe that after the prescription, surgical instruments, etc., etc., had been sent out, our hearts failed and we thought it not expedient to trust it in the hands of country practitioners. I writ out another prescription three weeks after the former to suspend it.

I am quite aware that this letter will be of no sort of use to you but I really have been and am so overwhelmed with the business of both departments that I must defer till tomorrow writing anything which you can either understand or read.[1]

Meanwhile his postbag was affording him certain proof of his elevation in the political hierarchy. Abbot, the Speaker of the House of Commons, wrote on 9 August to offer congratulations and recommend a protégé to the goodwill of the Irish Office. This was the first of a rapid swelling flood of letters seeking patronage, pressing claims, and quoting promises, which was to encompass him for the next six years. But there were other correspondents less exigent. His friend Lord Desart expressed a wish that he would treat Desart as his country home in Ireland. His colleague Bunbury sent a line of felicitation and a hope that he would find his new situation more agreeable than he appeared to expect. Old William Yates penned from Bury not only his congratulations but, even more thoughtfully, a cheque to be laid out as his grandson considered fitting. The Rev. J. Hargreaves, his old tutor, now installed by Sir Robert at Shenstone near Tamworth, promised to find a servant for him and to look after his dog Dash, who was to be left behind in Staffordshire. Wellesley Pole came up to town to induct him into the mysteries of the Irish Office. On 13 August he attended a meeting of the Privy Council at Carlton House to be sworn in along with his friend and colleague Fitzgerald; and towards the end of the month he went down to Liverpool's country residence, Combe Wood, to prime himself with the cabinet's views on Irish matters and to discover if possible what their intentions were concerning the pledge of the House of Commons to take the question of Catholic disabilities into consideration the following session. In a succession of letters to the Duke of Richmond that were already

[1] Goulburn, II/13.

easier and unreserved, he sent the latest news of the war in Spain
(Salamanca on 22 July had shattered Marmont and earned Welling-
ton a marquessate), and inveighed in lively tones against those
supporters of Perceval who so soon after his death had begun to
equivocate on the Catholic question.[1] Whatever other doubts
Richmond might have had, he must have been reassured even before
Peel's arrival that he was not being sent a 'Catholic', and possibly
not a timid man either. But time was rapidly running out. On 28
August Peel left London and though he probably stayed a night at
Drayton to say goodbye to his father and his more bantering schoolboy brothers, Holyhead and the Irish Channel came at last and on the
evening of Tuesday 1 September 1812 he set foot in Dublin.

[1] Richmond, 1882, 1887.

# THE GOVERNMENT OF IRELAND

Dublin in September was out of season. With the courts not sitting, the theatres closed, and many families away, the second city of the United Kingdom was apt to strike strangers at this time of the year as unusually desolate. But even in season Dublin was no longer the crowded and fashionable metropolis it had been scarcely more than a decade earlier. It was still the *entrepôt* for the bulk of Irish trade, despite the growing competition of Belfast; but the abolition of the Irish parliament in 1801 had cut at the roots of its existence as a social and political centre. Before the Union some three hundred Irish M.P.s and almost as many peers and bishops resided in Dublin during the session. Twenty years later that imposing array had shrunk to little more than fifty, and many of the great mansions that had brought dignity and opulence to the Irish capital, such as Leinster House and Powerscourt House, together with the Houses of Parliament themselves, were passing into the hands of government departments, banks, or public institutions. Dublin society was already taking on the provincial appearance provided by merchants, manufacturers, shopkeepers, and professional men. Even the theatre had fallen into temporary decay and the Dublin stage that had known Garrick, Foote, Macklin, and the incomparable Mrs. Siddons, was still awaiting the revival under Kean, Macready, and the Kembles.

Yet it was undeniably a capital city, and the broad paved and gravelled vistas of Sackville Street recently graced by Nelson's lofty column, Gandon's magnificent Customs House, the new front of Trinity College, the Four Courts, the Castle, and the two cathedrals of Christ Church and St. Patrick, could challenge the architecture of almost any city of its size in Europe. Moreover, the constant presence of scarlet uniforms, the clatter of horse detachments, the sound of fife and drum, the bustle of activity round the

Castle, the familiar sight of the Viceregal coach, were a perpetual reminder that Dublin was the seat of administration even if its legislature had ceased to exist. The contrast was all the more powerful therefore between the riches and poverty, the fine houses and wretched slums in the same street, the commodious shops and swarms of beggars, that presented themselves to the curious gaze of every Dublin visitor. Around the great town houses of the nobility, among the narrow streets and alleys of the centre of the city, in the crowded liberties south of the river, were breeding grounds of misery, disease, riot, and drunkenness. If, as is probable, Peel came by the regular packet from Holyhead, he would have landed at the South Wall and his first sight of Dublin would have been the swarms of ragged children and the litter of slums and filthy tenements that lined the waterfront between the Pigeon House and the city. Had he come from the landward side, he might have noticed another sight: the barriers that had been raised at the time of the '98 rebellion still standing on the outskirts of the capital.[1]

The appointment of a new Chief Secretary and his arrival in Dublin attracted little attention in Ireland. In the narrow circle of official men at the Castle there had been considerable criticism at the bestowal of the two posts of Secretary and Chancellor on such young men as Peel and Fitzgerald. Both were under thirty and Peel indeed was still short of his twenty-fifth birthday.[2] But this was a prejudice which time alone could mend. In the wider sphere of Irish public opinion, however, there was little interest in either the new Secretary or his youthfulness. The official announcement of his appointment, dated from Dublin Castle on 4 August, appeared in the *Dublin Gazette* two days later and was copied in the course of the next few days by most of the other Dublin newspapers. But the item was pushed into obscurity by the news of Marmont's defeat at Salamanca; and even Peel's arrival in September passed virtually unnoticed except by the *Dublin Correspondent*, which optimistically hoped from him 'a greater sensibility to public approbation than some who have preceded him'.[3] In the provincial newspapers the

---

[1] For Dublin at this date see esp. C. Maxwell, *Dublin under the Georges* (1946) J. C. Curwen, *Observations on . . . Ireland* (1818), II, 103-32.

[2] Richmond, 478, 494 (Richmond to Liverpool, 7, 15 August 1812).

[3] *Dublin Correspondent*, 5 September 1812.

change of Secretary was either ignored entirely or briefly appended to the news of Fitzgerald's appointment in September. Fitzgerald, as an Irish landowner, inevitably received the major share of press comment; and the possibility, to which some of the Irish papers devoted eager attention during August, that Wellesley would come to Ireland as Lord Lieutenant, bringing Huskisson with him as his Secretary, contrived to surround the appointment of 'Mr. Peele' with an air of relative impermanence and unimportance.[1] Indeed it was another two years before Irish newspapers and private Irish correspondents even contrived to give his name a consistently correct spelling. It was therefore with a certain degree of unobtrusiveness that the new Secretary began his labours at the Castle.

Fortunately he struck up from the beginning an easy and friendly relationship with the man whose opinion mattered most, the Lord Lieutenant. In a letter to Wellington on 17 September 1812, in which he deplored the loss to Castle society of the Pole family, the Duke of Richmond added nevertheless that 'Peel, who has succeeded Pole I like very much'.[2] Richmond had not taken very seriously the objections to Peel and Fitzgerald on the score of their youth. He had been only forty-three himself when appointed Lord Lieutenant in 1807, and his station and habits in life predisposed him to a tolerant view of such departures from the conventional. He had done some soldiering in the West Indies and had sat in the House of Commons as a member for Sussex under Pitt. He was a sportsman, a cricketer, a patron of the prize-ring, and as Colonel Lennox he had achieved distinction by fighting a duel with a prince of the blood, the Duke of York. Both he and his duchess, a daughter of the Duke of Gordon, enjoyed their Viceregal position in Dublin and maintained it with stateliness and hospitality. His portrait in Dublin Castle shows a small thin-featured man, like an athlete on whose spare and active frame comfort and good living were beginning to tell. As both friends and enemies were well aware, he was fond of the wine-bottle and his too frequent excesses exposed him in the savage warfare of contemporary politics to damaging public criticism. It was also true that he was conscious of his weakness and made, at any rate while Peel was in Ireland, efforts to overcome it even though opportunities for a relapse presented themselves with tempting frequency. Partly

[1] *Dublin Correspondent*, 1, 5, 25 August 1812.    [2] Richmond, 1820.

perhaps because of the pleasures of the table, his health was not strong and he also had some trouble with his eyes. But to his staff at the Castle he was a good and kindly superior. His stout Protestantism, open expression of which he largely suppressed at the desire of the cabinet, endeared him to the ring of equally stout Protestants who surrounded him; and his intemperance, if a fault, was his only fault in their eyes.[1]

Of the other officials at the Castle the most important were the Lord Lieutenant's three legal advisers. Manners, the Lord Chancellor, once described as looking like the ghost of Charles I, was an English importation. Reputed a bad lawyer, he was by way of compensation a good Protestant and a devoted shooter of woodcock; in political matters he was said to be influenced by William Saurin, the Attorney General. In 1812 both were in their middle fifties but Saurin was a product of the Irish bar. The son of an Ulster Presbyterian minister and grandson of a Huguenot refugee, with his harsh foreign features and black eyes glittering under shaggy brows, Saurin brought both intelligence and fanaticism to the Protestant party at the Castle. He had headed the opposition of the Irish lawyers to the Union in 1800 and later became one of the most violent opponents of Catholic emancipation. The third member of the legal triumvirate and the only true Irishman among them, was Charles Kendal Bushe, who like Saurin was a Trinity College man. Broad-shouldered, a little corpulent by the time Peel knew him, with long intelligent face, he impressed people most by his bright blue eyes, mellow voice, and witty conversation; politically he was inclined to be more liberal than his two colleagues. Whatever their private views on the appointment, the official circle at the Castle together with the small Protestant society of Dublin, showed a typically Irish hospitality to the new Secretary and in a letter to Croker he gave a picture of the round of entertainment into which he plunged on taking up residence in Ireland.

> I have scarcely dined once at home since my arrival. I see no great prospect of it for some time to come, excepting with about twenty-five guests. I am just opening upon the campaign, and have visions of future feasts studded with Lord Mayors and Sheriffs Elect. I

[1] cf. Gregory to Peel, April 1813 (40196 fos. 1, 40).

fancy I see some who think that the Government of England have
a strange notion of Ireland when they put a man here who drinks
port, and as little of that as he can. The Governor of the Bank
remarked with horror that I was not fully impressed with the
necessity of toasting the glorious memory.[1]

Peel at this date was clearly not 'Orange Peel' in Protestant eyes,
nor indeed ever except in the journalistic abuse of Catholic agitators.
But his sobriety was a matter for remark in a country where hard
drinking went hand in hand with a disconcerting readiness to offer
and accept the satisfaction due from one gentleman to another. Mrs.
Orby Hunter, an old London acquaintance, wrote in September to
offer Peel the hospitality of her nephew's house in Co. Meath,
promising 'good shooting and a well-aired bed' and assuring him
that 'he will not be under the necessity of drinking more than he
likes. She mentions this, knowing him to be a moderate man.' As
within the same month she wrote again asking for patronage to be
bestowed on a *protégé* (which Peel politely refused), such invitations
were perhaps better avoided, however moderate the drinking.[2] One
of the first lessons for an official man in Ireland was never to accept
favours from casual acquaintances.

Hospitality, however, both in the giving and receiving, was
something which could not be avoided in his position. But he was
not unprovided with the means to entertain on the scale expected
of him. Certainly his official salary was not as large as was fondly
imagined by his younger brothers at Rugby who looked forward
with anticipation to sharing in some of the financial rewards of his
office. An early letter from John, written on behalf of himself,
Jonathan, and Lawrence, apparently went unanswered in the first
rush of business and pleasure. John accordingly wrote again, pointing
out that when Robert earned £4,000 a year he had made them rich
and handsome presents. Now with double that amount he was the
only one who had not given them something. 'But still hoping,'
added the schoolboy moralist with despondent indifference to sense
and spelling, 'some latent spark of generosity dwindles in you
bosom, I again implore your beneficence.' This second petition at
last secured a response from their busy elder brother, who promised

[1] *Croker*, I, 47.    [2] 40221 fos. 245, 340.

to increase their allowance on condition their father gave his consent, as he knew he was very strict on that point.[1] It was true, however, that his salary was now higher than when he had been at War and Colonies, even if the maintenance of two residences and the obligations of official hospitality made his new office an unusually expensive one. The salary of the Under-Secretary in the Colonial Department was £2,000 per annum at this period; that of the Chief Secretary to the Lord Lieutenant amounted with certain miscellaneous fees to over £5,000. Moreover, he was not without a few additional perquisites. The first item of business when Peel was sworn in at the meeting of the Irish Privy Council on 5 September 1812 was to read and sign the wine warrant whereby as a member of the Council he was entitled, under an Act of Charles II, to import into the country free of duty, three tuns of French wine and one butt of sack.[2]

As Chief Secretary he had not only official apartments in the Castle but also the Secretary's Lodge in Phoenix Park. This pleasant residence had been built by Blaquiere, one of his predecessors, in the last quarter of the eighteenth century, and was still unmarred by the Victorian additions of later Chief Secretaries. It was a low two-storeyed structure, flanked by projecting bow-fronted wings, facing south across lawn and sunk fence to the parkland beyond. At the back were fruit and flower gardens, peach-trees under glass, and a small demesne of grassland; and in the cellars over £2,300 worth of wine and other commodities which he took over from Pole.[3] There were other more markedly Irish characteristics in this sylvan retreat. The drawing-room ceiling showed signs of falling in; the sanitation was singularly old-fashioned by English standards; and the deer were continually wandering into the garden from the surrounding park. While Peel was away in England for the 1813 session an extensive work of repair and renovation was begun which lasted until 1816. Privies and cesspools were excavated, water-closets installed, a garden engine and pump erected, the suspect drawing-room strengthened by columns in imitation marble, and the demesne wall raised to keep out the deer. At the same time additional luxuries were added in the way of hot-bed frames, peach-houses and 'Graperies', and a dairy. In all some £1,600 at

---

[1] 40605 fos. 57-9.     [2] S.P.O., Irish P.C. Minutes.     [3] 40221 f. 262.

least, and probably more, were spent in improving the amenities of the Secretary's Lodge.[1] Other encumbrances he found there, such as 'an old man, who is a sort of heirloom together with his wife, at my lodge. . . . He was employed, at least he fancied he was, in my stables', were less easy to deal with. This particular one Peel tried, a little gracelessly, to get appointed as a stamper in the Irish administration.[2]

## II

The Chief Secretary had other things to do, however, than dine with the Lord Mayor and gaze apprehensively at his drawing-room ceiling. Even before he left England he knew that the cabinet were meditating the dissolution of parliament and a fresh appeal to the country; and his first letter from the Prime Minister warned him to begin collecting information in preparation for that event. The decision was kept secret until the last minute, in case an improvement in the king's condition necessitated a change of plan;[3] though the government could not have been unconscious of the advantages to be gained by springing a surprise on their opponents. Nevertheless, there were sound arguments for a premature dissolution. The reconstruction of the cabinet was finished and all immediate chances of a reconciliation with Wellesley and Canning had gone. As Bathurst idiomatically expressed it, everything was now afloat and they must fight on their own bottoms.[4] It seemed a propitious moment to go to the country. The war news was good: Madrid had been entered, Astorga captured, and the siege of Cadiz raised. The harvest had been abundant and Ireland was temporarily quiet. Accordingly on 29 September the unexpected announcement of a dissolution was made in an official proclamation from the Prince Regent. A week earlier Liverpool had sent Peel notice of the event, together with a prudent warning to observe the new stringencies imposed by Curwen's Act in any dealings which might implicate the government.

Within a month of landing in Ireland, therefore, Peel was not

[1] Details of the repairs, etc., to the Secretary's Lodge will be found in 40188 f. 269; 40286 f. 181; 40196 f. 119; 40202 f. 92.
[2] 40288 f. 202.     [3] 40181 fos. 1-2 (Liverpool to Peel).     [4] Richmond, 1300.

only facing his first general election, but he himself, as far as Ireland was concerned, was also in charge of it. It was made clear that his duty was to get as many ministerial supporters returned as was possible, without exposing himself to detection in any illegal operation—'bound', as he light-heartedly expressed it to Croker, 'to secure the Government interests if possible from dilapidation, but still more bound to faint with horror at the mention of money transactions'. It was a role that demanded some delicacy; already, on 17 September, he had written to Arbuthnot, the Patronage Secretary at the Treasury, for advice on the technique of arranging electoral bargains with borough patrons and would-be candidates without any absolute mention of pecuniary considerations. 'You cannot conceive how useful all information on this subject will be to me.' But Arbuthnot had his hands too full in England to assist his apprentice colleague in Ireland. In the end it was the Prime Minister himself who took on the task of initiating his former Under-Secretary into the complexities of electoral management.[1] There were, however, some saving features in the situation. Through fear of Curwen's Act, the government decided that all official men would have to find constituencies free from any imputation of direct purchase; and when Peel came to warn government supporters (five days before the official announcement) of the imminent dissolution, he found that there was in fact less to be done in the way of timely management than he had anticipated. In the counties it was chiefly a matter of writing to friendly landowners to stimulate their zeal. In the boroughs there were few places where specific arrangements had not already been made between the interested parties without reference to government. In two or three constituencies only did the opportunity present itself of finding a seat for unattached government candidates. For the most part Peel found himself playing an ancillary role in the curious medley of negotiations, bargains, compromises, and foregone conclusions that constituted the bulk of an Irish general election in that period.

Nevertheless, there was much to be done in the way of correspondence and interviews, and in allotting the small sums of money placed at the disposal of the Irish executive for electoral purposes. Here the Lord Lieutenant, with his wide knowledge of Irish

[1] 40221 f. 391; 40280 f. 32.

personalities, connections, and property, and his calm good sense, was of considerable assistance in conveying information on the intricacies of contests and the latest shifts of position and opinion. Though the government took a limited part in direct electoral arrangements, it was nevertheless active in assisting favoured candidates with the well-tried instruments of patronage and influence. At one degree more remote from the scene of the conflict, Liverpool and Sidmouth sent news of private negotiations in England with individual peers and magnates, and injunctions to secure the support of various friendly Irish landowners for candidates in whom they took a special interest. The Chief Secretary was asked to secure Lord Clancarty's backing in Galway for Richard Martin; Sir Edward Denny's and Justice Day's in Tralee for Herbert; and the Castle support for Falkiner in Dublin county.[1] There were the inevitable confusions and disappointments. Lord Desart was given a quiet return at the Cornish borough of Bossiney under the favour of Lord Mount Edgecumbe and the government, only for the government nominee for his borough of Kilkenny to discover that it was far from being the safe thing it had been reputed.[2] At one point an even more delicate situation arose. Lord Charleville, who controlled the borough of Carlow, allowed it to be known that if he received encouragement for his hopes of an English peerage, he would offer a free return for the constituency to the government. The Lord Lieutenant promised to communicate with the Prime Minister but warned him that there would be the greatest difficulty in complying with the suggestion. When the matter was referred to Liverpool, there came back, much to the satisfaction of the Lord Lieutenant and the Chief Secretary, a decided negative. 'I am particularly solicitous to avoid adding to engagements of this description. You must do the best you can without the promise of an English peerage.' In the end their political virtue was rewarded. Lord Charleville decided, notwithstanding, to return a government candidate for Carlow in the hope of realising his ambition later on.[3]

[1] 40182 fos. 1, 12, 15 (Sidmouth to Peel August-October 1812).
[2] 40181 fos. 11, 16; 40280 f. 54.
[3] He died in 1835 with his object unrealised. The relevant correspondence is mainly printed in *Peel*, I, 42-3, with the omission of proper names. The originals are in 40280 fos. 54-72; 40181 f. 15. See also *The Marlay Letters* ed. R. W. Bond (1937), pp. 233-5 where Carton should read Carlow.

For magnates who ought to have supported the government but did not, the reverse side of governmental power was exhibited. In sending in his initial report of the decisions in the uncontested constituencies, Peel adverted sharply to the shocking behaviour of Lord Waterford. He had supported Newport, an opponent, against Bolton, a good friend; he and the Beresford family controlled two members, Marshall from whom the government would never get a vote, and Lord George Beresford, who held a lucrative position in the administration; and he had declined contesting Dungarvan against Colonel Walpole. In the face of this catalogue of misdemeanours, the Irish executive had retaliated by withdrawing from him the whole of his patronage.[1] It is not perhaps surprising that Peel wrote to Arbuthnot in October, that 'this sort of business is so new to me that my head, like yours, is rather apt to be confused'.

To add to his distractions there was the question of his own parliamentary seat. In conformity with the cabinet's ruling on the election of 'official persons', he abandoned any thought of another return for Cashel—'the risque would be too great for a person in my situation.'[2] Yet he was unwilling to increase the difficulties of a hard-pressed government by requesting one of the few seats at the Treasury's disposal. Instead Sir Robert, and Peel's brother-in-law the Rev. William Cockburn, undertook to find him a less dangerous constituency in England. After negotiations with a Mr. Maitland at the end of September, Peel was elected on 7 October for the Wiltshire borough of Chippenham, Cockburn deputising for the absent member in the traditional chairing ceremony. The return for Chippenham was, however, as much a financial transaction as that for Cashel, and gave rise to greater private difficulties than the Irish borough would probably have done. His father had committed himself to the bargain on the understanding that it would be for a single election only; and further acquaintance with the internal politics of the borough convinced him that to attempt to establish a permanent interest at Chippenham would be a costly business. Maitland, however, asserted that he had put up Peel's name for Chippenham only on the assurance that election would be followed by an outright purchase by his father of the property in the borough.

[1] 40280 f. 66.    [2] ibid., f. 36.

When Peel was in London in December he had, as he told Sir Robert, 'a very unpleasant interview' with Maitland, in the course of which the latter claimed the immediate payment of £4,000 in return for a guarantee that £1,000 would be returned for each year the new parliament fell short of its usual maximum of six. Old Sir Robert, on the other hand, as a cautious businessman, proposed that the £4,000 should remain in a joint account until the dissolution of parliament, Maitland to recover £1,000 for each year over the first two that parliament lasted. It was an unedifying wrangle and Peel was clearly embarrassed by the imputation of bad faith. In private he advised his father to submit the case to friends of both sides for decision.[1]

However, there was solace in the fact that the elections were over, that he himself was returned once more, and that the government on the whole had strengthened their position. As far as Ireland was concerned, the cabinet's main hope had been not to lose any seats and this modest ambition had been more than achieved. On 28 October Peel was able to report a gain of five seats, a loss of three, and, of the contests still undecided, a probable gain of three against one loss. A number of new members, and the independent character of others, made exact calculation impossible; but neither the Castle nor the government in London had reason to be dissatisfied with the Irish results.[2] Goulburn indeed, a close and partial friend, wrote flatteringly to say that 'you have gained much honour, and I only wish that Arbuthnot had done half as well in England'. But even in England matters had not gone ill and at the beginning of November Liverpool wrote that they had gained there the difference between thirty and forty seats as a result of the dissolution. A particularly gratifying feature was the decided feeling for the government exhibited in the more popular elections; for many persons thought, and some said, that the principal object of the cabinet in bringing on a general election had been to weaken the Canning-Wellesley party. Croker, mortified perhaps by an unsuccessful contest for Down and the failure of the Castle to afford him any financial assistance, commented sharply to Peel on the folly of the government and on the certain failure of any attempt to 'keep down Canning'. He

[1] 40222 fos. 5, 20, 64; 40223 f. 142; 40280 f. 117.
[2] cf. Peel's reports to Liverpool, 40280 fos. 35, 66, 72.

estimated that his party would number not less than forty in the House of Commons. Croker, however, though holding office as Secretary to the Admiralty, was regarded with some suspicion at the time and Peel had already been warned by Robinson to be on his guard when writing to him.

His reply to Croker's letter allowed no misconception as to his own loyalties.

> I hope we may fight out this battle as we have fought out many others; there was a time when I should have had less fears and when perhaps, from every private and public feeling, I should have seen our little champion go forth with his sling and with his sword, and bring down the mightiest of his enemies, and felt prouder in his triumph; but there never was a time when I felt more determined to do all I could to support the Government on its present footing and on the principles on which it will meet Parliament. If I understand, as I believe I did, the offers made to Canning, I think they were fair ones, as he himself must have thought when he accepted them, and as to keeping him down, the Government know his power too well not to wish to have it exerted in their favour.[1]

If there had, in fact, been any likelihood that in a general sense Canning might have 'seduced' Peel in 1810, it was clear that by 1812 the gap had perceptibly widened. In any case, the impressive estimate of Canning's parliamentary strength was dismissed as flat exaggeration by Liverpool when Peel mentioned the subject to him. Croker, he replied in a letter of 7 November, was entirely misinformed. The most favourable calculation he had seen did not give the Canning-Wellesley party more than twenty or twenty-five.

Nevertheless, Liverpool was well aware of the danger that would continue to exist so long as Canning remained a political guerilla of genius on the flank of the formal parliamentary contest between government and opposition; Canning's seductive arts were not likely to be confined to one person only on the ministerial side of the House. As the Prime Minister wrote to Peel,

> Our danger is not from Opposition, but evidently from the third parties headed by Lord Wellesley and Canning, who will represent

[1] *Croker*, I, 46.

themselves as holding the same opinions as we do on all popular topics, who will say that they have as much right to be considered as the successors of Mr. Pitt's party as ourselves, and whose object will consequently be to detach as many of our friends as possible. The practical question in the House of Commons for the next session will be, Who are the true Demetriuses? and on the issue of that question the fate of the Administration will in a great measure depend.

A great deal therefore rested on the parliamentary manœuvres of the new session. The Canningites could only hope to defeat the government in conjunction with the main whig opposition, and that in itself could be turned to their disadvantage. At the same time, it was Liverpool's policy to persuade as large a body of supporters as possible to commit themselves in the government's favour on some major question of national policy. Until such an issue should arrive, he was anxious not to discourage even the neutrals or luke-warm 'friends' in parliament of whom Peel had already made some acquaintance in Ireland.

The new parliament was summoned at the end of November. Peel, faced with the prospect of a double sea-crossing before Christmas and mounting arrears of work, pleaded for leave of absence until the new year. But the Prime Minister was adamant and on 24 November, the actual day of the opening of parliament, Peel embarked with George Dawson, on the *Spencer* packet for Holyhead. In the event there was little call for his parliamentary services. The business before the House was mainly financial and the opposition was still in the process of reorganising their forces after their losses in the general election. Nevertheless, he detected a considerable feeling among them in favour of Canning and told the Lord Lieutenant that he anticipated a strong effort by the 'Catholic' party when the session got under way. On Monday 28 December, after a tedious passage of twenty-six hours, he was back in Dublin.

### III

With a general election, a parliamentary meeting, and three channel crossings behind him, Peel had already compressed a considerable amount of experience into the five months that had passed since his appointment. He was now able to settle to the routine of work and travel that was to be his life for the next six years.

The structure of Irish government in the early nineteenth century was relatively simple. The Lord Lieutenant governed, assisted by a Privy Council. Under him was the Chief Secretary, and through the Secretary were controlled the armed forces in Ireland, the revenue departments, and the other offices and boards which constituted the standing civil service of the country. The simplicity of the administration was the key to what was its outstanding feature: the centralisation of power in the hands of the Viceroy. Not only was all ordinary administration and the bulk of Irish patronage, including legal and ecclesiastical appointments, under his control but in his direction of the armed forces and the financial departments he combined a degree of power scarcely paralleled by any formal office in the English government. He was in fact the immediate source of sovereign power in Ireland; the legal and not infrequently the political mainspring of governmental action. But if the Lord Lieutenant was in miniature an Irish constitutional monarch, though of the eighteenth- rather than of the nineteenth-century type, his Chief Secretary was a combination of Prime Minister, Home Secretary, First Lord of the Treasury, President of the Board of Trade, and Secretary for War. It was, even allowing for the smaller scale of Irish affairs, an extraordinarily varied and testing office. Goulburn in 1821 called it 'one of the most difficult and laborious offices under the Government' and though something must be allowed for the fact that he was himself about to take up that office, it remained true that the Irish Secretaryship was a remarkably effective device for making or breaking the career of a young politician.

In its evolution the office was an illuminating example of the practical development of administrative and political power along natural channels. With little status or inherent strength, it was yet the post of greatest authority and responsibility under the Lord Lieutenant. In theory it was a private Viceregal nomination and the only formality necessary was an announcement in the Dublin Gazette and a notification to the Post Office to secure free franking of mail. In practice, even before the end of North's ministry in 1782, it had been recognised as an appointment of such consequence as to require the approval if not the actual decision of the British government. One annoying result of this constitutional vagueness in Peel's position was the uncertainty whether he would need to seek parliamentary re-election when re-appointed under a new Lord Lieutenant. On Richmond's retirement in 1813 Peel consulted Liverpool on the question. The Prime Minister could give no clear ruling, nor could the Speaker of the House of Commons, but the English Attorney-General and Solicitor-General delivered an opinion in favour of vacation in those circumstances. This was particularly vexatious in view of the difficult situation at Chippenham; and though his father assured him that he would cheerfully undergo the expense of another election, Peel's thoughts turned to Carlow where government influence might secure a return without undue expenditure.[1] However, in the end no one pressed the issue and he remained in office without having to submit himself once more to the costly verdict of the polls.

If there was some uncertainty about his legal position, however, there was none about his real power. The office of Chief Secretary had first been brought into prominence when the Lord Lieutenant emerged as the efficient head of the Irish executive after the rule of the 'Undertakers' in the middle of the eighteenth century. Though no longer the manager of an independent legislature, he was for half the year the standing representative of the Irish executive in London. If the Union had partially diminished his legislative importance, his executive independence in relation to the Lord Lieutenant had been sensibly increased. To the cabinet he was the expounder and defender of Irish policy in the House of Commons in an age when Ireland was moving into the front line of British domestic problems. It was inevitable, therefore, that he should increasingly rank in their minds as possessing an importance equal to that of the resident Lord Lieutenant who never left the country. After the appointment of Peel and Fitzgerald, the Prime Minister reminded Richmond that he should always communicate with them on matters of patronage. 'They will have the labouring oar of Irish business in the House of Commons and it is very desirable as I am sure you will agree that the arrangements should be

[1] 40181 fos. 45-7; 40183 f. 172; 40231 f. 120; Richmond, 305.

satisfactory to them.'[1] Only the personal vicissitudes of the Chief Secretaries themselves had prevented the office from assuming greater importance by 1812. In the dozen years that elapsed between the Union and the date of Peel's appointment, there had been no fewer than nine Chief Secretaries. One of these, Nicholas Vansittart, never went over to Ireland at all; and another, Sir Arthur Wellesley, fought a campaign in Spain while still holding his Secretaryship. Peel had succeeded to an office of great potentialities, but its potentialities had scarcely been realised by his predecessors.

The administrative power of the Chief Secretary, however, derived solely from the authority of the Lord Lieutenant and was inseparable from it. Though he had in fact been appointed by the Prime Minister and acted as the spokesman of the Irish government in parliament, in Ireland his importance was that he constituted for most purposes the sole channel for the executive power of the Lord Lieutenant. It was because he represented the sovereign authority in Ireland that his office enjoyed a kind of primacy in the Irish government. Of this fundamental aspect of his position Peel had early occasion to be aware in the difficulties that arose over the position of Fitzgerald and the Irish Exchequer. By the financial clauses of the Act of Union an adjustment of the financial responsibility between the two countries was made on a temporary basis until the two Exchequers could be amalgamated. Until then there existed a separate Irish Treasury and a separate Irish Chancellor. Under John Foster, a member of the powerful Louth family, who was Chancellor in 1804-6 and again in 1807-11, the Irish Treasury had endeavoured to make itself largely independent of the Lord Lieutenant. It was for that reason that the office of Chief Secretary and Chancellor of the Exchequer had been united under Pole in 1811. When the two offices were divided again in 1812, Fitzgerald soon discovered that he was in fact little more than the chief fiscal officer of the Irish government. The Lord Lieutenant was in actual control and Peel as Chief Secretary communicated directly with the Irish revenue departments in his name, besides administering the treasury patronage.

These discontents came to a head the following summer when Fitzgerald formally laid his resignation before the Prime Minister.

[1] 38328 f. 43, undated but from position September 1812.

But as Peel frankly told him, and repeated to Liverpool afterwards, he could not advise the transfer of control over the revenue departments to the Irish Treasury. The authority of the Lord Lieutenant must be paramount; and nothing could be more objectionable than the creation of a divided authority in a country situated and governed as Ireland was. With this view the cabinet entirely concurred. 'The unity of the Government in Ireland under the Lord Lieutenant,' wrote Liverpool in October 1813, 'must be preserved; the Chief Secretary is the channel through which the power and the patronage in Ireland must flow.' The issue, as Peel argued to both Liverpool and Fitzgerald, was not between the Chief Secretary and the Chancellor of the Irish Exchequer, but between the Chancellor and the Lord Lieutenant; but in practice, as Fitzgerald realised and resented, Lord Lieutenant and Chief Secretary were the same. The Prime Minister's solution of the problem was to ask the Secretary to take on both offices as his predecessor had done. But this Peel was unwilling to do. While he was in Ireland it was not impossible, but he told Liverpool that during the session he could not venture to undertake the whole parliamentary business of Ireland. In these circumstances Liverpool turned to the project foreshadowed in the Act of Union. In 1815 a select committee on the consolidation of the two Exchequers was set up and in 1816 the separate Irish Treasury abolished. Fitzgerald, whom Liverpool with his usual conciliatoriness had persuaded to remain in office up to the end, was offered but refused the post of Vice-Treasurer for Ireland under the new Act. 'He has certainly considerable abilities,' the Prime Minister wrote characteristically to Peel, 'but he is unfortunately deficient in two qualities more important in the concerns of life than any talents, *judgement* and *temper*.'[1]

In the Irish administration, therefore, the Secretary was unique not because of his separate office but because he wielded the Vice-regal authority delegated to him by the Lord Lieutenant; and this concentration of power added considerably to the strength and flexibility of the system. Yet unlike the Lord Lieutenant, who resided permanently in Dublin, the Secretary was absent from Ireland half the year in attendance on his parliamentary business. This periodic and prolonged absence in England threw a particular

[1] 40181 fos. 43, 81, 83; cf. *Peel*, I, 109-13.

responsibility on the Under-Secretary for Civil Affairs. In the early part of the nineteenth century there were two Under-Secretaries, in charge respectively of the civil and military departments of the Chief Secretary's office. The military department was a specialised and largely routine branch concerned with military finance and the Irish yeomanry. During Peel's Secretaryship the business of the department was reduced; though until the retirement in 1819 of the Military Under-Secretary, Sir Edward Baker Littlehales, the formal separation continued. The department for civil affairs, on the other hand, reflected the Chief Secretary's ubiquitous interest and authority; and the Civil Under-Secretary was one of the half-dozen men who constituted the real government of Ireland. Whether the Chief Secretary was in Dublin or London, he could find no more valuable henchman or more informative correspondent than his Under-Secretary. In the absence of the Chief Secretary, moreover, the Under-Secretary was thrown into direct contact with the Lord Lieutenant. He interviewed important visitors and was frequently called into consultation with the unofficial Irish cabinet—the Lord Chancellor, the Attorney-General and Solicitor-General—which advised the Lord Lieutenant. He was, as a later Lord Lieutenant expressed it, the channel of communication between Viceroy and the various Irish authorities, military, civil, and ecclesiastical, the depositary of the most confidential business of the government; 'the man, in short, upon whom must rest, during at least eight months of the year, the details of the administration'.[1]

A vacancy arose in this appointment almost immediately after Peel arrived in Ireland. The existing Under-Secretary, Sir Charles Saxton, was anxious to retire and it was thought advisable for his successor to be in harness before Peel went back to England again. Lord Sidmouth had mentioned a Mr. Hawthorne of the Board of Enquiry; Richmond was strongly in favour of an Irish official, Gregory; Peel's first thought was to sound his friend Beckett, the Under-Secretary of the Home Office. When Beckett showed no inclination to shift, however, Peel was ready to let the Lord Lieutenant decide between the two candidates already in the field. Richmond had his way and Gregory was appointed Under-Secretary in the Civil Department in October 1812. William Gregory

[1] *Peel*, III, 183-4.

was the younger son of a Galway landowner who had made a fortune in India with the Company. He had been educated at Harrow and Trinity College, Cambridge, and later read law at the Inner Temple. Returning to Ireland, he became in succession Surveyor of Skerries in 1795, M.P. for Portarlington in the Irish parliament of 1798, Commissioner for examining loyalist claims in 1799, Secretary to the Inland Navigation Board in 1800, and Commissioner of Excise in 1810. He had married into the influential Trench family, his wife being Lady Anne, the daughter of Lord Clancarty, who brought with her both aristocratic connections and a stiff Protestant outlook. In education, experience, and family, therefore, Gregory seemed eminently suitable; and he possessed in addition excellent manners and presence, a point which Richmond thought very material in view of the frequent absences of the Chief Secretary.[1] In many respects the selection proved an admirable one. Without any brilliance of intellect, Gregory was an intelligent, educated man with clear-cut views and a sense of humour. He gave his opinions firmly on persons and events, and though always courteous, handled his superiors with ease and confidence. In his work he was active and vigilant, and with his great experience of Ireland and the Irish character, was sensibly sceptical about all reports of rebellion, crime, and conspiracy until proof was forthcoming. Nevertheless, underneath the outer layer of official sophistication was a firm and unchanging core of Anglo-Irish Protestantism which gave his office so long as he held it a clear uncompromising stamp. Colonel Blacker, writing after Gregory's retirement, said 'the office has not been so well filled since he was removed from it. He was a perfect gentleman, as well as an excellent man of business, possessing a knowledge of the country and its gentry in general which in no small degree facilitated despatch.'[2] With the Chief Secretary he developed a personal friendship which lasted long after Peel left Ireland, and the disparity in their offices was amply balanced by the difference in their years, Gregory being the older man by twenty-two years. In the correspondence between the Lord Lieutenant, the Chief Secretary, and the Under-Secretary more than anywhere else was to be found the realities of Irish executive policy.

[1] Richmond, 1810. For Gregory's earlier career see 40193 f. 33.
[2] Blacker, VI, 114.

As his own private secretary Peel first appointed George Dawson, his old college friend, and himself an Irish landowner with property in Dublin, Co. Kerry, and Cavan. In August 1815 Dawson became M.P. for Co. Derry and was replaced by Sydney Streatfeild, a clerk in the Irish Office in London; but his connections with Peel were not thereby severed. In October 1815 Peel wrote to tell Gregory that George Dawson was going to marry his sister Mary. He had not, he added with an elder brother's surprise, the remotest idea of his intention.[1] When the wedding took place the following January, the links between the two families became closer still. Mary came to Ireland with her husband and Dawson was in London during the parliamentary session.

## IV

For the Chief Secretary himself attendance at Westminster was a substantial ingredient in the compound of labours that made up his office; and for him, as he had already discovered, there were no excuses for absence. Even the physical journey to London was a tedious matter. Holyhead, nominally some seven hours' sailing from Dublin, in winter sometimes took fourteen hours to reach, and the lack of a pier at Dunleary (not commenced until 1817), bad roads in Wales, and the failure of horses and carriage springs, added to the miseries of travel. Even more exasperating was the custom of holding short sessions before Christmas with a recess in January just long enough to deprive him of a decent justification for remaining in London. In his first two years of office Peel crossed the Irish Channel nine times, usually in the stormy season. When faced with a renewed summons in September 1814 he not unnaturally shrank from the prospect of coming across for yet another short autumn session in which, if the experience of 1812 and 1813 was a guide, it was unlikely that he would either vote or speak. Yet such considerations weighed little with his superiors and the Chief Secretary was obliged to set a good example. Each journey meant a gap of about a week in the regular flow of his correspondence, but once he arrived in London, the purely mechanical part of his work was alleviated by the existence of the Irish Office in Queen Street. All

[1] 40289 f. 182.

routine letters between the two governments passed through this office and an abstract and register was made of the incoming and outgoing letters. It is probable that other documents accumulated there too, since the permanent head of the office, Sir Charles Flint, was advising Peel in 1812 to have duplicate papers filed at Queen Street to facilitate answering parliamentary questions; and the office acted as a useful agency for the Irish Secretary in such a diversity of tasks as arranging for the publication of Irish items in the London press, reporting on the progress of Irish legislation in the House of Lords, and taking delivery of parcels of Irish salmon destined for Peel's table.

The Irish Office was intended both as a place of business and as an official residence; but Peel was early engaged in finding a more comfortable bachelor retreat for himself during the long months of the parliamentary session. His house in Little Scotland Yard was given up when he left the Colonial Office and in January 1813 he took Vansittart's house at 36 Great George Street for one year with an option to purchase. At the end of his tenancy, however, he moved to 12 Stanhope Street, off Park Lane, which remained his London home for the next decade. With his election to White's Club in December 1813, his London *ménage* was almost as well ordered as in Dublin. In his official life, however, Peel soon discovered that the framework of Irish administration was not noticeably designed with a view either to his comfort or efficiency. The clerks in his department on both sides of the water were on occasion both dilatory and careless. In February 1813, following a foolish error in which a routine letter for signature had superannuated not the retiring but the certificating officer, he asked Gregory to administer a sharp rebuke to the staff of the office in Dublin. The Under-Secretary did so, but with little visible effect on the hardened officials of the Castle. 'I am sorry to say it was not received as I expected and wished,' he admitted to Peel. 'The very cool indifference with which the matter was treated I confess has annoyed me very much.'[1] Next year it was Flint's turn. 'The constant mistakes which have occurred in the Acts of Parliament respecting Ireland are proof that sufficient attention is not paid to insure accuracy,' wrote Peel severely. 'I know not whose duty it is to prevent such inaccuracies, but I know that it

[1] 40195 f. 144.

is of the utmost importance that they should be prevented." Nevertheless, the effect of the new Secretary's brisk reforming temper gradually had its influence and in small matters he managed to infuse a great degree of efficiency into the domestic economy of his department. In 1816, for instance, he arranged with Flint for two London newspapers, the *Morning Chronicle* and the *Courier*, to be sent to him regularly by express. The same year he turned his attention to the defective and long-neglected Chief Secretary's library and made provision for its improvement and future security. He applied to Flint for volumes of the parliamentary sessions papers for 1807-14 and English Record Commission papers, and in the end a supply of the missing documents was obtained from Speaker Abbot.[1]

Outside his own department he found that little could be done in the sphere of Irish business unless he saw personally to its execution. Sidmouth, the Secretary of State under whom he nominally worked, maintained a routine correspondence on patronage, law and order, military matters, and trade, but showed little desire to initiate or control policy. It was from Liverpool rather than from the Home Secretary that he secured as a rule most support in time of need; though in the nature of the situation the Prime Minister could only give occasional attention to Irish problems. Yet legislation for Ireland was necessary, even if it had to be conducted through the parliament of the United Kingdom; and in the early nineteenth century the House of Commons was already beginning to find Irish affairs tedious and incomprehensible. Apart from the inflammable topic of Catholic emancipation, it was not easy for the Chief Secretary to interest his senior ministerial colleagues, still less the parliamentary Whips, in the details of Irish administration—police, magistracy, finance, potatoes, whiskey, and linen—that formed the substance of his legislative interests. Creative and energetic though Peel was anxious to be, he was constantly frustrated by finding his proposals shelved until the dog-days at the end of session, and then being left to his own resources to whip up attendance in a thin and jaded house. In July 1814 he made a rueful reference to the fact that people were accusing him of bringing in more bills than any other hundred members combined, and choosing the last possible moment

1 40215 fos. 180, 301; 40294 f. 79; *Colchester*, II, 588-91.

of the session for their introduction.[1] But it was in a more serious mood that he wrote to Arbuthnot in May 1817 pressing for better attendance in the House of Commons on the Irish Insurrection Bill and telling him that the last time it was discussed he had been left by almost every person holding English office and had to trust to personal friends and personal applications to make up his majority.[2]

There were, it is true, a hundred Irish members in the Commons, most of whom were supporters of the government. But they were not always present and even when they were, they exhibited little of that discipline which constitutes nine-tenths of political effectiveness. Part of Peel's duty was to supplement the work of the leader of the House in whipping up attendance among Irish supporters. Indeed the Chief Secretary was even expected to supervise the movements of those Irish M.P.s who belonged to the opposition. In October 1814 Sidmouth was asking him to keep an eye on the Irish members and, if opponents should begin to embark for England, to ensure that friends were despatched to London in the proportion of at least two to one.[3] But geographical obstacles, combined with the native indolence of the Irish gentry, operated as powerful deterrents. It was difficult to induce Irish members to make the journey to Westminster before Christmas and Peel suggested to Liverpool in October 1813 that it should not even be attempted, since those who did attend the pre-Christmas session would make it an excuse for not appearing again. A year later he wrote to Vansittart that 'it can hardly be expected that Irish members will undertake two journeys to London in the course of one session for the purpose of giving us their support'.[4] Irish members would clutch at any plausible excuse for postponing their departure. First they would wish to remain until after Christmas; then they would point out that the winter season was the time of greatest distress and disorder when their presence in the countryside was most needed; and finally they would plead the claims of attendance at the Easter court sessions as a further reason for remaining at home. Even those from whom the government might fairly expect to secure willing support showed a remarkable talent for procrastination. As Castlereagh observed to Peel at the start of his Secretaryship, 'our official friends from

[1] 40287 f. 98.   [2] 40293 f. 85.   [3] 40182 f. 124.   [4] 40285 f. 56; 40287 f. 169.

Ireland' were generally 'very relaxed' in their discipline.[1] The Lord Lieutenant in May 1816 was compelled to advert with some severity to the case of Mr. Webber who, having been brought in for Armagh city early in the month expressly to stiffen the Protestant ranks in the Catholic emancipation debate, still showed no signs of attending to his parliamentary duties and instead remained in Ireland to bargain with the government for his services.[2]

The Irish government in fact could urgently compel only its office-holders to attend parliament and even these on occasions needed some blunt speaking from the Chief Secretary. In the spring of 1815 Peel had to send personal letters to no fewer than three official members of the Irish administration, McNaghten, Odell, and Lord Henry Moore, urging their presence in parliament.

> Your absence [he observed to Odell is] not merely the loss of an individual vote. The friends of Government who are not in office presume from the non-attendance of those who are, that the business is not very pressing, nor indeed can it be expected that those who have no official connection with the government will put themselves to the inconvenience of leaving Ireland, while those intimately connected with it by office remain there.[3]

Support for Irish measures from Irish M.P.s was therefore spasmodic and incalculable. 'Receiving ten times as many favours as the English members,' wrote Peel in 1813, '[they] do not give us one-tenth of their support.'[4]

In theory the government controlled a mass of patronage which could be put to political use; and both at the time of the Union and later one of the prime arguments for the retention of Irish patronage by the Lord Lieutenant was that without it the administration of Ireland could scarcely be carried on. But in practice the area of patronage that was effectively in the hands of the Castle was extremely small. Military, judicial, and ecclesiastical appointments were in any case largely withdrawn from political considerations; and apart from newly created posts, government patronage in boroughs and counties was by custom put at the disposal of the local M.P.s if friendly to the ministry. Only in Dublin was it expressly

[1] 40181 f. 150.    [2] 40192 f. 117, cf. *Peel*, I, 226.    [3] 40288 f. 60.    [4] *Peel*, I, 73-4.

reserved for the government and even there the pressure of applications and the long waiting-lists deprived the system of flexibility. The old eighteenth-century habit of regarding patronage as a social perquisite rather than a political contract still persisted; and in the relatively smaller governing class of Ireland there was an inevitable tendency for single families to monopolise the patronage of their districts with only a faint sense of any reciprocal obligation. Flagrant opposition could be met with appropriate measures by a strong-minded administration. Open attempts at corrupt bargains and even proffers of bribes to subordinate officials, though not unknown, could be rejected by an executive which had its own self-respect as well as public opinion to consider. But sloth, indifference, occasional fits of independence, fair promises, and lax performance, though just as ruinous to administrative discipline, were not so easily open to suitable penalties. The character of the Irish gentry was not the least of the problems that confronted the Irish government.

To newcomers from England, where public opinion was already hardening against the indiscriminate bestowal of places and honours for political reasons, the avid and unscrupulous pursuit of patronage by the Irish aristocracy and gentry was apt to be a repellent phenomenon. There was in fact a perceptible gap between the political morality of the two countries. In England the greater wealth and solidity of the nation had emancipated society from undue dependence on court and administration. In Ireland the Protestant caste had been permanently conditioned to look almost solely to the state for support and nourishment. This Irish reliance on government made an early impression on Peel's mind.

> There is a disposition in Ireland [he wrote to Flint in the spring of 1814] which I will do all in my power to check, to refer everything to 'Government'. . . . I think the majority have the same idea of the Government which the natives are said to have of the East India Company. They attach to the Government all the attributes of omnipotence which it is peculiarly disposed to exert in every species of job and fraud and peculation.

Flint, while heartily agreeing that this was one of the worst and most prominent features of Irish life, added pessimistically that 'if you can even succeed in *checking* it, you will be rendering Ireland a most important service. But you will find it a Herculean task.'[1] This parasitic attitude extended not only downward to the trading and commercial classes but upward to those already in the public service. Peel found that every official man, not content with the favours of government for himself, 'thought he had the right to quarter his family on the patronage of the government',[2] an assumption which he found even more repugnant than the clamorous exigencies of outsiders. It was a practical commentary on this aspect of administration that a formal indexed Application Book was kept in the Chief Secretary's office, containing the names of about a hundred political clients, in which the existing patronage enjoyed was entered on the left page in red ink under the name of the individual and the objects he had still in view on the right page in black. This list, which included M.P.s, peers, and judges, constituted the essential basis of the government's support in Ireland.[3]

It was difficult enough to extract from this system the full political value which on the executive side constituted its sole redeeming feature; to dispense with it was impossible. All that the government could hope to do was to check its excesses and, by refraining from too automatic a distribution of favours, to instil some notion of reciprocal service into its beneficiaries. On the death of a great magnate there was invariably an unseemly scramble for the honours and perquisites he had gathered into his hands; and such occasions furnished a useful opportunity for the executive to spread out wider the area of obligation. 'It must be the interest of Government,' wrote Peel to Gregory in 1815 on the reported death of Lord Muskerry, 'not merely to promote the success of a single candidate for a County by the distribution of its patronage but to conciliate as much goodwill as it can without losing sight of the interests of its chosen candidate.'[4]

When county and borough M.P.s protested unreasonably against the Castle's disposition of patronage in their district, they were liable to encounter a discomfortingly rigid attitude on the part of the Chief Secretary. There was an early clash between Peel and the Dowager Lady Clare, the widow of Lord Chancellor Fitzgibbon and the mother of the second Earl of Clare.

[1] 40214 f. 203; *Peel*, I, 119-20.    [2] 40332 f. 11 (Peel to Goulburn).
[3] 40296; 40297.    [4] 40288 f. 61.

Lady Clare is in town [reported Gregory in December 1812] frantic that the nomination of the Sheriff for the county of Limerick should be given to the Chief Baron. She showed me what is called by her, your very impertinent letter to Odell. Unless she gains this point her son is to go into opposition. She is to have an interview with the Duke of Richmond as soon as he returns from Castletown.[1]

Three years later a dispute over the same office threatened even more severe consequences. Odell called on Peel in June 1815 and asked in turn for the nomination for the sheriff of Limerick. He argued that his interest was distinct from that of Lord Clare and professed not to understand why the county patronage was withheld from the county member. On pressing the Chief Secretary in rather a peremptory tone for an opinion on his chances of getting the nomination, Peel told him flatly that he thought he had not the remotest hope. At that Odell left the room in a state of utmost indignation and promptly lodged a complaint with Liverpool and Sidmouth. This availed him nothing and though he talked of resigning from his post on the Irish Treasury Board, in the end he prudently held back from this act of sacrifice.[2]

More reasonable approaches met with more conciliatory treatment. When Lord Ormonde in 1815 offered his support and that of his two brothers to Lord Liverpool, provided a satisfactory arrangement could be made about the patronage of Co. Kilkenny, Peel advised the Prime Minister to reply that while the government were not indifferent to Lord Ormonde's support, they could not purchase it with promises of exclusive patronage; but that without defining the degree of consideration he would obtain, he could be assured that his views would be given due weight by the Irish government. In private Peel urged Lord Desart, the rival magnate in Kilkenny, to come to some accommodation with Lord Ormonde; and when in November Ormonde applied for the shrieval nomination for the following year, Peel told Desart in confidence that it would be necessary to give it to him. Desart, who had nominated for the three previous years, was obviously sore at being passed over; but he was obliged to admit that as he had one vote and Ormonde controlled three, it was impossible to make an equal

[1] 40195 f. 20.          [2] 40289 fos. 101, 125.

distribution of the patronage between them.[1] Not all Irish peers were as tactful or as powerful as the Marquess of Ormonde. A hint was conveyed to Peel in April 1816 that Lord Donegal would be prepared to return a government candidate for Belfast in return for the promise of the next ribbon of St. Patrick for himself and a baronetcy for Sir Stephen May. 'I laughed at such a monstrous proposition,' reported Peel to the Lord Lieutenant, 'and said he might return whom he pleased.'[2]

Colleagues and friends presented as embarrassing a problem as the more frankly opportunist applicants. Croker emerged from an unsuccessful contest for Downpatrick with a burden of unfulfilled promises which harassed not only his but Peel's life for the next six years. But though conscious of his importunity, he did not on that account relax his petitioning. 'Oh, my dear Peel, the horror of refusing a friend is nothing at all to the horror of asking a friend', he wrote in August 1813. To which Peel lightly replied, being for once able to meet the request, 'Oh, my dear Croker, it is very pleasant to receive an application with which you can without difficulty comply.'

More illustrious figures than Croker called for no less tact. By a complicated Act passed in 1793 the Irish government was limited to a sum of £1,200 per annum for additions to the Irish pension list until the total was reduced to under £80,000. The death of the Duchess of Brunswick, who enjoyed a pension of £5,000 on the Irish establishment, brought the list below the statutory total in 1813, and the Duke of Richmond at once proceeded to increase his awards for the year from £1,200 to £3,300. Peel, with some justifiable doubts on the precise legal position and a politic regard for the economists in the House of Commons, not only indicated his reluctance to the Lord Lieutenant but the following year even brought Sidmouth into the discussion. Even if the statute was clear, he had strong objections both to some of the specific proposals put forward and to the general policy of spending up to the limit of the pension fund as a matter of course.

I think [he wrote to Richmond from London] the Pension Fund ought to be applied (and in this country I believe it strictly is) to

[1] 40216 fos. 283, 303; 40289 fos. 38, 189.     [2] 40290 f. 224.

the support of persons who have either rendered a service to the public, or who are nearly related to those who have, and to enable those who have rank and title, and no means of maintaining them, to live at least with decency.[1]

The matter of pensions was in fact the most delicate point in the relationship between the Lord Lieutenant and the Chief Secretary, since the awards were in a peculiar degree the personal gift of the Viceroy, while on his Secretary fell the task of defending the pension list against the critics at Westminster. With Richmond's successor, however, he soon won acceptance of his views and from the start of the new Viceroyalty the annual pension awards were kept down to a figure very close to the previous limit of £1,200. Lord Whitworth cheerfully submitted his list to the Secretary's scrutiny and in more than one instance withdrew proposals for new pension additions. 'I am as anxious as you yourself can be,' he wrote to Peel in 1816, 'that we should be justified in all our words and works'. When he showed some remorse at some of his early grants, one to an impoverished sister and the other to the widow of his nephew, amounting in all to £700 per annum, Peel was quick to reassure him. 'I really think you have nothing whatever to accuse yourself of in the distribution of the Pension Fund,' he wrote back in May 1816. 'I do not think there are any three years in the whole period of the Irish history during which so honest a use has been made of it.'[2]

In the lower reaches of patronage, among such posts as gaugers, tidewaiters, and tax collectors, the difficulty was as much to find vacancies as to decide between rival claims. As in England there was a vast pressure on all minor official posts, and vacancies were often booked up two or three years ahead by lists of applicants kept by the various government departments. A curious but convincing proof of this was cited by Peel to Fitzgerald in 1814.

> When Lord Wellington was here as an aide-de-camp, he lodged at the house of a Mr. Dickson, a shoemaker. Mrs. Dickson had a son, who by some accident or other bore a much stronger resemblance to Lord Wellington than to Mr. Dickson. In favour of this young

---

[1] 40282 f. 29, partly printed *Peel*, I, 100.    [2] 40191 f. 215; *Peel*, I, 275.

man (who I believe is no doubt Ld. W's son) he wrote to Lord Whitworth, on the latter's first arrival in this country, earnestly entreating the appointment of this young man, who was educated in Trinity College and is properly qualified for it, to some situation of about £200 a year, with a reasonable hope of further advancement according to his merits—'to be put on the ladder' was his expression. A year has elapsed; of course Lord Whitworth has every good disposition towards him; but he has not put his foot upon the first step yet.[1]

When such an administratively important office as the Collectorship of Excise at Cork fell vacant, Peel saw to it that a fitting professional appointment was made in the person of one of the Surveyors-General of Excise, who had, as he disarmingly explained to the local magnate, 'no other claims than those of merit'. But with the whole host of Irish applicants on his back, he could do no more with the lesser situations than reject corrupt bargains, punish fraud, and ensure that the flow of patronage was as far as possible channelled through those who had earned it by their votes in parliament. He did so with often a humorous indifference that at least added some flavour to a flat and tedious traffic. 'I do not think your son can make a more inefficient member of the Board of Stamps than Mr. T. has done,' he wrote to Gregory in 1816. 'I am perfectly ready therefore to acquiesce in the exchange.' On an application for an increase in pensions he minuted—'A modest request! Use my name as you please in discountenance of it. R.P.' On the recommendation of somebody described as an honest man for a coast officer's post: 'Pray reward him then—*rari nantes in gurgite vasto*.' On a letter from Baron Smith: 'I would rather give Judge Smith five gaugers' places than receive one letter from him.'[2] But this flippancy merely masked his complete antipathy to what he once called 'the vortex of local patronage' and its attendant evils. 'I am quite tired of and disgusted,' he wrote to Whitworth in 1817, when pressing for disciplinary action against a government official, 'with the shameful corruption which every Irish enquiry brings to light.' Irish patronage and Irish administration together formed a school of human nature in which even the youngest official rapidly matured. The constant

[1] 40287 f. 141, printed with omission of names in *Peel*, I, 161.
[2] For these and similar examples see *Letter-Box*, pp. 282-3; *Peel*, I, 271ff.

canvassing, the bluster and deceit, the tendency of Irish suitors to claim silence as an assent and a friendly word as a promise, taught Peel habits of official caution and reserve. He made himself a rule 'on which I invariably act, of avoiding by civil expressions, assurances of good will, etc., the encouragement of those sanguine hopes which it is in Ireland so much more easy to raise than to gratify'.[1]

One special aspect of Irish dependence on government, as useless and irksome as it was costly, was the subsidised Irish press.[2] When Peel came to Ireland he found that six newspapers in Dublin alone were receiving money from the government. The bulk of the payments came from the proclamation fund and were nominally on account of advertisements and proclamations inserted in the press by the government. The system was extravagant and, though mainly designed to attract and retain newspaper support, had no marked success. When supplying details of expenditure under the proclamation fund to Peel for parliamentary use in May 1813, Gregory added despondently, 'but what can you say in defence of the system, except that your adversaries expended larger sums in the same way'.[3] Nevertheless, though press expenditure by 1813 had been materially reduced, it still remained one of the more dubious aspects of Irish administration. Several of the editors were in receipt of government pensions and certain newspapers were additionally financed from secret funds. Two of the Dublin papers, the *Patriot* and the *Correspondent*, received an annual subsidy of £500; and a third, the *Dublin Journal*, one of £300. As the secret service fund, normally used for this purpose, was limited to £5,000 and had to meet many other calls, the government was often hard put to it to find the necessary money.

While the connection lasted, the government papers were used by the Secretary's department for various purposes: to correct false statements in the opposition press, to give publicity to specific items of information in the government interest, and to print parliamentary speeches on the government side, together with an occasional inspired article, some written by Peel himself, in support of the Castle policy. But the blunders, extravagances, and jealousies of the government newspapers formed a heavy price to pay for

40294 f. 160.    [2] cf. A. Aspinall, *Politics and the Press* (1949), ch. iv, v.
0196 f. 145.

these moderate services, and the Castle editors proved a trouble-some, quarrelsome team. In May 1813 the *Dublin Journal* inserted a fictitious announcement of a protest by the Catholic Board against the proposed Catholic Relief Bill, a journalistic device that made Peel threaten to withdraw proclamations from the paper entirely. In June the *Correspondent* refused to print a speech of Peel's because a copy had gone first to the *Patriot*.[1] On another occasion the editor of the *Hibernian Journal* let off, as Gregory reported to Peel, 'a flaming puff upon both of us, for which he shall get a jobation'; and a similar reproof came from Peel for what he considered a malicious personal attack by the *Patriot* on the eminent Irish whig, Sir John Newport.[2]

There was every reason, therefore, for Peel to take a critical view of the subsidised press. The *Patriot*, costing the government £1,500 per annum for its miserable daily circulation of 750 copies, came under his particular condemnation. In April 1815 he was urging Gregory to complete the arrangements for ending the connection with the newspaper. 'I estimate the value of its services so low, the amount being certainly a minus quantity, that whatever we can save from the present expenses of the establishment will be more than clear gain.' He was willing to make some provision for the proprietors so long as his eye was no longer offended by 'this execrable paper'.[3] The following year he showed an almost equal alacrity in proposing the discontinuance of the subsidy to the *Dublin Journal*, which was struggling along under Giffard's editorship, with a revenue of £2,490 and an expenditure of £2,430. 'The account,' he wrote to Gregory, 'would be more fairly stated thus—gain to himself £60, loss to the government, £1,400, and in point of injury and discredit, as much more. I had always a difficulty in putting an end to the paper because I thought it had been a source of considerable profit to him.' Relieved of such compunctions, he now instructed Gregory to withdraw the proclamations as soon as he could, with an offer to Giffard of an additional £100 per annum from the secret service fund in compensation.[4] Nevertheless, the government newspapers were as difficult to detach as Irish place-hunters. Not only was the *Dublin Journal* still writing on the government side in 1818, but Peel was still representing to Gregory in that year the desirability of

[1] 40197 f. 56.    [2] *Peel*, I, 114-16.    [3] 40288 f. 167.    [4] 40290 f. 177

extinguishing the *Patriot*. The editor, Comerford, had just been drowned and it seemed a suitable opportunity, as Gregory hard-heartedly expressed it, to let the *Patriot* sink with him. At that date the paper was still annually receiving £500 from the Secret Service fund and two sums of £800 and £260 from the Proclamation fund, as well as the pension of £200 for its proprietor Corbett.[1] The Irish subsidised press led a charmed if eccentric life of its own.

Part at least of the reason for the continuance of the Irish government newspapers—almost it seemed against the will of the Irish government—was that they performed however ineffectually a defensible function. Deprived of press support, the Irish executive would have been deprived of almost their only general means of disseminating information and argument. Even as it was, the Irish newspapers with the largest circulation, such as the *Freeman's Journal* and the *Dublin Evening Post*, were in the hands of the nationalist opposition; and to maintain their footing in the face of such competition the subsidised newspapers had to compromise with the needs of their public more frequently than their paymasters always approved. To have left government advocacy to the voluntary efforts of a free and independent press, would merely have meant that the government had no press advocates at all. Moreover, the bitter and unscrupulous character of press warfare in that period left no place for impartiality and little for truth. Without some newspaper protection of their own, the government would have been naked under a daily torrent of libel and abuse. In the conditions of 1812, with Catholic agitation running high and the continental war still being desperately fought out, that was not a situation which any Lord Lieutenant or Chief Secretary could contemplate with complacency. As late as 1816 Peel told the House of Commons that one of the causes that unquestionably contributed to disturbance and outrage in Ireland was the press of that country. 'What,' he asked, 'could be said in favour of a press which never sought to enlighten the public mind, which never aimed at the dissemination of truth, which never endeavoured to correct the morals or improve the happiness of the people? On the contrary, the most studious efforts were made to keep alive and foment discord, and the malignant influence of the worst passions.'[2] Inevitably, therefore,

[1] 40205 f. 167; 40295 f. 25.     [2] *Speeches*, I, 62 (26 April 1816).

Irish administrators were caught between impatience at the crude and sordid instruments at their disposal and anxiety not to be left completely without support in the unequal warfare with Irish nationalist feeling. Between the horns of this dilemma the subsidised press contrived to preserve its expensive, threatened, and disreputable existence.

## V

The key to the efficiency of the Irish administration lay in the relationship between the Lord Lieutenant and his Chief Secretary. Without harmony between them, there could be no unity in the government; and without unity there could be no strength. Moreover, within that highly personal relationship, the role of the Lord Lieutenant was in no sense that of a cipher. His office was to a considerable extent what he chose to make it and much depended on the temperament and experience of the man himself. A Lord Lieutenant of three or four years' standing, a Lord Lieutenant of sagacity or strong character, could easily outweigh a Secretary newly appointed or lacking either administrative skill or political talent. The relationship between the young Peel and the middle-aged Richmond in 1812-13, the one beginning and the other ending his term of Irish service, was one in which the balance of authority naturally lay with the older and more experienced man. It is true that an easy confidence soon sprang up between them, and Richmond was always mindful of the need to delegate responsibility to the official who toiled at 'the labouring oar' in Westminster. An illuminating example of his attitude was provided by a letter he wrote to Peel in March 1813 on the controversial issue of the Maynooth grant. After canvassing considerations of public expediency on one side and personal predilections on the other, he added cheerfully at the end, 'you see, I give one opinion as a public man and another as a private man, so that take which course you please, you may decidedly quote me as perfectly agreeing with you. You will be a better judge on the spot than I am.'[1] Nevertheless, despite this happy relationship, it represented a decided enhancement of Peel's position when the Duke of Richmond finally laid

[1] 40185 f. 190.

down his office in August 1813. It was the Secretary now who was armed with seniority and experience, and the new Viceroy who had his Irish apprenticeship to serve.

Richmond had been in Ireland over six years, the longest period of any Lord Lieutenant in the first half of the nineteenth century, and he had been served by no fewer than four Secretaries. His rule coincided with some of the most difficult and depressing years of the war, and had seen the first serious renewal of the Catholic movement since the Union. It was a proper as well as a considerate act on Peel's part when he wrote to urge that a special mark of approval, such as a letter from the Prince Regent, should be sent on the occasion of his retirement.[1] His successor was an elderly experienced diplomat, Lord Whitworth, whose wife was a step-daughter of Lord Liverpool. The traditional and symbolic ceremony of inauguration took place in Dublin on the evening of 26 August 1813. Lord Whitworth on arrival at the Castle was received by the outgoing Lord Lieutenant in the Presence Chamber and was thence led in state to the Council Chamber. His commission as Lord Lieutenant was read by the Deputy-Clerk to the Hanaper; the oath of state administered by the Lord Primate of Ireland, the Arch-bishop of Armagh; and the declarations required by law repeated and subscribed. Peel as Chief Secretary next read the royal letter directing the Sword of State to be delivered to the new Lord Lieutenant. The Duke of Richmond formally handed over the sword, together with the insignia of the Order of St. Patrick, and immediately withdrew from the chamber, to leave Ireland accord-ing to custom at the earliest possible moment. Whitworth, now legally Lord Lieutenant, took his place at the Council board and—a touch of the incongruous to which the members of the council were inured—his wine warrant was then read and signed. There was on this occasion a representative attendance of the Privy Council: two archbishops and a bishop, the two Lords Chief Justice of King's Bench and Common Pleas, the Attorney-General, the Solicitor-General, Peel, Fitzgerald, General Hope, and three Irish peers.[2]

The new Lord Lieutenant was in some respects a self-made man.

---

[1] 40284 f. 121. In response Sidmouth wrote a handsome letter to the Duke of Richmond.

[2] S.P.O., Irish P.C. Minutes.

He had been first a soldier and then, through the influence of his patron the Duke of Dorset, a diplomat, representing the United Kingdom in Poland, Russia, and France. He was ambassador in Paris at the time when the Treaty of Amiens was broken off and the famous scene between himself and Napoleon took place in the Tuileries. In appearance he was a handsome florid man. His manners were polished; and gossip credited him with a past of some gallantry. In Dublin he was rumoured to have been one of the great Catherine's lovers when minister in Russia in 1789-1800, a distinction which is unlikely to have lowered his prestige in the Irish capital. Creevey had a less edifying story of an affair with a Russian lady who deserted her husband, supported Whitworth with her own money, and finally came to England in the expectation of marrying him.[1] Whether this was true or not, Whitworth in fact married in 1801 the widowed Duchess of Dorset, reputed to be one of the wealthiest matches in the country, and brought her with him to Ireland in 1813. Described as the haughty duchess, she has been given a reputation for snobbery and imperiousness, and her husband represented as being, through age and indifference, largely under her management.[2] There is perhaps malice in such a portrayal. Lord Whitworth gained immediate approval by his agreeable manners and appearance; and Lord Sheffield reported in November 1813 that 'the Duchess, who is unaffected and pleasing in her manner, will be very popular'.[3] Certainly there was no trace of any strain in the relations between Peel and the inhabitants of the Viceregal Lodge a short way across Phoenix Park. Even before the arrival of the Lord Lieutenant in Ireland, Peel had formed a favourable impression of his new chief. 'All that I see of Lord Whitworth,' he wrote to Richmond in June 1813, 'convinces me that his appointment is a good one. I rather hoped that [the Marquess of] Huntly would have had the offer. . . . He would have been an excellent Lord Lieutenant. Next to him, I think Lord Whitworth is the best that could have been selected.'[4] To Goulburn he wrote in September that though he missed the Duke of Richmond and the Lady Lennoxes, Lord Whitworth would do admirably and a better successor could not have been chosen.[5]

[1] *Creevey Papers*, p. 67.  [2] cf. C. O'Mahoney, *Viceroys of Ireland* (1912), 213 ff.
[3] Foster (Sheffield to J. Foster, 4 November 1813).  [4] Richmond, 1417.
[5] Goulburn, II/13 (19 September 1813).

His relations with Peel certainly bore no mark of senility or indolence. With less knowledge of Ireland than Richmond, he had the better trained mind; and his correspondence reveals a cool and acute intellect. At the outset he was clearly feeling his way in the labyrinth of Irish politics and personalities; but as time went on his early scepticism and tolerance gave way to a closer apprehension of the inherent dangers and difficulties of the Irish scene. He was, moreover, not without a reserve of stubbornness on certain issues. When in 1816 Peel discovered that Liverpool and Castlereagh had virtually promised an Irish peerage to a cousin of Canning, Whitworth threatened to resign rather than sanction such a step. 'I really think,' wrote Peel privately to Fitzgerald, 'he would not stay ten days here after Canning was gazetted.'[1] Yet underneath his normally firm and urbane exterior, there was perhaps a need for friendliness and companionship not satisfied elsewhere and his relationship with Peel was from the start unusually warm and affectionate. When they were separated he kept up a constant correspondence with his Chief Secretary irrespective of official forms and necessities. He had no news, he wrote in December 1813, but 'I have a gratification in scribbling to you and you must indulge me'. Again in 1816: 'I have a pleasure in talking with you which I cannot resist, so you must bear with me.' When in 1814 Peel hinted at retiring if he could not get satisfaction from the cabinet in the case of Judge Fletcher, Whitworth wrote back in even more pressing terms. 'I cannot without great alarm contemplate the possibility . . . of your being induc'd to adopt a measure which would deprive me of my most substantial comfort and consolation in this country.' In such circumstances it was natural that Lord Lieutenant and Chief Secretary soon looked on Irish matters with a single eye. 'You estimate so purely the state of this country,' wrote Whitworth in July 1814, 'and are so anxious to provide the best means of preserving its tranquillity, that I can have nothing to do but to approve as I do most cordially of all your proceedings.'[2]

The four years spent in Ireland by Lord Whitworth and his duchess were scarred by a personal tragedy of a kind that was not infrequent in an age when riding for pleasure and utility was an ordinary part of living for most men in the middle and upper

[1] 40291 fos. 91, 121.   [2] 40187 f. 170; 40189 fos. 5, 169; 40191 f. 56.

classes. On 14 February 1815 the duchess's son, the young Duke of Dorset who had just attained his majority, fell while hunting near Kilkenny. The horse rolled on him and he died within half an hour. Peel was in London and Gregory wrote to him immediately with the news: 'the Lord Lieutenant is quite wretched; she, poor soul, has cried much during the night but for several hours she could not be brought to believe her son was dead'. Peel at once sent back what Whitworth described to Gregory as 'a most feeling and amiable letter . . . It gave us both great comfort. What an excellent Creature he is!'[1] The Viceregal Lodge was being repainted at the time and was uninhabitable but Peel made the practical suggestion that Lord Whitworth and the duchess should retire from the Castle to the comfort and privacy of his own Lodge. The offer was gratefully accepted and immediately after the Duke of Dorset's body was sent to England for burial, his parents took possession of Peel's 'airy and cheerful drawing room' and the sheltered walks in the lodge garden. The Lord Lieutenant was anxious, however, to take the duchess to England for a period of rest and Peel saw the Prime Minister and the Home Secretary on 18 February to get permission for him to leave Ireland for that purpose. This was naturally granted but it entailed recourse to the traditional machinery of Lords Justices to carry on the government of Ireland in the Lord Lieutenant's absence. Appointed at a Privy Council meeting on 13 March, they consisted of the Primate, the Lord Chancellor, and the Commander-in-Chief of the forces, Sir George Hewett. It had originally been suggested that the Lord Chief Justice should be the third member, and Peel argued tenaciously in his favour with a wealth of historical and legal detail. But the three great law officers of the crown in Dublin were opposed on principle to a combination of political and judicial functions, and the Secretary's opinion was overruled. The same evening Whitworth and the duchess embarked for England, the Lords Justices by precedent not being sworn in until the Lord Lieutenant was not only on board but actually out to sea.[2]

The timing of Whitworth's absence from Ireland was unfortunate.

---

[1] *Letter-Box*, pp. 57-61.

[2] For the Duke of Dorset's death, the absence from Ireland of the Lord Lieutenant, and the appointment of Lords Justices, see 40190 fos. 18-76; 40288 fos. 64-78; 40200 fos. 20-273; Irish P.C. Minutes; *Letter-Box*, pp. 56-86.

The Viceregal couple were met at Holyhead by the news of Napoleon's escape from Elba and at every stage on their journey to London, where they arrived on 17 March, they received in Whitworth's trenchant words, 'formidable accounts of the Ruffian's progress'. For a month Peel and the Lord Lieutenant conferred daily in London on the news from Ireland and still more on the news from the continent. At one point it was decided that if necessary Peel should go to Dublin for a while, to be relieved by Whitworth when his parliamentary duties compelled his return to Westminster. Even in 1813 Whitworth had been apprehensive of French diversionary efforts in Ireland, and the news of the allied entry into Paris in 1814 had been received with particular relief by the Irish government. Now the old excitement and disaffection had returned, and reports from all over Ireland spoke of the general joy of the poorer classes at Napoleon's reappearance in France. It was an additional misfortune, in the eyes of authority, that the news coincided with Eastertide, when as Gregory dryly expressed it, 'the lower orders testify their faith and piety in Drunkenness for two days'. Though the Irish government discounted the wilder rumours of general insurrection, they did not neglect elementary precautions. At Peel's suggestion the correspondence of the French consul was opened in the post, though nothing suspicious was discovered; the military authorities and the Dublin police were kept on the alert; and a watch kept on Mrs. Arthur O'Connor, the wife of the former leader of the United Irishmen who had entered French service in 1804. The risk of disorder was all the more alarming since the British government was obliged to withdraw 5,000 troops from Ireland to reinforce the small British army in Flanders. Peel and Whitworth, doubly concerned for the state of Ireland in their absence, represented to Sidmouth the dangers of stripping the country of its regular troops; but the cabinet's decision to run the minor risk of weakening Ireland rather than the major one of depriving Wellington of reinforcements could not seriously be opposed. The Lords Justices, however, protested vigorously from Dublin at this drastic diminution of the forces at their disposal. Gregory, who worded the despatch, took care nevertheless to accompany it with a private letter to Peel in which he expressed his conviction that there was no organised conspiracy or danger of general rebellion in Ireland, and that it would simply be playing Napoleon's game to allow mere rumour and disaffection to detain British troops at home.[1]

Reassured, despite their anxieties, by this opinion from the man they trusted most in the Irish executive, Peel and Whitworth stayed in England and busied themselves instead with plans for calling out some of the more efficient Irish yeomanry units to relieve the remaining regular forces of their security duties. In the latter half of April Whitworth even went down to the country for a week, and it was not until 12 May that he was back once more at the Castle. A couple of weeks later he wrote cheerfully to Peel that 'everything is going on so smoothly here, barring Murder, Rape, and Robbery, that there can be no necessity for hurrying you away from London'. The Lords Justices, it appeared, had acted in his absence on a kind of self-correcting principle. Manners, the Lord Chancellor, who was inclined to fuss and panic, had been kept steady by the Primate; and General Hewett had been sensible and efficient on all matters except the yeomanry.[2] There were in fact numerous arguments, both military and legal, against using the yeomanry for general service, all of which duly found their way to the Chief Secretary's desk. But Peel's response was brisk and masterful. 'Littlehales tells me of difficulties about pay, deficiency of estimates, etc.', he wrote to Gregory on 17 June. 'I shall advise him to cut the Gordian knot. I have no notion of being prevented by the letter of an Act of Parliament from averting any serious evil to the State or depriving it of any great benefit.' When in June the cabinet took the further decision to send Wellington every available regular soldier in the country, Peel procured authorisation for embodying the Irish militia. But he continued to argue against putting the Insurrection Act into force without 'urgent and imperious necessity'.

As the armies drew together in Belgium, however, there was a renewed wave of rumour and the *Dublin Evening Post* in particular gave prominence to all reports of French successes. Waterloo was fought on 18 June and on the 20th Peel was able to send off from London the first unconfirmed report of an allied victory. Two days later he was able to follow this up with what Whitworth described as 'most interesting and most animating particulars of the great and glorious victory of the ever-memorable 18th. I am not,' continued

[1] *Letter-Box*, p. 81.  [2] 40190 fos. 76, 86, 104.

the Lord Lieutenant, 'sufficiently collected to be able to write with any degree of composure.' The news was celebrated in Dublin with a salute of guns, an illumination, and a *feu de joie*; and the police were ordered to clap into the watch-house what Whitworth described as 'blackguards running about the streets in the night denying the Victory and asserting that Bonaparte was the conqueror'.[1] The danger was over. It was the end, as it proved, of the long period stretching back to James II and the Boyne in which Ireland had been not only England's weakness but France's opportunity; and, what was more the concern of Englishmen, the end of the war with which they had lived for nearly a quarter of a century. Peace was to bring its problems no less than war; but for a brief moment the laurels of victory could be savoured while they were still green and fragrant.

For Peel, after the strain of the preceding three months, it was an exhilarating occasion and he profited from the general festive spirit by obtaining leave from Whitworth to visit Paris before resuming his duties at the Castle. This was a project he had meditated earlier, though it had been put aside when Napoleon's escape made it more probable that, if Peel left London at all during the session, Dublin rather than Paris would be his destination. The report that Wellington was about to enter Paris renewed his thoughts of a continental trip and together with Fitzgerald and Croker he set out at the end of the session. Travelling by way of Dover and Boulogne they reached Paris on 11 July where their eyes were gladdened by the sight of the Life Guards patrolling the boulevards as they were accustomed to do at Charing Cross in time of riot. They saw most of the notabilities, Wellington, Castlereagh, Talleyrand, Fouché, the King of France, the Emperors of Austria and Russia, Marmont, Masséna, and a bevy of other French marshals; and on 19 July they dined with Wellington, when Peel had the honour of sitting next to the Duke and hearing all the details of the battle. On their way back they spent a couple of days with the Duke and Duchess of Richmond at Brussels. On the second day they drove out in pouring rain to see the field of Waterloo. All the way from Brussels the *pavé* was strewn with broken weapons, articles of clothing and equipment, and the bones of horses; and they found the battle-field itself still littered with the

[1] 40190 fos. 187, 192.

untidy and melancholy debris of war: scraps of clothing, caps, helmets, torn paper, empty cartridges and cannon-wadding, with here and there the raw mounds of mass graves. People were still searching for mementoes but there was little left to find. The Belgian peasants had been over the ground like harvest gleaners, and were offering their plunder for sale at a steadily mounting tariff. Peel bought a handsome French cuirass for two napoleons and Croker a cross of the Legion of Honour.

Early in August Peel was back at last in Dublin, having had a passage of thirty-three hours from Holyhead in the teeth of a westerly wind with a shipload of passengers, the men all sick and the women and children maintaining a running chorus of lamentations and appeals to the stewards—'ludicrous enough for half an hour,' he wrote subsequently to Croker, 'but, like other good things, wearied by constant repetition'.[1] It was his thirteenth crossing of the Irish sea.

---

[1] For this continental trip see *Croker*, I, 61-76.

# CHAPTER

# 5

# AGITATION AND ORDER

The legal position of Roman Catholics in Britain in the eighteenth
century was one of considerable complexity. This was due partly
to the mass of piecemeal legislation on the subject; partly to the
circumstance that some of the more important restrictions were
imposed not by way of prohibitory statutes but by specific tests.
Various offices and civic privileges, including voting at elections and
sitting in parliament, were or could be made liable to oaths such as
those of allegiance and supremacy to which a practising Roman
Catholic could not with good conscience subscribe. In Ireland,
where the status of Catholics had been depressed even lower than
in England by the legislation of William III's reign, a series of Irish
statutes mainly between 1777 and 1793 had redressed the balance.
Catholics could practise their religion, establish schools, enter the
legal profession, dispose of property, vote at elections, become
magistrates, and in general hold most civil and military appointments. But they remained debarred from the high political and legal
posts in the Irish government; the offices of judge, king's counsel,
governor and sheriff of counties, and generals on the staff; membership of parliament or the Privy Council; and a few others of less
importance. By the beginning of the nineteenth century, therefore,
the Roman Catholics in Ireland, and for most practical purposes
those in England and Scotland also, were no longer penalised as
subjects for the profession of their religion. Nevertheless, the
constitutional formula established at the Revolution of 1688-9 of
'a Protestant King in a Protestant State' was still largely intact. It
was from the state in its institutional aspect that the Catholics were
still excluded. The controversy over Catholic emancipation centred
on this fundamental issue.

The Union of 1800 and the inability of Pitt to carry either his cabinet or his sovereign with him on the policy of emancipation, transferred the issue from Irish to British politics; and for the next thirty years it remained the most disruptive of all domestic problems. In 1809 Perceval had persuaded the king not to exact pledges against emancipation from Grey and Grenville if they entered the cabinet, on the grounds that their junction with ministers known to be adverse to the measure would itself be the best guarantee that they would not bring it forward. Liverpool, less advantageously placed, had taken up the attitude in 1812 that while not permanently opposed to emancipation, he did not consider the time had yet arrived when a settlement of the question could be made that would satisfy Catholics and still provide security for the Protestants. His government was based collectively, therefore, not so much on hostility as on neutrality towards Catholic claims. Ministers were left free as individuals to follow their own views and inclinations, and officially at least the government Whips were not put on for Catholic debates. It was true, as Canning realised, that without the active support of the government, the question could hardly be carried successfully through both houses of parliament. But the absence of organised government opposition, and the known sympathies of several government members, invited an almost annual trial of strength. Consequently Catholic emancipation proved an irritant in every ministry up to 1830, hindering and dividing men who might otherwise have worked together, and clogging all the leading politicians with an inescapable record of public commitment on a major controversial issue.

For the Irish executive this neutral attitude on the part of the ministry was a peculiar embarrassment. As long as it was the policy of the cabinet as advisers of the crown not to propose any change in the laws affecting Roman Catholics, the Irish government was bound to administer the law as it stood. Yet Ireland was the one part of the British Isles where those laws were likely to encounter serious political opposition, since only in Ireland did the majority of the population belong to the Roman Catholic faith. Admittedly the Irish government itself was not entirely united; Fitzgerald was favourable to Catholic claims, and Bushe not unsympathetic. But the central core of officials, from the Lord Lieutenant down to the Civil Under-Secretary, was composed of supporters of the Protestant establishment. Indeed, in a direct sense they were guardians of that establishment; and without that protection it could not long have survived. Even the large number of public offices, mainly in the administration of the law, for which Roman Catholics were legally eligible, were in practice overwhelmingly in Protestant hands; and administrative policy in Ireland deliberately maintained this inequality. It was not merely through the law but through their political dominance of the executive that the Protestant party upheld the Anglo-Irish ascendancy. Peel himself would hardly have been chosen for Chief Secretary had he not also belonged to that party. In his family, opposition to Catholic claims was almost a religious faith, and Peel entered on politics with convictions on that issue which had been formed in his earliest boyhood.[1] There was therefore a striking contrast between the preponderance of Protestant feeling in the official corps at Dublin Castle and the neutrality of the cabinet, and between the Protestant administration of the law in Ireland and the divided counsels in the House of Commons. Of the weakening effect of this dualism Peel became conscious very early in his Secretaryship. On the question of the Maynooth grant he wrote to Richmond in March 1813:

> All this difficulty arises out of the unfortunate state of the Govt. as far as the Catholic question is concerned. I always thought that to throw open a question of that kind, perhaps the most important one that concerns the domestic policy of the country, and to leave each individual to take his own course upon it, was a very impolitic measure, and one which would involve the whole Govt. and particularly the Irish Govt. in daily embarrassment.[2]

Nevertheless, it was doubtful whether Liverpool, or anyone else, could have kept an efficient cabinet together except on the principle of neutrality. The Irish government was accordingly left in the difficult position of administering a system which was under constant attack in parliament and on which cabinet ministers themselves notoriously disagreed.

Ireland itself, of course, was a country of three religions. All had their particular problems for the government; all gave rise to

[1] Peel, *Life*, p. 105.    [2] 40281 f. 112.

troublesome and obstructive political movements. If the Irish executive was at bottom a Protestant one, it was not infrequently forced by the exigencies of administration into a position of opposition to the wilder manifestations of all three religions with which it was confronted. There was a Castle policy which came into collision with all the partisan activities of the deeply divided society over which it presided. The Church of Ireland, by reason of its state establishment and close connection with the government, enjoyed the greatest security and power; it enjoyed also a greater measure of independence than was usually thought. Political motives played little part in the appointment to the Irish episcopacy. Vacancies on the bench of bishops were inevitably the subject of close consultations between Lord Lieutenant, Chief Secretary, Prime Minister, and Home Secretary, but they were filled with regard to the needs and wishes of the establishment rather than of the Irish executive, even though, as Richmond remarked once to Peel, many people would not credit that.[1] Partly in consequence of this autonomy the Irish bishoprics were monopolised by Anglo-Irish aristocratic families to an extent that called down the ironic criticism of the youthful Chief Secretary.

> It must be admitted that the Bench in Ireland is rather overstocked with men of Birth. There are the Bishops of Kildare, Kilmore, Derry, Killaloe, Raphoe, Cork, Ferns, and Elphin, who are all men of noble families and 3 of the Archbishops also—the brother of Lord Bute, one brother of Lord Middleton, and the third uncle to Lord Waterford. It cannot be supposed for a moment that noble birth is a disqualification for the Bench, but it is perhaps desirable to make it less a recommendation to preferment than in former periods it has been in Ireland. [2]

Richmond, to whom this passage was addressed, agreed that it would be better to place some clerics on the Irish bench whose character might defend the government from the imputation of creating bishops for political reasons. But he added characteristically that he did not feel such motives had in fact weighed with him and if people chose to examine the situation of those he had recommended, that would become evident.[3]

[1] 40186 f. 120.      [2] 40283 f. 102 (8 June 1813).      [3] Richmond, 1408.

Yet if bishops were not part of political patronage in the more offensive sense, their own views on appointments and promotions within the Church were not above suspicion. Both Lord Lieutenant and Chief Secretary were plagued by ecclesiastical suitors who pressed for patronage on distinctly secular grounds. A later Lord Lieutenant, indeed, roundly declared in 1818 that 'the whole system of Church preferment as conducted, or rather as is wished it should be conducted here, is disgraceful and so I told my Lord Bishop of Kildare'.[1] The Castle found itself in consequence engaged in a running battle for the purity of Church patronage against the solicitation of its spiritual heads. Balked sometimes of what they conceived to be their just pretensions, Irish bishops in turn did not always lend to the Castle that degree of political support which government usually expected. 'That larder of the lean earth, Bishop A.,' wrote Peel disrespectfully to Croker at the time of the Trinity College election in 1818, 'would do nothing for me because his son did not get (what he did not deserve) the Deanery of Derry.'[2] Nevertheless, in such behaviour the Church of Ireland was merely reflecting the ordinary attitude of the Anglo-Irish governing classes towards government perquisites; and however distasteful the contrast between the spiritual offices and the materially-minded incumbents, the problem was only part of the general battle against corruption.

The Presbyterians of the north constituted a religious organisation whose pretensions if more modest, and more easily evaded, were of a totally different nature. Though their Protestantism was as fervid as could be wished for, they were little disposed to support either the Anglican establishment or the Castle authorities. Memories of their own legal disabilities were still tenacious, and there was a recent and by no means totally extinguished tradition of democratic republicanism which was opposed to aristocratic English rule almost as much as to Roman Catholic domination. Yet to a limited extent the Presbyterian Church itself was established, or at least endowed and supported by the state. The *Regium Donum*, a grant from the crown for the assistance of the Presbyterian clergy dating back to

[1] Lord Talbot, 6 May 1818 (40194 f. 249).
[2] 40295 f. 90. The only Irish bishop in 1818 whose name began with A was Nathaniel Alexander, Bishop of Down and Connor.

the seventeenth century, had been periodically increased until by
1803 it amounted to £14,000, an average of £75 for each minister;
and at the time of the Union plans had been canvassed for strengthening the connection between the government and the Synod of
Ulster, and for establishing a training college in the north for
Presbyterian students. In 1814 the Belfast Academical Institution,
built by voluntary subscription but receiving an annual grant of
£1,500 from the state, began in fact to train students for the Presbyterian Church and to agitate for the right to grant degrees. This
development was on political grounds highly unwelcome to the
Irish executive. The settlement of 1800-4 had included, as part of the
implicit bargain, the establishment by the Ulster Synod of new
regulations requiring a degree as an indispensable qualification for
its ministers, and enjoining an additional year's residence in Glasgow
for its ordinands. This high educational standard not only was the
justification for the increased state grant, but furnished in the view
of the government some guarantee that the Presbyterian ministry
would not fall into the hands of a narrow Ulster republican faction.

The proposal to give the Belfast Academy the faculty of granting
degrees seemed to threaten the whole basis of this relationship.
Castlereagh, as member of the government and still more as head
of perhaps the most influential Anglo-Irish family in Ulster, took a
leading part in opposing what he described to Peel as 'a Bastard
Institution ostensibly for Academical purposes . . . but in fact
establishing a Junta, which might be turned to the most oppressive
and mischievous ends' under the leadership of the redoubtable
Dr. Drennan. While Castlereagh in the winter of 1816-17 was
meeting representatives of the Synod and using his considerable
powers of persuasion in the north, Peel and Fitzgerald were receiving
a delegation from the Belfast Academy in Dublin. Castlereagh's
views were clear and forcible, and he expressed them at great
length to  the Chief Secretary. Indeed, at the outset he did not
hesitate to advise Peel to use the power of withholding the *Regium
Donum*—'purify the Mass by defeating a democratick effort'—in
order to maintain the university degree qualification. Peel while
expressing his general agreement and assuring Castlereagh that his
activities in Ulster could only assist the government, was more
cautious on the point of tactics.

I so fully concur with you as to the importance of identifying as far as possible the *Protestant* Body of this country, and of preserving a Union between the government and all constituent members of it without distinction, that I think matters should have proceeded very far indeed before the Government pledges itself irrevocably to withdraw the *regium donum* even from the refractory members.

Though he would rather deal with a ministry of regular university graduates, he added sensibly, if he had to deal with a race of Dr. Drennans, he would rather have them as stipendiaries than independents. When he and Fitzgerald met the Academical deputation, they declined to put forward any positive suggestions on behalf of the government and contented themselves with observing that it was inexpedient either to turn the Academy into a college or to connect it with the Presbyterian Church or to make an alteration in the existing mode of qualification for the ministry.[1]

In March 1817 Peel conveyed to the Belfast Academy the formal view of the government that it was not advisable at that time to establish a collegiate institution in northern Ireland; and that certain alterations were necessary in the existing organisation of the Academy, in particular in the control exercised through trustees by a body of proprietors who had no academic qualifications other than subscribing to the funds of the Academy. He proposed therefore that visitors should be appointed by the crown to act with the trustees in the management of the institute's affairs and in the appointment of professors and other officials; and he invited the proprietors to send a delegation to discuss details with him previous to the introduction of the necessary legislation to amend the Act of incorporation. The letter was considered by the proprietors at a meeting in April and was in effect rejected. The only concession made was an offer to give the Irish government a veto on the appointment of professors and other teachers. The *Ulster Register*, a radical Cobbettite emancipationist magazine, edited by the notorious Jack Lawless who later joined O'Connell, congratulated the North on this 'triumph over an insolent and audacious attack on its religion and independence' and spoke of Peel's letter causing such a reaction in

[1] For the correspondence between Castlereagh and Peel see 40181 fos. 211-49; cf. McDowell, *Public Opinion*, pp. 55-6.

Ulster as would sweep away both the letter and, it was hoped, the writer. But it took more than journalism to deflect the Chief Secretary. From England a fortnight later he wrote warningly that the government would withdraw its support unless drastic changes were made in the conduct of the Academy. This failing to produce the required effect, the threat was carried out and for some years the state grant was withheld. Thus in the event Castlereagh's advice was accepted, though not until negotiations had proved the impossibility of compromise between the Irish executive and the unbending Presbyterians of the north. It is not surprising that the *Ulster Register*, on the occasion of a congratulatory address to the Chief Secretary, wrote critically in October 1817:

> Mr. Peele seeks the establishment of a political and religious ascendancy in Ireland incompatible with the happiness or permanent peace of the people. We speak of Mr. Peele with much respect, viewing him as a man of considerable talents but we cannot hesitate to lament that such talents should be wielded against the rights and harmony of Irishmen.

Language such as this was indistinguishable from what was said, though for different reasons, by the more moderate Catholic papers.[1] But at least the danger of setting up a Presbyterian Maynooth had been averted.

If neither Episcopalian nor Presbyterian opinion showed much willingness to conform to Peel's conception of a general union of Protestants with the government, the more extreme version of common Protestant hostility to Catholicism was in turn a source of serious difficulty to the executive. It was one thing to base the state on the Protestant minority; a different matter to allow that minority to provoke the greater mass of Catholic Irish into lawless retaliation. This was the real problem of the Orange societies. Originally a product of the disturbed period of the 1790s, the Orange lodges had continued as a federated society of semi-militant Protestants, enjoying the patronage and support of many prominent Anglo-Irish families. The secret nature of their ritual, and the fact that oaths were administered to new members, made it at least questionable whether

---

[1] *Ulster Register*, 4 April, 3 October 1817; 40292 f. 131; 40293 f. 26.

they were not infringing the law; and the ease with which Orange celebrations, especially at the Twelfth of July, could degenerate into faction fights, made the lodges an obvious ground on which to attack the Irish executive. Yet Peel was surrounded with men, from the Prime Minister down to Gregory, in whose eyes the zealous loyalty of the Orange lodges outweighed considerations of administrative efficiency and impartiality. Peel was cooler and more detached in his appraisement. Indeed it was a mark of his prudence that on first going to Dublin he had altered the orange facings on his servants' livery that were customary at Drayton.

But prudence alone was inadequate. The periodic discussions in parliament and the elementary needs of law and order in Ireland made the Orange lodges a perpetual object of attention. As early as June 1813 Charles Wynn moved in the House of Commons for an enquiry into 'certain illegal societies under the denomination of Orangemen'; though a personal attack on the Duke of Richmond by Sir Henry Montgomery for giving 'inflammatory speeches at midnight orgies' enabled Peel to confine his intervention in the debate largely to a vindication of the character of the Lord Lieutenant. In fact, however, the government had already been endeavouring to prevent the spread of the Orange societies to the yeomanry and militia, and only the previous March Peel had ordered a commanding officer of the militia to be reprimanded for sanctioning the formation of a lodge in his unit.[1] But this was merely touching the fringe of the problem; and in October he was obliged to call Liverpool's attention to the growing animosity between the lower classes of Catholics and Protestants in northern Ireland.

The combinations of Orangemen and Ribbonmen (as the Catholics call themselves) are increasing their numbers respectively. We feel it, I assure you, a most difficult task when anti-Catholicism (if I may so call it) and loyalty are so much united as they are in the Orangemen, to appease the one without discouraging the other.

Liverpool, while unhopeful that the topic could be kept out of Parliament, expressed a firm disinclination to allow any legislation on the subject that should not apply to all associations of a political

[1] 40281 f. 119.

character and not merely to one which had as its purpose 'the maintenance of the Protestant establishment in Church and State'.[1]

Nevertheless, the situation appeared more complex than this to the Chief Secretary actually engaged in the task of administering Ireland. The following summer, in the month preceding the annual Orange celebrations of July, he brought the subject to the notice of his new Lord Lieutenant.

> The cause of the evil, which is of course to be found in the bitter animosity that exists between the two religions, particularly among the lower classes, makes the remedy proposed almost hopeless. Any direct interference either of the Legislature or of the Government to suppress those feelings would, I think, be worse than useless. . . . But as regards persons under the control of the Government, I confess I think there is a material difference. If they meet as yeomen, and offer just cause of offence to their Catholic brethren, and we do not interfere to prevent it, we are in fact little less than a party to it.

Certainly, he continued, the government could scarcely wish to see the lower classes in northern Ireland united, since that could only imply the adoption by Protestants of Catholic principles 'and therefore a cordial concurrence in hating the British connexion'. He hoped they would always be disunited. 'The great art is to keep them so, and yet at Peace or rather not at war with each other.'[2] His fundamental objection to the Orange lodges was that they formed a para-military organisation outside the control of the government. As he wrote to Gregory in July 1814,

> The more I think upon the subject, the more am I convinced that even the most loyal associations in Ireland for political purposes are dangerous engines. . . . There are many phrases applied to the Association of Orangemen which are of much too military a character to suit my taste. Regiments and Colonels and Captains, etc., do not sound well to my ear when applied to societies not under the control of Government.[3]

[1] 40181 f. 49; *Peel*, I, 122.    [2] 40287 f. 34, partly printed *Peel*, I, 158.
[3] 40287 f. 98, partly printed *Peel*, I, 159 (22 July 1814).

This critical attitude may not have been without its effect, for the same month Gregory was desired by Dr. Duigenan, the prime representative of militant Protestantism among the Irish M.P.s, to inform Peel that a few weeks earlier the oath had been universally abolished in the Orange lodges of Ireland.[1]

In November 1814 the topic was once more raised by the opposition on a motion of Sir John Newport calling for papers relating to the Orange Associations of Ireland. Peel met the attack by seconding the motion with a speech in which he not only cleared himself of charges of receiving and answering addresses by Orange societies, but defied the mover to produce any evidence of government partiality in their dealings with the societies. But though he was able to adduce the abolition of the Orange oath as a sign of increasing respect for the law, he admitted that abuses had taken place in the associations. In July 1815, when Sir H. Parnell moved for a commission of enquiry, came the last major parliamentary attack on the Orange societies during Peel's Secretaryship. But ill-supported by any cogent reasoning, and brought forward late in the session, the motion was easily defeated by Peel in a thin House. The studied neutrality of the executive in its handling of the Orange problem had at least the merit of making it difficult for the parliamentary opposition to fix responsibility for Orange excesses on the Irish administration. To have done more was scarcely possible. In the prevailing climate of sympathy with the principles of Orangism in both the English and Irish executives, Peel would have found it beyond his powers to secure the dissolution of the lodges.

## II

The administrative problem formed by Protestant activities in Ireland, however, could hardly be weighed in the balance against those provided by the Roman Catholics who composed perhaps as much as five-sixths of the population. The Roman Catholic Church itself, with its hierarchy of four archbishops and twenty-two bishops, was aloof and independent, and its titles were not officially recognised. In consequence the Irish government were singularly

[1] 40199 fos. 27, 191.

ill-informed on the numbers and organisation of the Roman Church in Ireland. Though it was believed, for example, that their religious houses were on the increase, Peel tried frequently but without success to obtain accurate figures of their regular clergy and the state of the monastic Orders.[1] At one point only was there formal contact between the Irish government and the Roman Catholic organisation. This was the College at Maynooth.

The Royal College of St. Patrick at Maynooth had been set up by act of parliament in 1795 in consequence of the suppression by the revolutionaries of the seminaries in France and the Low Countries to which intending Irish priests had usually been sent. An annual grant of £8,000 was made by the state to support the establishment and this was raised during the Grenville administration to £12,000 despite a warm opposition on the part of Perceval. With the change of government, however, this was reduced once more in 1808 to £9,250. The College was superintended by a body of Visitors including the Lord Chancellor of Ireland, the Irish Chancellor of the Exchequer, and a number of Irish judges; and in Peel's day it accommodated some two hundred students with a staff of about ten professors. In November 1812 the trustees of the college wrote formally to Fitzgerald asking for an increase in their grant to make possible a larger number of students and an improvement of the existing system of education. A sum of £1,200 was estimated for this purpose, part of which was to be provided by the trustees from endowments, leaving £700 which it was hoped would be granted by parliament. Fitzgerald himself and the Chancellor favoured the request. The Lord Lieutenant was decidedly hostile. With Perceval he believed that the Maynooth grant was bad in principle, and that it ought at least not to be increased. If, he told Peel, he thought £700 would satisfy the Catholics or their Protestant friends, he would grant it; but he did not, and were he in the House of Commons he would vote against it. Peel, still feeling his way in his new position, consulted various members of the cabinet and as usual discovered a diversity of opinion. Liverpool thought the request could be granted without departing from Perceval's argument that the college might be improved but not extended. 'He had formed no very decided opinion upon it,' Peel reported in February 1813 to the Lord

[1] Peel to Abbot 25 December 1816 (*Colchester*, II, 591).

Lieutenant, 'but was, I own, to use the modern phraseology, more inclined to "the liberal" than I expected.' Vansittart was dubious but evasive; Sidmouth against; Castlereagh favourable; but all were anxious to put the responsibility back on the Irish executive.

Peel himself saw obvious embarrassment in personally opposing or amending a measure proposed by Fitzgerald and supported by other members of the government, and he sought Richmond's advice on the best course of action. He agreed with the Lord Lieutenant that if the object was to satisfy the Catholics, 'there is not a hope, not the most distant one of attaining it'. Nevertheless, the crucial point was whether, on behalf of Richmond and himself, he should oppose the addition if it seemed clear that such an opposition would be fruitless. Any attempt by the whigs to secure the higher figure of £13,500 should, he thought, be resisted to the last; but the addition proposed by the trustees seemed too trifling to warrant the risk of defeat. Richmond conceded gracefully and gave his Secretary *carte blanche* to decide his actions as the situation demanded. 'I think you rather lean towards giving way,' he wrote back sympathetically in March, 'if it can be fully explained that we do not give up the principle.' When the time came, Peel advised the Lord Lieutenant that there was no chance of successfully resisting some increase in the Maynooth grant and that it was therefore politic to accept the £700 addition as a means of preventing anything larger. That was not, he concluded, a good argument if the issue was important but 'it is hardly worth while perhaps to give up office on the Maynooth grant.'[1]

Further than this, however, he was not prepared to go. This was manifest in February 1818 when Dr. Everard, the titular bishop of Cashel, made a private approach to the Irish government with a proposal that £1,000 should be annually granted by the state to subsidise a special house for ten young priests from Maynooth to preach to the lower orders in Ireland their moral and religious duties, and obedience to the law. Gregory, with whom the bishop had an interview, was clearly taken by the personality and frankness of Everard, and was inclined to look favourably on the scheme. Peel, however, after further enquiry into the details of the proposal satisfied the Lord Lieutenant of the expediency of rejecting it. Even

[1] 40281 fos. 72, 111, 285; 40185 fos. 88-92, 190; Richmond, 429, 1420.

Gregory, while admitting that he was attracted by the prospect of securing some understanding with the Catholic clergy, acknowledged the difficulty of establishing the requisite machinery.[1] Even apart from the obvious pitfalls in Everard's ingenuous proposals, the character of the Maynooth clergy hardly afforded much hope for the success of such a venture. All observers[2] concurred in their view of the profound changes worked in the Irish Catholic priesthood by the substitution of Maynooth for the old seminaries of the continent. In the days of the *ancien régime* the colleges of Douai, St. Omer, Coimbra, and Salamanca, had produced a recognisable type of continental-trained priest—well educated, urbane, royalist, and authoritarian. The Maynooth seminarists, drawn almost exclusively from the poorer classes, imperfectly educated, knowing nothing of society outside Ireland, went back to their parishes, as a later Lord Lieutenant expressed it, 'with the bitterest feelings of the Partizan and the grossest habits of a Peasant'.[3] The Catholic bishops of Ireland in Peel's day were still of the old school; but the growing nationalism of the inferior Irish clergy was not the least important factor in the ultimate success of O'Connell's Catholic movement.

In a wider sense, however, Catholic education was one of the earliest problems with which the Chief Secretary concerned himself. At the time of his appointment in 1812 the Commissioners of Education in Ireland were preparing a report recommending the creation of a new Board for the superintendence of lower education in Ireland which should include Roman Catholics. Peel raised the matter privately with Liverpool and Sidmouth on his first visit to England in the late autumn. In January 1813 he opened up a formal correspondence on the subject with the object of discovering whether the government would in fact sanction a system of general education in Ireland without distinction of religion or, indeed, one in which the Protestant religion would not necessarily form part. His own view was that without the admission of Catholics to the Board nothing effectual could be accomplished. But he held to the

---

[1] 40205 fos. 47, 80, 152.

[2] cf. O'Connell before the Select Committees of the two Houses of Parliament on Ireland 1824-5, (4, 11 March 1825); *Sheil Memoirs*, I, 275-6; *Creevey Papers*, pp. 517, 522.

[3] Duke of Northumberland to Peel 1829 (40327 f. 70).

principle that the parochial schools should continue to educate their scholars in the religion of the state, that is to say, the Protestant faith; and that entirely new schools should be set up for Catholics. 'I think,' he wrote to Saurin in April, 'we should guard with care every institution that we have for the instruction of the Protestants . . . but I am equally impressed with the necessity of forming the new establishments, which may be founded for the general education of the poor, on as liberal a scale as possible.' In the spring of 1813 he was repeatedly urging on the government the need to take into consideration the whole question of Irish education. But with parliament the battle ground for the political claims of Roman Catholics, and the co-operation of the Roman hierarchy in Ireland more than doubtful, the time was hardly propitious for such a controversial issue. He brought in and passed a limited bill, creating a new board for endowed schools; but the wider scheme for national education foundered on innumerable obstacles. The perpetual dilemma which for the next half-century was to clog all questions of educational reform, and not merely in Ireland, was clearly pointed out by Saurin. The Roman Catholic Church would not concur in any system of education except one controlled by themselves; and the establishment of a non-confessional system of education was one from which all Churches and religions recoiled. The rise of an organised movement of Catholic agitation put it out of the question, however, even to attempt at this time the fundamental task of Irish elementary education.

'The Catholics of this country,' wrote Peel to Sidmouth in October 1813, 'may be considered as divided into four classes—the clergy, the lower orders of the people, the moderate and respectable part of the Catholics, and the violent party, with O'Connell and Scully at their head.' It was in fact a feature of the Irish Catholic movement when Peel became Chief Secretary that it was deeply divided on questions of organisation, tactics, and personalities. In the years after the Union a leading part in organising petitions for emancipation had been taken by the Catholic aristocrats, Lord Fingall, Lord Gormanstown and other men of moderate views, who continued to be prominent until 1811. But an increasingly important role in the agitation movement was played by Catholic barristers, Scully notably from the start, and others like O'Connell a few years later. Behind the scenes a gradual struggle for leadership developed which turned largely on matters of organisation and policy. Self-appointed committees of leading Catholics were open to criticism from below, but any attempt to form more representative bodies came up against the Irish Convention Act of 1793. This Act, originally designed to make illegal the organisation of the United Irishmen, prohibited the election or appointment of assemblies purporting to represent the people or any description of people under the pretence of preparing public petitions or other addresses to the crown or parliament. Aggregate meetings, so-called, were a means of escaping this danger, since in theory they were gatherings of the total body of Irish Catholics. In practice the aggregate meetings, usually held in Dublin, tended to be composed mainly of Catholics from Dublin city and county with at most a sprinkling of provincials. Even so, they were too cumbersome for regular use and could only effectively act through permanent or *ad hoc* committees.

A general representative Catholic committee had been set up in 1810 and though, following judicial action by the Irish government, it formally dissolved itself the following year, it was shortly after reconstituted at an aggregate meeting and assumed the name of the Catholic Board. It disclaimed any representative status and as a measure of legal protection was annually dissolved and renominated.[1] Yet at the same time the body of Catholics were in sharp disagreement over the nature of the relief being sought on their behalf. Grattan in 1808 had put forward a proposal to give the crown a negative control, or veto as it became known, on the appointment of Irish Catholic bishops; and he claimed that he had for this the support of the Irish clergy. In Ireland, however, a considerable agitation developed against the veto and it was finally condemned at a synod of Irish Catholic clergy. By 1810 it was clear that the Irish hierarchy would have nothing to do with emancipation on these terms. The Catholic aristocracy, both in England and Ireland, were still in favour of a compromise and showed dissatisfaction at the manner in which Lord Fingall's policy and leadership had been thrown overboard by the organised Catholic movement in Ireland. Though the Board officially adopted the clerical attitude on the question of the veto, it continued to possess an aristocratic minority

[1] Memorandum on the Catholic Board, May 1814 (40198 f. 82).

who thought that the prospect of early emancipation was being sacrificed on the altar of ecclesiastical and nationalist intransigence.[1]

The year 1813 saw all these crosscurrents and divisions fully exposed. By its resolution of the previous year, the House of Commons was pledged to consider the Catholic question; and a long controversy, lasting most of the session, began in February when Grattan moved for a committee on the claims of Roman Catholics. After a hard debate he passed his motion by a majority of forty and in March the House proceeded as a committee of the whole to consider the specific resolutions he brought forward. In May his bill received a second reading and went into the committee stage. A great part of the discussion on the bill revolved round the securities it ought to embody, and Canning prepared a list of amendments to strengthen it in this vital particular. As it issued from committee the bill contained a clause giving the crown, on the advice of a mixed board of commissioners, Protestant and Catholic, a power of veto on the appointment of Catholic bishops and deans. On 24 May the House again resolved itself into a committee to consider the amended bill and following a strong speech from Abbot the Speaker, it was defeated by the narrow majority of four votes in one of the fullest divisions ever recorded, 247 to 251. A brief note scribbled by Peel on half a sheet of paper at 2 a.m. in the House of Commons brought the welcome news to the Lord Lieutenant.[2]

In these parliamentary proceedings the Chief Secretary for Ireland, both from his office and his convictions, felt bound to take a part even though he could not rival such established orators as Grattan, Canning, and Plunket. Indeed he was early struck by the lack of feeling on the Protestant side and the poor opposition made to Grattan's original motion for a committee. One of the first surprises of the session was a speech from Pole on 1 March in which he not only supported Catholic claims but claimed to have urged them on the government when in office. This remarkable volte-face, coupled with a jibe at the way in which his two successors, Fitzgerald and Peel—his two halves as he described them—were themselves divided on the question, stung Peel into a lively though

---

[1] Wyse, *Catholic Association*, I, 144-65; McDowell, *Public Opinion*, pp. 87-92.

[2] Richmond, 1173. A very full report of the debate was printed as a pamphlet. (London 1813, J. J. Stockdale.)

necessarily impromptu reply. 'We are not more at variance with each other,' he observed, speaking of himself and Fitzgerald, 'than the right honourable gentleman is with himself. . . . In personal unity we cannot represent him, but in discordance of sentiment we are competent to the task.' The body of his speech was, however, a criticism of the lack of any effective security in the plan outlined by Grattan, and he wrote the following day to Richmond that though he was ready to remove certain anomalies in the existing system, the main structure he would leave untouched.

At no time and under no circumstances, so long as the Catholic admits the supremacy in spirituals of a foreign earthly potentate, and will not tell us what supremacy in spirituals means,—so long as he will not give us voluntarily that security which every despotic sovereign in Europe has by the concession of the Pope himself, I will not consent to admit they are excluded from privileges for which they will not pay the price that all other subjects pay, and that all other Catholics in Europe but themselves consent to pay.[1]

Though he ruefully admitted that in the heat of action he had omitted some points in his reply to Pole, he received a cheerful letter back from Richmond praising his speech as 'particularly good' and describing the general astonishment in Dublin at Pole's reversal of opinions. Nevertheless, as the great debate continued, he found little cause for satisfaction. He told Richmond that there was no *esprit de corps* among the Protestants;[2] and what irked him as much as the steady succession of defeats was the half-heartedness on his own side. On the second reading of Grattan's bill on 13 May, no one at all except Duigenan appeared anxious to speak against the bill until Ryder and himself determined that if no one else did, they at least would rise to prevent the indignity of the bill passing in silence. Accordingly he got up at a late hour and in a brief speech again attacked the bill for the absence of any real securities in its provisions.

It was impossible to look at the situation of Ireland, where the Roman Catholics so greatly preponderated in number, and where

[1] 2 March 1813. The original is in Richmond, 427; the version in *Peel*, I, 76 has minor inaccuracies.
[2] Richmond, 433 (10 March), partly printed in *Peel*, I, 79.

there were such distinct interests, without feeling alarmed at the consequences of such unlimited concession. . . . How could they hope, when it was admitted that there were four million Catholics and only 800,000 Protestants, to maintain the Protestant ascendancy?

The emphasis on the question of securities was tactically sound, for it was precisely this issue which even then was splitting the Catholic movement in Ireland; and in proportion to the success of the attempt, under Canning's inspiration, to insert greater securities in the bill, the Irish Catholics openly began to repudiate the measure which he and Grattan were endeavouring to obtain for them.

The Veto in fact raised an issue of greater significance than merely that of securities. If safeguards for Protestantism could only be obtained by imposing a formal administrative control over certain aspects of Roman Church organisation in Britain, that control in itself would represent a revolution in the religious policy of the state. It implied not merely a formal recognition of the Roman Church but a direct constitutional relationship with it that involved the crown and the executive government with the Papacy and the Irish hierarchy. The Catholics in Ireland instinctively reacted against any scheme of emancipation that would subject them to Protestant and Erastian control; but it was an equally powerful instinct on the part of the English Protestants that led them to reject a settlement which for the first time since the Reformation would establish a legal position for the Roman Church within the pale of the constitution. The liberalism of Canning and his followers was leading in effect to something that was incompatible with the structure of the existing Protestant state; and had their proposals been accepted, it would have meant, however indirect the method, a revolution in constitutional principle. It was this failure on the liberal side fully to comprehend the implications of what they were suggesting, that led to the repudiation of their plan by both Protestant and Catholic Church parties. Indeed, as soon as the amended bill was printed, Peel sent a copy over to the Lord Lieutenant with the observation that it would give no satisfaction to the Catholics. He himself thought the veto on the appointment of Catholic bishops useless as well as vexatious. It was not, he told Richmond, the power of any one ecclesiastic that was to be feared, however disaffected or disloyal. The real danger was the general strengthening of the Catholic community. 'What security have we that they or the great majority of them will not continue to act in a body, will not render their interest distinct from those of the Protestant population in Ireland, and will not use every privilege they may now receive to promote it.'[1]

In the event the Roman Catholic bishops in Ireland formally declared against the ecclesiastical clauses of the Relief Bill, though unknown to them the bill had already been defeated, and their decision was conveyed to the clergy and laity in a subsequent pastoral letter. Nevertheless, Peel was concerned about the reaction in Ireland of the parliamentary defeat. He could not omit from his calculations the possibility that Protestant rejoicings on the one side, and Catholic disappointment on the other, might result in further agitation and illegalities on the part of the Catholic Board; and he instructed Gregory accordingly to spare no expense in procuring intelligence of their proceedings. If the Secret Service money were inadequate, he wrote on 26 May, there should be no scruple in looking to other funds; it would be false economy not to get the best possible information. Gregory set to work immediately and with success. In June he told Peel that he was hoping to get the services of one of the Catholic Board itself and asked for approval of a payment of £300 per annum with an increase for good service and suspension for bad. The name of the man concerned he prudently abstained from committing to paper. It would, he said, be dangerous and needless since Peel did not know him, but he assured the Chief Secretary that 'he is a man of peculiar qualities adapted for the undertaking', a moderate who mixed habitually with the most violent of the movement.[2] From that time on Gregory received direct reports on the activities of the Board from one of its own members.[3] It was true that the proceedings of the Board were normally carried on in public, with both police and reporters present, but some meetings were in private and Gregory's informer must have provided an

---

[1] 40283 f. 56, partly printed *Peel*, I, 85.
[2] 40283 f. 67; 40196 f. 255; 40197 f. 52.
[3] cf. 40198 f. 227 (May 1814): 'my correspondent is of the Committee'.

additional assurance to the Irish executive that they would not be taken by surprise.

The danger that impressed itself more and more on the Castle officials was that the moderate aristocratic wing of the Catholic movement would abandon the unequal struggle against clerical and popular feeling, and that control of the movement would fall entirely into the hands of the extremists. Gregory thought that though O'Connell was now ostensibly the leader of the intransigents, he was in fact only a creature of Scully whom he described to Peel as 'the Master Mover of all the violence'.[1] Early in June the Under-Secretary raised with Peel the possibility of suppressing the Board; but this was not easily accomplished by legal means. All the chief officials in the Irish government, including Peel, agreed that the activities of the Board should be scrutinised to see whether they could be brought under the operation of the Convention Act. Yet though it was clear that it represented the Catholic body, there was considerable doubt whether that could be proved in a court of law. The Irish executive in fact was in the difficult position of a constitutional government seeking to repress political agitation by legal means against all the ingenuity of the Catholic barristers and the partisan votes of a Dublin jury. Peel himself came to the conclusion that it would be necessary to ask parliament for fresh powers to put down the Board, but that the time was hardly ripe for such a step. Of the ultimate necessity of intervention, however, he had no doubt. 'We must not only crush the Board,' he wrote to Gregory in June 1813, 'but must destroy the seeds of future boards, committees, and conventions.'

For the rest of the year, therefore, the government contented itself with a close watch on what the Board was doing. Some members of the Irish executive, notably the Attorney-General, thought that the violence of O'Connell and the extremists would in the end bring about their own defeat; and the government press in Ireland carried on a campaign designed to bring about that end. At the same time an opportunity presented itself to attack the *Dublin Evening Post*, the principal press organ of the Board. Magee, the editor, had already been successfully prosecuted for a libel on the Lord Lieutenant in 1813, and when the paper printed in August the

[1] 40197 f. 79 (27 June 1813).

resolution of a Catholic meeting at Kilkenny, condemning his trial and libelling in turn both the government and the administration of Irish justice, Magee was again prosecuted. Not only did Peel believe that the government was right to employ the limited judicial means at its disposal, but he hoped in this particular instance to force into the open the agitators, especially Scully, who was the author of the offending resolutions. The trial, which began in November but was not finished until February 1814, was chiefly remarkable for Magee's repudiation of the speech of his counsel, O'Connell, and for the open breach between the newspaper and the Catholic Board which followed Magee's conviction. All this gave grounds for hope. Clearly if the Board expired through its own folly and fanaticism, it would be a much more satisfactory conclusion than any arbitrary closure at the hands of the government.

During the winter of 1813-14 Peel was hopeful that this might prove to be the issue of all their troubles. But his optimism gradually waned and when he went back to England in the spring of 1814 it was evident that the Irish government was not prepared to be quiescent much longer. In April Peel was asking Gregory to secure more information about the precise status of the Board, and early next month he raised with the Prime Minister the possibility of amending the Convention Act so as to bring the Catholic Board within its compass. But Liverpool and Sidmouth, justifiably anxious after the narrow escape of the previous session not to start another Catholic debate in the House of Commons, were decidedly averse to such a step. This was an unpleasant check, since Peel was acutely conscious of the embarrassment of proceeding against the Board after an interval of two years and without recourse to fresh legis-lation. The only excuse could be, and it was indeed partly true, that the government had exercised forbearance from policy and dis-cretion. Nevertheless, he was of the opinion that forbearance could not be continued indefinitely and that if the Board did not change its tone or dissolve itself, the government would have to act under the existing law.[1] The legal officials in Dublin were disinclined to any action without the sanction of the cabinet, and the Lord Lieutenant himself was clearly perturbed by Liverpool's non-committal attitude. His energetic Chief Secretary in London, however, assured him in

[1] 40286 f. 151 (Peel to Whitworth 7 May 1814).

positive terms that the cabinet had no desire to discourage the Irish government and wished indeed to leave the decision, manner, and time entirely to its judgement. Fortified by this the Lord Lieutenant put in train preparations for the issue of a proclamation dissolving the Board. His advisers in the Castle were by no means as resolute as the Chief Secretary. The Chancellor was weak and vacillating; Bushe was inclined to give the Board a longer respite; and only the firmness of Saurin carried the little Irish junto through to a resolve to act.

The decision to dissolve the Board was taken on 10 May. Between that date and the issue of the proclamation there was a delay of over three weeks, largely caused by the famous Quarantotti letter and its effect on the Irish Catholics. The division of opinion among Catholics in Ireland and England over Grattan's bill of 1813 and the question of securities, had been complicated by the position of the Pope as a virtual captive in French hands. Nevertheless, attempts to secure an expression of his views were so far successful as to lead in 1814 to the despatch of a letter from the Congregation of Propaganda in Rome to Dr. Poynter, the Apostolic Vicar in London. In the absence of the Cardinal Prefect, who was with the Pope in France, the letter was signed by the acting vice-prefect, Monsignor Quarantotti, and it came in the form of a rescript enjoining Catholics to receive the bill with gratitude. The letter was known in Dublin on 3 May and caused an immediate sensation.[1] It was promptly and violently attacked by clerics and laity alike on grounds of policy and defective authority. Nevertheless, it was not entirely clear what the final outcome would be and one of Gregory's informants told him that a meeting of Catholics was in preparation to subscribe to a declaration approving the rescript. The Catholic Board itself a little later decided to discontinue its regular meetings until the Catholic bishops formally expressed their opinion on Quarantotti's letter. Though Gregory was sceptical of any real alteration in the Catholic attitude, and inclined to suspect that there had been a leakage of the government's intention to dissolve the Board, it was obviously an inopportune moment to proceed to any drastic action. In the meantime a draft proclamation, running to

---

[1] Wyse, *Catholic Association*, I, 166 ff.; McDowell, *Public Opinion*, pp. 92 ff.; Broderick, *Holy See*, pp. 21-2.

two close pages of quarto, was sent over to London for Peel's comments. A lively correspondence followed. Peel was anxious for brevity and taciturnity, and thought that the reasons for issuing the proclamation should be held in reserve. But the Chancellor held that some explanation was necessary and in its final form the proclamation was a compromise both as to length and content. On 27 May the Irish bishops met at Maynooth and came to a resolution that the Quarantotti rescript was not mandatory. The proclamation, already postponed once, was again held up in view of a meeting of the Board announced for 2 June when it was still hoped in the Castle that it might dissolve itself. But the proclamation was finally signed on 3 June and issued the next day.[1]

After all the hesitations and delays, the news of the issue of the proclamation seemed to Peel in the nature of a triumph. To Gregory he wrote with candour that the proclamation of peace with France the previous month had not given him a tenth of the satisfaction which the proclamation of war against the Board had done; and to Whitworth he declared that it would constitute 'quite a new era— to use a fashionable phrase—in the policy of the Government'. Opinion among the Protestant Irish members was all in its favour and even the supporters of emancipation raised no voice against it. The long forbearance of the Irish government had in fact served to gather opinion on its side and the timing of the proclamation had been excellent. In the event the mere issue of the order dissolving the Board was enough. Weakened and discouraged as it was, it put up no resistance to the Irish executive. For the remainder of Peel's Secretaryship the organised Catholic movement ceased to be an influential force in Irish politics. When attempts were made at the end of the year to revive the Board, Lord Fingall held aloof. The following year saw a split among the middle-class Catholics, with Sheil and the moderates on one side, O'Connell and the clericalists on the other. The Catholic Association founded by the anti-veto party in 1815 failed to accomplish any tangible ends, and had a rival in the moderate Catholic party led by Lord Trimlestown. From 1814 to 1822 Catholic agitation in Ireland was at its lowest ebb. If Peel looked on the successful challenge to the Board in 1814 with personal satisfaction, it was not without some justification. Of all

[1] 40198 fos. 183-288 (Gregory to Peel); 40286 fos. 178-219; 40188 fos. 98-200.

the members of the government he had shown the greatest constancy and resolution; first in waiting until the time was ripe, and then in guiding the Lord Lieutenant past the doubtings of his own advisers and the discouraging neutrality of the cabinet to the final and successful act.

But though Catholic agitation was temporarily arrested, O'Connell remained; and more was to pass between the two men before Peel left Ireland. For some nine months after Peel became Chief Secretary he had not received much notice from the opposition either in the press or in public speeches. But the opening of the debate on Grattan's bill and the clash with Pole in May 1813 brought Peel's name before the Irish public and the Irish agitators. O'Connell in a speech of 29 May at the Catholic Board made up for any previous neglect and did it in a manner peculiarly his own. A curious but characteristically Irish mixture of shrewd Kerry farmer, devout Catholic, and Benthamite radical, O'Connell had a dangerous gift of popular oratory. This, in the heady atmosphere of Irish gatherings, was constantly leading him into extravagances of speech which were in striking contrast to the underlying caution of his real nature. A speech early in May 1813 on Princess Caroline, indirectly attacking the Prince Regent, had required Peel's personal efforts at Carlton House to dissuade the Regent from demanding an immediate prosecution. Three weeks later it was Peel's turn to be pilloried:

> That ludicrous enemy of ours . . . 'Orange Peel'. A raw youth, squeezed out of the workings of I know not what factory in England, who began his parliamentary career by vindicating the gratuitous destruction of our brave soldiers in the murderous expedition to Walcheren, and was sent over here before he got rid of the foppery of perfumed handkerchiefs and thin shoes . . . a lad ready to vindicate anything, everything.

This was smart hitting but it called for no reply on Peel's part. In August he was cited as a material witness in the first Magee libel case and though he was not called upon to give evidence, he spent two days in court watching the proceedings. It was the first time he had seen O'Connell in action and he found the experience an interesting one. O'Connell, whom he thought 'an eloquent and vulgar speaker', used the court as a platform for scurrilous abuse of the Attorney-General and was more libellous, Peel thought, than his client had ever been.[1] The encounter could only have strengthened his views on the necessity of ultimately suppressing the Catholic Board on which O'Connell was already a prime mover.

In May 1815, a year after the dissolution of the Board, a debate arose in the House of Commons on Sir Henry Parnell's motion to consider Roman Catholic petitions. In the course of it Peel made use of quotations from O'Connell's speeches to the Board to illustrate his argument that the Irish Catholics had been completely opposed to the Emancipation Bill of 1813. The references to O'Connell were quite factual and contained no criticism of the Irish leader whom he described indeed as possessing the confidence of the Irish Catholics to a greater degree than any other person. O'Connell nevertheless took offence and at a Catholic meeting in July made the pointed comment that Peel was too prudent to abuse him in his presence. So far Peel had ignored O'Connell's increasing attacks on his political conduct. To Saurin who in the spring of 1815 had advised legal proceedings he replied, 'I should be inclined to go as far as I could, consistently with my duty, to avoid a prosecution of O'Connell.' But this was a different and personal matter and though Peel's absence on the continent at that date enabled him to ignore the imputation on his courage, it made it difficult to do so a second time. At an aggregate meeting on 29 August, however, O'Connell declared that Peel had traduced him in a place where he was privileged from being called to account; and calling upon the police reporters present to record his words, he added with studied deliberation, 'Mr. Peel would not dare, in my presence, or in any place where he was liable to personal account, use a single expression derogatory to my interest or my honour.' In the society in which Peel and O'Connell moved, this was a challenge to which between private individuals there could be only one answer. In Ireland, which was notorious for the levity of its duelling habits, it was an even greater provocation than it would have been in England. Unless O'Connell was betrayed into a piece of bravado he subsequently regretted, his language could only have been intended to intimidate Peel into silence or bring on, as the phrase went, an affair of honour. Coming from O'Connell,

[1] 40284 fos. 39, 85, 95.

the insult was peculiarly venomous. Not only was he the older and more experienced man—forty years of age to Peel's twenty-seven—but he was an excellent shot with a pistol, from long practice, it was said, in shooting the curs that came round his horse's heels when riding on circuit through the Irish countryside. Moreover, and this was a circumstance that gave unusual force to his words about Peel, in February of that very year he had killed d'Esterre, a member of the Dublin Corporation, in a duel which itself had arisen from a political controversy.

If he thought that the Chief Secretary would be intimidated, however, he had mistaken his man. On 31 August Sir Charles Saxton had an interview with O'Connell on Peel's behalf. The evasive answers he received from O'Connell and his friend Lidwill were printed in the *Correspondent*, whereupon O'Connell in turn published a letter complaining that Peel and his second 'preferred a paper war'. This at once provoked a direct challenge from Peel and it was agreed after some delay that to avoid the intervention of the Irish authorities a meeting should take place at Ostend. Peel, Saxton, and a Colonel Brown arrived at the rendezvous on 15 September. O'Connell, who at his wife's instance had been put under recognizances in Dublin, travelled more slowly and with less secrecy, arriving in London three days later. By this time the English press was full of the affair and though the Home Office failed to intercept Peel, the police arrested O'Connell in London the morning after his arrival. From the start the unusual circumstances of the case had procured for it a publicity that soon bordered on the absurd; and as the newspapers in England and Ireland redoubled their reports and comments, a just note was struck by the *Dublin Evening Post* when it observed severely that by long custom 'the first report of a Duel should be the report of a pistol'. Even more embarrassing was the way in which the partisans of the two principals increasingly gave the matter a political and even religious aspect. At the outset there was general admiration and support for Peel's conduct among his friends at the Castle, including the Lord Lieutenant; and later expressions of approval came from persons in England as different as Liverpool and Sidmouth on the one hand, Croker and William Peel on the other. Peel himself, according to all observers, was extraordinarily cool and self-possessed. As was to be apparent later in his life, a personal crisis had the effect of stringing him up to an unusual pitch of strength and collectedness. Croker, who slipped down to Maidstone to see him on his way to France, reported to Gregory that 'he was in the finest spirits and as unaffectedly gay and at his ease as when we were going to Dover two months ago on our tour to Paris'.[1]

But three weeks later, travelling about in the Netherlands with Saxton, furtively and *incognito*, with police warrants out for his arrest, he was placed in a hapless and exasperating situation. On 24 September, the day after he heard of O'Connell's arrest, he wrote to Gregory from Bruges asking whether he would be put under restraint if he returned to Ireland. By the time his letter arrived he had been away from his official duties for the greater part of a month and the Under-Secretary's reply was couched with sound sense and a salutary briskness. He told Peel he had put himself in the right and his adversary in the wrong; and that there was nothing more to be done. He would and indeed ought to be bound over on his return; it would be most unjust if O'Connell were put under penalties and not Peel. But it would be folly to ruin everything by a false step.

> I really feel more uneasy about you [he concluded] than on the day you left Ireland. I could then plainly see the course you intended to pursue; I am now blinded and unable to calculate on your intentions. I hope to have my fears soon removed and that they may be groundless is the anxious wish of yours very sincerely,
>
> W. GREGORY.[2]

The characteristic family obstinacy of which Peel possessed his full share, had in fact taken him past the point which good judgement and his official duty could justify. By contemporary standards, and the ethics of duelling can hardly be considered except by contemporary standards, he could not have acted at the outset otherwise than he did. But the time to stop was probably when the judicial

---

[1] *Croker*, I, 77.

[2] 40201 f. 243, partly printed *Peel*, I, 199. Peel eventually returned to England via Ostend (40215 fos. 126, 135). Details of the duel affair can be found in 40266 fos. 295 ff.; Richmond, 269 ff.; *Bathurst*, pp. 385-6; in the Irish press, esp. the *Dublin Evening Post*, 2 September-5 October; and various pamphlets, e.g. *The Rt. Hon. Robert Peel or Daniel O'Connell Esq.* (Dublin 1815).

authorities in Dublin intervened to prevent an immediate encounter. Peel's courage and honour had been vindicated and it was not his fault that O'Connell could not meet him. Peel's stubbornness, however, which surprised his friends as much as his coolness had delighted them, broke out again in a sequel the following November. Lidwill and Saxton, as was apt to happen with seconds, had got themselves into a quarrel over disputed versions of the transactions in September. The two men met in November at Calais when Saxton missed and Lidwill fired in the air. Peel, who had taken offence at certain comments passed on him by Lidwill, followed Saxton to Calais in the hope of exacting reparation. After some confused negotiation between the seconds (Colonel Brown for Peel and Major Lidwill for his brother) an apology was drawn up on Lidwill's behalf and the matter petered out in a vague and unsatisfactory manner.[1] But by this time his friends thought that Peel was acting with little sense of what was owing to himself or his position. Croker, to whom he wrote in confidence before leaving Dublin, told him frankly that all reasonable men would advise him to treat Lidwill with silent contempt.[2] Peel himself was scarcely happy at the outcome.

> I am no doubt annoyed [he wrote afterwards to his friend the Earl of Desart] at my name being mixed up in cursed publications and rejoinders and statements with the names of two men whom I believe to be cowardly liars. I should be miserable if I were not supported by a consciousness that I have acted throughout in a straightforward manner, and with as good a will to meet both my adversaries as it was possible to entertain.

He was left with an immediate feeling of dislike and contempt for O'Connell which was revived by what happened several years later. In 1825 O'Connell's second, Bennett, came to Colonel Brown and offered an apology from his principal for his remarks about Peel's speech in 1815 and his subsequent comments. Peel sent back a handsome reply, saying that if he had not long ago ceased to have

---

[1] 40266 f. 295 (original documents and pamphlets). See also the pamphlet *Point of Honor* (Dublin 1815).

[2] 40183 f. 306 (14 December 1815); *Croker*, I, 78.

any feelings of personal hostility and resentment over the incident, O'Connell's behaviour in making the communication could not have failed completely to extinguish them. The news of this *amende honorable*, as always seemed to happen in Irish affairs, later became public and O'Connell was taunted with having 'crouched' to Peel. His defence was that he had made the apology in the hope of propitiating Peel on the Catholic question then pending in parliament. Even if he had outgrown the old animosity of 1815, this was something which Peel could never understand or forgive. For his own part O'Connell retained for the rest of his life an inveterate and irrepressible dislike of Peel.[1] Politically they always found themselves opposed; temperamentally they were antipathetic; and O'Connell, the older man, had twice on a personal matter been put in the wrong.

### III

The organised Catholic agitation which had been brought to an effective halt in 1814 was a specialised political movement threatening the structure of the Anglo-Irish Union as it had been created by the Act of 1800. Behind the façade of meetings, petitions, boards, and committees, however, was another Ireland whose problems were less susceptible of easy definition and for which remedies were as difficult as the causes were obscure. No Chief Secretary could be in office for more than a few weeks without realising that Ireland was a country of endemic violence and lawlessness. This in itself constituted the chief justification for the existence in Ireland of a separate local executive under the Lord Lieutenant. 'In a large part of Ireland,' wrote Cornewall Lewis twenty years later, in words equally applicable to the period of Peel's secretaryship, 'there is still less security of person and property than in any other part of Europe, except perhaps the wildest districts of Calabria or Greece.'[2] England and Ireland were not only two societies but they were different to a degree which few Englishmen who had no personal experience of Irish life could understand. The short sea-route from

---

[1] cf. art. on O'Connell by W. H. Gregory (*Nineteenth Century*, XXV, 588-9, April 1889).
[2] Lewis, *Local Disturbances*, Introduction.

Holyhead was a passage from one stage of civilisation to another.

Pouring into the Castle, month after month, from county after county, the teeming correspondence on the 'state of the country' afforded *prima facie* evidence of conditions which were not merely absent in England but could scarcely be comprehended there. A few examples may suffice. Waterford 1812: 'the people complain of being unprotected and the gentlemen of being unsupported. . . . The system of terror is not to be described in words.' Cavan 1813: 'yeomen are in general the most daring smugglers in this county'. Waterford 1813: 'assassins are to be hired very reasonably as has already appeared in trials'. Clare 1814: constant faction fighting among the lower orders, 'in fact they are perfect savages'. Westmeath 1814: 'this county is at this moment at the mercy of an armed bloodthirsty seditious banditti'. Antrim 1814: 'in the night some ruffians took up the corpse [of an Orangeman], smashed the coffin, disfigured the body, and left it . . . about half a mile from where it was interred'. Waterford 1814: 'at present the payment of rent is merely at the tenants' own discretion'. Limerick 1815: 'this country does not want a Peace Preservation Bill, as they have no peace to preserve; it wants a Peace Restoration Bill'. Tipperary 1815: 'it is almost impossible to bring any offender to justice in this county who has money or influence, as gentlemen will take the most unwarrantable steps in their favour'. From magistrates, peers, landowners, clergy, police officers, and military commanders, came a steady stream of reports whose contents seemed endless and unvarying: attacks on revenue officers and tithe collectors, private vengeance, burning of houses and ricks, robbery of houses and mail-coaches, plundering of food, theft of arms, intimidation and assault, murder, rape, mutilation, abduction, maiming of cattle, riot, nocturnal assemblies, firing on sentries, killing of stragglers on the line of march, rescue of prisoners, and assassination of hostile witnesses.[1] There was truth as well as irony in Peel's remark in 1814 to Goulburn that if he stayed much longer in Ireland he would be so familiarised to murder and robbery that he would never get used to an uninterrupted state of tranquillity.[2]

[1] For quotations and other refs. in this para see S.P.O., State of Country, 1796-1831 (MS. Calendar).
[2] Goulburn, II/13.

In Ireland, of course, it was more than customarily expedient to sift the evidence laid before the executive authority. Until the end of the war there was a constant suspicion, not entirely unreasonable in view of Ireland's recent history, that disorders in the Irish country-side were part of an organised conspiracy aiming, with French assistance, at the overthrow of the whole system of government. Whitworth himself, who was peculiarly sensitive to the Napoleonic danger, thought in the autumn of 1813 that France was bound to attempt some incitement to rebellion in Ireland. 'I have no doubt that France is cutting out work for us at home and that the Priests are instructed to incite their flocks to every kind of outrage against the Protestant,' he wrote to Peel in October; and again in the same month, 'it is so evidently the interest of the French government to give us occupation that we may give them some credit for any attempt to that effect'.[1] But this was no more than supposition. The more settled opinion in the Castle was that there existed no danger of an organised rebellion and that there could not be one without foreign aid; though, as Gregory pointed out, if there was any probability of such aid, thousands of Irishmen would be ready to join.[2] But if such thoughts could be entertained by the sober officials of the government, it was inevitable that more fearful and less responsible individuals in the rural parts of Ireland were sometimes ready to accept even more extravagant notions. Reports came from Athlone in March 1813, for example, of widespread conspiracy with delegates from other counties and swearing of oaths of allegiance to Bonaparte.[3] In the summer of 1814 the magistrates of Co. Kildare were convinced that there was a regular system in their county of administering oaths, frequent meetings, and organised plans for imminent insurrection. Troops were sent to the district and on 5 June a house in the town of Kildare was surrounded and seven alleged conspirators seized. First reports spoke of captured documents affording proof of intended rebellion, with mention of an Executive Directory and requests from delegates from other counties for arms and ammunition. This information was at once sent to Peel at the Irish Office in London and a fortnight later it was included in a formal letter from the Lord Lieutenant to the Home

---

[1] 40187 fos. 69, 74.
[2] Gregory to Peel, 10 March 1813 (40195 f. 212).      [3] *ibid.*, f. 252.

Secretary. But in fact there was grave doubt whether the document described had ever existed. Gregory subsequently informed Peel that the military party saw no papers in the room and that Mills, the magistrate concerned, was not observed seizing any. As the case against the prisoners rested solely on Mills's evidence the Attorney-General and Solicitor-General decided not to prosecute and ordered their release.[1] This 'Kildare conspiracy' was one of the items which Peel had been intending to use in parliament as proof of the need to renew the Insurrection Act, and its early exposure prevented what might have been a serious embarrassment.

There were in fact alarmists in every section of the Anglo-Irish governing classes; and in the letters coming into the Castle a clear tendency was discernible to make the best of both worlds. Either riot and outrage took place, or if they did not and all was quiet this very quietness was regarded as suspicious evidence of organisation and conspiracy. On the subject of French agents and dissident Catholic priests, in particular, the reports from the provinces were apt to be exaggerated and prejudiced. No real evidence came before the government that the disturbances between 1812 and 1815 were in any way fomented from abroad; and though the county correspondence over the whole period of Peel's Secretaryship contained a good deal of generalised assertion of the disaffection of the Roman Catholic clergy, it also furnished some specific instances of their loyalty, their co-operation with the civil authorities, and their attempts to discourage lawlessness. This in itself, even for a Catholic priest, needed some measure of moral and physical courage. 'It is a melancholy truth,' wrote one correspondent from Waterford in July 1814 'that a Catholic clergyman whatever may be his inclination, cannot speak against any prevailing view in his Parish without injury to himself.'[2] One of Peel's best informants, the Earl of Desart, a Kilkenny landowner and a level-headed if sympathetic observer of Irish provincial life, gave an instance to Peel of a Roman Catholic priest organising his parish to suppress all disturbances; and in another letter emphasised the absence of any political element in the con-federations of peasantry in his district. 'On the contrary the oaths they exacted here in almost every recent instance and the outrages

[1] 40199 fos. 25, 154; S.P.O., Private Official, f. 189.
[2] S.P.O., State of Country.

perpetrated appear to have had their origin in the desire to prevent
the taking of land at advanced rents away from the old tenants, or in
private malice.'[1] In fact an almost equal and probably more justified
feature of the county correspondence were the complaints against
the supineness and inefficiency of local magistrates. This in turn
created another difficulty for the authorities in Dublin. The absence
of reports of disorder did not necessarily imply that all was quiet;
it might only mean that the magistrates and gentry did not wish to
draw governmental attention to their particular county. As Desart
wrote to Peel in the winter of 1813-14 about his own district,
'matters are there sometimes represented as worse than they are in
order to call for assistance, and sometimes as better than they are to
excuse inactivity'.[2] When to such notorious evils as the intimidation
of witnesses was added the equally notorious defects of the Irish
magistracy, the task not even of enforcing law and order but merely
of obtaining accurate information on which to act was one of constant perplexity to the Irish government.

Yet with exaggerations reduced and alarms ignored, the state of
the Irish countryside was still a sombre spectacle to any official who
had concern for the basic elements of justice and peace. Periodically
while Peel was Irish Secretary came reports of singularly barbarous
incidents which were verified by irrefutable evidence and which in
their ugliness made a profound impression on his mind. One of these
was sent by Desart himself in January 1813. At Carrick-on-Suir,
on the borders of Tipperary and Kilkenny, four men broke into the
house of Mr. Lawrence. All four in succession raped his daughter
before her father's eyes and departed with fourteen shillings taken
from the house. Two men were arrested and identified by the
Lawrences, who in order to secure their own lives took up residence
near the local barracks. Miss Lawrence even offered to go into gaol
and stay there until the assizes. In the meantime some financial
assistance was necessary for the family and Desart arranged for
fifteen shillings a week to be paid to them which he hoped to
recover from the government.[3] Another incident was reported to
Peel by Gregory in April 1813. A small farmer in Co. Westmeath,
named Geoghagan (or Gahagan), was visited by men seeking arms.

[1] 40216 fos. 98, 181 (July–December 1813).
[2] ibid., f. 172.     [3] ibid., fos. 84-7.

He resisted; two men were killed at his door and a third was found dead nearby the next day. The government gave Geoghagan a reward of £100 and the grand jury at the next assizes raised a private subscription for him. But ever since the attack he received constant threats and was obliged to live in a state of continual defence. Then, while talking to his friends near the door of his chapel after attending Mass one Sunday, he was shot from behind. It was Palm Sunday and hundreds were present; but no one made any attempt to apprehend or pursue the attackers. A military surgeon from Athlone removed one pistol ball from his back though another remained lodged there, and the man eventually recovered. The parish priest solemnly cursed the assassin from the altar, in consequence of which the priest himself was threatened and notices were posted throughout the county denouncing any who attended his chapel.[1]

In Co. Westmeath again there occurred in November 1813 a crime which Lord Castlemaine described as the most savage in all his experience of Irish disorders. A man named James Connell had given evidence in a prosecution against certain persons for administering illegal oaths. Before the trial he had been kept in gaol for greater security and when he came to Dublin for the assizes, Peel saw him and cautioned him against returning to his own county. Nevertheless, after staying at Lord Castlemaine's residence for a while, he finally went back home. A short time afterwards a body of men broke into his house at night. Connell's body was afterwards discovered thrown on a dungheap outside with a pitchfork sticking in his breast and his body battered flat with stones. Inside was found his wife with her eyes hanging out on her cheeks, a pistol ball having passed through the front of her head between the temples. At the trial it was proved that the gang which committed the crime was composed of delegates from three adjoining parishes, specially appointed to carry out the murder.[2] A few months later, in May 1814, Gregory sent Peel 'as frightful an account as the annals of Irish violence can produce'. At Kilmagarry near Kilkenny, eight men entered the house of a Mr. Butterfield, ate and drank all they could

---

[1] 40196 fos. 14, 36, partly printed *Peel*, I, 121.
[2] S.P.O., State of Country (Westmeath 1813); 40197 f. 253; 40198 f. 21; *Speeches*, I, 27-8; Blacker IV, 365 (written long after the event and inaccurate in some details).

find, demanded money which they got, and then raped his wife and daughter. They next went to the house of a Rev. Mr. Sutton from whom they stole a gun and £95. Sutton was then taken outside under guard while those within raped his wife. The whole party escaped without detection.[1] In 1816 John Foster sent Peel an account of the murder of a whole family in Co. Louth. A man named Lynch, with his son-in-law Rooney, had prosecuted three men for having broken into his house at night. On his evidence they were convicted and hanged. The following October a body of men rode up to his house at Reaghstown, surrounded the building and set fire to it. Lynch, Rooney, his wife, two children, two maids, in all eight persons, died in the flames.[2]

One last instance may be given since it made such an impact on Peel's imagination that seventeen years afterwards he was still able to quote it to the House of Commons. It occurred the same year as the Lynch murders. When relating the story to Croker, who had asked for material bearing on the state of Ireland, Peel began with unusually savage irony, 'you must give a specimen,—one specimen, —of the humanity of the poor suffering oppressed natives of this country who are trained up by their priests in the paths of religion and virtue, and are only driven to the commission of outrage by the tyranny of their landlords or the insulting triumphs of Orangemen'.[3] A man named Dillon had given evidence against persons charged with Whiteboy offences on which they were found guilty and executed. He took refuge in Dublin with his family but eventually returned to his home in Co. Limerick. One night about a dozen men broke into his house, dragged him from bed and killed him outside the door with pitchforks. His wife, knowing her turn would come next, threw a piece of dry turf on the fire and told her eldest daughter, aged fourteen, to remember the faces of the men when they entered to fetch her. When they came she struggled as long as she could while the child watched in the firelight. Then they forced her out and killed her over the body of her husband. When it was

---

[1] 40198 fos. 156-9.

[2] Foster (J. Foster to Peel, 30 October 1816); S.P.O., State of Country (Louth 1816); cf. *Ann. Reg.* 1816, Chron. 175.

[3] *Speeches*, II, 641; 40291 f. 173, printed *Croker*, I, 91. The statement that the Dillons were Catholic was corrected in a subsequent letter (*ibid.*, f. 183).

all over and the girl went to seek shelter with neighbours, she was told 'by all the people in the neighbourhood' to whom she applied that she could go to the devil. A number of men were subsequently arrested, and mainly on the evidence of the daughter nine of them were convicted and hanged. Four others offered to plead guilty on condition of transportation for life. Peel himself, as he told the Commons in 1833, remained haunted by such 'scenes of atrocity and suffering'. Years later he was still active in protecting the survivors of the Dillon case. A local clergyman, the Rev. F. Langford, had been instrumental in securing the arrest of the band of murderers and though his own life was thereby endangered, he claimed no reward except to ask that one of his sons should be provided for in the Church. In 1828 Peel, when Home Secretary, wrote to the then Lord Lieutenant on his behalf and the following year a living was found for him. At the same time Peel asked for enquiries to be made about the fate of the elder Dillon girl. The reply that came back provided a happier conclusion than was usually found in this dark side of Irish life. She had been apprenticed to a milliner and when she married received a dowry of £50 from the government. Since then she had gone with her husband to India.[1]

What in fact confronted the government in Ireland was not crime in the ordinary sense but a species of intermittent social warfare. It was this which explained the peculiarly repellent nature of many of the incidents that came to Peel's notice. One feature of the lawlessness rife in Irish society was the presence of innumerable secret societies and confederations among the peasants. The Whiteboys, a title often used generically to indicate the whole system, was originally a peasant movement against enclosures which started in the middle of the eighteenth century and gradually embraced all activities against landlords and tithes. The Ribbonmen were an offshoot of the Catholic Defenders revived after the 1798 rebellion. The Thrashers was the name given to a Connaught movement in the first decade of the nineteenth century. As peasant resistance and intimidation flared into activity and temporarily died away under equally temporary repressive measures, more and more names were added to the list of Irish secret associations. Some were derived from some practice or peculiarity of its members. The Carders, for

[1] 40325 fos. 175, 182; 40326 f. 117.

example, lacerated the backs of their victims with the wire brushes used for carding wool. The Shanavests and Caravats were said, perhaps with less certainty, to take their names from articles of clothing: shanavest, an old coat; and caravat, a cravat (possibly in the grim sense of the hempen cravat, or hangman's noose). Many were simply invented appellations: Rockites, Peep O'Day Boys, Terry Alts, Moll Doyle's Sons, Levellers, Dingers, and Dowsers.[1] But Whiteboyism was a general movement with one clear general aim: to wage war on landlords and tithe-collectors, to intimidate any who aided or even compromised with their opponents, and to revenge any action taken against their members. Many of the worst crimes were acts of reprisal, though in turn the knowledge of these reprisals served as a means of indiscriminate intimidation; and the prevalence of rape was perhaps less due to any personal lusts than to a cold-blooded desire to inflict a peculiar pain and degradation on an entire family.[2] The worst penalties were reserved for informers; and partly because of the ferocious intimidation, and partly because of a natural peasant solidarity, one of the principal problems for the judicial authorities was to obtain witnesses. Working in the context of a hostile or terrified population, the Irish legal system was ordinarily defective and often totally suspended.

To the average Englishman the endemic lawlessness of Ireland and the silent refusal of the mass of the population to co-operate with the authorities, presented a situation which lay outside his experience.

> In Tipperary [wrote Peel to the Prime Minister in January 1816] we are . . . making a terrible but necessary example under the special commission we have sent there. There have been thirteen capital convictions for offences amounting to little short of rebellion, and fourteen sentenced to transportation for the destruction of a barrack. All these sentences will be carried into execution without mitigation. We find convictions attended with so many difficulties that we are obliged to be very sparing in the extension of mercy. . . . You can have no idea of the moral depravation of the lower orders in that county. In fidelity towards each other they are unexampled, as they are in their sanguinary disposition and fearlessness of the consequences.

[1] S.P.O., State of Country, *passim*.     [2] Lewis, *Local Disturbances*, p. 226.

Liverpool replied sympathetically but unhelpfully. 'In truth Ireland is a political phenomenon—not influenced by the same feelings as appear to affect mankind in other countries—and the singular nature of the disorder must be the cause why it has hitherto been found impracticable to apply an effectual and permanent remedy.' Being English and Protestant, Peel could not help thinking sometimes that the phenomenon was in part at least facilitated by the nature of the Irishman's religion. At the end of the same year he told Abbot that in view of the remorselessness of Irish crime and the disregard of oaths, it was difficult not to be satisfied that the prevailing religion of Ireland acted as an impediment rather than as an aid to civil government.[1]

Nevertheless, the law existed and Peel saw it as his first duty to enforce it. From the start of his secretaryship the state of the country impressed itself on his mind as a matter calling for urgent attention from the government. On returning to Ireland after the parliamentary session of 1813 he wrote in strong terms to Beckett, the Under-Secretary at the Home Office, asking for militia reinforcements from England.

> The country is in a very distracted state in many parts. Do not suppose that I have caught the infection from the numerous alarmists with whose exaggerations I am daily inundated, but it is very very difficult to conceive the impunity with which the most horrible crimes are committed in consequence of the fears even of the sufferers to come forward to give evidence. . . . I have no apprehension of any serious or well concerted attempt at commotion but I assure you that the force we have is hardly sufficient to enable us to preserve ordinary tranquillity in many parts.[2]

In the succeeding weeks he turned his mind to the possibility of fresh legislation to deal with the problem. The old Insurrection Act passed during Wellesley's secretaryship, giving summary powers to magistrates to arrest persons found abroad at night and to impound arms, had been repealed in 1810 and Lord Whitworth was reluctant to inaugurate his Viceroyalty by applying to parliament for its renewal. Other more constructive measures, such as a strengthening

[1] *Colchester*, II, 591.    [2] 40284 f. 154 (18 August 1813).

of the Irish police force, needed time for preparation if they were to prove successful. Though Peel originally thought of proposing a new Police Bill in 1813 he deferred it in the end because he had been unable to give it adequate consideration. Meanwhile he began to collect information on the subject from sources in Ireland. Some measure would be necessary in any case since the existing Act regulating the Irish county police, such as they were, expired in the spring of 1814.[1] No immediate steps were taken therefore during the autumn session of 1813, but the onset of winter brought the problem forward with renewed urgency and Whitworth admitted in November that when Peel returned it would be necessary to give it the serious consideration of the government.[2] Even the sober-minded Gregory was becoming alarmed and anxious for the government to take a stiffer line. Westmeath was in a particularly disturbed state and petitions had come in from that district for a re-enactment of the Insurrection Act. Discussions during the Christmas recess bore fruit and in January 1814 a formal letter was sent to Sidmouth over the Lord Lieutenant's signature stating emphatically that 'the ordinary operation of the law is considered completely inadequate to the preservation of tranquillity throughout the country' and giving notice of a probable request to strengthen the legal powers of the Irish executive and magistracy relating to the public peace.[3]

When Peel returned to England at the end of March he began preparations for the introduction of two bills. The first was for a renewal of the Insurrection Act, as a temporary measure at least, to arm the executive with extraordinary powers in time of emergency. The second was for the establishment of a special police force to act in disturbed districts as a reinforcement to the efforts of the magistracy and the local county police. The latter, the old baronial constables familiarly known as 'Barneys', were in practice as inefficient and useless as their counterparts in England, the parochial constables or 'Charleys', and scarcely entered into any administrative calculations of the forces at the disposal of the law. The Lord Lieutenant heartily approved the idea of a new police force for Ireland. 'A numerous Police establishment on the footing proposed by the bill and plenty of troops,' he wrote optimistically in April,

[1] 40285 f. 86.     [2] 40187 f. 119.     [3] S.P.O., Private Official 1811-23, f. 168.

'would enable the magistrates to do their duty and keep this country in perfect peace and tranquillity.'[1] But Peel had to encounter considerable obstruction from the cabinet. There was a reluctance on their part to countenance a renewal of the Insurrection Act, and the mere word 'police' was sufficiently novel and unpopular in contemporary England to make Liverpool and some of his colleagues shrink from such an administrative innovation. Moreover, the war in Europe was coming to an end and it could plausibly be argued that it would be better to wait until peace conditions were restored before taking any drastic measures. As usual, Irish affairs were pushed back to the end of the session; but this delay was not altogether disadvantageous. It enabled Peel both to mature his preparations and also to make some assessment of the situation in Ireland after the armistice agreement was signed.

Early in June Gregory was busy collecting material for Peel to use when introducing his Police Bill. He himself was a warm supporter of the new police. Though less sanguine as to the permanent prospects of restoring order, he had litle patience with those members of the cabinet who wished to forbear a little longer before introducing another Insurrection Act. 'I wish,' he wrote roundly to Peel in May, 'the Forbearers were obliged to pass one month with their wives and daughters in any of the disturbed counties.'[2] Peel, however, picked his way cautiously among the doubts and hesitations of the English government. Early in June he told Gregory that he was going to postpone the Police Bill to a later period in order to see the effect of the fall of Napoleon, and would not press for the renewal of the Insurrection Act. On 18 June he wrote to Saurin that as it seemed impossible that the cabinet would consent to both bills, he would concentrate on passing the Police Bill and include in it some of the more useful clauses of the older Act.[3]

Less than a week later, on 23 June, he rose to introduce the Peace Preservation Bill, as his police measure was innocuously entitled. Armed with Gregory's material, he devoted a large part of his speech to a description of the state of Ireland that rendered the bill necessary, being careful to preface his remarks with an assurance that

[1] 40188 f. 20.    [2] 40198 f. 215.    [3] 40286 f. 223 ; 40287 f. 41.

he should rely only upon documents the authority of which could not be questioned. He would not quote the verbal or written communications which had been made to government which, though in many instances were well founded, yet in others might be liable to a suspicion that they were exaggerated.

He mentioned, among other examples of Irish lawlessness, the Connell case in Westmeath of the previous November. He emphasised the advantages of giving magistrates a means of repressing disturbances without recourse to military assistance—'the frequent use of soldiers in that manner made the people look upon them as their adversaries rather than their protectors'—and expressed an anxiety to have the measure he was about to produce regarded as a permanent part of the law of Ireland, distinct from any extraordinary powers which the Irish government might have to seek from parliament. There was a ready assent in the Commons to the introduction of the bill and to the principle of permanency which Peel thought of particular importance. It passed rapidly through the House, receiving its second reading without opposition on 1 July.

Heartened by the general approval for his Police Bill, Peel immediately determined to carry out if possible the whole of his original programme. On 24 June he sent to Gregory for a fresh budget of evidence of more recent date that could be used to justify a stronger, if temporary, measure. Any sworn information on nocturnal assemblies, organised robbery of arms and infliction of torture, he wrote, would be very serviceable. The hesitation of the cabinet was the most serious obstacle he had to overcome. On 5 July he saw Liverpool, Sidmouth, and Castlereagh, and pressed hard for a revival of the Insurrection Act, preceded if necessary by a secret committee of the House in which documents could be produced. Liverpool was against any action; Castlereagh, though sympathetic, feared the reaction on British diplomatic prestige at the forthcoming Peace Conference. But strongly backed by Sidmouth, the energetic Chief Secretary in the end received permission to attempt to secure a renewal of the Act on his own statement of the case in the House of Commons, avoiding as far as he could any reference to general disaffection in Ireland. This was not quite the method he would have chosen, but after a brief reflection he made up his mind to try the experiment. In view of the peace conference and Castlereagh's necessary absence abroad, the cabinet thought it improbable that parliament would be called together in the autumn. In that case, if he missed the summer session of 1814, there would be no chance of fresh legislation until the following spring. In such a situation Peel characteristically chose the course of boldness.

On 8 July he rose once more in the House to propose a renewal for three years of the old Insurrection Act of 1807-10, which as he pointed out was itself a revival of an Act of the Irish parliament of 1796. He admitted frankly that it was an evil that such a measure was necessary; but the House had to choose between comparative evils. This was a measure only designed as a reserve power, to be applied when all other means had failed; and he presented an array of fresh evidence, including an ugly case in which a man, his wife, and two daughters, had been 'carded', to justify placing these emergency powers in the hands of the Irish government. As was foreseen, there was more opposition to the second bill than to the first. Some critics objected to the late period in the session at which it was introduced; others argued that it would be preferable to appoint a committee to examine generally the state of Ireland before accepting the necessity of such an extraordinary measure. But with Castlereagh, Fitzgerald, and other Irish members supporting him, Peel overrode all objections. The House in general was clearly not unkindly disposed, and he determined to make the most of the favourable moment. 'I feel strongly inclined,' he wrote to Whitworth on 13 July, 'to resist any innovation whatever, however plausible, and to keep the screw as tight as we can.'[1] To Gregory he had already described the salutary effect of the evidence he had provided on the minds of the English country gentlemen. 'Though I fear,' he added dryly, 'it will not encourage them to settle with their families in Ireland.' The screw-tightening policy was successful and both bills passed the Commons without amendment. Sidmouth in the House of Lords had a still easier passage and by the end of July the Peace Preservation Act (54 Geo. 3 c. 131) and the Insurrection Act (54 Geo. 3 c. 180) were both on the statute book. It was Peel's first essay in major legislation and he was pardonably gratified at

[1] 40287 f. 82 (passage omitted from *Peel*, I, 149).

the outcome. It had been almost entirely his own battle and the critical decision to proceed with the Insurrection Act completely so.

By the terms of the Peace Preservation Act the Lord Lieutenant was given power, when disturbances existed in any part of Ireland, to 'proclaim' the disturbed district and to appoint to it a salaried superintending magistrate in charge of a body of up to fifty special constables. The superintending magistrate received £700 per annum; the ordinary constables £50. It was envisaged that they would normally be appointed for twelve months at a time, but special provision was made for a bonus payment if the restoration of peace enabled the establishment to be disbanded at an earlier period. The cost of the establishment was to be met by a special levy on the district where it was set up. In framing this plan it is possible that Peel was guided to some extent by the precedent of Wellesley's reorganisation of the Dublin police in 1808, which in turn derived from an Irish measure of 1786 based on an abortive English bill of 1785. By this scheme Dublin had been divided into a number of districts, to each of which was assigned three magistrates, with a chief magistrate having his office in the Castle. Each division had a fixed number of police and there was also a mobile horse and foot patrol. In all some eight hundred police were available to keep order in the Irish capital. But the Dublin police were not entirely satisfactory and both the Lord Lieutenant and Gregory were agreed on the need to overhaul their organisation.[1] In Peel's plan there were three principal features: the creation of a new kind of magistrate, a professional salaried official who would have no legal connection with the district to which he was sent; the organisation under his direct control of a full-time body of police for the prevention of disorder; and the imposition of the financial charge on the districts in which these measures were enforced. The last provision was intended as much as a deterrent as a measure of economy. Indeed, in September 1813, a correspondent in Tipperary had already suggested to Gregory the expediency of inflicting some sort of penalty on disturbed areas that might shake the 'cold indifference' of local inhabitants to the disorders around them.[2]

An additional establishment of salaried magistrates meant to most

[1] 40188 f. 238, Whitworth to Peel, June 1814.
[2] S.P.O., State of Country, Corr. (Tipperary 1813).

of the active Irish public an extension of political patronage and before the bill was through parliament shoals of applications began to stream into the Castle and the Irish Office in London. But Peel was determined that his new force, from magistrates down to constables, should be kept free from patronage and local influence. 'If the present or any other Government make a job of it, they will most grossly betray the confidence which parliament has placed in them,' he wrote to Saurin in July, 'and shamefully sacrifice the best interests of the country to the worst.' How much in earnest he was to avoid any imputation of jobbery was seen when the appointment of an unsuitable magistrate, suggested by the Lord Chancellor and accepted by Gregory, was promptly overruled by Peel and the Lord Lieutenant.[1] A few magistrates already in government service were singled out for the new posts and Peel hoped to secure some of the brigade-majors in the Irish militia on the recommendation of the Commander-in-Chief. For his constables he looked to discharged N.C.O.s and men from the regular army and militia, accustomed to active service and good discipline. The class above all to be avoided were 'the servants of our parliamentary friends'. The pay he was offering being higher than the rates in the services, he thought that a sufficient number of good men would be attracted into the new force. When Richard Willcocks was appointed a chief magistrate in September, even a political opponent like Lord Donoughmore was moved to congratulate the government on their obvious determination to exclude political considerations and make efficiency the sole test of appointments.[2] Peel was all the more incensed therefore when Fletcher, one of the Irish assize judges and a whig by connection, in the course of a long political address to the Grand ury at Wexford, satirised the new Peace Preservation Act as a measure for providing jobs for government supporters. With considerable warmth and more than a touch of the tenacity he was to show the following year over O'Connell, Peel not only busied himself with the publication of an elaborate counter-statement, but with the approval of the Lord Lieutenant and his advisers took up with the cabinet the question of proceeding against Fletcher in parliament. But Sidmouth and Liverpool were wisely reluctant to engage in a party quarrel on such flimsy grounds, and though

[1] 40201 fos. 19, 47.      [2] 40189 f. 120.

Whitworth feared at one point that Peel might go so far as to resign on the issue, in the end the matter was allowed to pass over without any official action.[1]

The new police came into action for the first time on 6 September 1814 when the barony of Middlethird in Co. Tipperary was proclaimed under the Act and a force of twenty constables, selected from discharged sergeants of cavalry with good conduct certificates, was sent down to Cashel under a superintending magistrate.[2] The effect was immediate and salutary. Not only did disturbances die down but there were early reports of a general anxiety among farmers and tenants to bring offenders to justice in order to avoid the tax on their district. In the proclaimed areas themselves, however, especially when the original disorders were quelled, there was a certain resentment against the expense of the police establishment, and possibly some jealousy on the part of the resident J.P.s against the police magistrates whom they were called upon to assist. Willcocks reported from Cashel in February 1815 that he was receiving very little help from the Middlethird magistrates, and that some of them were trying to get the Insurrection Act substituted for the Peace Preservation Act. The cost of the police establishment, according to Willcocks's reckoning the following month, did not amount to more than $10\frac{1}{2}d.$ per acre.[3] Even so, it became evident that in order to escape the financial burden of the Peace Act, many magistrates either refused to petition for assistance when disorders broke out, or when matters became too serious to be dealt with locally, asked for the Insurrection Act to be applied instead.

There was a particular instance of this in Louth where several baronies were proclaimed under the Peace Act in the autumn of 1816. After some disagreement a majority of magistrates at the end of October petitioned for a withdrawal of the police on the grounds that peace had been restored. Then, eleven days later, as a result of the Lynch case, they petitioned for the Insurrection Act.[4] The financial clauses of the Peace Act were in fact so unpopular as to militate against the efficiency of the Act itself. Moreover, the parts of Ireland where there were fewer magistrates and gentry, and

---

[1] ibid., fos. 129, 169, 173; 40287 fos. 158, 188; 40182 f. 126.
[2] Colchester, II, 515ff.    [3] S.P.O., State of Country (Tipperary 1815).
[4] Foster (Peel to J. Foster, 17 November 1816); State of Country (Louth 1816).

consequently a greater degree of lawlessness, were also the poorer districts, least able to bear any extraordinary expenses. Accordingly, in March 1817, Peel proposed an amendment to the Act allowing discretion to the Lord Lieutenant in Council to direct that part of the expenses for proclaimed districts should be met from public funds. As it finally passed, the amendment introduced an additional measure of flexibility in the employment of magistrates and police in adjacent districts, and allowed up to two-thirds of the cost of police establishments to be defrayed by the Exchequer. By that date the Act had been applied in six instances: once in Louth, Clare, and Cavan respectively; and three times in Tipperary. The remission of tax now made possible was a substantial saving to the local rate-payers, even if the full proportion was not always granted. The cost, for example, of the police establishments in the baronies of Middle-third and Clanwilliam, Co. Tipperary, from March to July 1818 totalled £2,827, of which one-third was paid by the Exchequer and the remainder divided equally between the two baronies. The force employed comprised the chief magistrate, his clerk, two high constables, and eighty sub-constables.[1]

It is clear that Peel had in mind the ultimate introduction of a general and permanent body of police in Ireland, with fixed stations in every county. The limiting factor in the early years of the Irish constabulary was a shortage of suitable men rather than any deficiency of will on the part of the executive. 'I frequently considered the possibility of introducing a general system of Police,' he told the Marquess Wellesley, then Lord Lieutenant, in 1822, 'and was more dissuaded from it by the fears of not being able to procure proper instruments than by any conviction that such a system was not highly desirable.' To create an establishment of stipendiary magistrates in sufficient number to cover the whole of Ireland would need forty or fifty men of good character and judicial training, and free from the local connections that bedevilled all branches of the Irish administration. 'I was more inclined,' he continued, 'to the establishment of a Body of Gendarmerie (to be called by some less startling name) who should act under the control of Superintendents constantly varying their stations and reporting to the Lord Lieutenant the mode in which the subordinate officers were employed by

[1] S.P.O., Finance, 4 August 1818.

the magistrates.'[1] This was not a mere afterthought. He told the House of Commons as early as 1816 that he regretted the imperfect nature of the Irish police establishment; that much good might be done in Ireland by a reform of the police; and that he should prefer an army of police to a military army. In 1814, however, such a force would have taken a long time to build up, even if he could have won the consent of the legislature to such a costly and un-English innovation. As it was, the first years of the Irish Constabulary were marked by a certain amateurish air scarcely avoidable in a force that was only gradually evolving the distinction between military proper and armed civil police. The system of recruiting constables locally and the temporary nature of their services in the disturbed districts were the chief difficulties which the force had to encounter. Efficient organisation and discipline, even common uniform, were all lacking in the early stages. The original Constabulary appeared in a wide array of military costume, some in scarlet cloaks with plumed brass helmets bearing the inscription 'Waterloo', some in hussar uniform with short cloaks, others attired as riflemen riding pillion, and commanded by officers equally splendid and equally heterogeneous in their dress.[2]

Nevertheless, the Constabulary secured some success even from the start, and though Peel asked for the re-enactment of the Insurrection Act for a further year in 1817, he was able to tell the House that it had only been applied once that year, and in 1816 not at all. The organisation of an Irish Constabulary on a regular national basis was not carried out until 1822, when Peel was at the Home Office and Goulburn Chief Secretary; and when Drummond passed his consolidating Act in 1836, Peel's statute of 1814 was finally repealed along with most of the earlier legislation relating to the maintenance of the peace in Ireland. Its work had been done, however, and subsequent legislation was essentially an enlargement of the original narrow foundations of 1814 and a rectification of the defects thrown up by experience. Peel's prophecy in 1814 that in eight or ten years he would be thanked not merely for providing a means of controlling present disturbances but for putting on the statute book a law intended for permanent operation, proved true in spirit if not in letter; and the term 'Peelers' by which the Irish constabulary rapidly

[1] 40324 fos. 41-4 (12 April 1822).　　[2] Curtis, *Irish Constabulary*, p. 5.

became known was a fitting popular recognition of their original begetter.

In one particular respect the constabulary of the Peace Preservation Act was of special value to the Irish government. Before they were instituted, the only effective instrument for enforcing law and order in the countryside was the military; and throughout Peel's Secretaryship the problem of obtaining an adequate military force was one that constantly exercised the minds of Irish officials. In time of war the troops were wanted elsewhere; in peace the tax-payer did not want them at all. As far as Ireland was concerned, there were three sources of armed strength: the regular troops on garrison duty; the yeomanry who came together for twelve days annual training under a small permanent brigade staff; and the militia who as a last resource could be called out and embodied on a semi-permanent basis. In practice both the yeomanry and the Irish militia were of limited value, and more reliance was placed on the English militia regiments which were sent to Ireland to replace or reinforce the regular units in the last phase of the Napoleonic wars.

The relatively large force of men maintained in Ireland during the war was in fact primarily engaged on police duties. As Whit-worth wrote to the Home Department in June 1814:

> it is scarcely necessary for me to state that the Military are now called upon for the performance of severe and unusual duties, that they are dispersed and detached throughout the country, and yet not sufficient to supply the many applications which are made for them, and in fact that they alone are enabled to perform the duties of the interior police of the country.[1]

Yet the nature both of the troops and of their employment gave satisfaction neither to the military authorities at the Castle nor to the magistrates in the disturbed areas. The Commander-in-Chief saw his small force of some 14,000 men violating all the rules of war and discipline by being dispersed in small detachments over the country; while the local gentry fretted at the military regulations which prevented these detachments from going out on duty except under a magistrate. Peel was in the position therefore of having to counter

[1] S.P.O., Private Official (Whitworth to Sidmouth, 27 June 1814).

complaints and criticisms from both sides. To Hewett, the Commander of the forces, he was obliged to point out that 'the army in this country is not stationed in it for those purposes for which an army is usually employed', and to Desart that

> there have been so many instances wherein the military have been improperly called forth and their services employed in the mere promotion of the private ends of individuals, that it is absolutely necessary to lay it down as a general rule that the military shall be employed solely under the personal direction of the magistrate who requires their aid.[1]

It resulted from this essentially police function of the army in Ireland that the coming of peace in 1814 made no real difference to the pressure on their services, and that the Irish government in 1815 could not entirely share the view of the British cabinet that the regular troops in Ireland were a strategic force whose most effective employment lay in Flanders. Even before hostilities ended in 1814 Peel and the Lord Lieutenant had been jointly pressing for the reinforcement of the troops at their disposal, and the cabinet decided in January to despatch to them all the remaining regiments of British militia that had volunteered for service in Ireland. When hostilities ended it was further agreed that the disbandment of the militia should take place slowly and that none would be withdrawn from Ireland until regular troops were available to take their place. The escape of Napoleon from Elba shattered these plans and the Irish government was faced in the spring of 1815 with the early departure of most if not all the regiments of the line for service in Flanders. Indeed, Sidmouth told Peel in June that every regular soldier in Ireland would have to leave. The only course open to the Castle in those circumstances was to mobilise some of the yeomanry and call out the remaining Irish militia. The proclamation to that effect was issued by the Irish Privy Council on 26 June, eight days after Waterloo. The sudden collapse of the war left Ireland therefore with a considerable armed force which, if not too large

---

[1] S.P.O., General Private (Hewett to Peel, 23 October, Peel to Hewett, 29 October 1815; Peel to Desart, 24 January 1817). Military (Desart to Peel, 10 January 1817).

for its domestic duties, seemed nevertheless to be of indefensible proportions both to the cabinet in London and to the Irish executive in Dublin Castle. The total strength of the armed force at the disposal of the Lord Lieutenant amounted to over 63,000, of whom about 22,000 were regulars.

Large as this force seemed on paper, however, the crucial point was the size of the regular element in it. In 1814 the Irish executive accepted the view of their military advisers that a total of 40,000 all ranks would be necessary as a peacetime establishment for Ireland. Though Peel was not sanguine that this figure would be accepted, he sent a reasoned memorandum on the subject to Sidmouth so that the opinion of the Irish government would at least be on record. As the embodiment of the militia in 1815 could only be a temporary feature, the Irish government were anxious not to be left with a regular force of much less than the establishment they suggested. The disorders in parts of the country during 1815, especially in Tipperary, caused in fact a considerable concentration of troops in the disturbed districts and it was not until 1816 that the task of effective demobilisation could be attempted. How necessary armed force was to the Irish executive power was almost comically illustrated in the spring of 1816, when the Board of Excise was obliged to apply for a piece of artillery of sufficient calibre to reduce the castle of Belkelly, near Lough Derg, which was garrisoned by manufacturers of illicit whiskey. In enclosing their report for Sidmouth's edification, Peel added wryly,

> there is a mixture of the melancholy and the ludicrous in this despatch, but it suffices to give some idea of what you may expect from the unassisted operation of the law, when sixteen men can defy it in this way, aided as it is by a Howitzer and 30 men. It is hardly necessary to assure you that we shall send no 32 pounder or take any other step for the reduction of the castle of Belkelly without due caution.

To Littlehales, the Military Under-Secretary, he wrote judicially 'it would be very wrong to begin battering with a 32 pounder without being perfectly clear as to the law, and to the inefficiency of any milder operation'.[1] Nevertheless the cabinet, faced with public

[1] 40290 fos. 77, 163-4 (March 1816).

demands for post-war economy, was under the imperative necessity of effecting reductions in all departments of administration, and Peel was too good a parliamentarian not to appreciate that the Irish government would have to make its contribution. Indeed he was himself annually faced with the task of defending the Irish military estimates in a House of Commons increasingly sensitive to any expenditure of public money that was not demonstrably necessary.

The military planners in Dublin, however, happily exempt from the political pressures of Westminster, proceeded to estimate for a continuation of the existing inflated establishment of the armed forces in Ireland. A memorandum from the commander of the forces envisaged for 1816 a force that was not only larger than that estimated for 1815 but 24,000 more than the theoretical peace establishment which the Irish government had approved in 1814.[1] Since Vansittart had already suggested in parliament a reduced establishment of 25,000 for Ireland, Peel was both embarrassed and annoyed at the extravagance of the Irish estimates. In a long letter to Littlehales he called sharply for a drastic revision of the offending document. At the same time both he and the Lord Lieutenant were opposed to the full reduction proposed by the cabinet and they were agreed that at any rate some of the militia would have to be kept on foot to supplement the regular forces. Their strong representations had some effect even on the harassed cabinet. Following a formal letter from Peel in November 1816, the Prime Minister and Sidmouth privately asked for his and Whitworth's estimate of the forces they would need. Peel then put forward a compromise plan for the retention of the existing regular troops, at that date about 25,000 men, until the end of the winter, and a reduction to 22,000 for the remainder of 1817; and this was finally accepted.[2]

General Hewett, the Commander of the Forces in Ireland, who had been extremely discontented with this arrangement, was succeeded by General Beckwith in December 1816. Even so, the Irish military estimates for the following year were still above what Peel thought were politically acceptable. The Chief Secretary was not prepared to accept silent opposition from the soldiers and in the spring of 1817 he sent to the military department a long questionnaire, covering ten sides of foolscap and ranging over the whole

[1] S.P.O., Military, 1816.    [2] 40181 f. 87; 40182 f. 247.

history of the military force in Ireland since the outbreak of war, which laid bare the significant increase over the pre-war strength of what was being proposed as the permanent peace establishment.

> In 1792 [ran his final question] there were no yeomanry and no militia in a year of peace, there was only a force of 9,500 men. In 1817, in a year of profound peace with a militia staff and with 30,000 yeomanry, why is it proposed to retain 23,000 rank and file? Let me know what additional military grounds there are which did not exist in 1792?[1]

Having extracted every economy from his subordinates, however, he proceeded, by a transition familiar to all parliamentary administrators, to take a high line in the House of Commons when defending the Irish estimates in the following May. He protested against taking 1792 as a criterion for the establishment in 1817, quoted his recently acquired information on the size of the Irish force in the eighteenth century, and declared that he found more difficulty in justifying the reduction of 3,000 than the retention of 22,000. One lesson, it is clear, he had mastered: to defend his subordinates in public and harry them in private.

In his own calculations, however, a factor of growing importance was the effect of the Peace Preservation Act and the new Constabulary in diminishing the need for a large military force. In telling General Torrens at the Horse Guards of the ability of the Irish government to reduce their establishment to 22,000 at the end of March 1817, Peel added that though they did not want the reduction, they would be more uneasy if they did not have in Ireland the powers of the superintending magistrates and their mounted police; and that he hoped to extend the police more generally throughout Ireland.[2] The work of economy went on steadily for the remainder of Peel's secretaryship, and in November the Irish government was able to inform Sidmouth that they did not think the peace of Ireland would be endangered if after the winter the effective regular force was further reduced to 20,000. In discussing the reduction with General Beckwith in December 1817, Peel pointed to the other means at the disposal of the government for preserving order—the

---

[1] S.P.O., Military, 22 April 1817.    [2] 40292 f. 112.

substantial yeomanry force still retained, the permanent militia staff, and the powers of the Lord Lieutenant under the Peace Preservation Act of establishing in disturbed districts a numerous and effective body of police.[1] In private he expressed to the Prime Minister his opinion that the Irish establishment might ultimately be reduced to 18,000. Ireland was not a soil in which either economy or efficiency readily took root, and both Chief Secretary and his former chief for different reasons could look with satisfaction on this particular achievement.

[1] S.P.O., General Private, 1814-21, fos. 261, 265.

CHAPTER

6

# LAST YEARS IN IRELAND

The alternation of his duties between Westminster and Dublin left little leisure for the Chief Secretary. Indeed, except for his Paris trip in 1815, Peel took no real holiday at all in these years. Brief occasional visits to friends near London, like the Duke of Richmond at Goodwood, or a few days at Drayton on his way to Holyhead, were all that could be spared from his limited time in England. But in Ireland almost every winter he was able to get away from his desk for a week or so, usually to join a shooting party at the country house of one of his Irish landowner friends. An expedition to Killarney which he planned in the autumn of 1813 was abandoned when he thought he would have to go to England to secure his re-election. But in 1814 he went up to Connaught in the north-west; at the end of 1816 he was at Farnham in Co. Cavan; and in the winter of 1817-18 in Monaghan and Cavan again. The Dalys at Dunsandle, Co. Galway, and Lord Farnham in Co. Cavan, had him as their guest on several occasions; and it was at Farnham in January 1818 that he shot 173 woodcock out of a total bag of 458 made by his party. He had seen something of at least three of the four Irish provinces, and though the object of his visits into the Irish country-side was clearly sport and relaxation, it is unlikely that he failed to make his own observations on the state of the Irish rural classes. Desart's criticism in 1818, therefore, that much as Peel had done for Ireland, it was 'not nearly half what you might and would have done if you had continued in your present situation and seen something of the interior of Ireland, and of those residents there who are occupied in its improvement and are little interested in giving false representations to men in power',[1] was in all the circumstances perhaps not entirely justified.

[1] 40216 f. 333 (22 June 1818).

Yet it remained true that the root of Ireland's evils lay in its social and economic structure; and though governmental administration was neither habituated nor equipped to deal with such fundamental problems, no one with an open mind could study Irish society for long without beginning to observe the depths of social chaos from which the more superficial if more striking social vices were nourished. Ireland was poor, over-populated, and dependent almost entirely on agriculture. The only exports of any consequence were linen and corn, and along with other Irish members Peel welcomed the Corn Law of 1815 as affording some sort of encouragement to Irish agriculture and drew attention to the need to encourage the trade in Irish butter which formed the third major item in the staple exports of the country.[1] But what Ireland needed was not so much a protective tariff for her relatively small export trade as a complete economic revolution; Dublin and Belfast were in no sense representative of the island as a whole. Ireland lacked large towns, important industries, and a thriving commercial life. Infertile, with much of its surface hillside and bog, it could barely support its population at subsistence level. Yet that population, for a generation before Peel came to Ireland, had been growing at an unprecedented rate. From a figure probably over rather than under four million in 1790, it was steadily rising to a total of nearly seven million at the 1821 census, a rate of increase higher even than that of contemporary England with all the wealth of industrialisation to aid it, and perhaps higher than any other country in Western Europe has ever experienced.[2] This social phenomenon had been made possible by the development of the potato as the staple crop of the Irish peasant. Yielding a far greater bulk of food to the acre than any cereal, the potato had secured a dominating position in Irish economy in the latter part of the eighteenth century; and from the start of the nineteenth the introduction of new strains, more prolific though perhaps more susceptible to disease, further augmented Ireland's chief food supply. Needing no capital and only unskilled seasonal labour, it enabled the peasants to marry young and rear large families. Potatoes and a little milk were enough to maintain strength and health without much addition to this simple and uniform diet. The

[1] Debate on agricultural distress, 22 March 1816, (*Speeches*, I, 54).
[2] Connell, *Population of Ireland*, contains a full discussion of this subject.

limiting factor was the soil itself, and as the population multiplied, with no employment except in agriculture, the pressure on the land became intensified.

There was in theory one outlet for Ireland's depressed and crowded population—emigration. But the feature of Irish emigration in these years was that it took place not from the impoverished areas of the south and west, but from among the relatively wealthier and more skilled artisan classes of Ulster. Six months before Waterloo was fought, in anticipation of the revival of large-scale emigration from Ireland across the Atlantic once peace returned, Peel was urging the adoption of means to divert the flow from the United States to Canada, where it would 'contribute to the strength and future defence of our own colonies' rather than furnish 'the means of annoyance already very formidable, which increasing population will afford to our neighbours in N. America'.[1] His own notion was a scheme of supervised emigration from Dublin, under the control of a government agent, and assisted by bounties for those proceeding to Canada. But other than judiciously worded paragraphs which he caused to be inserted in the Irish press, little was done. A year later a return made to him of emigration to America in the preceding three-year period showed how correct his prognostication had been. In 1814 there had been no emigrants; in 1815 the figure was 1837; and in 1816 it was 6171. This time he wrote direct to the prime minister, drawing his attention not only to the 'large and increasing extent of emigration from Ireland to the United States' but to the fact that it was almost entirely from the north of Ireland. A reduction in the dense and under-employed population of southern Ireland could be nothing but a benefit to the country; but 'I think this diminution of the Protestant population very unfortunate, and I think it still more unfortunate that not only Ireland should lose so many industrious and valuable inhabitants, but that the United States of America should reap the advantage.' How encouragement could be given to them to stay in the Empire he did not presume to say. 'I know it could not be without considerable expense, but I much doubt whether the saving of that expense at present would prove true economy in the end.'[2] The policy of

[1] 40288 fos. 41-2 (January 1815).
[2] 40192 f. 176; 40291 f. 99, partly printed Peel, I, 233.

empire development and assisted emigration was still in its pioneer days, however, and in the political state of 1816 few proposals that involved additional and novel forms of government expenditure were likely to win the cabinet's approval. It is clear, nevertheless, that his two years at the Colonial Office had not been without some effect in widening the horizons of Peel's political imagination. When the great famine of 1846-7 produced the first mass exodus of Irish peasantry the traditional route they followed led them to the United States. Until then, emigration did little to solve the fundamental problem of Irish rural life: the struggle for the land.

Centuries of uneasy Anglo-Irish relations marked by conquest, rebellion, and confiscation, had seen the ownership of most of Ireland pass into the hands of an Anglo-Irish aristocracy. The same long historic process had produced among the larger proprietors the evils of absenteeism; a division of interests between Ireland and England; a lack of close personal supervision; and a reluctance to invest capital in a country that was distant, alien, disturbed, and often dangerous. In the social gap thus created came agents, middlemen, and rack-renters, to add to the burden of rent on the tenant, while decreasing the profit of the proprietor. It was true that Ulster formed a striking contrast to the other three Irish provinces, and that many exceptions had to be made to any general indictment of Irish landowners. Peel could count in his own circle of friends men like Desart, J. L. Foster, and Fitzgerald, who were humane, enlightened, and resident landlords. But the system was too strong for individuals to break and Ireland remained a country which economically as well as politically retained many of the appearances of a colonial possession. Landlord neglect, however, was only one side of Irish rural society. Even the best of reforming landlords had to encounter a silent social pressure from the peasantry which was capable of defeating any attempt at improvement. It needed no special perspicacity to see that what Irish economy needed was a consolidation of holdings and the investment of capital in large-scale farming; but every element in Irish society conspired to prevent such a policy being realised. The political value of a numerous tenantry that could vote in their master's interest at the county elections led to the toleration and sometimes to the deliberate multiplication of peasant holdings; and the frequent canvassing of measures to abolish the 40s. freehold vote in this period was primarily with a view to its economic results. But the major obstacle to agricultural reform lay in the Irish peasantry themselves.

Impoverished and half-illiterate, cunning and lawless, the Irish in many parts of the country looked upon the land less as the absolute property of an owner than as an historic tribal possession from which at most they had only been partially dispossessed, and over which the alien landlords had been only partially established. In the subsistence economy to which they were accustomed money played an insignificant part. The only wealth was land and the only remedy for an increase in the community was a subdivision of land. Fathers divided their holdings for their sons, and sons for grandsons. Tenants gave sub-leases though they did not lease the original land themselves, and left land in their wills though they did not own it. The relationship between landlord and tenant became in reality a relationship with a semi-autonomous community; and legal rights were choked by a tenacious and vegetative growth of purely social usage. Against this the landlords as a class were powerless. Their nominal tenants were only the leaders of a multitude of settlers on their land; and at the expiry of a twenty- or thirty-year lease a landlord might find thirty or forty tenants installed where he had originally let the land to one.[1] The only remedy for such a situation was eviction; and eviction was the one measure certain to evoke the savage retaliation of social warfare: threats, physical intimidation, and, in the last resort, assassination. But as often as not peasant, racial, and religious solidarity ensured that, even without bloodshed, no one would come forward to take up land from which any family had been expelled. In fact the period from Waterloo to the Irish famine was not characterised by any widespread or continuous efforts at ejection on the part of the landlords. Anxious as most of them were to prevent the further sub-division of their estates, they found it impossible to make headway against the universal resistance of the Irish population. Consequently, since capital and consolidation offered the only chance of prosperity for Irish agriculture, the bulk of the Irish peasantry in the south and west continued to live not only on the margin of subsistence, but in utter dependence on a single vulnerable crop. All the other features of Irish rural life—the poverty,

[1] cf. Lewis, *Local Disturbances*, pp. 319ff.; *State of Ireland* 1824-5.

idleness, and lack of incentive, the endemic shortage of money, the bitter resistance in times of scarcity to all the financial demands made upon the tenant class in the shape of rent, tithe, county rate, parochial rate, and priests' dues—flowed from this central desperate situation.

## II

The coming of peace in 1815 made it almost inevitable that parliamentary scrutiny should occasionally be turned to a consideration of the state of Ireland. A government which asked the legislature for a Peace Preservation Act, a renewal of the Insurrection Act, and a military establishment of 25,000 men, was bound to be faced with some awkward and searching questions. Indeed, in order to justify these measures at all, it had been necessary to draw the attention of parliament to the peculiar conditions existing in the sister island and to convince honourable members, as Peel once remarked, that they knew as much about Ireland as they did of Kamchatka. If the House of Commons was not the most qualified body to deal with Irish business, that was after all a penalty of the Union.

> I believe [wrote Peel to Gregory in 1816] an honest despotic government would be by far the fittest government for Ireland. But while you have any deliberative assembly, in which every member is at liberty to bring every subject under consideration, how are you to deal with such a body? . . . Judge of the trouble of managing Irish affairs in such an assembly and of the absurdity of supposing that you can withdraw them from notice and discussion.

Even at the time of the passing of the Peace Preservation Bill in 1814, there had been an evident desire on the part of some members to embark on a full discussion of Irish problems; and once the prestige of victory which had carried the government through 1815 had begun to fade, a renewed attack was made by the opposition. Early in March 1816 Sir John Newport, one of the leading and most respected Irish whigs in the House of Commons, gave notice of a motion for a general enquiry into the state of Ireland; and a parallel motion was introduced in the House of Lords by the Marquess of

Buckingham, a relative and follower of Lord Grenville. The prospect of a set debate on Ireland in both Houses was not a pleasant one for the Irish executive. No discussion of Irish affairs could fail to bring up the Catholic question, and any mention of that problem was calculated to create confusion and trepidation in the counsels of the cabinet. But even apart from the religious issue, Ireland could afford enough material to last a whole session. Pensions, police, army, tithe, finance, justice, education, and crime, offered a vast field over which the opposition members could range endlessly; and the fact that lengthy enquiries, issuing in lengthier reports, had already taken place on many of these topics, would not prevent the House of Commons, if it felt so disposed, from again traversing the same familiar ground. Moreover, there were some aspects, such as the administration of justice, which the Irish government could scarcely defend, and if they could not defend, would have to offer to reform. Peel's instinct was to resist the motion altogether, and he remained convinced that no good could come of any general and unrestricted inquest on Irish affairs. But his characteristic caution almost at once proposed a more politic line of defence, and when writing to Lord Whitworth he suggested the possibility of a particular enquiry into the disorders in specific counties that had led to the application of the Insurrection Act. Not only would this provide a manageable subject for examination, but it concerned an aspect of Irish life as widely removed as possible from sectarian animosities, and one in which the actions of the Irish government had no reason to fear publicity.

With this attitude the Lord Lieutenant concurred, and though some members of the Irish government from the seclusion of Dublin Castle were disposed to fight the issue, Peel's constant argument that tactical concession must be made in order to achieve parliamentary success overcame the resistance of his more militant colleagues. The cabinet in any case offered no encouragement for an heroic policy. When Peel was called into cabinet consultation at the end of March over Buckingham's motion, it was clear that Liverpool and his fellow ministers were strongly impressed with the need to accept enquiry into particular Irish problems with a view to discovering a remedy for what were, after all, notorious evils. Peel laboured to impress on the Prime Minister the danger of a purely political inquest; but as he reported afterwards to Whitworth, 'I fear, however, some enquiry we must have, though no good can come from it. . . . I am satisfied to resist enquiry, but then if I am beaten, I should like to resign, and not submit to the humiliation of being forced into such a measure.' The debate in the House of Lords came on first, and though Liverpool successfully resisted the motion for a committee of the whole House, Peel was not altogether pleased at the arguments used by some ministerial speakers to defeat an immediate enquiry, since he thought they virtually admitted the necessity of a future one.[1] However, the main battle was in the House of Commons and he busied himself in the remaining weeks with preparations for the forthcoming debate.

The exact wording of Newport's motion, which called for an examination of existing evils and the adoption of 'other wholesome and efficacious remedies' for the state of Ireland, seemed to him designed to extract from the government an indirect pledge on Catholic emancipation and thus inveigle Castlereagh and other emancipationist members of the front bench into supporting it. He turned his mind accordingly to the framing of a counter-motion which would have the opposite effect, and a fortunate postponement of the debate provided him with time for reflection. A meeting of the leading ministerialists in the Commons held at Castlereagh's house approved his suggestion and it was settled that Peel should rise immediately after Newport with an amendment to the motion expressing regret at the state of Ireland and asking for information both on recent disturbances and the measures taken to deal with them. It was generally agreed that many on the government side would not consent to a mere negation of Newport's motion; and the amendment, as Peel somewhat cynically reported afterwards on 8 April to Whitworth, 'would give every man an opportunity to fire off his speech on Irish affairs, which people are more anxious for generally than for the perusal of the papers they require'.[2] If the amendment was carried, it was decided that Sidmouth would formally call on the Lord Lieutenant to provide a connected account of the nature and extent of present and previous disorders in Ireland. One gratifying feature of the meeting was that Castlereagh showed every disposition to oppose a motion which he, like others, thought was framed to embarrass him personally, as well as all those members

[1] 40290 fos. 183, 188, 192.    [2] *ibid.*, f. 202.

of the government who had ever spoken in favour of Catholic claims.

With parliamentary tactics now decided, Peel turned at once to the amassing of the necessary material. Mobilising with practised assurance the resources of his office, he wrote to Gregory on 9 April:

> I should like to make enquiries with respect to some portion of the country, and I know none where more impartial sources of information could be found than Tipperary, and I should also select this part of the country on another account, namely that as it is the most disturbed, the presumption is that the peasantry are as badly off as in most other districts. The sources from which I would propose to collect information are Willcocks, Wills, and Wilson [chief magistrates under the Peace Preservation Act] and it would probably be extracted from them in answer to such questions as the following.

What followed was a long list of minute questions on land-holding, rent, wages, diet, support of the aged and infirm, lease and other tenures, marriage, casual employment, morals, manners, housing, fuel, and middlemen, covering three sides of quarto paper.

> Have the goodness to write a line to Willcocks, etc., explaining to them my object and requesting them to add any other information which they may think valuable, and which they may have acquired in other parts of Ireland. For instance I should like to know very much whether much difference prevails between the state of the people in Longford and Westmeath, and that in Tipperary. To this they would be competent to speak. Wills must know a great deal, but unfortunately he thinks himself rather a fine writer. I would give a great deal for his facts but nothing for his eloquence.[1]

Willcocks's report on Tipperary, even more massive than the questionnaire which elicited it, was forwarded on 20 April in time for the Newport debate on the 26th.

While the chief magistrates were collecting information, Peel moved ahead to the next step, and, even before the debate came on,

---

[1] 40290 f. 205; 40202 fos. 277, 286; partly printed *Letter-Box*, p. 95, including the reply sent by Willcocks.

he suggested to Whitworth that a start should be made in collecting the material that the Irish government would be called upon to produce should his amendment be successful. Provided the information was made available, he offered himself to put it in proper shape to lay before parliament. On the tender point of Irish judicial administration, which had come under heavy fire in the House of Lords and which he had already warned the Lord Chancellor would be one of the subjects of debate in the Commons, he wrote for advice to Saurin. The most vulnerable aspect was the position of the sheriffs. The existing practice of appointment by the government, Peel felt, could not be defended in view of the great political influence they wielded in Irish county affairs. But nomination by the Irish judges, with a bench that included political partisans like Fletcher, he thought almost equally open to practical disadvantage. To the professional opposition of the Irish legal officers he paid little attention.

> The Chancellor thinks I am nervous upon some matters in which I am not personally concerned [he wrote to Gregory] and he is perfectly right. I am more than nervous when I consider the probable consequences of a Committee to enquire into the state of Ireland when I reflect that I could not select a Committee upon which, from the very necessity of putting upon it certain individuals in office,—Lord Castlereagh, Fitzgerald, Pole, etc.,—I must not insure an immense majority of persons pledged on the Catholic question.

It was therefore armed and prepared at all foreseeable points that he rose on the evening of 26 April to reply to Sir John Newport's long historical review of the evils from which Ireland had suffered since the end of the sixteenth century. Peel began with an acknowledgement both of Newport's moderation and of the reasonable desire of the House to know the conditions in Ireland which made an establishment of 25,000 men necessary in time of peace. But he asked what sort of enquiry, and how defined and restricted, would best suit the situation. 'He was still inclined to think that the difficulties and evils which encompassed Ireland formed a Gordian knot which could not be cut and which only the gradual lapse of time could unravel.' Then he turned to an account of the actual disorders in specific parts of Ireland: Tipperary, Kings County, Westmeath, Limerick, Cavan, and Louth. It was hard to give a precise description of the disorders; they differed from county to county. He had been in some where it was impossible to find men more tractable and obedient. The Irish people had been frequently misrepresented; in their dealings with each other they were faithful, honest, and chaste. But in some parts there was a 'general confederacy in crime' and judicial records showed 'such a settled and uniform system of guilt, such monstrous and horrible perjuries' as could not be found in the history of any other civilised country. The causes of many Irish evils were historical—conquest and confiscation—and these could only be cured by the passage of time, a kind and paternal system of government, and an extension of education. Similarly English commercial restrictions had stifled Ireland's economy, cheapened her land, and had caused among the peasantry sub-division of holdings, reliance on potatoes, early marriage, and over-population. 'He was perfectly aware that the food of the poor in Ireland was inferior, and he sincerely wished that it were possible to find any means of giving him better, and a better place in which to enjoy it. Nothing would be more calculated to seduce them from idle and vicious habits.' As to specific complaints against the administration, he gave a pledge that in future the appointment of sheriffs should be placed in the hands of the judges, though he did not think a general revision of the magistracy a practicable reform; and he ended with a brief and mainly non-committal review of Orange lodges, the Irish press, the 40s. freehold franchise (which he suggested was partially responsible for many social evils), Catholic emancipation, and education.

It was, and was clearly intended to be, a general survey of the whole complex of Irish affairs, designed to indicate difficulties rather than to suggest any sovereign remedy. Its sober tone was reflected in the debate which followed. Fitzgerald and Castlereagh supported Peel, while among the opposition speakers Plunket delivered what Peel thought was a factious, uncandid speech, and Grattan tended to lay the blame for Ireland's disorder on her commercial state. The discussion as a whole seemed to Peel dull and uninteresting, and though his amendment was carried by 187 votes to 103, he was not very satisfied at the division. However, the challenge had been resisted and there was material consolation in the fact that there would be little further interest in any Irish debate for the remainder of the session. As he had anticipated, there appeared no real demand for the information on Ireland that the House had agreed to request. Nevertheless, Gregory and his staff busied themselves up to the middle of May preparing a mass of evidence on Irish lawlessness since 1813; and early the following month a formal despatch, containing what Gregory described as 'the bloody catalogue of crimes', was sent off to Lord Sidmouth.[1]

If Peel had formulated no policy for Ireland, he had at least shown the merit of realising the depth and intricacy of the problem, particularly the part played by the economic condition of the Irish peasantry. But the more specific, if perhaps more superficial, question of Catholic disabilities was one to which the political world in general found it easier to pay more attention. It was a clear issue, readily apprehensible, already prominent in the public eye, and susceptible of immediate legislative solution. Less than a month after the Newport debate, Grattan moved that the House should take Catholic claims into consideration the following session. He was supported by Castlereagh, and though Peel spoke briefly both to argue against the motion and to emphasise that Irish disorder arose from various causes 'not even remotely connected with the political disabilities of the Catholics', the motion was only lost by the narrow margin of thirty-one votes. Unimportant as the debate was in the general history of Catholic emancipation, it was not without some significance for Peel's own career. In these latter years of his Irish secretaryship, circumstances were already impelling him into the front rank of the Protestant party in the House of Commons. His Irish experience had not only confirmed his original attitude towards Catholic claims, but had drawn his attention, however tentatively, towards other more dimly discerned features of the Irish problem. At the same time his official position as chief representative of the Irish government, and his embarrassing relationship with Castlereagh whenever the Catholic issue was debated in the lower House, placed on him at this early stage in his political life the necessity of an explicit formulation of his views. It was inevitable that in such a situation he would speak his mind. His own temperament made it

[1] 40203 f. 4.

difficult for him to hold back on an issue where he held firm opinions. Intellectual conviction in Peel was a prelude to action. At the same time the Protestants in the Commons were discouragingly short of able spokesmen. Most of the ministers and politicians who were prominent opponents of Roman Catholic claims sat in the House of Lords. In the Commons, though the Protestants never lacked numbers, they had few men of ability to put up against Canning, Castlereagh, Grattan, Plunket, Parnell, and Newport. Indeed, John Leslie Foster, one of the more influential Irish government supporters, wrote in 1817 that Peel and Manners Sutton were the only two men of outstanding talent to take a lead on the Protestant side.[1] In a party so ominously lacking in established reputations, leadership was a distinction less likely be be achieved than to be thrust upon one.

The debate on Grattan's motion in 1816 made Peel acutely aware of the political poverty of the side to which he belonged.

> The Protestant cause [he wrote to Lord Whitworth the day after the debate] has fallen into the hands of lukewarm or timid or incompetent men. Can you conceive that within ten minutes of the division our friends proposed that we should not divide, fancying we should be in a small minority. . . . Grattan, Parnell, Mathew, Hippisley, Castlereagh, had spoken; not a single Protestant had said a word, and I determined therefore, to take a part which others with more weight might have taken, and to divide the House at any rate. . . . The result was a majority of thirty, to our great surprise and satisfaction.

This preliminary success, casual and unpremeditated as it was, made it almost unavoidable that at the next great trial of strength on the Catholic issue Peel should be regarded as one of the main pillars of the Protestant cause.

In 1817 a major attempt, the first since 1813, was made by the emancipationist party in the House of Commons to re-open the question of Catholic disabilities. Basing himself on the Catholic petitions presented to parliament in the previous session, and on a renewed application by Irish Roman Catholics to bring their case

[1] Foster (J. L. Foster to J. Foster, 26 April 1817).

before the legislature, Grattan introduced a motion for a committee
of the whole House to consider the laws affecting Roman Catholics
in Great Britain and Ireland, with a view to final and conciliatory
adjustment. The issue of the year before had been primarily whether
the House should pledge itself prospectively to such a debate. The
issue now was once more the direct principle of emancipation. A
parallel motion in the House of Lords, moved by Lord Donoughmore, marked the importance of the occasion. As in 1813, it was
impossible to tell beforehand what the outcome would be. No
calculation based on the strength of the government was applicable
here, since the majority of influential ministers in the Commons
favoured the motion, and the ordinary apparatus of government
influence could not readily be brought into operation. But Leslie
Foster noted an unusual degree of apathy among the Protestants,
and it was evident that many of their leaders, while preparing for
the contest, were already anticipating defeat. The division in the
Lords was safe enough, but the House of Commons was a different
matter. Foster reported that 'persons very high in Government
really believe that the House will go into a Committee'. Indeed,
up to the time when the division actually took place, the little group
of leading Protestant Irish members with whom Peel habitually
worked thought that Grattan would carry his motion by about five
votes. Nevertheless, they were determined not to be beaten without
a fight, and before the debate came on, they consulted together on
tactics and speakers. It was agreed that Foster should open on their
side, and Peel also took pains to secure the services of Webber, who
on Duigenan's death the previous year had succeeded to the blue
riband of Irish Protestant representation, the membership for the
borough of Armagh. These preparations were the more important
since in the event it was on this small Anglo-Irish group, together
with Bathurst, that the entire burden of the Protestant cause fell.

The debate on Grattan's motion took place on the evening of
9 May 1817 and Peel reserved himself for the crucial place of last
speaker on the Protestant side. His speech was not only one of his
most outstanding parliamentary achievements, but in its indirect
consequences one of the most fateful for his own career. As a contribution to the actual debate it owed much of its powerful effect to
the precision with which he related his arguments to the detailed

proposals put forward by the other side and to the actual administrative problem before the government. He took his chief stand on Ireland and his whole effort was directed to showing that the proposals were obnoxious to those whom it was designed to relieve, and calculated only to weaken the union and the Protestant establishment and to strengthen without conciliating the forces in Ireland hostile to them. It was an effective line of attack, for the difference between Peel and his opponents was not that they willed two different ends but that they differed on the means of attaining the same end. They thought that their proposals would preserve the Union; he did not. Yet in elaborating his arguments he was led on to a general expression of opinion which was opposed to emancipation in any form and at any time. He achieved in fact the feat of both destroying his adversaries' particular policy and also suggesting that no policy they could bring forward was likely to succeed. Not only was their chosen position broken but all alternatives denied them. But in winning this dialectical success, he also denied to his own side any room for manœuvre. His case in the last analysis was a pessimistic one, for it rested on the presumption that there was a political and religious cleavage between the majority of the Irish population and the rest of the British Isles which could not be immediately, if ever, overcome. It was not, for all that, a necessarily false presumption but it offered as a consequence no alternative to the existing policy of the government. Essentially, therefore, it was a purely defensive speech despite the attacking language in which it was clothed.

He opened with a detailed and devastating criticism of the weakest part of the emancipation case. It was agreed by Grattan and his supporters that securities were indispensable and they admitted that it was the common practice of European states to enter into agreements with the Papacy to obtain such securities from the Roman Catholic Church within their dominions. But in Ireland the Roman hierarchy and the body of Catholics had rejected the controls proposed in 1813 and there was no reason to suppose that they would accept the 'domestic nomination' of bishops suggested on this occasion. Indeed, as Peel pointed out, the security arrangements now put forward lacked the authority either of Rome or of the Catholic bishops; and all past experience made it certain that they would be repudiated by those whom it was hoped to assist and conciliate. That being so, the whole argument that a final and satisfactory settlement of the religious problem could be secured collapsed at the start. Even if the House were agreed that the new proposals were fair and expedient, the indispensable support from the Roman Church necessary for their success would not be forthcoming.

The next step in his argument was a consideration of the proposals themselves. The issue here was one of fundamental principle. It was in fact whether the Protestant system of Church and State set up at the Revolution should be altered or not. 'We are now discussing,' he warned the Commons, 'the respective merits of two systems for the government of a great country.' The case for altering the constitution was grounded on the state of Ireland and on the assumption that political equality for Roman Catholics would solve, or at any rate ease, the problem of administering Ireland. It was essentially therefore a controversy on the best way of governing Ireland. The opposition asserted that Ireland had been misruled in the past, and drew the conclusion that to rule it well in future necessitated the grant of emancipation. Was that either a logical or practical conclusion? Peel denied that it was. 'We may regret this misrule and its consequences, but what we have to determine is this:—circumstanced as Ireland now is,—by what course of policy shall we best promote the interests of the empire at large?' If the issue were one of governmental policy, the argument must address itself to that. There were, he suggested, four ways of dealing with Ireland that could be envisaged: the legal proscription of Roman Catholicism; the legal establishment of Roman Catholicism; the existing system; and the system now proposed. The first two could be dismissed out of hand, since there was no political support for either. In that case the issue narrowed to a choice between the present settlement under which Catholicism was tolerated but the Established Church and the higher public offices reserved for Protestants; and the modified system proposed by the emancipationists whereby the religion of the Protestant minority was to retain its privileged position but all posts in government except that of Lord Lieutenant were to be opened to the Catholic majority. It was the essence of Peel's case that of the two, the existing system was the one most likely to preserve the union between the two countries and ensure stability and harmony between the minority and the majority into which Irish society was divided.

Having arrived at this decisive point, Peel turned to Ireland for the matter of his fundamental argument. It was not that under the existing system Ireland was stable or contented, but that the proposed changes would make her even less so. The object of emancipation was presumably to open up to the Roman Catholics of Ireland the share of political power to which their numbers, talent, and education might seem to entitle them. If they secured that share, would the situation remain there? Would the Irish Catholics rest permanently satisfied with the limitations, restrictions, and anomalies which would still confront them as a result of the continuing Anglo-Irish connection?

> Do you think that when they constitute, as they must do—not this year or the next, but in the natural and therefore certain order of things—by far the most powerful body in Ireland—the body most controlling and directing the government of it—do you think, I say, that they will view with satisfaction the state of your Church or of their own?

Clearly they would not, and it would be unnatural if they did. But if so, the effect of emancipation would merely be to render less defensible a position which would still be under attack: 'We are told that we cannot stop where we are; I answer that we are more likely to stop where we are, than we shall be if we advance to the point to which we are invited.' It was true that there was still the special argument based on the difficulties of governing Ireland under the existing form of union. Concession, it was said, would tranquillise Ireland. This view he challenged outright. Emancipation would confer no benefit on the mass of the Irish people; it would make no difference to the state of the peasantry. Privileges would be given to the Catholic aristocracy and middle-classes; but nothing would be done for the lower classes. As for the Roman clergy under whose influence the peasants would continue to live, they would suffer an absolute loss of privilege and independence as a result of the restrictions proposed as an integral part of emancipation. With the clergy fettered by new and unwelcome regulations, and the peasants no better off than before, was there any real hope that the predictions of concord and tranquillity would be realised?

He reviewed finally the anomalous position which would be created by the admission of Roman Catholics to nearly all—but not quite all—important offices of state. There was an anomaly in proclaiming the essentially Protestant character of the constitution and then admitting Catholics to it; in opening more offices to Roman Catholics and still debarring them from some. There was a political inconsistency in a settlement that would allow a Catholic Chief Secretary to be appointed as adviser to a necessarily Protestant Lord Lieutenant; a Catholic Secretary of State as responsible minister to a necessarily Protestant monarch. 'In all this I see nothing that can lead to harmony—nothing that can constitute a final and satisfactory settlement—nothing but a wild and irreconcilable contradiction of principles.' Religious disunity was deep and irrational in its origins; uncertain and unpredictable in its effects. That alone should make them pause before any rash innovation. Under the constitution they had inherited from their ancestors they had enjoyed more liberty, more glory, more character and power, than had been the lot of any other country in the world. If any man was undecided on the issue, he concluded, he should before he cast his vote at least 'weigh the substantial blessings which he knows to have been derived from the government that *is*, against all the speculative advantages which he is promised from the government that is *to be*'.

To Foster, listening from the benches after his own by no means insignificant effort earlier in the debate, it was 'a most admirable speech, better delivered, I think than anything since Pitt's time'.[1] Canning, who rose almost immediately after, spoke of its 'consummate ability'; and Ward, though a Canningite, thought it said all that could be said on that side, and said it as well as possible. A humbler but none the less valuable witness, and one engaged on the opposite side, told Plunket several years afterwards in 1821 that he had been attending Catholic debates in parliament for forty-two years and that the most unpleasant moment he ever experienced was

[1] For Foster's part in the debate see Foster (J. L. Foster to J. Foster, 25, 26, 29 April; 2, 19 May 1817).

Peel's display in 1817.[1] Certainly it made an immediate effect on the House. Peel was told afterwards that his speech had influenced the votes of thirteen members. If it had accomplished this, it had been decisive, for in the division that followed Grattan's final speech the motion was defeated by 221 votes to 245, a majority of twenty-four. There is no doubt that the Protestants had expected defeat, and their joy was correspondingly great. The faithful Goulburn urged Peel the day after the debate to allow his speech to be printed—'we must have the speech and if you will not indulge us, we must exert our memories'.[2] Cyril Jackson wrote up from Felpham enclosing a laudatory note from the Speaker on Peel's performance; and other congratulations came in from his friends, including his old chief, the Duke of Richmond, together with prophecies of the high station in politics which he was bound before long to fill. The Grand Jury of Dublin presented their thanks to 'the Rt. Hon. Robert Peel and the glorious majority of the House of Commons'; the Corporation of Dublin wished the honour of having him sit for his portrait; and Gregory wrote for copies of the speech to distribute among their friends in Ireland. To this flattering request Peel acceded and on 20 May twenty copies were sent off to various destinations: Lord Whitworth, the Duke of Richmond, a number of Irish officials, peers, and prelates; and (a pardonable domestic touch) four to the Tamworth News Room.[3]

It was an occasion which would have justified feelings of pride in any politician. In a debate graced by Castlereagh, Canning, and Grattan, by common consent Peel had carried off the laurels of victory. He wore them modestly enough, however. In his despatch to the Lord Lieutenant he made no mention of his speech other than the bare inclusion of his name in the list of those who took part in the debate; and his first thought was to restrain the Irish government from any undue exultation over the unexpected triumph of the Protestant cause. But whatever his private behaviour, in public estimation he had placed himself at the head of the Protestant party in the House of Commons; and in less than a month that distinction was confirmed by an honour too gratifying to refuse however onerous it might be to maintain.

---

[1] *Plunket*, II, 68 (the date given is 1816 but this is clearly a slip).
[2] 40265 f. 99.      [3] 40293 f. 72; 40204 f. 137.

## III

In the spring of 1817 Charles Abbot, Speaker of the House of Commons and M.P. for the University of Oxford, retired after several attacks of illness that caused the adjournment of the House in March and April. A year or two earlier the choice of a successor at Oxford might have seemed to lie between Canning and Vansittart. Neither perhaps was completely satisfactory. Canning was an outstanding supporter of Catholic emancipation and in any case had never entirely lived down the distrust created by his political actions between 1809 and 1812. Vansittart, the more orthodox, was also infinitely the inferior man in point of talent, and his evangelical Protestantism and patronage of the Bible Society made him not altogether acceptable in some High Church Oxford circles. Other names had been mentioned, including Peel's. The university had given him an honorary degree in 1815 and the cordial welcome he had received on that occasion could only have strengthened any ambition he or his friends in Christ Church might nourish for the supreme mark of Oxford's favour. But until May 1817 Canning was outwardly in a strong position. He was a friend of Cyril Jackson and had staunch supporters at Christ Church in the new Dean, C. H. Hall, and his former tutor, Pett. He had made his peace with Liverpool, and had returned from his Lisbon embassy in 1816 to join the cabinet as President of the Board of Control. In experience and talent he had few equals in the political world, and none among the limited number of politicians to whom the university would have to turn for a rival candidate. Moreover, he wanted the seat desperately. His own constituency of Liverpool was large, and if not personally costly, in many respects irksome to a busy minister. From 1811 if not earlier he had turned his thoughts to Oxford and on four separate occasions he had sounded Abbot on the possibility of his retirement and his own prospects as successor.[1] The last of these enquiries was as recent as 26 April 1817, and it is clear that Canning was also in touch at this date with his friends at Christ Church. Abbot himself was a Christ Church man, and if the unwritten convention was followed whereby the college claimed one of the two Oxford seats, another Christ Church man would succeed

[1] *Colchester*, II, 328, 374, 478, 610.

him. Almost everything depended on the attitude of the college, therefore, and in the middle of May Dean Hall assured Canning that the Common Room would certainly be in favour of his nomination.[1] Ostensibly the government would be neutral, but it was highly probable that Liverpool would discourage any other member of the administration from contesting the seat if Canning were nominated.

Yet the delicate balance of influence and prestige had shifted perceptibly during the month of May 1817. The great Catholic debate had raised Peel's reputation for the first time to a national level and had done nothing to strengthen Canning's. At the triennial celebration of the Pitt Club on 28 May Peel was asked to take the chair, and Canning's refusal to attend that ultra-Protestant gathering further emphasised his disagreement on the religious question. On the evening of the dinner Abbot finally sent his written resignation to the Prime Minister, and the following day wrote to the Vice-Chancellor of Oxford, the dean of Christ Church, Canning, Manners Sutton who was to be his successor in the Speakership, and a few others to inform them of his decision. Sometime during the same day, 29 May, Peel heard of the Speaker's intended resignation but gave the matter very little thought. On 30 May it was generally known that the Speaker was to retire that day and on going down to the House at half-past four, the usual time when business began, Peel was accosted by a large number of members, all anxious to know whether he was going to be a candidate for the vacancy at Oxford. Faced by this unexpected but highly flattering development, Peel left the House and wrote a hurried note to old Dean Jackson, asking for his counsel. Later in the evening he wrote to Lloyd, and made up his mind to send Dawson, his brother-in-law, down to Oxford to get advice and information. Within a few hours, however, these tentative preliminaries were overtaken by events elsewhere. At seven o'clock on the morning of Saturday, 31 May, he received—indeed, was probably awakened by—a brief note from an unheralded caller.

> My dear Sir,
> Allow me to see you directly; I am come to you express.
> Yours,
> C. LLOYD.

[1] *Bathurst*, p. 434 (Liverpool to Bathurst, 31 May 1817).

When Lloyd was shown in, the urgency of his business was soon explained. He brought with him a letter from Dean Hall, conveying the 'anxious wish' of the Chapter and Common Room of Christ Church that Peel should allow himself to be nominated for the vacancy in the representation of the university.[1]

The news of Abbot's resignation had reached Christ Church on the morning of Friday 30 May.[2] The Dean, Dr. Hall, summoned the available officers of the college for an immediate conference, and when they assembled, proposed Canning for the vacancy. In this he was supported by Barnes, the Sub-Dean, and by one of the Censors, Goodenough, but opposed by the other Censor, Corne, and by Lloyd. Corne had to be in the examination schools that morning and in consequence the meeting broke up early without a decision. When deliberations were resumed in the afternoon Corne, who had already expressed the opinion that Canning's nomination would not meet with the approval of the majority of the college, now said positively that not only could he not support Canning, but he would have to resign his Censorship if his nomination were adopted. As the next Censor would be Lloyd, the Dean abandoned the struggle. The question then was whether anyone at all should be put forward. Discussions continued intermittently during the evening and Barnes, who had invited the Vice-Chancellor and various heads of Houses to dine with him that evening, was continually called away from his guests to join the conversation. At one point Barnes suggested Vansittart but he was soon set aside in favour of Peel. Two members of the Chapter who were present, Van Mildert and Laurence, heartily concurred in this choice, and it was agreed that Lloyd should immediately set off to London to communicate to Peel the wishes of the College. Between nine and ten in the evening there was a formal meeting of the Chapter in the Common Room, to hear the Dean read Abbot's letter of resignation and learn the results of the deliberations of the officers of the college and the Chapter. Peel's name received a unanimous assent. Indeed, as Barnes

[1] 40265 f. 248; 40267 f. 225; 40293 fos. 95-6.
[2] Twiss (Eldon, II, 295) states that earlier intelligence of the vacancy was sent down to Oxford by Lord Eldon and his brother Sir William Scott in the hope of stealing a march on the Canning party. Abbot's letter, written on the 29th from London, arrived by first post on the morning of the 30th, cf. letters from Barnes and Smith to Abbot (Colchester, III, 5-6).

almost unwillingly confessed to Abbot afterwards, there was almost 'a sort of enthusiasm about it' among the resident members of the college.

Peel himself needed little time to make up his mind and in his reply to the Dean assured him that no object on earth would be so gratifying as to be the representative of the University of Oxford. His first action was to go round to tell the Prime Minister whom he found still in bed. For Liverpool the emphasis in Hall's letter on the unanimity of the college relieved him of some embarrassment since only the day before Canning had told him that if Peel was called upon to stand, he had no right to expect him to refuse. He asked Peel, therefore, to go at once to Canning and show him the Dean's letter.[1] This Peel did, first calling on Vansittart who received the news with his usual cheerful equanimity and wished him joy. When Canning was told, he seemed to Peel surprised and un-prepared (as well he might be) for the event. But whatever dis-appointment he felt, he concealed it from his younger rival and added to his congratulations the comforting observation that the issue was decisive as far as Christ Church was concerned and he did not suppose that there would be serious resistance in other quarters. This judgement proved to be correct. Though Lloyd, writing daily and sometimes twice a day from Oxford in a character-istic mixture of joy, excitement, and anxiety, reported various alarmist rumours, Peel's candidature could scarcely have met with greater approval. Indeed, with everything at Oxford 'going on in the most pleasant manner' as he described it, Lloyd's main anxiety was to secure an official contradiction of a report in the *Morning Chronicle* of 2-3 June that Peel's candidature was a political plot between Eldon and Peel to lay the foundation of a new 'No Popery Administration'; and he implored Peel to ensure that the govern-ment-inspired newspapers refrained from talking of the election in terms of Protestants and Catholics. Hardened by five years of Irish public life, Peel took these journalistic attacks more coolly than the nervous and inexperienced Lloyd.[2] Meanwhile the machinery of resignation, nomination, and election went smoothly on, and on 10 June Peel was elected unopposed as member for the university.

There can be no doubt that even if the election had been con-

[1] *Bathurst*, p. 434.     [2] 40266 fos. 148-51.

214

tested, Peel would have won an easy victory. Deprived of the support of his college, Canning could never have secured enough strength from the rest of the university to offer a hope of success. It is also clear that Peel's public eminence as chief parliamentary spokesman of the Protestant party was the principal reason for the ready approval in the university as a whole and among the university voters in the country. As a Worcestershire clergyman expressed it when offering his support to Peel, 'we are all, Sir, greatly indebted to you for that weight of argument by which when the House of Commons was in a state of portentous equipoise, you inclined it in behalf of "Protestant Ascendancy" '.[1] But if this general feeling accounted for the popularity of his candidature, it was to his college that he owed the circumstances of being candidate at all; and it is by no means certain that the same predominant sentiment was responsible for his selection as ensured him, when selected, success.

Writing to Peel on 2 June Lloyd was insistent that his speech and in fact the whole Catholic issue was not mentioned in the college discussions that preceded his nomination, and that no one either privately or publicly took notice of his views on that question.[2] The real choice before the college was in fact whether to nominate Canning or not; and if not, whether to select another candidate from among the other former members of the college. Canning was proposed and rejected; but it is at least questionable whether his attitude on Catholic emancipation was the decisive factor in his rejection. Oxford itself was divided on the question and Canning had other claims to consideration. But in a matter as personal as the university representation was at this period, his character and reputation were bound to be of major weight in deciding the issue. Discussing with Peel in 1825 the reasons why the university did not choose Canning, Lloyd said categorically that 'they did not believe in the sincerity, the consistency, the honesty of the man. This opinion, right or wrong, was the cause of his rejection. The Catholic Question had nothing to do with it. . . . It was the character of Canning not his measures which stood in the way.'[3] This was written by a man hostile to Canning, eight years after the event. But Cyril Jackson, a

---

[1] 40266 f. 176 (from the Rev. J. Shaw, vicar of Bengeworth, Evesham, formerly of Lincoln College).

[2] ibid., f. 149 (MS. slightly torn but sense is clear).     [3] 40342 f. 207.

friend of Canning, and writing at the time, expressed almost
identical views. In a letter to Abbot on 5 June 1817, and clearly
referring to Canning, he observed:

> I should fear that another friend of ours will have been greatly
> disappointed, yet I may say to you (*but to you only*) that I have
> frequently, indeed always when he has brought up the subject, told
> him what the event would be. That the Dean would not be able to
> carry even Christ Church for him; and that, in the rest of the
> University, he had no chance whatever. I did not say things so
> plainly as I might have done, for the truth is (I say it only to your-
> self) that I never knew a man so thoroughly disliked (or *even more*)
> as he is at Oxford. But I put the matter to him as plainly as I could
> without being very offensive, and entreated him not to expose
> himself to certain defeat.[1]

It was round Canning, rather than Peel, that the real issue of the
Oxford election of 1817 revolved; and Peel came in on his rival's
unpopularity rather than on his own somewhat accidental reputation
as Protestant champion. He had in fact been very fortunate, as more
than one person behind the scenes of university politics privately
observed. 'Such a combination of time and circumstance,' remarked
Barnes, the Sub-Dean of Christ Church, 'could scarcely have been
imagined by his most zealous friends.'[2]

But fortune is an ambiguous and Delphic goddess. Older and
longer heads might perhaps have questioned the wisdom of a young
politician, so clearly destined for a high public career, taking upon
himself the peculiar responsibility of the representation of Oxford
University before he had reached the age of thirty. It is true that
Peel himself in all his utterances showed only a sense of extreme
pleasure and an almost unduly modest awareness of the singular
honour done to him by his university.

> If I succeed, I shall have attained the paramount object of my
> ambition [he wrote with unusual effusiveness to Jackson] one to
> which I should have looked forward as the ample reward of a long
> political life. And I trust in God that my success, though it may

---

[1] *Colchester*, III, 3-4.    [2] *ibid.*, p. 6.

make me undervalue the usual objects to which political men aspire, will stimulate me to those exertions by which alone I can prove myself worthy of the confidence which the most distinguished body on earth has been pleased to confer on me.

There is in this more the ring of the prize scholar than of the man of the world. Less than a decade had passed since Jackson had presided, alarming and impressive, over his undergraduate days; and these tutelary relationships cannot all at once be shaken off on quitting the quadrangle. But deep in his reserved nature Peel clearly felt an emotional attachment to Oxford that still coloured his view of the men who spoke in her name. If so, he would not be either the first or the last Oxford undergraduate to carry into adult life the bittersweet enchantment of adolescence. Even when writing in more sober terms to Dean Hall, he said that his election for Oxford had given him more satisfaction than he had ever felt or could ever feel again. Indeed, in his first mood of exhilaration when discussing the future with Lloyd on the morning of 31 May, he even thought of resigning office if he were elected.

In all this scene of happiness and congratulation, the one reflective and warning note was struck by Lloyd. In a curiously prophetic letter written on 1 June, he examined Peel's new relationship with the university with an intelligence and insight that was in striking contrast to his agitated notes about the *Morning Chronicle* and *Courier*. He began with an expression of pleasure at the virtual certainty that Peel would go forward to an unopposed election. 'Nobody but yourself and Dawson can feel the joy which I do; it has been to you the high object of a noble and honourable ambition; to me it has always been the object of my dearest wishes and most anxious hopes.' Then, on the quixotic notion of resignation from office, he hinted at the extent to which Peel's official status as well as his 'attachment to the Tory principles and the true interest of the Church of England' had served to recommend him to the university. But there was a further and stronger point he wished to make. The Oxford tradition was to elect a man for life, but unlike most of his predecessors Peel was a professional politician rather than an independent representative. It rested with himself therefore whether that tradition would be maintained.

Now, Oxford, it may without argument be assumed, will never vary from the principles of Mr. Pitt; the attachment to them seems to me at this place to increase with time. So far then I think certain that any person who is a strenuous defender of those principles will hold his seat for ever. Now I would simply ask, whether any man of 29 years old, can say positively that if he is left entirely to his own single opinion, this never can happen during the space of 40 years, which is (you see) the time I allow you to sit as our representative. But if you are a member of an Administration founded entirely on those principles, your own prejudices will coincide with all your best principles, and your conduct never can change. It is change and versatility in any way which will at any time injure the reputation of the members for the University in the University itself.[1]

To assume the permanence of Pittite principles for the next forty years argued a certain unworldliness in Lloyd's political outlook. Yet he knew his Oxford, and in voicing the opinion that the university wanted representation for its views, and not merely an eminent politician as its representative, there can be no doubt that he spoke for the mass of university electors. In accepting the university seat Peel had put his political career under bond; but such a mortgage on the future seemed in 1817 to offer little risk. To the public at large, judging hastily or indifferently, Oxford's choice of Peel seemed but another instance of the good luck that had so far attended him. But whether the Oxonians had chosen Peel because of his Protestantism or because they identified his principles with those of Mr. Pitt, the fact remained that his new constituents cherished expectations from him of a kind unknown to the simple and venal voters of Cashel and Chippenham.

IV

So long as Peel was Chief Secretary for Ireland, however, he had an administrative preoccupation which left him little time for academic speculations. The spring and summer that saw the great Catholic debate and the university by-election had brought to the Irish executive problems as pressing and anxious as any that Peel had encountered during his years in Ireland. His first act as member for

[1] 40266 f. 145.

Oxford was to support in committee an extension of the Insurrection Act, and the topic which dominated his correspondence in the preceding month was the danger of famine. It was to the realities of the cottar's cabin rather than those of the college Common Room that his mind was turned in the early summer of 1817.

In August 1816 Peel had written hopefully to Sidmouth of the relatively tranquil state of Ireland. Though the condition of the lower classes was no better, yet there were fewer acts of violence and the causes of disaffection and disturbance had diminished.[1] In less than eight weeks this prospect clouded over. During the summer and early autumn the weather was unusually wet and though there was a brief respite in the latter part of September, the rain and gales recommenced with added force from the beginning of October. The oats were seriously damaged; the wheat smutted and spoilt; and the bread made from the new flour was partly uneatable. Children would pull out wet unwholesome lumps from the inside of the loaf and throw them at the walls where they stuck like putty.[2] Worst of all, the potato crop was gravely affected. The tubers were under-sized and the flesh soapy and unpalatable. To the shortage of food was added the threat of shortage of fuel for the oncoming winter. The peat, on which the peasantry were as dependent for firing as on potatoes for food, had not been cut in any great quantity and was so wet that it could not be burnt without several days of fine weather in which to dry it. On 9 and 10 October Peel wrote to the Prime Minister and Sidmouth to warn them of the gloomy prospect of the harvest and the melancholy reports coming from all over the country. Yet he confessed that there was little that the government could do at that stage. Exhortation to economy might have the disastrous effect of causing hoarding and shortage; while the prohibition of distilleries, a measure invariably demanded at every onset of distress in Ireland, was not an expedient which Peel viewed with any satisfaction. It merely resulted in the importation of spirits from England and Scotland, encouraged the growth of illicit distilleries in Ireland—'the greatest curse we are inflicted with'—and would, he thought, probably use up twice as much grain as the ordinary

[1] 40291 f. 139, partly printed *Peel*, I, 228.
[2] Curtis, *Irish Constabulary*, p. 7 (author's childhood recollection).

processes of the legal distilleries.[1] The cabinet were no better prepared with remedies. Liverpool, Sidmouth, and Vansittart were agreed that stopping the Irish distilleries was useless unless accompanied by a similar prohibition in Great Britain. But this would be unpopular with the agricultural interest and could not therefore be proposed; nor could trade in spirits between England and Ireland be prevented. All that was done consequently was to authorise Peel in December at his own request to make a grant of £2,000 to the poor of Dublin in the name of the Prince Regent.[2]

By the nature of Irish rural economy, the worst famine period came in the spring and early summer when the diminished supplies of the previous year had been eaten up and the new harvest was not yet ready; and it was for the spring of 1817 that the government waited with increasing apprehension. Peel left Ireland at the end of January and by the beginning of March was anxiously waiting for documentary evidence of the apprehended scarcity of food in Ireland to be sent to him from Dublin so that he could lay the facts before the cabinet. Instead he received a series of alarmed but not very illuminating letters from the Lord Lieutenant. It was necessary, thought Lord Whitworth, to stop the distilleries and to distribute money so that the work of seeding the land could proceed. Flour, potatoes, and coal were exceedingly dear, in consequence of contrary winds and rough weather, and he felt it almost obligatory to do something about the export of potatoes. Peel arranged to see Liverpool and other members of the cabinet on the subject of Irish distress but he wrote with some asperity to Gregory on 6 March that 'general information may satisfy me that such apprehensions are justly entertained, but I must have precise information to enable me, or others whom I may consult, to judge of the measures which it may be expedient to adopt'. He had convinced himself that the prohibition of distillation was a delusive expedient. Indeed, only the previous day, on a motion by Maurice Fitzgerald, he had argued cogently in the House of Commons that 'the proposed measure would not save one barrel of corn'. But it was evident that the Lord Lieutenant was not equally well informed on the subject. As for the export of potatoes, Peel himself observed to Gregory that he was not aware

[1] 40291 fos. 186, 196.
[2] 40181 fos. 77, 85; 40182 fos. 228 (printed Pellew, *Sidmouth*, III, 151), 230.

of any great export from Ireland to England, though he was under the impression that potatoes were frequently shipped to Dublin from Liverpool. On this and other material points he asked Gregory to obtain precise information. 'I cannot, advised and informed as I at present am, form any judgement satisfactory to myself upon the subject. Let me hear from you without delay on this most important question.'

Meanwhile, he saw the Prime Minister on 7 March, and attended a general meeting at the Board of Trade the following day at which Liverpool, Sidmouth, Castlereagh, Vansittart, Robinson, and several of the leading Irish members were present. There was general agreement on the severity of the crisis, and a disposition to waive any ordinary principle in order to alleviate distress; but the difficulty was to ascertain the best mode of affording relief in the absence of detailed information. Hampered though he was by inadequate knowledge, Peel wrote the same day a long and painstaking despatch on the complex economic factors involved in such matters as the prohibition of exports and distilleries, the difficulties under which the Irish peasants suffered in not possessing money to purchase food from elsewhere when their own crops failed, and the possibility of direct governmental distribution of food in case of actual starvation. As Donegal was the area most distressed he suggested that a qualified person should be sent down there to prepare a detailed statement of the situation which he could present to the authorities in London. In the event his criticisms were more than justified. On calling for a return of the Irish potato trade between the two countries from January to March 1817, Gregory discovered that 391 tons had been exported and 967 tons imported. The communication of these figures to Peel brought back a merited rebuke.

> I cannot tell you how much embarrassed I am. . . . After having had a meeting of the Government . . . and seriously discussed the policy of immediately prohibiting the export of potatoes from Ireland, I must now inform those who attended that meeting that the imports into Ireland exceeded the exports from it in the last two months in the proportion of three to one. I must beg of you to consider the peculiar difficulties of my situation. I am here between three and four hundred miles from the seat of the Government for which I am acting. If I receive a letter from Ireland upon any subject

of importance that requires immediate decision, I must act. . . . I cannot call for explanation or wait for authentic documents, as men in public situations in this country can do. With all the subordinate departments at hand, their references do not take as many hours as mine take days. The presumption too must be that those on the spot can judge of the necessity better than I can.

Under the impact of these brisk despatches the officials in Dublin Castle gradually took hold of the situation. Two reports on the food situation in Co. Donegal, written on 19-20 March in the approved Peelite form of answers to a specific questionnaire, reached him probably before the end of the month.[1]

In that region, barren, mountainous, and thinly populated, the produce of oats was always scanty and even potatoes barely sufficient. As a result of the failure of last year's harvest there was a great shortage of food; fuel was scarce; and the distress among the poorer classes very great. There was little illicit distilling of spirits owing to the lack of fuel and the unwillingness of farmers to part with their grain. Existing stocks of potatoes were almost used up and the poor were living exclusively on meal. Their distress, however, arose not merely from the bad harvest, but also from the chronic want of employment and consequent lack of money with which to purchase food from other parts of the country. Meanwhile, officials were sent to the northern ports to gather information on relevant food imports and exports; the duty on imported rice and maize was suspended for one year; and the distillers were urged to use only inferior grain and sell to the government any supplies fit for human consumption. Gregory was authorised by Peel to take £2,000 from Civil Contingencies for a general relief fund; and arrangements were put in hand for the importation of seed oats for distribution in the famine areas where there was a likelihood that the acute shortage would impair the prospects of the following harvest. The latter measure, owing to the dishonesty of contractors and perhaps inadequate means of inspection, was less successful than it promised. The first arrivals of seed oats in northern Ireland had an encouraging effect, but by mid-April Whitworth was reporting

[1] S.P.O., Trade and Industry, P. Singer to Commissary General (endorsed 'read, R.P.'), March 1817.

that for every cargo of good oats, there were three so bad as to be almost useless for any purpose. Though in the end the financial loss to the Irish government was not very great, the seed-oats speculation, as the Lord Lieutenant termed it, was unfortunate throughout.[1]

The crisis of the famine came in June, in the last weeks before the start of the 1817 harvest. Rainy weather at the end of May brought forebodings of another bad year, and reports from all over Ireland told the same tale of present scarcity and future apprehension. The distress was particularly severe in the north-west, in Kildare and Meath, and in Galway. Food transports were held up and robbed. In Dublin butchers and bakers shops were attacked and pillaged, mainly by mobs of women and boys. Large numbers of beggars migrated to the capital from the impoverished country districts. In Galway riots took place to prevent oatmeal being sent to the northern market. The firms concerned offered to sell their stock to the local relief committee but the committee lacked the necessary funds to make the purchase and the authorities in Galway consequently petitioned the Lord Lieutenant to avoid further disturbances by prohibiting the movement of meal and potatoes from the district.[2] The famine conditions in fact brought with them a widespread threat to local law and order, and at one point the government considered calling out part of the yeomanry. Peel, who early in June again saw the Prime Minister about the distress in Ireland, redoubled his efforts. He was given powers to draw on the Treasury for any necessary sums of money for Irish relief, and he suggested to Whitworth that the government should place the money for local charity in the hands of the parish clergy and the Roman Catholic priests. For relief in kind he proposed setting up soup kitchens and drawing up to £50,000 in the first instance for the purchase of biscuit from Bristol and Liverpool. For the proper supervision of famine relief he advocated the establishment of a government Commission which would receive information, subscribe to local relief funds, and distribute food. With this went the familiar warning that no suspicion of jobbery must attach to the commission. 'Put a Quaker or two,

---

[1] For the activities of the Irish government in the winter of 1816-17 see esp. 40193 fos. 82-267; 40203 fos. 259, 265; 40292 fos. 170, 174, 186.

[2] S.P.O., Trade and Industry, June 1817.

a Catholic or two, let it be quite clear there is no party, no government view in the appointments.' The Irish government, which had produced from its own counsels nothing more helpful than a proclamation calling on the wealthier classes to discontinue eating potatoes and to reduce their horses' oats, hastened to put these suggestions into effect. By the end of the month they had expended some £14,000 of the indefinite sum put at their disposal, mainly in small sums of £40 or £50 to the more distressed parishes; and it became evident in the course of their relief campaign that the distress was caused much more by shortage of money among the poor than by any actual shortage of food in the country.[1]

In contrast to the negative policy of the Lord Lieutenant and his local advisers, Peel's insistence on positive relief measures—the distribution of money (amounting in the end to £37,000) and the procuring of food—marked him out during the 1817 famine as the one member of the Irish government who had penetrated any distance into the heart of Ireland's social and economic troubles. The relief measures undertaken at his instance, combined with the precautions against disorder and a welcome return of fine weather at the end of June, enabled the Irish authorities to keep control of the situation; and with the promise of an abundant harvest the danger finally passed away. Indeed, the prominent part played by the government in bringing relief to the peasantry at the period of most acute suffering, followed by the gradual improvement as the first crops of the 1817 harvest became available, earned it as near a measure of popularity as it was possible to obtain. There was undoubtedly an element of the fortuitous in this, and Peel admitted to the Prime Minister in the autumn that 'the people attributed their relief in a much greater degree to the intervention of Government than they ought to have done'. Nevertheless, the crisis had been surmounted and before the onset of the winter there was a heartening abundance of both food and fuel in the country, together with a relatively greater absence of disorder than had been experienced for many years.

Yet the year 1817 was a portent. It was the first substantial failure of the potato crop since Ireland had become dependent on that one staple food; and with the famine had come typhus fever from which

[1] 40204 f. 225; 40194 fos. 13-85; 40293 fos. 109-14.

perhaps as many as fifty thousand died. Spreading to the over-crowded slums of the towns, it took on the proportions of an epidemic, of which Dublin and Cork became the centres of contagion. In September 1817 Peel called for the preparation of a report from the medical authorities throughout Ireland on the nature and origin of the disease. All agreed in tracing its origin to poverty, scarcity, and unwholesome food; and, with more accuracy, its rapid spread to the general habits of the peasantry and the great number of itinerant beggars. From March onwards the incidence of the disease began to decline. Nevertheless, in April 1818 Peel joined Newport in moving for a select committee to enquire into the prevalence of contagious fever in Ireland with a view to providing against its recurrence and securing adequate support for hospitals dealing with the disease. A sum of £15,000 was voted for the care of fever patients, and Peel told the House that if this proved insufficient, he would not hesitate to increase it from other funds. 'I think,' he wrote to Sir Edward Baker in May 1818, 'before the summer comes a great exertion should be made to put down the fever. If it costs £20,000 I care not; the money will be well expended when the distribution is entrusted to those who compose the Fever Committee.' Throughout 1818 the Irish government was still endeavouring to stem this aftermath of the famine. Grants were made to Dublin hospitals; prisons and barracks converted into infirmaries; and aid given for the establishment of fever hospitals in country districts. An Act passed in 1818 empowered the setting up of local Boards of Health with authority to isolate typhus patients in hospitals and disinfect houses and clothing. But not until 1819 did the epidemic die down, and even then it was checked rather than suppressed.[1]

V

The 1817 famine showed Peel at the height of his powers as Irish Secretary. With equal knowledge and greater imagination than the permanent officials of the Castle, he was nearer grasping the realities of the Irish problem than perhaps any other man in public life; and his foresight, energy, and readiness to override conventional policy

[1] Chart, *Ireland*, pp. 122, 280ff.; Connell, *Population of Ireland*, pp. 228ff.

and governmental regulations wherever a certain and practical advantage was to be secured, made him even when three hundred miles away in London the real mainspring of Irish executive action. There were, it is true, limits both to the extent and the character of the measures which he was prepared to advocate. He held no sanguine views on the possibility of finding an immediate or general remedy for Irish unemployment. To those who pressed for large-scale schemes of public works, he replied that what was being undertaken was already commensurate with the needs of the country and that the government had done as much as was politic to encourage the construction of roads, canals, and public buildings. If private enterprise found no profit in further development, he doubted the policy of government intervention.[1] In the face of the prevailing administrative tradition, the economical restrictions imposed on government by public opinion, and the untrustworthiness of local Irish officials, it would in fact have been virtually impossible for a large programme of public works for Ireland to be accepted at that time. But within the limits of what was practicable and what could be made acceptable, there were few possibilities which he left unexamined. Certainly in eliciting information and stimulating action, he used the instruments at his disposal to the limits of their capacity. By 1817 he had perfected his technique of administration: the collection of factual information by means of carefully prepared series of specific questions to the men most likely to have access to the knowledge he wanted; the testing of generalities, opinions, and advice by reference to the facts; the prudent choice of agents; caution and scepticism in coming to a decision; and energetic action once the decision was reached. Few things are more striking in his dealings with his subordinates than his insistence on facts. Not only were facts the basis of sound administration, but facts were the best arguments to lay before the legislature. 'There is nothing like a fact,' he wrote to Gregory in June 1814 when applying for another budget of recent information with which to reinforce his argument for the Peace Preservation Bill. And again in April 1816—'facts are ten times more valuable than declamations'.[2]

[1] cf. his letter to Lord Cloncurry (*Cloncurry Recollections*, p. 286), September 1817.
[2] 40287 f. 53; 40290 f. 205.

The time had now come, however, when the end of his Irish labours was in sight. In the end Peel's Irish Secretaryship over-lapped three Viceroyalties; but in a special sense his real Lord Lieutenant was Lord Whitworth. He had welcomed him to Ireland, served him throughout his years of office, and saw him depart. Between the two men had grown up a close personal and political confidence which made the Irish administration of 1813-17 a model of unity and efficiency. The original arrangement with the cabinet had been that Whitworth should serve for three years; but in 1816 he consented to stay on until the following summer so that his successor could arrive in the quiet period that followed the close of the season in Dublin and the end of the parliamentary session. To his evident pleasure Peel willingly agreed to remain with him until he laid down his Lord Lieutenancy. But from several points of view it seemed appropriate to Peel that he should go out of office with Whitworth. In a long and singularly outspoken letter to Lord Liverpool in October 1816, he strongly advised the appointment of an Englishman to succeed him, on grounds of the utter necessity of having a Chief Secretary with 'no private interests to attend to, and no private friendships and partialities to gratify', from the imputation of which even the most upright Irishman could scarcely hope to be acquitted. Moreover, if a new and inexperienced Viceroy were saddled with an Irishman as his Secretary, it would inevitably mean that 'the Secretary will be Viceroy over him', with all the foreseeable friction that would ensue from such an unbalanced relationship. From that point of view, he added dispassionately, 'I may be considered almost in the same light as an Irishman'; and he concluded consequently that it would be pleasanter for the new Lord Lieuten-ant in many respects to have a new Secretary.

The Prime Minister was clearly regretful at this decision; and since Peel was prepared to conduct Irish affairs at any rate during the next parliamentary session, he thought it would be inexpedient to choose his successor before parliament rose. The whole question therefore was postponed until a more seasonable date. By the follow-ing summer further reflection had caused Peel to change his mind. The session of 1817, which saw his great triumph in the Catholic debate and the Oxford election, ended with a singular compliment to the quality and success of his Irish administration. On 30 June an address was presented to him, signed by fifty-nine Irish M.P.s, paying tribute to his conduct of the executive affairs of their country and expressing their hope that he would continue in office under the new Lord Lieutenant. James Daly was the principal promoter of this letter, but as J. L. Foster told his kinsman, John Foster, it would 'have been signed by almost all the Irish members but for his Protestant spirit which has induced several of the opposition to shrink back. Had it not been for this, I am convinced that even Newport would have signed it.' He added that 'I am certain it will not influence Peel to stay but it is a compliment which must highly gratify him.'[1] But Foster's certainty was not perhaps quite infallible. More than most politicians would have been, Peel was touched by the personal regard which such an unprecedented document displayed; and in writing to his old mentor, Lloyd, he went so far as to say that the address was 'the chief motive that led me, contrary to my own wishes and inclination, to abandon my intention of quitting the office of Chief Secretary at the same time that Lord Whitworth relinquished that of Lord Lieutenant'. But there were undoubtedly other considerations. The administrative awkwardness of Viceroy and Secretary leaving simultaneously was a practical objection which outweighed all theoretical considerations. The new Lord Lieutenant, Lord Talbot, was anxious for Peel to continue and Liverpool made no secret either of his distress at the prospect of his leaving Ireland or of his earnest hope that he would stay on not only to smooth the way for Lord Talbot but also to superintend the government's Irish interests in the next general election. At the beginning of June, with Whitworth still in office, it was clear that Peel was ready to carry on for some time longer after the end of the session; and early in July it was finally settled that he would return to Dublin for a further unspecified period.

It was not until the afternoon of 9 October 1817 that Lord Talbot arrived in Ireland. For the second time Peel took his part in the elaborate ceremonial that surrounded the installation of a new Lord Lieutenant. A messenger stationed at the Pigeon House brought notice of the approach of the Viceregal yacht. The Lord Mayor and county sheriffs met Lord Talbot at the entrance to the city and brought him in state to the Castle. There he was received by the

[1] Foster, 6 June 1817.

outgoing Lord Lieutenant in the Presence Chamber and conducted in procession to the Council Chamber where the Privy Council was already assembled. Then followed the reading of the commission, the oath, the handing over of the Sword of State, the retirement of Lord Whitworth, while outside came the crack of cannon, the answering volley from the detachment of Foot drawn up on College Green, and the shrill note of the state trumpeters.[1] But for Peel the occasion was very different from that of 1813. Then he had been at the start, now he was at the end of his Irish administration. Five years of office had turned him almost into a routine Irish official and he could look with detached and critical eye on the new Lord Lieutenant. The choice of Lord Talbot had not been one that commended itself to either Peel or Lord Whitworth. As early as March 1816 his name had been mentioned as the probable successor in Ireland, but Whitworth who knew him well, and thought him an honest and well-intentioned man, saw in his Irish family connections and still more in those of Lady Talbot a radical objection to putting him at the head of affairs in that country. The force of these arguments, however, was more apparent to Irish than to English officials, and Liverpool persisted in his choice.

To Lord Talbot in person, however, there were few positive objections, and his lively unconventional manner secured him an early popularity in Dublin. A stout jovial man, looking (according to Colonel Blacker) like a jolly good-humoured farmer,[2] he rode clattering into Dublin from Phoenix Park each day attended only by a groom, to the displeasure of the precisians on his staff; though, as Peel observed privately in a letter to Whitworth, since it was estimated in the Castle that he rode nearly nineteen stone, he was more to be envied than his horse.[3] He was soon on friendly terms with Peel and the two men had a common passion for shooting which was reflected in their correspondence. Succeeding as a newcomer, however, to the close personal system built by Whitworth, Peel, and Gregory in the preceding four years, Talbot found it difficult at first to grasp the informal and confidential pattern of relationship among his immediate staff. There was an awkward

---

[1] See details of ceremonial approved by Peel, 10 September 1817 (S.P.O. Privy Council Papers; Irish P.C. Minutes).
[2] Blacker, VI, 129; cf. Talbot's portrait in Dublin Castle.　　[3] 40194 f. 125.

incident in May 1818 when Talbot, relying on Peel's earlier report of the cabinet's views, refused to assist Croker in his Trinity College election. Peel in fact had written subsequently to Baker to inform him that the cabinet had changed its view and that Croker was to be supported; but the Lord Lieutenant was unwilling to take that as authority for disregarding Peel's previous despatch. The Chief Secretary had to write from London to explain that he was accustomed to regarding letters from Baker or Gregory as dictated by the Lord Lieutenant and similarly his answers to them as intended for the Lord Lieutenant. Sometimes, he added, he would write to Talbot on matters not mentioned to the Under-Secretaries, but he never sent communications to the Under-Secretaries which were not as a matter of course to be laid before the Lord Lieutenant.[1] Wherever the fault lay, such a confusion would not have arisen under Lord Whitworth.

By May 1818 it was known definitely that there would be a general election in June, and Peel wrote to Talbot to announce his positive decision 'to close my Irish campaigns with the present Parliament with which I commenced them six years since, in the year 1812'. But he told Lord Liverpool that as his successor might not want to take office until after the election, he would return to Ireland at the end of the session to assist Talbot during that period. Though expressing a friendly regret at the news, Talbot was clearly not surprised at this final determination. He had never expected to keep Peel for long, and prepared himself cheerfully to wait for the cabinet's choice of a successor. In the circumstances it was inevitable that 1818 should be the quietest session in Peel's period of Irish office. With parliament and his secretaryship expiring together, he was more concerned to wind up the affairs he already had on hand than to embark on any fresh legislative efforts. Indeed, his major speeches of the session were concerned not with Ireland but with his father's bill to shorten the hours of labour in the cotton factories. His advocacy of this measure brought him letters from such unusual correspondents as the cotton spinners of Warrington and from as far afield as Ayrshire. The most effective contribution he made to the discussions on the bill came on 27 April 1818. There was in this debate a curious social contrast between Lord Stanley,

[1] 40194 fos. 255-63; 40295 f. 108.

M.P. for Lancashire and heir to the historic Derby earldom, who led the opposition to the bill, and Peel, himself the son of a cotton-spinner, who argued in favour of legislative interference to protect children in factories, and gently ridiculed the claims of cotton mills to exceptional salubrity which had been advanced by some of the opponents of the measure. But this interesting addition to his parliamentary record was outside the line of official conduct, and was perhaps mainly prompted by filial duty. As far as Irish administration was concerned, his chief preoccupation in his last year of office was the supervision of retrenchment and reform in the Irish government departments.

The enforced abandonment of the income tax in 1816 as well as the general mood of the country had made it essential for drastic reductions to be made in governmental expenditure in the immediate post-war years; and Ireland was as good a grove as any for the economists' axe. In the spring of 1817 a general enquiry was afoot into the existing sinecures in the Irish administration and the means of reducing their number; and Peel was kept busy in London with attendance on the finance committee and frequent consultations with Liverpool and Sidmouth. While assuring Peel of his hearty co-operation in cutting down official expenditure, Gregory pointed out, nevertheless, that 'in many articles of expenditure we are more sinned against than sinning, having no control by which we can correct the abuses (perhaps frauds would be more applicable) committed'.[1] This in fact was one of the major difficulties. It was not enough to detect extravagance; the obstructions both legal and personal in the path of reform had also to be removed. When in 1816 an attempt was made to reform the extortionate system of fees diverted to deputies in the Irish Clerk of Pleas office, the machinery favoured by Lord Sidmouth was the tardy and doubtful procedure of the Irish law courts, followed in all probability by a delaying appeal to the House of Lords. Peel, straining his position to the furthest point, begged the Home Secretary to discuss the matter with Liverpool and Castlereagh before confirming that decision. But elsewhere the Chief Secretary could use his authority to secure quicker and more effectual results. His own constabulary, the Protestant charter schools, the notorious scandal of the Dublin

[1] 40203 f. 327 (22 March 1817).

Foundling Hospital, all came under his vigilant review, as well as the more central departments of the government. In the latter the mor e practicable method of retrenchment, for obvious personal and administrative reasons, was a gradual compression of establishments, rather than any sudden disbandment. From the end of 1817 the Irish Revenue Boards were instructed to report specifically, whenever a vacancy occurred, whether it was absolutely necessary to fill it, and if so whether it was possible to appoint a civil servant whose existing post was marked for abolition. In this way, Peel wrote to Croker in February 1818, half the offices that had become vacant were promptly discontinued and the remainder filled by victims of economies elsewhere.[1] In other departments there was the same story of reduction and saving. At the Yeomanry Office, which in 1814 had employed eleven clerks and three other staff, the establishment in 1816 was five clerks and three others, or almost exactly the same as had sufficed in 1796, though the rise in salaries still left the total pay roll half as much again as before the war.[2]

In the second week of June 1818 Peel returned to Ireland to superintend the general election. Electoral politics were never long absent from his correspondence in any year. Even in 1817 he had been intermittently active in securing the influence of various members of the government for various Irish candidates and from May onward his postbag was full of electioneering topics. Once he was back in Dublin the final stages of management began, and with the ease of long familiarity with Irish connections he embarked on the task of recommending individuals, canvassing borough-patrons, appealing to country magnates, composing differences, and suggesting compromises. Dealings with friends like Foster, Clancarty, and Lord Farnham offered no difficulties. Lord Hertford, however, who took umbrage at Leslie Foster's preference for the archbishop's seat at Armagh over Hertford's borough of Lisburn, had to be placated; and an even more serious defection by Lord Shannon, who without warning transferred his support at Cork from the government candidate, had to be referred to the Prime Minister. But in the preliminary survey he sent off to Liverpool on 22 June he was able to hold out a cheerful prospect of some gains in strength, especially in the Irish counties. Twelve days later, with the majority of the

[1] 40294 f. 145.    [2] S.P.O. Finance 1818-20.

Irish elections decided, he reported to Arbuthnot that though there would be probably a loss on balance in the boroughs, the government would gain six and lose only one of the county seats. The final returns bore out the accuracy of this forecast and when the lists were drawn up of the Irish members elected for the new parliament, seventy-one were marked down as government supporters.[1] Croker, aided by some active canvassing on his behalf by Peel, fought a desperate battle against Plunket for the Trinity College representation, in the course of which he sent a constant stream of superfluous information to the Chief Secretary. He failed in the end by four votes.[2] But the government had only reluctantly been induced to support his candidature and the result was in no sense a severe defeat to them. Peel could look with satisfaction on his political stewardship when he rendered up his accounts; and a burst of hot dry sunny weather at the close of July seemed symbolic of the serenity of the Irish situation as he made his preparations for departure. To his old parliamentary opponent, Sir John Newport, he wrote a graceful and cordial letter of farewell to which Newport replied equally gracefully, as one duellist saluting another. All that remained was to see his successor safely installed before he left.

When Lord Whitworth had reached London after his retirement in October 1817 he had found the cabinet, as he expressed it, quite at sea as to a successor for Peel. Inevitably there were rumours about Peel's intentions, some as early as the spring of 1818, and mindful perhaps of the circumstances of his own appointment, Peel asked the Prime Minister in May not to decide on his successor until Lord Talbot had been given an opportunity to write to him on the subject. But Talbot appeared to have no strong positive views and on 18 June Liverpool informed Peel that the post had been offered first to Huskisson, who had declined, and then to Charles Grant, who had accepted. Grant, like Huskisson, was a 'Catholic'; but, as Peel pointed out to Talbot, this was an objection which applied to nearly every one whose name might have been considered for the secretaryship. The Lord Lieutenant, if not enthusiastic, accepted the decision with good grace. By the middle of July it was public knowledge that Peel was retiring and that Grant would succeed him.[3]

[1] 40295 fos. 114-64; 40298 (List of Irish members elected 1818).
[2] 40184 f. 140ff.     [3] 40181 f. 135; 40295 fos. 78, 93, 132; 40194 f. 121.

In contrast to his arrival six years earlier, there were few Irish newspapers of any substance that did not take the occasion of Peel's departure in 1818 to comment on his character and policy. Whatever else he had done, he had put an impress on Irish administration that had been equalled by perhaps no previous Chief Secretary and certainly by none since the Union. Party distortions and animosities were of course not absent in the general public comment. On 23 July the Dublin Corporation presented an address to Peel which included a reference to his maintenance in the imperial parliament of the Protestant constitution of these realms. The *Freeman's Journal* and the *Dublin Evening Post* omitted this passage in their reproduction of the text and were thus enabled to give to their readers a more flattering interpretation of Peel's printed answer than would otherwise have been possible. Indeed, the *Evening Post* went so far as to say that

> We are persuaded, if ever there was an enemy to Catholic Emancipation, from principle, Mr. Peel is the man; and we are equally persuaded, that as he is a man of a strong and penetrating mind, he will, if Emancipation be not granted in the meantime, become, in a few years, its advocate. It is clear, his heart is with the Catholics of Ireland, and their Cause must be as bad, as it is in reality good, if his understanding shall not be ultimately convinced. But whether it be or not, the People of Ireland should treasure the Legacy he has bequeathed to them.[1]

Of more direct importance, perhaps, was the long review in the *Patriot*, running over four issues, of Peel's general administration. Since the *Patriot* was a government paper, it is probable that the material for the article was supplied by the Castle, perhaps by Gregory; and it can be reasonably taken as the official view, which could not have been far from Peel's own view, of the significant aspects of his work in Ireland.

After a preliminary survey of the difficult situation in the country at the time of Peel's arrival, the reviewer argued that the first major problem confronting him was the Catholic Board. Between the alternative policies of endeavouring to crush it by every means possible, or treating it with leniency while preventing any positive

[1] 25 July 1818.

breaches of the law, Peel had chosen the latter. The result had been that men of character, wealth, and influence had left the Board and it had degenerated into a vulgar popular club. Though Peel had been adverse to Catholic claims, he was not influenced by enmity towards them; and if he had kept the opposition from power, he had disappointed the selfish claims of the ministerialists, and rebuked the bigotry of Protestants. The second great problem had been disorder and outrage, caused less by the agitation of demagogues than by the more real social evils. 'It is a truth, and it would not be patriotic to conceal it, that in many instances the tenantry were neglected.' What was to be done? The pacific exhortations of the Roman Catholic Church were counterbalanced by incendiary speeches from Dublin and every town in Ireland. People could not be educated in a day and so it was imperative that strong measures had to be taken in strong cases. Violent districts were proclaimed and everything done to punish outrage and disorder. It became in the interest of the proclaimed districts not only to bring offenders to justice but to prevent others from offending. The country was restored to peace, and though a general period of distress and famine followed, which compelled England to suspend the Habeas Corpus Act, Ireland remained in honourable contrast.[1]

By the time the last of these eulogistic articles appeared, Ireland and its endless problems were no longer exercising Peel's brain. He had been in office without a break for eight years, six of them in the most harassing situation, physically and mentally, that government had to offer short of the Prime Minister's post itself. He had worked as no other Irish Secretary had worked; and he was tired and sated. There were rumours that he was to be promoted to cabinet office; but his friends knew better. He was leaving Ireland, he told Desart on 18 June, 'but not as the world supposes for the purpose of being appointed to other office. I always intended to resign my present office at the close of the parliament at the commencement of which I undertook it. I am tired of it.'[2] To Croker, who had described to him in foolish and perhaps highly coloured language how Lord Yarmouth had been speaking of Peel for the premiership, he

---

[1] *Patriot*, 16, 23, 25 July, 6 August 1818; cf. the similar views in the pamphlet *The Peel Administration* (Dublin 1818).

[2] 40295 f. 134.

answered, 'Fudge. I am thinking of anything but office and am just as anxious to be emancipated from office as the Papists are to be emancipated into it.' He continued with a burst of his old youthful liveliness:

> A fortnight hence I shall be free as air—free from ten thousand engagements which I cannot fulfil; free from the anxiety of having more to do than it is possible to do well; free from the acknowledgements of that gratitude which consists in a lively sense of future favours; free from the necessity of abstaining from private intimacy that will certainly interfere with public duty; free from Orangemen; free from Ribbonmen; free from Dennis Browne; free from the Lord Mayor and Sheriffs; free from men who pretend to be Protestants on principle and sell Dundalk to — the Papist of Cork; free from Catholics who become Protestants to get into Parliament after the manner of —, and of Protestants who become Catholics after the manner of old —; free from perpetual converse about the Harbour of Howth and Dublin Bay haddock; and lastly, free of the Company of Carvers and Gilders which I became this day in reward of my public services.[1]

His only interest now was to make his departure by the beginning of August. In compliance with his urgent request, Grant arrived in Dublin on 24 July. Peel persuaded his own private secretary, Streatfeild, to stay on in the same capacity with Grant, and was thus enabled to leave the whole of his files of private correspondence behind in Dublin for as long as the new Chief Secretary needed them.

On 29 July he attended his last meeting of the Irish Privy Council, a placid deliberation in which the only item of business was the discharge from quarantine of a sloop from Alicante laden with a mixed cargo of liquorice roots, wine, and cane reeds.[2] The same evening he was guest at a select dinner party given by Sir Charles Vernon, the Castle Chamberlain, at his cottage in Phoenix Park, attended by Grant, Fitzgerald, Gregory, Saurin, James Daly, and Viscount Allen. On Monday 3 August 1818, the day of his formal resignation from office, he arrived at Belfast and, taking ship at Donaghadee, crossed over to Scotland.[3] The low green coastline of County Down was the last he ever saw of Ireland.

---

[1] *Croker*, I, 116.     [2] S.P.O., Irish P.C. Minutes.
[3] *Faulkner's Dublin Journal*, 5 August 1818.

# THE PLEASURES OF
# PRIVATE LIFE

Peel's departure from Ireland in 1818 as clearly marked a period in his life as his departure from Oxford in 1809; and as he had done nine years earlier he celebrated his release from toil by a holiday in the Highlands of Scotland. Indeed, the visit was perhaps more a conscious repetition than a coincidence, since he returned to exactly the same district that he had before traversed with his solitary steed. But the old undergraduate days were long past. He was thirty, M.P. for Oxford University, and a politician of some note; and this time he relaxed in comfort and congenial company. With a small party consisting of his brother William, Colonel Yates of his mother's family, and James Daly from Galway, he took the castle of Cluny in Inverness-shire among the mountains of Badenoch. The Spey ran through a pretty valley before their door, and behind them the fir woods rose to snowclad peaks where the eagles soared in the distant sky. For six weeks they ranged over thousands of acres of hillside, forest, loch, and stream, with Jacobite Macphersons as their guides, unshod Highland ponies as their transport, and no civilised society for ten miles around. Hind, hare, grouse, partridge, ptarmigan, snipe, and wild duck offered a sportsman's paradise by day, and in the evening when they returned, Peel's own cook was there to rejoice their hunters' appetites. 'I really left Clunie with regret,' wrote Peel afterwards to Croker, when giving him an account of the expedition. 'There was so much novelty in the mode of life, so much wildness and magnificence in the scenery, so much simplicity and unaffected kindness among the people.'[1] In October he came south, staying in Yorkshire for ten days with Lord Grantham, before

[1] *Croker*, I, 117; *Peel*, I, 287.

going on to Drayton. There he remained for a short time, planning a visit to Oxford to see his constituents and a brief trip to Paris with Vesey Fitzgerald before the start of the parliamentary session.

It was a long leisurely period of rest after the incessant activities and responsibilities of the last six years, and he was in no mind to bring his holiday to a premature end. He attended parliament, but Arbuthnot, the Treasury Secretary, noted with some sourness that he gave too many dinners and rarely stayed late in the House. Friends like Croker and Fitzgerald might proclaim his virtues and prophesy advancement to even higher spheres in the political firmament, but the subject of their praises continued outwardly unmoved. Nevertheless, even if Croker's talk of Peel for the premiership was only Hibernian hyperbole, most politicians would have admitted that Peel had brought himself within reach of the cabinet. It was unlikely, therefore, that so long as he was a member of parliament he would be permanently left without offer of employment; and that he had no intention of abandoning an active parliamentary career was soon evident. At the start of the new session he moved the re-election of his friend Charles Manners Sutton as Speaker, and five weeks later came to the rescue of the ministry on a more doubtful issue. The death of Queen Charlotte in November 1818 had made it necessary to appoint the Duke of York as custodian of the aged king and the government proposed to transfer to him the official salary of £10,000 formerly granted to the queen for that duty. Despite the reduction from £100,000 to £50,000 of the general grant for the royal Household at Windsor, Tierney (who had succeeded Ponsonby as leader of the whigs in the Commons) sought to remove the Duke of York's salary from the Civil List entirely and throw the expense on the private revenues of the crown. On 22 February 1819 Peel intervened in defence of the ministry, making what Greville described as one of the four good speeches in the debate. Not only was his compact, detailed argument of great assistance to the government but it was also clear proof that if the cabinet had lost an Irish Secretary, they had gained an invaluable free-lance supporter, disengaged from departmental responsibilities and able to range over the whole field of parliamentary business.

In private, moreover, he was trying to improve his debating powers by studying the formal art of ratiocination; and it was typical that it was on reasoning rather than on rhetoric that he laid the emphasis. 'Pray tell me,' he wrote to Lloyd only three days after his speech in the Tierney debate, 'what you consider the best specimen, not exactly of reasoning, but of that part of reasoning which is occupied in confutation of your adversary's arguments.' He continued with a passage that threw some light on his own reading.

> I want, as I have often told you, from reading much of polemics, to endeavour to form some general principle of arguing and reply. Locke touches upon the subject, but he leaves it directly. Chillingworth is capital, but he is too close, and sets about it much too logically for these times. I find much the best reasoning in divinity —disputatious reasoning I mean. There is an answer of Warburton to Boyle and Shaftesbury (prefixed to the 'Divine Legation', I think), that is good. I do not want to read for information on the subject; at least that is not my chief object. What I want is subtle reasoning in reply. I care not if the book is on alchemy. There is not half reasoning enough in politics—not half. Burke's speech on the Nabob of Arcot's debts is good, for he sets out with a distinct enumeration of the arguments of his opponents.

A man who was prepared to read alchemy in order to improve his powers of debate was clearly not without ideas on his own future.

But while Peel endeavoured to strengthen his forensic talents, he also found work of another kind to do. Since the arbitrary abolition of the income tax in 1816, the finances of the state had been on a permanently insecure basis. Faced with an insuperable gap between revenue and expenditure, Vansittart had resorted to borrowing and raids on the Sinking Fund; and the attention of the opposition was in consequence increasingly devoted to attacks on his not very reputable budgets. Moreover, with government financial policy inevitably affecting the state of the money-market, the specialised questions of currency and banking came under searching and often hostile examination. To many persons the acute post-war deflation, the fall in wages and prices, unemployment in industrial areas, distress among farmers, all seemed connected in some way with the manipulation of loans, discounts, and currency, at the hands of the Bank of England and the government. But if that opinion was commonly held, the remedies put forward were various. The war-time suspension of cash payments had been carried into the peace, though as a professed temporary expedient rather than as permanent policy. In the meantime the Bank privately sought to prepare the way for a return to cash payments by restricting its note issue. Yet this policy in itself, in the conditions of post-Waterloo England, aroused loud complaints; and there was a widespread conviction that by its operations with currency and credit the Bank was amassing wealth at the expense of the rest of the community. Both agriculturalists and middle-class radicals like Attwood of Birmingham saw in the restriction of paper currency a source of continuing economic depression, and they pressed for a looser, more inflationary, money policy.

As against the inflationists, who included Sir Robert Peel in their number, Horner's Bullion Committee of 1810 had tried even in wartime to obtain an immediate return to the gold standard, and a whig-radical economist school was becoming a powerful element in the House of Commons. Ricardo, the greatest economic theorist of the day, who entered parliament as member for Portarlington in 1819, had argued in 1816 in favour of a return to payment in specie at fixed prices and he supported the growing attack on the privileged position of the Bank of England. Under Tierney's leadership the whigs began to declaim, in language similar to that of Cobbett, against the 'money party' of financiers, fundholders, and stock-jobbers. The repeated assertions of the Bank of England directors that they were preparing for an abandonment of the wartime system received substantial confirmation by the resumption in 1817 of cash payments for notes not exceeding £5 in value. Nevertheless, the government secured a further postponement of the full return to the gold standard. When in 1819 yet another postponement was announced, this time until 1820, there was a general parliamentary revolt. Caught between the views of the Bank directors and the pressure of exasperated public opinion, the cabinet accepted at the beginning of February a proposal to appoint an immediate parliamentary committee of enquiry. The committee, chosen under government influence, included Castlereagh, Vansittart, Canning, Huskisson, and Robinson. Peel also expressed a wish to Arbuthnot, the Treasury Secretary, to serve on the committee, and after consultation between Arbuthnot and the Prime Minister it was decided to propose him as its chairman.[1]

Peel approached the work of the committee with an open and critical mind. In 1811 as a young member he had voted in favour of Vansittart's resolution on the efficacy of paper currency against the views of Horner's Currency Committee which had recommended a resumption of cash payments within two years. But he did not profess any particular knowledge of the subject and was determined on a thorough examination of the evidence before forming any views. Indeed, when asked by the government whether he would consent to become chairman, he made it clear that his vote in 1811 had been taken without full consideration of the subject and that he must reserve the right to take a course unfettered by either his previous action or the opinions of any members of the government.[2] 'I conceive,' he wrote to Lloyd, 'my chief, perhaps my only qualification, for the office for which I have been selected by the committee, is that I have not prejudged the question, am committed to no opinion upon it, and shall be therefore at least disinterested in the result of our investigation.' But he was impressed by the general absence of prejudice and party feeling in the committee, and by the general desire to get to the bottom of an important and complicated problem. The committee began to take evidence on 11 February and continued until 1 May. On all of the twenty-five occasions Peel was present in the chair, listening to a long and distinguished train of witnesses that included the Governor, Deputy-Governor, and directors of the Bank of England, bankers and brokers like Baring, Rothschild, and Gurney, economists like Ricardo, and merchants like John Gladstone. When interviewing an anti-bullionist, he told Lloyd, he interrogated as though he belonged to the opposite school; with a bullionist exactly the same.[3] In addition he studied the report of the Bullion Committee of 1810, pamphlets such as that written for the occasion by Copleston of Oriel and dedicated to him, and countless other articles and documents engendered by the same prolific subject. Reading all this matter with the same attention, as he said, that he would give to the proof of a proposition in mathematics, he was early persuaded that the system of paper money had

[1] Earl Stanhope, *Conversations with . . . Wellington* (1889), p. 288.
[2] *Speeches*, II, 696.  [3] 40342 f. 30.

resulted in a depreciation of the currency, an increase in the price of bullion, and an unfavourable rate of exchange in the foreign markets. In this, along with the majority of the committee, he differed sharply from the official view taken by the Bank of England. Nevertheless, he was of too practical a mind not to foresee concrete problems in any attempt to enforce economic doctrine, however susceptible of mathematical demonstration. In particular the prospect of future repayment by the state and by the taxpayer, in the new and appreciated currency, of debts contracted under the old depreciated currency, impressed him as one of the most formidable obstacles the committee would have to face.

Once the theoretical arguments in favour of a return to gold had been accepted, however, the real problem became one of method. It was the difficulties encountered here that had in fact been responsible for the repeated postponement of the final decision in previous years. In 1817 the Bank of England, relying on its post-war accumulation of cash and bullion, had begun a tentative return to cash payments in the anticipation that this would facilitate an early and complete resumption of payments in specie. As far as the British public was concerned, this hope had been justified; but financial operations on the continent finally caused the exchange to fall below par with the result that it became profitable to export gold. Not only did the Bank's gold reserves begin to decline sharply but, even more disturbingly, most of the gold currency issued left the country. In order to stop this continuing drain of gold and to allow the Bank to build up its metallic reserves again, the committee issued an interim report on 5 April foreshadowing an early resumption of cash payments, but recommending the immediate passage of a bill to restrain the Bank from all payments in gold until its full report had been received and studied by the House of Commons. In a brief speech the same day Peel brought in a bill to give effect to the interim recommendation and it passed through all its stages before the end of the evening. Nevertheless the ability of the Bank to resume cash payments depended less on the amount of bullion in its possession than on the state of foreign exchange and the relation between the market value of gold and its mint value. This by its nature was not easily amenable to legislation. Yet in view of the permanent advantages of the gold standard, which though variable was less subject to fluctuation than any other system that could be devised, the committee drew up what it hoped would be an effective plan for a gradual removal of all restrictions. At the same time it accepted the view of the Bank directors that a partial repayment to the Bank of advances made to the government on exchequer bills and other securities was a necessary preliminary to such a step, and that in future there should be some regulation by law of the amount of advances made by the Bank to the government. Part at least of the Bank's trouble had been Vansittart's endless borrowing.

On 24 May Peel introduced the main report, which he had himself been responsible for writing, in a speech which in its length and closely-knit detail was perhaps the most difficult he had ever had to deliver. After a tribute both to the impartiality of the committee over which he had presided, and to the principle if not the timing of the report of Horner's committee of 1810, he emphasised the need for a clear decision on the issue of a return to a metallic standard. If that first point were conceded, a number of alternative methods were conceivable which he dealt with in turn before coming to the specific recommendation of the report. A resumption of cash payments could not, he argued, be made before the period suggested by the committee in view of the high market price of gold and the loans made by the Bank to the government. To repay public loans, not at a fixed price, but according to the current value of gold would be a fraud on the public creditor. The committee had agreed with the view of the Bank that some partial repayment of government loans should be made. But the time had come when the nature of the relations between the government and the Bank should be changed. The Bank should cease to regard itself as the institution to which were peculiarly entrusted the financial and commercial interests of the community; and the House of Commons should recover the authority it had so long abdicated. He then proceeded to an historical retrospect of the great epochs in British history that had coincided with a restoration of the value of British currency and to an eloquent vindication of the bullionist school of thought. He ended with a passing reference to his father's different views on paper currency—'the necessity he felt of opposing himself to an authority to which he always had bowed and he hoped always should bow with deference'—and to his own process of conviction—'he felt himself called upon to state, candidly and honestly, that he was a convert to the doctrine of regarding our currency which he had once opposed'. The 'conversion' was not perhaps from any strongly held previous opinion and few were likely to take seriously his youthful vote for Vansittart in 1811. But it was part of Peel's nature, once convinced, to pay tribute to the force of the intellectual demonstration that had led to his conviction. A more hardened politician might have refrained from such a gesture even while adopting the arguments.

In the circumstances no great opposition was possible to the principle of the bill. Though there was discussion on the details of the successive periods of time recommended by the committee and on the question of the repayment of government loans, the fact remained that the broad demands of the critics had been met and that if any surrender had taken place, it had been on the part of the Bank. Ricardo himself, though not an advocate of cash in preference to ingot payments, could with reason claim a victory for his principles over the forces of timidity and obscurantism. The real issue in fact had not been whether to return to the gold standard. The leading economists in the government—Liverpool and Huskisson—and the repeated sense of parliament were all in favour of that. The question was the technical one of when, and how, to put the principle into effect. On 26 May the House unanimously approved a series of resolutions embodying the recommendations of the committee; and a bill giving them force moved easily and rapidly into the statute book. It proved to be a singularly quiet passage for an Act which settled an issue of controversy in the past and was to raise controversy in the future. For Peel it brought enhanced reputation and personal satisfaction. It was a task peculiarly to his liking: the examination of the evidence, the enunciation of principle, the devising of method, the translation into law. Moreover, he had avoided either identifying himself with the opposition or behaving as a mere governmental spokesman.

By the provisions of the bill the Bank was required to furnish in exchange for notes ingot gold in quantities of not less than sixty ounces at the rate of £4 1s. 0d., the current market price, from February 1820; at £3 19s. 6d. from October 1820; and at £3 17s.

$10\frac{1}{2}d.$, the former mint price, from May 1821. From May 1823 it was to pay its notes in the legal coin of the realm. In this way, by first attacking the price of gold and the exchange rate before coming to the actual issue of gold coinage, it was hoped to overcome the problems of the transition period. In effect, 'Peel's Act' of 1819, together with another statute of the same session which forbade the Bank to make advances to the government without parliamentary authority, laid the foundations of the British currency system for the remainder of the century. The return to gold proved easier than had been anticipated and in 1821, two years before the statutory period, the Bank began to cash small notes up to £5 in the new gold coinage, sovereigns and half-sovereigns, which had been authorised in 1816.[1]

Apart from his work on the currency committee, Peel did not take a great share in the debates of the session. In part this was due to accident, since in May 1819, in the last great effort of his career, Grattan once more opened up a full-scale debate on the Catholic question. It was an occasion on which Peel was inevitably expected, and indeed was prepared to play a leading role on the Protestant side. He was perhaps the more inclined to be active in the question since he had some reason to suspect a close collaboration on the tactics of the debate between Canning and Plunket, despite the fact that the one was in the government and the other formally belonged to the opposition. It was believed on Peel's side that the policy of the Catholic party was to exhaust the strength of their opponents on the first night of the debate and put up a solid platoon of their own speakers on the second. When the debate came on, therefore, hardly a man rose on the Protestant side other than Leslie Foster. Peel's own instinct, despite the dissuasion of his friends, who pointed to the row of Catholic orators still in reserve, was to wait until the last minute and then, if no one came forward, to speak himself. He did in fact rise, but in a moment of great confusion, and sat down again. Plunket was following similar waiting tactics and the result was that the question was put and the debate terminated the same evening without either speaking. After considerable wrangling and disorder a division was finally taken, and Grattan's motion was defeated by

[1] P.P. 1819, III (*Cash Payments*); Clapham, *Bank of England*, II, ch. 1; *Early Railway Age*, pp. 263-4.

two votes (241-243).[1] There was little satisfaction for Peel in such a hollow victory. Indeed, he began to look with some foreboding on the outcome of the struggle. 'Notwithstanding the result of the debate,' he wrote unhopefully to Gregory, 'I shall pursue the course I invariably have pursued and offer, I fear a very unavailing, but a most sincere and uncompromising resistance to a measure which will, I believe, establish Roman Catholic ascendancy in Ireland.'

His only other contribution to debate in the session was little less unsatisfactory. The work of Brougham's predominantly whig-liberal Education Committee of 1816 and 1818, originally starting as an enquiry into the education of the poor of the metropolis, had enlarged its scope to include all charitable endowments, including some of the public schools, and there was some talk even of the universities being affected. A bill founded on the report of the 1818 committee had passed the Commons, despite the efforts of Robinson and Peel to exclude Harrow, but had been drastically altered in the House of Lords. In 1819 the government itself introduced a Charitable Endowments Bill, embodying many of Brougham's proposals but excepting endowments with special visitors. When Brougham, though welcoming the bill, opposed this particular omission, Peel took the opportunity of making a general criticism of Brougham's committee and what he considered to be the unjustified scope and methods of the enquiries it had undertaken. There had been a good deal of dissatisfaction at Brougham's activities but the timing and detail of Peel's attack were not the happiest. Brougham answered impromptu with a long and savagely sarcastic speech; and though Fitzgerald and Castlereagh gave some cover, the weight of subsequent speakers was against Peel. It was characteristic, nevertheless, that despite the rough handling he had received from one of the greatest masters of invective then in the Commons, he stubbornly held his position and persisted at the end of the debate in asserting his view that Brougham as chairman and the committee as a whole had followed their investigations to a point never envisaged by the House when they were appointed.[2]

In August he was back in the Highlands with Lord Apsley and Colonel Yates, shooting grouse at the invitation of the Duke of

[1] Williams, *Rickman*, p. 209; *Croker*, I, 134-5.
[2] *Hansard* XL, 1296-1344 (23 June 1819).

Gordon's son, the Marquess of Huntly. Their headquarters, at Pitmain, was only some ten miles farther down the Spey valley from Cluny Castle and the weather was so hot that it was almost impossible to do anything until the evening. In the first seven days they were out they shot over seven hundred grouse, though the heat made it difficult for the game to reach Edinburgh in edible condition. As for sending a brace or two to Gregory in Dublin, 'I am afraid,' wrote Peel, 'of inflicting a box full of maggots on you.'[1] But the sultriness was not only in the weather. The fluctuations in employment and wages had already in 1818 caused strikes and disorders in Lancashire and other districts, and from the start of 1819 radical agitators were at work in Lancashire, Yorkshire, and the Midlands, organising a widespread political movement with demands chiefly centred on a repeal of the Corn Law of 1815 and a democratic reform of parliament. Participating in the agitation, though deprecating and sometimes startled by the inflammatory language of some of the more radical speakers, were some of the middle-class dissenters and manufacturers, and a few provincial editors. In July a mass meeting in the unrepresented town of Birmingham elected a radical Staffordshire neighbour of the Peels, Sir Charles Wolseley, as their 'legislatorial attorney and representative' in parliament. Stung by this final demonstration, the government arrested Wolseley and issued a proclamation against seditious meetings. The radicals at Manchester, who had planned a similar staging of an 'election', organised in its place a mass meeting to petition for parliamentary reform which was to be addressed by the great demagogue, Orator Hunt, in St. Peter's Field. An unwise use of local yeomanry was made to arrest Hunt, and cavalry were sent in to extricate the yeomanry. By the evening of 16 August Hunt was in gaol and eleven people including two women were dead or dying. Within a week 'Peterloo' had passed into the vocabulary of the English nation.

During the remainder of the summer, meetings and petitions of protest were organised all over the country, and when parliament assembled in November it was in an atmosphere of anger and alarm. The opposition in both houses called for an enquiry into the conduct of the Manchester magistrates. The government countered with the

[1] *Letter-Box*, p. 130.

introduction of six bills designed to strengthen the maintenance of order and limit the freedom of political agitation. Two dealt with unauthorised military training and the possession of arms; one with the regulation of public meetings; and the remainder with the evasion of existing press laws by semi-periodical political pamphlets and with the more effectual prosecution of seditious libel. All six passed into law before parliament rose for the Christmas recess, and under the generic epithet of the 'Six Acts' gained a notoriety which their content hardly justified. Part at least of their provisions conferred powers with which few modern governments have been able to dispense; and other sections merely endeavoured to make more effective the enforcement of existing statutes. But the wide and some-times anarchic tradition of British liberty was still engrained in the public mind, even though the unprecedented growth of industrial population in the unpoliced and in some places virtually un-governed communities of the North and Midlands was creating out of that tradition a growing threat to law and order. The revulsion of feeling at the recent killing of civilians at Manchester tended, moreover, to overcloud any impartial examination of the measures among the public at large. It was difficult to isolate the Six Acts from the general political movement of agitation in the country. By opponents of the government the Acts were represented as at best a barren enunciation of rule by force, and at their worst a deliberate and partisan attack on the principles of constitutional liberty.

At the start of the session Peel was present at an official dinner given by Castlereagh at which a preliminary account was given of the legislation to be brought forward by the government; but a bout of illness prevented him from taking part in the earlier debates on the Six Acts.[1] It was not until 2 December that he intervened in the discussions on the Seditious Meetings Bill, which imposed a series of close limitations on the traditional right of political assembly. With certain specified exceptions public meetings for the purpose of discussing grievances in Church or State were severely restricted in size, composition, and object; and meetings designed to secure an alteration in the law otherwise than by act of parlia-ment, or that were calculated to bring into hatred and contempt the

[1] *Ward Memoirs*, II, 27, 40.

crown, the government, or the constitution, were prohibited under penalties of up to seven years' transportation. The ministry accepted during discussion in parliament the principle that it should be a temporary measure only, and it was passed for a period of five years. It was perhaps the most sweeping of the encroachments on the liberty of the subject made by the Six Acts, and it was this bill that Peel characteristically chose as the occasion for demonstrating his support of executive government. He began with a reasoned and uncompromising defence of the magistrates of Manchester, a town as he reminded the House with which he was connected by ties of birth and early acquaintance. He asked first that they should be judged not against the background of the events of 16 August but of the months and years preceding. The history of agitation and projected disorder in Manchester went back to 1817 and the magistrates would have been answerable for their conduct had they not taken precautions. If a similar meeting were to be held, they would be bound to proceed as before; and deplorable as the loss of life was, he said flatly, 'were he to enter into a comparative estimate of the two evils . . . he would say that he believed on his honour that the loss of lives was the less evil'. The magistrates could not prevent the meeting with the two or three constables at their disposal; nor could they send troops to prevent the peaceful approach of thousands of men with banners and leaders from the surrounding towns. The government had done right to congratulate the Manchester magistrates, if there were to be any hope in future of finding men ready to do a difficult duty in the face of danger and criticism. 'He would appeal to the civil commotions in this country, he would appeal to the history of the civil commotions of France, and he would ask, What on those occasions had been the effect of ill-timed rigour and what had been the effect of ill-timed concession?'

Then, turning to the provisions of the bill itself, he pointed to the evidence of 'a great abuse of popular rights' calculated to bring down destruction on the constitution. It was absolutely necessary that immediate and powerful measures should be taken to check the dangers confronting the country. It was easy enough for the upper classes to protect their interests; it was the middle and lower classes living in the centre of disorder and disaffection who needed the protection of the state against an intimidation that rendered absurd any talk of popular liberties. It was asked to what the discontent and changed habits of the people were to be attributed. 'In those districts which were called manufacturing districts, a change had taken place in their manners, and habits, and feelings, and he confessed that he found it much more easy to point out the cause of those disorders than to devise the means of preventing them.' He refused to believe that the discontent was due to the defective state of the representation or to misgovernment by ministers. The distress and the agitation were local manifestations; they existed only in manufacturing towns where a population had grown up, lacking the social ties and habits that characterised the rest of the country, and subjected to great and constant alternations of prosperity and poverty. They were open to the arts of political agitation and by their concentration in one place could readily combine for political purposes. Because the districts in which they lived were more populous, a more effective civil power was called for; yet civil power was notoriously deficient in such places. These were the causes of disorder, though he could not point to a remedy. But the choice was between two evils—the restriction of valuable rights or general anarchy and confusion.

Both argument and analysis carried weight, even among the whigs, and if he offered no easy solution for the discontents, as was emphasised even more clearly in a brief speech he made a week later on the state of the manufacturing districts, he was not singular in this. Nevertheless, for all his strong words in the House, Peel was disturbed at the breach that seemed to be opening up between the government and the nation. Talking with Plumer Ward just before the meeting of parliament, he observed that the lower classes had changed their attitude towards parliament a great deal in the last few years, and added that he thought Hunt was a very clever fellow.[1] He seemed cheerful enough about the government's parliamentary prospects but it is clear that the wider problems remained in his mind during the remainder of the winter.

Do not you think [he wrote to Croker in March 1820] that the tone of England,—of that great compound of folly, weakness, prejudice, wrong feeling, right feeling, obstinacy and newspaper

[1] *Ward Memoirs*, II, pp. 24-5.

paragraphs, which is called public opinion,—is more liberal, to use an odious but intelligible phrase, than the policy of the government?

There seemed to have come about, he thought, a curious situation in which public opinion, with more actual influence on government policy than ever before, was never more dissatisfied with the share it possessed. 'It is growing too large for the channels that it has been accustomed to run through.' Moderate reform could not in his view be in the long run resisted; and if that were so, it appeared probable that whigs and tories would unite to carry it through rather than let the radicals have their way.[1]

It was a confused and despondent time in English public life. In January 1820 the old forgotten king died at Windsor, and the accession of the Regent to full regal dignity brought to an issue the long-standing estrangement between him and his wife. In February came the barbarous plot to assassinate the cabinet known to posterity as the Cato Street conspiracy; in March took place the general election necessitated by the demise of the crown; and in April an outbreak of radical agitation in Scotland led to a clash between yeomanry and armed rioters at Bonnymuir. The laurels of Waterloo had long since withered; and though Wellington himself had been brought into the cabinet as Master-General of the Ordnance, the Liverpool ministry was approaching the nadir of its fortunes. Ministerial changes were thought likely, and Wellesley Pole told Ward that Peel would be the first to be provided for, though he added fretfully that he had made a mistake in leaving Ireland, where he had such a following, and that the Irish party had since fallen to pieces.[2] But it was an inauspicious season for a fresh point of departure in public life. Moreover, Peel had acquired a stronger motive than ever before for wishing to remain detached from political office.

## II

In February 1820 Peel reached his thirty-second birthday, wealthy, successful and still unmarried. He was one of the more eligible

[1] *Croker*, I, 170.    [2] *Ward Memoirs*, II, 47.

matches in London society but so far no woman's name had been connected with his; nor had any whisper of scandal or dissipation detracted from his reputation. Though he was too strongly endowed with aesthetic sensibility to be indifferent to sexual attractions, his ethical and intellectual instincts always appeared in control of his emotions. There is no reason to suppose that the appearance was false. His father had not married until well past thirty. Until then he had been wedded to his factory and the pattern of the elder Peel's life was repeated in the son's. From the age of twenty-one, when he left Oxford, all his energy and emotion had gone into his work. What recreations he had were of a hard physical masculine kind and the company in which he habitually moved was that of men. Long hours at his desk, even longer on the benches of the House of Commons, left him little opportunity, even if he felt the need, for the softer sensuousness of women's society. Too fastidious to be a rake, and too busy to have thought seriously of marriage, he remained one of the steadily declining number of bachelors in his personal circle of friends. He was not for that reason less an object of interest to women; and the more leisurely social life he led in London after his retirement from office gave them sufficient opportunity to try their seductive arts.

Pretty feather-headed Lady Shelley was introduced to Peel for the first time at a house party she gave at Maresfield at the end of January 1819. Impressed by the enthusiasm with which his friends spoke of him, yet seizing on the one vulnerable point of his plebeian origin, she had looked forward to their meeting with anticipation, though woman-like had made up her mind to dislike him. In the event she found her guest something of an enigma among the hard-drinking, hard-spoken aristocrats that her husband usually brought to the house. 'At first sight he displeased me. He spoke of shooting and country pursuits in a condescending manner; and his parade of good breeding and attention, a parade to which an Englishwoman is unaccustomed in a man of talent, disappointed me.' However, his attentiveness had the effect that might have been expected, and with a serene assurance she soon decided that he was the English Metternich. 'He has a foreign *tournure de phrases* which I delight in, and yet in an Englishman it had at first displeased me. An observation of Mr. Peel's as to Englishwomen's tendency for satire, threw new light upon me; for I could not deny that I had met Mr. Peel with a determination to criticise, rather than to admire him.' They talked of such literary matters as the identity of Junius and the authorship of the Waverley novels; and Peel described some of the legal cases he had known in Ireland during his secretaryship, including the Dillon case and the Louth murders of 1816. At breakfast he entertained the company with an anecdote of Sir Frederick Flood, the Irish M.P. for Wexford, at the time of the Corn Law riots in 1815. Having been mishandled by the crowd, he related, Flood made his way into the House of Commons to complain, swelling with anger and importance. 'Mr. Speaker, I appear before you, literally torn into four quarters. (Shouts of Hear! Hear!) I have been seized by the mob. They wanted to know my name. Mr. Speaker, I *scorned* to equivocate. I tould them my name was Waters.' 'I wish,' added Lady Shelley enthusiastically, 'I could render justice to the humour with which Mr. Peel told this story.'

Mr. Peel in fact had made a conquest and since he was approved by the great ladies who dominated Almacks, it was not long before they met again at that ultra-fashionable rendezvous. 'Wednesday's Almack's was very pleasant,' recorded Lady Shelley happily on 17 March. 'I talked a great deal to Mr. Peel, who came to me with the greatest *empressement*. He is a most delightful person.' On 22 November she dined at Peel's house, the only woman present in a company that comprised Vesey Fitzgerald, Grant, Huskisson, Beckett, Lord Westmorland, and Sir George Warrender. It was a situation that most women would have found flattering, even though the conversation ran mainly on politics and the sins of the radicals. Nevertheless, with six male chaperons, Peel was in no danger of compromising either the reputation of his lady guest or his own; and it is unlikely that Sir John Shelley saw much cause for alarm.[1] In fact, Almack's and private dinner parties notwithstanding, Peel's affections were already irretrievably engaged elsewhere. Ireland, which had done so much to shape his public career, had also been fateful in his private life.

When Peel first went to Dublin in 1812, the second-in-command of the Irish military forces was a certain General John Floyd. From the age of eleven, when he had been given a cornetcy in Elliott's

[1] *Shelley Diary*, II, 16–21, 34, 90.

Light Dragoons, to the time of his death in 1818—due appropriately enough to gout in the stomach—Floyd's career had been an epitome of a professional officer's life in the era of the Napoleonic Wars He was born in 1748, the son of a Captain Floyd of the 1st Dragoon. Guards who was killed on active service in Germany. Taken into the Light Dragoons for his father's sake at a tender age, young Floyd saw service in the Seven Years' War, fought at the battle of Emsdorf, and from his proficiency as a cavalry officer was later given command of the 23rd (19th) Light Dragoon Regiment raised for service in India in 1781. He fought in the wars against Tippoo Sahib and commanded the cavalry forces at Seringapatam in 1799. In 1800 he returned to England with a considerable reputation as a cavalry leader and a not inconsiderable fortune derived from his Indian appointment and the spoils of war. In 1801 he was promoted lieutenant-general and two years later was sent to command the Limerick division in Ireland. He made his final step to full general in 1812 and was given the sinecure post of Governor of Gravesend and Tilbury the following year. In 1816 he was created baronet and he died at the age of seventy a few months before Peel retired from the Irish Secretaryship. When in India he had married Rebecca Juliana the daughter of Charles Darke, a merchant of Madras, by whom he had four children: a son, Henry, who chose his father's profession and served in the Peninsula and at Waterloo; and three daughters—Miranda, Julia, and Flavia. Little is known of Rebecca Floyd, and other than the euphonious Christian names which she bestowed on her daughters, little survived of her presence and personality after the return to England. The family settled at Chalk Farm, Farnborough, and there in January 1802 the children caught scarlet fever. Flavia, the youngest, succumbed before the end of the month. Mrs. Floyd, nursing her son, caught the disease and died on 1 February. The two other girls had been sent away to friends and relatives, though one was brought home again very ill on 26 January. General Floyd and some of the servants were affected but all in the end recovered.[1]

For a while the orphaned family were looked after by an aunt at Bromley, Kent, but in July 1805, only a couple of months before Sir Robert Peel undertook a similar venture, the widowed general

[1] G.M., LXXII, Pt. I, 185 (1802).

married again. Unlike the second Lady Peel, however, General Floyd's second wife was a brisk, worldly Irishwoman who took charge of the fortunes of her two step-daughters with a competent hand. She was the widow of Sir Barry Denny of Tralee, Co. Kerry, and with her native Irish connections she easily made a home for her husband and his family at the various stations in Ireland to which he was successively posted. Blacker described the pair of them in a racy passage. General Floyd, with his 'broad and jolly red face' was a

> gallant veteran . . . one of the real old school as far as being, I believe, the last officer in the service who adhered to blue breeches. Yet he adopted not the pigtail of that school either, but wore his hair in a short closed kind of one buckle like the lowermost story of a coachman's cauliflower wig, and I imagine his little triangular hat was the last of that cut. With all that he woo'd and won one of the finest women of the day, the comely Lady Denny. Whether the blue breeches or the rupees which fill'd the pockets of them that took the fancy of the gay widow let others decide; at all events she made him an excellent wife.[1]

By match-making criteria she also made an excellent stepmother. In November 1815 Miranda made an eminently suitable marriage with Major-General Fuller of the Coldstream Guards; and with Henry already embarked on his military career, there remained only Julia to be provided for.

In the last years of his Irish service General Floyd was in Dublin, and though on his appointment as Governor of Tilbury he set up his domestic establishment in London at Mansfield Street, off Portland Place, the link with Ireland represented by Anna Denny was not severed. As was almost inevitable in the circumstances, Peel while Chief Secretary made the acquaintance of General Floyd's family, probably even before the appointment to Tilbury in 1813. Indeed, since the Governorship needed no personal attendance, there was little haste for the Floyds to move to England. Certainly by 1817 Lady Floyd was on terms of close friendship with Peel's sister, Mrs. Dawson, and with her stepdaughter had evidently been guests at the Secretary's Lodge. The acquaintanceship was perhaps even closer,

---

[1] *Blacker*, IV, 157.

since at some date, probably at the end of 1816 or early in 1817 when Lady Floyd and Julia were in Ireland, they undertook to find some ice-pails in Dresden china to match Peel's dinner service: and he was unusually attentive to them on their departure from Dublin. Lady Floyd did not forget the commission and after many months delay she wrote in December 1817 to report on some recent importations from France which she thought might serve his purpose. 'Miss Floyd agrees with me in thinking they are very much in the style of your service.' Julia was mentioned again towards the end of the letter.

> Miss Floyd joins me in requesting that you will remember us and that you will believe that we never do or can forget your kindness to us at Dublin. Few persons occupied and stationed as you, Mr. Peel, would have thought of so many signs of shining good nature ... [illegible] ... we were almost last away. I therefore feel it most particularly, it was in my native land and all my friends were gone. Sir John Floyd begs you will accept his best compliments, and dear sir, believe me, sincerely and faithfully yours,
>
> A. FLOYD.[1]

The Floyd ladies' choice of china being approved, a purchase was made and in February 1818 when Peel was in London, Lady Floyd offered to send the articles round should he be unable to call; but she threw out the careful suggestion that if he were in the neighbourhood of Mansfield Street on a given day, Mrs. Dawson would be drinking tea with her and perhaps Mr. Peel might find it convenient to call at that time. Peel duly called, though not in all probability for the sole pleasure of seeing his sister, and from that date onward the relationship between himself and Julia steadily ripened. It was typical of Peel's reserve, however, that the subject which touched his personal feelings more deeply than anything else, left least trace in his correspondence and went unrecorded by his friends.

Julia Floyd had been born in India in 1795 and at the age of twenty-five was not without experience of social life of a wider kind than that afforded by subalterns at regimental balls or Irish squireens. With her oval face, dark ringlets, and a fine neck and

---

[1] Lady Floyd wrote a vile hand and in the sentences after 'Dublin' some words are conjectural. Her letters are in 40272 f. 233; 40274 fos. 61, 80.

shoulders set off by the still surviving high-waisted Regency fashion, she was an acknowledged beauty. Even the future Tsar Nicholas enrolled himself among the circle of her admirers when he visited England at the end of 1816. Twenty-eight years later, when he was again in England, Queen Victoria was to note, without visible sympathy, how faithful he was to that early attraction.[1] Another of her followers, more eligible as a suitor if less distinguished as a person, was the dashing and popular Hughes Ball, known from his great wealth as 'The Golden Ball'.[2] But it was to Robert Peel in the end that she surrendered her heart. He at one point, according to family tradition, had some misgivings whether she would be able to abandon her gay society world for the severer climate of a working politician. 'You are my world,' she is said to have replied, and the devotion implicit in the words was no more than the literal expression of her feelings. The two of them, both motherless since childhood, possessed deep and untouched springs of affection which were not unsealed until they met each other. On the 2nd or 3rd of March 1820, when less fortunate politicians were intent on their electoral position, the decisive step was taken and they became engaged.

In the interval before the wedding the strict proprieties were observed. Julia took up residence with the Dowager Countess of Clermont in Berkeley Square, while Peel went off in self-imposed exile at Bognor with his sister Mary. A note written to his 'dearest Julia' from Stanhope Street on 14 March while his carriage waited at the door, implored her not to forget her promise to write should anything occur, and ended 'with unceasing love, ever ever yours, Robert Peel'. His first letter from the seaside, written the following day, began with the unwise premiss that having no news he would not supply the deficiency with 'impassioned declarations' of love and admiration, as such declarations were easily made and often insincere; and 'I am so satisfied that they are so unnecessary to convince you of the ardour and constancy of my attachment to you, that I purposely avoid them.' The ethics of engagement, and perhaps a feminine obliquity in Miss Floyd, deprived him of anything but a

---

[1] *Letters of Queen Victoria*, ed. A. C. Benson and Viscount Esher (1908), II, 15.

[2] *Reminiscences . . . of Captain Gronow* (1889), II, 90. Hughes Ball found consolation a few years later by marrying the Spanish dancer Mercandotti.

few brief and unsatisfactory lines from his Julia in reply; and the days passed in an unhappy contrast between the dullness of his external life, as he toiled over empty shingle beaches with Mary or turned the pages of a book with vacant eye, and the ferment of his emotions within when he wrote to the beloved one of whom in reality he knew so little.

I hope you take delight in the wildness and magnificence of Nature [he wrote on 22 March, with an obvious recollection of his Scottish haunts] as well as in the calmer beauties of cultivated scenery. You see I put quite out of the question long ranges of brick walls and tracts of stone pavement, which many young ladies would think infinitely preferable to either one or the other. I do not want you quite to agree with me in having a particular admiration for the sterility and solitude of a rocky, uninhabited wilderness; I will be content if you will think a very high mountain, with a rude craggy outline, a splendid and awful sight, but I am sure you have much too pure a taste not to think so.

He had at least the minor consolation that his own family highly approved the match. His elder sister Elizabeth told her husband that only one thing on earth was wanting to make her completely happy, and that was Robert's marriage with Julia Floyd; and despite uncharitable gossip, which after the manner of human nature was carefully brought to the notice of Julia, Sir Robert Peel himself received with pleasure the news of the engagement. He showed it in his usual practical and munificent fashion. As a marriage endowment for Julia and any children she might have by his eldest son, he set up a trust fund of £100,000 in 3% Consols, the trustees being the Earl of Pembroke, Sir Henry Floyd, George Dawson, and William Peel. Malicious reports of his father's disapproval of his choice, however, touched Peel at his tenderest point; and the mixture of indignation and lofty pride with which he assured Julia of their falsehood led him into a somewhat self-righteous and involved expression of feelings.

My dearest Julia,                                   (Bognor, 17 March 1820)
    My father is, as I knew he would be, made perfectly happy by my letter of Monday last. I was sure that he preferred you to any other

person whom he had ever seen. He says that nothing shall be wanting on his part to promote the happiness of our union. You recollect the story that was told you that he did not like you. If the iniquity of our enemies had been half so great as their malice, surely they might have invented something more plausible than they have done. All they have fabricated is not only without foundation, not only at variance with but in direct contradiction to the truth. We wish to take no revenge but it would be inconsistent with candour and fair dealing to pretend to be on terms of friendship or even intimacy with them. I forgive them, for they have afforded me a proof of your generous confidence in me which without their artifices I never could have had. I do not mean that I ever could have doubted it but without them it never would have been put to the test of a severe trial. . . .

I hope there will be a letter from you to Mary tomorrow morning. Do not I keep my promise of writing to you without formality?

Ever my dearest Julia most truly and affectionately yours,

ROB. PEEL[1]

However, apart from this expression of moral indignation, he showed himself in other respects a more natural and human lover, teaching his little nephew Robert to pronounce the name of Julia, and forgetting in the absorption of his letters to London that he was temporarily disqualified from using a parliamentary frank.

As time went on, moreover, he lent himself to moderate distraction, perhaps not too unwillingly; for the role of a sighing lover is not capable of indefinite prolongation. He drove Mary to Chichester to see the 'humours of a contested election', and later they made an excursion to Goodwood—a melancholy visit, for the last time he had been there was as guest of the Duke of Richmond, and only the previous year had come the news of his sudden death in Canada. 'I never knew a man,' he informed Julia, 'of whom it could be said, with so much justice, that he was always anxious to find an excuse for the misconduct of his friends, and to put the most charitable construction on the acts of every human being.' Peel was in a mood himself to see all his friends in a rosy colour, for in forwarding to Julia a warm letter of congratulation from Goulburn, he assured her that 'of all the men with whom I was ever acquainted, he

---

[1] Peel MSS.

approaches the nearest to perfection'. This benevolence was not, however, extended to his material surroundings. They went to see Arundel Castle, but Peel was determined to find no consolation anywhere. It was a long drive and a wet day; most of the castle was modern and all in bad taste; it was completely uninhabited and partly stripped of its furniture; there were no fires; and they saw preparations for a funeral both at the lodge at which they entered and that by which they left. But time saw out even the longest days and on 30 March he wrote his last letter from the seaside, full of anticipation at being rejoined to 'her who is dearer to me than all the world beside'.[1]

He returned to London to find that his engagement was now generally known, and received a teasing letter of congratulation from Lady Shelley, wondering whether he would still be in possession of his liberty when next she saw him and whether it was true that he had boasted that his future wife was no politician. The new parliament assembled in April and sat throughout the summer to November, the latter part of the session being taken up with the sordid business of the Bill of Pains and Penalties introduced by the government under pressure from George IV for the dissolution of his marriage. But Peel had neither time nor inclination for parliamentary attendance, least of all on such a topic. In May he was paying £1,080 for a string of seventy-eight pearls as a present for his bride[2] and the wedding itself took place on 8 June in the drawing-room of 45 Upper (West) Seymour Street, near Hyde Park, where Lady Floyd had moved after the death of her husband.[3] Their honeymoon was spent at Mickleham in Surrey, on the Dorking road, where Peel had rented a country house; and from there the young couple sent their first letters to Lady Floyd, writing together on one sheet of paper as though to symbolise the unity of their happiness.

*My dear Lady Floyd,*

I must write you one line to thank you for the beautiful table which you were good enough to send to Mickleham, and I am sure you will forgive me for not having written it to you before. We find this place as comfortable as could have been expected. Thank

---

[1] Peel, *Letters*, pp. 28ff.     [2] Goulburn (misc. papers).
[3] *Ann. Reg.* 1820, Chron. 559; H. B. Wheatley, *London Past and Present*, III, 236

God Julia is quite well, and I cannot wish her anything better than that she should be as happy as I am. Ever most truly yours, my dear Lady Floyd,

ROBERT PEEL

*My dear Mamma,*
    My Robert says truly that I am well but he does not add what I do, which is that I believe myself to be the very happiest of all human beings. I am thank God united to a thoroughly aimiable Man and one *whom I adore, for whom* I would willing risk existence itself. I can not write more at present. Give my love, my best love to my dear Henry, my Aunt etc., etc., and Believe me ever

Your very affectionate<br>JULIA PEEL

I was going to write Floyd.[1]

Later in the summer they went down to Drayton, where Julia charmed old Sir Robert and demonstrated a not total inaptitude for country pursuits by making her first essays in gardening; while at other times Robert drove her round the countryside in a tilbury behind a high-spirited hunter. In September they were on the continent, despite Peel's indifferent health earlier in the year, and his father's patriotic suspicion of foreign doctors. They had every reason to be happy as they lingered out the last autumn weeks of their bridal year. He had secured the one element so far lacking in his life, the complete possession of a woman he loved and the warmth of a wife and home; and she was with a man she adored and respected. Peel was not a man to speak much about intimate matters even with friends, but when he and Julia at last took up residence again in London they could all see his pride and affection.

    The one faint cloud on their early married life was Julia's stepmother, known to the Peels as the 'Dowager'. Talkative, unabashed, and with an Irish eye for favours from above, Lady Floyd spent a good deal of time after 1820 in forwarding the interests of her stepson, Sir Henry. In pursuit of that and perhaps other ends she hovered on the fringe of the Peels' family circle in a manner that caused her son-in-law peculiar annoyance.

[1] Peel MSS.

Is it not extraordinary [he wrote sarcastically to his wife, having been met on his return to town in August 1823 by an immediate note from Lady Floyd] what information she has of our movements. The gentleman she met at dinner must have been someone actually employed by her to look out for our arrival. Only observe that the gentleman has his eyes so peculiarly constructed that he not only sees me arrive at half past six but sees me arrive 'for three weeks'. How a person coming to London for three weeks differs in appearance from one coming for ten days, I do not know.

In a letter the next day he mentioned the subject again. 'I send you another epistle from her Ladyship. What a torment she is. I really cannot conduct such a correspondence as that which would delight her—eternal bickering, explanation, reconciliation. I have therefore taken no notice of her last.' The acerbity of these comments was not due merely to prejudice on Peel's part. Julia was equally sharp-tongued on the subject of the Dowager.

> I have purposely avoided the Dow. [she wrote to her husband, when left alone at Stanhope Street in December 1824] until last night when I succeeded in getting rid of further importunities to take tea at her house by asking her for just two hours, to ours. . . . The conversation was almost entirely of America, and she quite bored me with reading pages descriptive of the outlandish scenery, but this was far better than suffering her to deal in insinuating mischief which I very soon put a stop to, but which she attempted more than once. I have ordered myself to be denied if she calls. I think her spirit of interference yet alive, though she does less to manifest it.[1]

In later years the principal trouble seems to have arisen over Sir Henry Floyd's financial difficulties. About 1825 the house in Mansfield Street was sold and the proceeds assigned to trustees; and five years later Peel was politely expressing regret to Lady Floyd at the embarrassment Sir Henry was in as a result of his own credulity, and at the same time stating firmly his inability to find employment for him in the public service.[2]

[1] Peel, *Letters*, pp. 46, 63; Peel MSS.  [2] 40401 f. 105; 40606 f. 55.

Irritating as Lady Floyd clearly was, she fortunately inspired a complete unity of sentiment in Robert and Julia Peel. They had, however, much to learn, as most young couples have. about their new relationship with each other, he perhaps more than Julia. Though seven years older and immeasurably more knowledgeable in men and affairs, he was singularly lacking in experience of women. By nature he was a sensitive person, and a young man in love (and in love Peel was a young man) is doubly sensitive. Julia was the first person, certainly the first woman, to whom he had exposed his soul, and he was therefore more vulnerable to the slightest feminine pin-prick from her than to blows from anyone else. When he once more returned to the busy professional life which he seemed to have abandoned in 1820, he was of necessity often if unwillingly absent from her. She on occasion could not withhold a tart remark about his social activities, and he at a distance could not prevent himself from suffering an exaggerated pain over trifles. 'I had a melancholy journey yesterday,' ran a characteristic passage in August 1823, 'leaving my own Julia and all that is dear to me behind me.' In a letter the very next day: 'Stanhope Street is very dull and dreary to me, more even than the office, for in Stanhope St. I see everything that reminds me every minute that I am alone.' Or again in December 1823 from Sudbourne, Lord Hertford's country house in Suffolk: 'if I could love you more, the sight of others and their odious ways would make me do so'. Yet he mixed with no apparent objection in sometimes questionable society, and not all their ways were found odious. It was on this visit that a wager was made between Lord Hertford and Henry Baring that Peel could not kill in the course of a day a pheasant, a red-legged partridge, a common partridge, a snipe, a jack-snipe, a woodcock, a wild duck, a rabbit, and a hare. Peel backed himself to the extent of three hundred guineas, began shooting at ten and had won the match before one o'clock. Betting on Peel's skill was a feature of that Sudbourne party, for on another morning he went out in pouring rain to decide whether he could get twenty brace of pheasant. He returned home at one, drenched but having won his bet, to the financial detriment of Baring who had again been the principal figure in the wagers. Huskisson had ventured a mild flutter of fifteen to ten against his colleague and also lost. 'He is an excellent shot,' he wrote to his wife, 'and has always been a lucky man.' Huskisson was neither, and there was perhaps a touch of involuntary envy in his comment.[1]

The following December Peel was again at Sudbourne in a company that included the Duke of York, Wellington, Croker, Arbuthnot, and various of their wives. The shooting was extremely good, but that once over, 'my pleasure is at an end'. Moreover, Lord Hertford being a notorious libertine, whose current mistress was Lady Strachan, Peel was shocked at the arrival at Sudbourne of Admiral Sir Richard Strachan in the role of *mari complaisant*. 'I must say I am pleased with the compliment which Lord Hertford paid to you,' Julia's husband wrote to her, 'by not asking you to this house. . . . He paid homage to your virtue and good name.' But Julia had not been altogether convinced. 'I do not understand,' she wrote, 'how the house at Sudburn which you used to describe to me as small and uncomfortable in bedroom furniture can accommodate such a very large party as the one now assembled within its adulterous walls.' Back came the reply with already a shade of pain. 'My dearest Julia, I have just received your letter, and I presume, as you consider the party here so perfect and fashionable, that my letter of yesterday may have surprised you.' But Julia could not resist a further barb. 'How will you bear to think of *one*, compared to *fifteen*. I know it is nothing in the scale.' Her husband was hurt and showed it in a ponderous masculine way.

> I should have but little satisfaction in the thought that anyone but myself had seen a letter from you to me, during my separation from you, in which there is such a sentence. . . . I will only remark upon this that I would suffer much rather than write such a sentence to you, at a time when I was absent from you. Is the repetition of the word 'fashion' meant to be severe? I only feel its injustice and unkindness if it is. Kiss my children for me. I hope they will always justly estimate my affection for them.

And to add point to the emphasis in the last sentence, he signed himself with unusual distance, 'I am, my dearest Julia, your attached husband, R.P.'

But these were mere spots on the sun that less obscured the light

[1] Peel, *Letters*, pp. 45ff.; Fay, *Huskisson*, pp. 119–20.

of their affection than revealed its intensity. Most of his letters to Julia flowed naturally and unclouded, and in no other of his writings did he show such a pleasant and unforced style, free alike from the routine jargon of office and the caution of official life. Take for example his description of Apethorpe and its owner, the Earl of Westmorland, written to his wife when at a house-party there in January 1833.

> The house is exactly like a small college in Oxford. It is a building about two hundred years old, built round a tolerably sized quadrangle which is large enough to be entirely of grass, a little field. Its equal in discomfort cannot be produced. [Nevertheless it possessed] a clergyman, a Dr. Bunney, who performs all the duties of the Groom of the Chambers, and some of those of the housemaid. His civility in showing *little conveniences* to the guests is amazing.

The whole party except for Peel and Croker consisted of relatives, —'Fanes and Chaplins with a gruff general of the name of Fisher'. The weather was wet; there was no shooting; and to avoid the solid family group of Fanes, playing whist round two tables in the drawing-room, Peel took refuge in the billiard room where Croker was playing with Lord Westmorland. Peel's bedroom, situated in a distant and lonely wing of the house, was reached at the second attempt after his candle had blown out halfway.

> Then came my bedroom, a room with family portraits, very dark by day, looking into the quadrangle. There are four doors open into the room, two of them into passages and staircases that lead I know not where. Another into a long sort of closet that has been cut out of the thickness of the wall, and seems occupied at present by nothing but spiders and rats. . . . I thought of you in the middle of the night, and how frightened you would be at the frolic of the rats in this long closet which goes round at the head of the bed.

His host, noticing a large and comfortable blaze in one of the bedrooms, had cautioned the servants against the danger of large fires.

> Conceive my horror after I had felt my way for quarter of a mile through cold blowy galleries and passages to find when I came to

bed at 12 o'clock, how Lord Westmorland's order had been executed in my room. The moment I opened the door out went the candle again, and well it might, for both the windows were wide open, and not a coal live or dead left in the grate, every one having been carefully raked out either on the hearth or on the floor.

His vignette of aristocratic country life, which could not be greatly improved even by the creator of *Jorrocks*, was rounded off by a description of the meal—a side-dish consisting of two whole infant pigs, with their accompanying trotters beside them,—and the sporting side of the establishment—'louts that are called game-keepers' and some remarkable spaniels, each with a muzzle to prevent it from eating the game and one leg tied up to prevent it from running too fast.[1]

While Peel was away he wrote almost daily to his wife, even in the press of business, and all his letters told the same story of his regrets at their separation and longing to be with her once more.

> Yesterday and the day before I dined alone at the Union Club [he wrote from London in August 1823] . . . today I mean to dine at home but I shall feel so solitary and dull without my dearest Love that I almost repent that I ordered dinner at Stanhope Street. I find it very lonely without you, my own Julia, and believe me, I sleep no better when I am away from you. . . . Tell me whenever you write exactly how you have been the whole day, my dearest, tell me whether you have had a headache, a sickness or have been, as I pray God you have been, perfectly well.

And from Sudbourne at the end of the same year: 'you know my darling that I wish you were with me and with what delight I shall clasp you to my arms on Sunday next. It would be difficult for me to say when I do not think of you. You are always present to my thoughts.' She, for her part, was equally constant and affectionate in her letters when they were parted. While at Stratfield Saye in January 1827 Peel complained of being dull for having been without a letter from her for two days running. 'It never happened before,' he added; and that was nearly seven years after their marriage.[2]

---

[1] Peel, *Letters*, pp. 139-43.
[2] Peel MSS., partly printed with some alterations in Peel, *Letters*, pp. 60, 95.

Political affairs entered little into their correspondence and when he did mention them it was mostly to give brief items of information. There was only occasionally any discussion of the matters which filled his daily routine, and when he sometimes passed on to her small pieces of confidential knowledge, it was with injunctions to mention it to nobody. What he needed and what he obtained from his wife was a respite from the world, and the constant refuge of her love and confidence. Julia Peel was not a *femme politique* after the manner of Lady Palmerston or Princess Lieven, nor did she even affect a knowledge of politics like Lady Shelley. She was content with the other half of her husband's life: marriage, the house, the children, friends, recreations, and holidays. His letters to her seemed almost deliberately to shut away everything else. Apart from his malicious little sketches of country-house life, which even so he cautioned her not to mention, the only activities he detailed with pleasure were his shooting, which she encouraged him to tell her about, and the little commissions for her or the house and garden which he undertook when in London. For the rest he wrote almost too critically of the boredom and unpleasantness of the society in which he found himself: the buffoonery of some, the loose-living of others. He had a special dislike of men who neglected their wives for the company of other women and was one of the few who were moved to any sympathy for the poor, foolish, short-sighted Duchess of Wellington, so openly abandoned by the great Duke for the attractions of sprightly ladies like Mrs. Arbuthnot and Lady Jersey.

Perhaps he dwelt on these things partly to reassure Julia; but it is hard to doubt that in so doing he was also expressing a side of his own nature. Happy in his own marriage and totally uninterested in any other woman, he took a puritanical view of the vagaries of less fortunate men and their feminine companions. 'What wickedness and what folly to undervalue and to be insensible to the affection of a wife', he wrote to Julia on one occasion. The very absorption of so much of his personal life in his home and family tended to make him more stringent in his judgements on others. Yet Peel was no outward purist, as his friendship with the Marquess of Hertford demonstrated. A man of pleasure, separated from his wife, Lord Hertford in the 1820s was a leading figure in society and through his electoral influence a peer of some weight on the tory side. It is true that he had not yet degenerated into the open profligacy which made his latter life a European scandal, and he was a person of undeniable wit and charm. As an Irish M.P. before his father's death in 1822, and as the close friend of Croker, who took upon himself unpaid the management of his estates, he came inevitably into contact with Peel, who enjoyed both his shooting parties and his company. 'I like him,' Peel wrote to Croker in September 1822. 'He is a gentleman and not an everyday one.' The references to Hertford in his letters to Julia were unusually gentle. In 1823 he sent her one of Hertford's notes. 'I have just got the enclosed from Lord Hertford, which is as usual very civil and kind. He never wishes to separate us. I have just told him we cannot be of his party.' At Hertford's death in 1842 Peel paid the debt of old friendship by sending his carriage to the funeral. Yet though many men took their wives to Sudbourne, Peel never allowed Julia to go.[1]

Quite apart from considerations of propriety, however, Julia was limited in her own social activities by the physical burden of a steadily growing family. Their first child, a daughter Julia, was born on 30 April 1821, eleven months after their marriage. A year later, on 4 May 1822, came the first boy, named inevitably Robert. Then followed four more boys in quick succession: Frederick in October 1823, named after his godfather, the Duke of York; William in November 1824; John Floyd in May 1827; and Arthur Wellesley, for whom the Duke stood godfather, in August 1829. Already by 1828 the problem of education for his flock was beginning to exercise Peel's mind, and in November he wrote to Lloyd for assistance. He wanted a clergyman as tutor for his five children, he explained. The three eldest could read and write, and understand the common rules of arithmetic; but the two youngest were very little advanced in anything. What was needed was someone who could devote the greater part of the morning to the tuition of the children in all ordinary branches of knowledge—reading, writing, arithmetic, Latin, and French—though if necessary a special teacher could be engaged for the last. It would not be convenient to have him as a resident in the house, but he hoped it would be possible for him to come daily and take charge of the children from nine or ten in the morning to four or five in the afternoon with an interval for

[1] Peel, *Letters*, ch. iii-iv.

dinner. Lloyd recommended a Mr. Tomlinson and after an interview with Peel at the end of November he was duly engaged.[1]

But there were other domestic considerations besides education.
In nine years Julia bore him six children and though her constitution
was fundamentally robust, she suffered frequently in the latter part
of this period from minor maladies, especially in 1825-6 and 1828, in
1830-1, and again in the twelve months following the birth of their
last child Eliza in April 1832. For a growing nest of young children,
and a wife whose health at times gave him anxiety, Peel thought it
essential to find peace and fresh air away from the smoke and fogs of
London. In 1821 he rented Lulworth Castle in Dorset, which besides
its seclusion and soft climate had the further advantage of sufficient
rough shooting to justify an occasional sporting party. In December
1822 Robinson, Palmerston, Huskisson, and Lord Melville were
down there—all keen sportsmen, so he told Goulburn, and enjoying
very good sport.[2] Later on the Peels began the habit of holidays at the
seaside. In 1824 he took Stone House, Broadstairs, for half a year;
and after a month *en famille* exploring the pleasures of Margate and
Ramsgate, and going by steamboat to London and back, he left the
children there while he took Julia off to Staffordshire. His father,
who had lived to see all nine of his children married and settled,
was now in his declining years finding the big house at Drayton that
he had built empty and oppressive. Every year, usually in the early
autumn, his eldest son paid him a visit, and whenever in the neighbourhood of Staffordshire he usually broke his journey for a day or
two rather than risk hurting his father's feelings. With increasing
age Sir Robert had become more demonstrative in his emotions. 'He
has more than once desired I would not forget to send you his most
affectionate regards,' his son wrote to Julia in December 1825. 'He
really loves you.' In that year they were on the Kentish coast again,
at Kingsgate near Ramsgate; early in 1826 Julia was at Brighton
with the children, and in the summer they again took a house on the
Isle of Thanet. Peel had more than once shown a desire to have a
place of their own to which they could retire, and when in 1827 Julia
expressed a casual wish to be even in winter at a nice house near the
sea, he thought seriously of purchasing a 'marine villa' overlooking
the Solent and the Isle of Wight. 'I stayed awake last night thinking

[1] 40343 fos. 303, 313, 321.     [2] Goulburn, II 13.

of the happiness we should enjoy together in a place of this kind with our little ones and not an earwig to molest us.' But nothing came of this pretty vision and for the summer of 1827 they again rented a house for the holidays, on this occasion Sir John Shelley's place at Maresfield, while Lady Shelley was abroad convalescing from an illness.[1]

The difficulty in buying a holiday retreat of their own was partly financial, for a great deal of Peel's disposable capital had gone into their new house in London. His bachelor residence in Stanhope Street, with only one guestroom, was clearly inadequate once his children began to arrive; and with the prospect of renewed political activity at the end of 1821, he wanted to find a suitable house in the neighbourhood of Whitehall. This did not prove easy, and it was not until a year later that an opportunity presented itself. Not far from his old residence in Little Scotland Yard, between Pembroke House and Montague House, was a row of old buildings known as White-hall Gardens, only a quarter of a mile from the Houses of Parliament and two hundred yards from Downing Street. They had long been scheduled for destruction by the Crown Commissioners and three new houses were built there early in the century. But the rest of the scheme was in abeyance until the remaining leases expired. In 1823 Peel bought the residential lease of one of the old houses, and Sir Alexander Cray Grant that of the adjoining one. The two owners agreed to proceed at once with the completion of the design for the improvement of Whitehall Gardens on condition of securing a crown lease from 1824 onwards. This was given and in 1823 the old houses were pulled down. Robert Smirke, the fashionable architect of the day, was engaged to draw up the plans for Peel, and with much self-volunteered advice from Croker, as ready on this as almost any other matter under the sun to deliver an opinion or sketch a draft, Peel's new house began to take shape early in 1824. Though on the same frontage as the other houses in the row, and forming in effect part of a terrace, Peel's house (No. 4) had its own individuality. Sixty feet wide, its striking feature was the great bow front rising the entire height of the building on one side, with triple windows divided by massive pillars on each of the three stories. A continuous balcony running the width of the house, and a broad columned

[1] *Shelley Diary*, II, 161.

porch, assisted in creating the florid appearance characteristic of much of Smirke's work and more representative of later Victorian architecture than the simpler Regency style favoured a generation earlier. On the garden front at the back was a corresponding bay, with steps leading down to a terrace which ran in front of the dining room along the remainder of the east side. In the interior, planned by Smirke in Grecian Doric style, the most notable room was the great gallery on the first floor, extending sixty-six feet from front to back of the house, rounded off by the bay windows at each end. Immediately below the gallery on the ground floor was Peel's library and a smaller waiting room leading off from the hall. A small garden at the back went down to the Thames whose broad waters still rose and fell over the ground where the Victoria Embankment now stands. From the bay windows of the gallery the visitor could look across the busy surface of the river to the arches of Westminster Bridge or north-east over the roof-tops to where the great dome of St. Paul's floated like a bubble in the London haze.

In December 1824 was signed the promised lease from the Department of Woods and Forests: an agreement for ninety-nine years at a yearly ground rent of £189 together with £19 6s. in lieu of land-tax. By that date the house was nearing completion. It cost in the end, or so it was said, £14,000; and if furnishings and the purchase of the original lease are taken into the reckoning, this figure is not an improbable one. In advances to the architect and builders alone during 1824 Peel paid out £7,500 in successive instalments. Expenses on this scale were more than an official salary could bear, and it may be true, as Greville recorded in March 1831, that his father came to his assistance. Even so, by the summer of 1825 Peel had so far outrun his resources that he was obliged to borrow £5,000 from his brother William which he did not pay back until five years later.[1] But the money was found and the house finished at last; and in the spring of 1825 they moved from Stanhope Street. In May he was sitting in his new library with the windows open to the garden where he had just been walking with Lord Liverpool, and writing to his absent Julia. 'Tell little Julia that the east wind had nipped her lilacs in the bud, and they are not so flourishing as when she left them. . . . I have been several times in your little

[1] 40606 f. 1; Goulburn, memo. by Peel 17 June 1825.

room. I do indeed think of you and long again to be at home, for that is my home where you and the children are.'[1] Neverthe-less, Whitehall Gardens was to be his London home until the end.[2]

## III

The long gallery of the house in Whitehall Gardens was not an empty embellishment. By 1825 Peel had already started the collection of pictures that was to be one of the great personal pleasures of his life. His interest in painting probably went back to his early years in Dublin, for when he went to Paris in 1815 Lord Whitworth had facetiously suggested that if he was in time for any plunder, he should try to get the picture by Paul Potter in the Louvre. His first recorded purchase, however, was the portrait of Monsieur Henry, Burgomaster of Utrecht, by Rembrandt, which he bought at a sale in Dublin in 1817 for the moderate sum of fifty-nine guineas. After his marriage he began systematically to acquire a set of paintings, mainly of the Dutch and Flemish school which the upheaval of the French Revolution and the Napoleonic wars was increasingly bringing on the London market. In 1821 he made at least four important purchases, including a Wynants and a Ruysdael; in 1822 over a dozen, among them paintings by Rembrandt, Jan Steen, W. Vandervelde and A. Vandervelde, Cuyp, and Teniers; and in 1823 as many again. One of the pictures bought in the latter year was a Wouverman, depicting a man loading a white horse with a faggot. On seeing it at Peel's house in July, Sir George Beaumont told him that he recollected being with Sir Joshua Reynolds when the painting was brought for his inspection. The great painter knelt down to examine it, and after looking at it attentively said, 'By God, if I were a young man, I would never rest till I had painted a picture like that.' More purchases followed in 1824 and 1825, among them Hobbema's *Château de Brederode*, for which he paid £1,400; and another by the same artist, (*The Avenue, Middelharnis*), showing a

[1] Peel, *Letters*, p. 69.
[2] For details of 4 Whitehall Gardens, see 40605, fos. 145-285; Goulburn (map and lease of December 1824): *Survey of London* (ed. M. H. Cox and P. Norman, 1930), XIII, 198-203.

village and avenue with sportsmen, which a Scotsman brought down from his native land knowing nothing about it. 'I gave him,' recorded Peel, '800 guineas for this the moment I saw it.' The year 1826 saw another large addition to his collection. In February he had the first offer of Count Pourtales' collection of Flemish pictures brought over from Paris by Smith and Emerson. Peel bought two by W. Vandervelde, a *View of Scheveling* and *A Storm*; one by A. Vandervelde, *Skating*; and one by de Hooge, paying a total of 2,100 guineas. In May, in a sale at Christie's, he paid even more for five pictures by Terborch, Metzu, Isaac Ostade, Hobbema, and Wynants. Thereafter the rate of his buying seemed to decrease, although he was constantly on the watch for interesting items coming on the market. At the Erlestoke sale in 1832, for example, he commissioned Smith, the Bond Street dealer, to bid for Reynolds's portrait of Dr. Johnson and a bust of Pope by Roubiliac. He had little hope of securing either, though he and Julia went down for the occasion and stayed at the Black Bear, the home of Sir Thomas Lawrence's childhood; but everything went auspiciously. 'People were buying gilt chairs and old china,' Peel related afterwards to Croker, 'and let me quietly buy my portrait and busts for £300 altogether.'[1] Alexander Baring was at the sale and instructed Smith, if Peel's maximum were exceeded, to buy the Reynolds at any cost for himself. Fortunately for Peel, it fell at 150 guineas, a hundred less than the limit he had given to Smith.

Among the outstanding items in Peel's collection were two famous paintings by Rubens, the *Spanish Hat* or *Chapeau de Paille*, to give it the misnomer by which it is commonly known, and the *Triumph of Silenus*. The first, having remained in the Netherlands since it was painted, was put up for auction in Antwerp in 1822 and eventually knocked down to a consortium of British dealers—Nieuwenhuys, Foster, and Smith—for about £3,000. Being, it was said, refused by George IV, it was put on show in London in 1823 and purchased by Peel later in the same year. The price was reputed to be over £3,000, though Greville was told only 2,700 guineas. According to the same authority, this sum—almost unprecedented for a half-length portrait—was paid by old Sir Robert. The *Triumph of Silenus*, once the property of Cardinal Richelieu and later of the

[1] *Croker*, II, 189.

Regent Orleans, was purchased from Smith for £1,100. A large and dominating canvas, it formed one of the more striking items in the gallery at Whitehall Gardens. Indeed, Dr. Waagen, the director of the Berlin Royal Picture Gallery who first saw it at Peel's house in 1835, thought it almost too massive for the delicate seascapes and interiors by which it was surrounded. Nevertheless, he was impressed by the skill and taste which had gone into the creation of Peel's collection.[1]

His growing reputation as a patron of the arts also brought Peel into the slowly developing field of art administration. The National Gallery was founded in 1824 and in 1827 Peel became one of the trustees. The brisk impact of his professional competence was at once apparent. Until that year there had been no formal meeting of the trustees, but within a few months of his appointment the Board held its first regular meeting. In a short time Peel's constant attendance and active interest made him the principal person to whom the officials of the Gallery turned in cases of difficulty. It was largely due to his influence that Eastlake was later appointed Keeper, and to Peel and Lord Monteagle was entrusted the selection of works from the Vernon collection. His views on policy were clear and sensible. 'We should give a preference,' he wrote to Eastlake, 'to works of sterling merit that may serve as an example to the artists of the country rather than purchase curiosities in painting.' In 1832 he urged parliament to provide funds for building a new gallery, in place of the old house in Pall Mall, riddled with dry rot, which housed the early collection. 'Of all expenditure, that like the present,' he told the Commons when supporting the official motion by Spring Rice, 'was the most adequate to confer advantage on those classes which had but little leisure to enjoy the most refined species of pleasure. The rich might have their own pictures, but those who had to obtain their bread by their labour, could not hope for such enjoyment.'[2] His political influence also served to protect the Royal Academy from the whims of George IV. At the beginning of 1830 the king, himself an enthusiastic patron of art, had the notion of changing the constitution of the Academy to allow the appointment as president of 'some distinguished amateur of the arts' with the

---

[1] Dr. Waagen, *Treasures of Art, etc.* (1854), I, 396ff.
[2] *Speeches*, II, 594; *Apollo*, July 1950 (art. *Sir Robert Peel*).

patronage vested in himself. Peel was completely opposed to any alteration in the tradition of choosing a professional painter as president of the Academy and went down to Windsor towards the end of January to discuss the subject. He told the king that he stood so well with the artists of the country, was so generally admitted to be the greatest patron that art had ever had in Britain, that it would be imprudent to risk that reputation by exciting other feelings. Soothed by this courtier-like approach, the king gave up his project. 'Well,' he said cheerfully, 'perhaps we had better not meddle with the Royal Academy.'[1]

In the selection of his own pictures Peel did not only rely on his growing knowledge and appreciation of the painter's art. He took expert advice and made use of several of the great London art dealers of the time—Buchanan, Emerson, Nieuwenhuys, and Smith. Of these the two most in his confidence perhaps were C. J. Nieuwenhuys and J. M. Smith. The former, of Anglo-Belgian descent, played an important part in bringing Dutch pictures to the London market, and it was from him that Peel secured the *Château de Brederode*, a Cuyp (cattle standing in water), a Gonzales Coques (family scene), and other paintings by de Vries, Van der Heyden, and W. Vandervelde, as well as the *Chapeau de Paille*. With Smith of Bond Street an even closer connection was formed and it was to Peel that Smith dedicated in 1829 his 'Catalogue Raisonné' of the Works of the Most Eminent Dutch, Flemish, and French Painters'. Peel obtained from Smith the *Triumph of Silenus*, and employed him as his agent at picture sales on many occasions. At the Fonthill sale in October 1823 Smith secured the Gerard Dow *Marchand de Gibier* for £1,330; and though the Franz Mieris *Lady feeding a Parrot*, for which Peel also empowered him to bid, remained unsold, Peel bought it for 350 guineas after the sale. It was through Smith also that in 1827 Peel commissioned a pair of seascapes from the Dutch marine painter Johannes Schotel, with careful directions as to subject and treatment so that they could be hung as companion-pieces to paintings already in his collection. In Peel's opinion Schotel's work was in no way inferior to that of the Vanderveldes, though the judgement of posterity has so far scarcely endorsed that comparison.[2]

[1] 40300 f. 309; *Peel*, II, 142-3.
[2] Sir Walter Armstrong, *The Peel Collection* (1904), pp. 30-2.

In later years the connection with Smith became less close Smith's fees seemed to Peel to be increasingly exorbitant, and in 1836 he wrote to tell the agent that he would no longer place any business in his hands, characteristically explained the reason, and enclosed an account from another firm of art dealers, Messrs. Seguier, for purposes of comparison. However, the breach was not absolute. Peel continued to figure in Smith's account-book for some more years; and they remained on friendly terms throughout Peel's life.[1]

Though Peel's collection was centred round the classical Dutch and Flemish painters, he was not indifferent to contemporary art. Besides Schotel, he also gave commissions to William Collins, the landscape and portrait painter. A scene of the seashore near Hastings, exhibited at the Royal Academy in 1825, was painted for Peel, who gave him 150 guineas for it; and he also commissioned at least two more works, including a frost scene exhibited in 1827, for 500 guineas. For the same sum, on the advice of Lawrence, he bought in 1827 Mulready's *Boy Firing a Cannon*, shown at the Academy that year. Benjamin Haydon was another contemporary artist to whom Peel was both patron and benefactor. In 1830 when Haydon, not for the first time, was imprisoned for debt, Peel intervened on his behalf and sent £10 to assist his wife in her immediate difficulties; and at the end of the year he commissioned him to paint *Napoleon Musing at St. Helena*. With David Wilkie, the Scottish artist, Peel came into even closer relationship. The acquaintance began in 1822 when Wilkie went to Edinburgh for the king's visit, hoping to find a subject suitable for a major canvas. Peel was anxious himself to have a painting as a memento of the occasion, but not being very pleased with the sketches produced by Wilkie the following year of the scenes in Edinburgh, he eventually chose a different subject which finally emerged as one of the artist's best historical paintings, *John Knox Preaching Before the Lords of Congregation*, bought by Peel and exhibited in 1832. For the sketches produced by Wilkie for the king, however, he had little commendation.

> I am heartily glad it is not ours [he wrote to Julia on 29 August 1823]. He has quite failed in his likeness of the King and never will succeed. He has made three different sketches in different attitudes but his

[1] Correspondence printed in *The Times*, 4 March 1937.

conception of the King's person and manner is not at all a correct one. Sir William [Knighton] was very much dissatisfied with the portrait and the King will be more so. He has chosen for the subject of his picture the delivery of the keys of Holyrood House by the Duke of Hamilton to the King. He has introduced several intended likenesses into the sketch but I defy you to guess one of them. This failure of course entirely spoils the picture. It makes it disagreeable.[1]

However, this did not prevent Wilkie's appointment the same year as Limner to the King for Scotland, in which Peel acted as perhaps something more than the mere official channel of communication; and for the rest of his career Wilkie was a constant correspondent of Peel's and made frequent suggestions for the purchase of paintings. When he died in 1841 Peel took the chair at a meeting called to subscribe for a monument to his memory, and spoke eloquently of Wilkie as a man and as a painter.[2]

But among living British painters Peel's greatest patronage went to Sir Thomas Lawrence. Their acquaintance began in 1820 when Lawrence painted a seated portrait of Sir Robert Peel; and during the next ten years he produced no fewer than fifteen paintings for Peel, all portraits. It was said that Peel asked him to produce a landscape but was refused; but the set of contemporary portraits he created for Peel more than made up for this refusal. Even before his long gallery with its red wallpaper was ready for hanging, Peel started his series of eminent figures in 'fine arts, sciences, war and law', as he once described it. Lord Eldon and Lord Stowell were the first for whom he secured Lawrence's brush, and in 1824 he was planning a continuation with portraits of Sir Walter Scott, Lawrence himself, Davy the scientist, and the Duke of Wellington. Lord Liverpool, Aberdeen, Southey, Huskisson, and Canning were added to the list in due course. Aberdeen's picture, Peel told his wife in 1830, 'certainly is the finest portrait in the world'; though other less partial observers were perhaps more impressed by that of Canning. With such an array of eminent subjects Lawrence's studio must have seemed at times almost like the cabinet offices. At one stage Wellington and Canning were being painted at the same

[1] Peel MSS.    [2] W. Bayne, *Wilkie* (1903), pp. 96-7, 145, 182; *Apollo*, loc. cit.

time, a circumstance which enabled Canning to hear a pleasant anecdote about his fellow sitter. Lawrence had originally begun to portray the duke holding a watch in his hand, waiting for the Prussians at Waterloo. Coming into the studio one day Canning found that the watch had been painted over and a telescope put in its place. On being asked the reason, Lawrence told him that as soon as the Duke had understood why the watch was there, he observed, 'That will never do. I was *not* "waiting" for the Prussians at Waterloo. Put a telescope in my hand, if you please, but no watch.'[1] Canning's own portrait was not finally completed until 1829, and Lawrence was still giving it some finishing touches shortly before his last illness. In a note of 3 June 1829 he asked Peel for a loan of the Speaker's mace and for his further assistance in 'standing for the raised hand, that there may be no record out of your own family of any other form being resorted to, for the completion of the portrait'.

Besides this set of contemporary celebrities, Lawrence was also commissioned by Peel to paint a number of family portraits. Julia Peel he painted twice. The first, a three-quarter length portrait in white drapery against a landscape, was exhibited in 1825. Though not perhaps among the artist's more inspired works (Lawrence was not a good painter of women), the husband of his subject could see no fault in it. He thought it, he told Lawrence, 'eminently beautiful. I wish for no alteration in a single fold even of the gown. I wondered how it was possible to blend so much of simplicity and modesty with all that is elegant and refined.'[2] But this was the lover rather than the connoisseur speaking. The second and better-known portrait of Julia, exhibited in 1827, was a kitcat designed as a companion piece to the *Chapeau de Paille*. Though Lawrence failed to rival the vivid physical personality of Susanne Fourment, the portrait was a bright, gay picture, not entirely unworthy to be placed beside the Rubens masterpiece. Attired in a large black hat with red plumes, with fur-lined purple cloak half-open to show the white gown underneath, with a red camellia in her bosom and heavily gemmed bracelets on her arm, Julia is shown at the height of her loveliness, her dark chestnut hair in ringlets, her brown eyes and

[1] *Macmillan's Magazine*, XXXI, 9 (Art. by Stapleton on Sir Robert Peel).
[2] G. S. Layard, *Sir Thomas Lawrence's Letter-Bag* (1906), p. 191.

regular features enhanced rather than obscured by the opulence of the costume and jewellery. Despite the probability that Lawrence infused something of the painter's art into the comparison, it is difficult not to credit that Peel's purchase of the *Chapeau de Paille* as well as his marriage to Julia Floyd owed much to an innate attraction to this particular type of feminine beauty. The following year, 1828, Lawrence painted their first daughter, Julia, then a child of seven, and already showing a clear resemblance to her mother. She was depicted seated against a landscape with a dog in her lap. The dog, 'one of the Duke of Marlborough's breed', was not a member of the Peel household, and was so shy that a naval A.D.C. of the Duke of Clarence had to be present during the sittings to keep it quiescent. The portrait of the first Sir Robert was in terms of painterly skill one of the most successful of all the Peel family pictures. It showed the old baronet seated in a chair, holding a paper, his hair curling and grey, the face strong and kindly, with large nose, strong mouth and chin, blue eyes and ruddy complexion. Finally there was one of Peel himself, shown at the Academy in 1825 and familiarised by its reproduction at the hands of the engraver Samuel Cousins, depicting Peel standing at a table with his left hand on his hip. It shows not only the elegance of clothes characteristic of Peel's early manhood, but also the growing maturity of the face with its strong slightly convex nose and determined chin beneath the upswept curling auburn hair.[1]

In the half-dozen years between November 1823, when Eldon's portrait was commissioned, and Lawrence's death in 1830, a not inconsiderable part of his work was thus undertaken expressly for Peel. Indeed, Lawrence received more commissions from Peel than from any other person apart from George IV, and it was with complete truth that Peel was described by the urbane academician on one occasion as 'the second patron of my pencils'. The total of fifteen Lawrence portraits which Peel acquired formed a large item in Peel's expenditure on art purchases in this period. He paid Lawrence 250 guineas for Wellington's portrait and the same for the first of

---

[1] The portraits of Peel and his father are in the possession of Earl Peel. The portrait of Julia Peel painted 1827 was sold by the fourth Sir Robert Peel about 1896 and is now in the Frick Collection, New York. See *The Frick Collection* (Pittsburgh 1949), I, 36.

Julia's.[1] Moreover, in the course of their transactions together Lawrence became his client's friend and adviser. Peel and his wife visited Lawrence's house at Russell Square, and the last time Lawrence went out to dine was at Whitehall Gardens on Saturday 2 January 1830. He had not been in good health during the previous few days and on returning from the Peels that night he complained of fatigue. He continued unwell the next day or two, was taken ill on the Wednesday and died the next day, 7 January. It was Peel who conveyed the news to the king; and at the funeral at St. Paul's a fortnight later he acted as one of the pall-bearers. In his will Lawrence directed that his collection of paintings which he valued at £20,000 should be offered in turn to the king, to Peel, and to the Earl of Dudley for £18,000. Since none of the three accepted the offer, the collection was sold by auction, but Peel managed to secure out of it two Vandykes and some drawings by Rubens.[2]

The main series of Lawrence portraits was transferred to Drayton after his father's death, and the central feature of the Whitehall Gardens gallery remained the Dutch and Flemish paintings. In its final shape the London collection comprised about a hundred pictures, half of which were hung in the long gallery and the remainder in the drawing-room, the dining-room (including five Reynolds portraits and one by Wilkie), and elsewhere in the house.[3] From 1830 the reputation of his collection was beginning to spread and Peel delighted to show visitors round his gallery and point out the special features of the different paintings. Greville, who met Peel in November 1833 at a house-party at Buckenham, went to see his pictures in the following March—'his collection,' he thought, 'is excellent, and does honour to his taste'. The compliment was not undeserved. However much he profited by the judgement of artists and art-dealers, Peel clearly had an appreciation of certain aspects, at any rate, of the painter's craft. He made himself a connoisseur in the sense of having a wide knowledge of art and artists, especially of the great Dutch and Flemish schools. His purchases were never indiscriminate; he knew what he wanted and was always ready to discard and exchange pictures for something better. He took advice and made much use of agents; but he could also act on his own

[1] 40605 fos. 422, 480.     [2] D. E. Williams, *Lawrence* (1831), II, 489-566.
[3] Goulburn (inventory of pictures at Whitehall Gardens, July 1850).

judgement. His taste in contemporary painting was perhaps more questionable, but this is a peculiar and uncertain field where more knowledgeable critics than he ever professed to be have shown their fallibility. But of the satisfaction he found in his pictures there can be no doubt. One of the few personal documents he left behind was a manuscript notebook, written in his own hand and obviously for his private use, containing a list of his pictures, with prices, dates of purchase, and various notes and details concerning them.[1] He had other aesthetic tastes. He attended concerts and formed the tolerably good library that a man of his education and means might be expected to have; but his paintings went deeper than any of these. For a man who spent a great part of his life reading and writing official correspondence, and listening to the endless flow of question, answer, and debate in the House of Commons, it was perhaps natural to find greater solace in the visual stimulus of pictorial art than in the abstractions of literature. Like his enjoyment of the country scenes and pastimes or the care he bestowed on his new house, his love of painting derived from the same strain, both sensuous and sensitive, that showed in the relationship with his wife. There were deeper currents in the calm and successful politician, as there had been in the cool good-natured schoolboy, than observers often realised.

Yet there had been little in Peel's upbringing to have implanted in him any special interest in art. It was a spontaneous and personal development and for that reason the more revealing. The artistic strain in the third Robert Peel was a notable departure from the utilitarian tradition of his father and grandfather; and Sir Robert Peel's generous assistance to his eldest son in building and adorning his house in Whitehall Gardens was all the more creditable since, as Greville justly observed, it was 'for objects which it might have been thought he would have under-valued'. Yet it would be a mis-conception of the puritan tradition in English life to deny any hereditary influence. It was not entirely out of keeping, for all Greville's remark, with the practical sense of his family that Peel turned to painting and architecture rather than to the abstract arts. An appreciation of artistic achievement that had colour and physical form was at only one remove from the ingenuity and effort that had

[1] Goulburn. The bulk of Peel's collection of paintings are now in the National Gallery to which they were sold in 1871 by the third baronet.

produced printed calico and spinning machines. Nor was it entirely accidental perhaps that Peel preferred the classical Dutch school with its robust realism, and its emphasis on contemporary humanity and the living landscape of towns, windmills, woodlands and ships, mirroring nature rather than swathing it in romantic or classical allegory or seeking to pierce through it to ineffable depths of passion and mysticism. Between the Protestant Dutch burghers that patronised Rembrandt and Jan Steen, and the Protestant Lancashire Peels was perhaps no very great distance. But if it is true that in every art-collector there is an imprisoned artist, then Peel's rigorous classical and mathematical training, followed without a break by entry on an active political and administrative career, had possibly prevented an even more surprising departure from the family tradition. Instead, the main stream of his emotions and energies was directed to the supreme art of all, politics. The medium was to be life itself, the canvas contemporary society. It is difficult not to believe that what constantly drew him back to public life, despite its personal animosities and perennial sordidness, was a deep pleasure in political creativity.

# 8

# BACK IN HARNESS

The affair of the 'Queen's trial' that in 1820 almost destroyed the Liverpool ministry was in itself an index of the weakness and un-popularity of the government. Lacking the confidence of the king, and without sufficient control of parliament, it allowed its prestige and authority to become the battleground of private and party animosities that could scarcely have taken on a more degrading form. After Caroline's departure from England in 1814 her mode of living had procured her a European notoriety; and by July 1819 the government was in possession of evidence which virtually established the fact of her continued adultery with the Italian, Bergami, whom she had made her chamberlain. From the moment of his accession George IV pressed frantically for a divorce which would prevent her from returning to England and taking her place as queen. The cabinet consented to the omission of her name from the prayers for the royal family included in the liturgy, but were reluctant to embark on public proceedings which would create an open scandal and provoke discussion of the king's own discreditable private life. As the months passed by, however, they were pushed inexorably towards the thing they dreaded by the passions of all the parties involved. The king, supported by his own favourites and advisers, continued to insist on a divorce and showed increasing hostility to the ministers when they hesitated. Brougham, the chief legal adviser to the queen, whom the cabinet endeavoured to use as an intermediary for contriving a private agreement, deceived both sides in the pursuit of some tortuous scheme of his own. Finally Caroline herself, prompted by extreme radicals such as Alderman Wood of London, in June 1820 took the disastrous step of coming to

England and setting herself up as the heroine of the London mob. All hope of a negotiated settlement having passed, the government introduced in July a Bill of Pains and Penalties in the House of Lords. From August to October the newspapers regaled the nation with the minute details of royal divorce evidence. In November the Lords passed the third reading of the bill by only nine votes and the government announced that they would no longer proceed with the measure. Immediately afterwards parliament was adjourned till the new year.

In point of reputation neither the king nor the queen had much to lose. The government had; and it was the government that emerged with greatest discredit, despite Liverpool's admirable handling of the difficult and distasteful proceedings in the Lords. The upper classes in England knew too much of the queen's private life to doubt her guilt; but they did not all approve of legislative action against a princess who had suffered a long series of slights and petty persecutions, and whose technical infidelities were at least no greater than those of her husband. George IV as an injured husband was in a singularly unconvincing role. The lower classes, partly because until 1820 the newspaper press in Britain had been silent about Caroline's life abroad, believed heartily in her innocence; and led on by irresponsible radical politicians, who even carried some of the whigs along with them in the general opportunism, the popular movement became an immense demonstration against the government. At the same time the issue deprived the cabinet of its most talented member. Canning, who had been opposed to the proceedings in the Lords, proffered his resignation in June, and though desired by the king to remain in office absented himself from the cabinet and travelled on the continent during the 'trial'. On his return to England in December he resigned his office on the India Board. The king, whose anger with his ministers had been increased by their failure to carry the bill, was already nourishing the idea of a change of government, and the defection of Canning, whatever its motives, seemed the final stroke. Indeed, only the lack of an acceptable alternative saved the ministry; for there was no alternative other than the whigs. Much as George IV had grown to dislike the Liverpool cabinet, he could scarcely bring in the party that had been championing his wife; and Canning showed no sign of joining the opposition.

Nevertheless, the storm seemed bound to break as soon as parliament assembled in January, and the depleted front bench in the lower House hardly appeared an adequate force with which to meet it. Apart from Castlereagh, on whom fell the main burden of representing the government, there was Vansittart, who rarely spoke except on his own subject; Bragge Bathurst, who was a nonentity; Pole, who lacked command either of himself or his audience; and Robinson, who was incapable of fighting.

On 15 December Croker had an interview with the king, who told him of Canning's retirement and of his own desire expressed to the Prime Minister that Peel should be asked to fill the vacancy. The same evening Croker called on Peel and warned him of what was in the wind. Peel had heard nothing and showed no enthusiasm.[1] The same day, however, Liverpool wrote from Wellington's country house at Stratfield Saye asking for an interview the following week. On 18 December the meeting took place and after explaining the course the government meant to adopt in the queen's affair, the Prime Minister formally offered him Canning's post of president of the Board of Control with a seat in the cabinet. Peel declined; though he did so in a friendly manner, and promised to keep the offer secret. He said he thought the government had been wrong in removing the queen's name from the liturgy and in refusing to pay her the customary honours on her return to England, thus prejudging her cause, when it was in fact intended to proceed against her in a semi-judicial manner by means of the Bill of Pains and Penalties. The case against the queen was now materially different; but as he had not initially supported the ministry, he did not feel he could take as high a line as they were now justified in doing, if only in self-defence, against their parliamentary critics. To join the cabinet at such a juncture would not be advantageous to the government or creditable to himself. 'I had no wish,' he recorded afterwards, 'to take a hostile part against the Government but to be enabled to express my opinions with respect to the proceedings in the case of Queen Caroline and to take a course unfettered by any official connection with the government.' He also added that he was in any case not very anxious for office, and that if a sense of duty should induce him at a later date to enter the ministry, he

[1] *Croker*, I, 175.

was indifferent what post he would take.[1] The cabinet, not unfairly, took his answer as holding out a prospect of ultimate union; and though Arbuthnot and Castlereagh were in favour of an approach to Lord Grenville, it was finally decided to make no further effort to strengthen the administration. It would be a mistake, thought Liverpool, to knock on too many doors. The vacancy left by Canning was filled by Bragge Bathurst, the Chancellor of the Duchy of Lancaster, as an interim measure until the fate of the government was decided in the ensuing session.[2]

Politicians who knew merely the bare fact of Peel's refusal, speculated in mundane fashion whether it was because he was still absorbed in his young and pretty wife, or because he thought the ministry could not stand.[3] It is probably true that in addition to political scruples, he had no great desire to return at once to the grind of office hours and compulsory parliamentary attendance. He had been married only seven months and Julia was expecting her first baby in the spring. Nevertheless, there is no evidence that he shared Canning's pessimism on the fate of the ministry; and he certainly had no intention of standing idly by to wait for the outcome of the parliamentary battle. He was prevented from being present at the debate on Lord Archibald Hamilton's motion of 25 January, condemning the omission of the queen's name from the liturgy, on which the government secured an unexpected majority of 101; but he intervened a fortnight later in the debate on Lord Tavistock's resolution criticising the whole course of proceedings against the queen. It was his first public utterance on the subject; and while he repeated what he had said privately to Liverpool— that he disagreed with the treatment of the queen in the interval before the Bill of Pains and Penalties was introduced—he argued the necessity of that measure. In view of the evidence in their possession, the ministers were bound to institute an enquiry, and an attempt to evade it would only have made an enquiry more certain. The only two ways open to them were by bill or impeachment; and the latter was juridically the more questionable of the two. The queen herself, however, he treated with careful restraint. His sharpest

---

[1] 40304 fos. 1-4, partly printed *Peel*, I, 298; *Bathurst*, 490 (Arbuthnot's account of the interview).

[2] Pellew, *Sidmouth*, III, 338.     [3] cf. *Colchester*, III, 202.

strictures were for the men who had led her on—'had seized her arm in order to shake the throne'—and for the popular opinion, 'fickle inconstant and ungrateful', which the supporters of the resolution endeavoured to make the criterion of parliamentary conduct. The debate was finished the next day, 6 February, and resulted in an even greater ministerial majority than in January. Peel's speech was not the most effective in the debate. That honour could be claimed by Castlereagh, who on the second evening gave a long exposition of the remarkable part played by Brougham in the negotiations preceding the introduction of the Pains and Penalties Bill. The value of Peel's action was that he came forward clearly and without reservation as an advocate of the ministry; and politicians searching for significant straws noted that at the same time he shifted his seat in the House of Commons from the upper isolated benches he had previously been occupying to his former place in the rear of the Treasury Bench.[1] The Tavistock motion was the crucial one for which the opposition mustered its full strength; and though a third effort was made a week later to restore the queen's name to the liturgy, the government again succeeded by a comfortable majority. It was clear that, all argument aside, the country gentlemen were not prepared for Caroline's sake to overthrow the ministers and let in the whigs.

The conclusion of the queen's affair, however, left the way open for a renewal of the old Catholic controversy, in which the fate of the ministry was not at stake and the issue in consequence more uncertain. Yet it was a controversy to which Peel was more committed than any other leading Protestant in the House of Commons. Despite the growing indifference of a large part of public opinion, it was impossible for him to abdicate from the position he had secured in 1817. Both his public record and his duty as member for Oxford University thrust him once more into the leadership. He took his place once more in the Protestant van, but with less immediate hope and a more profound sense of the ultimate victory of emancipation than ever before.

On 28 February Plunket introduced a motion for a committee of the whole House to examine Roman Catholic disabilities. His speech was in large measure an analysis of Peel's arguments four years

[1] Buckingham, *Memoirs*, I, 121; *Ann. Reg.*, 1821, History 15.

earlier and was indeed directed personally at him. It had the perhaps intended effect of bringing Peel to his feet for a prompt reply. Yet it was noticeable that his language was unusually restrained, and some at least of his supporters thought that he showed a consciousness of the defensive position into which the opponents of emancipation were now being forced.[1] Early in the speech he assured the House that 'he had never viewed the question but as a choice of evils; nor had he been ever satisfied with the alternative proposed; but it had grown out of the anomalous state of society which he found pre-existing'. Nevertheless, he was bound to state his convictions. The principle of exclusion of certain classes of subjects had been inaugurated at the Revolution. It was not merely a question of Catholics but of dissenters and Quakers. It was not merely a question of political danger, but of the actual position of the Established Church. 'In making laws to govern this moral and religious country, was he to exclude from his notice all considerations of religion?' It was this that justified the legal monopoly of the legislature and high public office by members of the Established Church. Having stated the groundwork of his case, however, he ended on a lower key. He did not think that the troubles of Ireland were due to the penal laws. If he thought emancipation would lead to concord in that country, he would be the first to hail its success; but no result of the debate could give him unqualified satisfaction. Though he was bound to hope for the success of opinions in which he honestly believed, that success would be mingled with regret at the disappointment of others. If emancipation was carried, no one would rejoice more, should his predictions be unfounded.

It was a personal confession rather than a rallying-call to a party; and not surprisingly there was some disappointment over it among his followers. It is unlikely that it swayed many votes. When the division took place Plunket's motion was carried by 227 to 221, a slender majority of six votes, but a majority all the same. Nevertheless, Peel continued to lead the opposition throughout the stages of the bill which Plunket subsequently introduced in March. Yet the little knot of Protestant speakers he headed—Sir William Scott, Bankes, and Wetherell—was a frail defence against Plunket, Mackintosh, Grant, Castlereagh, and Canning; and every step in the progress

[1] *Colchester*, III, 218.

of the emancipation measure received the support of the House by majorities that tended to increase rather than diminish. Indeed, an amendment by Peel in committee to exclude Roman Catholics from the Privy Council and judicial offices was negatived by nineteen votes, and one by Goulburn to exclude them from governorships of the colonies by forty-three. Tenacious to the end, however, Peel made one final effort at the third reading on 2 April with a speech that was considerably more forthright and compelling than that of February. If now, he argued, they were about to adopt a new system and grant political power, it would be necessary to consider what should be the relationship between the Catholics and the State. It was no obscure sect, but the Church of the greater part of Europe, and though the Protestant establishment in England was not in danger, the position in Ireland was far different. There a kingdom, only united twenty years ago to the rest of Britain, was separated from it by a great span of history. 'In the Catholic island we had to maintain a Protestant establishment.' By the bill the representative part of Ireland was certain to become Catholic, and attempts by the Protestant majority in parliament to control Irish representation would only prolong and deepen religious animosities. There were securities in the bill but those securities had been denounced by the Roman Catholic clergy of Ireland, and he ventured to prophesy that they could not be put into execution. It was because the bill would not have the effect of consolidating England and Ireland, or of uniting British subjects, that he was bound to oppose it.

It was an effective speech; but it would have been more effective had it come at the beginning instead of at the end of the bill's progress. As it was, the third reading was passed by nineteen votes. For the first time the House of Commons had given its approval not only to the principle but to an actual measure of emancipation. It was a portent that no subsequent proceedings could obscure. The bill, it is true, was later defeated in the Lords, where Liverpool, Eldon, and Sidmouth all strongly opposed it. Yet how long the upper House could continue to resist a movement that had secured the support of the House of Commons was a question which from then onward continued to haunt the intellectual champions of the Protestant cause. With a declining interest on the subject among the people at large, and a growing conviction in favour of emancipation among the political community, there could in the end be only one answer.

The Catholic debates, while they obscured, did nothing to cure the intrinsic weakness of the government in the House of Commons. The difficulties encountered there in the latter part of the session on such matters as corn, currency, legal reform, and finance, once more emphasised the urgent need for a reinforcement of the Front Bench. Already in March there had been some discussion in ministerial circles of a general reshuffle which would put Vansittart innocuously at the Board of Control, Peel at the Exchequer, Canning at the Admiralty, and Melville at the Home Office in place of Sidmouth who was anxious to retire. On the surface the scheme had much to recommend it but it encountered an unexpected and curious opposition from Castlereagh. He objected to the proposal to make Peel Chancellor of the Exchequer on the grounds that it was in peacetime one of the most important positions in the cabinet and that Peel's possession of it would seriously diminish Castlereagh's influence as leader of the House of Commons. He brought forward other factitious, and not altogether just arguments, such as Peel's inexperience in financial matters and his failure to give steady support to the government during the session; but it was clear that the crux of his attitude was that Peel might raise a party round himself in the Commons and overthrow the authority of the leader of the House. The project in consequence hung fire; but during April Canning lent his support, perhaps not quite disinterestedly, to the move for putting Peel at the Exchequer and Liverpool himself was still disposed to favour the idea. About the beginning of May, however, the matter was discussed once more between Liverpool and Castlereagh, and in the face of the latter's reiterated view that Peel's appointment would 'make an opposition' in the Commons and so weaken rather than strengthen the government, the Prime Minister finally put the matter out of consideration. To credit Peel of all people with disloyalty and factious ambition was a remarkable attitude for Castlereagh to adopt. One rational explanation might be that he feared the enhancement of the Protestant interest in the government if Peel, commonly regarded as the head of that party in the Commons, were given one of the great offices of state. Yet the same consideration could equally well have occurred to Canning, who nevertheless supported Peel's promotion; and in any case Liverpool's government was expressly based on the principle of disregarding the Catholic issue in ministerial appointments. Vansittart, who held the post of Chancellor and sat in the Commons, was also a Protestant; and if Castlereagh's estimate of the intrinsic importance of the Chancellorship of the Exchequer was correct, his objection held the unspoken implication that he could dominate Vansittart but not Peel. It was evident that Castlereagh was greatly disturbed by the discussion of changes in the cabinet, and perhaps the true explanation of his otherwise not easily comprehensible hostility to Peel is that his mind was already infected with the psychopathic distrust and persecution-mania that was to bring tragedy only a year later. As leader of the Commons and heir to the premiership, however, his views could not be overridden; and the possibilities of reconstructing the cabinet on a firmer basis were thereby considerably restricted. By the middle of May Liverpool had made up his mind not to offer Peel the Exchequer but to attempt a more modest arrangement under which Melville was to move to the Home Office, Canning to take his place at the Admiralty, and Peel to be offered the Board of Control.[1] Even this, however, encountered difficulties at every point.

Canning's resignation in December had revived the king's old suspicion that he had been the queen's lover, and he now conceived his personal honour involved in refusing to readmit him to the cabinet. He disliked the prospect of Sidmouth's retirement, and in this he was supported by Eldon, who expressed his own intention of resigning if Sidmouth left the government. Few of the ministers in fact shared Liverpool's zeal for recalling Canning. With Peel the plan met with equally little favour. At the end of May the Prime Minister sent for him and, as he told Croker afterwards, 'made him an offer of Cabinet office but that it was done in a strange shuffling hesitating sort of way, that nothing specific was offered, but that he conjectured from the style and the expressions, that Lord Liverpool referred, in his own mind, to the Board of Control'. Peel refused in terms as vague as those in which the offer was made. He assured Liverpool that he was well disposed towards the government but from the state of his health he had no great wish to take office. However, before he left, he said he would like to know what

[1] *Arbuthnot Journal*, I, 82, 89-94.

cabinet changes were in contemplation and what office was to be offered to him, before he made any final answer.[1] To Croker he explained that as he had refused before when the government was in danger, it would be shabby to accept now that the vessel had righted itself. More important still, he did not think he could be of much use in that particular office, not having much taste or turn for debate unless obliged by his departmental duties to take part. However, the door was not entirely closed, and it was not until 4 June that Peel went to Liverpool and made a clear verbal refusal of the India Board. The Prime Minister asked whether that would apply to anything else he should offer; but Peel observed that there would be time enough to decide when an offer was made. He thought Liverpool was peevish and embarrassed, and was inclined to believe—what others had already concluded—that the Prime Minister was acting not altogether straightforwardly.

There was, in fact, some reason for Liverpool to show signs of strain. His advocacy of Canning had led to unpleasantness with the king; and he had become involved in a brush with Sidmouth over the question of a lucrative sinecure for the latter's son in which the king had taken Sidmouth's part. Peel's refusal was the more awkward since the Board of Control was the one post to which Canning had made it clear that he would not return; and until Canning's future was decided, it was not easy to offer Peel any alternative. At the same time he still had to reckon with Castlereagh's jealousy. In his mood of morbid suspicion the Foreign Secretary showed some resentment that the Prime Minister had not specifically mentioned the Board of Control to Peel at their first interview and was inclined to suspect that Liverpool wished to return to the original plan of reconstruction. Finally there was a not altogether ungrounded fear that the king would press for Peel's immediate entry into the cabinet as a means of excluding Canning. In a defensively written letter to the king on 10 June Liverpool told him that Peel's refusal had been chiefly on grounds of health; and that he personally could not feel that Peel's position could be impaired by the acceptance of a post which both Canning and Harrowby had held after being Secretaries of State. What, indeed, were Peel's precise motives in declining the Board of Control was a subject of much speculation

[1] *Arbuthnot Journal*, I, p. 97.

among his friends. It is unlikely that he had invented the pretext of health. He had not been well the previous year and there were renewed symptoms, chiefly of inflammation of the eyes, in 1821 and 1822. Eight years of incessant manuscript correspondence, following hard on his intensive reading at Oxford, had left their mark on even his unusual physical endowments. He told Liverpool that his eyes were so bad at times that he could not read at all by artificial light and very little during the day.[1] It is also probable that he was ruffled by Liverpool's devious behaviour. Yet almost certainly the chief deterrent was the character of the post offered to him. Unlike most other departments of state the India Board provided little scope for creative work. Perhaps he remembered a phrase from the past: 'nor any, at any time, but what is really efficient and of high consideration'. Cyril Jackson was dead but his words were still good. Goulburn frankly regretted Peel's decision; Croker and Manners Sutton were more inclined to accept Peel's view of the special disadvantages of the only post he had been offered, though still sorry that he had declined it. But Peel kept his own counsel. To Bathurst, the elder statesman of the Liverpool cabinet, who had written to press him to join the ministry, he replied on 1 June with friendly generalities.

> Many considerations induce me to prefer, I am afraid, I must say, idleness to the occupation of public life, but believe me that the want of a sincere goodwill towards the government, or of strong personal regard for those who compose it, is not among the number. Your letter alone would persuade me not to act precipitately, but I think I shall never persuade myself to exchange Cannon Row[2] for Lulworth as a summer residence.

Trying to wring some drop of significance from this, Bathurst sent the letter to Wellington for his opinion on whether it constituted a refusal of a particular office or a general refusal. The Duke was not given to psychological subtleties and professed to see nothing very indicative in the final antithesis. Indeed, he expressed the opinion that Peel would probably accept if his friends used their influence or even remained neutral. In fact all his friends seemed to have favoured his accepting. Croker, moreover, without any authorisation, went

[1] *ibid.*, p. 97.     [2] Where the India Board was located.

so far as to inform Bloomfield, the Keeper of the Privy Purse, that Peel's refusal was limited to the India Board, and even further in telling Melville that what Peel really wanted was the Exchequer or the Home Office. This instance of Croker's incurable meddling would have secured him little gratitude from Peel; but in any case Liverpool was not prepared at that juncture to make any appointment that might exclude Canning or alienate Castlereagh.[1]

In the end the king had his way, though he built a bridge for his adversary by offering to make Canning Governor-General of India within a year, if that would gratify him. Liverpool's wife died in the middle of June and harassed almost to the point of collapse the Prime Minister finally agreed to defer a decision. The rest of the cabinet busied themselves with alternative plans to bring in some of the Grenville connection. They were not prepared to make the immediate return of Canning a matter of confidence, and indeed would have been prepared if necessary to go on with Liverpool. The summer of 1821 saw the coronation, the death of Caroline, and the unhappy bungling over the arrangements for her funeral procession through London. But by the autumn tempers had cooled on both sides. The king told Castlereagh that he would be prepared to admit Canning to the cabinet as a temporary measure while awaiting his appointment to India. By November the breach between the court and the Prime Minister, which had been steadily widening ever since 1820, seemed closed at last.[2] On 26 November Liverpool and Castlereagh (now Lord Londonderry) went down to Brighton to lay before the king their plans for the reconstruction of the cabinet. This time the arrangements went through without a single obstruction. Lord Hastings was desirous of leaving India and Canning was prepared to replace him. At home the government had secured the support of the Grenvillites. Though Lord Grenville was now too old and indifferent for office, his party formally joined the government. The Marquess of Buckingham received a dukedom and Charles Wynn went to the India Board. For the rest, Sidmouth thankfully resigned the Home Department but retained a seat in the cabinet. As his successor there could be only one man. The question was whether he would at last accept. Peel was not without warning

[1] *Croker*, I, 186–91; *Bathurst*, 497–8; *Hobhouse*, pp. 58–62.
[2] *Geo. IV Letters*, II, 466–76.

of what was coming. Three times during November Croker had written to him expressing his certitude that in the forthcoming negotiations with the king, Peel's name would be approved as a successor to Sidmouth.[1] On 28 November came the expected summons. This time it was a formal written offer in the king's name of the seals of the Home Department. 'I should hope,' ended the Prime Minister, with perhaps an intentional significance, 'that this office, from the nature of the business which belongs to it, would not be unacceptable to you, and I need not, I trust, say how gratifying it would be to my feelings to be again placed in the relation to you of habitual intercourse and confidence.'

There was no hesitation on this occasion. The messenger that brought Liverpool's offer to Lulworth started back the same day with Peel's acceptance. After a reference to 'the habits of retirement in which I have indulged since I quitted Ireland, and the happiness of my domestic life', and an assurance of his attachment to the ministry whether his name had been considered for office or not, Peel continued:

> As however, the offer has been made to me, and as my health is so far improved that I can on that account make no objection to public life, I will not prove myself unworthy of that signal confidence with which the King has honoured me, by either yielding to the fears of my own unworthiness, or by taking that course which if I consulted merely my private inclinations, I might probably have preferred.[2]

After three and a half years of 'idleness' he was back in the saddle once more, and Julia was to have her first experience of what it was like to be a minister's wife.

## II

One of Peel's first thoughts was for his own family. His brother William had entered parliament in 1817, having through the good offices of the government and the payment of about a thousand pounds expenses by Sir Robert, succeeded to Lord Desart's seat at

[1] *Croker*, I, 216-17.    [2] 38195 f. 104, quoted *Peel*, I, 300.

295

Bossiney. Though chosen to second the address in the king's speech in 1819, he had so far made no mark on the House of Commons, apart from gaining some notoriety at the contested election for Tamworth in 1818 when he and his father secured both seats against the opposition of Lord Charles Townshend. It was the first time that the Peels had monopolised the representation of the borough. The Townshend party were resentful and accused Sir Robert of going back on a previous assurance; and Mr. Floyer, a local magistrate, published some libellous letters reflecting on Sir Robert's dealings with a Tamworth bank that had failed in 1816. William Peel at one point challenged Floyer to a duel, and after another publication by Floyer in October 1818, followed him down to Worthing with George Dawson, his brother-in-law, and threatened to horsewhip him. For this Peel and Dawson were eventually fined and imprisoned for one month by the King's Bench in 1820. But the Peels later secured satisfaction for this when they won a libel action against Floyer and saw him sentenced to a fine of £1,000 and three months' imprisonment in the Marshalsea. As might be expected, these events roused considerable feeling in Tamworth, and at the next election, in 1820, old Sir Robert retired rather than face another contest like the last. Townshend and William Peel were returned unopposed, and with a peaceful division of the borough, harmony was restored. Indeed, William Peel—young, handsome, high-spirited—secured more genuine popularity in the town than his father had ever done; and being resident at Bonehill, near Tamworth, was better known to the inhabitants of the town than his elder brother.

It was this active and volatile young man whom Peel thought to divert into more official habits by appointing as Under-Secretary at the Home Office. In part this may have been prompted by consideration for his father, who was anxious that William should take advantage of the general change in the ministry to begin his administrative career. William went down to Lulworth to visit his brother and while there Robert broached the matter to him. He explained that though the official duties were light, the parliamentary duties were important and considerable; William would be acting as his right-hand in such matters as attendance at committees and conducting business in the House. He added that the work would be

difficult at first, and nothing but experience would make it less so;
but he would do all in his power to assist him, and there was a
material difference between having his principal in the House of
Lords and having him at his side in the Commons. William, proud
and touchy like most of his family, misunderstood the emphasis on
the difficulties of the office and his own inexperience, fired up, and
declined the appointment. When Peel shortly after went to Drayton
and explained what had happened to his disappointed father, the
old baronet in turn took fire. In the course of an unhappy domestic
scene, he told William that he had shuffled through life; that he
had given up the Church, the law, and now politics; and that he
had now lost one of the finest opportunities that could have presented itself. He added finally that he took William's failure to
secure a position in the government as so great a reflection on himself that he could no longer attend parliament.[1] It was a sudden
manifestation of the hot temper that underlay the Peel character;
but by that time the damage was done, and Peel had already
appointed George Dawson to the vacancy. As he had explained to
his brother, there was a special need for haste since in all probability
the Prime Minister would make some suggestion to facilitate his
own general parliamentary arrangements, and Peel was anxious to
be able to say with truth that the post had already been filled.
Dawson's predecessor, Henry Clive, had been notoriously incompetent and he had no wish for another of the same kind to be foisted
on him for political reasons. It was clear that Peel was determined to
surround himself with men on whom he could rely; and the remainder of his small team was chosen with equal care. Henry
Hobhouse, Sidmouth's efficient and diligent Civil Under-Secretary,
he asked to remain in his post. 'I offer you in return,' he wrote, 'my
entire confidence.' Finally, now that Grant was relieved of the Irish
Secretaryship, Peel secured once more the services of his old private
secretary, Sydney Streatfeild, who continued with him until his
death some four years later.

For the rest he found himself with a staff of fourteen clerks, a
précis-writer, a librarian and various porters and domestic officials, an
establishment smaller than the joint civil and military departments

[1] 40605 fos. 121ff., docketed quaintly by Peel 'mon père et mon frère
Guillaume'; *Peel*, I, 304.

of the Secretary's office in Ireland and considerably smaller than the Treasury. In January 1822 Sidmouth had already complained that 'the whole strength of the establishment has been insufficient to carry on the current business of the office'. Even so they were inadequately housed. One of Peel's earliest tasks was to transmit to the Prime Minister a memorial from his clerks on the state of the apartments they occupied. He confirmed from his own inspection that the rooms were 'dark, incommodious, and unwholesome. I am informed that several of the clerks have suffered so much in their health, in consequence of the closeness of the rooms, and the unpleasant smells which ascend from the lower apartments, as to render a frequent absence from their duty necessary.' Little seems to have been achieved by this first approach, however, for in March and again in May 1822 Peel had to write to Arbuthnot in more emphatic terms on the same subject, the last letter saying forcibly that something must be done without delay.[1] Probably something was done in the end, but this glimpse of the narrow domestic atmosphere in his department is indicative of the restricted range of administrative activity in early nineteenth-century government. The Home Office, by its own nature, was one of the most central of the great departments of state; but its actual functions were primarily concerned with the preservation of law and order; and there had been little attempt under Sidmouth to extend or deepen these traditional duties. The exiguous clerical establishment that the Secretary had at his disposal reflected the relatively narrow field of his power. The responsibility was, however, none the less because the instruments of policy were so limited. The Home Department was a notoriously troublesome and difficult office; and the supporters of the ministry were as pleased as the cabinet at getting a man of proved administrative ability to fill it. Moreover, the circumstance that the new Secretary would be in the House of Commons was in itself a considerable advantage. 'Peel . . . is of the greatest use in Parliament,' wrote E. B. Wilbraham at the beginning of April, 'and saves Lord Londonderry and Van. much speaking and explanations, as he is concise and clear in what he says.'[2] Peel himself was less enthusiastic, and his prompt acceptance of Liverpool's offer in November did

---

[1] 40340 fos. 1, 3; H.O. 43/31, (12 January, 27 February 1822).
[2] *Colchester*, III, 250.

not mean that all his original scruples had vanished. 'I fear,' he confessed with curious deprecation to Lord Stowell not long after-wards, 'I cannot look upon my intended appointment as a fit subject of congratulation. It will compel me to make very painful sacrifices; and I am almost overpowered by the fear that I have undertaken what is beyond my strength.'[1]

On 17 January 1822 he formally received the seals of his depart-ment from the king and the same day was sworn in as Secretary of State at a meeting of the Privy Council in London. At the end of March Canning was appointed Governor-General of India and began the long round of farewells to his friends and preparations for his departure. Before quitting the House of Commons, where for a quarter of a century he had played so notable a part, he had one final fling at the Catholic question. Though Plunket, the acknow-ledged leader of the emancipationist party, had probably little thought of proposing any measure so soon after the defeat of the previous session, Canning raised the issue again in what Peel de-scribed to Saurin as 'a new, and I think, extraordinary and objection-able shape'. At the end of April, in a speech of great oratorical appeal and considerable historical learning, he moved for leave to bring in a bill to admit Roman Catholic peers to the House of Lords. Peel met the motion with a direct negative. True to his habit of rebutting his opponents' arguments one by one, he first embarked on an historical disquisition to disprove Canning's thesis that there was a clear distinction between the reasons for disqualifying Roman Catholics from the upper and lower Houses respectively. Then, with greater practical persuasiveness, he pointed to the absurdity of taking up one branch of Catholic disabilities after the question had been considered as a whole the previous session and notice given that it would be raised again in the next, and when nothing was said as to securities. He asked merely that the issue of the peers should be postponed until the whole question, including securities, should once more be introduced. The motion, nevertheless, was carried by five votes and a bill founded on Canning's proposals subsequently passed through all its stages. Though Peel spoke briefly on the second reading, the bill passed the third reading without debate or division only to suffer the expected defeat in the Lords. As a measure

[1] Pellew, *Sidmouth*, III, 395.

of Catholic relief it was something of a curiosity; and Canning's historical theories were an equally curious departure from the usual emancipationist arguments. Nevertheless, its success in the lower House demonstrated the wide political support for the cause it represented, and placed Peel for the first time in the position of a cabinet minister speaking and voting against his senior colleague Castlereagh, as well as against Canning.

Even apart from the Catholic question, however, the 1822 session found him, as was inevitable, more often on his feet and talking on a wider variety of topics than he had ever faced before, even in his busiest days as Irish Secretary. His speeches between February and July cover fifty closely printed pages on such miscellaneous subjects as agricultural distress, opening of letters in the post, assaults on a city sheriff, the salt tax, the queen's funeral, the treatment of Hunt and other prisoners in Ilchester gaol, the office of Postmaster General, gaol deliveries, the currency, the criminal laws, the Aliens Act, the Irish Constabulary, resumption of cash payments, parliamentary reform, Scottish newspapers, and Irish distress. One notable aspect of the session's activities which touched him personally was the opening of a major controversy concerning the return to the gold standard in 1821 under what was already beginning to be called 'Peel's Act'. The resumption of cash payments had been accompanied by a general fall in prices, including those of foodstuffs. Trade began to recover, industrial unemployment declined, and at long last the revenue showed some buoyancy, with unexpected surpluses in 1820 and 1821. The change had started even before the 1819 Act had begun to operate and could only partly have been influenced by it. Nevertheless, by the midsummer of 1822 wheat had dropped to half the price it fetched in January 1819. The country gentlemen were invaded with alarm at the fall in agricultural prices, and they associated their difficulties with the new currency policy.

In the 1822 session the discontented agriculturalists were a force to be reckoned with. 'We are to have a tremendous session,' reported Peel to Goulburn as early as January, '—agriculturalists in an uproar, and the cabinet is considering what is the largest tub to throw out to this very troublesome whale.' But his own views were clear. 'I believe nothing can be done for their relief. But as the revenue is flourishing, trade in a very prosperous state, and consumption increasing, time will bring a remedy.'[1] The whale was hardly likely to be consoled by this. Though not a party in any political sense, and drawing their strength from both sides of the house, the agriculturalists did not need much in the way of organisation or leadership to make their voice heard in an assembly formed predominantly of landowners. Moreover, any movement against official policy was bound to attract interested supporters. Radical whigs like Brougham and Burdett lent their aid to the malcontents and Attwood provided them with the tempting theory that an inflationary paper currency would see the restoration of high prices. The government duly offered their tub in the shape of a repeal of the malt tax, a renewal of the committee on agricultural distress, and finally a revision of the 1815 Corn Law. But tariffs and low taxes could not alone produce high prices, and there was an increasing tendency to look to a depreciation of the currency as the most certain escape from the farmer's difficulties. The battle in the Commons was mainly fought on the government side by Castlereagh and Huskisson; but 'Peel's Act' and Peel's name were so constantly called in question that he had frequently to intervene in defence of the policy laid down by the 1819 committee. The government held its ground; but by the end of the session it was evident that corn and currency had been added to Catholicism in an alliterative trinity of troubles likely to beset politics for an indefinite period to come.

The end of the session brought the new Home Secretary no respite, for the king had made plans for a royal visit to Scotland. The previous year he had gone to Ireland, accompanied by Sidmouth as Secretary of State. Now it was Peel's turn and on 4 August he set out with Julia (to whom their first son had been born three months earlier), and his private secretary Streatfeild. They stayed three days at Tamworth on their way north and arrived at Edinburgh late on the evening of 10 August, taking up their residence at Melville Castle. The king, coming by sea, attended by a squadron of five other vessels, was due to arrive on 12 August; but it was not until two days later that his yacht, the *Royal George*, arrived in Leith roadstead towed by two steamboats. The weather was wet and blustery and the royal party spent an uncomfortable night on

[1] Goulburn, II/14.

board before making their ceremonial landing on the 15th. Proceeding in state from Leith, through quiet but curious and respectful crowds, the king passed on to Holyrood Palace where he was presented with the regalia of Scotland and received an address from the Lord Provost and magistrates. Peel, who with the Duke of Montrose and Lord Melville was in attendance on the king, reported to Liverpool that everything passed off admirably and that the king was astonished at the numbers, especially on Calton Hill, that had collected to watch the procession. The royal party then went on to Dalkeith Palace and Peel returned to Melville Castle. He was in little heart for festivity. His eyes were again giving him trouble and towards the end of the visit, indeed, he took to wearing a green shade to protect them. But there was greater cause for low spirits than this. On the afternoon of the king's arrival, Wednesday 14 August, he went out to the royal yacht to pay his respects to the king. He had scarcely returned when he received a hasty letter from Lord Liverpool, informing him that Castlereagh had committed suicide two days earlier and begging him to break the intelligence to the king. Peel at once returned on board the *Royal George* with the tragic news. It was not entirely an unexpected shock to the king, for when he had taken leave of Castlereagh the previous week he had been struck by his peculiar manner and wrote to Liverpool to warn him that 'Londonderry's mind was gone'. Wellington had made a similar observation and drawn the same conclusion. It was in fact a terrible and distressing end to a notable career. For a decade Castlereagh had combined the duties of Foreign Secretary and leader of the House of Commons in a period of abnormal strain in both external and domestic affairs. Underneath the cool and dignified exterior, and his flat, odd, but sensible oratory, was a proud and vulnerable nature; and in the summer of 1822 came the last blow. He was, or thought he was, being blackmailed with charges of homosexual practices; his mind became clouded by a mania of persecution and fear; and on the morning of 12 August he cut his throat. 'What a conclusion to such a life,' wrote Liverpool in obvious anguish in his letter to Peel. 'May God have mercy on his soul.'

But politics could not wait on personal feelings and the effect of Castlereagh's death on cabinet arrangements was a question that at once came uppermost in people's minds. Liverpool's first impulse was to come to Scotland, but on reflection he judged it more prudent to remain at his post. Instead he wrote to the king to assure him that no immediate decision need be taken and that the whole matter would be kept in abeyance until his return. At Holyrood on 19 August the king told Peel confidentially that forty-eight hours earlier he had written to the Prime Minister on his own initiative to the effect that the arrangements with regard to Canning and India were to remain unchanged, and that there must be no delay in completing them. He added, 'I hope you think I have done right.' But Peel refused to commit himself and excused himself from an observation on the letter or anything connected with it. In his reply to the king's letter Liverpool was equally evasive, but he wrote urgently to Peel asking to see him as soon as he returned from Scotland, if possible before the king's arrival, and to bring Melville with him. Other politicians, with less responsibility, were less restrained. Croker wrote on 14 August to retail a conversation with Huskisson which pointed at two conclusions: that Canning would rather take office at home than go to India, and that he would willingly concede to Peel the leadership of the House of Commons. This in itself was hardly credible and two days later Croker wrote again to confess that Huskisson's judgement had been at fault. Canning had returned to town and told Huskisson explicitly that if offered Castlereagh's place both at the Foreign Office and in the Commons, he would accept it; but he would not accept any higgling or reservation. Peel thanked Croker for the information but declined to comment. 'There are some subjects on which one does injustice to one's feelings by saying anything,' he ended, 'and our departed friend's death is one of them. I bitterly deplore it.'[1]

Meanwhile, in Edinburgh, the programme laid down for the king's visit proceeded on its appointed way. On Saturday, 17 August, there was a *levée* at which the king appeared in Highland dress. 'I had some doubts on this point,' Peel dryly reported to Liverpool, 'but I dare say it has greatly pleased the Highlanders.' On Monday was the reception of addresses; on Tuesday a Drawing-Room; on Wednesday a select dinner-party and evening concert; on Thursday a procession from Holyrood to the Castle attended by

[1] *Croker*, I, 227-33; 40319 f. 48.

a great concourse of kilted clansmen; on Friday a cavalry review at Portobello; on Saturday a civic dinner at Parliament House. Though he was inevitably called upon to receive deputations and answer addresses and petitions, Peel kept himself in the background of the public events. 'I shall be heartily glad when these ceremonies are over,' he wrote to Liverpool. 'I am not very well, and little disposed after what has so recently happened to join in the general festivity.' The procession to the Castle he watched privately from the pavements under the towering tenements of the old town in the company of Sir Walter Scott. As they walked up High Street his distinguished companion was enthusiastically greeted by his fellow-countrymen in the crowd who probably had little notion of the identity of the tall stranger beside him. He excused himself from the civic banquet on the Saturday on grounds of indisposition, and his toast was given *in absentia* by the Lord Provost. The weather continued miserable, with intermittent rain and fog, which could have done nothing to lighten his health or spirits. But he was kept hard at work until the end, replying to loyal addresses from such varied sources as the Faculty of Procurators, the county of Forfar, and the Edinburgh Chamber of Commerce; advising on the propriety of the king's attendance at a Presbyterian service in St. Giles's; checking attempts by the king's physician, Sir William Knighton, to set himself up as private secretary; discussing with the king who should take Castlereagh's place at the Congress of Verona; and urging on the Scottish judges a reform of Scottish criminal law. One of his last letters was to Sir Walter Scott, thanking him for his contribution to the success of the visit and asking him to convey the royal appreciation to the Highland chiefs and their followers who had given the scene 'so peculiar and romantic a character'. To the novelist Peel had in fact taken a great liking, and emboldened by his cordiality Scott raised the question of returning to Scotland the old cannon, Mons Meg—a matter which Peel duly broached with Wellington the following September. On 29 August the king re-embarked and on a Scottish summer afternoon of mist and rain the *Royal George* passed rapidly out of sight down the Firth of Forth to the noise of cannon from ship and shore.[1]

[1] 40304 fos. 55-7; 40306 f. 16; 38195 fos. 114, 120; Lockhart, *Scott*, VII, 62-79, 83; *Edinburgh Evening Courant*, 12-31 August 1822.

Though unable to leave until the day after the king's departure, Peel made his way south as expeditiously as possible and arrived at Stanhope Street on Sunday night, 1 September, to find that Liverpool was anxiously expecting him. The interval for counsel was short, for the king landed at Greenwich the same day and he had already, according to Hobhouse, suggested to Peel while in Scotland that he should become Chancellor of the Exchequer and take the lead in the House of Commons. Liverpool, for all his assurances to the king, had been moving in an opposite direction. He had held discussions at his country house, Combe Wood, with Bathurst and Wellington; he had allowed talks to take place between Arbuthnot and Huskisson, Canning's friend and confidant; and his instinct to retain Canning in the government had been given further impetus by a letter to Wellington from the Duke of Buckingham hinting at a withdrawal of the Grenville party if Canning were not given office. It was essential, however, first to see Peel and discover his views. Peel also had been given time to reflect. As soon as he arrived in London he tried first to see and then wrote to his friend Manners Sutton, the Speaker.

*Monday morning, Sept. 2, 1822*

The question may be put to me, what I think and feel with respect to Canning's accession to the government. I intend to answer that I should be ashamed of myself if I personally threw a difficulty in the way of it, or of his being placed in any situation which the Government might think it for the interest of the country that he should fill. . . . As to his being leader of the House of Commons, I must fairly own that he being so would be no personal disappointment to me; and if it were, I should think it quite unworthy of me not to submit to it. I shall, as I have always done, conduct the business of my own office, and conduct it in and out of Parliament in the way I think best; and he must be both a bold and vain man who is dissatisfied with either the share or the importance of that business which the Home Department devolves upon him.

To Liverpool, when he saw him, he spoke in the same strain. He would do what his colleagues thought most conducive to their general interests; he had no wish to lead the House of Commons, nor to decline it, if it was thought better he should undertake it.

Of this latter offer the prime minister made no mention to the king. Instead he proposed in the name of himself, Wellington, Bathurst, and Westmorland, that Canning should succeed to Castlereagh's position. The king, however, was not prepared to be overridden so easily, and seemed at one point even to contemplate a break-up of the cabinet rather than give way. In this he was not without external support. Sidmouth when consulted advised him to make Peel leader of the House, and fill the Foreign Office with some one other than Canning. Eldon probably expressed himself even more strongly to the king against admitting Canning to the cabinet; and the Duke of Newcastle wrote to Peel, Eldon, and Liverpool, to much the same effect. When he had his own audience, however, Peel simply stated his readiness to acquiesce in what was thought best; and added, if Hobhouse is to be believed, that he was indifferent to ambitions for office and preferred the pleasures of private and family life. The last sentiment was not uncharacteristic; and tired, ill, and depressed as he was after his Scottish visit, he probably felt all the greater distaste for the intrigues and rivalries of political personalities.[1]

In the end, however, and largely through Wellington's sensible masculine influence, the king yielded. On 8 September Liverpool received the royal assent to the new arrangement. He wrote at once to give Peel the news even before communicating with Canning. 'I think it due to you on every account and not the less so, from your handsome and disinterested conduct throughout the whole business.' By 13 September all was over and Peel could write cheerfully to Croker that Canning was to succeed to Castlereagh; and, what was more important, he and Julia were setting out for Lulworth the next day. It was a relief to have the issue settled, and he could feel with justice that he had come through the crisis with enhanced credit among his colleagues. Yet the situation had not been an easy one, and in all the circumstances his attitude of complete passivity had been the only safe and wise course. Though, as he told the Speaker, he had no political difference with Canning except on the Catholic question, that in itself was a formidable division; and the clash of two political careers could easily supply what was wanting. Moreover, there were some politicians who out of dislike of

[1] *Hobhouse*, pp. 94-7; *Geo. IV Letters*, II, 535 n.1.

Canning rather than love of Peel, were prepared to set up the two men as personal opponents. Sidmouth in fact had told the king that Peel and Canning could not go on indefinitely together, and that when Liverpool retired, it would be imperative to choose between the two. Neither man, however, lent himself to that manœuvre. Indeed, only the preceding April Canning had told Croker that 'to Peel especially I feel it quite impossible to do justice, for a frankness and straightforwardness beyond example, and for feelings for which I own I did not before give him credit but which I hope I know how to value and to return.'[1]

Even so, no amount of straightforwardness could surmount the disagreement on Catholic emancipation; and with every prospect of a renewal of that question the following session, Peel was faced once more with the difficulty of working under a leader who would be speaking and voting against him on that issue. In the peace of a Sunday morning at Lulworth towards the end of September he disclosed his inner thoughts to Goulburn.

I never had a doubt as to what I *ought* to do, in regard to the late arrangements. I therefore was spared the pain of any consideration, being perfectly satisfied that what is right, must inevitably be politic. I think with you, that that which has been done, is the best that could be done, but even the best, is not unmixed good. I should conceive that in the *Vox Stellarum*[2] for March next there might be a safe general prophecy of much perplexity and debate in Parliament.[2]

But March was six months ahead and in the meantime there was congenial work at hand in his own department.

1 *Croker*, I, 223.
2 Francis Moore's, better known as Old Moore's, *Almanac*.
3 Goulburn, II/13 (22 September 1822).

# CHAPTER

# 9

# LEGAL REFORM

At the time when Peel took over the Home Department, the English criminal law had for over a generation been attracting the attention of reformers.[1] That reform of some sort was desirable could hardly be denied. In theory England had one of the severest penal systems in Europe; in practice it was lenient, defective, and haphazard. Some two hundred offences (no one precisely knew) were punishable by death, most of which had been created piecemeal and arbitrarily in the century and a half since the Restoration. Yet the absence of any efficient police organisation, the obsolete formalism of judicial procedure, the influence of juries, and an increasingly liberal attitude by judges and crown advisers, had produced what Romilly not unfairly described as a 'lottery of justice'. Many criminal offences went undiscovered; many indictments failed on purely technical grounds or on the sympathies of jurymen; and many capital convictions were followed by commutation or reprieve. In practice executions were normally confined to cases of murder, sexual crimes, burglary and robbery, forgery, and horse stealing. Nevertheless, the general liberal movement of thought in Europe exemplified by Rousseau, Montesquieu, and Beccaria, had its effect on Britain; and the work of pioneer reformers like Eden and Howard was carried on in the early nineteenth century by Romilly, the whig lawyer who had been Solicitor-General in the Grenville administration of 1806. A number of influences combined to give impetus to the campaign for criminal reform which he led from 1808 onward: the professional views of lawyers and jurists, the religious humanitarianism of the Quakers and evangelicals, the intellectual current of Benthamite utilitarianism, and the small body

[1] See Radzinowicz, I, 97ff.

of radical whigs in parliament. Above all, the House of Commons provided Romilly with a secure platform for his advocacy and a sure method of bringing pressure to bear on government and public opinion. Even before the end of the war his efforts had won the support of the lower House. It was the House of Lords, where Eldon and Sidmouth added the weight of executive authority to the innate conservatism of the peers, that remained the persistent obstruction to any significant alteration in the law.

Romilly committed suicide in 1818, but his work was taken up by Mackintosh and Buxton, and in 1819 a motion for a committee of enquiry was carried against the government by a majority of nineteen. The report of that committee, of which Mackintosh was chairman, not only provided a careful and comprehensive view of the state of the criminal law, but submitted a large plan of reform to the attention of parliament. In particular it recommended the repeal of a number of obsolete or redundant statutes; the abolition of the death sentence for certain cases of larceny from shops and houses; and a reform of the forgery laws. Bills to implement these proposals met, however, with determined resistance in both Houses, and only the least important—those dealing with obsolete statutes—passed into law, and then in severely mutilated form. The one exception to this tale of failure was the limitation of capital punishment for shop-lifting to offences involving property of £15 in value in place of the previous amount of 5s. The arrival of Peel at the Home Department, however, materially altered the position of reform and there was now some prospect that the government would lend its aid to the movement. Nevertheless, in an effort to pledge the House of Commons to the principle of reform, Mackintosh on 4 June 1822 moved that next session the House should take into consideration 'the means of increasing the efficacy of the criminal laws by abating their undue rigour; together with measures for strengthening the police, and for rendering the punishment of transportation and imprisonment more effectual for the purposes of example and reformation'. Peel briefly opposed the motion on the technical grounds that he hoped to bring in measures dealing with the police and prisons, and was awaiting a report on transportation; but on the general principle of the resolution, he assured

Mackintosh that should he feel disposed to take up the subject in detail the following session, 'he should not find in him a predetermined opponent'. In deference to Peel's objections the clauses concerning police, transportation, and prisons were omitted; the remainder was passed by sixteen votes in a relatively small House.

The reference to the police in Mackintosh's resolution was interesting since it was a point on which Peel substantially differed from the Romilly-Mackintosh school of reformers. Indeed, it might well have been inserted as a concession to his views and in order to win his support.[1] In general the whig legal reformers put their trust in an amelioration of the criminal law as the surest method of enforcing it. It was because the law was so severe, they argued, that its practical operation had become so ineffective and uncertain. Restore the approval and confidence of the public, and the law would once more be carried out. To the notion that the law might be more effectively enforced if there were a reformed and efficient police, they exhibited in general a notable repugnance. If in this they were partly influenced by a dislike of putting stronger instruments of power in the hands of the government, they were also manifesting a deep-rooted popular prejudice which character-ised all parties and all classes. An efficient police seemed inconceiv-able to the mind of early nineteenth-century England except as an arbitrary and oppressive engine of executive tyranny. The tradition of English liberty, so admired in its political aspect by continental observers, was in its social context a tradition of public and private behaviour, free in Paley's words, from 'inspection, scrutiny, and control', and subject to the action of the law only after an offence had been committed. The ferocious paper clauses of the old English criminal law were matched by the anarchy of the society whose excesses it endeavoured to stem. Traditional habits and institutions provided for the most part a workable framework of law and order except in time of distress or political excitement; but in the teeming streets of London, in the new industrial areas that had either out-grown or from the start were outside the older borough adminis-tration, in the wrecking and smuggling population of the coastal districts, and in the itinerant beggars, gipsies, and vagabonds that

[1] Radzinowicz, III, 371.

310

infested the countryside, there were large social elements that had almost escaped from government regulation.[1]

Nevertheless, it was almost the settled conviction of Englishmen that this was the price of liberty, and that the price was not too high. Ever since Henry and John Fielding had expounded the need for an efficient police in the middle of the eighteenth century, there had been one parliamentary committee after another to consider the problem; and occasionally an outstanding shock to the public conscience such as the Gordon riots of 1780 or the Ratcliffe Highway murders of 1811 seemed to presage some effective action. But once the initial spasm of excitement was past, the solid weight of opposition to a police system effectually blocked all attempts by individuals to secure a change of principle. The one great piece of police legislation in the period, the Middlesex Justices Act of 1792, was in essence a reform of the magistracy; and the police organisation established by the Act was too small and decentralised to have any perceptible effect on the state of the metropolis. The public at large preferred to place their hopes of social amendment on the progress of religion and morals, on private associations for discovery and prosecution of felons, and on such characteristic Georgian manifestations as the Society for the Suppression of Vice. Even in its attitude to crime, contemporary England was profoundly individualistic and libertarian.[2]

Yet in an age when the very word 'police' was only just passing into the English vocabulary, there were isolated figures that had tried to develop a different approach to the problem of crime. Patrick Colquhoun, a former Lord Provost of Glasgow, who moved to London and became one of the magistrates under the 1792 Act, had elaborated a theory of preventive police which was one of the first serious contributions to the science of penology. His conception of 'police' was the wide contemporary definition that embraced the whole system of public regulations and agencies for the preservation of the morals, order and comfort of civil society; and his classic *Treatise on the Police of the Metropolis* (1795) had virtually nothing to say on the technical problem of creating a full-time professional

[1] cf. evidence on *Police of Metropolis* (P.P. 1816, V) and *County Constabulary*, (P.P. 1839, XIX).

[2] cf. Radzinowicz, III, 1ff.

body of police in the more modern derivative sense. But in his advocacy of a centralised police authority separate from the judiciary, and in his insistence on the primary need for the prevention and control of crime rather than on its punishment, he exposed the essential principle of later nineteenth-century development. Colquhoun retired in 1818 and died two years later, undistinguished and unrecognised. Yet if he had failed to command general attention for his views, his idea of 'preventive police' had entered the phraseology of experts; and in Jeremy Bentham for one he had gained an appreciative adherent. The Benthamites, however, were as yet a small and isolated group and their influence was confined to an intellectual *élite*. Between Colquhoun's generalised concepts and the practical realisation of an efficient London police force was a wide and apparently insuperable chasm. The state of the metropolitan police continued to be the subject of fitful parliamentary enquiries, but they had little purpose or principle behind them. In the year of Colquhoun's retirement a committee which, for a change, did consider the implications of a preventive police system, concluded that it would be 'odious and repulsive', and incapable of execution.

As an expression of popular feeling this was accurate enough; but Peel was never noticeably influenced by popular prejudices. His instinct, as always, was to ascertain the facts and draw the right conclusions. A decade of office had ingrained in him an administrative outlook, and at the Home Department he had a direct responsibility for law and order. Ireland had been an ample education in the subject of crime, and as author of the Peace Preservation Act he hardly shared the views on police common among politicians as well as the public. Moreover, recent events in London had reinforced the conviction that the lawlessness of the London mobs needed some corrective. The rioting at the time of the queen's trial; the popular and successful demonstrations at her funeral, despite the forcible action of the military; more disquieting still, the unrest among some of the troops stationed in London; all these were fresh in the minds of the cabinet. Stung by an attempted mutiny in one of the Guards battalions, Wellington himself in 1820 had drawn up a memorandum in which he expressed the incidental opinion that the government should form 'either a police in London or a military corps which should be of a different description from the regular military force'. It is not surprising that when Peel took office the question of police reform was one of the first to which he turned his mind. Indeed the government itself had given a promise the previous session that the matter would continue to be kept under enquiry. On 14 March 1822 in a brief and carefully moderated speech he moved for a select committee on the police of the metropolis. He refrained, on grounds of his short period in office, from expressing any further views; but he emphasised 'the paramount importance of the subject, and its intimate connection with the criminal juris-prudence of the country', and expressed the hope that the committee would prosecute its enquiries with the one view of 'obtaining for the metropolis as perfect a system of police as was consistent with the character of a free country'.

His cautious approach, in view of the past history of similar committees, was understandable. His own committee, chosen from those who by their associations or interests might be expected to have special understanding of the problem, comprised twenty members: reformers like Grey Bennett, Fowell Buxton, Mackintosh, Holford; on the government side George Dawson, William Peel, and the Solicitor-General; whigs like William Lamb, Spring Rice, and Francis Burdett; and two London aldermen, Thompson and Wood. Peel himself was chairman, but despite his influence the committee followed exactly in the footsteps of its predecessors. It elicited much useful information about the existing organisation of the London police; it made one or two suggestions for minor improvements; but on the only issue that counted, it recorded a flat negative. Its report, presented on 17 June, refused to recommend a wider freedom of action or any other measures calculated to facilitate the work of the police. The conclusion came in a classic passage:

> It is difficult to reconcile an effective system of police, with that perfect freedom of action and exemption from interference, which are the great privileges and blessings of society in this country; and Your Committee think that the forfeiture or curtailment of such advantages would be too great a sacrifice for improvements in police, or facilities in detection of crime, however desirable in themselves if abstractedly considered.[1]

[1] P.P. 1822 IV (*Police of Metropolis*).

The one merit in the report (it was perhaps the one thing Peel as chairman was able to secure) was that the issue was plainly stated and the naked choice offered to parliament and the public. There can be little doubt that the result was a disappointment to Peel. Whatever his own views had been at the commencement of the enquiry, and he had told the House that they could only be 'crude and imperfect', he had convinced himself what the choice should be. Even before the report was published, when speaking in the Commons on Mackintosh's resolution of 4 June, he expressed his complete concurrence with the need to adopt a vigorous system of police. 'God forbid that he should mean to countenance a system of espionage; but a vigorous preventive police, consistent with the free principles of our free constitution, was an object which he did not despair of seeing accomplished.' For the time being, however, the question had to be shelved until circumstances were more propitious and a more sympathetic committee could be formed. There remained the larger problem of legal and administrative reform of which, in a sense, the reform of the police was only an offshoot.

## II

The concentration of the whig and humanitarian reformers on the obvious and dramatic issue of capital punishment tended to make them neglect not only the question of preventing crime but also such administrative problems as secondary punishments and legal procedure. It was a feature of Peel's work at the Home Office that he approached the problem more cautiously but over a wider front. Any considerable reduction in the scale of major punishments, for example, would necessitate an effective system of secondary punishments; that in turn raised the question of the adequacy of the existing prison system. The innumerable gaols, prisons, and Houses of Correction throughout the country were subject to no central direction and were often ill-managed. They varied in accommodation and discipline; many were brutal and corrupt; and they were insufficient to deal with the growth in population and the increase in crime. Prison reform, however, was a matter on which Peel could secure a substantial and articulate support. The work of the eighteenth-century reformers such as Howard, Blackstone, and

Eden, had long drawn attention to the abuses of the system; but the abuses still persisted and it was not until Romilly began his campaign that the combination of radical enlightenment and evangelical Christianity was able to make headway against the general inertia and disorganisation of county and civic authorities.

By 1820 the pressure of public opinion and the disclosures of the statistical returns presented to parliament from 1815 onwards had brought the legislature to the brink of action. In the last year of Sidmouth's tenure of office a bill prepared by a parliamentary committee had been accepted by the government. It was in the hands of William Courtenay, M.P. for Exeter, and when Peel took over the department he left the bill in his charge though he made it clear that he approved whole-heartedly of its provisions. The bill was rejected by the House of Lords, but it was understood that Eldon would bring in a similar bill immediately on the reassembly of parliament in 1823. When Hobhouse reminded the Lord Chancellor of the matter at the end of December, however, his reception was not encouraging. Eldon told him that the judges and law officers had not been consulted about it; there was no indication how far the counties could bear the new charges imposed on them by the bill; many of the peers were critical of it; and Eldon himself was too busy to do more than merely introduce it. Peel wrote back a soothing letter, pointing out that the bill was supported by all the ministers in the House of Commons, and that the government was pledged to bring in legislation for the consolidation of the prison laws and improvement of prison discipline. He was anxious, therefore, to learn Eldon's sentiments on it, though he had no wish to throw on him the burden of conducting such a bill through the Lords.[1] His conciliatoriness had its effect, and the Gaols Act (4 Geo. IV c. 64) passed into law in the course of the 1823 session.

In placing it on the statute book Peel had acted more as a midwife than as parent. Nevertheless, it was the first time that the government had taken responsibility for a measure of national prison reform; and the measure itself was a landmark in the history of penal legislation.[2] It was, firstly, a great consolidating statute, dealing with previous acts as far back as the reign of Edward III; and, secondly, a great reforming statute, introducing most of the principles of

[1] 40315 fos. 83-5, 108.  [2] cf. S. and B. Webb, *English Prisons* (1922), p. 73.

enlightened prison administration advocated by a generation of penal reformers. It provided for the establishment of a common gaol or house of correction in every county or riding, and in London, Westminster, and seventeen other towns and cities, to be administered by local magistrates and paid for out of local rates. The justices in session were to report to the Home Secretary on their proceedings under the Act; visiting justices were to carry out inspections at least three times each quarter and to report on their visits to Quarter Sessions; and a general report on a prescribed form was to be made annually to the Home Department. A detailed system of prison discipline, including medical and educational provisions, was to be uniformly adopted; and the keepers of prisons were to report to Quarter Sessions on the enforcement of the rules. Two further Acts, one in 1823 (4 Geo. IV c. 47) and another in 1824 (5 Geo. IV c. 85) showed Peel's continuing interest in the problem. The first of these enabled convicts under sentence of transportation to be employed on public works in any of the colonies; and in fact by 1826 some three or four hundred men were already at work in the Bermudas. The second, besides remedying some omissions and defects in the Gaols Act of 1823, extended the scrutiny of the Home Department to some hundred and fifty prisons and Houses of Correction in the smaller towns not covered by the earlier Act. Magistrates in those districts were enabled to send prisoners to the county gaols and contract for their maintenance there; they were given facilities for the construction or repair of their own prisons; they were required to report any action they took under the statute; and where no action was taken they were obliged to make annual returns on a printed schedule of the prisons under their care. Finally an elaborate code was laid down for the classification and separation of the prisoners in the institutions specified in the 1823 Act, and any magistrate was empowered to visit them at any time.

In this early handling of the problem of imprisonment it is clear that two issues were present in Peel's mind. One was the provision of a regulated and efficient system of secondary punishments. In opposing a motion in April 1823 to abolish the punishment of whipping, he told the House that 'it was peculiarly incumbent upon those who advocated the necessity of mitigating the severity of the penal code, in respect to capital punishments, to beware of rendering such an experiment impracticable, by narrowing too much the scale of minor punishments'. Under adequate safeguards, and for certain classes of offenders, he defended both whipping and the treadmill. 'Solitary confinement was, in his opinion, a much more rigorous punishment and one which was much more likely to break the spirit, than moderate whipping.' As for the treadmill, he told the Commons in February 1824, he had made a minute enquiry into the health of the prisoners so punished; and if increased weight was an indication, the effect could not have been injurious. Peel's other objective was to bring under some degree of uniformity and control at least the more important of the medley of different institutions and special jurisdictions into whose hands a prisoner might fall. It was admittedly a first attack on the problem. Only a certain number of prisons, though they included most of the larger ones, came under the regular scrutiny of the Home Department; and the management and inspection of them was left to the local magistrates. Nevertheless, a uniform set of principles was prescribed, and something had been done to initiate some kind of central supervision. The further step of enforcement by direct inspection was one that was scarcely practicable at that date. Without a body of prison inspectors in the pay of the Home Department—indeed, without something of a revolution in the accepted functions of that department—it was impossible to achieve any greater degree of discipline or centralisation. Yet public opinion, still apt to look upon any extension of governmental power as oppression, and any increase in the number of government servants as corruption, would hardly have tolerated such an innovation. The science of penal reform and social administration was in its infancy; but at least a start was made and the mere fact that information was now reaching the Home Office which had not reached it before was a sensible stimulus to local authorities.[1]

Peel himself was certainly aware of the difficulties of the problem and the limitations of what he was able to achieve. To Sydney Smith, himself a convert to the efficacy of the treadmill, who had written to him poking fun at the ostensibly deterrent effect of transportation to Australia, he sent a long letter on the subject in March 1826.

[1] Radzinowicz, I, 570-1; Webb, *op. cit.*, p. 107.

I admit the inefficiency of transportation to Botany Bay, but the whole subject of what is called secondary punishment is full of difficulty; a difficulty arising mainly, I regret to add, from the vast harvest of transportable crime that is reaped at every assize. I can hardly devise anything as secondary punishment in addition to what we have at present. We have the convict ships, which at this moment hold four or five thousand convicts employed in public works. There is a limit to this, for without regular employment found for convicts, it is worse even than transportation. Solitary imprisonment sounds well in theory, but it has in a peculiar degree the evil that is common to all punishment, it varies in its severity according to the disposition of the culprit. It is a punishment which requires too delicate a hand in the enforcement of it to be generally available. To some intellects its consequences are indifferent, to others they are fatal.

Public exposure of convicts at work on the common highways, he thought, would rightly revolt public opinion. As for long terms of imprisonment without hard labour, there was already the example of 'the Penitentiary with room for eight hundred penitents'. When they were given normal diet, their lot in the winter season was 'thought by people outside to be rather an enviable one'. When their diet was reduced, the result was an outbreak of fever which emptied the prison either by death or by the precautionary removal of its inhabitants. The present occupants were therefore again living more comfortably than was consonant with strict penitence. 'The real truth is,' he concluded, 'the number of convicts is too overwhelming for the means of proper and effectual punishment. I despair of any remedy but that which I wish I could hope for—a great reduction in the amount of crime.'[1]

There remained the task, more complicated, more controversial, and more publicised, of legal reform. A long letter to Lord Liverpool, written from Lulworth on 12 October 1822, showed the spirit in which Peel, after nine months' experience of his new department, was preparing to tackle the problem. After assuring the Prime Minister that everything was in train as far as the Home Office was concerned for cabinet discussions on all the measures likely to come up the following session, he dealt first with the question of

[1] *Peel*, I, 401-2.

Scottish law reform. While in Edinburgh with the king he had seen the heads of the Scottish courts and urged them to consider earnestly the application especially to Scottish criminal law of the kind of alterations being successfully agitated in England. In the present temper of public opinion, he told them, practices could not be defended merely because they were established. There were many features of Scottish law repugnant to English feeling; and though it might be proper to retain them, their retention could only be justified by examination and discussion.

> If the arguments in favour of the existing practice are better than the arguments in favour of the proposed changes, or if they are as good, I assured them we could maintain it, but if upon consideration we ourselves feel that they are not tenable, I tried to convince them that it was the best policy to take to ourselves the credit of the reform, and that by being the authors of it, we should have the best chance of prescribing limits to the innovation.

Since then he had written to the Lord Advocate suggesting a specific reference to the chief judges of the Scottish courts on all proposed alterations. It was equally necessary for the English ministers to make up their minds on the course to be pursued in the House of Commons when the question of the reform of the criminal law was raised in pursuance of Mackintosh's resolution the previous session. It would be advantageous, he thought, to consider the whole question in detail—

> not to argue as if there was some Criminal Code which must be maintained in all its integrity, but to look at all the offences which are now punishable with death, to select those (if there be any) which can be safely visited with a mitigated Punishment, and to be prepared to assign our reasons for maintaining the Punishment of Death, in each case in which it ought to be maintained. I really do not think there is, when the question is looked at in its details, any irreconcilable Difference upon points of real importance, between the reasonable advocates for the mitigation of the Criminal Law, and the reasonable defenders of it.[1]

[1] 38195 f. 120, printed Yonge, *Liverpool*, III, 215.

Much depended, of course, on Peel's definition of what was important and what was reasonable; but it was at least clear that he wished to approach his task in a constructive manner, and to make legal reform a practical and not a political issue.

The question of law in Scotland was one of unusual delicacy for the Home Department since it involved mediation between the time-encrusted Scottish legal system, safeguarded by the Act of Union, and the rising tide of whig-liberalism both south and north of the border. Yet there can be little doubt that Peel was right in urging that the position must be re-examined by the Scottish judicial authorities themselves, if they were not to have reform thrust on them from without. Already in 1819 the Scottish burgh system—narrow, corrupt, and self-perpetuating—had attracted the attention of parliament, and a motion for a committee of enquiry had been carried against the government. Though the ministers had ignored the evidence produced, this negative attitude could not be indefinitely extended to every year and every aspect of the legal structure in Scotland. The election of Kennedy of Dunure in 1818 as M.P. for Ayr brought a distinguished representative of the Scottish liberals into the House of Commons; and his marriage to a daughter of Romilly ensured for him a close connection with the main law reform party in England. The Scottish system of jury nomination by judges was the first point selected for attack. Kennedy's first effort in 1821 found little support, but a bill he introduced in 1822 met with better success. Though opposed point-blank by the Scottish Lord Advocate and by Lord Binning, the real fate of the measure was dictated by Peel, who argued for the retention of nomination subject to a right of peremptory challenge of up to five jurymen without assigning cause on the part of each of the parties to the case. As amended on these lines in committee, the bill passed into law.[1]

The major effort of the Home Department, however, was directed to the Commission on Scottish legal procedure. Peel's letter to the Lord Justice Clerk in October 1822, besides requiring him to consult the heads of the Scottish courts together with Hume, the nephew of the philosopher and the leading Scottish legal writer of the day, also enumerated a series of questions in Peel's habitual

[1] cf. H. Cockburn, *Memorials* (1856), pp. 384-8; *Ann. Reg.*, 1822, pp. 91-2.

administrative manner, relating to the powers of judge and jury, and any specific reforms needed to protect the position of defendants in criminal cases. As a class, judges are rarely characterised by an excessive zeal for change, and in the face of the traditional independence of the Scottish judiciary, it was all the more requisite for Peel to move warily. 'Scotch law officers are, as I know by experience, very sensitive animals,' he wrote to Liverpool in November 1825,[1] and they needed tactful shepherding down the road of reform. Nevertheless, the Home Secretary's private persuasions had their effect, and in July 1823 a bill was passed setting up a commission to enquire into the forms of process in the Scottish law courts. Besides the leading Scottish judges, the commission appointed under the Act included four English lawyers, of whom three later became judges and the fourth, Courtenay, is better known by the title of the Earl of Devon to which he succeeded in 1835 Their enquiries, which created keen interest among Scottish lawyers, issued in what Cockburn called the 'invaluable statute of 1825'.[2] With the unanimous authority of the Commission behind it, the government was able to withstand the inevitable opposition to the measure in Scotland; and Peel himself, perhaps deliberately, took little part in the subsequent parliamentary proceedings.

Another, even more intractable, legal problem was successfully shifted to a commission of enquiry in these years. This was the reform of the Court of Chancery, whose delays and expenses had for some time been the target of considerable criticism. The root of the trouble lay in the defective judicial staffing of the court and its consequent inability to deal promptly with the volume of equity work coming before it. The defects of the organisation were aggravated by the defects of the Lord Chancellor. Though a good lawyer, Eldon was temperamentally slow in delivering his opinions. At the same time he was reluctant to submit to any major alteration in the court over which he presided. Up to 1823 the campaign against the Court of Chancery had been conducted with pertinacity but no great skill or success by M. A. Taylor, the whig M.P. for Durham. In that year, however, it was taken over by a more formidable antagonist, John

[1] 38195 f. 184, wrongly attributed in K. G. Feiling, *Second Tory Party* (1951), p. 325.
[2] Cockburn, *op. cit.*, pp. 409-10.

Williams, the member for Lincoln, a lawyer and later judge of the Queen's Bench. To a more expert knowledge of the subject, he added a severe personal criticism of Eldon himself; and his efforts were materially aided both by other opposition lawyers and by the organ of intellectual whiggery, the *Edinburgh Review*. The situation before the Home Department was a complex one, for part at least of the movement for Chancery reform was inspired by a desire to discredit Eldon, who with Sidmouth represented the main unyielding and unreforming element in the government. Yet from Peel's point of view, as he had demonstrated in the matter of Scottish law reform, the essential task was to gain the co-operation of the existing judicial authorities in effecting reform, rather than to enforce it on them. It was well enough for the opposition to use the state of Chancery business as a stick with which to beat the Lord Chancellor. Yet if the object was to secure changes by way of enquiry and legislation, that simple and artless procedure was scarcely sufficient. Peel's policy was therefore twofold: to defend Eldon against attack from without and at the same time to coax him into sanctioning an effective enquiry into the problem. To the latter, indeed, he found Eldon in no way insuperably opposed. The delays in Chancery were not due to lack of assiduity on the part of the Chancellor; and if in specific cases he deliberated too long, he was in no personal sense responsible for the general volume of arrears. The work of the court had immeasurably increased; the nominal list of causes awaiting decision included some not ready for presentation; and delays were sometimes caused by the parties themselves or their legal advisers. Straightforward and industrious in his professional work, Eldon felt keenly the attacks repeatedly levelled against him; and in 1823 he had already signified in the House of Lords his readiness to appoint a commission to enquire into what improvements could be made in the working of the Court of Chancery.

With the prospect of renewed hostilities in the House of Commons, the Lord Chancellor was anxious to secure adequate expression of his views in the lower House. Unwilling to ask favours from Canning, he turned for aid to Peel. 'I hope,' he wrote on 10 February 1824, 'you will be so good as to take some care of the Court of Chancery in the House of Commons. It is not possible to go on in my office, the object of constant attack which will never cease till the present Chancellor is removed. He is a nuisance therefore to the Administration.' Peel replied immediately and sympathetically, and eleven days later attended a private conference with Eldon and several lawyers to prepare a defence against Williams's forthcoming attack. It was agreed that Peel should meet the critics by moving for a commission of enquiry, such as Eldon had suggested the previous session; and Eldon lightened Peel's task by consenting to the inclusion in the commission of Sir William Grant and Lord Redesdale, both legal reformers, and accepting the principle that one of the objects of the enquiry should be to discover the proportion of work that could be withdrawn from the Lord Chancellor.[1] Both these, in Peel's opinion, were material concessions which he hoped would ensure a favourable majority in the division.

On 24 February Williams brought in his motion for a committee to enquire into delays and expenses in the Court of Chancery with a speech which, like his previous one of 1823, referred in considerable detail to a number of cases in chancery that seemed to justify the enquiry he proposed. He was answered immediately by Peel with a long speech in which, though he quoted Oliver Cromwell on the danger of quarrelling with lawyers, he defended Eldon's position point by point. Emphasising the great increase in the business of the court since the days of Hardwicke, he cited figures to prove the multiplication of appeals to the House of Lords, of lunacy orders, of bankruptcy commissions, and bills filed in court; and the steady rise in the amount of property contested by suitors in chancery which had continued unchecked from 1740 onwards. The business of chancery, he concluded, had multiplied four or five times and when Eldon's judicial and political duties were also taken into consideration, this in itself amounted to 'a complete vindication of the Lord Chancellor as far as related to the question of delay on his part'. He then went on to inform the House that the Chancellor had himself advised the appointment of a crown commission to examine the state of the Court of Chancery; and that although there would be grave disadvantages in severing the judicial and political functions of the Chancellor, there might be considerable advantages in enquiring into the question of delays and expenses in his court.

[1] Canning Papers, Peel to Canning, 22 February 1824; Twiss, *Eldon*, II, 487; *Peel*, I, 360.

There was no objection to the principle of enquiry proposed by Williams, but he suggested that a commission composed of judges, lawyers, and other technically competent persons would be a better instrument of reform than a committee of the House which would be bound to have the appearance of sitting in condemnation on the Lord Chancellor. In a personal defence of Eldon he quoted figures to disprove the charge of disproportionate fees levied by him, and in a telling description of his rigorous hours of employment, concluded that

> when, as was really the case, that individual had for a period of two and twenty years denied himself every indulgence, shunned every pleasure, and secluded himself from the society of the world, in order to devote his whole time to the performance of his public duties, it would be the most unjust thing possible to make it a matter of crimination against him, that he was not able to compass the whole of them.

The speech was completely successful. Abercromby and Brougham, who followed on the opposition side, both advised Williams to withdraw his motion; Lord Stowell, the head of the Admiralty Court, came out of the House of Commons in tears at Peel's eloquent and affectionate defence of his brother; and Eldon himself was rendered happy and grateful. Nevertheless, Peel had not intended his vindication of Lord Eldon to be a ground for delaying a fundamental examination into the undeniable inadequacies of the Court of Chancery. Shortly afterwards the commission of enquiry was created, including in its members the Lord Chancellor himself, the Vice-Chancellor, the Master of the Rolls, and various Masters in Chancery, barristers, and M.P.s. Peel took an active interest in the composition of the commission, showing an anxiety to see on it qualified persons independent of the government, and suggesting names like Stephen Lushington, the whig legal reformer, and R. P. (Bobus) Smith, the brother of Sydney, and an independent M.P. for Lincoln.[1] Moreover, when the commission entered on its work, Peel did what he could to urge it towards a conclusion. In the following year the opposition renewed their criticisms, and in June

[1] 40315 f. 135 (March 1824).

1825, at the end of the session, Burdett carried a snap motion calling for a return of undecided cases in chancery in the previous eighteen years. The motion was of no practical value, except in driving Eldon towards thoughts of resignation; but Peel made it clear to the Prime Minister that he could only resist similar motions in future if the report of the commission was completed and laid before parliament as soon as it reassembled. This steady pressure, reinforced by a personal letter from Liverpool, had its effect. By December Peel, who felt some personal responsibility for ensuring that the report would be available at the start of the 1826 session, was able to tell Canning that a satisfactory arrangement had been made. He was assured that the report would be ready for the opening of parliament and that the whole of the evidence would be appended to the report; and he had made preparations for its immediate printing so that it could be circulated before a debate came on.[1] This time-table was not strictly adhered to, but at the end of February 1826, some four weeks after the beginning of the session, the report of the Chancery Commissioners finally appeared. Peel wasted no time in instituting legislative proceedings. At his request the Attorney General Copley, as principal law officer of the government in the House of Commons, took into his charge the task of framing measures based on the recommendations of the commission, and in May a bill was introduced to regulate the practice of the Court of Chancery. The comparative lateness of the session, however, and the additional complication of various financial provisions involved in the bill, resulted in a postponement to the following session.

The cabinet were by now fully aware of the political dangers of any further delay, and Peel received support from the Prime Minister, the Chancellor of the Exchequer, and Courtenay, one of the members of the commission, in endeavouring to remove all the remaining obstacles to legislative action. Part, perhaps, of the difficulty sprang from Eldon himself. Seventy-five years of age, and harassed by his consciousness of personal hostility, he found it hard to turn his mind from the routine of work to considerations of reform. Indeed, he complained to Hobhouse that he was half dead from fatigue, and could not possibly carry on the daily administration

[1] Canning Papers, Peel to Canning, 15 December 1825.

of the law and also employ himself in correcting it.[1] A renewed contemplation of retirement, however, was cut short by the death of Sir Robert Gifford, whom he had wished to succeed to the Great Seal. Copley became Master of the Rolls, and Eldon consented to stay on for a while, rather than expose the government to the embarrassment of having two new equity judges. Meanwhile the course of chancery reform continued to be beset by fatalities and delays. Copley's bill, re-introduced in February 1827, was held up by the political crisis resulting from Liverpool's illness and it was not until Eldon had retired that a fresh start could be made. A series of orders in 1828 put into effect some of the recommendations of the commission, but the main work of chancery reform was left until after 1830.[2]

## III

The work of the Scottish and the Chancery Commissions was primarily concerned with technical questions of judicial procedure and organisation which had necessarily to be delegated to legal experts, even though the pressure to initiate and expedite enquiry came from the politicians. Between these two specialised fields of reform, however, lay the great expanse of criminal amendment and consolidation which Peel was determined to keep in his own hands. In his letter to Liverpool of October 1822 he had drawn the Prime Minister's attention to the decision of the House of Commons to take into their future consideration the state of the criminal law; and early in the new session he made it known to Mackintosh that he was ready on behalf of the government not only to state their attitude but to originate measures putting those views into effect. As Mackintosh was anxious, however, to bring forward resolutions in conformity with the pledge he had secured from the House the previous session, Peel was content to leave the initial moves to him. On 21 May 1823 Mackintosh submitted nine resolutions to the House of Commons, seeking approval for the abolition of capital punishment for forgery, larceny in shops, dwelling-houses and ships,

[1] 40315 f. 259.
[2] For Chancery reform, see Twiss, *Eldon*, II, 487-502, 561-5, 572-6, 586; III, ch. lxiii; cf. also W. Holdsworth, *Hist. of English Law*, I, 442-5.

and for stealing horses, sheep and cattle, together with the repeal of a number of obsolete statutes such as the Waltham Black Act of 1722, and the abolition of certain obsolete practices. Most, if not all, of these changes had been recommended by the 1819 committee.

Peel replied with a long and carefully prepared speech which for the first time made public his detailed attitude to the problem of criminal reform. He began with a reference to the resolution taken by the House in 1822.

> When he opposed himself to giving that pledge, he proposed to take into consideration the whole question of the criminal laws and to have the alterations projected stated specifically to the House. That was a pledge he was now ready to redeem. He conceded the proposition of the necessity of some amendment. There could be no necessity for him and the hon. and learned gentleman to debate that point. The real question between them was only as to degree.

Nevertheless, there were certain aspects of Mackintosh's proposals of which he was critical. He disliked the method of securing assent to general resolutions instead of specific bills; and he could not accept the principle that a rigid and uniform enforcement of penalties was a necessary improvement. A discretionary power in the executive, he held, was always expedient. There were many crimes from which Mackintosh did not propose to remove the death penalty that in practice were handled with greater or less leniency according to the circumstances of the case. For arson, burglary, murder, and rape, there had been only one execution in every ten convictions during the previous sixteen years; yet this disproportion between the offence and the maximum penalty prescribed by law, so far from being a defect, was a factor that operated beneficially on the criminal himself. No less an authority than Montesquieu had observed that where robbery was always punished by death, murder would be its certain accompaniment.

Then, turning to the specific propositions before the House, he laid down the detailed policy which the government was prepared to follow. Taking the report of the 1819 committee as his basis, he enumerated four classes of crime for consideration. The first were crimes which the committee had recommended should be left as misdemeanours at common law. Twelve of these were at that time subject to capital punishment. Four had already been repealed; and he proposed to do away with capital punishment for the other eight, most of which were crimes under the Waltham Black Act. The second class consisted of crimes which, though dangerous and pernicious, ought in the view of the committee to be punished by hard labour or transportation. To the abolition of the death penalty for most of these he was prepared to agree, though he would except the statutes against abduction of women, embezzling, and harbouring returned convicts. The third category was larceny. For stealing in shops and on navigable rivers and canals he was prepared to remit the capital punishment. In view of the increasing prevalence of stealing from dwelling-houses, however, he was not ready to alter the law in these cases. Finally, in the matter of forgery, he did not propose any change and the numerous exceptions which Mackintosh himself had deemed necessary to any mitigation of the death penalty for this offence, had convinced him that it would be inexpedient to alter the law in any respect. A reform was all the less necessary, he argued, in view of the decline in executions for forgery which had accompanied the return to cash payments. Other matters, such as horse and cattle stealing, and the legal consequences of suicide, which Mackintosh had brought in additionally to the recommendations of the 1819 committee, he thought too important to deal with incidentally and advised the House against taking any precipitate step.

In his final summing-up, Peel stated his readiness either to bring in bills on those cases of larceny he had mentioned, or to support them if Mackintosh preferred to introduce them himself. He also proposed to bring in measures to relieve judges of the necessity of pronouncing the death sentence when it was unlikely that it would be carried into effect; and minor legislation providing for expatriation and hard labour in the colonies in place of banishment. He ended by formally moving the previous question and secured a majority of ten (86-76) on the first of the nine resolutions; the remainder were then also negatived. But that was only a technicality. In effect Mackintosh had secured the approval of the government for the greater part of the 1819 resolutions and it was clear that the Home Department would itself now take the lead in reforming the criminal code. This in itself represented a complete transformation of the prospects for the criminal reform movement. The only point of interest was how fast and how far Peel would go.

If there was any residue of doubt in the minds of Mackintosh and Buxton, it must have been allayed by the prompt passing of five Acts in the two months that remained before the end of the 1823 session. One of them (4 Geo. IV c. 53) carried out two of the three larceny reforms which Romilly and Mackintosh had long urged: the abolition of the death penalty for larceny to the value of 40s. in shops and from ships in navigable waterways. A second (4 Geo. IV c. 54) repealed the Waltham Black Act. A third (4 Geo. IV c. 46) abolished the capital penalty for such miscellaneous crimes as breaking river-banks, cutting down hop-vines, destroying the Bedford Level, impersonating Greenwich pensioners, and stealing or destroying textiles and textile machinery. A fourth (4 Geo. IV c. 48) enabled judges to withhold formal sentence of death in all capital convictions except murder; and the fifth (4 Geo. IV c. 52) abolished the old barbaric custom of burying suicides on the high-road with a stake driven through the body. Two circumstances were noteworthy in this rapid fulfilment of Peel's pledges to the House of Commons. Not only did he carry out his promise of specific reforms, but he also included in the crimes for which the death penalty was no longer prescribed a number (such as the destruction of textiles and textile machinery, and embezzlement from naval stores) which had not been included in any previous scheme of reform. The other feature was the speed and silence with which these reforms, some of them agitated for years, passed through the barrier of the House of Lords into the statute book under the authoritative seal of the Home Office initiative. With a reforming Home Secretary the citadel of legislative inertia had been finally outflanked.

So at least it must have appeared to the reformers on the opposition benches as they witnessed, for example, the peaceful repeal of the Waltham Black Act which only three years earlier had been rejected by the House of Lords at the instance of Lord Eldon. Yet to conclude that the mere acquiescence of the Home Secretary in the principle of legal reform was in itself decisive would be to undervalue both the strength of the opposing forces and the administrative skill with which Peel undertook his task. For him the problem was not only to decide on reform but to translate those decisions into legislation. The 1819 committee, and indeed Romilly, Mackintosh, and Buxton themselves, had tried to take the government and the legal authorities by storm; Peel saw his work as one of persuasion. The uneventful passage through the legislature of such controversial and pioneer measures was only made possible by careful preparation beforehand; above all, by enlisting the knowledge and influence of men who directly or indirectly would be the final arbiters. What the whig legal reform movement had lacked was organisation; it was that which Peel made it his primary business to supply. In Hobhouse, his Under-Secretary, he had a coadjutor to whose services, as he on more than one occasion made clear to the House of Commons, he could not sufficiently pay tribute. Another invaluable assistant was Gregson, a barrister on the northern circuit, who became his chief legal adviser and played a leading part in drafting his bills. Well served as he was in his own department, however, he also realised the necessity of securing the co-operation of the judges. One of the principal defensive arguments that had been developed by Eldon and Sidmouth in resisting the reforms pressed on them by the opposition, was the need to secure the approbation of the judicial bench for any major changes in the law which it was their duty to administer. Peel saw to it that no such argument could be used against the measures he brought forward. Drafts of Home Office bills were circulated for comment by the judges, and professional advice was received from such eminent members of the bench as Bayley, Hullock, Holroyd, Burrough, and Gaselee. From the Lord Chief Justice, Lord Tenterden, he obtained assistance, both technical and political, which alone went far towards ensuring success. Not only did Tenterden devote, as Peel told the House in 1826, to 'the minute examination of these measures all the leisure which he could spare from the immediate pressure of his judicial duties', but he acted as Peel's collaborator in conducting some of his most important measures through the House of Lords.

For all this, perhaps, there was a price to pay. Co-operation pre-supposed assent, and assent could not always be expected to be unconditional. The legal profession in general, and the judges in particular, could hardly bring themselves to move with the rapidity desired by either the critics on the opposition benches, or such sections of the public as were interested in the problem. Yet to Peel's mind, cautious and sure, it was of greater consequence to create an agreed maximum of consent over a wide field of legal reform than to risk obstruction and defeat by pressing forward immediately to the furthest visible objective. If at certain points he stopped short of what he might conceivably have achieved, the very care and thoroughness with which the ground already traversed had been prepared inevitably imposed their own limitations. As Peel acknowledged, in a speech of 1827 on the consolidation of the criminal laws,

> he had another motive for proceeding gradually and slowly in this matter. It was necesssary to carry along with him all the instruments engaged in the administration of justice, for if too many changes were suddenly made in the laws of daily and ordinary occurrence, and if what was declared law were not executed well, no advantage would result to the country. . . . He would be content if, by his humble efforts, a gradual reform could be effected in our criminal law, without leading to any great practical inconvenience.

The very confidence he inspired assisted in disarming opposition. Judges do not often compliment law reformers, but Lord Tenterden paid an unusual tribute when he told the House of Lords in 1827 that 'it was fortunate for the country when a gentleman of comprehensive mind, not bred to law, turned his attention to the subject, for those who were bred to the law were often, by habit, dull to its imperfections'.[1]

Nevertheless, in winning the esteem of the legal practitioners, Peel did not entirely neglect the theoretical writers. He acknowledged in 1826 the debt he owed to W. O. Russell, whose best-known work, the *Treatise on Crimes*, had been published in 1819 and who offered a number of suggestions for Peel's consideration. An even greater theorist than Russell also gave Peel the benefit of his views during these years. At the date when Peel entered the Home Department Jeremy Bentham was seventy-four and most of his published work had already appeared. Yet his interest and activity remained unsubdued. In 1823 he had assisted in founding the

---

[1] Quoted Radzinowicz, I, 589 n. 84.

*Westminster Review* as the organ of the philosophic radicals, and a few more products of his pen were still to come. As the greatest theorist of his day in the field of ethics and jurisprudence, he could hardly be indifferent to the legal reforms being undertaken by the Home Secretary and, being Bentham, did not hesitate to make his own views known in his own inimitable style. Between the two men there could, at the outset, be little sympathy. Peel approached his work as a practical administrator in the spirit of the passage from Bacon that he once quoted to the House of Commons: 'the work which I propound tendeth to pruning and grafting the law, and not to ploughing up and planting it again; for such a remove I should hold indeed for a perilous innovation'. Bentham on the other hand started from first principles and wished to see a codification of the law that would replace rather than reform the mass of haphazard, chaotic legislation on almost every subject that confronted the legal reformers of the early nineteenth century.

Correspondence between Peel and Bentham passed at least as early as the autumn of 1826, the first topic of discussion being the magistracy. Bentham favoured the multiplication of ordinary magistrates and the maximum accessibility of justice. Peel, on the contrary, as he made clear in a letter of February 1827, maintained the view that at any rate in London it would be better to establish stipendiary magistrates at a reasonable salary rather than leave judicial functions to men who would serve either for a low salary or without payment at all. He took the opportunity, however, to pass a compliment on the observations which Bentham's nephew, Mr. George Bentham, had sent to him. Thus encouraged, the philosopher extended his work of proselytisation. The following month he sent Peel one of his own works, adding severely that 'according to Mr. B. and those who think with him, an adequate as well as authoritative definition of everything men are liable to be hanged for, or otherwise punished for, is a *sine qua non* in a penal code'. The Jury Act (6 Geo. IV c. 50) which Peel had passed in 1825 was the next to receive attention.

7 April 1827.

*Jury Packing Act.*

Sir,

    *Jury packing* is now my theme. In the passing of that Jury act on which your name is stampt, which of two objects, *abolition* or *establishment*, was the one really aimed at, I declare myself with all sincerity utterly unable to determine.

To enlighten Peel's darkness he enclosed an extract from his Constitutional Code (ch. ix para 16 supplement) entitled *Use of Lot as an instrument of selection*, and requested that Peel should decide whether to bring in amendments himself or prepare to receive them from some more or less hostile quarter. 'This is the 7th of the Month. From and after the 12th silence will be regarded and acted upon as a declaration of indifference.' Peel replied, as might have been expected, that he was not prepared to bring in a Jury Bill of the type favoured by Bentham. It is not surprising that the correspondence languished for a while or that Bentham expressed himself critically in private on what he considered to be Peel's timid and feeble handling of law reform.[1]

But before Bentham's long life closed in 1832 their relations became more personal and more cordial. In March 1830, following a statement[2] in the House of Commons by Peel of his intention to consider the defects in the practice of courts of law, Bentham sent him a long letter, rallying him on his conversion to the cause of reform.

> What is this I see? One of his Majesty's Principal Secretaries of State become a Reformist? a Law Reformer in good earnest? . . . Sir, you have passed the Rubicon. Your foot is on the career that leads to the ends of justice. . . . You, Sir, even you are fallen into the same pit with me.

In more serious vein he assured Peel of his complete support in such an undertaking as lay before him. Against remuneration by fees and the system of factitious expenses and delays, arguments might be found that would 'afford some facility to the operation of pulverising any objection which lawyer-craft might venture to oppose to the measure you have embraced'. The letter, dictated by Bentham because of his 'approaching blindness', ended 'believe me

[1] 40391 fos. 83, 87; 40393 fos. 65, 148, 156; cf. Radzinowicz, I, 574 and n. 24.
[2] On 9 March with ref. to Welsh judicature.

to be with cheering hope and unfeigned respect, Sir, yours Jeremy Bentham'. Several letters followed in March and April. Peel explained his intentions with regard to regulating fees in courts of justice and promised to send a copy of his bill when it was presented to parliament. Bentham, having learned that the Home Secretary had been enquiring whether there was any work by Bentham on the subject of transportation, referred him to his *Panopticon* and added an account of his project for the Millbank penitentiary—'official aptitude maximised, expense mimimised' . . . 'the Prisoners I should have made as tame as—yes, more tame than—lion was ever made; yes, and by the same principle—the all-affectionate one, *kind usage*'. In reply, Peel told Bentham that he was familiar with what had passed in connection with the parliamentary report on the *Panopticon* but expressed a desire to see Bentham's observations on pauper management. A copy, the only one in Bentham's possession, was sent to the Home Secretary at the beginning of April with a promise of a further printed copy in a few months' time.[1]

Despite Bentham's earlier criticisms and perhaps a permanent difference in their approach to the problem of legal reform, it is clear that by this time the relationship between the two men had grown much more friendly. Even before 1830 Peel had sent copies of his projected bills to Bentham and on occasions he visited the 'sage of the law', as he described him to the Commons in 1831, at his house in Queen's Square Place, Westminster. Bowring, one of the editors of the *Westminster Review*, has recorded seeing Peel walking with Bentham in the latter's garden, perhaps on one of his famous 'anteprandial circumgyrations', discussing law reform under the shadow of the house where Milton had lived while secretary to Oliver Cromwell.[2]

The Jury Act of 1825 which had been the object of Bentham's strictures in 1827, was the first great legal consolidating measure to which Peel turned his attention. The legislation of 1823 had constituted in his view an immediate alleviation of the criminal code where reform seemed most urgent and on which general agreement was already established. The Juries Regulation Bill which he

[1] 40400 fos. 94, 104, 134, 149, 151; Bentham Papers 33546 f. 124 (1827) wrongly attributed to Sir Robert Peel.

[2] *Recollections of Sir John Bowring*, ed. L. B. Bowring (1877), pp. 300, 338.

introduced in March 1825 represented the first calculated attack on the general state of the law. If it should prove successful, he told the House, he hoped that the principle of consolidation would be extended. 'It was impossible to contemplate the vast mass of laws in our statute books, without feeling that great advantage might be derived from extending the principle. The criminal code should be the first.' The Juries Bill indicated the technique which the Home Secretary had evolved in dealing with the problem. Scattered over the statute books were eighty-five Acts relating to the empanelling of juries. He proposed to consolidate them in one clear and intelligible Act, removing obscurities, repealing obsolete and redundant statutes, and resolving contradictions. At the same time he also proposed certain reforms and additions. The responsibility for drawing up lists of common jurors was removed from parish constables and given to the church wardens and overseers; a more distinct definition of qualifications was required; and appeals were to be heard at petty and not quarter sessions. An even more important change was the method of selecting special juries by means of registration and balloting, to be optional in civil and compulsory in criminal cases and when the crown was a real or nominal party. These changes were generally welcomed by the House. The ease with which the bill passed through both houses, indeed, was sufficient encouragement to essay an even more far-reaching reform.

A year later to the day, 9 March 1826, after long and careful preparation, Peel introduced the first of his great measures for consolidating the criminal laws. A general revision of statute law in this field, though formerly mooted, had never taken place, and a parliamentary committee of 1796 had drawn attention to the fact that parliament had suffered the question to sleep for a hundred years. 'What I propose is to break this sleep of a century; of more than a century indeed, for thirty years have passed away since the report of 1796 and each successive year has added its own heavy encumbrances to the statute book.' His proposals fell under two heads: the consolidation of the law relating to theft, and the improvement of certain aspects of criminal justice. Theft was selected in the first instance because it constituted the most important class of crime, amounting in 1825 to six-sevenths of the total number of criminal charges. The statutes dealing with it numbered about ninety-two, dating from the reign of Henry III to the sixth year of George IV, and frequently intermingled with widely different matters or related to specific or local crimes rather than possessed of any general application. That great bulk of confused legislation was now reduced to the compass of thirty pages. The first end aimed at was the enunciation of a general principle where it had, by hasty and slovenly legislation, been imperfectly applied; the strengthening of the law in cases where its own cumbrous procedure hampered proof; and the abatement of penalties that were unnecessary or unduly rigorous. The other great object was to render more efficient the general administration of criminal law. Under this heading came a reorganisation of procedure in the various stages of criminal prosecution from the coroner's inquest in cases of murder and manslaughter to final proceedings in courts of assize; in particular the introduction of safeguards against prosecutions being quashed on purely technical quibbles and defects.

On the broad question of criminal reform, Peel admitted that some critics might say he was proceeding too cautiously and too slowly, and allowed, for example, that if he was legislating *de novo* he should relieve private individuals by the institution of a Public Prosecutor. But he thought it would be unwise to force too many changes in rapid succession on the existing framework of law without adequate deliberation and perhaps without the necessary concurrence of the judicial authorities themselves. Even so, it could hardly be said that the progress of legal reform of late years had been too slow. The consolidation of the laws relating to prison administration; the mitigation of capital punishment; the revision of laws dealing with transportation and crown pardons; the corrections of abuses in writs of error; the recent Juries Act: all these, he claimed, constituted a record of advance since he had held office that indicated no indisposition on his part to review and improve the administration of criminal law. He ended with a full and explicit tribute to the various persons, from Hobhouse to the Lord Chief Justice, who had given him their advice and assistance, and a revealing if perhaps unwise reference to his 'legitimate ambition to leave behind me some record of the trust I have held, which may outlive the fleeting discharge of the mere duties of ordinary routine, and that may perhaps confer some distinction on my name, by connecting it with permanent improvements in the judicial institutions of the country'.

This long speech, adorned with quotations from Bacon, and illustrated by statistics of prosecutions and convictions, and by detailed examples of the erratic working of the law, received the general applause and approval of the House of Commons. Canning described it to the king as 'a speech of rare ability, temper, and information.'[1] Despite, perhaps because of, the unpolitical character of its subject-matter, it confirmed Peel's growing reputation as a reformer. A year earlier, when the two whigs Tierney and Moore had been discussing Peel, the former commented on the popularity he had gained by his Jury Act and added that he was the only reformer of the day.[2] This was unfair to some of Peel's colleagues, but it was a measure of the prestige he had won for the Home Department. The speech of 1826, printed copies of which he sent to various friends and collaborators, elicited tributes which went beyond the usual conventions of courtesy.

> You have made [wrote Lord Chancellor Manners from Dublin] the office of Secretary of State for the Home Department of infinitely more consequence than it has ever been in the hands of any of your predecessors. The well managing of our foreign affairs and interests may be more striking and brilliant; it is by no means more substantial or more important.

But the lesser men were not forgotten. In enclosing a copy of his speech to Hobhouse, Peel wrote generously that 'I cannot send you this without assuring you that I feel that the chief merit of the works to which it refers belongs to you.' Another copy found its way to his old college friend James, now rector of Flitton in Bedfordshire, who corresponded with him from time to time on various country topics.

There was, nevertheless, still much ground to be covered before the two bills presaged by his speech of 9 March passed into law. Both were brought in before the end of that month and sent to committee. The bill for improving the administration of justice, from its nature highly detailed and technical, evoked a considerable amount of discussion but no special opposition and received its

---

[1] *Geo. IV Letters*, III, 142.    [2] Moore, *Memoirs*, IV, 292.

third reading at the end of April, to become law the same session (7 Geo. IV c. 64). A separate motion, however, was made by George Lamb to allow counsel for defendants in cases of felony to address the jury upon the evidence. The lawyers in the House were divided on the issue—Williams, Twiss, Scarlett, Brougham, and Denman in its favour, Tindal and the law officers of the crown against. Peel admitted that the arguments on each side were as evenly poised as the weight of legal authority, but concluded that with such conflicting views it was not worth making a change, particularly in view of the protection afforded to prisoners by the need for unanimity in the juries' verdicts. On a division the proposal was rejected by a large majority.[1] It was another reminder that without the goodwill of the Home Department it was not easy to pass legal reforms even through the Commons.

The other measure Peel brought forward was the bill to consolidate and amend the laws relating to larceny and certain other offences affecting property. It failed to reach the statute book during the 1826 session, though this delay was due not to any opposition in the House but to second thoughts on the part of the Home Secretary himself. When the House came to consider the details of the bill in April, Peel proposed that it should go into committee *pro forma* only, so that the bill could be reprinted, and then stand over for reconsideration. The principal difficulty, he explained, was that the section of the laws dealing with malicious destruction of property was so intimately connected with theft, that it would be preferable to leave it under review in its amended form until the following session. Meanwhile, private discussions with the Lord Chancellor indicated some of the points on which his mind was engaged. In a letter of 14 April he suggested to Eldon the propriety of raising from 1s. to 5s. the distinction between grand and petty larceny, and of changes in the law relating to larceny from dwelling-houses. 'It is so desirable,' he wrote, 'to retain the capital punishment when the offence of stealing in a dwelling-house [is concerned] that I cannot help thinking it would be desirable to raise the amount, the stealing of which makes the offence capital, from forty shillings to five pounds.'[2]

[1] Debate of 25 April 1826.
[2] 40315 f. 252 (14 April). No year given but from position 1826.

When in February 1827 he again brought the subject before the House, he had disentangled the complex problem confronting him into four bills which in their entirety went beyond the original plan of the previous session. As he explained at the outset, his intention was less to propose fundamental changes in the criminal law than to proceed gradually in the course of improvement and avoid too much experiment. Even so, it was his wish 'to abolish every part of the criminal statutes that could not with safety be acted on, and to accommodate the laws relating to crime to the present circumstances of the country and the improved state of society'. The four bills he introduced were for the consolidation and amendment of laws relating to theft; the amendment of laws relating to malicious injury to property; the consolidation and amendment of laws relating to remedies against the Hundred; and finally the repeal of statutes rendered obsolete by the first three bills. Under the first heading he proposed to abolish the distinction between grand and petty larceny,[1] and to affix a common maximum punishment of transportation for seven years to a first, for life to a second offence. He also proposed to raise the limit of capital punishment for stealing from dwelling-houses from 40s. to a higher amount, later fixed at £5. The total effect of the changes envisaged would be to remove a hundred and thirty statutes from the book, and to consolidate the law of theft into less than thirty pages. In May he introduced a fifth measure to abolish certain obsolete institutions such as benefit of clergy in cases of felony, to simplify legal phraseology, and to lay down general rules for the whole body of criminal law. As in previous years the House of Commons responded with approval and encouragement rather than criticism, and by the end of the session all five bills[2] passed into law.

In his 1827 legislation, as in his earlier reforms, Peel had three objects in view: simplification, consolidation, and mitigation. What was achieved under the first two headings alone constituted a massive reform. It involved not merely the mechanical process of collecting under one head the confused mass of statutes and parts of statutes dealing with different classes of crime, but the more

---

[1] i.e. theft of articles of over and under 1s. in value respectively, the first being a capital offence.
[2] 7 & 8 Geo. IV cc. 27-31.

339

difficult task of simplifying, pruning, discarding, and amending the unplanned legislative accumulation of centuries. Though he did not aim at, in fact specifically rejected, the creation of a code of criminal law on the French, or indeed on the Benthamite model, what was accomplished represented in its scope and thoroughness a fresh point of departure in the history of English criminal law. His work under the third heading, however, was of necessity more cautious and more temporary, for it involved a question of policy on the crucial problem in criminal reform: the extent to which capital punishment could at that date safely be repealed for various offences. Much was done, of course, even here. In addition to the abolition of the death penalty for specific crimes, as in 1823, its scope was considerably restricted in 1827 by such measures as the raising of the limit of 40s. to £5 for stealing from houses; by a much narrower definition of the term dwelling-house in cases of burglary and housebreaking; by a relaxation of penalties for accessories after the fact in capital offences; and by a considerable mitigation of the law relating to malicious injuries to property. The abolition of the distinction between grand and petty larceny also made a sweeping reduction in the number of capital offences. This, however, was a formal rather than an actual change since in practice the death penalty was scarcely ever inflicted for grand larceny. Finally the abolition of benefit of clergy provided the opportunity for imposing a uniform secondary penalty for a large number of felonies. Except where a felony had been specifically made a capital crime, it was to carry in future a punishment of seven years' transportation or two years' imprisonment.

These changes in the penal system did not, as Peel was aware, satisfy all the demands of the humanitarian reformers. They represented, however, the limit to which he thought it prudent or practicable to advance in 1827. In his speech of 22 February in that year, he refused to give a theoretical opinion whether it might be necessary to go further in reducing capital punishment.

He never was an advocate for the infliction of capital punishments. . . . Willing as he felt, however, to reduce the amount of capital convictions, he advised the House not to be led away too far by mistaken feelings. If parliament were to proceed too rapidly to overthrow the existing enactments, a strong prejudice might arise in the country against measures that were intended for the public good; and thus the great object of justice and humanity might be defeated.

In thus stating his attitude he also drew the attention of the House to the record of capital punishments carried out during his own term of office at the Home Department; and it was indisputable that the administrative powers of reprieve and commutation in themselves represented a powerful limitation on the nominal severity of the law. Despite the increase both in population and capital convictions, there was a marked decrease in the number of executions carried out in the 1820s compared with the period 1810-17.[1] But for the time being Peel preferred to retain a relatively severe system of capital punishment combined with a wide administrative discretion, rather than proceed at once to an absolute reduction in the number of capital offences. In this he was influenced not only by the practical advantages of gradual reform, but by the startling and unwelcome increase in crime which had taken place since the first changes in the criminal law in 1823. Already, in his speech of 9 March 1826, he had emphasised the unsatisfactory trend of criminal statistics. In the seven years ending December 1816 there had been 47,522 criminal commitments in England and Wales; for the period of seven years ending December 1825 the corresponding figure was 93,718. Other comparisons between the two periods were equally discouraging. Convictions were 29,361 in the first; 63,418 in the second. Capital sentences were respectively 4,126 and 7,770; though it was a mark of the more merciful administration of justice that of these, 536 had been carried out in the first, and only 579 in the second period. Part of this increase was due to the rise in population; but only part. A committee of 1828 which compiled a similar table of comparative statistics for criminal commitments in England and Wales (excluding London and Middlesex) for the period 1811-17 and 1821-7, found an increase in commitments of 86 per cent and in convictions of 105 per cent. Even allowing for such factors as the growth of population, possible improvements in the detection of crime, and greater readiness of the public to prosecute and of juries

[1] Radzinowicz, I, 590 n. 85.

to convict, it was difficult to avoid the conclusion that crime was absolutely on the increase.[1] Moreover, the increase was not so much in the major offences, such as murder or highway robbery, as in the middle range of offences which provided the main area of contention for the humanitarian reformers.

Faced, therefore, in the country with all the appearances of a rising tide of crime, and in the Commons with a legislature that would not sanction any radical reform in the police system, Peel deliberately set himself against any further reduction in the severity of the penal code. At the same time he rarely lost any opportunity of reminding the Commons of the interdependence of the three topics of crime, police, and penal reform; and of the futility of pursuing reform in isolation from the other aspects. In discussing offences against property in March 1826 he made the observation that property in England was more exposed than elsewhere as a result of 'the freedom of action which is allowed to every man by our law, the absence of any control upon that action through the medium of police establishments, like those which exist in many countries, empowered to act upon vague suspicions and preventing by unceasing vigilance the commission of offences that would otherwise be completed'. In the same speech he ascribed the relatively more satisfactory nature of the criminal statistics for London and Middlesex, compared with the rest of the country, to the efficiency of the police establishments in the metropolis acting under the direct superintendence of the Home Secretary and devoting their whole time to their duties. In April 1827, in a discussion on the interference of the military in the Carlisle election, he pointed out that the whole civic force in Carlisle at the time amounted to two constables and that what was needed was not a body of volunteer constables but 'a well paid and united police'. The following month, in defending the use of spring guns by market-gardeners near London, he gave it as his opinion that it would be better if the market-gardeners took into their pay a sufficient number of ordinary constables. But he stressed the fact that while major crimes were diminishing, offences against property had greatly increased, and that this could only be ascribed to the defective state of the police in the neighbourhood of the metropolis. From these public utterances alone it was obvious

[1] Radzinowicz, I, pp. 588-9.

342

that Peel had never regarded as a permanent defeat the check administered in 1822; and four years later he was ready to make another effort. At the end of 1826 he gave notice of an enquiry into the state of the police in the districts surrounding the metropolis; and in private he was writing to Hobhouse that 'the continued increase of crime in London and its neighbourhood appears to me to call for some decisive measure'. With the legislation of 1827 he felt he had travelled far enough down the road of progressive legal amelioration. If five years of penal reform had merely resulted in an increase in secondary crime, it was time to turn once more to the creation of a preventive police.

CHAPTER

# 10

# PUBLIC DISCONTENTS

In the large and intractable matter of crime, the issue was one not of political principle but of legal and administrative methods. There was, however, another aspect to the task of preserving law and order which was considerably more complicated and embarrassing. Poverty, unemployment, and industrial disputes periodically produced their inevitable disorders; and in the rough and un-regulated society of early nineteenth-century Britain, disorders constantly overflowed into crime. Yet individual infringements of the law could not easily be detached from the local conditions which bred them, and those conditions formed a social and economic rather than a legal problem. Even from the legal point of view, however, the situation was made intrinsically more complex by the state of the law affecting industrial relations. The older statutory legislation regulating the relations between employer and servant, some of it dating from the Elizabethan period, had been allowed to fall into disuse; and by the time of the Napoleonic wars non-intervention was not only the received doctrine but the actual practice of the constitution. Confederations of workmen existed wherever trade and industry had grown up on any significant scale; but the existence and activity of these early unions had no legal basis, and had indeed to contend with severe legal restrictions. Combination in restraint of trade was a common-law offence, punishable as conspiracy and subject to heavy penalties; specific statutes existed forbidding unions of workmen in certain trades; and in 1799 the government had passed a general Combination Act. As amended in 1800, this Act prescribed a variety of minor punishments for workmen combining to secure higher wages, shorter hours, or a decrease of work, or wilfully and maliciously trying to dissuade or intimidate men from accepting or staying at work, or employers from providing work. It was made an offence to collect, receive, or give money for combinations of workmen or for strike action. The Act also forbade similar combinations of employers, and provided for arbitration in cases of disputes over wages and work.

The Acts of 1799-1800, however, scarcely clarified the situation. The clauses dealing with employers were virtually a dead-letter, and the Act itself was not as severe in its penalties as the old laws against combinations. In a desire to make summary convictions before magistrates legal, and to preclude the long delays possible under the common-law procedure, the government had imposed a maximum penalty of three months' imprisonment. Compared with the already existing penalty of seven years' transportation, this was a relatively innocuous deterrent. Not surprisingly, therefore, Pitt's Combination Act never became the main statutory barrier against trade unions. Except when speed of conviction was sought, it was on the common law of conspiracy, or such indirect means as statutes prohibiting secret oaths and the Treason and Sedition Act of 1799, that the employers were as likely to rely as on the Combination Act proper. But few employers could be perpetually at war with their workmen, and in many cases either from policy or prudence they came to terms with the unions. In fact, as every one with experience of industrial conditions knew, the growth of the trade unions could not be halted. Operating secretly, camouflaged in public-houses, disguised as sick clubs and benefit societies, they spread through the country as part of industrial expansion itself; and with techniques of meetings, delegates and federations, learned from masonic lodges, radical clubs, and dissenting chapels, they constituted an obscure but tenacious network of organisation which was feared and suspected by many of the governing classes. If employers had wealth, the men had numbers; and though the penalties of the law, when it could be enforced, were sometimes savage, the men had methods of their own—arson, vitriol-throwing, gunpowder, and assassination—even more ferocious.[1]

Industrial disturbances tended, therefore, to be a compound of private economic disputes, genuine distress, semi-illegal organisations, potential disorder, and specific crime, which required a degree of discriminatory handling on the part of the local magistrates

[1] cf. Aspinall, *Trade Unions*, Introduction.

and ultimately of the Home Department itself. Peel's first year in office provided him with early practice in this difficult branch of administration. In April 1822 there was trouble in the industrial district of Monmouthshire—strikes, rioting, and interference with the transport of coal to the iron and tin works. The magistrates applied for three companies of infantry, which were sent down to them early in May. In June came reports of fresh disorders in the Forest of Dean and not until July were the troops withdrawn from the area. Almost at the same time there were disturbances in Staffordshire near Wolverhampton, and a detachment of infantry was despatched there in May. Though two companies were withdrawn at the end of the month, a third was left in the district as a precaution. In October the discontent moved further north. The 'keelmen' of Newcastle-on-Tyne, who took coal in keels or lighters to the ships in deep water, came out on strike and were joined by many of the ordinary ships' crews. The strikers assembled in boats on the river and obstructed navigation, especially traffic in coal. Nearly ten weeks passed before they consented to return to work. At the start of the disturbances the mayor of Newcastle called in military aid, and these troops were later reinforced by three naval vessels and a number of marines stationed at South Shields.

All these outbreaks of disorder produced a crop of communications from employers, magistrates, clergy, civic authorities, and peers, from which the Home Department had to make its own assessment of the situation. The variety of witnesses was itself an advantage, for not all the correspondents were sympathetic to employers or blind to the grievances of the men. If manufacturers and colliery owners professed astonishment at the unreasonableness of the operatives, there were usually a few more disinterested local observers to point out the unreasonableness of the employers. The Home Secretary was not left in ignorance of the reduction of wages and the extension of the illegal practice of paying wages partly in kind ('tommy' or 'truck' as it was called), which had started the trouble in Staffordshire; and the Duke of Northumberland himself wrote more than one letter to emphasise the peaceful behaviour of the Newcastle keelmen in all respects save trying to prevent others from carrying out their work during the strike. In return the Home

Department continued to enunciate its settled policy of non-intervention in purely economic disputes. Magistrates were encouraged to act with energy and determination, to apply the remedies already prescribed by law, and to use the final sanction of military force only in extreme circumstances. Both for administrative and judicial reasons the military detachments sent into the disturbed areas were not allowed to be divided by their commanders into small parties for the defence of individuals or private buildings, and were only so employed under the direct orders of a magistrate. Invariably the emphasis was laid on the primary responsibility of local authorities, and the enforcement of law on all parties. For the rest the Home Department was studiedly neutral.

> Mr. Peel without entering upon the question whether more or less wages ought to be paid (which is a matter of contract between masters and their workmen) is only solicitous that the peace of the country should not be broken in consequence of disputes arising out of this question. And tranquillity having (as he trusts) been now restored, he is anxious by means of the punishment of the ringleaders, to deter the illdisposed from attempting a renewal of the disturbance by the effect by the hands of the law [of] the terror which he is always sorry to see imposed by military force.[1]

But the law was a two-edged weapon. In July 1823 he sent a sharp rebuke to magistrates at Frome who had been persuaded by master-manufacturers to issue warrants enabling constables to enter houses and impound raw material belonging to them on the looms of the weavers. 'Mr. Peel directs me to remark,' wrote Hobhouse, 'that however desirable it may be to preserve the property from deterioration, it is vastly more important that the magistrates should act strictly within the line of their authority and . . . he thinks the tendency of the measure you adopted is rather to foment than to allay the existing discontents.'[2] The caution was not perhaps without effect, for though eighteen of the striking weavers at Frome were sent to hard labour, the magistrates also imposed a fine of £20 on an employer for paying wages in truck; and their professed determination to administer the law impartially against all offenders

[1] H.O. 41/7/32 (20 May 1822).    [2] Printed Aspinall, *op. cit.*, p. 376.

was warmly approved in a second letter from Hobhouse at the end of the month.[1]

The following year, apart from some slight trouble at Sunderland in the early summer, was a relatively tranquil one; and from July 1824 to August 1825 the Home Department enjoyed a halcyon period of freedom from the acute industrial distress that called for intervention by the central authorities. The main cause of this was, of course, the general improvement in commerce and manufacture, and the consequent decline in unemployment. This period was, however, marked by a major change in legislation affecting trade unions principally brought about by Francis Place, the radical tailor of London and (in his own view at least) uncrowned king of the working-class movement. Ever since 1819 there had been a campaign, led by Hume in parliament and in the press by McCulloch the economist, for the repeal of the Combination Laws; and though the Benthamites made the question peculiarly their own, the ground was prepared for them by the increasing acceptance by informed opinion of the general doctrine of non-interference in economic policy. As early as 1822 Huskisson had expressed himself in favour of a parliamentary enquiry and in 1824, with the full support of Huskisson and Grant, the President and Vice-President respectively of the Board of Trade, a committee was finally appointed. Hume managed the committee; Place managed the witnesses. There was no report; but a series of brief resolutions was agreed on, and at the end of the session a bill passed through parliament almost without debate. The old Combination Laws disappeared, and workmen were given the right to combine for wages, hours, and work, and to persuade others to join them, subject only to a maximum penalty of two months imprisonment for threats of violence or intimidation. The Benthamites argued, and being doctrinaires believed in the argument, that the Combination Laws had produced the combinations, and that in a free society the workmen would once more act as individuals. Place professed to believe this, too; but his attitude was perhaps slightly equivocal since he knew that the working men expected the repeal of the Combination Acts to result in an immediate and appreciable rise in wages. The general liberal expectation,

[1] For the industrial disorder 1822-3 see H.O. 41/7/1-94; Aspinall, *op. cit.*, pp. 352-79.

however, was that the workmen would gradually accept a free market in labour and employment, controlled by the same iron laws of economics that governed other commodities.

The actual result, if unexpected, was entirely natural. In the west of Scotland a large number of spinners and weavers at once went on strike, bringing the cotton industry almost to a standstill from August 1824 to January 1825. More significant still, the strikers organised openly as never before. Public meetings were held; delegates appointed; terms fixed on which to negotiate with the masters; and conditions laid down for the conduct of workmen. Later in the year there was a series of strikes among textile workers, colliers, and other miscellaneous trades in Lancashire and the midlands to secure higher wages. The shipwrights and seamen in London and the north-east followed their example during the winter with consequent considerable dislocation of the coastal trade. The general demand for higher wages was frequently accompanied by conditions which struck contemporary opinion as novel and tyrannical: a closed shop for union men; restrictions on the number of apprentices and the use of machinery; the dismissal of unpopular foremen; and limitations on the total of men employed. Among the rules of the unions now visibly springing into activity all over the country were entry fees for union membership, forced levies on wages, affiliations of different unions for common action, control of stocks held by employers, and restrictions on work done by union members. The wave of strikes produced by the newly-won legal freedom produced, perhaps inevitably, a number of brutalities, mostly directed against non-unionists or blacklegs imported by employers. Two murders occurred and many were injured in Ireland; a Lancashire miner was beaten almost to death; a Glasgow weaver pistolled in the back; and seamen were attacked and driven ashore at Sunderland. Appeals by Hume to strikers in Lancashire and Scotland went unheeded and it became evident, almost before the end of the year that saw the repeal of the Combination Acts, that the situation could not be left as it was. From the reports streaming in to the Home Department it was clear that if the problem of the unions was not dealt with by Huskisson as an aspect of trade and industry, it would soon have to be considered by Peel as a matter of law and order.

At the end of March 1825 Huskisson moved for a new committee, and confessed at the same time that he had not examined the 1824 Act with sufficient care when it had passed through the House. He was supported by Peel in a short speech giving examples of restrictive and illegal union practices in London and Dublin. The system of delegation, observed the Home Secretary, was 'an excessive and infamous tyranny' and was in complete contradiction to any notion of free trade. 'The fact was that there existed the strongest necessity for a law to repress combinations, a law which should equally bind masters and men.' Peel had in fact already been taking some preliminary soundings in the matter. On 24 March, five days before the debate, he had written to the law officers of the crown to enquire what power would exist for repressing combinations of workmen if that part of Hume's Act were repealed which prevented prosecutions at common law. Copley's reply was to the effect that the common law procedure was defective owing to the delay and expense. A week later, after the new committee had been appointed, Peel instructed the law officers to draw up a bill to amend the provisions of Hume's Act, enclosing at the same time a copy of the evidence laid before the Committee of 1824. He also wrote to Goulburn in Ireland for information about Irish unions and suggested that union witnesses might be sent over. In the new committee neither Hume nor Place was able to rig the proceedings as they had the previous year. Both were displeased and not inclined to credit Huskisson and Peel with anything but a desire to serve the ends of employers. In fact the amendment to the 1824 Act which resulted from the 1825 enquiry was strikingly moderate. The committee reported in June and a bill founded on its recommendations became law early in July. No fundamental alteration was made to the principle of the legality of trade unions *per se*; but a maximum penalty of three months was fixed for persons who by violence, threats, or molestation tried to make others quit or refuse work, join unions, or contribute to union funds, or to force employers to alter their mode of carrying on business or employing men. Convictions under the 1824 Act had required two witnesses; the 1825 amendment allowed conviction on the evidence of one, with appeal to Quarter Sessions. The object of the new Act, as is obvious from its provisions, was not to make illegal either trade unions, or collective bargaining, or strikes, but merely to prevent the abuse of collective power and to defend individual workmen and employers.

With this Act on the statute book Peel hoped that the excesses of 1824-5 would be a thing of the past. As he wrote to Leonard Horner in November,

> I think the law with regard to combination as it at present stands, is founded upon just principles and I believe it will ultimately be as effectual as law can be. Men who . . . have no property except their manual skill and strength, ought to be allowed to confer together, if they think fit, for the purpose of determining at what rate they will sell their property. But the possession of such a privilege justifies, while it renders it more necessary, the severe punishment of any attempt to control the free will of others. A conviction of the uselessness of such attempts will, however, be much more service-able than the fear of their punishment.

At the same time he was prepared to sharpen the law if it seemed necessary. In Scotland, where simple combination was previously punishable only at common law, and the connection between combination and individual acts of intimidation not always easy to trace, there was a case for further legislation. It had been suggested to the Home Secretary by a Glasgow magistrate as early as 1823, that the operation of Ellenborough's Act of 1803, making stabbing, cutting and wounding a capital offence if committed in circumstances that would have made it murder if death had ensued, should be extended to Scotland. Peel now took the opportunity to put this suggestion into effect, adding at the same time a special clause on vitriol-throwing, for which the cotton-spinners of Glasgow had gained since 1820 an unpleasant reputation.[1] But vitriol was a weapon used by workmen against other workmen. There was nothing in this to derogate from Peel's claim when replying to Hume in the House of Commons on 30 June that 'ministers had never felt the slightest inclination to attend to the interests of the master, and to neglect those of the workmen'.

Indeed he could have cited his own administration of the Factory Acts to support this claim to impartiality. As early as February 1823

[1] For the passing of the 1824-5 Acts, see Aspinall, *op. cit.*, xxv-xxx and pp. 366, 392; Ramsay, *Peel*, pp. 74-82.

magistrates in Manchester were asked by the Home Department whether the provisions of the 1819 Act were being observed in the factories under their supervision. In May 1823 Peel circularised the Clerks of the Peace in Lancashire and Cheshire drawing their attention to the failure of the magistrates in those counties to comply with the section of the Act of 1802 (42 Geo. III c. 73) for the appointment of visiting magistrates for cotton-mills, and requiring a return of the names of those appointed at the following summer sessions. When the magistrates in Quarter Sessions had been finally brought to do their duty, their reports not surprisingly indicated a considerable laxity in the observance of the law on the part of the mill-owners. The stimulus from above, however, resulted in a flood of reports reaching the Home Department in 1824 which at least provided some picture of what was actually happening in the cotton industry. The conditions of child-labour varied widely from good to indifferent and sometimes thoroughly bad. Petty infringe-ments of the laws protecting the children were almost universal; bad cases were rare; but there was a general reluctance to bring any breach of the law into court. In this there was an evident connivance between masters and men. Nevertheless, the detailed information called for by a circular from the Home Office in August 1823 on such matters as hours of labour, meals, ages of children, and clean-liness of factories, was in itself a mode of securing a better regard for the law; and though many magistrates were palpably lukewarm in their zeal for the enforcement of factory legislation, a noticeable feature of the returns made to the Home Office was the activity of clergyman-magistrates who by their position were more free from private economic interests and by their calling more disposed to concern themselves with social problems in the industrial areas. In cases of extreme negligence the Home Department was quick to exert pressure. In October 1823, for example, the visiting magistrates of the Hundred of Leyland in Lancashire reported to their colleagues that in no case were the provisions of either the 1802 Act or the 1819 Act (59 Geo. III c. 66) being observed in the employment of factory children. When in February 1824 their report finally reached the Home Department it received immediate attention. Hobhouse wrote forthwith to say that Mr. Peel relied on the magistrates to take steps to inflict the penalties of the law in all cases where those penalties had been wilfully incurred. Nor did all the magistrates show dilatoriness or lack of zeal. At Rochdale the same month the magistrates on their own initiative served a printed notice on cotton-mill owners warning them that in future the law would be enforced and penalties inflicted for infractions of the Factory Acts. From the Home Office correspondence it was evident indeed that before 1823 there had been a general neglect of duty by both magistrates and factory-owners; it was equally evident that under the energetic administration of the department after Peel's arrival a decided improvement began to show itself.[1]

Wilful disobedience and obstruction continued, of course, to be encountered. It was met by an increasing severity of tone from Whitehall. When the law had for so long been a dead-letter, it was impossible to expect an immediate observance of all the regulations. But deliberate and gross defiance of the law brought a sharp reaction. In March 1823 the Home Secretary called on the Mayor of Maccles-field and another magistrate to provide a full account of a case which had occurred the previous November, when a large number of informations laid against cotton-mill owners for offences against the Factory Acts had been abandoned because of the non-attendance of witnesses, said to be due to intimidation on the part of their employers. Five years later, in February 1828, the visiting magistrates of Wigan reported that there were considerable abuses in the cotton-mills of that town which the court of Quarter Sessions had no power to remedy. Peel had letters sent to the two offending owners, William Wood and Thomas Darwell, informing them in precise language of the illegalities they were committing and conveying the Home Secretary's expectation that they would at once cease. Much of the difficulty at Wigan was that the acting magistrates in the borough were themselves mill-owners, and Peel took care to communicate with the Rev. Jonathan Brooks of Everton, the magistrate who had brought the case to his notice, telling him what had been done and requesting him to keep the Home Office in-formed should the law continue to be broken by the Wigan manu-facturers. In fact the infringements went on and became the subject of complaints from John Doherty, the secretary of the cotton-spinners union, in the following spring. This time a sharp letter was

[1] H.O. 43/31; 43/32; 44/14.

sent to the magistrates of Wigan, enclosing a copy of Doherty's communication, and reminding them of what had passed the previous year. 'I am now desired by Mr. Peel,' ran the concluding part of the Under-Secretary's letter, 'to inform you that if further breaches of the law are reported to him, he shall think it his duty to introduce a bill into Parliament for the purpose of giving to the magistrates of the county a concurrent jurisdiction with the magistrates of Wigan.' Doherty was informed of this letter and was asked to communicate again with the Home Office should he or his society obtain information of further offences. Incidents like these went some way towards justifying the continuing prejudice of the governing aristocracy against the appointment of mill-owners as local magistrates. Peel himself was primarily concerned with upholding the law irrespective of class or wealth. Nevertheless, for a Home Secretary, at the instigation of a trade-union official, to resort to the threat of such an extreme coercive measure against a body of magistrates was a remarkable example of the official disinterestedness which informed Home Office policy.[1]

Both the sources of Peel's information and the executive powers at his disposal were, of course, inadequate. Without a centrally controlled and salaried inspectorate, early industrial legislation was difficult to enforce even though its existence afforded a standard of behaviour. But if local magistrates were not always either active or impartial, there could be no doubt of the Home Secretary's views and policy. He co-operated with J. C. Hobhouse in 1825 when the whig politician was preparing his Cotton Mills Regulation Bill and supported the measure in the Commons, though he recommended him to confine its effects to making his father's bill really operative. As an administrative measure it came within Huskisson's province rather than Peel's; but, as Hobhouse himself recorded, the Home Secretary was in no sense disposed to offer any opposition to the bill.[2] He disliked on principle intervention in the free play of industrial activity; yet, as he had argued in 1818, there could be little question of freedom in connection with child-labour. In the wider field of industrial relations, however, what he wished to foster in the raw industrial society of his day was greater liberty and greater

[1] H.O. 43/31; 43/35; 43/37; cf. Ramsay, *Peel*, pp. 72-4.
[2] Broughton, *Recollections*, III, 95, 98-9.

order. It remained to be seen whether the working-class movement would, or even could, be built up on principles that were exclusively voluntary or humanitarian; or whether indeed employers, with their smaller numbers and greater influence, could be prevented from making private agreements among themselves to fix wages and prices. Though not a doctrinaire, Peel was sufficiently imbued with the notion of 'free trade' in its contemporary sense, that is to say freedom in all economic processes, to dislike both sets of combinations. However, as he pointed out to the Commons in March 1825, if they were conceded to the men, they could scarcely be denied to the employers. Yet the mere existence of combinations and counter-combinations was a provocation to disorder, and it was with disorder that he was immediately concerned.

## II

The industrial and financial boom that had been growing since 1819 came to a sudden end in 1825. There had been a spate of new joint-stock companies; much capital had been loaned abroad, especially to South America; and by the autumn the over-strained economic structure began to give way. From October onward there was a mounting rate of bankruptcies; many important country banks broke; and in December the Bank of England came within a hairsbreadth of suspending cash payments. Inevitably the English banking system, with its striking disparity between the monolithic Bank of England enjoying a monopoly of joint-stock banking on the one hand, and the eight hundred small uncontrolled country banks on the other, came under sharp criticism; and the criticism was given point by the relative ease with which the Scottish banking system, based on the great chartered banks with a ring of smaller joint-stock banks around them, had weathered the financial storm. It was inevitable too that parliament would ask for an enquiry, and Liverpool himself was ready with plans of reform. He thought much of the trouble could be attributed to the over-issue of notes of low denomination by country banks; and he was anxious either for an extension of joint-stock banks in England, which meant abandonment by the Bank of England of its monopoly, or for the establishment by the Bank of country branches of its own. Two bills introduced early in the 1826 session embodied the cabinet's solution. By the first the issue of notes under £5 was forbidden, and those already in circulation were to be withdrawn by 1829. By the second joint-stock banks were authorised outside a radius of sixty-five miles from London, and the Bank of England was given permission to set up branches in the provinces. As was to be expected, the issues involved aroused considerable controversy, and the parliamentary debates on the two bills lasted intermittently until May. In the Commons the brunt of the battle was borne by Huskisson, Peel, and Canning. Indeed, even before the session started Peel had been drawn into a discussion of the problem. In December 1825 Attwood of Birmingham, came up to see him in London with a letter of introduction from Sir Robert, and though the younger Peel had no faith in the remedy of increased small-note circulation which Attwood and his father prescribed, he took his visitor to see both the Prime Minister and the Chancellor of the Exchequer. In private he wrote to his Staffordshire neighbour and county M.P., E. J. Littleton, that 'I fear we have been working too fast, building too fast, importing too fast'. However, he drew the comfort that the crisis must result in a review of the English banking system and its establishment on more rational principles. Littleton encouraged him in the view that the solid country bankers had been sufficiently alarmed to accept some measure of control; and in January, in a letter to the same correspondent, Peel threw out the suggestion that a joint-stock system, such as the Scottish one, would probably give more security to the public than any obligation on the country bankers to deposit securities with the government.

When the debate opened the following month on the Bank Charter and Promissory Notes Bills, Peel expressed a firm conviction that the whole banking system of the country must be put on a sounder footing. In a speech of 13 February he attacked the country banks for contributing first to inflation by over-issue and then to crisis by equally exaggerated reductions; and he held up the Scottish system as a model to be followed. The worst effect of the financial crisis, he went on to argue, was always felt by those least able to bear it—the working classes who alternated between periods of high wages and periods of deep distress. For their sake alone no pains should be spared to find a remedy for the financial fluctuations which harassed the country. To the issue of small notes as a factor in producing instability he attached only marginal importance. This was perhaps wise; for there would have been an obvious superficial illogicality in criticising the small-note issue of the English country banks and at the same time praising the Scottish banks who not only issued £1 notes in abundance but now embarked, in a famous campaign led by Peel's friend Sir Walter Scott, on a struggle to retain that privilege. The government took refuge from the Scottish storm in a select committee of both Houses, and Peel found himself chairman of the Commons committee on the banking system of Scotland and Ireland. Its report, which he presented to the House at the end of May, prudently refrained from making any recommendations for major changes of policy in either country. But on the crucial matter of a reform of the English banking and currency system the government was in earnest; and a feature of the 1826 session was the energy with which the cabinet ministers in the Commons made common front against the government's critics.

The crisis, however, went even deeper than was at first anticipated. In the early months of the year, while the depression was at its worst, there was strong pressure on the government from the City and from many of its own supporters to relieve the shortage of money by the issue of exchequer bills. This the cabinet refused to do on the grounds that the market for exchequer bills was already overstocked, and that the proposed remedy would only increase the government's and the country's financial difficulties. Instead they forced on a reluctant Bank of England an agreement whereby the Bank would advance up to three millions on the security of actual goods in the hands of firms and individuals. Between the pressure in parliament and the reluctance of the Bank, the government was for a time in a critical position, and at one point Canning announced in the Commons that the government would resign rather than give way. Croker informed Wellington, then on a diplomatic mission to Russia, that Liverpool had expressly authorised Canning to make this announcement. Whether this was so is perhaps doubtful. Certainly Peel knew nothing of such an explicit decision; though the Prime Minister did remark to Peel and others in conversation that as he was personally pledged on the issue the best thing would be for him to retire and leave the rest of the cabinet to carry on the government. Disquieted by this language of desperation, Peel went privately to Liverpool afterwards and told him that it would be folly for the minister who presided over financial matters to retire at a time of financial crisis; and dishonourable to allow one member of the cabinet, and that the head, to make himself a sacrifice for the others. He for one, he added, would regard Liverpool's retirement as a dissolution of the ministry.[1] The surrender by the Bank at the end of February averted the crisis, and in the event the cabinet's firmness was justified. Not much more than half a million was actually advanced by the Bank on security, and though bankruptcies continued to run at a high rate during the remainder of 1826, by the summer the money market had recovered its stability.[2]

Finance and currency, however, formed only one aspect of the 1826 depression. There was another and more human side with which Peel as Home Secretary came into closer contact than perhaps any of his cabinet colleagues. As he had reminded the Commons in February, the worst sufferers from the depression were the labouring poor, caught in the tides and whirlpools of economic forces which neither financiers nor politicians had yet learnt to control. Panic and instability in the financial world meant stagnation and bankruptcies in trade and industry, and those in turn meant for the workmen short time, lowered wages, unemployment, hunger, and riot. The widespread industrial unrest that filled the correspondence of the Home Department in 1826 was heralded in the preceding summer by a renewal of the troubles with the seamen's union at Sunderland. Forcible attempts to prevent ships from sailing with non-union crews led to a clash with a troop of dragoons and the death of five civilians. Peel acted with promptitude. Two naval vessels were sent to patrol the mouths of the Tyne and Wear; and he promised to recommend a free pardon to any accomplice willing to lay evidence against any rioters actually concerned in a statutory offence. His efforts were evidently not matched by a corresponding vigour on the part of the local magistrates and at the end of the month he warned them that he would withdraw military assistance unless they made more exertion to enforce the law and bring offenders to justice.

[1] 40306 fos. 174, 182, 184, partly printed *Peel*, I, 394-8.
[2] For the 1825-6 financial crisis see also Clapham, *Bank of England*, II, 98-109 and *Early Railway Age*, pp. 272-5; *W.N.D.* III, 117, 143, 209; *Ann. Reg.*, 1826, ch. i, ii.

'Unless the law be steadily and vigorously enforced,' he wrote on 31 August, 'against all those by whom such acts of violence are committed, no other measures such as the detachment of the military or the stationing of ships of war in the port will be efficacious.' When a week later the shipowners suggested that the Treasury Solicitor should prosecute the rioters, Peel replied that he saw no reason why they should not do it themselves at their own expense. Later in the year he sent a party of marines to reinforce the ships of war at Newcastle, but the disorder at Sunderland dragged on until the autumn. In November, indeed, there were attacks by the rioters on the soldiers stationed there.[1]

The disturbances in 1826 began in February with rioting at Macclesfield. In March the Marquess of Londonderry was writing to the Home Department about distress in the north-east and combinations among the colliers. The same month the magistrates called in troops to assist in handling the disorders at the Abergavenny ironworks; and more troops were sent at the end of the month to Hinckley in Leicestershire. By April the disorders were spreading rapidly through the great industrial area of Lancashire. Reports of rioting, machine-breaking, and general subversion came in rapid succession from Accrington, Blackburn, Rochdale, Manchester, Bolton, Burnley, and Clitheroe; and the unrest soon threatened to spread over the Pennines into Yorkshire. Six people were killed in a clash with troops at a mill near Bolton in April; another was killed in an attack on a factory at Bradford in May. Elsewhere there were riots in places as far apart as Norwich, Macclesfield, Carlisle, and Trowbridge. In June there was trouble in Peel's own county of Staffordshire; in July the seamen of the north-east ports were restive once more; and acute distress was reported in the Glasgow and Paisley areas. The worst rioting and destruction of property took place in Lancashire. In the Blackburn and Manchester areas large armed mobs assembled in the last week of April and, despite the efforts of the military, went round for several days attacking mills and breaking machinery. It was estimated that in the course of a week about a thousand power-looms belonging to sixteen firms were destroyed. At Blackburn it was said that not a single power-loom was left standing in a six-mile radius of the town.[2]

[1] H.O. 41/7/103-14.     [2] *Ann. Reg.*, 1826, pp. 63-8.

In this welter of distress and violence the Home Department's first task was to stiffen the morale of the magistracy and local inhabitants on whom the main shock of the disturbances fell. Letters from the department repeatedly emphasised the need for local authorities to take precautions and exercise initiative; to prosecute offenders whenever they could be brought to trial; to look first to their own efforts and depend on the use of troops only in absolute necessity; and to send full, prompt, and accurate information on the disorders both to the Home Secretary and to the local military commanders. There was praise for good work and constant reminders that the best method of protecting mills and machinery was for the masters to arm their own workpeople in self-defence. In June Peel wrote to the Bradford magistrates warmly approving the policy they had adopted of not recommending a military guard for any mill where the owners themselves had made no preparations against attack. At the same time, however, he steadily strengthened the forces available for keeping order. At the start of the disturbances an additional regiment was stationed in Lancashire and further reinforcements were despatched at the end of April. More troops were sent north from London at the beginning of May, travelling on the Grand Junction Canal; and others ordered across from Ireland to Liverpool. The command of the Northern District was for the time being put in the hands of Sir John Byng whose experience and local knowledge would, it was hoped, be valuable in the difficult circumstances under which the troops were operating; and a temporary headquarters was set up in Manchester. The tactical deployment of troops was left to the commanding officers in the localities, to whom the magistrates were told to apply. But Peel sent a special request to the Duke of Wellington to strengthen the artillery force in Lancashire and to make arrangements with the Ordnance Board to enable local commanders to supply weapons for the defence of isolated mills.

Meanwhile, he did not relax his own precautions. Early in May he was asking about the state of the workmen and the possibility of outbreaks at such danger spots as Wolverhampton, Sheffield, Birmingham, Coventry, Leicester, Trowbridge, and Warminster. At the beginning of June the Home Department was taking anticipatory measures in South Wales in view of reports of wages disputes between the ironmasters and their men. One of the standing handicaps of the central authorities was lack of precise knowledge of what was actually going on in the industrial districts. Unwilling to neglect any source of information, Peel sanctioned the use of spies by the military commanders in the north and told Foster, one of the principal Manchester magistrates, that the Home Office would reimburse any expenses incurred in securing private intelligence on the disaffected elements in his neighbourhood. But he issued a warning against provocative action, showed considerable scepticism towards the reports that came into the department from these sources, and refused to authorise any prosecution based on their statements.[1] Prevention rather than suppression was, indeed, the main object of Peel's policy and he tried to instil the same attitude in the minds of provincial authorities. He made a point of congratulating Lord Grantham, whose yeomanry had played a leading part in the prompt dispersal of an incipient riot at Bradford in May; and of writing to the mayor of Leeds to praise the preparations made in his town to resist disorder. Even when the worst of the rioting was over, he wrote to Lord Liverpool on 9 July asking that no reductions should be made in the number of troops stationed in the disturbed areas. It was essential, he argued, to prevent any impression that the strong measures taken in the spring were only temporary. There was no immediate prospect of increased employment for the working classes and it was imperative consequently to keep a powerful military force on foot there.[2]

As his letter to the Prime Minister illustrated, Peel did not confuse symptoms and causes. The disorders arose from unemployment, poverty, and starvation, and though his main task was to repress disorder, he knew there could be no permanent security until the economic causes of the unrest were removed. 'At home the prospects are gloomy enough,' he wrote privately to Goulburn on 22 July. 'The great cause of apprehension is not in the disaffection but in the real distress of the manufacturing districts. There is as much forbearance as it is possible to expect from so much suffering.' To another correspondent he had written earlier in the summer that

---

[1] See the extracts from H.O. correspondence printed in *English Historical Documents*, XI (ed. A. Aspinall and E. A. Smith), 374; and in Ramsay, *Peel*, p. 66 n.
[2] 40305 f. 192.

'though it is found on the present, as on former occasions, that the mischief is not actually committed by the most distressed, yet the existence of that distress enables the ill-disposed to effect outrages which they cannot find the means of perpetrating when the manufacturers are in a more flourishing condition'.[1] In the meantime the only palliative was direct relief and in this he took an active part. As early as 24 April he was able to announce a contribution from the king of £500 to augment a sum of £900 raised locally to relieve distress in the Rochdale area; and similar amounts were sent at the same time to meet the distress in the Craven district of Yorkshire (where his own ancestors were said to have originated) and in the area round Bolton. In May he was able to notify further grants from the royal bounty: £1,000 for relief in Glasgow, £500 for Paisley. By 8 June all the funds placed at his disposal were spent, the balance having been sent to the general distress fund administered by a committee sitting at the London Tavern with which Peel was in constant communication. In the second half of July this committee was distributing £5,000 weekly in relief money. Nevertheless, at a meeting on 24 July Liverpool, Robinson, and Peel advised them to continue spending the remaining £57,000 left in their hands and assured them that when it was exhausted, the government would support a further appeal for funds. To direct encouragement of industry by means of government subsidies—what he described to Goulburn as 'quackery'—Peel was opposed both by theory and instinct. His main hope was to tide over the next few months until the country righted itself.[2] Writing to the Bishop of Chester, a member of the London Tavern Committee, on 24 July, he expounded his attitude more fully.

I fear that nothing effectual can be done until trade shall revive by the complete exhaustion of the present stock on hand excepting by direct pecuniary relief. I should not *a priori* have thought it possible that so much good could have been done and so much evil averted where the number of sufferers has been so great by the expenditure of little more than £60,000. Gloomy as the present prospect is, I confess I am sanguine enough to hope that the period not of complete but still of material relief is not very distant. The

[1] H.O. 41/7/201 (6 May 1826); *Peel*, I, 415.
[2] 40332 f. 74 (21 July 1826), original in Goulburn.

stock in hand of manufactured goods in London is certainly very low. In the home trade which is the great source of employment there must shortly be a revival. The importation from abroad of the raw materials of our manufacturers was so unusually great during the year 1825 that I fear it will be a considerable time before we shall recover from the lassitude caused by that extravagant exertion.[1]

The cabinet, like Peel, was against any large-scale government intervention in economic affairs as distinct from a temporary alleviation of the worst distresses; but like him also, they were determined to act vigorously within their own limited sphere to meet the crisis.

Just as financial instability had raised the question of the Bank of England, so poverty and unemployment brought up once more the larger question of the Corn Laws. Petitions for repeal from workmen and manufacturers alike poured into the House of Commons at the start of the session of 1826; and in April Whitmore, the whig M.P. for Bridgnorth, moved for a committee to consider a revision of the Corn Laws. The agriculturalists were alarmed and the cabinet embarrassed, for though they thought that there was a case for modification, they had announced on the first day of the session that they would not bring up the question that year, which was in any case the last of the 1820 parliament. Huskisson said with justice that it was worse than useless for the House to discuss the matter unless they were prepared to go through with it; but he pledged himself to take the first favourable opportunity of introducing the subject in the new parliament. Nevertheless, the increasing distress in the spring and early summer drew attention to the existence in bonded warehouses at Hull, Liverpool, and other ports of some 250,000 quarters of wheat in the immediate vicinity of the stricken areas. In May the government proposed to parliament that this bonded corn should be allowed to come on the market subject to a duty of 10s. a quarter on wheat and proportionate rates on other cereals; and they asked for discretionary power during the recess to admit foreign corn. Both proposals, though eventually carried, met with stubborn resistance from the agriculturalists, particularly the proposal to allow corn from abroad. The government was accused of inconsistency, of claiming unconstitutional

[1] H.O. 41/7/299.

powers, of acting on mere expectation, and of wishing to undermine the existing Corn Laws. It was only after a guarantee had been given that the amount admitted would be limited to 500,000 quarters during a period of two months, that the second proposal was approved. As in the financial debates, the ministry encountered some of the most bitter opposition from the ranks of its usual supporters and was aided by many of its usual opponents; and as before, the small knot of ministers in the Commons worked indefatigably together in defence of the executive policy against a confused, divided, and angry House.

Peel's major intervention came on 5 May, when the resolution for discretionary power to admit foreign corn was debated in committee. He denied having any prepossession either for the landed or the manufacturing interest, to both of which he was connected by important ties. But he asked for the attention of members to be given to the distress of manufacturers and the mass of unemployed in the industrial districts. How were they being supported at that moment? By the charity of their neighbours. What folly it was to contend that lowering the price of corn and increasing the amount of food which that charity could purchase would not assist the unfortunate classes who had no means of their own. It was said that to adopt this measure was to make a dangerous concession to infuriated and destructive mobs. 'Sir, there are two sorts of courage which may be displayed in respect of them: there is the courage of refusing to accede to such demands at all; and there is another kind of courage—the courage to do that which in our conscience we may believe to be just and right, disregarding all the clamour with which these demands may be accompanied.' He rejected flatly the insinuation that the disorders had been caused solely by lack of precaution, and told the House that months ago, in anticipation of such disturbances, he had doubled the forces available in the Northern District without any application from the authorities there. If disorders had broken out, they had also been repressed; and he instanced Yorkshire, where despite the widespread distress there had been scarcely any outrages and the working classes had borne their privations with fortitude and forbearance. All that the government was asking was for power to prevent public calamity, a power for the general safety of the people, which left untouched the question of a permanent and satisfactory settlement of the Corn Laws for which he anxiously hoped.

When the time came, the government's foresight was justified, since to the unemployment and poverty of 1826 was added the additional misery of a bad harvest. The wheat crop was average, but a drought in July and August seriously diminished the yield of the other grains, as well as potatoes and pulses. By the beginning of September the price of oats had reached the level at which importation was allowed, although the system of quarterly averages prevented the government from taking action under the existing Corn Laws until mid-November. A cabinet had been fixed for 5 September, but in the latter part of August the reports on the bad harvest prospects, especially in Scotland and Ireland, convinced Peel and other ministers still at their departments in London at that unfashionable season that they should have an earlier meeting. The responsibility for the rearrangement of business fell on Peel. By 21 August he had settled on Tuesday 29 August as the day for the cabinet, and had asked the king for a council meeting the same week. He himself had little doubt what their action would be, for simultaneously he requested Huskisson to prepare the necessary forms for opening the ports so that there should be no further avoidable delay.[1] Faced with reports of a prospective deficiency of one-third in the oat-crops of England, Scotland, and Wales, the cabinet did not hesitate. By Order-in-Council on 1 September the government opened the ports for oats, rye, peas, and beans, and summoned parliament for a pre-Christmas session to secure indemnity for their action. By that time the disorders were past their peak, though the distress continued especially in Lancashire and Scotland throughout the winter, and a steady trickle of reports came in from all over the country of strikes, turn-outs, disorders, and illegal union activities.

But at least there had been no Peterloo, no Six Acts, no widening of the gulf between the state in its institutional and legal aspects and the people as represented by the starving weavers of Bolton and Paisley. The workmen had revealed themselves as singularly free from the wild political ambitions instilled into them seven or eight years earlier by the Radical demagogues; and the public in general

---

[1] Goulburn, II/16, Peel to Goulburn, 1 September 1826; Canning Papers, Peel to Canning, 21 August 1826; 40300 f. 157.

had shown a much greater appreciation than in 1819 of the economic circumstances underlying the disorders. If the government had been inhibited by current economic doctrine from embarking on any wide schemes of state assistance to industry, it had shown a clear sense of impartial executive responsibility in its handling both of the Bank of England and of the agriculturalists in parliament, even at the cost of annoying many of its own supporters. In this general framework the Home Department under Peel had played a central part. Much damage had been done, and several lives had been lost; but at only one stage, in Lancashire at the end of April, had it looked as if the situation might get out of hand. By its nature, military force is a repressive rather than a preventive agency; and it was the only force which the Home Secretary had at his disposal. Yet what was remarkable was the skill and restraint with which that force was used; the absence of any wanton bloodshed; and the success of the central and local authorities working together in preventing a spread of the Lancashire disorders into the neighbouring industrial areas of Yorkshire and the midlands. The efforts of private charity had been stimulated and augmented by the state, and precautions taken against famine. Above all, the attitude of the Home Department, throughout the period of disorder, had been informed and humanised by the constant realisation that the problem with which it was faced was fundamentally one of human suffering.

# DEADLOCK IN IRELAND

When Peel took the seals of the Home Department in January 1822, only three and a half years had passed since he left Dublin Castle. In that short period there had been considerable changes in the composition and character of the Irish executive. The relative order and peacefulness of 1818 had broken down once more and his immediate successor in the Chief Secretaryship had shown himself utterly incompetent. The pious, humanitarian, and 'Catholic' Grant was not only a wretched man of business, but he was out of sympathy with the Lord Lieutenant and most of the senior officials at the Castle. When in London on a private visit in 1821 Talbot told Sidmouth that he had no confidence in his Chief Secretary and indicated his wish for a replacement. The Home Secretary laid the problem before the cabinet in November and it was resolved to make a clean sweep, replacing both Grant and Talbot. Adequate as the Lord Lieutenant might have been with an efficient Secretary, he had lost so much authority himself in Ireland that Liverpool thought it would be better to remove him at the same time as Grant and so avoid any appearance of discrimination. With so many other posts in the government changing hands at that juncture both men could be withdrawn without apparent reflection on their conduct. The problem was to find replacements. For the Lord Lieutenancy the cabinet considered three candidates: the Duke of Wellington, Lord Hopetoun (better known to the public as Moore's second-in-command, General Hope), and the Marquess Wellesley. The first seemed too eminent for such an exile; the appointment of the second, a professional soldier, might emphasise too much the gravity of the Irish problem; and it was finally settled, with some misgiving, that Wellesley was the least exceptionable of the three. His defects as an administrator, however, were notorious, and it was thought essential, if he went to Ireland, to furnish him with a capable Chief Secretary. The cabinet's choice fell on Goulburn, and it was not until his consent had been secured that an approach was made to Wellesley. Goulburn accepted with considerable hesitation; Wellesley with 'quite eastern ecstasy'; and the two oddly assorted drivers took over the reins of the Irish government a few weeks before Peel went to the Home Office.[1]

The changes in Irish administration did not, however, represent an entirely straightforward executive reconstruction. Liverpool's mind in particular had already been travelling towards certain wider conclusions of a kind which perhaps made it unduly easy to persuade himself and others of the abstract need to terminate Lord Talbot's viceroyalty. For some time he had been anxious for an understanding with the Grenvillites, and the main obstacle to such an understanding was Irish policy. An overture was made to Plunket as early as the spring of 1821, and when negotiations with the Grenvillites were resumed in the autumn of the same year, Liverpool told Fremantle that it was now possible for the government to keep the Catholic question in a state which would give preponderance to neither of the contending parties. Technically the Prime Minister was only reasserting the principle of neutrality on the Catholic issue which had characterised the cabinet since 1812. But the junction of the Grenville party with the government in 1821 implied to many observers that a fresh spirit was being infused into the old formula. Wellesley was too much an individualist to be classed as a member of any party, but he was on close terms with the Grenvillites and as a 'Catholic' his appointment to Ireland was as welcome to them as that of Goulburn was unwelcome. Though it was no business of the Lord Lieutenant to promote any alteration of the law, it was at least Wellesley's proclaimed intention to administer the law in a liberal and conciliatory manner; and the significance of the first 'Catholic' appointment to the Lord Lieutenancy since the Talents administration of 1806-7 was underlined by the further decision to replace Saurin by Plunket as Irish Attorney-General.[2] Saurin was given the offer of the vacant post of Lord Chief Justice but declined, and Bushe was promoted in his place.

---

[1] *Bathurst*, pp. 522-5; *Letter-Box*, p. 128.
[2] Buckingham, *Memoirs*, I, 232-53; *Plunket*, II, 85-6.

In these arrangements Castlereagh was anxious to obtain the previous assent of Peel and Goulburn, but there is no evidence that they were consulted. The Prime Minister was in fact committed to Plunket's appointment and an awkward situation might have been created by asking for Peel's opinion without being certain before-hand that it would be favourable. Liverpool's delicate balancing policy rested on an adjustment of persons and offices, rather than on any explicit attempt to secure agreement on questions over which it was clear that the various members of the cabinet could hardly be expected not to differ. By the time Peel became Home Secretary the reconstruction of the Irish executive had been completed, and all he could do was to write a warm personal letter to Saurin conveying a hope that the change in his situation would not affect his regard or diminish his confidence. Official propriety prevented the Home Secretary from any further expression of opinion but in privacy to Saxton he wrote that 'I doubt whether he [Saurin] has felt disappointment more deeply than I have.' It remained to be seen whether the conduct of Irish affairs by the 'Protestant' Peel and Goulburn and the 'Catholic' Wellesley and Plunket would lead to any greater harmony than had existed between the 'Protestant' Talbot and the 'Catholic' Grant.

In the interval since 1818 Peel had not lost his interest in Ireland and even before he went to the Home Office his library contained a notable section on Irish affairs. As Chief Secretary he had started to collect tracts and pamphlets on the subject, and in 1820 he had commissioned W. S. Mason, the secretary of the Records Commission in Dublin, to compile for him a representative collection of books on Ireland. As finally completed, Peel's Irish library comprised a hundred and twenty-five books, uniformly bound in green morocco, covering most aspects of Irish society: eleven on antiquities, twenty-seven on history, five biographies, twenty-six topographical, twenty-five statistical surveys, twenty-six on travel, and five on finance.[1] The formation of this collection was a clear indication of his continuing interest in the Irish problem. Since the Union there had in fact been no Home Secretary with Peel's experience of Irish matters; none so well informed; and none so

---

[1] *Bibliotheca Hibernica or a Descriptive Catalogue of a Select Irish Library collected for the Rt. Hon. Robt. Peel* (Dublin 1823).

prepared to take an active part in the direction of Irish policy. Indeed, the Home Secretary had more of the knowledge and experience of an Irish official—as he had remarked to Liverpool in 1816—than the newly appointed Lord Lieutenant and Chief Secretary in Dublin Castle. It was a position which might have had its inconveniences; but he told Goulburn in the first month of office that he was determined not to embarrass the Irish government with communications respecting patronage arising from his long connection with Ireland, though he would have to answer them and frequently transmit letters to Dublin.[1]

It was evident from the start, however, that the new Home Secretary was going to give abundant attention to the Irish part of his duties. He read the Irish newspapers; indeed, he was obviously keeping a closer watch on the Irish government press than the Chief Secretary himself. In December 1824, for instance, Goulburn found himself in the invidious position of receiving copies of the *Patriot* from London for his perusal and attention.[2] A year earlier Gregory had received instructions to send to the Home Office all Irish publications bearing on public affairs.[3] Peel's first act on taking control of his department was to write to Wellesley expressing the 'strongest attachment to Ireland and the sincerest desire to cooperate with you in the promotion of her welfare', and he added (perhaps in view of the known taste of his correspondent for admiration) an unusually flowery compliment to 'that union of energy and talent which has enabled you in not less exalted stations to triumph over the most appalling difficulties'. Two days later he wrote in more practical language to suggest the expediency of informal correspondence between them, and invited the Lord Lieutenant to send him any confidential communications he wished at any time. The following month, remembering perhaps the confusion into which Lord Talbot had fallen, he told the Lord Lieutenant that there was no need to acknowledge all his communications and that he would take it for granted that Goulburn would keep him informed of everything that passed in parliament and anything of interest that was not the subject of official correspondence.[4]

---

[1] Goulburn, II/13 (18 January 1822).
[2] 40330 f. 252, original in Goulburn, 6 December 1824; cf. *Peel*, I, 353.
[3] 40334 f. 75.    [4] 40324 fos. 5, 15.

Energy and informality, however, were the last qualities likely to appeal to the former Governor-General of India, and the regular flow of letters to Dublin from the new Home Secretary was in marked contrast to the scattered and haphazard incidence of vice-regal despatches. A long letter from Peel on 12 April 1822, covering eleven sheets of paper and every important aspect of Irish policy, was briefly acknowledged by Wellesley's private secretary, who explained that the Lord Lieutenant was ill, that the despatch had been read to him, that Lord Wellesley thanked him, concurred in his views, and would write later.[1] As time passed it became clear that Wellesley's habit of 'writing later' was almost psychopathic. In November 1824 Peel told Goulburn that some months had elapsed since he had heard from Wellesley on any subject whatsoever. 'There is nothing more difficult than to induce the Lord Lieutenant to write,' replied the Chief Secretary a few days later. 'It is his misfortune to have had the reputation of an able writer and a great statesman. To preserve this he considers and reconsiders every point until the moment is past when a knowledge of his sentiments would have been useful.' When he did write, moreover, he was apt to do so without consulting either Goulburn or Gregory. The following month Goulburn told Peel that he never saw the Lord Lieutenant's despatches until after they had been sent. Wellesley's mode of procedure was to call on everyone around him for their opinion, to state at length his own views, and then after due deliberation compile his own despatch. He was, thought Goulburn, extremely sensitive to any criticism and accordingly offered no opportunity to anybody for suggesting amendments to what he had written.[2] Even Goulburn's mild temper began to show signs of strain and in July 1826, in a private note to Peel from Cambridge, he expressed the gloomy conviction that on return to Dublin he would find the Lord Lieutenant 'as unreasonable and absurd as at any former period'.[3]

The Chief Secretary was not the only official at the Castle to feel the aloofness and inattention of Lord Wellesley; Gregory was another sufferer. After the intimate footing on which he had lived with both Chief Secretary and Lord Lieutenant in the days of Peel and Whitworth, the civil Under-Secretary now found himself

[1] *Ibid.*, fos. 35, 47.    [2] 40330 fos. 218, 235, 304.    [3] 40332 f. 44.

kept at arm's length by a Viceroy who scarcely seemed aware of his existence. After he had been in Dublin for five weeks, he had still had no conversation with Gregory. They had only met once in a private room and that was at a dinner-party given by the Lord Chancellor. Gregory, not unnaturally in view of Saurin's dismissal, drew the conclusion that his own supersession was intended. Peel cautioned him on no account to resign, but a year later Gregory's thoughts were still turned in that direction and Peel asked Goulburn to represent to him on public grounds the embarrassment which his resignation at that juncture would produce.[1] The atmosphere gradually lightened and, indeed, when Gregory raised with the Lord Lieutenant the advisability of his retiring on the accession of Canning's ministry in 1827, Wellesley advised him against any hasty decision. Nevertheless, it was clear that the old standing which Gregory had enjoyed in the Irish executive before 1821 was never recovered.

Throughout his period of office the Lord Lieutenant like an aging and jealous actress continued to inflict his temperament on everyone around him. The most damaging and exasperating of his traits was the unreasoning favouritism he showed to his illegitimate son, Edward Johnston, whom he brought with him to Ireland and installed as his private secretary. This was embarrassing enough, but in 1825 Wellesley made his domestic situation even more complicated by marrying Mrs. Patterson, discreet, beautiful, American, and a Roman Catholic. The king exploded with Protestant anger at the news that on the Sunday after the wedding Mass had been celebrated at the viceregal lodge in Phoenix Park. 'That house is as much my palace as the one in which I am,' he told Peel in a private interview before the Privy Council on 11 November, 'and in my palace Mass shall not be said.'[2] But in fact the trouble came not from the new Lady Lieutenant but from the egregious Johnston who, after a temporary absence, was restored once more to favour and confidence and soon began to create discord not only in official circles but between Lord and Lady Wellesley. Dublin gossip was regaled with reports of violent domestic warfare; Lady Wellesley

[1] 40334 f. 5; 40329 f. 61.
[2] 40331 f. 184, original in Goulburn (Peel to Goulburn, 12 November 1825); cf. also fos. 164, 178-80, 211, 233.

was clearly unhappy; her husband was always being announced as indisposed, and was undoubtedly ill and excitable.

> Since Johnston's re-establishment [Goulburn wrote to Peel in January 1827] I hardly ever see him [sc. the Lord Lieutenant]. Gregory never is admitted. . . . The torment that this fellow is to me is not to be described—not that he directly interferes but that he gives rise to a jealousy in the mind of the Lord Lieutenant which makes a long discussion and necessarily a written one the prelude to every, even the most trumpery, proceeding.[1]

Peel, however, was helpless to provide a solution. He had already taken up the matter with Liverpool and the Duke of Wellington, but neither thought that anything could be done.[2]

That this disjointed Irish executive lasted nearly six years could only be attributed to the political necessities of Liverpool's cabinet on the one hand, and to the steadiness and efficiency of Peel, Goulburn, and Gregory on the other. Even before he formally took up office, Peel wrote privately to Gregory with a glowing recommendation for the new Chief Secretary.

> As a public and private character I know not a single defect in him. He is prepared to give you his utmost confidence, to consult you on everything, and I have assured him that you will give him all the assistance in your power. . . . I hope often to hear from you. You know you may trust me with the most private communications.[3]

The long-standing friendship and confidence between the Home Secretary on the one side, the Chief Secretary and civil Under-Secretary on the other, was a fact of integral importance in the government of Ireland between 1822 and 1827. Not only did it offer a guarantee that the more important half of the machinery would work well, but it enabled Peel to guide and assist the inexperienced Goulburn to an extent which might not have been practicable with another man. At the start of their collaboration, in January 1822, when Goulburn sent half-apologetically a long letter

---

[1] 40332 f. 266.
[2] Goulburn (Peel to Goulburn, 9 January 1826; Wellington to Peel, 7 January 1826).
[3] 40334 f. 3.

of discussion and enquiry on Irish affairs, Peel begged him in reply not to think that any questions he might put to Peel would be troublesome. On any matter on which his opinion was asked he would do the best he could and would not be dissatisfied if Goulburn did not agree. Out of the store of his own experience and knowledge, however, Peel did not merely answer questions that were put to him but was constantly offering advice, suggestions, and encouragement. In September 1822 he was reminding Goulburn of the need not only to confer with the Lord Lieutenant on matters likely to come up for discussion in the following year, but to announce specifically what their intentions were, especially in view of the regrettable practice of postponing Irish measures until the end of the session. Two months later he was writing on the complicated subject of Irish tithes.

> There may be strong reasons for commuting tithes in Ireland, which reasons do not apply to England, but any measure which *forcibly* deals with tithe property in Ireland, must affect the same description of property here. I always expected therefore that you would require from the king's government here a decision on the principle of the measure in question.

There followed in characteristic style a long list covering three quarto pages of searching questions on the operation of the proposed bill, together with requests for concrete information and examples. Goulburn's reply, extending to seven sides of paper, evoked from the Home Secretary the comforting observation that the time they spent in examining the question, and in anticipating and obviating objections, was well spent; and that if he seemed to be suggesting difficulties, it was with a desire to improve and not defeat Goulburn's plan. The detailed criticisms and arguments which followed this preface filled a letter twice as long even as that of Goulburn.[1]

Another illustration of the Home Secretary's technique in handling his subordinate came in October 1823.

> *My dear Goulburn*, You forget nothing connected with your public duty, therefore it is useless to remind you. But by writing I

[1] 40328 fos. 9, 12, 129, 252, 277.

shall discharge from my mind two or three subjects which occasionally recur to it when I am revelling in the delightful contemplation
of Irish affairs and Irish debates.

With that disarming introduction came a practical discussion of the
linen trade and the possibility of government assistance to extend it
to the south of Ireland; parish schools; the obligations of moral duty
and political expediency on the Church of Ireland to make provision for the education of the poor in every parish; and the need
to do something to enforce clerical residence—'such men as Mr.
Henry Maxwell, drawing enormous sums from Irish livings, and
leading a profligate life at Boulogne, are the real enemies of the
Establishment'.[1] Goulburn, a sound if not brilliant administrator,
lacked neither energy nor intelligence; but dealing with a difficult
country and beset by personal obstacles in the conduct of the Irish
administration, he stood in need of all the strength that Peel could
supply, and there were times when his spirits perceptibly flagged.
Indeed, in November 1825 he described his position to Peel as 'the
most disagreeable office under the government'. But the Home
Secretary was always prompt to supply aid and comfort. He supported Goulburn in resisting what the Chief Secretary thought
were Plunket's inordinate requests for patronage on behalf of his
friends and relations; and when Goulburn showed him in July 1826
a tiresome and vexatious letter he had received from Lord Wellesley,
Peel returned a light and cheerful answer suggesting that much of it
had obviously been written under the influence of personal pique.
In fact, faced with Irish famine, Irish polemics, the temperament of
the Lord Lieutenant, and the acquisitiveness of the Attorney-
General, Goulburn was as near to despair in the summer of 1826 as a
man of his steady character was ever likely to come. So depressed
was he that in April of the following year he told Peel that it
would be useless for him to remain in Ireland if Peel abandoned the
Home Office.[2]

Few Irish Secretaries had an easy passage in the first half of the
nineteenth century; but Goulburn, even apart from his unhappy
relations with the Lord Lieutenant, had more than his fair share of

[1] 40329 f. 187, original in Goulburn, 28 October 1823.
[2] 40332 fos. 11, 44, 46, 321.

difficulties with which to contend. In his first year of office he was confronted with a partial famine over most of Ireland as a result of the failure of the potato crop the previous autumn. With experience of the 1817 famine behind it, however, the Irish government was active as early as April 1822, preparing to meet the distress with measures based on Peel's policy of 1816-17. Galway, Mayo, and Clare were among the worst affected areas and it was a mark of Peel's imaginative vigilance in distant London that in June he suggested the despatch of someone to the western isles since there was a danger of severe privation existing among the inhabitants of those remote areas without the fact coming to the knowledge of the Irish government.[1] The food situation remained a source of recurrent anxiety, for though the 1822 potato crop was good, there was another bad harvest in 1823. The oats fortunately were more abundant in that year, but the potatoes were deficient to the extent of a quarter and in some districts a third of what was thought necessary for the maintenance of the population. Like Peel before him, Goulburn was faced with the dilemma of either letting the situation develop naturally or starting to make purchases of food on behalf of the government with the consequent danger of forcing up prices and encouraging wasteful consumption of stocks already in private hands. Peel, in a despatch of 19 November 1823, was disposed to refrain at the moment from accumulating government stocks. He agreed that to do so would protect the administration against the criticisms of foolish people in the House of Commons, but he thought that to run the risk of such criticisms was better than to create public alarm and private improvidence. He doubted whether the government could act in secret, and if their commercial activities became known, it would raise the price of corn and stimulate speculation. There was no doubt that enough food existed in the United Kingdom to feed everyone until the next harvest, and government action could not increase that amount. His advice was, therefore, for Goulburn to overhaul the machinery of relief so that it could begin to operate, when necessary, with greater expedition than in 1822.[2]

The threatened danger passed over, and it was not until the generally bad year of 1826 that the Irish government, like that of

---

[1] 40328 fos. 69, 80, 100.     [2] 40329 fos. 199, 225.

Great Britain, had to meet a serious social and economic crisis. The commercial panic affected Dublin, where there was a curious mixture of strikes and unemployment, complicated by an outbreak of typhus almost as bad as that of 1817-18. In the country districts the wheat harvest promised well, but oats and barley had partially failed. Preoccupied though he was with the situation in England and Scotland, Peel did not forget Ireland. Thinking with justice that Goulburn would need 'a little oil', he arranged in July for him to draw up to £4,000 for fever expenses and another £3,000 to relieve industrial distress. A further sum of £500 came in the king's name for the poor of Dublin, and with all these funds at his disposal Goulburn was hopeful that he would be able to tide over immediate difficulties. Nevertheless, the reports on the oats and potato harvest continued to be pessimistic, and the prospect of renewed famine in Ireland was one of the considerations that prompted Peel to press for an early meeting of the cabinet at the end of August. He had asked for a memorandum on the state of Ireland to be prepared for the meeting originally fixed for 5 September and it was Goulburn's discouraging reply that brought him back to town to confer with Liverpool. 'If the worst shall happen,' he wrote to Goulburn on 17 August, '—that is, if the potato crop shall entirely fail—I fear that there will be no alternative but that most distressing one—the direct interference of government.' He pressed the Chief Secretary to ensure in that case the establishment of a responsible agency for administering relief—above all, no 'jobbing local committees'.[1] Meanwhile, he discussed with Wellington ways and means of meeting the crisis. The Duke calculated with military precision that in the event of full famine, £8 million might be necessary to support something like four million peasants for eight months. Peel, more sanguine and perhaps more realistic, doubted whether there would be a demand for as much as a million pounds solely for Ireland.[2]

In the event the worst anticipations were not realised. Though the early potatoes were scanty, the main crop held out. Relief of some kind was unavoidable, but Peel, as always, was determined neither to commit the government to a general and demoralising policy of

---

[1] 40332 fos. 65, 74, 76; 40300 f. 157; Goulburn, II/16, Peel to Goulburn, 14, 17 August 1826.
[2] *W.N.D.*, III, 385, 390.

public expenditure nor to allow the Irish landlords as a class to evade the burden of responsibility for their own tenants. To Lord Cloncurry, who wrote gloomily to him on the unemployment and inadequate means of subsistence among the Irish people, he replied briskly on 7 September that his own information did not confirm the tenor of Cloncurry's report. It was acknowledged, he went on to say, that England owed it to justice as well as interest to save Ireland from famine and pestilence; and England had already done much both in grants of public money and by private subscription and voluntary aid. But it was not for the English public to take on itself the discharge of obligations which justice and moral duty, if not strict law, imposed on the landed proprietors of Ireland.[1]

Questions affecting the rights and duties of the Anglo-Irish governing class were in fact in the forefront of Irish policy in Peel's early years at the Home Office. No advantage had apparently been taken by the cabinet of the appointment of Wellesley and Goulburn at the end of 1821 to have a general discussion with them on Irish policy before they departed to Ireland. In his first long policy despatch to the Lord Lieutenant in April 1822,[2] however, Peel raised a large number of points for Wellesley's consideration, including two that were to loom large in all Irish discussions for the next few years: tithes and magistracy. On the question of tithe, the Home Secretary confessed that he had never been satisfied with any of the plans so far put forward; and in any case it seemed unlikely that there would be any proposals for a general settlement of the question that session. With the magistracy the dilemma seemed to be between retaining men who were demonstrably unfit or leaving some districts without an adequate provision for the administration of the law. However, he threw out the suggestion that if some fresh scheme were adopted, an entirely new Commission of the Peace for Ireland might have to be drawn up. Both problems, however technical in form, were of wide political significance. The one raised the issue of Church property and the extent to which it should be subjected to state direction; and the other the crucial administrative issue of maintaining order and justice in the most lawless part of the British Isles. During the summer of 1822 a start was made on plans for the reform of the magistracy, but the Irish

---

[1] *Cloncurry Recollections*, p. 287.     [2] 40324 f. 35.

government showed no signs of evolving a satisfactory solution of the tithe problem. A palliative measure was introduced enabling tithe proprietors to lease them for a term of years to the tenants of the lands on which they were chargeable, but it was clear that something much more efficacious than this had been expected by the House of Commons. James Daly and other friendly Irish members were persuaded by Peel in June to postpone their own motion, but it was only by a majority of seven that the government were able to defeat a move by Hume and Newport to commit the House of Commons prospectively to a discussion of the problem the following session.[1] It was increasingly evident that if the property basis of the Church of Ireland was not altered by the government, an attempt would be made by the opposition; and, possibly, not without success.

For the ensuing session the Prime Minister was anxious to be better prepared, and in October he was urging Peel to ensure that the Irish executive had everything in train. It was essential, thought Liverpool, that they should prepare a plan for Irish tithes after full discussion on both sides of the water, so that it should not be left to the unpredictable chances of a parliamentary committee. With the urgency of these Irish problems Peel was in full agreement. On the question of the magistracy it had already been settled between himself, Goulburn, and the Irish Chancellor that the new reign provided an excellent cover for drawing up a completely new commission in which the number of Irish J.P.s could be reduced and the unsatisfactory ones eliminated. By the end of the year the revision of the list had been completed and a fresh commission was issued embodying a considerable number of changes. Tithe, however, was a more delicate question since it could not be disentangled from the question of similar Church property in England and required therefore a decision on principle from the cabinet.[2] A tentative plan for tithe commutation was submitted to Liverpool by the Lord Lieutenant and received an initial scrutiny in the cabinet at the end of November. Peel was not satisfied, however, that the subject had received a thorough examination and he plunged into an exhaustive

[1] Debate of 19 June 1822.
[2] 40304 f. 80; 38195 f. 120 (printed Yonge, *Liverpool*, III, 213ff.); Goulburn, II/13, Peel to Goulburn, 5 September 1822.

correspondence with Goulburn on every aspect of the tithe question which carried on until Christmas.[1] By the beginning of February 1823 heads of proposals were received from Ireland, and after consideration by the cabinet were drafted by Peel's instructions in the form of a bill. His apprehensions about the feeling that would be engendered in parliament by interference with Church property were fully realised. An attempt by Hume on 4 March to gain parliamentary sanction for the principle of state disposal of Church property was easily defeated. Nevertheless, Goulburn's bill itself contained a clause whereby, if the incumbent and vestry differed over the appointment of an umpire, the Lord Lieutenant was empowered to appoint a commission to make a composition based on the quantity and nature of the land in the parish. This clause was sharply criticised in committee both by those who thought the clergy would be unduly favoured and by those who disliked any notion of compulsion in relation to Church property. In the end the 'compulsory clause' was abandoned and the bill as passed simply made provision for voluntary commutation when jointly requested by the incumbent and the vestry. The bill was introduced in the House of Commons by Goulburn, and Peel took no great share in the main proceedings connected with it except to defend it in its amended form against the efforts of Fitzgerald and Wetherell to have it withdrawn entirely. In committee, however, he said he could not consent to any principle of compulsion unless the rights of the Church were secured and expressed the hope that the clause would be omitted from the bill. It is possible that as M.P. for Oxford University he felt a certain delicacy in his position. Certainly he was from the start very sensitive to the implications of Irish tithe reform for the whole position of the Established Church in England; and Abercromby went so far as to say that the dropping of the compulsory clause was solely attributable to the Home Secretary's position as university member.[2]

The Irish Tithes Composition Act was perhaps no more than a straw in the wind, presaging the ecclesiastical storms of the following decade. What more immediately confronted the Irish government was an angry domestic scene in which political and religious partisanship soon reached a height almost unprecedented since the Union.

[1] 40328 fos. 252-77.     [2] *Hansard* N.S., IX, 805, 810, 991.

Following the lax administration of Talbot and Grant, the arrival in Dublin of a Lord Lieutenant ostentatiously pledged to a policy of conciliating Roman Catholics aroused rather than assuaged sectional animosities. Such early acts as the prohibition of the annual ceremony of decking King William III's statue on College Green on 4 November, the anniversary of his birthday, roused the indignation of the Orangemen; and the 'bottle incident' which followed, when a rowdy demonstration took place against Wellesley in a Dublin theatre, was only one of a number of indications of outraged Protestant feeling. At the same time, however, there were ominous signs of a renewal of Catholic agitation. For all his liberalism Wellesley could not escape from the responsibilities of a system still in principle anti-Catholic; his attempt to hold a balance between the two parties merely resulted in exacerbating both. It was not long before his government was falling back on a series of ineffectual judicial measures against both sides. In 1824 it was decided, without reference to Peel, to prosecute O'Connell for having expressed in public the hope that 'another Bolivar might arise to vindicate the rights of the Irish people'; this at the very time when Canning was proceeding to a recognition of the revolted South American republics. Almost at once a second decision was taken, again without consulting the Home Department, to prosecute a prominent Orangeman, Sir Harcourt Lees, for calling on the Protestants of Ulster to arm themselves against the Catholics. Since the Irish executive had embarked on both actions before he could intervene, Peel made the best of the situation by giving his firm and unqualified approval to the men on the spot. 'I thought it but fair,' he explained characteristically to Wellington in January 1825, '(before the issue could be known) to commit myself personally to the support of what was at least well-intentioned.' In fact the trials ended in acquittals for Orangeman and Catholic alike. Plunket, as Liverpool dryly observed, was very unfortunate in his prosecutions.

Even with closer collaboration with the authorities in England Plunket's lack of forensic success continued. In January 1827 Wellesley wrote to Peel recommending the prosecution of Sheil for a speech delivered at a Catholic Association meeting and printed in the Dublin *Morning Register*. At the same time, the Lord Lieutenant added, the Irish law officers would like to have the professional opinion of their English brethren. Peel acted with caution; he submitted copies of the speech to the English law officers and also sent details to Liverpool, who was at Bath, and to Canning, who was at Brighton. The law officers and the Prime Minister were unanimous in thinking that a good case for prosecution had been made out. Canning, however, expressed certain doubts on the legal aspect. Before replying to the Lord Lieutenant, therefore, Peel showed Canning's letter to the law officers and asked them to reconsider the case in the light of his objections. They, however, adhered to their previous opinion and were supported by the Lord Chancellor. The need for a speedy decision now becoming urgent, Peel put the Lord Lieutenant in possession of all the facts, including Canning's dissentient view, and added for his own part that, trusting in the legal unanimity in both countries, he was prepared to take his full share of responsibility in advising the prosecution.[1] Armed with this sheaf of expert opinions, Plunket brought Sheil to trial and secured a true bill from a Dublin jury in February. Sheil's counsel obtained a postponement of the hearing until the next commission. In the interval Canning succeeded as Prime Minister, and when Sheil's case came on, the Irish government, acting on instructions from the cabinet, withdrew their prosecution.[2]

The real difficulty facing the Irish government in these years, however, was not so much the behaviour of individuals as the rising tide of feelings on both sides. Gregory went so far as to say in January 1823 that in all his long residence in Ireland he had never known the same violence of party animosity as then existed; and two months later he wrote gloomily to Peel that Ireland deserved its fate. 'The false pride and abject servility of the higher orders are more disgusting than the squalid poverty and sanguinary ferocity of the lower.'[3] Wellesley, who during 1822 had combined suggestions to dampen Orange Society activities with exaggerated expressions of alarm at the existence in Dublin of secret Catholic committees, pressed in November for an extension to Ireland of the Act of 39 Geo. III against treasonable and seditious societies. Peel viewed this proposal with little favour, particularly as it seemed as if the Act

[1] 40324 fos. 276, 287; Canning Papers, Canning to Peel, 29 January, Peel to Canning, 30 January 1827.
[2] *Sheil Memoirs*, I, 322-47, 359-60.     [3] 40334 fos. 27, 38.

would be used merely to suppress the Orange lodges. Not only would it leave the general situation in Ireland still difficult, but the Orange party would feel their loyalty was doubted and the Catholic party would be all the more encouraged.[1] At the same time he expressed to Gregory his conviction that the real security for Protestantism in Ireland was the support of English public opinion, which was worth more than all the Orange lodges that could ever be founded. That support, however, would have to be earned.

> In this age of liberal doctrine, when prescription is no longer even a presumption in favour of what is established, it will be a work of desperate difficulty to contend against Emancipation, as they call it, unless we can fight with the advantage on our side of great discretion, forbearance and moderation on the part of the Irish Protestants. If the worst should come to the worst, that forbearance and moderation will not have been thrown away.[2]

As always, there was parliament to be considered. In the spring of 1823 Abercromby gave notice of a motion on Irish secret societies, clearly aimed at the Orange lodges, and though the cabinet decided to resist the motion *pro forma*, Peel was authorised to state that Wellesley had already recommended a measure against secret societies and that the government was prepared to consider the introduction of a bill for that purpose at an early date.[3] This concession, announced by Peel during the debate of 5 March in studiously vague terms, was sufficient for its purpose and Abercromby withdrew his motion.

The difficulty was to know what kind of measure could be introduced; and with Goulburn tied during session to London, the constant embarrassment was lack of information. On 20 June 1823, in anticipation of a renewed discussion of Irish affairs in the Commons, Peel sent over a despatch to Dublin by special messenger, requesting a report on the recent state of the country. It was then exactly four weeks since he had last heard from the Lord Lieutenant. Wellesley, explaining somewhat stiffly that for the avoidance of inaccuracies and for the greater maturing of judgement he had decided to extend to one month the interval between his despatches,

[1] 40324 f. 101.    [2] 40334 f. 34, partly printed *Peel*, I, 341 (5 April 1823).
[3] 40324 fos. 131, 139.

answered with unusual punctuality on 22 June with voluminous
details thankfully received by the Home Secretary. To the two main
points in the despatch Peel replied a week later. On the question
of an increase in the military establishment, he said, the cabinet
concurred with him in thinking that it would be best not to arouse
anxiety by asking for additional credits until the fact of an emergency
could be proved; and on the question of wider legal powers to deal
with societies, the law officers were quite clear that the provisions of
60 Geo. III cap. 6 (the 1819 Act regulating public meetings) applied
to Ireland. Would that statute, together with the Irish Convention
Act, he asked, enable Wellesley to deal with the situation without
introducing fresh legislation so late in the session?[1] The session of
1823 ended, therefore, with no more than a renewal of the Insurrection Act for one year. Between endemic crime and renewed agitation
the prospects for Ireland were as discouraging as they had ever been.
Even the new police, set up in 1822, scarcely redressed the balance.
One of Goulburn's chief objects in instituting an extension of Peel's
constabulary was to infuse some vigour into the local magistracy.
As late as November 1823 he told Peel that it was a substitute rather
for the old rural constables than for the regular forces in Ireland,
which he thought would need to be maintained at the existing level
of about 21,000 for some time.[2]

## II

In the first two years of its existence, the attention of Wellesley's
government was diffused over a wide miscellany of Irish discontents.
From 1824 onward its apprehensions were increasingly focussed on
one specific source of agitation, the renewed movement for Catholic
emancipation. Two events were responsible for this rapid change of
attitude. The first was the founding in 1823 of the Catholic Association; the second the decision in 1824 to raise funds for the Association by a regular national subscription, the so-called Catholic Rent.
After preliminary work by Sheil and O'Connell the plan of the
Association was approved at an aggregate meeting on 10 May 1823.
Leading Catholics, including members of the old Catholic Board,

---

[1] 40324 fos. 165-225.
[2] 40329 f. 218; cf. 40333 f. 84 (Goulburn to Peel, 30 December 1829).

were asked to join and within a few days some sixty or seventy members were enrolled and a constitution drawn up proclaiming their intention of adopting all legal and constitutional means to secure Catholic emancipation. For the remainder of the year the new Association, with its weekly public meetings over a book-shop in Capel Street—derided by its opponents as the Popish Parliament— seemed to present no special danger. Meanwhile, however, a committee had been set up to study organisation and tactics, and in February O'Connell brought forward a scheme for organising small subscriptions from as many Catholics as possible in the 2,500 parishes of Ireland. The target aimed at was £50,000, which was to be spent partly on the furtherance of public agitation in Ireland and England, partly on support for Catholic religion and education.

From that moment the fortunes of the Catholic Association took a decisive turn. Neither the principle nor the name of the 'Catholic Rent' was new. What was unprecedented was the skill and success with which the reinvigorated Catholic leadership built up a national organisation for its collection. By the summer of 1824 some 4,000 collectors' books were in circulation; by the autumn the weekly amount received was over £300; and £1,000 was already invested by the Association in government bonds. By March 1825 the Rent had risen to nearly £2,000 in one week and investments to £13,000. The funds thus accumulated provided a basis for action of a kind never before achieved by the Catholics; but the political importance of the Rent was even greater. It gave to the Catholic movement for the first time a national organisation and a national interest; and it achieved a major success in linking the Dublin agitators, the Catholic peers and gentry, the clergy, and the peasants, in a common interest and a common aim. The redoubtable Bishop Doyle of Kildare and Leighlin joined the Association as early as 1823 and was followed by other members of the hierarchy and parish clergy. The bulk of the financial subscriptions, it was true, came from the towns. The poverty-stricken countryside displayed far less willingness to contribute, and on occasions there was recourse to various methods of persuading or coercing reluctant contributors. But the significant development in the rural areas was the growing habit of making collections at chapel doors on 'Rent Sunday' and the active participation of the priests as treasurers and propagandists for the funds.

O'Connell had aimed at raising money; he found himself with the most formidable instrument for national agitation that British history had ever known.[1]

Within a few days of the founding of the Association at the aggregate meeting of 10 May 1823, Peel was apprised by Wellesley of the new development. The Association, as the Irish authorities realised, was studiously legal in its constitution, but Peel pointed out in his reply that a body not illegal in origin might become so by its actions and he advised a close watch on its proceedings. Gregory, who took the precaution of writing to Peel himself, despite the Lord Lieutenant's announced intention of doing so, thought that the Association was merely the old Board under a new name assumed to evade legal penalties; and little happened for some time to disprove that assumption.[2] Peel took care, however, to study the newspaper reports of the Association's activities, and in November he was asking Goulburn about the names and numbers of those who attended its meetings and the attitude towards it of the Catholic aristocracy and clergy. He suggested also that something should be done to discountenance the publicity given to what he still called the 'Board'. 'Surely the government papers as they are called in Ireland (I suppose from doing mischief to the Government) need not publish the debates of the Catholic Board? The *Press* is what makes the Board and their debates of the least consequence. Studious silence upon all that concerns the Board would be the best policy.' But Goulburn's reply was what the Home Secretary, from his own experience of the subsidised Irish press, might have anticipated. So many readers of the government papers were interested in reports of the debates that sales would be prejudiced if they were omitted.[3] From the Lord Lieutenant all this time came little guidance. A despatch of 28 January 1824 on the state of Ireland contained much detail but no constructive policy. When, at the end of the letter, Wellesley adverted to the imminent expiry in August of the Insurrection Act, it was merely to say in his usual oblique fashion that it would be imprudent to come to any positive resolution on a

---

[1] Wyse, *Catholic Association*, I, 209ff.; Reynolds, *Catholic Emancipation*, pp. 14ff., 55ff.; *Life . . . of O'Connell*, ed. J. O'Connell (Dublin 1846), II, 398ff., 478ff.

[2] 40324 fos. 149, 156; 40334 f. 51.

[3] 40329 fos. 211, 217, 222; Goulburn (Peel to Goulburn, 14 November 1823).

subject of such vital importance and still less would he be prepared to advise the government to offer to parliament any decided opinion on its renewal.[1] This was both characteristic and useless. Fortunately there were other hands at work in Dublin. By the spring of 1824 Gregory had organised secret sources of information on the Association's activities and at the end of April sent a long annotated list of its members to London. Previously composed mainly of barristers, journalists, and merchants, it was now being joined by the Roman clergy; and the recent institution of the 'Rent' was one which Gregory viewed with considerable alarm. This was not because of the intrinsic sums involved but, as he explained to Peel, because he thought it 'the most efficient mode that could be devised for opening a direct communication between the Popish Parliament and the whole mass of the popish population'.[2]

Gregory was noticeably more pessimistic about the state of the country than he had been before Wellesley's arrival. For this there were good grounds, but it was also true that he was unhappy about his reduced status in the Irish government and this may have influenced his outlook on public affairs. He may also have helped unconsciously to colour the Home Secretary's attitude, since Peel probably put greater trust in his knowledge of Irish affairs than in that of any other member of the Irish executive. Certainly the marked increase in the activities of the Association in the spring of 1824 brought about a sharper note in Peel's letters to Ireland. It was impossible, he wrote on 14 April, to regard its proceedings without anxiety and apprehension; the publicity attending them counter-balanced the insignificance of the persons concerned. He suggested that Goulburn should confer with Wellesley and Plunket on means to suppress the Association. If it did not contravene the Irish Convention Act, would it be advisable to strengthen the law? If the Orange lodges broke the law, they also should be made to conform, or be included in any new law that might be thought necessary. Goulburn duly saw the Lord Lieutenant—it was the first time that they had discussed the possibility of measures against the Association —but Wellesley showed some hesitation and wanted to seek legal opinion before expressing his own views.[3] Nothing happened until

---

[1] The despatch is in H.O. 100/211.
[2] 40334 fos. 87, 94, 112.     [3] 40330 fos. 35, 39.

after Easter, when Plunket arrived in London with a draft of a bill to suppress dangerous confederacies, one of the professed objects of which was to put down the Association. Wellesley himself, however, preserved an official silence, and Peel for one did not get the impression from Plunket that the Irish government was convinced of the immediate necessity for such a measure. The cabinet discussed the problem on more than one occasion, but seemed in some doubt whether the bill submitted would answer its proclaimed purpose. Moreover, on 11 May Althorp pressed for a committee on the general state of Ireland and the government was obliged to counter with Peel's tactics of 1816, conceding a limited enquiry into specific recent disorders. In these circumstances it seemed advisable to delay for the moment any new restrictive legislation.

Irish policy continued to drift in this desultory fashion for the remainder of the summer. The Lord Lieutenant showed an inclination to hark back to measures forbidding Orange processions, but declared that no major decision could be taken in view of the differences among his own advisers and the absence of any clear directive from the cabinet. Goulburn meanwhile had private talks with some of the Orange leaders to discourage lawlessness among their followers. With this course of action Peel warmly concurred, though he was at pains to point out that the cabinet was anxious to suppress all partisan activities, and that the Lord Lieutenant was mistaken if he sensed any disinclination on the part of ministers to put down illegal societies. The difficulty was to find efficient means of doing so, since failure in such an attempt would have unfortunate consequences. By the end of October Goulburn himself was becoming alarmed at the gathering strength of the Association. The situation seemed to him to have materially worsened since he left London. The Association had increased in numbers and influence. Many of the gentry, both Catholic and Protestant, looking to the need for popular support at the next election, had joined the movement, together with numbers of clergy who whether from inclination or fear thought they could not stand aside. The part played by the priesthood in collecting the Rent in itself ensured that the Association would have to be taken seriously. What was most alarming, however, was the progressive tendency for the whole country to be organised and united under the leadership of the

Association. Party feeling was inflamed and magistrates overawed. 'It is not concealed also that whenever an election shall take place, the people will be placed in opposition to their landlords and such members only returned as shall please the Association.' The long despatch, covering fourteen sides of quarto, in which the Chief Secretary expounded these views was written on 27 October. It ended with an expression of hopelessness at finding an adequate remedy for the evils it detailed. Suppression by law would simply result in the re-emergence of the movement under another name. Something might be done by prosecuting the publishers of their proceedings. But Goulburn's main object, he confessed, was simply to bring the subject thus early before the Home Secretary.[1]

Peel was not unprepared for this communication and it was clear to him that the time had come for a radical decision on policy. He sent a copy of Goulburn's letter to Wellington and on 6 November replied at length to the Chief Secretary with a preliminary review of the various courses open to the government. An attitude of delay and opportunism, while offering some advantages, was not in his view commensurate with the real dangers confronting them. Prosecutions would scarcely lessen the influence of the Association, though it would remove the impression that the government connived at its activities. Mere reprobation in parliament would be useless—'the Association would beat us at a scolding match'. The existing law could be enforced, but only if the Association had violated it in such a way as to justify prosecution. A new law could be passed, either of a general nature that would include the Association, or one specifically aimed at the Association by name. Both were open to objection. The first could be evaded; the second, especially if it involved giving a wide discretion to the executive, would be subject, and perhaps justly so, to constitutional criticism. The main value of an appeal to the legislature would be the attention it would draw to the danger of the situation. 'If the discussion did nothing but bring matters to an issue, if it merely advanced the development of this drama by one act, it would do something.' Peel was not alone in thinking that something would have to be done. The Duke of Wellington prophesied civil war if the Association were not put down, and later in November the king wrote a

[1] *ibid.*, fos. 111, 123, 145.

stiff letter to Peel referring to the activities of the Association as 'intended rebellion'.[1]

One immediate stumbling-block, however, was the Lord Lieu-tenant. Peel had already heard through Goulburn that Wellesley was now saying that he had not shrunk from vigorous measures but that others had different views and the responsibility did not rest on him. This on enquiry turned out to be a reference to the incident of the previous session when the cabinet had failed to take up Plunket's draft bill. A subsequent memorandum from Wellesley dated 20 November confirmed that in his view at least he had intimated to the government through the Irish Attorney-General in the spring of 1824 the necessity for special legislation to suppress the Association and that the cabinet had decided against him. This retrospective version of events surprised and annoyed both Goulburn and Peel. 'On this as on all other occasions of difficulty,' wrote the Chief Secretary acidly, 'he is always the first to impute the difficulty to others.' Peel, waiting impatiently for an official communication from Wellesley, replied with equally sharp strictures on the Lord Lieut-enant's evasion of responsibility in simply sending over complicated bills without any expression of his own views on the subjects with which they dealt. 'This is not a manly and straightforward course and it leaves you and me in a situation in which we ought not to be placed.' He told Goulburn that if the Lord Lieutenant did not soon give his opinion on the Catholic Association, he would write to ask for it. Almost at once, however, Wellesley's memorandum arrived under cover of a letter from Goulburn and the cabinet at last had before it some expression of the Lord Lieutenant's views. Though Wellesley announced that the division of opinion among the Irish law officers made it impossible for him to act under existing law against the Association, he gave it as his clear conviction that without new legislation the evil would continue to grow. He promised, moreover, to write to Peel as soon as fresh legal advice was obtained. This was satisfactory as far as it went, and while awaiting the promised viceregal despatch, Peel urged Goulburn to take stock of the forces at his disposal and ensure that the Irish government was prepared for extreme emergencies. From the tone of his letters it was

[1] *ibid.*, fos. 161, 163, originals in Goulburn, partly printed with verbal errors in *Peel*, I, 346-9.

apparent that the Home Secretary was strongly impressed with the dangerous state of Ireland even though Goulburn pointed out that the danger was not of a general rising but of sudden and local disorders against which there could be no anticipation. The Catholic Association in itself presented only a framework of national organisation in which a future leader might emerge to foment rebellion.[1]

On 6 December Wellesley wrote a private letter to Peel, deprecating any early meeting of parliament to discuss the Irish question and making the startling observation that 'when Parliament shall meet, some preliminary enquiry will certainly be necessary previously to any legislative enactment on the subject of the Association'. The notion of submitting the question of executive action against the Association to a parliamentary committee shocked the Home Secretary and he at once wrote off a reasoned but strong protest against that mode of procedure. Such an inquest conducted by such a jury would in his view create delay and argument, add no new information, and merely take away from the government its constitutional responsibility and all appearance of character and firmness from whatever action might eventually be taken. He was prepared to wait until the last possible moment before taking a decision, but should action be necessary he wished to make an immediate announcement in the king's speech at the opening of session. Before his letter arrived in Dublin, however, Wellesley's official despatch of 10 December had been sent off, formally conveying the opinion of the Lord Lieutenant that the question of fresh legislation or fresh coercive powers for the Irish government should be referred for preliminary enquiry to the parliamentary committee on Ireland appointed the previous session.[2] With this despatch before them, the ministers began their consideration of the state of Ireland at a long cabinet on 14 December. Peel was in favour of a strong measure, undertaken on the responsibility of the government without reference to the parliamentary committee on Ireland. With this opinion the cabinet agreed, and while the Irish executive plunged precipitately into simultaneous prosecutions of O'Connell and Harcourt Lees, Peel concerned himself with preparations for a bill to suppress the Catholic Association. His own view remained that it

[1] 40330 fos. 161, 171, 173, 194, 205, 218, 230, 269, 352.
[2] See Peel-Wellesley correspondence 6-11 December 1824 in H.O. 100/211.

ought to be a general Act against all political confederacies, including the Orange societies; but, as he told Goulburn, he was no lawyer and the details of the measure were so full of technical pitfalls that it would have to be put in the lawyers' hands. He urged Goulburn to come over with the Attorney-General a week before the start of session so that they would be prepared with details on the first night. The cabinet was to assemble in London on 20 January and he wanted a draft to lay before it by that date. At the beginning of the new year he had discussions on the draft with Copley and Wetherell, the English law officers, and with better news arriving from Ireland he was able to take a few days off before the opening of session which he employed in thinning Palmerston's pheasants in Hampshire. 'As the massacre is postponed and O'Connell and Sir Harcourt have paired off,' he wrote in more cheerful vein on 9 January 1825, 'I shall go down to Palmerston at Broadlands for two or three days.'[1] His momentary pique at Wellesley's devious conduct in November had dissipated, and he was anxious for all members of the government in England and Ireland alike to work together with cordiality and confidence.

The decision to keep the measure in the hands of the government, and the care devoted to its preparation, were more than justified by the hostile reception of the bill in parliament. An announcement of the ministers' intention was made in the king's speech, and on the second day of the session Goulburn gave notice of his bill to amend the Acts relating to unlawful societies in Ireland. The debate opened on 10 February and for four successive nights was bitterly contested by the opposition. By the end almost all the available speaking talent on either side had been called up: for the government, Goulburn, Leslie Foster, Peel, C. W. Wynn, Plunket, Dawson, Robinson, and Canning; for the opposition Abercromby, Parnell, Denman, Tierney, Spring Rice, Mackintosh, Lushington, Newport, Althorp, Burdett, and Brougham. Peel, speaking on the first evening, delivered a speech pitched in his lower, more specifically debating, key. A great deal of his time he devoted to a detailed examination and refutation of various points raised by the opposition speakers who had preceded him. But he stressed two particular points:

[1] 40330 fos. 310, 372; 40331 f. 27; Goulburn (Peel to Goulburn, 14 December 1824), printed with wrong date and minor errors in *Peel*, I, 353.

the activity of the Catholic Association in interfering with and over-awing the work of the local Irish magistracy, and its deliberate assumption of political authority even to the point of imitating the forms and regular sittings of the House of Commons. If people suffering from grievances set up unconstitutional associations to decide on the proper mode of redress, he argued, there was an end to the representative and legislative functions of parliament. 'Parliament would abandon its duty if it allowed any body of men to act independently of its authority, and only according to their own free pleasures.' His speech, though competent, was not one of his better efforts, nor was it one of the outstanding performances in the debate.

In fact, the concern of the opposition was less for the details of the bill than for the general cause of Catholic emancipation; and a further diversion of interest was created by the tendency of some of their speakers to turn the debate into a personal attack on Canning and the Grenvillites for having changed their coats on entering the ministry. Canning, making on the last night what was perhaps the finest contribution to the debate, devoted the last part of his long speech to an eloquent vindication of his consistency and pointed to Peel, sitting on the bench beside him as member for Oxford University, as a living symbol of one of the sacrifices he had made for the Catholic cause. 'He laid hold of Peel's shoulder awkwardly,' related J. C. Hobhouse, 'and wished him "a long possession of the mistress he had lost". Peel, who was apparently not prepared for the familiar wishes of his colleague, shrugged his shoulder and looked uncomfortable.'[1] Goulburn's motion was carried by a large majority, and the remaining proceedings on the bill in the lower House were concluded before the end of the month. In its passage through the Commons, however, Peel had a brush with Brougham. In a sharp exchange which developed over some Catholic petitions against the bill presented by Brougham on 17 February, Peel had drawn attention to the laudatory address presented by the Association to Hamilton Rowan, 'an attainted traitor' of the United Irishman movement, when he was made member. There happened to be present at the debate, sitting under the gallery, O'Connell, Sheil, and other members of the Association who had come across to present the

[1] Broughton, *Recollections*, III, 87-8.

petitions. Furnished on the spot with information from these Irish experts, Brougham was able to make a telling reply. To the triumphant cheers of the opposition he announced that Rowan had subsequently been pardoned, made a magistrate, and actually received at Dublin Castle. Peel flushed and looked discomfited but after the division he surprised his opponents by congratulating Brougham on his speech and adding that of course he had felt very much what Brougham had said about his reference to Rowan. Burdett explained away this action by saying that Peel was too stunned and stupefied by the blow to know what he was doing; but Burdett's understanding of his fellow-men was not perhaps of the finest.[1] In the end, however Peel shared the honours of the encounter. On application to Ireland it transpired that Rowan had not in fact been admitted to the magistracy, and Peel was able to use this information with effect in the debate on the third reading.

Goulburn's bill received the royal assent on 9 March. By its terms any body of persons acting in redress of grievances in church or state, or intervening in judicial proceedings, renewing its meetings for more than fourteen days, or collecting or receiving money, was declared unlawful, the Act to remain in force for four years. Its effects were immediate but transitory. The Catholic Association disbanded and the collection of 'Rent' was for a time discontinued. But shortly after the close of the parliamentary session an aggregate meeting in Dublin set up a committee to consider further action and in July was formed the New Catholic Association with the self-proclaimed programme of not acting in any way which would be inconsistent with the recent statute. Framed with lawyers' skill, the provisions of the new association were either negative or innocuous, and with a supreme gesture of tongue in cheek, the committee responsible for its constitution proceeded to instruct the Catholic movement on the mode and object of procedure, now that 'petitions to parliament must of course be altogether unconnected with the New Catholic Association'.[2] Given the constitutional framework in which both sides were acting, it was clear that the subtle Irish barristers of the emancipation movement could always contrive a legal method of pursuing their agitation by some means or other.

[1] Broughton, *Recollections*, 88–90; Sheil, *Memoirs*, I, 222–6.
[2] *Ann. Reg.*, 1825, pp. [43–5.

Nevertheless, the Act of 1825 was not without a crippling effect and though the partisan feeling aroused by the earlier Association still manifested itself in popular meetings throughout the country during the remainder of the year, the government was satisfied with what had been accomplished. The event to which it looked forward with greater anxiety was the general election due to be held in 1826. As early as September 1825 Goulburn anticipated contests in eight certainly, and possibly eleven, of the Irish counties, and was convinced that in some at least of them—Waterford, Mayo, Kilkenny, and Cavan—the influence of the priesthood would be brought to bear on the electorate in opposition to the gentry. 'The protestant interest in this country is the support of the government,' he wrote pessimistically to Peel, 'I ought rather to say, of government and of British connection, and wherever that shall be defeated, as it will be in many instances, you will have an immediate political opponent.' All the signs, he thought, pointed to a corrupt, disturbed, and unpleasant election.[1]

When it came, the general election, fought in the middle of the famine year 1826, went a long way towards fulfilling these depressing predictions. It was not the first time the Roman Catholic clergy had intervened in elections, and most informed observers of the Irish scene were convinced some years beforehand that if it came to a direct collision of appeals to the Irish peasant, Catholicism and the priests would beat property and the Protestant landlords.[2] What was new and impressive in 1826 was the extent to which the influence of the Catholic Church was exerted and the significant success which that influence obtained. The Irish boroughs, with their small oligarchical corporations, were virtually immune from popular pressure; but the large freeholder electorate of the counties offered an open field for clerical and demagogic influence. Not since the Union had the organised forces of Irish Catholicism played the part they did in the election. Catholic support was instrumental in electing candidates in Co. Dublin and Roscommon. In Waterford, Louth, Monaghan, and even Westmeath where Gregory had been hopeful of success, the freeholders deserted their landlords and

---

[1] 40331 fos. 147-9.
[2] cf. evidence of Anthony Blake and J. L. Foster to Committees of both Houses (*State of Ireland*, I, 407, 452).

returned emancipation candidates.[1] Waterford was the stronghold of the Beresfords, but Lord George Beresford was weakened by the rivalry of Villiers Stuart, a relative of the influential Duke of Devonshire. When confronted with the sight of his own tenantry being marched against him by O'Connell and a Catholic priest, the Rev. Mr. Sheehan, he abandoned the unequal contest before the close of the poll. In Louth, the Foster country, where Leslie Foster entered on a contest with a promise of five-sixths of the votes, he found his supporters melt away like snow in the spring. Sheil came down to aid the campaign; committees on behalf of his opponent, Alexander Dawson, were set up in every parish; and priests visited every Catholic elector. The clergy preached against Foster in chapel and Sheil told the freeholders that it was a choice between 'the distress warrant and the cross'. When the poll started priests took up their stations to watch their flock do their duty. The result was a widespread defection by the Foster supporters even on their first vote, and an almost universal one on their second. Dawson, who in normal circumstances could only have counted on about 120 votes, received 862; and of the 250 votes promised to Foster by Lord Roden, only ten were actually cast in his favour.[2]

To Goulburn the outlook following on the election seemed as bleak as could be well imagined. Never had religious animosities run deeper; never had the priests and agitators been so triumphant. O'Connell was master of the Catholic clergy, and the clergy masters of the Irish people. On them would depend the fate of the country in the ensuing winter: hardly a consoling situation for the Irish executive after four years of endeavour to reduce party feeling and preserve to Roman Catholics the full enjoyment of their legal rights. Gregory, while noting that some of the most ferocious elections had been those in Galway and Kerry, where no religious differences existed, agreed nevertheless that if Catholic influence continued much longer, the result be a transfer of the choice of M.P.s 'from the landed proprietor to the Popish priest'.[3] Leslie Foster, who had scraped into second place in Louth by a margin of five votes, described with mortification the swagger of the priests, the insolence of the tenants, and the popular feeling that 'stick to your

---

[1] cf. McDowell, *Public Opinion*, pp. 104-5.
[2] 40388 f. 7.     [3] 40334 f. 178; *Peel*, I, 416.

priests and you will carry all before you'. Sir George Hill, writing from that venerated shrine of Protestantism, Londonderry, said bluntly that the present situation could not be endured. The Catholics were united as one man, and common safety justified counter-associations. Under the initial impact of these tidings of gloom from Ireland, Peel tried to preserve a balanced judgement and even to extract what grains of comfort were discernible in the general scene of alarm and defeat. To Sir George Hill he wrote on 16 July that 'I am not so sure as some are that the priests have triumphed over the landlord. They have carried the tenantry in some counties by a *coup de main*. I doubt whether there may not be a powerful reaction. . . . Six or seven years is a long interval of sobriety after the drunkenness of an election.'[1] To Foster he speculated in much the same strain, though he touched on a more fundamental dilemma when he added that the old question remained—whether these things were merely the result of artificial distinction and disqualification, or were due to something more ineradicable in the nature of Catholicism in a country like Ireland. 'It would be a greater relief to my mind than I ever hope to enjoy,' he confessed, with a rare disclosure of his inner doubts, 'to be persuaded that the removal of the present disqualifications will be a cure for the present evils, and at the same time leave Ireland under a Protestant government.'[2]

But the remainder of the summer brought no grounds for a more hopeful view of Irish prospects, and in October he thought it necessary to remind Goulburn once more of the need to take precautions. Various considerations, 'the event of the last elections tending to dissolve the bond between landlord and tenant', the approach of winter, the violence of Catholic demagogues—all were arguments for making every kind of preparation. As always, he felt it was best to err on the side of overcaution. What was the strength of the regular forces in Ireland? What was the actual size of the police force? What was the state of their efficiency, their fidelity? If means of defence ought to be strengthened, let them be strengthened. On this aspect at least Goulburn was reassuring. With a force of some 20,000 regulars, the Irish government had adequate means of preserving order; and there were in addition some 4,000

[1] 40388 f. 66.　　　[2] *ibid.*, f. 62, printed with minor errors *Peel*, I, 413.

police which at need could be reinforced by about 1,500 revenue and waterguard officers, and 1,200 militia staff. Of the present loyalty of both troops and police there was little doubt; they were too roughly handled by the mob to have any affection for them. Yet it was a disquieting circumstance that so many of them were Roman Catholic. If rebellion broke out, reinforcements would be needed but they could quickly be brought over from Lancashire.[1] In the event, the Irish establishment so far from being increased, actually diminished. The decision of the cabinet in December to prepare an expedition to Portugal resulted in a call for a draft from Ireland; and though clearly taken aback by the summons, Goulburn made an attempt to comply by holding in readiness two regiments already under orders to leave for India in the spring.

At the end of the year the Lord Lieutenant revived, but in his characteristic evasive way, the question of prosecuting the Catholic Association. Without expressing his own opinion he merely transmitted the opinions of the Irish law officers, together with a brief note saying that he was too ill to do more than refer Peel to the Chief Secretary for certain relevant details. By the time his communication was received in London, Goulburn had already left for Ireland, and Peel was obliged to write with renewed exasperation for further information.

> How is it possible that we can form an opinion on the policy of prosecuting the Association [he enquired on 15 December in a private note to Goulburn] on such documents as those which I have hitherto received? Pray write to me your own opinion, confidentially if you please, on the whole subject. Collect as far as you can what is the opinion of Lord Wellesley, if he has formed any at all.

The latter request was not easy to fulfil. Goulburn on his return had found Johnston in greater power than ever, and experienced constant trouble in getting the Lord Lieutenant to discuss at length any matter of importance. His immediate impression was that Wellesley wished to throw on others the responsibility of acting or refraining from action. However, he collected further information on the

[1] 40332 fos. 154, 174, partly printed *Peel*, I, 420-1.

Association to send off to Peel, subjoining his own opinion that there was no reason to depart from the decision taken a year earlier not to prosecute. The influence of the Association had declined and it was proving less easy to collect the rent. The real danger came from the general activities of the Catholic agitators in the country, and still more from the quasi-independent exertions of the priesthood, who having demonstrated to themselves their own strength would continue to exercise it. Eventually, some three weeks after his return to Ireland, Goulburn managed to extract the views of the Lord Lieutenant. They turned out to be after all, like those of Plunket and Goulburn, against a prosecution.[1] With this belated conclusion Peel and the other cabinet ministers thankfully concurred. Seven weeks later the sudden illness of the Prime Minister broke up for ever the uneasy team of officials and ministers that had ruled Ireland since the start of 1822. But for Peel it had been an unsatisfactory five years. In the triangular relationship between Wellesley, Goulburn, and himself, he could only guide and stimulate policy, not enforce it. Though in higher office, he had less direct power; and the fact remained that he had done more for Ireland between 1812 and 1818 as Chief Secretary than between 1822 and 1827 as Secretary of State. That was not his fault; but compared with his work in England, the Irish pages of his Home Office administration formed a relatively barren chapter. Implicit in that lay an uncomfortable moral.

[1] Goulburn, II/16, Peel to Goulburn, 15 December 1826, enclosing note from Wellesley to Peel, 5 December 1826; 40332 fos. 205, 209, 211, 213, 227, 241; partly printed *Peel*, I, 428ff.

# THE END OF LORD LIVERPOOL'S ADMINISTRATION

The reconstruction of Liverpool's administration after 1821 had given it a renewed lease of office. With the Grenvillites detached from opposition, the loss of Castlereagh made good by the retention of Canning, Peel at the Home Office, Robinson replacing Vansittart[1] as Chancellor of the Exchequer in January 1823, and Huskisson appointed President of the Board of Trade the following April, the government took on an increasingly workmanlike appearance. The additional number of efficient cabinet ministers in the House of Commons redressed the balance of executive authority which had become dangerously uneven after Canning's resignation in 1820, and as leader of the House he could afford to take a less prominent part in debate than his predecessor had done. Yet for all that a certain air of looseness and disunity persisted. To some extent this was due to greater activity in government policy. More things were being attempted by ministers than were thought possible or desirable in the half-dozen years after Waterloo, and the liberal, reforming, free-trade tendencies of the new members of cabinet were given a wider scope. At the same time the Catholic question seemed more open than for many years. It was a change of atmosphere rather than of policy. The Grenvillites and Canning himself had entered the ministry on the old principle of neutrality. If there was an impression abroad that a change had taken place, it was because the movement for emancipation was stronger than ever before and the inclusion of so many emancipationists in the government had aroused the expectation of partisans.

[1] Vansittart became Chancellor of the Duchy of Lancaster and entered the upper House as Lord Bexley.

To Peel neither the junction with the Grenvillites nor Canning's succession to Castlereagh had been a source of serious apprehension. As long as Liverpool remained Prime Minister, he had a guarantee that the Catholic question would remain officially in abeyance. Yet if his position was clear, it was not always comfortable. There was an early example of this when in a debate on Catholic petitions in April 1823 Burdett charged the ministry with being a compromise administration in which both sides had sacrificed their principles. Wynn, defending the place of the Grenvillites in the government, replied that they had been given at least one pledge, that of just, impartial, and conciliatory administration in Ireland; and that the pledge had been carried out. The remark was unfortunate in its silent reflection on the preceding Irish executive. Peel felt obliged to deny briefly that he had entered into any compromise and temperately rejected any conclusion that might be drawn from Wynn's statement. Next day he wrote in private to Wynn to the same effect. This courteous but significant disagreement between two members of the government was, however, overshadowed by a violent scene in the Commons the same night when Brougham, after a fulsome compliment to Peel's consistency, accused Canning of 'monstrous truckling for the purpose of obtaining office', and was promptly given the lie direct by the leader of the House.[1]

All this was unpleasant, even though under the reproaches of the opposition the ministers were as likely to draw together as to fall apart. But it was not only from parliament that the cabinet's agreement to differ came under fire. Agitated by the growth of the Catholic Association, and disquieted by the feeling that his own attitude was being misrepresented, the king in November 1824 warned Peel that if its activities continued, he would no longer consent to leave the Catholic issue an open question in the cabinet. The threat, if seriously intended, was capable of destroying the whole basis of the government. Peel, by the king's command, showed the letter to the Duke of Wellington and the two ministers conferred on the course they should follow. Peel was considerably perturbed and felt that he must either put the communication before Liverpool or return it to the king. Wellington was less disposed to take any action; he thought that the king would be offended if it

[1] Debate of 17 April 1823.

were sent back and begged Peel to do nothing without further reflection. Arbuthnot, however, with a clearer understanding of its dangerous possibilities, advised the Duke privately that the letter should be shown to the Prime Minister. To him, as to Peel, it was obvious that the king's message would be known by too many people for its existence to be kept secret from Liverpool indefinitely. Wellington accordingly wrote to Knighton, and Peel was rescued from an embarrassing situation by a note from the king on 24 November directing him to lay the letter before the Prime Minister, with whom he proposed to discuss it. Liverpool received the document quietly and agreed with Peel that the best course was to do nothing for the moment and keep its contents private. Before Liverpool's interview, however, Peel secured an audience himself and begged the king to make no declaration but let matters stand on their old footing. The advice was followed and nothing was said to Liverpool by the king that indicated a wish to press the matter further. Nevertheless, it was one more reminder of the narrow edge of policy on which the cabinet was treading in the most controversial problem of the day.[1]

The king himself was in other respects not the least of the personal embarrassments that beset the government; and Peel as Home Secretary had a more than ordinary share of the king's waywardness to encounter. Much of this arose over the contentious and painful matter of capital executions. In the clever, indolent, sensual personality of George IV there was a strong vein of kindliness and sentiment; and he was peculiarly open to the private influences of irresponsible favourites. There was a typical incident in May 1822 over the first Recorder's report which Peel had to present as Home Secretary. It contained eight capital sentences for burglary which were duly confirmed. Subsequently, in response to the king's request, one was commuted; but Peel declined to recommend any further intervention. On the night before the executions were due to be carried out, he received a letter from the king, reprieving by name one of the condemned, a man of good family, and directing Peel to select two others for mercy. Peel postponed all the executions for forty-eight hours and summoned a cabinet to consider the issue.

[1] 40300 fos. 17, 21-2; 40306 fos. 72-81, partly printed *Peel*, I, 349-51; *Arbuthnot Journal*, I, 357-8.

As a result the king's action was overruled, though one of the other prisoners, a young boy, was recommended for reprieve; and with this George was forced to agree.[1] A similar instance occurred a year later when Lady Conyngham, the king's companion, induced him to write on behalf of a young man named Mills who was under sentence of death for uttering forged notes. Peel had already been in anxious consultation with the Lord Chancellor on this very case. Not long before, a reprieve had been granted in almost identical circumstances and forgers had already been quoting that act of clemency as an inducement to young men to pass notes for them. The Home Secretary stood firm therefore and—according to Hobhouse—was ready if necessary to offer his resignation. But the king once more gave way and the Duke of Wellington undertook to dissuade Lady Conyngham from any further interference in judicial administration.[2]

When piqued, George IV could vent his displeasure in small but irritating ways. Pressed by Peel in July 1825 to hold a council for hearing the Recorder's report, the king suddenly brought forward the date of the meeting from 8 August to 2 August. 'It will put Mr. Peel to some inconvenience,' he wrote maliciously to Knighton, 'which I hope may tend towards its being a useful lesson to him for the future.' Whatever the value of the lesson, there was certainly inconvenience.[3] Even apart from the business of Privy Council meetings, Recorder's reports, and reprieves, the nature of Peel's department necessarily brought him into constant correspondence with the king on what were often trivial though confidential matters. Fortunately the king's mercurial temperament prevented him from bearing a grudge for very long, and for the most part the routine business between the monarch and the Home Secretary was despatched peacefully and efficiently with periodic expressions of approval from the king. Indeed, in October 1823, when the head of the Board of Works had incurred the king's displeasure, Lord Liverpool delegated to Peel the invidious task of composing the difference. The offending official was induced to compile a letter of apology which, when suitably edited by Peel, resulted in the

[1] 40299 fos. 68-73, printed *Peel*, I, 315-17; *Hobhouse*, p. 87.
[2] 40299 fos. 241-3, cf. *Peel*, I, 317; *Hobhouse*, p. 104.
[3] *Geo. IV Letters*, III, 116-17.

pacification of the king and the writer's rescue from instant dismissal.[1]

If the Home Department required its due share of tact and forbearance in dealing with exalted personages, it also enabled Peel to be of assistance to his close friends and relatives. While he was Home Secretary he was joined on the benches of the House of Commons by two of his brothers. William sat as M.P. for Tamworth and despite the unhappy incident of 1822 Peel was sounding the Prime Minister four years later on the possibility of transferring Dawson so that William Peel could succeed him as Under-Secretary in the Department. Nothing could be done immediately but in May 1826 Peel was able to send the welcome news to his father that William was about to be introduced to active public life by an appointment as commissioner for the affairs of India at a salary of £1,500 per annum.[2] The gazetting of the post followed a month afterwards. In the general election of the same year another Peel was launched into parliamentary life. Sir Robert was anxious to find a seat for Jonathan that would not cost more than £1,500 and yet afford enough business to keep a young man from idleness. He became candidate for Norwich, a manufacturing constituency and also a very corrupt one, and though in the end the return cost his father substantially more than the figure first named, Major Jonathan Peel was successful in a contested election. The Home Secretary himself added his meed of influence by going to Norwich and dining with the mayor and guilds. There was also talk of finding a constituency for Edmund Peel. Unlike most of his family he was in favour of Catholic emancipation, and so disqualified for such a strong tory and Protestant stronghold as Norwich. His elder brother suggested Leicester, where an expenditure of £1,500 or £2,000 might secure his return. Nothing came of his plan, however, and when Edmund finally entered parliament it was in 1831 as member for the Staffordshire borough of Newcastle-under-Lyme.[3] Even Lawrence, the youngest of the brothers, was not overlooked. He was taken into employment by Peel at the start of his tenure of the Home Department, nominally as private secretary but in fact doing little or nothing since Peel already had the competent Sydney Streatfeild

[1] 40299 f. 240; 40304 fos. 159-69; partly printed *Peel*, I 339-40.
[2] 40305 f. 156; 40386 f. 257.  [3] 40387 fos. 12, 78; 40386 fos. 241, 257, 276.

with him. But patronage was so scarce, even for a Secretary of State, that Peel could find no vacancy elsewhere to which he could be appointed.

Fortunately Lawrence found occupation for himself in July 1822 by marrying Lady Jane Lennox, a daughter of Peel's old chief, the Duke of Richmond. This was the second daughter-in-law of that name to enter the Drayton family circle, for William in 1819 had married Lady Jane Moore, a daughter of the Earl of Mountcashel. The coincidence of Christian names provoked a pleasantry from the king. 'The Peels,' his Majesty was said to have observed, 'have still a hankering after the Jennies.' John, Sir Robert's fourth son, a Christ Church undergraduate destined for holy orders, also spent some time with his eldest brother. 'He is, as it appears to me,' wrote Lloyd somewhat donnishly in March 1822, 'much improved by his intercourse with you—improved, that is, in sentiment; for I still wish that you could give him a freer air, a manlier manner, and an unoiled head.'[1] Three years later Peel was trying to interest Lord Liverpool in the task of finding some preferment for this clerical dandy. Employment rather than emolument was the object his brother had in view, since John would have ample provision for his material needs; but Peel thought sufficiently highly of him to assure the Prime Minister that he would distinguish himself not merely as a preacher but 'by the most unremitting attention to all those daily duties of a minister which are sometimes overlooked'. Clerical patronage, as Liverpool took care to point out, was largely monopolised by that 'great leviathan', the Lord Chancellor; and in the end, probably on behalf of his father, Peel bought John a living at Handsworth in Warwickshire for £17,000. Eventually in 1828 the Lord Chancellor provided a living at Stone in Worcestershire, and within a few months offered for good measure a stall at Gloucester; though this was refused by Peel on the grounds that he had a half-promise of a stall at Worcester from Wellington.[2]

Peel's efforts were not confined to his own immediate family. While he was Home Secretary he took the trouble to search out his cousin Lawrence Peel, the son of his uncle Joseph, who was then living an obscure life as a young and studious barrister in the Temple. Peel asked what his prospects were at the Bar and whether he could

[1] 40342 f. 69.     [2] 40307 f. 58; 40316 f. 7; 40607 f. 71.

be of any assistance to him in his profession. Lawrence Peel, a whig in politics like his father, and conscious moreover of the distance between himself and his eminent cousin, was too proud to accept the offer of help. Yet he was not oblivious to the generosity that had prompted the overture; nor was Peel unappreciative of his cousin's independence. When on appointment as Advocate-General to Bengal in 1840 Lawrence came to make his farewell, Peel reminded him of their interview sixteen years earlier and said with emphasis, 'remember you owe nothing whatever to me, and all to yourself'.[1] With a closer friend on his own side of politics Peel had in the end more success. When it was decided at the end of 1822 to promote Huskisson, then Commissioner of Woods and Forests, to the Board of Trade, Peel tried to secure the vacancy thus created for Vesey Fitzgerald. This Liverpool was unwilling to do since he wished to offer the post to Arbuthnot as a reward for his fourteen arduous years as Secretary to the Treasury. What Fitzgerald really desired was a diplomatic post; but Peel's enquiries in this direction also proved fruitless. He was not in any case an easy person to place in the ordinary routine of political life. Upright and honourable as he was, he did not possess the physical strength or temperamental solidity of a professional politician. He had already, in 1820, undertaken a diplomatic mission to Sweden, but lack of financial means made it necessary, he told Peel, for him to have a peerage if he went abroad again since he could not in those circumstances keep his seat in the House of Commons. Though not unfriendly to his wishes, Liverpool and Canning were not able to meet these requirements immediately. On the other hand, Fitzgerald refused both the vice-treasurership of Ireland and the vice-presidency of the Board of Trade. Peel, however, continued to keep his claims before the government and in the summer of 1826 Fitzgerald was appointed Paymaster-General with the additional bestowal of the dignity of a barony on his mother to which in due course he would succeed.[2]

Charles Lloyd was another of Peel's friends who benefited from his official position. In 1822 he had been appointed Regius Professor of Divinity at Oxford and could therefore, on academic grounds at least, reasonably look to further advancement. In February 1826,

---

[1] Peel, *Life*, pp. 62-3.
[2] 40304 fos. 98-100, 218; 40322 fos. 35, 37, 60-4, 80, 103, 111-16, 146.

when there seemed a likelihood of a vacancy in the see of Oxford, Peel wrote privately to the Prime Minister on his behalf. After detailing his professional claims, he asked Liverpool, other considerations being equal, to give some weight to Peel's connection with Lloyd and with the university.

> More than this, I do not ask, and you will not, I am sure, consider this unreasonable, particularly when you bear in mind that I hold an office, the duties of which are as irksome as those of most others of its rank, but which has not yet afforded to me (excepting in regard to the office of Under-Secretary of State) the means of promoting or obliging a single friend.

Lloyd, to whom he sent a copy of this letter, replied frankly and gratefully. He wanted the Oxford bishopric because it alone would enable him to carry on his work of founding a strong school of theology at the university; thereafter anything that would offer a comfortable and rewarding retirement. Both he and Peel lived in a society which accepted without much question the need for external assistance in the pursuit of a public career and saw little virtue in affecting an indifference to that fact. When, a year later, in January 1827, the Bishop of Oxford lay dying at last, Lloyd sent a long letter containing a statement of his claims; and Peel once more addressed himself to the Prime Minister. Liverpool was hesitant; he thought Lloyd had already received rapid promotion and could afford to wait. Moreover the king was interested in a vacancy which would occur if Liverpool's own candidate for Oxford, Dr. Gray of Durham, was elevated to the episcopal bench. Peel replied, with some sharpness, that he would not have recommended Lloyd unless convinced of his fitness, and expressed pointed surprise at the notion that the interests of Oxford would be better served by the promotion of Gray than by that of Lloyd. 'I have written to him temperately,' he reported to Lloyd, 'but as it is the only letter of the kind, the only letter at all of an unpleasant nature, which I ever addressed to him in my life, he will not misunderstand it.' Undoubtedly it made Liverpool pause. The king suggested the appointment of Copleston, the Provost of Oriel and a strong Canningite, whom Lloyd had already mentioned as his chief rival in Oxford for the post. The

Prime Minister in return proposed that he should consult the Bishop of London before coming to a decision. Bishop Howley of London, himself a former Regius Professor of Divinity at Oxford, cast judicious doubts on Copleston's soundness on certain important questions; and the king, presented with a choice between the two Oxford candidates, decided in favour of the orthodox Lloyd. At the same time, other moves on the ecclesiastical chess-board allowed the Prime Minister to satisfy the king's own interest in the matter. A timely vacancy allowed the Bishop of Bristol to be translated to Lincoln, and Dr. Gray to make his required departure from Durham. On 9 February 1827 Peel wrote to announce the good news.

> If you knew the anxiety which I have felt respecting this appoint-ment for the last two or three days (which has, however, tempted me to do nothing unworthy of your station or mine) you would also know the full extent of my esteem and affection for you. Lord Liverpool will write to you by this post. Answer him, as he really deserves to be answered, very warmly.[1]

Peel's concern for Oxford was not, however, confined to the high plane of the episcopacy. Besides keeping up a steady flow of corres-pondence on elections and on church and university appointments, he took a more than conventional interest in the university's more academic activities. In 1822 he provided £50 to support an exhibi-tion at Christ Church for four years. In 1825 he wrote to Lloyd with the suggestion that Oxford should emulate Cambridge in doing something to improve and enlarge its colleges and make room for more undergraduates. 'If every college in Oxford is pressed for want of accommodation, and many more members would enter if they could be admitted, why not consider at least the expediency of making such additions as are required by the growing opulence and increasing numbers of the country?' He thought that it would be relatively easy to raise the necessary money and offered to make himself responsible for any parliamentary legislation that might be required. But Lloyd's reply, in characteristic Oxford style, was critical and discouraging. It was clear that the Home Secretary's spirit of enterprise was not expected to extend to the university which

[1] 40342 fos. 322-8; 40343 fos. 2-5, 14, 22, 24; 40305 fos. 265, 273, 283, 309; 38195 f. 192; partly printed Peel, I, 438 ff.

furnished him with his seat in the Commons.[1] In 1826, however, Peel acceded with pleasure to a suggestion from Cooke, his old examiner in the schools, that he should institute an annual gold medal for mathematics similar to that which not many months before he had founded at Harrow for the Latin prize.

At the general election of that year his return for Oxford passed without incident. A few months earlier there had been talk of putting Canning up for the other seat. Heber, who had succeeded to Sir William Scott's place at a by-election in 1821, had proved a failure in the House and resigned at the beginning of 1826.[2] In view of the rumours about Canning, Peel wrote to enquire from Lloyd but added that he wished to be able to say that he had expressed no views on the choice of a successor to Heber. The Prime Minister, however, told Peel that Canning would not become a candidate unless there was a strong movement in his favour; and though Copleston was active on his behalf, the feeling against him in such old-fashioned colleges as Magdalen, Queen's, Worcester, and St. John's, remained unshakeably hostile. Pett of Christ Church went so far as to write to Canning on the possibility of his nomination but encountered so discouraging an attitude that he broke off the correspondence. Peel remained carefully neutral, and indeed asked Lloyd to make it clear to Pett and Copleston that he had done nothing that might interfere with the choice of Canning. In the end nothing came of the Canning movement and a more decorous if undistinguished choice was made in the person of T. G. B. Estcourt of Corpus Christi College. At the general election Peel and Estcourt were re-elected without opposition. In his official notification of the result, Jenkyns, the Vice-Chancellor and Master of Balliol, expressed on behalf of the university 'the entire confidence with which from a recollection of the past, we commit our interests to your hands'; and Peel in reply referred to their choice of him as 'a strong incentive to the steady maintenance of those principles, the avowal of which recommended me at an early period of my political career to the favour and confidence of the University'.[3] These courtesies aside, the value of a quiet return for a busy minister was inestimable. The session of 1826, beginning with the Bank of England crisis and pursuing its crowded course through the

[1] 40342 fos. 196–8, misdated in *Peel*, I, 385.

[2] According to Professor A. Aspinall, he was a homosexual who went abroad to escape prosecution.

[3] 40387 fos. 142–4.

consolidation of the criminal laws bill, chancery reform, the banking committee, Irish famine, English disorders, Catholic agitation, and the Irish elections, had placed an unusually heavy strain on the Home Secretary. He told Lloyd in May that he was fagged to death by all his exertions, and the summer months that followed gave him little respite. But when he paid a visit to Oxford in the autumn term and dined in college, he seemed in excellent spirits again. 'They were all delighted,' wrote Lloyd afterwards, 'and I have heard of nothing but Mr. Peel's good humour and good company.'[1]

Dining in company, whether at home or away, was part of the professional life of a rising politician; and when he had moved into his new house in Whitehall Gardens, Peel was able to dispense hospitality on a grander scale than at Stanhope Street. During the parliamentary session he took his share with other ministers in dining and wining government supporters; and at the height of the agitation over foreign corn at the beginning of May 1826 he was able to report to Canning that the country gentlemen who had dined with him seemed in very good humour.[2] The end of the year, however, when the London season had started but the parliamentary session was not yet fully under way, provided opportunity for more leisured and less political occasions. When Sir Walter Scott came down to London in November 1826, he was invited to a succession of meals by members of the cabinet. He dined first with the Duke of Wellington in a party that included Peel and his wife, the Arbuthnots, Croker, and Fitzgerald. Next he was entertained by Croker at the Admiralty along with no fewer than five cabinet ministers, Canning, Huskisson, Melville, Peel, and Wellington; though their guest thought privately that so many eminent men together tended to freeze the conversation. Two days later it was Peel's turn, and with Scott he invited Lord Liverpool, Wellington, and Croker. 'The conversation very good,' noted Sir Walter approvingly this time, 'Peel taking the lead in his own house, which he will not do elsewhere. . . . Should have been at the play but sat too long at Peel's.' Sir Thomas Lawrence was also present at the dinner; and the guests admired in the long gallery the celebrated *Chapeau de Paille*.[3] In December the Austrian *chargé d'affaires*, von

[1] 40342 f. 381.     [2] Canning Papers, Peel to Canning, 8 May 1826.
[3] Lockhart, *Scott*, IX, 47-52.

Neumann, was invited to Whitehall Gardens for another of Peel's dinners. Among the company were Lord Harrowby, Canning, and Huskisson; and Peel produced for his guests' inspection an autograph letter of Napoleon, given by Talleyrand to Wellington and by him presented to Peel. Its interest was personal as well as historic, for it was an instruction to Talleyrand on the handling of Lord Whitworth in the negotiations which ended with the rupture of the Treaty of Amiens in 1803.[1]

All that was history now and most of the actors in it departed from the scene. It was five years since Napoleon ended his life at St. Helena, an insignificant and forgotten figure; Lord Whitworth at the age of seventy-three had died in 1825 at his home in Kent. Peel himself, within a few years of his fortieth birthday, was already on the verge of middle-age. A decade stretched between the realities of 1826 and the carnage of Waterloo; and in politics the last decade is always the longest.

## II

Yet one thing seemed constant in politics, the agitation for Catholic emancipation. The angry debate of April 1823 had ended in a complete collapse of the opposition effort to force the issue that session. After the tirades against Plunket and Canning, a number of opposition members, including Burdett, Hume, Hobhouse, and Wilson, withdrew from the debate and all further discussion was indefinitely postponed. Nevertheless, a limited motion was introduced by Lord Nugent, the opposition member for Aylesbury, to place the English Roman Catholics on the same footing as those in Ireland by admitting them to the franchise and to certain public offices. On 28 April a number of leading Protestants in the House of Commons, Peel, Dawson, Sir George Hill, Lord Clive, Bootle Wilbraham, Sir Edward Knatchbull, and others, met at the London house of Henry Bankes, the great Protestant member for Corfe, to discuss what their attitude should be. Peel told the meeting that he and Lord Liverpool were in favour of enfranchising the English Roman Catholics but not of placing them in a position superior to that of the Protestant dissenters by exempting them from the Test

[1] *Diary of P. von Neumann*, ed. E. B. Chancellor (1928), I, 141.

and Corporation Acts. It was preferable, he considered, to leave both to the protection of the annual Indemnity Acts if they infringed the law respecting offices.[1] When the debate came on, Nugent at Canning's suggestion divided his proposal into two bills. The first, for admittance to the franchise, was supported by Peel in the Commons[2] and passed without much difficulty, though Bankes criticised the inconsistency of allowing Catholics to vote and yet excluding them from parliament. In practice the disqualification of Catholics from voting at elections depended on the administration of oaths which might or might not be enforced. Peel argued on more realistic lines that the English Catholics were too few to affect any election result even in Lancashire; that at the moment their exclusion was irregular and arbitrary; and that it was better even to make an absolute prohibition than leave the law in its present state. As for Bankes's argument, he pointed out that there were innumerable classes of persons qualified to vote but debarred from sitting in parliament, including the whole body of the Anglican clergy. In the matter of admittance to office, he said he was ready to support the extension to English Catholics of the same rights as those enjoyed by the Irish Catholics, subjecting them in the same manner as Protestant dissenters to the operation of the Indemnity Acts. The bill went to the House of Lords and there, though supported by Liverpool, Harrowby, and Melville, it was lost by a majority of seven largely as the result of strong opposition from the Lord Chancellor and Lord Redesdale. The second bill, making English Roman Catholics eligible for certain offices, passed the Commons but was withdrawn before it reached the upper House. An effort by Lord Lansdowne in the House of Lords the following year to revive both measures met the same fate.

The central issue of emancipation, after lying dormant through 1824, was brought once more before the Commons in 1825. In the discussions early in the session on Goulburn's bill to suppress the Catholic Association, Canning and other 'Catholic' supporters of the bill had taken care to distinguish between their hostility to O'Connell's organisation and their continued advocacy of emancipation. For the latter the prospect was as encouraging as it had ever been. It was two years since there had been any major battle in

[1] *Colchester*, III, 280-1.     [2] 28 May 1823.

412

parliament on the subject, and in the intervening months there had been a small but noticeable strengthening of the Catholic party in the House of Commons. Canning was at the height of his powers and reputation as Foreign Minister, and the passage of emancipation would have crowned the commanding position he had built for himself since the death of Castlereagh. At the same time Peel was proportionately conscious of the ebbing of Protestant support. 'There is little feeling, I think, in this country,' he wrote to Gregory in March 1825, 'upon the [Catholic] question. People are tired of it, and tired of the trouble of opposing it, or thinking about it.'[1] Nevertheless, he saw in the general apathy no reason for abandoning his own attitude, and prepared without much hope for a renewed struggle. The tactics of the emancipation party were more subtle than before. Three distinct measures were proposed: the relief of Catholic disabilities; the establishment of a connection between the Roman Church and the state by a scheme for the payment of their clergy; and the abolition of the 40s. freehold franchise in the Irish counties. The two last provisions, the so-called 'wings', were offered as securities to set the Protestant mind at rest.

On 1 March 1825 Burdett moved for a committee of the whole House to consider the laws affecting Roman Catholics. He spoke with unusual moderation and conciliatoriness, and his whole argument went to decry the danger to be expected from liberated Catholicism or from the political changes that emancipation would entail. Canning, Plunket, and Brougham supported the motion and were opposed by Leslie Foster, Wetherell, and Peel. The question, observed the Home Secretary, had been placed by Burdett on three grounds: positive treaty, natural rights, and expediency; and he proceeded to examine the three arguments in turn. On the historical discussion of the Treaty of Limerick he did not spend much time; nor on the question of natural rights. The real question, he asserted, was whether there was sufficient reason for maintaining the existing laws. 'I come then to what, in fact, is the main point, and which has reference to the circumstances of Ireland; and I ask first, whether the power sought can safely be granted; and whether, if granted, it will conduce to tranquillity.' It was because he did not believe that it would promote tranquillity in Ireland or lessen religious animosities

[1] 40334 f. 118.

that he opposed it. The civil disabilities of Irish Catholics were not the cause of Irish disorders. The history of those disorders lay far back in the past; and the substantial concessions made to Roman Catholics in 1793 had not ended them. With Ireland constituted as it was, with the religion of the minority the religion of the state, and the property of the minority twenty times that of the majority, a removal of technical disabilities in itself would not end Ireland's internal troubles. The Irish Catholics would constantly endeavour to recover the power they had lost by overturning a system which they viewed with other eyes than the English. Then, taking up a phrase which had been used against him by Burdett in 1823, he gave him an explicit answer.

> I am not afraid of the Pope, nor of the Pretender; but I am afraid of a powerful internal party in this country, of whom great numbers are dissatisfied, as they must be, with our principles of religion; and I can never think they can be fit to enact laws respecting the established religion. When I hear that the nature of the Roman Catholic religion is changed, I must say, after a pretty accurate review of what has been passing in Ireland—and I say it in no unfriendly spirit —that that church would have consulted its own dignity much better if it had avoided several publications that have lately appeared.

He quoted from a pamphlet by Bishop Doyle, the famous J.K.L. of the Irish movement, where the writer had acknowledged that 'emancipation would only lead a passage to ulterior measures', and added that such language persuaded him that if their disabilities were removed, the Catholics would still not be satisfied.

It was a speech of moderate length, clearly and sharply setting out the fundamentals of his creed; but the tide was running against him and Burdett's motion was carried by thirteen votes. The division was decisive as far as the House of Commons was concerned. A series of resolutions embodying the principal terms of the relief measure were carried in committee and a bill founded on them introduced before the end of March. Peel opposed *pro forma* the first reading on 23 March but reserved his main effort for the second reading in April. In the meantime he had private discussions with Gregory on the question of securities. It was obvious that they were being offered as a kind of compensation for the removal of Catholic disabilities, and he thought many Protestants, despairing of the defeat of the main measure, would be inclined to accept the 'wings' as valuable concessions. Peel was by no means convinced that they did in fact constitute any equivalent advantage. He was uncertain whether the removal of the 40s. franchise would weaken or strengthen Protestant influence; and though it was a plausible argument that payment of the Catholic clergy would provide a means of control over them, he could not blind himself to the fact that it would in effect create another established church in Ireland which might not limit its ultimate claims to mere payment of stipend. Whatever his conclusions, he would soon have to face the alternative of either accepting or rejecting the proffered securities. Before coming to a decision he wrote to Gregory for his views, and those of men like Clancarty, Foster, and Saurin, on the value of the two wings in circumscribing the effects of emancipation. Gregory's opinion was that payment of the clergy would make them more powerful without decreasing their independence, and that it would be madness to establish the Roman Catholic Church without securing the right of nomination to its offices. The disfranchisement of the 40s. freeholders, on the other hand, was a proposal frequently made on grounds quite unconnected with religion, and he was inclined to regard it as a desirable step. In Galway and Kerry, the two most Catholic counties, he thought it would make no difference whether the qualification was 40s. or £10; in the other counties it would produce a better class of voter. On the general issue he could not refrain from expressing a kind of funerary elegy. 'That our cause is falling, is deplored by no one man more than by you and if it falls, you will remain regarded as its ablest and most uncompromising defender.' Clancarty and Saurin, with whom Gregory had communicated, also wrote. Saurin, inveterate to the last, said roundly that the whole bill was a fraud on parliament and the public, and denounced the use of the Indemnity Acts to evade a law which the promoters of emancipation did not dare openly abrogate.[1] How far the Protestant cause seemed failing was shown by a rumour which went round London in March and even appeared in the press, to the effect that the cabinet had decided to take up emancipation

[1] 40334, fos. 118, 135, 140, partly printed Peel, I, 369.

as a government issue and Peel had resigned. The story created alarm in Oxford and Peel was obliged to reassure Lloyd that there was no truth in any suggestion that the Prime Minister was wavering in his views.[1]

When he spoke on the second reading of the bill on 21 April he said almost at the start that he did not attach much importance to the two securities that seemed to influence many others, and would therefore persist in giving his decided opposition to the main bill. The fears of Anglicans were justified, for it was no longer a question of admitting Catholics to a share of political privilege, but of setting up a qualified establishment for the Roman Church. Technical alterations in the Oaths of Supremacy and Abjuration made no difference to this situation. 'As to the incorporation of the Roman Catholic clergy with the state, he would fairly own that he objected to it, not because they believed in the doctrine of transubstantiation but because he could not reconcile himself to the operation of that civil influence which he believed to attach to their religious system, and which held sway over the temporal conduct of mankind.' He was asked, he continued, whether the law could continue on its present footing. That was a question he was not at the moment prepared to determine. He was anxious to allay grievances and relax the penal code. He would make all reasonable concessions to Catholics while maintaining the Protestant character of the throne, the parliament, the church, and the judicial bench; but more he could not relax. As for securities, especially the proposed board of Catholic bishops to act in various advisory and administrative capacities, the whole history of attempts in the past to secure Catholic concessions had shown their fruitlessness. 'On this point, he would say, that if the great measure were once conceded, he would infinitely rather place all its details upon a principle of generous confidence, than fetter them with a jealous and ineffectual system of restrictions.' In subsequent discussions on 26 and 29 April, he argued against the abolition of the 40s. franchise on the ground that there was no evidence that its removal would benefit the Protestant cause; and briefly, but equally firmly, against the payment of Catholic clergy. In his opposition to the wings, however, he found even less support than against the principal measure; and meanwhile that

---

[1] 40342 fos. 213, 216, cf. *Peel*, I, 372; 40305 f. 20.

measure moved steadily through the Commons. The third reading, when Peel rose—as he said, perhaps for the last time—to express his continued resistance to the bill, took place on 10 May and was carried by 248 votes to 227.

The triumphal progress of Burdett's bill was accompanied behind the scenes by a protracted crisis in the cabinet. As early as 1 April the Prime Minister raised with Wellington the question of his own retirement if, as he anticipated, the second reading of the bill passed the Commons. He agreed that it would still be possible to throw it out in the Lords, but that would only be in the nature of an expiring effort. Meanwhile, there was the matter of Peel. If he resigned, how could Liverpool fill his post, which in the circumstances would be the most important office of state, when he himself had it in con-templation to retire?[1] Liverpool's apprehensions concerning Peel were justified. Faced in the Commons with the opposition of all four of his cabinet colleagues—Canning, Robinson, Huskisson, and Wynn—and encountering one defeat after another on every aspect of the relief bills, Peel in the end came to the conclusion that his position was an embarrassment both to the government and to himself. After the final defeat on Leveson Gower's motion for the payment of Catholic clergy on 29 April 1825, he went to the Prime Minister and tendered his resignation. The crisis that Liver-pool had foreseen a month earlier was at hand, and on 30 April he wrote to Bathurst to join him, Peel, and Wellington, for a dis-cussion on what was to be done. The meeting of this inner group of ministers took place on 1 May at Fife House. The Duke, less con-cerned with religious principle than with finding a way out of present difficulties, laid before his colleagues a plan for settling the Catholic question which involved a formal agreement with the Papacy, the establishment and endowment of the Roman Catholic Church in Ireland, and governmental supervision of higher eccle-siastical appointments.[2] This proposal, remarkable both in its detail and its timing, made little impression on the other three ministers. Peel said it was full of difficulties and he was obviously unwilling to take any responsibility for such a step. Liverpool was more concerned with the effect on the cabinet of the existing situation. Indeed, it was clear that if Peel went, the Prime Minister would go too. The calm

[1] *W.N.D.*, II, 435.    [2] *ibid.*, 592.

and influential Bathurst, who did more than was ever suspected by the public to keep together the discordant elements of Liverpool's government, was against desperate remedies. But Liverpool was not to be assuaged or diverted. How, he wrote agitatedly to Bathurst on 4 May, could he replace Peel—'it must not be an *ordinary man*. A moment's reflection will convince you that the man cannot be found'. The crisis could not be averted much longer. 'Whenever *the crisis does come*, the *Protestants*' cause must go to the *wall*'; and in the meantime he would only have earned obloquy by not retiring with Peel. Bathurst in turn asked Wellington to use his influence and accordingly on 7 May the Duke had a long talk with Peel, pointing out that statesmen should not act on personal feelings and that if he resigned it would break up the ministry. Peel, while admitting that likelihood, said nevertheless that he had made up his mind. He was alone in his views among the House of Commons ministers and had the mortification of seeing them allied on this point with the most extreme opponents of the government. He told Liverpool afterwards that Wellington had been both kind and reasonable but that honour and consistency forbade him to remain in office.[1]

It was expected that the Catholic bill would be rejected in the House of Lords on 16 May, and Peel and Liverpool apparently agreed to send in their resignations immediately afterwards. The Prime Minister hoped that the king would then send for Canning. Whether the remainder of the cabinet would accept him as leader was a different matter; and the entire disintegration of the ministry seemed imminent. The key to the position was, however, in Peel's hands; for the Prime Minister admitted privately to Arbuthnot that if Peel could be induced to stay, he would do likewise. Renewed pressure was therefore brought to bear on the Home Secretary. After the third reading of Burdett's bill, Bathurst himself took a hand. 'I cannot answer to myself,' he wrote to Peel on 16 May, 'not to entreat you to reflect upon the consequences. Your resignation will occasion Lord Liverpool's. His will cause the dissolution of the government. He must justify his resignation by the necessity which yours imposes upon him, and upon you alone therefore rests the responsibility.' He asked Peel finally to consider what the effect would be on the Church of England, on the king, on the university

[1] *Arbuthnot Journal*, I, 393-5.

he represented, and on the public which at that moment was doing him justice for the firmness with which as the single minister in the House of Commons he had maintained his opinions. Difficult as Peel's position was, it was not a sufficient reason for retiring. 'You will find that public men who have by their resignations exposed the country to great trouble and sudden convulsions, are not easily forgiven. The public confidence in them is shaken in a way which is not soon recovered.'[1] Under this formidable battery of argument the resolution of the Home Secretary began to give way. What was supremely clear to him was that if he resigned he would bring down the government and that the only conceivable successor to it was a ministry under Canning pledged to bring in Catholic emancipation. The contingent danger was in fact more ominous than his own immediate difficulties.

Meanwhile the crisis took an unexpected turn. Immediately after the bill (opposed in a sensational speech by the Duke of York, the heir presumptive to the throne) had met its expected defeat in the House of Lords, Canning requested a special cabinet meeting on the Catholic question; and he told Liverpool privately that he thought it could no longer be left in abeyance.[2] The Prime Minister once more consulted Wellington, Bathurst, and Peel. Bathurst was prepared to let Canning resign and stand the consequences; but the Prime Minister, whose partiality for Canning was notorious, was as loth to face the prospect of his retirement as he was Peel's. Nevertheless, the Catholic question could only be kept in abeyance if all the ministers were agreed; and if any chose to make it a cabinet issue it was hard to see how the ministry could continue. But events did not take so implacable a course as the tired and harassed Liverpool feared. When the cabinet met on 20 May, Canning stated his view that the government could no longer remain neutral on the issue. The Prime Minister pointed out in reply that any other decision would alter the whole basis on which the government rested, and it was finally agreed to defer consideration of the matter for a few days. When on 24 May the cabinet again met to discuss Canning's explosive proposition, Peel said outright that he would enter into

---

[1] *Bathurst*, pp. 579-81; *Peel*, I, 374.

[2] Canning Papers, Canning to Liverpool, 18 May 1825; *Arbuthnot Correspondence*, pp. 77-8.

no compromise and if necessary would resign. But the rest of the cabinet, even 'Catholic' ministers like Robinson and Melville, showed no desire to follow Canning's lead; and two days later, when they met to consider Irish policy, Canning acknowledged defeat. He said he did not wish to break up the ministry and was content to have vindicated his right to raise the question in cabinet. Peel and Liverpool told their colleagues that had the majority in the House of Lords been smaller, they would have thought it incumbent on them to resign. But in fact the crisis was over. Now that the danger from the Catholic side had been averted, it would have been highly inconsistent to have started difficulties on the Protestant side. Peel agreed therefore, to remain in office until a new parliament had pronounced on the Catholic question. Having coasted perilously past its Scylla and Charybdis, the ministry floated out once more into smoother waters. With no resignations and still agreeing to dis- agree, the Liverpool ministry had survived once more.[1]

Nevertheless, the crisis had been more severe than the public realised. The Protestant party in the cabinet was now on the defensive, and in the last resort it had been the indispensability of the Prime Minister that had prevented an open breach. Even so, the balance of power in the legislature was precariously poised; and though the Lords had killed Burdett's measure, another majority in the Commons for emancipation would almost certainly force the cabinet out of its neutrality. Even if Canning had mistimed his action, the logic of his argument was undeniable. The only imme- diate question, however, was the tactical one of dissolution. Welling- ton was in favour of an early election, partly to take advantage of the strong but transient wave of Protestant feeling in the country, partly because he was reluctant to expose the sorely strained cabinet to another session with the existing House of Commons. Liverpool characteristically preferred the milder course. If they could all agree, he thought, to keep both the Catholic question and corn suspended during the next session, it would be unnecessary to have a premature dissolution. In fact there was little enthusiasm for a general election in 1825 even among the Protestants. It was settled in the end that parliament should run its normal course and that the Catholic question should not be raised, or even supported, by any of the

[1] *Hobhouse*, p. 115; *Bathurst*, pp. 583-4; *Arbuthnot Journal*, I, 398-401.

ministers.[1] Everything was to be left to the verdict of the polls. The short session of 1826, the last of the parliament elected in 1820, saw therefore no formal renewal of the emancipation question; and if corn became a subject of acrimonious debate towards its close, this was due to the action of the government rather than of the opposition. The general election fought in June presented the customary series of desultory local combats, rather than any grand clash of parties or principles. Nevertheless, if Catholic emancipation was not a general issue, the Protestant party did in fact increase its numbers. Hobhouse, the Under-Secretary, calculated that it had gained some thirty-two seats in the lower House. Even the limited contact with popular feeling afforded by the unreformed electoral system served to strengthen the Protestant spirit among the legislators. If educated opinion in England was preponderantly in favour of giving civil equality to Roman Catholics, the old *No Popery* animus in the population at large was still unexpired. The claims of toleration, justice, and expediency were opposed not for the first time by a deep historical emotion.

Within the cabinet there was, meanwhile, the leaden calm of temporary truce. In private many dissatisfactions and animosities were ready to come to the surface. Though the Duke of Wellington had been largely instrumental in securing Canning's re-admission to the cabinet against the wishes of the king in 1822, his opinion of the Foreign Secretary had cooled rapidly. He disliked his policy abroad, he distrusted what appeared his systematic attempts to curry favour with the king, and he was jealous of the unusual degree of influence that Canning seemed to possess over the Prime Minister. Ready as he was, therefore, to see a settlement of the Catholic question under Lord Liverpool, he would certainly have retired if Canning had become chief minister in 1825. Peel himself shared something of the widespread attitude of suspicion and distrust towards Canning. As early as the autumn of 1823 he had told Arbuthnot that though he did not mind doing business with Canning in the cabinet, and they were always very civil with each other in the House of Commons, yet Canning was the sort of person with whom he would be very sorry to have a *tête-à-tête*. He, too, noted Liverpool's undue reliance on Canning's opinion

[1] *W.N.D.*, II, 463, 482, 499, 562.

even when he raised departmental matters with the Prime Minister with which Canning had nothing to do. In this there was perhaps a twinge of personal resentment, for Peel could not help regarding himself as being in a special relationship with Liverpool, who had been his official superior in every post he had held since he entered politics. Insensibly therefore, his own feelings towards the Prime Minister began to cool, and increasingly isolated as he felt in the group of ministers in the lower House, he began to move into closer contact with the Duke of Wellington. The events of 1825 increased these small and almost invisible shifts of position within the cabinet. To Arbuthnot, the Duke's great personal friend, Peel expressed his dissatisfaction in an unwonted fit of irritation towards the end of April 1826. Because he would not intrigue—he said—with Knighton and the king, he was completely out of favour at court. Lord Liverpool he rarely saw, since the Prime Minister saw as few people as possible; and he was forced back therefore on his mere departmental duties. Despite these personal annoyances, however, Peel did not allow his conduct to be guided by other than public considerations. His displeasure was as much with Liverpool as with Canning, and though he did not trust and therefore could not personally like Canning, the only political issue that separated them was the Catholic question. He sympathised with much of the emotional feeling against Canning in Wellington's circle, but prudently refrained from committing himself on what his conduct would be if Canning became Prime Minister.[1]

That contingency might occur sooner than could be expected, for Liverpool himself was near the end of his physical and mental powers. Attached though he was to Canning, he found it increasingly difficult to stem his ebullient activity, and began to look back with nostalgic regret to the serene days when Castlereagh was leader of the Commons. In part his lassitude was due to purely physical causes, and a severe illness in December gave him premonitory notice that he could not hope much longer to stand up to the strain of office. Robinson, who was anxious to leave the Exchequer, offered to come into the Lords to relieve him of some of his work. But Liverpool, pessimistically anticipating in any case the dissolution of his ministry over the Catholic question in the course of the

[1] *Arbuthnot Journal*, I, 271, 285, 321; II, 21-2, 29.

new session, thought that any change in the principal cabinet offices would merely hasten its destruction. Nevertheless, that did not prevent other members of the administration from discussing a possible reshuffle of offices. When Peel was at Sudbourne in December, Arbuthnot told him of Robinson's wish to retire, and Peel expressed his readiness to move to the Exchequer if necessary. He would prefer, he said, to remain where he was, but the difficulties of the post which deterred Robinson would be his main inducement to take it. He also added that he did not think the king was really attached to Canning, and that only a short time previously George had said to him what a misfortune it was that he had not thoroughly understood Peel's attitude before they parted at Edinburgh in 1822; that all the misfortunes that had since happened might then have been averted.[1] In Arbuthnot's mind was the fleeting thought that it might prove possible to construct a post-Liverpool ministry in which Peel and Wellington, rather than Canning, would play the leading part. But there is no evidence that Peel was indulging in any such speculation. The difference between his position and that of the Duke was in their attitude towards the Catholic question; and in that respect Peel's *alter ego* in the cabinet, despite all transient irritations, was Lord Liverpool. Indeed, in the following February Mrs. Arbuthnot was complaining that 'he and Mr. Peel talk together upon the Catholic question till they persuade each other they must be driven out by it. Mr. Peel is perfectly sincere and moreover would be very glad to go.'[2]

## III

The brief session of the new parliament before Christmas 1826 was held primarily to legalise the steps taken during the autumn to admit foreign corn. In December an additional distraction was provided when the cabinet announced the despatch of an expeditionary force to Portugal to defend the government of Donna Maria against her uncle Miguel and his Spanish supporters. On both issues the ministers successfully vindicated their action. Nevertheless, there was difficult

[1] The reference was to Peel's stated readiness at that time to undertake the lead in the House of Commons, an offer which Liverpool did not mention to the king.
[2] *Arbuthnot Journal*, II, 69-70, 79; Yonge, *Liverpool*, III, 437-41.

water ahead. In the corn discussions the ministerial spokesmen had made it clear that they intended to introduce changes in the Corn Laws after Christmas, and the Catholic party after their victory in 1825 were determined to bring up the emancipation issue at the earliest moment in the new House of Commons. Parliament met after the adjournment on 8 February 1827, and on 5 March Burdett moved to take the Catholic laws into immediate consideration. Four days earlier Canning had introduced the ministerial plan for a sliding scale of duties on foreign corn to operate when the home price reached 60s. a quarter in place of the existing fixed duty when the price reached 80s. The debate on this controversial subject was fixed for a week later. But by that time the Liverpool ministry which had governed the country since 1812 had received a mortal blow.

Since the summer of 1826 the Duke of York had been seriously ill with dropsy, and though an operation was performed in September it was recognised almost at once that his malady was likely to prove fatal. 'It was from the beginning,' Liverpool observed to Peel in August, 'the breaking up of a constitution worn out by a busy, active, and luxurious life.'[1] With the enormous physical vitality of the Hanoverians he lingered on to the end of the year; and as late as December he was busy on details of the Portuguese expedition. But it was obvious that the end could not be delayed much longer. Peel, who saw the Duke for the last time on 27 December, was shocked by his appearance and the following day went back to Arlington House to persuade the doctors to issue some sort of bulletin which would prepare the country for the inevitable news. Calling there on the evening of 5 January he was told by Sir Herbert Taylor that the Duke's last moments were rapidly approaching, and soon after ten o'clock the same night he received the intelligence of his death.[2] After the body had lain in state at St. James's, the funeral took place at Windsor on the evening of 20 January.

In the interval there was a brisk exchange of letters between Peel and Wellington on the question of the vacant post of Commander-in-Chief. The Duke had reason to think that the king did not wish him to succeed; and Peel, to whom Arbuthnot conveyed his

[1] 40305 f. 212.
[2] Canning Papers, Peel to Canning, 28 December 1826; 5 January 1827 (misdated 1826), 8 January 1827; *Ann. Reg.*, 1827, p. 452.

424

apprehensions, raised the matter with the Prime Minister. To Liverpool he expressed the direct opinion that Wellington ought to succeed to the Duke of York and the Prime Minister agreed that no other person could possibly enter into consideration. It was clear that some notion of appointing another prince of the blood had been passing through the king's mind; and equally clear that Wellington was highly gratified by Peel's prompt and unreserved championship of his claims. Peel was invited for a shooting party at Stratfield Saye towards the end of the month and Wellington proposed that they should go over together to Windsor for the funeral and return again after the ceremony.[1] On 20 January Peel travelled up from Hampshire with Huskisson, Arbuthnot, and Beckett, arrived about six in the evening, and dined with other cabinet ministers at the house of Canon Long. After eight o'clock the heralds summoned them to the Chapel Royal and for nearly an hour the company, including most of the cabinet and the three royal dukes, waited in the gloom and draughts of a side-aisle. It was a bitterly cold night and there was no carpeting on the stone floor. Old Eldon, who had only just recovered from an illness, took Peel's advice and prudently put down his cocked hat to stand on.[2] Others were not so fortunate and the Duke of York's funeral was long remembered for the crop of illnesses which followed among the mourners. The Duke of Sussex, the Duke of Montrose, Lord Rosslyn, Wellington, and Canning, all went down with severe colds immediately afterwards; and according to the gossips the common soldiers (who had no doubt been paraded for hours before) died at the rate of half a dozen a day. 'I presume,' wrote Canning to the Duke of Wellington nine days later, '. . . that Mr. Marsh or whoever filched the cloth or the matting from under our feet in the aisle, had bets or insurances against the lives of the Cabinet.'[3] Canning himself was one of the chief victims and throughout February he remained seriously ill with cold and rheumatic fever at Brighton.

[1] 40340 fos. 116, 120; 40305 fos. 252, 254, partly printed Peel, I, 433ff.; 40306 f. 214.

[2] See Peel's letter to his wife, 21 January 1827 (Peel, Letters, p. 93). Stapleton, who was present, later claimed the credit for this sage counsel for Canning (Stapleton, Canning, p. 578).

[3] W.N.D., III, 574; Creevey's Life, pp. 233-4; Correspondence of . . . Lady Williams Wynn, ed. R. Leighton (1920), p. 356.

The unexpected fatality, however, came the following month to one who had not been present at the funeral. On the morning of Saturday 17 February Lord Liverpool's servant found his master lying unconscious on the floor of his breakfast-room. He had evidently had a stroke, and though he recovered under medical treatment, his right side remained paralysed, his speech was inarticulate, and it seemed already to some observers that his public life was finished. Peel was immediately informed and, after despatching a messenger to the king at Brighton, he sent a hurried note to the Duke of Wellington, who was one of the few cabinet ministers in town. There was a ministerial meeting in the afternoon, and as a result of its deliberations Peel left for Brighton the same evening with a report from Liverpool's doctors. He had already written to Mrs. Canning, asking her to break the news at her discretion to Canning, and promised to call the next morning. He arrived at the Pavilion soon after ten o'clock to find the king suffering from a sharp attack of gout and not unnaturally distressed by the news from London. He asked Peel what was the best course to pursue and was advised to decide nothing at the moment but wait until Peel had seen Canning. A note from Mrs. Canning, who had already conveyed the news to her husband, had reached him on his arrival at Brighton, and the following morning, Sunday 18 February, he visited his slowly convalescing colleague. The two men agreed on the need to do nothing that would indicate to the public that there was no hope of Liverpool's recovery and to proceed with the government business in the Commons in the ordinary way. Peel then returned to the king and told him of the conclusions to which they had come. Shocked and irresolute, George readily fell in with this course and at midday Peel sat down to write off a report to Wellington. The fresh medical bulletin which reached Brighton in the afternoon was still unsatisfactory; and as the king was alone in the Pavilion, even his private secretary Knighton being detained by illness in London, Peel decided to remain over the weekend. This precaution was justified. The king became increasingly agitated and finally summoned Peel in the middle of the night and asked him to send instantly for the Duke of Wellington. Peel represented that nothing more could be said or done at that moment, and that a precipitate message for the Duke to come down to Brighton would only create public alarm. After talking for over an hour the king finally consented to wait. Next morning he agreed once more to postpone any action until further information on Liverpool's condition was available. After one more call on Canning, therefore, Peel returned on Monday evening to London where the remainder of the cabinet had already been assembling. In a private discussion a couple of days later the Duke and Peel decided that it was not their business to offer advice to the king on the choice of a successor to Lord Liverpool and that no step should be taken until the king had made that choice.[1]

Because of Canning's illness, Peel was already acting as temporary leader of the House. On 12 February he had moved the official address of condolence to the king on the death of his brother. A few days later he spoke in support of a government motion to increase the allowance to the Duke of Clarence, now heir presumptive, against a lively whig opposition. The main business before the Commons was, however, the old combination of corn and Catholics. The date originally fixed for the government's corn resolutions was 26 February. This was now postponed to 1 March by which time Canning assured Peel he would be fit to attend. The Catholic debate was a more delicate matter. Already in early February Burdett had been in communication with Canning about suitable dates for the corn and Catholic resolutions, and Liverpool had been obliged to remind Canning that in his absence Peel was in charge of government business. With this Canning acquiesced and on 13 February Peel had been able to tell him that the 26th had been fixed for corn and 1 March for Burdett's resolution. Canning's continued ill-health now made necessary another postponement and Burdett agreed to 5 March as the new date for his debate. All arrangements were completed by 23 February, on which day Canning was so far restored to health as to visit the king at the Pavilion. He found him, he wrote afterwards to Peel, in a calmer frame of mind than he had expected and satisfied that 'our joint advice' had been entirely proper.[2]

[1] *W.N.D.*, III, 596-7; Canning Papers, Peel to Mrs. Canning, 17, 19 February (latter dated Monday morning 11.30, wrongly endorsed 18 February), partly printed *Peel*, I, 448-50; Stapleton, *Canning*, p. 581; *Arbuthnot Journal*, II, 82-5; Aspinall, *Canning Ministry*, pp. 1-2.
[2] 40311 fos. 247, 249, partly printed *Peel*, I, 450; Canning Papers, Peel to Canning, 23 February 1827; E. J. Stapleton, *Correspondence of . . . Canning* (1887), II, 261-9.

After Canning introduced the corn resolutions there was an interval of a week before the House went into committee to discuss them. As was to be expected, a number of agriculturalists objected to any tampering with the absolute prohibition on foreign wheat under 80s. a quarter; but criticism also came from those who thought the new tariff proposed by the government was not low enough. Between the extremists on both sides, the majority of the House were inclined to think that the ministers were pursuing a safe middle course, and the bill made its way through committee without much difficulty. Its transit was eased by the government's concession of some small increases in the protective duties originally proposed for barley and oats. The second reading was carried by a substantial majority on 2 April and the third on 12 April. Peel's main contribution came in the debate on 8 March when the House went into committee. He argued that what was proposed was little more than a return to the system in force from 1774 to 1815; and that the recent alteration in the currency and consequent fall in prices made a modification in the 1815 Act absolutely necessary. The effect of the ministerial measure would, he hoped, prevent speculation and secure a more constant price in good and bad years alike which would benefit the farmers as much as any class in the community. The Catholic debate took a more unexpected turn. The results of the Irish elections and the renewed activity of the Irish Association had inspired the emancipationists with the belief that they could gain another triumph like that of 1825; and the issue of the debate was anticipated with far greater interest than the fate of the corn resolutions. The only new feature was the attention drawn by Protestant speakers, notably Peel's brother-in-law Dawson, to the part played by the Catholic priests in the Irish elections of the previous year. For the rest, all the old arguments were rehearsed once more. After twenty years of continual discussion it was beyond human wit to find anything original to say. The interest of the debate was in its result, not its matter. Moved by Burdett on 5 March, the resolutions were debated for two nights and no fewer than 548 members voted in the final division. The leading figures on both sides reserved themselves for the second evening: Newport, Plunket, Brougham, and Canning for the motion; Copley, Peel, and Goulburn against. Peel's speech, which followed Plunket's and

428

was answered by Brougham, like those of many others was no more than a refurbishing of his arguments of 1825; though the reference in his peroration to the loss sustained to his side by the illness of the Prime Minister made a sympathetic impression on his audience. After Canning had wound up the debate, the division took place: for the motion 272, against 276. The result was decisive, and the parallel motions intended to be moved by Lansdowne in the upper House were abandoned without a discussion.

This victory, gratifying as it might have been to Peel in other circumstances, was overshadowed by the continuing cabinet crisis. He told Arbuthnot privately in the House of Commons on 9 March that when he spoke on the Catholic motion it was with every expectation of having to resign the following day; and that the result of the debate left the political situation as difficult as ever. In view of the defeat of Burdett's motion, it would be open to Canning to postpone any immediate proposals for a solution of the Catholic problem, and take over the ministry on the old principle of neutrality. He added, however, that he would need to talk with the Duke on the line they would follow. The Arbuthnots were nettled at Peel's apparent assumption that Canning was bound to succeed to the premiership, and in consequence Arbuthnot wrote to him next day describing Wellington's attitude to the problem and begging him when they met to discuss openly and freely the Duke's own claims to the succession as well as those of Canning and Peel. When on 12 March Peel and Wellington considered their position, the Duke said unreservedly that he did not think that he could remain in the cabinet under Canning, and suggested putting a Protestant peer—Rutland, Clancarty, or Bathurst—at the head of the ministry. Peel was doubtful; he said he would serve under Bathurst or the Duke himself, but not under the others that had been mentioned; and added—a trifle optimistically if he was correctly reported —that Canning would probably not object to serving under Wellington. But he insisted that, glad as he personally would be to quit office, they would not be acting fairly by the king if they abandoned him and so forced him into the arms of the whigs.[1]

Towards the end of March Lord Liverpool showed the first signs

[1] *Arbuthnot Journal*, II, 87-9; *Peel*, I, 452.

of recovering political awareness. He asked his wife what the result of the Catholic debate had been, but negatived her tentative suggestion that he would soon be able to return to work.[1] Meanwhile, the king made no move to end the deadlock. Wellington went down to Windsor on 22 March but was merely told that the matter should be left until the Easter recess. The cabinet held the following day to hear the result of his mission found itself with nothing to discuss except the details of the corn bill. Canning had already suggested to Peel on the day of Wellington's visit that if nothing emerged as a result of it, the cabinet might have to consider the expediency of a direct approach to the king; and Peel himself found it hard to believe, in view of the allusions being made in parliament to the state of the ministry, that the king would not take the opportunity of raising the matter with Wellington. Before the end of the month, however, the cabinet urged that some communication should be made to Lady Liverpool on the subject of her husband's retirement and eventually the king received from her on Liverpool's behalf a formal resignation of office. It was increasingly evident that if nothing were done soon, not only would parliament grow restive but more irresponsible advisers would seek to influence the king. Indeed, Lord Lowther had written to Knighton as early as 27 February to point out that Wellington and Peel were the props of the old established principles on which the government was based, and to hint that the Duke should become Prime Minister with Peel as leader of the Commons.[2] On 25 March the Duke of Newcastle went down to see the king at Windsor and assured him of the support that would be forthcoming from a large body of peers for a Protestant administration. But though the king declared himself heart and soul a Protestant, even Newcastle could sense a certain evasiveness in his attitude. There was also some activity on the other side. Shortly after Liverpool's stroke the whigs held a meeting and agreed to support Canning if he became Prime Minister. Fortified by this news Canning told Knighton on 3 March that he could manage both the corn and the Catholic question if his hands were free. In terms of age, seniority, and parliamentary experience, indeed, Canning had better claims than any to succeed to the premiership. Everything, however, depended on the king; and among all the diverse counsels that came to him, the one point to

[1] *Croker*, I, 366.     [2] *Geo. IV Letters*, III, 201.

which George still clung was the preservation of his consistency as a Protestant monarch.[1]

On 27 March Canning and Wellington were summoned to Windsor and the following day the king had talks with both of them on the position of the government. Wellington told the king he must choose between Peel, Canning, or some third person under whom both would serve. When George threw out the suggestion that the cabinet might elect a leader from their own number, the Duke replied that he could not himself advise the king whom to select. The choice was his own—'it was the only personal act the king of England had to perform'.[2] With Canning there was a rather more delicate fencing-match. Canning's ironic advice that the king should consult his own feelings and form a purely Protestant ministry was, as both men knew, an impossibility. But while offering assurances, he refused to make pledges on his course of action if he became Prime Minister; and the king showed equal reluctance to commit himself to a ministry headed by a Catholic. The upshot was that Canning drafted a formal minute to the cabinet, conveying the royal desire for a continuation of the ministry and by implication leaving the choice of a Protestant peer as its head to the cabinet itself. The king now expressed a wish to see Peel. A note from Canning written from the Royal Lodge on 29 March warned him of the summons and asked him to leave the House of Commons for a brief interview the same evening when Canning returned to London. When they met, Canning told him what had passed at Windsor and there was an open and friendly exchange of views. Peel made it clear that he wished the government to remain on its old footing and was perfectly ready to serve under Canning in the Commons. But he pointed out that there was an insuperable difficulty in his remaining Secretary of State for the Home Department under a Catholic Prime Minister because of the close connection between the two offices.[3] In all the speculation and intrigue of the preceding month, Peel had been given ample time to contemplate what his action should be in any future reconstruction of the ministry; but this was the first time he had formally expressed to anyone the

---

[1] *ibid.*, pp. 204-11.      [2] *Colchester*, III, 500-1.
[3] Memorandum on Change of Government, April 1827 (Goulburn, II/20); Stapleton, *Canning*, pp. 582ff.

conclusions to which he had come. Even though Canning had made
no specific offer, Peel felt it right to leave no doubt what his attitude
was. 'I will tell you without reserve what are my feelings as to my
particular situation; they dictate to me retirement from office, if His
Majesty should select you to form an administration.'[1] If disappointed, Canning appreciated the straightforwardness of the
reply. 'What his ultimate decisions may be—or *might* be—I cannot
say,' he wrote to Knighton. 'But it is impossible to do more than
justice, by any expression of mine, to the frankness and generosity,
and *self-denial* of his declarations.'[2]

Next morning Peel called on Wellington, who was in a highly
suspicious frame of mind and convinced that his own attitude had
been misrepresented by Canning in his interview with the king.
Peel then departed for his audience at Windsor, which had been
fixed for twelve o'clock. When he arrived the king mentioned to
him the memorandum for the cabinet which Canning had drafted.
Apart from his conviction of the futility of such a manœuvre, Peel
objected in principle to the choice of a Prime Minister being thrown
into the hands of the cabinet; and the king agreed therefore that if
Canning shared those doubts, he should be at liberty to withhold the
document. The more critical part of the interview bore on Peel's
personal position. It is clear that it was discussed and it is probable
that it was on this occasion that Peel told the king that if Canning
became Prime Minister, he would feel bound to retire. The king,
however, was not yet ready for such a drastic solution. If he had by
that time virtually made up his mind that Canning must be appointed, he still hoped that the compromise character of the Liverpool *régime* could be transmitted to the new government and that
Liverpool's mantle of Protestant guarantor could be assumed by
himself. All this was put down in a letter he sent to Peel the following day. After observing that he could not open negotiations with
other members of the cabinet until some progress had been made in
the talks between Canning and Peel, he added with emphatic
underlinings,

the point of consistency on the Protestant question rests between

---

[1] Quoted by Peel in House of Commons, 1 May 1827.
[2] Aspinall, *Canning Ministry*, p. 43.

the King and Mr. Peel. The King, on the one hand, considers himself Mr. Peel's guarantee, and on the other hand, Mr. Peel is the King's. So that no means, let the Government be formed as it may, can be ever practised with a view of carrying the Catholic question, or of injuring the Protestant Constitution of the country.[1]

Time was now running short. On 30 March, when Canning announced that the king proposed to fill the vacancy created by Liverpool's illness, Tierney tried to extract a pledge that the new arrangements would be made public before the Easter recess; and Sir Thomas Lethbridge put down a notice for 6 April praying the king to appoint an administration that would be unanimous on the questions affecting the vital interests of the Empire. During the next few days Canning had several interviews with Peel and Wellington. To the Duke he suggested the installation of Robinson as Prime Minister with a peerage. This proposition, which would have given Canning the virtual authority of head of the government in the lower House, the Duke refused to consider. To Peel he offered a peerage with the lead in the House of Lords, or a transfer to the Foreign Office. He also mentioned his own failing health and the probability of Peel's early succession to the premiership. Peel, however, did not waver from his position. Two points seemed to him conclusive: he could not sanction by remaining in office the great political advance of the Catholic party which would result from the substitution of Canning for his old leader, Liverpool; more specifically, his position as Home Secretary, which he did not wish to change, obliged him in many respects to be the legal instrument for the acts of the Prime Minister. Agreement between them on such a fundamental question as Catholic claims was therefore virtually indispensable. All Irish affairs passed through the hands of the Home Secretary. Every warrant for a peerage, appointments to every political and ecclesiastical office in the gift of the crown, were signed by his hand. There was consequently a complete deadlock. On 5 April the king came to town and on the following day had talks with both Canning and Peel. To the king Peel said that he could not advise any attempt to form an exclusively Protestant

[1] 40300 fos. 191–4, printed with some errors *Peel*, I, 457–8.

government, and would not even be party to such an attempt. He also said that he himself was out of consideration as head of the government since Canning obviously could not be expected to acquiesce in such an arrangement; and he repeated his own wish to remain in the Commons with Canning as leader in a ministry that would be a continuation of Lord Liverpool's. On 9 April, at the king's request, Lord Eldon called on Peel to ascertain whether any change had taken place in his view that he would be unable to serve in a ministry of which Canning should be head. Peel had not changed his views and told the Chancellor so. But he was anxious to make his position completely clear both to Canning and the king. He therefore set down his attitude in writing and sent it to Eldon, who showed it the same day to the king.[1]

The most notable feature of this formal statement was Peel's insistence that only the Catholic question prevented his co-operation with Canning as Prime Minister, and that if the ministry as a whole could be kept together under Canning he would give it a general support.[2] The practical weakness of Peel's attitude, as he well realised, was the difficulty of finding any Protestant peer of sufficient talent and prestige to take the government, leaving Canning in his old position as leader of the House of Commons. To Peel there seemed only one person capable of filling that role, and when at the king's request he again saw Canning, he proposed to him that their differences should be solved by the appointment of the Duke of Wellington. For Canning, of course, this was no solution at all. He was confident of his own appointment as Prime Minister and his only object was to retain as many as possible of his Protestant colleagues. Next day, 10 April, both ministers had interviews with the king. Peel went first at half-past one to report on the failure of his mission to Canning. All possibilities except one had now been exhausted and the king at last took the final and inevitable step. That afternoon he commissioned Canning to prepare a plan for the reconstruction of the government. The phrase was vague, but it could only mean in practice that Canning was to consider himself the first minister. By six o'clock Canning was back at the Foreign Office and immediately asked Peel to come to him. When Peel

[1] *Speeches*, I, 547.
[2] *Peel*, I, 460-3; Twiss, *Eldon*, II, 589-92; *Geo. IV Letters*, III, 217.

returned home from the Commons at half-past seven he found the note waiting for him and offered in reply to call at nine. But Canning who was busy writing and paying visits to other members of the government called instead at Whitehall Gardens the same evening.[1] Neither man could have expected much from the interview. While Canning expressed a hope that Peel would be able to join him, he said he feared that Peel would not be prepared to give any answer other than that already given. With this Peel agreed, but added that he would retire in perfect good humour, would not seek to influence anybody else, and out of office would support the same principles on which he had always acted. Two days later, on 12 April, when Canning was formally installed as First Lord of the Treasury and Chancellor of the Exchequer, he sent in his resignation. It was one of many: Wellington, Eldon, Westmorland, Bathurst, and Melville, from the cabinet; Goulburn in Ireland; and dozens of other holders of minor offices and household appointments, including Lord Londonderry, the Duke of Montrose, the Duke of Dorset, and the Marquess of Graham. Some of these Canning knew must take place; but he could scarcely have been prepared for the shoal of resignations that greeted the announcement of his appointment as Prime Minister. To many of his supporters it looked as though a concerted effort had been made to wreck his administration before it had even started.

In fact there had been no cabal. Wellington disliked and distrusted Canning, but he had made no attempt to exclude him from the premiership and there was no predetermined plan of resignation by the Protestant members of Liverpool's ministry. Indeed, there had been a singular absence of any discussion between other members of the cabinet on what their course should be. Lord Melville, as late as 11 April, had the impression that only Peel would resign; and Bexley, who first offered and then withdrew his resignation, did not know of the decisions of Peel and Wellington until after they had been communicated to Canning. From what Wellington had told him, Peel knew it was unlikely that the Duke would remain in office under Canning; and on 7 April he heard from Arbuthnot that Melville would not join a ministry from which his Protestant colleagues were excluded. But he kept himself deliberately

[1] *W.N.D.*, IV, 16; Canning Papers; *Peel*, I, 463-4.

aloof from his fellow ministers in the hope that the old government would substantially be kept together. What active plotting had been done against Canning was not by the professional politicians but by the great Tory peers like Rutland and Newcastle. Nevertheless, the combination of those intrigues on the one side and on the other the prompt defection of half Liverpool's cabinet as soon as Canning became Prime Minister, provided overt justification for charges of attempts to coerce the king and of personal spite against the minister of his choice. Wellington's resignation, not only from the cabinet, but from the command of the army; the decision of Melville, though a Catholic, to go out with his Protestant colleagues; all these circumstances added to the bitterness of the secession. At bottom, as became increasingly evident, it was not merely Protestant feeling but a general dislike of Canning's foreign policy, and more fundamental still, a deep distrust of the man himself, that was responsible for the dramatic rupture of Liverpool's cabinet.

It was significant that Peel, who resigned on the single issue of disagreement over Catholic claims, escaped almost entirely from the accusations made against his other retiring colleagues. Certainly in the confused days of mid-April some of the back-benchers in the Commons were not even clear why Peel would not stay in office, in view of the announcement that Canning was to continue the mixed system of Lord Liverpool; and Goulburn wrote to him on the 16th to urge that he should make public his reasons for leaving the government.[1] But Peel kept his explanations for the meeting of parliament after the recess. When on 1 May he gave an account of his resignation to the House of Commons, he placed his case entirely on his own uniform and convinced opposition to Catholic emancipation, on Canning's equally uniform advocacy of that measure, and on the incompatibility in the relationship between Home Secretary and Prime Minister when in disagreement on such a crucial point of policy. He denied any personal hostility, citing his own conduct on Castlereagh's death in 1822 as evidence; and he mentioned his proffered resignation in 1825 to illustrate both the embarrassment he had experienced as the only Protestant minister in the House of Commons and the special connection between his department and

[1] 40332 f. 319.

that of Lord Liverpool. He then dealt with the circumstances of his resignation, and defended himself and his outgoing colleagues against charges of 'concert and cabal' or attempts to dictate to the king. Finally he made a reference to his regret at ending his public services and to his own record in office.

> I may be a Tory, I may be an illiberal, but the fact is undeniable that when I first entered upon the duties of the Home Department, there were laws in existence which imposed upon the subjects of this realm unusual and extraordinary restrictions; the fact is undeniable, that those laws have been effaced. Tory as I am, I have the further satisfaction of knowing, that there is not a single law connected with my name which has not had for its object some mitigation of the severity of the criminal law; some prevention of abuse in the exercise of it; or some security for its impartial administration. I may also recollect with pleasure, that during the severest trials to which the manufacturing interests have ever been exposed, during the winter of the last two years, I have preserved internal tranquillity, without applying to the House for measures of extraordinary severity.

The Duke of Rutland, writing to Lady Shelley a week later, criticised this peroration as 'too much trumpeting forth of his own publick services'.[1] It is probable that it made a similar effect on others.

If Peel was proud of his achievements, it was not without some degree of justification. But the feelings which prompted this reference to his work in the Home Department probably went deeper than mere pride. Conscious of the growing discredit of his uncompromising Protestantism among the younger and more liberal generation of his day, conscious too of the reactionary prejudices that stimulated much of the opposition to Canning, he wished to remind his audience that whigs and Canningites had no monopoly of liberalism and that an opposition to Catholic claims was not necessarily the mark of obscurantist 'pig-tail' toryism. He was aware that many politicians would willingly have put him forward as the leader of a general party against Canning. On 20 April he had sent Bishop Lloyd copies of his correspondence with Canning on resignation, but Lloyd declined to show them to the Dean or to

[1] *Shelley Diary*, II, 156.

other members of Christ Church because of the declaration they contained of his agreement with Canning on all public questions except emancipation. It was, the bishop told him, precisely that with which Lord Mansfield and others found fault, since there were many points on which they did not wish him to agree with Canning.[1] But Peel refused to be moved into a general attitude of tory intransigence. If party labels were once more to be affixed on all politicians, he at least would wear his with a difference.

If that reminder was only half understood by his hearers, he was at least able to clear himself on the principal issue. Reporting his speech to the king, Canning described it as 'upon the whole very satisfactory as to himself and perfectly respectful towards your Majesty. For his colleagues he was generally thought to be not quite so successful.'[2] Wellington, in his own explanatory speech the following day in the House of Lords, said that Peel was 'unanimously acquitted' of charges of intrigue and deserting the king. George IV himself, though he could not have been flattered by Peel's evident reluctance to trust to the royal Protestantism as his 'guarantee', was not unduly offended. When Peel returned his seals at an audience on 30 April, the king told him that he was sorry at his resignation, that he considered him as much a friend as a minister, and that he himself was as firm a Protestant as ever. To this Peel replied that his power of serving the king depended entirely on preserving his public character and that it was inconsistent with that character to serve in a ministry of which Canning was head. A fortnight earlier, when still sore at what he considered his desertion by those who had originally persuaded him to take Canning as a minister in 1822, the king told Londonderry that he could understand the resignation of some of the Protestants. 'Peel, for instance, is a man of the highest integrity and honour, and respected by the whole country; rich in reputation, rich in domestic happiness, rich in wealth, wanting nothing. He steers himself above every petty consideration.'[3] The Canningites themselves—Bagot, Binning, Howard de Walden—were agreed in recognising the justice of Peel's resignation and the clear difference between his motives and conduct, and those of the ultra-tory opposition. Tierney, indeed, writing as early as 16 April, said that Peel was

---

[1] 40343 fos. 46, 52, 54, partly printed *Peel*, I, 477-81.
[2] *Geo. IV Letters*, III, 225.     [3] *W.N.D.*, III, 633.

spoken of in the highest terms by all parties; and added a few days later that no Protestants were anxious to come forward to take the Home Department and so put themselves into comparison with 'what all the world has admired as manly and candid in Mr. Peel'.[1]

Canning, the figure round whom all these controversies circled, was equally friendly and understanding. Though regretful at Peel's decision, he had realised from the start of the crisis that it was almost inevitable. But there had been nothing either in their previous relationship or in the circumstances of their parting to suggest that Peel had been influenced by any motives except political principle in resigning his office. As cabinet colleagues they were on cordial if not intimate terms and their intercourse had been remarkably un-reserved. Peel kept Canning informed of Irish affairs and did not hesitate to show him Goulburn's confidential communications. Canning in return regularly submitted current diplomatic documents for Peel's perusal. When the Home Secretary disagreed, he did so openly. In August 1823, for example, he had written to Canning from Lulworth to dissent from the project of sending troops to Portugal. It could not be done with secrecy and speed if parliament was to be consulted, and he thought that it ought not to be done without such consultation. Or again, in September 1825, when expressing his views against Lord Clanricarde (Canning's son-in-law) and in favour of Lord Farnham for a vacancy in the Irish representa-tive peerage, Peel added 'I prefer writing to you without reserve (although I write respecting so near a relative) rather than conceal my opinion'.[2] In foreign affairs, indeed, there was little at issue between them. To the outstanding measures of Canning's policy— the recognition of the South American colonies and the Portuguese expedition of 1826—he had given full support; and on one occasion, at the end of the 1825 session when Canning had left the Commons, Peel himself made a reply to criticisms from Alexander Baring on the government's attitude to the South American republics and the Foreign Enlistment Act. Only a short time before Lord Liverpool's illness Peel told one of his relations that when he went to a cabinet meeting on any matter of importance, he generally found himself anticipated by Canning in the view of the subject he had formed and

[1] Bagot, *Canning*, II, 380-91.
[2] Canning Papers, Peel to Canning, 5 August 1823, 5 September 1825.

that Canning advanced the very reasons which had influenced his own mind but in better language than he himself could have done.[1] Canning endorsed all this in his parting letter to Peel on 15 April.

> It is a pride as well as a comfort to me to know that, but for the point of honour which forbids your serving in any government from the head of which you differ on the Catholic question, you would willingly have continued to sit by my side in the House of Commons, and to share with me the defence of all those other great questions, and of all those principles of external and internal policy, with respect to *all* of which (with the single exception of that *one* question) we agree as entirely and cordially as it is possible for any two individuals to agree in the concerns of publick life.

Though Peel took exception to the phrase 'point of honour' and insisted that his motive was one of public principle, he accepted all the other implications of this passage and even expressed his deep regret at the severance of their connection and his inability to continue his co-operation with Canning 'in the conduct of public business, with the same cordiality and good will with which I have hitherto acted in concert with you on all points save the one which now compels our separation'.[2]

The arguments Peel had used with Canning, with the king, and with the House of Commons, were convincing as a public explanation of his retirement. Yet there were aspects of those arguments which in greater privacy were no less cogent in deciding his conduct. If he had acted as an individual in the crisis, it was because he felt himself to be an individual in the cabinet. He headed no group; he could not control the actions of such men as Wellington, Bathurst, or Eldon; still less could he lead, even if he wished, the ultra-tory members in either House. They might consider putting him forward as minister; but had he accepted, he would have been the figure-head of a faction rather than the acknowledged leader of a large party. Equally so, had he joined Canning, he would still have been an individual with no power beyond his personal influence of controlling cabinet policy. He could not predict what Canning might in future do on the Catholic issue; and he did not trust Canning to

[1] Peel, *Life*, p. 152.
[2] 40311 fos. 308, 313, printed with verbal errors *Peel*, I, 464-8.

maintain perpetually the balanced inactivity of Lord Liverpool. Indeed it might be impossible for Canning to do so; and if another Catholic crisis arose, Peel would be obliged to retire in circumstances infinitely more painful and acrimonious than those of 1827. Severed from his old colleagues, estranged from his new, he would be open to charges of clinging to office for its own sake; and failing to anticipate the natural and inevitable outcome of a Canningite ministry. Though he made his initial decision on personal grounds, he scarcely expected his to be the only resignation; and the action of most of his Protestant colleagues, however unconcerted, confirmed both the rightness of his own decision and the certainty that Canning would move into close connection with the whigs.

Even before Canning's ministry was properly formed, Peel suspected that there was a secret understanding with the opposition and that despite the anti-Canningite temper of Lord Grey, the whigs would gradually be inserted into office.[1] That Canning, deprived of half Liverpool's old cabinet, should look to the whigs for reinforcement, was natural enough; but since Peel could not have prevented his former colleagues from retiring, it was equally natural that he should regard the development of events as a justification of what he had done himself. 'Thank God, I never had a doubt as to what course I individually ought to pursue, and never have had a moment's repentance that I did pursue it,' he wrote on 20 April to Lloyd. 'Every hour's reflection confirmed the first impulse of feelings to which, however, no reflection could have persuaded me to act counter. *Depend upon it, I was right.*'[2] And to Gregory he wrote the same day, 'my answer to Canning contains the general grounds on which I retired from office but it gives a very imperfect view of the difficulties with which I should have had to contend in remaining'.[3] The choice before Peel, as before the other Protestants in the ministry at the beginning of April 1827, was not an easy one. Either they could collectively bargain with Canning for guarantees, or they could individually protect themselves. In the first case the charge of cabal would have been justified; in the second they were bound to act with great personal caution.

[1] Goulburn, II/16, Peel to Goulburn (April 1827) undated but while still in office.
[2] 40343 f. 52.    [3] 40334 f. 183.

Peel chose the latter course and chose it promptly and unequivoc-
ally. In consequence he came through the crisis with less reflection
on his motives than any of his colleagues. But even for him there was
a painful personal aspect to the formation of Canning's ministry in
the breach which it created between himself and Croker. Both as a
member of the government and as a supporter of emancipation
Croker had every title to regard Canning as the natural and desirable
successor to the premiership. Being Croker, however, he could
not refrain from advancing those views to both Wellington and
Peel almost immediately after Liverpool's stroke; and incidental
circumstances connected with Lord Hertford's pending mission to
Russia subsequently threw him into close contact with Canning in
the critical period preceding the break-up of the old cabinet. During
March he had several interviews with Canning on Hertford's behalf,
and their conversations tended to end in more general discussions
of the political situation. These interviews attracted some comment,
not all of it friendly, and Croker made matters worse by a sudden
cessation, as soon as the king's intention to replace Lord Liverpool
was announced, of his customary visits to the Peels. On 6 April,
becoming aware of the interpretation others were putting on his
activities, Croker wrote to Peel to explain that though he had done
nothing that would affect their private friendship, he had thought it
better in view of his situation with Canning not to intrude on Peel.
With this attitude Peel agreed and indicated that he had no wish to
discuss the political position. Nevertheless, Croker made two subsequent attempts, before and after accepting Canning's invitation to
remain as Secretary to the Admiralty, to have an interview with
Peel. When this was refused he wrote a long letter, detailing
the various phases of his dealings with Canning and denying that
he had tried to procure support for him up to the day (14 April)
when he himself accepted office. Peel replied briefly and frigidly,
refusing any discussion, and on 20 April Croker wrote once more,
repeating his assertion that he had not deviated from the truest and
most anxious friendship for Peel and lamenting the interruption to
their relationship.

A greater contrast could scarcely be afforded than in this correspondence. Croker's vindicatory letters were long and laboured;
Peel's replies were those of a hurt and offended man, rebuffing

overtures that for him could only increase the painfulness of the situation. How much Croker said to Canning and how much Peel suspected can only be surmised. But it is evident that Peel like other politicians knew in general of Croker's activities. As he wrote the following autumn, he discontinued relations with Croker because of the part he had reason to believe he was taking in the arrangements connected with the dissolution of Liverpool's ministry and that as Croker, in consequence of Peel's 'unreserved communications', was in full possession of Peel's opinions and fixed intentions in 'certain contingencies', he thought he had a right to expect from him 'a total abstinence from any interference, direct or indirect, in what was passing'. This, if unreasonable, was at least intelligible. Croker's defence, set down subsequently in his diary, was that he believed Peel would in fact consent to stay on in office. This was both unnecessary and unconvincing. There was no reason why Croker should not wish well to Canning and do what he could to assist the formation of his ministry; and he was probably honest in desiring a regrouping of Liverpool's old cabinet under their new leader with Peel as successor-designate. But it does not explain the sudden interruption in his visits to Peel nor his own inconsistencies. To Peel he wrote that he had reason to expect from their conversations before and after Liverpool's attack that Peel would quit his office; in his diary he cited some flimsy incidents to justify his opinion that at some stage Peel changed his mind on the question of serving under Canning. To Peel he said he was not surprised at his resignation; in his diary he wrote that he was more surprised than the public in general. It is difficult to believe that Croker was in fact surprised, though he was probably disappointed.

Peel on the other hand undoubtedly set the claims of friendship very high; yet given the character of the two men, it is easy to understand his reaction. Croker had an indiscreet tongue, an itch for advancing opinions on every topic, and an Irishman's talent for draping awkward facts with his own sanguine fancy. In view of the closeness of their previous relations, Peel might well feel uncomfortable at the thought that Croker was closeted with Canning, busy with fertile schemes even before Canning was asked to form an administration. Compared with the studied isolation and reserve that marked the behaviour of Peel and those of his colleagues who retired with him, Croker's actions seemed indecent and unnecessary. Peel's decision to refrain from any discussion with him on the crisis and even to decline an opportunity for personal explanation, was both a measure of self-defence and a mark of disapproval; and the more Croker plunged into apologies and explanations the more disastrous and unconvincing they became. The puritanical rigidity of the one and the Hibernian tortuousness of the other caused a breach for which there was never perhaps any real justification. But superficial as the episode was, it sharply illuminated two very different personalities. The following autumn Croker sent an appealing letter asking for a return to their former friendship. Though the tone of Peel's letter was cool, he said he was perfectly ready to bury in oblivion the causes of misunderstanding and that nothing would more contribute to that, when they met, than a total oblivion of politics also.[1]

## IV

In the last week of February 1827 Canning had been informed that the bulk of the whigs under Lord Lansdowne were ready to support him even if he were not immediately in a position to carry the Catholic question. As soon as he had received his commission to form a government, he opened negotiations for their support. The resignation of so many members of Liverpool's ministry left him indeed with no alternative. He retained, however, both his freedom of action as Prime Minister and the principle of a 'mixed' government; and except for Grey the reluctance of the whig peers to join him on these terms was overcome by pressure from their own supporters. In its final shape the new cabinet contained twelve 'Catholics' and only three 'Protestants'—Lyndhurst, Bexley, and Anglesey. One of the greatest difficulties, as Canning had foreseen, was to fill the Home Department; and it was found impossible to discover a Protestant to take it. Lansdowne in the end was nominated successor, but as he was unwilling to be responsible for the choice of the Protestant executive which the king desired for Ireland, Sturges Bourne was put in as caretaker until the end of the session. It was not

[1] For the Peel-Croker correspondence see 40319 fos. 225ff., 252-6, partly printed *Peel*, I, 468ff.; *Croker*, I, 362ff.; Aspinall, *Canning Ministry*, pp. 54, 107.

a strong ministry, but the wonder was that Canning had been able to form a ministry at all in the face of the violent opposition to him; nor was it in any sense a party ministry. Tory Protestants like Herries and Holmes remained in minor office; some whigs agreed with Lord Grey in thinking that a coalition with Canning without a pledge on emancipation was a betrayal; some Catholics were in opposition; and there were many independent and uncommitted members.[1]

Nevertheless, the press as well as the bulk of middle-class opinion was on Canning's side; and there was probably a strong enough tradition in the House of Commons in favour of 'the king's government' to ensure that he would be given a fair trial. What he needed was time in which to allow his heterogeneous ministry to cohere, and time to prepare the ground for a settlement of the Catholic question. Those things could not be achieved in the remaining months of the 1827 session. Between the beginning of May, when parliament reassembled, and the beginning of July when it was prorogued, there was no direct trial of the strength of the new government; and neither side perhaps desired it. Nevertheless, there was a good deal of angry bickering in both Houses which was not improved by the unwonted irritability of the Prime Minister. The government speakers, following Canning's line, cast doubts on the circumstances under which half the cabinet had simultaneously sent in their resignations. Some of the opposition, including George Dawson, insinuated that a corrupt bargain had been made between Canning and the whigs. Peel himself on 3 May was moved by a speech of Brougham's to enquire on what principles the new ministry rested. What, he asked, was to be done on the question of parliamentary reform? What was to be done about Lord John Russell's motion for a repeal of the Test and Corporation Acts? Canning, misunderstanding the implications of these queries, replied with some resentment that he would oppose both those measures; and Peel rose to explain that he had intended no reflection on the Prime Minister, though he insisted on his right to enquire the principles of the government before giving it his confidence. In a subsequent debate on 11 May he declared himself perfectly satisfied with Canning's explanation of the new ministry's policy, and

[1] Aspinall, *Canning Ministry*, Introduction, xlv-liii.

disclaimed any intention of offering a factious opposition. Peel's own criticisms were directed to the whigs for abandoning their own principles in order to take office; and it was left to one of the independent country gentleman, Sir Thomas Lethbridge, to attempt a forthright opposition to the ministry as a whole.

In both Houses, in fact, the leading men in opposition held aloof from the attacks on Canning mounted by the lesser members, and in one particular instance Peel positively discouraged an attempt to embarrass Canning. The question was one of a direct appeal to the king on the Catholic issue. In the middle of April George IV had declared to the Archbishop of Canterbury and the Bishop of London that the new cabinet would have to be neutral on the matter of emancipation, and that he would insist on the Lord Lieutenant, Chief Secretary, and Lord Chancellor in Ireland being Protestants. The statement soon became widely known and when parliament re-assembled Lord Mansfield gave notice of an address to the king praying him to declare his intention of maintaining the Protestant ascendancy. When he consulted Peel, however, he found little encouragement for these tactics. Peel took the strict constitutional view that the king's statement to the bishops, not being made on the advice of responsible ministers, was not binding; and that it would be wrong to encourage people to place any reliance on a personal objection by the crown to a measure 'which after all, the King's ministers might advise him to grant'. Lord Mansfield in consequence withdrew his motion.[1]

For the remainder of the session Peel's activities were marked by an absence of any resentment or hostility. By agreement with Sturges Bourne he carried on with his bills for the consolidation of the criminal law and brought them to a successful conclusion. The Corn Bill, which had passed the Commons before the recess, was amended in the Lords at the instance of Wellington to prevent foreign corn being taken out of bond until the price of the home produce reached 66s. a quarter. It was not a party majority; nevertheless, in the view of the government the alteration destroyed the principle of the bill and it was therefore abandoned. In its place Canning brought in a temporary measure to cover the period up to May 1828. In doing so he expressed some irritation at Wellington's

[1] *Colchester*, III, 486-8, 497, 503-4.

446

action and suggested that he was merely the tool of a general intrigue against the government. In speaking on the temporary bill, Peel defended the Duke against these charges, and denied point-blank that the amendment in the Lords was a party measure. 'He was on such terms of confidential intercourse with him, that he knew the Duke would not have done a formal political act without at least having apprised him of it, were it intended as a party pro-ceeding.' He thought that some permanent measure, based on a compromise with the Lords' amendment, could have been devised; and he would have preferred it even at the price of lengthening the session. However, he supported Canning's proposal, which was accepted by both Houses. The corn question, like the Catholic question, was thus postponed to the following year.

By July 1827, therefore, Canning's ministry had barely begun to gather any momentum. The initial difficulties had been mastered but it would take all Canning's courage and talents to master those which remained. Yet the prospect was not unhopeful. If the Corn Bill defeat was vexatious, it was probable, as Peel had suggested, that a reasonable compromise could be worked out the next session. On the Catholic issue the ministry was still divided, but the balance had swung unmistakably to the side of emancipation and the substitution of Canning for Liverpool was a factor likely to be decisive at long last. The chief stumbling-block was the king, but it was not an irremovable one. If George IV had shown some anxiety for the fate of the Protestant cause, he had been even more stung by the attempt of the great aristocracy to place a veto on his choice of minister. In Canning's skilful hands he could almost certainly be coaxed into acceptance of emancipation when the time was ripe. In spite of his stipulation that the Irish executive was to be placed exclusively in Protestant hands, Wellesley had continued as Lord Lieutenant and the vacancy caused by Goulburn's resignation had been filled by a 'Catholic' whig, William Lamb. The number of serviceable Protestants at Canning's disposal was in fact so small that the principle of a 'balanced' as distinct from a 'mixed' government was impossible to maintain. The real difficulty lay perhaps not in the king but in the growing claims of the whigs. Out of power for twenty years, they had many men in their ranks hungry for office; and in proportion as Canning depended on their strength of numbers, they were likely to raise the price for their support. There was already a move to bring Lord Holland into the cabinet, and Brougham, one of the main architects of the coalition on the whig side, had received no office. Moreover, there must have been many whigs like Grey who had opposed, or like Althorp who reluctantly accepted the union with Canning that thought it only justifiable if it led not only to emancipation but to a general liberal policy;[1] and the whig conception of liberalism, as Peel had already pointed out, was beginning to include such measures as a repeal of the Test Act and parliamentary reform, to which Canning had pledged his opposition.

How far Canning would be able to stand out against the pressure of his new allies was a matter for speculation; but he was already a sick and tired man. On the last day of the session, 2 July, when coming away from the House of Commons, Peel met him in Westminster Hall. They shook hands; Canning turned round and for a quarter of an hour walked up and down the hall on Peel's arm in friendly conversation.[2] It was the last time they saw each other. During July Canning's health grew worse and towards the end of the month he accepted the Duke of Devonshire's offer of his villa at Chiswick in order to convalesce. There his condition rapidly deteriorated and a midnight bulletin issued on 5 August gave a clear warning of imminent danger. Next day his condition was unchanged and on 7 August Peel was one of those who went down to Chiswick to make personal enquiries.[3] Canning died early the following morning in the same house that had seen the close of Fox's life twenty-one years before.

[1] cf. attitude of Duke of Bedford, Lord Milton, and Ellice (Aspinall. *Canning Ministry*, pp. 212, 257, 259).

[2] Stapleton, *Canning*, p. 595.

[3] L. T. Rede, *Memoir of George Canning* (1827), p. 552; cf. *Peel*, II, 2. This throws some doubt on the allegation in Stapleton, *Canning*, p. 596, of Peel's 'inexplicable conduct' in not sending to enquire when Canning was ill or attending the funeral. It is true that on the day of the funeral (16 August) Peel was at Maresfield with his family; but it had been announced that the funeral would be private and that the coffin would be attended only by relatives, a few private friends, and those of his official colleagues who were in town. 'A strict line was drawn,' wrote Binning afterwards, 'colleagues, relations, physicians, secretaries, and some four or five intimate friends . . . were summoned to Downing Street'. (Bagot, *Canning*, II, 424.)

# 13

# THE DUKE'S CABINET

On the death of Canning many observers reasonably expected that the coalition which he had brought together would at once fall apart, and that the king would revert to the alternative which had faced him in the spring. But the events which had taken place since Liverpool's illness had created a logic of their own. The men who were scarcely warm in office showed no desire to vacate; and the king, having secured a ministry, even though it was now headless, was not anxious to expose himself so soon again to the troubles and fatigues of cabinet-making. Moreover, his lingering resentment against the seceders of April was strong enough for him to relish rather than otherwise the prospect of leaving them a little longer in the cold of retirement. Lord Goderich was promptly offered the post of Prime Minister; and the old cabinet was confirmed in power on the understanding that Catholic emancipation would remain an open question and that there was no intention of bringing forward a measure of parliamentary reform. Huskisson succeeded Goderich at War and Colonies, and took the lead in the House of Commons; and after some obstructiveness from the whigs, Herries became Chancellor of the Exchequer. It was clear that the king had no intention of strengthening the whig element in the cabinet. The question was whether Goderich would be able to resist a pressure which even Canning had found a drain on his energies in the closing weeks of his life.[1]

Of all these events Peel was a rural spectator. He was in London, preparing to move with Julia and the children to Maresfield, when the news of Canning's death reached him. 'One forgets all differences and dissensions now,' he wrote quietly to Arbuthnot the same day. It was the greater shock since Peel had been told the previous day

[1] *Geo. IV Letters*, III, 275-84.

that Canning's condition had shown a slight improvement. But with *The Times* speaking of vultures hovering round Canning's remains, and insinuating that former ministers had come up to town to be present in case of his death, Peel's instinct was to leave Whitehall as soon as possible for the privacy of his Sussex holiday retreat, the high-chimneyed gabled house near Uckfield with its ornamental grounds and classical statuary which he had rented from the Shelleys for a season. There he was kept informed of what was passing by Arbuthnot, Hardinge, and his neighbour in Whitehall Gardens, Sir Alexander Grant. Wellington himself wrote bluntly on 12 August that 'there are no two men in England whom his Majesty would not prefer to have about him to those two whom the public voice indicates, namely yourself and me'. Less than a week later, however, the Duke received a request from the king to resume command of the army which his professional feelings made it difficult for him to refuse. Arbuthnot and others thought the Duke was wrong to lend his reputation as a prop for the uncomfortable remnant of Canning's ministry; but Peel, to whom the Duke immediately sent the correspondence, did not think that Wellington's military duty would allow him to refuse. As for himself, he was prepared a trifle cynically to believe that the king had made his exclusion from office a *sine qua non* when appointing Goderich. 'It is very natural in a man,' he wrote to Arbuthnot, 'and particularly when that man is a king, to hate another who declines to trust him.' Since he doubted whether the Duke and himself could in any case have formed a strong government, he was content to look on at the struggles and intrigues provoked by the appointment of Herries as Chancellor of the Exchequer.[1]

The summer passed in a drift of rumours about the dissensions in the cabinet, the intransigence of the whigs, and the tearful misery of the Prime Minister. In September the Peels paid their customary visit to Drayton and in November they were back again at Maresfield. On 18 November Peel called on his old friend Abbot, now Lord Colchester, at his seat at Kidbrooke near Tunbridge Wells. Colchester told his visitor that nothing would give him greater satisfaction than to see him as leading minister in the Commons with Wellington as head of the government. To this Peel listened

[1] 40340 fos. 166–74; 40306 fos. 274, 276; *Peel*, II, 2–13.

silently but with no mark of dissent. 'He professed, very unaffectedly, to disclaim all ambition for power, or the common appendages of office, but did not disclaim such a situation if really called upon by the country.'[1] In December came a brief but not unimportant contact with Huskisson. William Peel had been retailing a story that Huskisson had declared it impossible for him to remain in office if Peel entered the ministry. Littleton, acting the role of peacemaker, sent to Peel a written denial by Huskisson and received a graceful note in reply. Peel said that he had not believed the story when he first heard it, and if he had, he would not have taken seriously a declaration made under the shock of Canning's death. Littleton forwarded the note to Huskisson. 'The perusal of it,' he wrote back to Littleton on 15 December, 'has gratified me more than I can tell you. It is everything that I could expect from good-feeling under the guidance of a sound judgement.' In less than two months the two men were colleagues again.

The rickety structure of the Goderich ministry collapsed at the beginning of the new year. On the surface the final causes of difference were the disputed chairmanship of the finance committee, over which Huskisson and Herries found themselves in an awkward personal disagreement, and the attempt by Huskisson and Lansdowne to secure the admission to the cabinet of Lord Holland, unknown to some of their colleagues and against the will of the king. Fundamentally, however, the government broke up because it still represented two discordant and rival factions which Goderich had not the wit or character to dominate. He had inherited Canning's problems but not the qualities which might have enabled him to master them. In December it nearly came to Goderich's resignation; but Harrowby refused the offer of his post and the king was still irritated by rumours of a coalition between the ultra-tories and Lord Grey for the purpose of destroying the government. Early in January, however, the initiative was taken from the king. Faced over the finance committee dispute with the probable resignation of either Huskisson or Herries, the Prime Minister cut the knot by resigning himself. He communicated his intention to the king on 8 January and was told to send for the Lord Chancellor. In turn Lyndhurst was ordered to summon Wellington. When he arrived

[1] *Colchester*, III, 526-9.

at Windsor the king said he wished him to form a government of which he should be head. The Duke made no pledges but said he would consult with others to find whether a ministry could be formed; and as soon as he returned to London in the evening he wrote to Peel.

[9 January 1828]

*My dear Peel*, I entreat you to come to town in order that I may consult with you, and have the benefit of your co-operation in the execution of this interesting commission. You will see that the whole case is before you for discussion. I have declined to make myself the head of the government unless upon discussion with my friends it should appear desirable, and excepting Lord Lyndhurst, who it must be understood is in office, everything is open to all mankind, excepting one person [Lord Grey]. I have sent for nobody else, nor shall I see anybody till you come.[1]

The only other stipulations which the king had made were that emancipation was not to be made a cabinet question, and that in Ireland the Lord Lieutenant and Lord Chancellor were to be Protestants; though he agreed that the government as a whole would have to include both Catholics and Protestants.

This letter reached Maresfield at midnight, and with a heavy heart Peel left the private peace of his family circle and travelled up to London in the early hours of the morning. The contrast between the personal happiness he was leaving behind him and the political turbulence which he was going to meet weighed on his mind; and he had no illusions about the difficulties ahead. To attempt to rely simply on a tory following in parliament was neither politically practicable nor personally acceptable; yet the task of piecing together the broken remains of the old Liverpool party, after the events of the spring and summer, was not one that could be faced with any confidence. He reached London at eight in the morning and two hours later was closeted with Wellington at Apsley House. He found the Duke in excellent shape, reasonable, friendly and anxious to satisfy; and the two men were agreed at once on the need to procure a strong support in the House of Commons and not rely on party

---

[1] *Peel Memoirs*, I, 11-12.

factiousness. How to secure that support was another matter. Peel said he was content to serve under Wellington and added that it would be of public service to have a name at the head of the government that might reconcile animosities and allay jealousies, though he hinted that it would be proper for the Duke to resign from the command of the army in those circumstances. He could not, however, advise an exclusively Protestant, still less an ultra-tory ministry. 'My view is,' he confided the same day to Julia, 'to re-unite the old Party which was in existence when Lord Liverpool's calamity befell him. I cannot undertake the business in the House of Commons without more assistance than the mere Tory Party, as it is called, would afford me.'[1]

Discussions at Apsley House continued for the next few days. Goulburn came to town on 10 January, Lord Bathurst on the 11th, and the circle of negotiations gradually widened. But the difficulties did not thereby diminish, and as Peel returned each night to the empty house at Whitehall Gardens his spirits continued to be low. The seceders of April clearly expected to return to office under the wing of Wellington and Peel, the most prominent of the resigning ministers, and the hope that some of them from age or tact would withdraw their claims soon waned. It was clear, however, that to make a government from the anti-Canningite politicians alone would only invite division and disaster. In a phrase of Peel's which Wellington quoted approvingly to Croker, it would mean going into the House of Commons with half a party to fight a party and a half.[2] Peel's own views were expressed in a memorandum written for the Duke soon after their first meeting. He did not think that a workable administration could be formed by an automatic reinstatement of those who had gone out in April. The alternative was to reunite the most efficient of Lord Liverpool's ministers, reinforced by others who might be ready to join a ministry under Wellington. In the House of Lords, he thought, the ministerial powers of debate should be strengthened by the addition of Aberdeen and Ellenborough; and in the Commons both Goulburn and Herries should be given cabinet rank. A policy such as this meant, of course, the

[1] Peel, *Letters*, p. 104, letter of 10th misdated by Peel 9 January (original in Peel MSS.).
[2] *Croker*, I, 404.

disappointment of many old adherents; it would equally certainly call down the criticisms of the uncompromising ultra-tories who saw in the Duke the incarnation of resistance to Canningite liberalism. All this Peel was prepared to face.

> I care not [he wrote privately to Gregory on 18 January] for the dissatisfaction of the ultra-tories. The country ought not, and cannot, be governed on any other principles than those of firmness, no doubt, but of firmness combined with moderation. . . . I must be quite sure that such men as Lamb have rejected *fair* offers before I can make common cause with inferior men, and commit the public service to their hands.

And again on 1 February to the same correspondent:

> What must have been the inevitable fate of a government composed of Goulburn, Sir John Beckett, Wetherell, and myself? Supported by very warm friends no doubt, but no [more] than warm friends —being prosperous country gentlemen, fox-hunters, etc., etc., most excellent men, who will attend one night, but who will not leave their favourite pursuits to sit up till two or three o'clock fighting questions of detail on which, however, a Government must have a majority. We could not have stood creditably a fortnight. I say this as a *raison de plus*. I for one, on other grounds, could not be a party.[1]

If the effort to recreate the Liverpool party failed, he was ready to make a fight in the House of Commons with what material was available until public business became impossible; but he had no real belief that such a fight would be successful. Moreover, on account of the financial measures and the mutiny bill, it was impossible to postpone or dissolve parliament.

The chief obstacle to reunion was created by Huskisson's temperamental scruples. Shy, irresolute, and unpopular with the country gentry, he was nevertheless the outstanding member of the Canningite group and an acknowledged expert on trade and finance. As early as 11 January he expressed to Peel the difficulties about his relationship with Herries, though to Wellington he had merely said

---

[1] 40334 f. 197, printed with slight verbal differences *Peel Memoirs*, I, 16-18.

that he must know the proposed cabinet arrangements before he could give his adhesion. A formal interview with Lyndhurst did nothing to narrow the gap; but Peel, to whom he reported what had happened, had a confidential and friendly talk with him on 15 January. As a result Huskisson agreed to consult his friends and followers to determine whether his difficulties could be removed by Herries' acceptance of some other post in the new cabinet. Their counsel was favourable, and on 17 January Huskisson informed Peel that he was ready to enter the ministry on the understanding that it was not the intention to appoint Herries Chancellor of the Exchequer and that Althorp would be proposed as a member of the finance committee. Ten days of negotiations at last had their reward.[1] By Sunday 20 January the final arrangements were complete; though for Peel late hours, anxiety, and wet cold weather brought their aftermath. Soon after his arrival in town he caught a cold which before the end of the month developed into whooping cough. However, he was satisfied that all that was possible had been done, and he was content to face the outcome of their efforts. For himself, once it was settled that Wellington was to be Prime Minister, there was no question of anything but the Home Office and the leadership of the House of Commons. Goulburn became Chancellor of the Exchequer; Bathurst returned as Lord President of the Council; Ellenborough came in as Lord Privy Seal; and Aberdeen at Chancellor of the Duchy of Lancaster. Of Goderich's cabinet, besides Lyndhurst, there remained Lord Dudley at the Foreign Office, Huskisson in the Colonial Department, Charles Grant as President of the Board of Trade, and Palmerston as Secretary at War. The major controversial issue was solved by compromise. Indeed, there was a general desire to avoid anything that might perpetuate the quarrels of the previous administration. Herries became Master of the Mint and was entrusted with the management of the government's business on the finance committee. The chairmanship of the committee was first offered to a Canningite, Sturges Bourne, and on his refusal was given to Parnell.[2]

The government thus retained a central and balanced character. Though the king had been anxious to retain some of the whig

[1] 40316 f. 5; 40395 fos. 21-3, 36-9, 46-8, 226; cf. *Huskisson Papers*, pp. 280-5.
[2] 40395 f. 226.

cabinet members, in the event none would take office. Lansdowne told Peel that he would not serve under an anti-Catholic Prime Minister and in the circumstances Wellington thought there was no purpose in making an offer to him. Without Lansdowne, neither Carlisle nor Devonshire would enter the ministry. Of the old tories, Eldon, Bexley, and Westmorland were deliberately omitted. Eldon, at the age of seventy-seven, was perhaps in any case scarcely eligible. Yet he was piqued at the failure to make him an offer and only partly mollified by the appointment of the ultra-Protestant Wetherell, another of the seceders of April, as Attorney-General. Wetherell was not indeed the first choice of the government; but Scarlett, though the king for private reasons was anxious to retain him, felt too closely connected with the whigs to continue under Wellington. Judging perhaps the degree of old Eldon's displeasure, Peel made it one of his first tasks when formally installed in office to write him a friendly and consolatory letter.[1] In Ireland Lord Anglesey, under the terms of a previous arrangement, succeeded Wellesley, and William Lamb continued, though a Catholic, as Chief Secretary. Among the lesser men Arbuthnot became First Commissioner of Woods and Forests, Vesey Fitzgerald Paymaster to the Forces, and George Dawson Financial Secretary to the Treasury, though none of these was in the cabinet. In Dawson's place, William Peel now consented to serve as Under-Secretary in the Home Department under his brother.

Despite the grumbles of the right at the inclusion of men like Huskisson and Dudley, and the inevitable party opposition of the excluded whigs, the new ministry offered on paper at least a reasonably effective coalition of central and moderate elements. If there were some like Bishop Lloyd who were uneasy at the spectacle of a professional soldier at the head of the government, there were other ministerial supporters who regarded him as a welcome and necessary restraining power on the unduly liberal proclivities of his chief coadjutor. When Peel had his audience on taking the seals of the Home Department, the king was pleased to treat him to what was later described by the royal pen to his confidant Knighton as 'a very strong lecture respecting his conduct both as to the past, as well as to the future'.[2] In this critical attitude to Peel's liberalism there can

[1] Twiss, *Eldon*, III, 28.     [2] *Geo. IV Letters*, III, 375.

be little doubt that George IV was exhibiting a temper found in less exalted political quarters. Rutland, for example, confided to Lady Shelley that he understood Peel was a liberal and he feared that Peel and Huskisson had been allowed too great a share in the formation of the Duke's ministry.[1] Wellington's government in fact was both a mixture and a compromise, and as such was open to much partisan criticism from those who were unlikely ever to have the responsibility of forming a ministry. But since 1812 every cabinet had been of this character. In the independent and undisciplined House of Commons of the early nineteenth century only a central coalition could hope to survive. If the ministries of Liverpool and Wellington were to the right of the centre, and that of Canning to the left, it was also significant that Liverpool, Canning, and Peel were all nearer to the centre point of politics than the bulk of their colleagues. To that extent Peel's insistence on a reconstruction of the Liverpool system derived from sound political instinct. Yet the prospects for such a coalition were far less promising than under Liverpool, and not merely because of Liverpool's departure from the scene. When the new cabinet for the first time dined together at Apsley House on 22 January, Ellenborough noted that 'the courtesy was that of men who had just fought a duel'.[2] Four Prime Ministers in less than twelve months had destroyed the sense of continuity and stability with which time had endowed the Liverpool ministry; the circumstances of the secessions from Canning in April and the collapse of the Goderich cabinet in January had created enmity and distrust among men who otherwise might have worked well together; and the whigs for the first time in twenty years had tasted power. The year 1827 had torn apart the old governing cadre and only the future could restore its unity. What was even more disastrous was that the schism of that year had not been offset by any solution to the outstanding political issues. Canning had not settled Catholic emancipation; Huskisson had not settled corn; and moving up from the background was the question of parliamentary reform. The events of the previous year had been purely destructive; and those problems still faced Peel and Wellington as they had faced their predecessors in office. All that had been demonstrated was the enormous difficulty of enforcing any firm and definite policy.

[1] *Shelley Diary*, II, 173.     [2] *Ellenborough*, I, 3.

Parliament reassembled on 29 January and the cabinet approached its first encounter with the legislature in a mood of studied agreement. In the first cabinet meetings of the previous week Wellington had accepted without pleasure the advice of his colleagues to resign from his post of Commander-in-Chief. The king's speech, containing the famous description of the battle of Navarino as an 'untoward event', was discussed; and though Peel thought the adjective might get the ministry into a scrape, it was finally decided to retain it, since Huskisson and his group approved. Peel expounded his view that since the government had no surplus revenue and would not be able to impose new taxation, the only practical policy was one of drastic economy. Huskisson won the support of the cabinet for his proposal that there should be a government Corn Bill on the principle of that brought forward by Canning the previous year.[1] In his new capacity as leader of the House of Commons, Peel gave a dinner to the more prominent supporters of the government on the eve of session to hear the king's speech. Thirty-two sat down at table in the long gallery at Whitehall Gardens beneath the Rembrandts, Rubens, and Vanderveldes; Croker, now restored to friendly terms, was present and thought the room looked very handsome.[2] The choice of members to move the address was tactful and symbolic. It was proposed by Cecil Jenkinson, the brother of Lord Liverpool, who assured his audience that the former Prime Minister had full confidence in the new ministry; and seconded by Robert Grant, the younger brother of Charles Grant, the Canningite minister. In his private suggestions to Jenkinson on the line to follow in his speech, Peel advised against any reference to recent animosities and mentioned only two public issues, Navarino and public finance, as fit for discussion. Indeed, with nearly all the House of Commons ministers necessarily absent until their re-election, there was more than ordinary need for avoiding controversy.

It was not to be expected that the opposition would exercise the same restraint. As Peel had forecast, there was criticism of the description of Navarino as untoward, and both whig critics and tory defenders of the phrase seemed at least to be agreed that it was Canning's whole Eastern policy that was at issue. Brougham signalised himself by heading an attack on Wellington as a potential

[1] *Ellenborough*, I, 6-9, 32.    [2] *Croker*, I, 406.

military dictator; and though Palmerston, in the absence of most of
the other ministers, was able to counter the attack with the announcement of Wellington's resignation of his post as Commander-
in-Chief, it was clear that the whigs would not easily abandon this
vulnerable point. When the newly elected ministers took their
places in the Commons, there followed the usual round of explanations and arguments on the dissolution of the Goderich ministry.
The whigs professed to be unable to understand how the Canningites
could with consistency retain their places in a Wellington government; and aided by Goderich's exculpatory speeches in the Lords,
they raked over the Huskisson—Herries quarrel to find evidence of
sinister intrigues by Knighton and Rothschild to keep Herries at
the Exchequer. The centre of controversy was Huskisson himself.
There was a public disagreement between himself and Wellington
on whether he had received 'guarantees' or merely general assurances on entering the cabinet; in public and in private he engaged in
a wrangle with Goderich on the precise details of the dissolution of
the late ministry; and simultaneously he was subjected to lengthy
reproaches from Canning's widow for having betrayed his master's
cause. The recriminations of the whigs he could afford to ignore,
since he had made up his mind on Goderich's resignation not to
serve with a purely whig administration;[1] but not the least painful
circumstance in his new position was the attitude of Canning's
personal circle of friends and relatives. Lady Canning, driven by the
unreasoning bitterness of a bereaved woman, incited others to join
her passionate attacks on those former followers of her husband
who had taken office with Wellington. Her son-in-law, Lord
Clanricarde, revealed in the House of Lords that Huskisson had
declared he would never sit in a cabinet with those who had per-
secuted Canning to death. In private society her nephew, Lord
George Bentinck, who had for a time served as Canning's secretary
at the Foreign Office, joined in the vendetta with all the violence
and ruthlessness that he brought to his more engrossing interests in
the Jockey Club and on the racecourse.[2] By an irony of fate
Huskisson was thus one of the first victims of the legend of the

---

[1] *Huskisson Papers*, p. 278.
[2] *Greville*, 25 February 1828; Bagot, *Canning*, II, 434-5; Aspinall, 'Last of the
Canningites' (E.H.R., L, 639).

'hunting down' of Canning which he himself had helped to shape.

In all these scenes Peel emerged as one of the few cool and influential figures. Not only was he the principal link between the Canningites and the rest of the cabinet, but he was assuming a position of general authority in the government that helped to give it some semblance of unity and direction. On 15 February, when moving the appointment of the finance committee, he took the opportunity to give a long review of the state of the public revenue. Though he disclaimed, as more properly belonging to the province of the Chancellor of the Exchequer, the task of estimating the probable future revenue, he did in fact offer a provisional forecast that the estimates for the coming year would be less than for 1827 by over a million pounds; and he assured the House that the ministry was imbued with a sincere desire to see economy in public expenditure carried to its utmost lengths. At a cabinet on 9 March when Wellington put forward his plan for a settlement of the Greek question, Peel took strong objection to the degree of suzerainty over Greece which it left to the Ottoman Empire, and headed a general movement of criticism supported by Palmerston and Dudley.[1] Four weeks later he was writing in authoritative tone to Dudley, the Foreign Secretary, on the need to intervene on behalf of the Greek citizens captured by Ibrahim Pasha in the Morea. 'Should not an immediate communication be made to Mr. Barker?'—'require him to send precise information'—'pray consider all this as soon as you possibly can'. Nevertheless, though a formidable second-in-command, he was not head of the government; nor could he provide the numbers in the division lobbies necessary to control the House of Commons.

The weakness of the government's position in the Commons was sharply illustrated before the session was a month old. Soon after parliament reassembled, Lord John Russell gave notice of a motion for the repeal of the Test and Corporation Acts. These old statutes of Charles II's reign made the holding of offices of profit or trust under the crown, and membership of corporations, dependent on taking the sacrament according to the rites of the established Church. The first, though aimed at Roman Catholics, was equally applicable to Protestant dissenters; the second was primarily

[1] Bulwer, *Palmerston*, I, 229–31.

intended to exclude them. Both had long since lost their efficacy and the operation of the annual Indemnity Acts regularly relieved dissenters from the penalties prescribed for their infraction. They remained on the statute book, however, as an historic symbol of the political monopoly of the Anglican Church. Bishop Lloyd, who urged Peel at the outset not to give way without first consulting the heads of the Church, argued for the maintenance of the distinction between religious toleration and the privileged position given to the Establishment in the sphere of civil rights. But Peel was not impressed, for House of Commons purposes, by the strength of an argument which depended on the fine difference between the sacrament as a qualification for office and as a test of fitness for office. In practice, as all knew, men took the sacrament when required for the sake not of religion but of office. The best argument—and he was speaking, he told Lloyd, 'of House of Commons arguments, of arguments for people who know very little of the matter, care not much about it, half of whom have dined, or are going to dine, and are only forcibly struck by that which they instantly comprehend without trouble'—was that under the existing system a kindly feeling had grown up between the dissenters and the Church of England, and that this happy relationship might actually have been promoted by a legal arrangement which gave the dissenters practical enjoyment of civil rights while recognising the predominant position of the Established Church.[1] It was a very English, very pragmatic attitude; and it was the attitude the cabinet itself finally adopted. Ellenborough asked Peel at a dinner on 23 February what his objections were to a repeal of the Test and Corporation Acts. His reply was that there was no practical grievance, and he would rather continue a system which gave tranquillity than risk opening old wounds. He added moreover, that if the statutes were repealed, it might prejudice the Catholic question and if he were in favour of emancipation he would on that ground alone oppose their repeal. When two days later the cabinet decided to oppose Russell's motion, it was precisely on Peel's Walpolean argument of *quieta non movere*. In addition, Huskisson, Ellenborough, and others specifically stated that they must also object to the motion on the grounds that it prejudiced Catholic claims.[2]

[1] 40343 fos. 140-2, 150.     [2] *Ellenborough*, I, 38-9.

Russell moved his resolutions on 26 February and was supported by Althorp, Brougham, and other whigs, and by representatives of the dissenting interest. They denied that even with the Indemnity Acts the dissenters were in fact relieved from all practical disadvantages; and on more abstract grounds contended that civil disabilities were only justified if a clear case of expediency were proved. The opposition on behalf of the government was expressed by Huskisson, Palmerston, and Peel. The first two stressed the inexpediency of tampering with one of the laws affecting Roman Catholics while the major issue was still in dispute. Peel, in a cool and balanced speech, developed the argument he had used with Lloyd and Ellenborough; and pointed to the presence of three Presbyterians in the cabinet—Aberdeen, Melville, and Charles Grant—as *prima facie* evidence of the insignificance of the formal restrictions on those Protestants who were not members of the Anglican Church. The one novel contribution to the debate was made by Sir Thomas Acland, who suggested that instead of annual Indemnity Acts the government should propose the suspension of the Test and Corporation Acts for specific periods, to be renewed until the time was ripe for a permanent settlement. On a division, however, the motion for a committee was carried against the ministers by 237 votes to 193, a majority of 44. Whether the narrow and unemotional ground taken by the ministers was the cause of their defeat is perhaps doubtful. Lloyd told Peel that some disappointment was caused at Oxford by his failure to champion the Establishment more decisively. But Oxford was not England, and even in Oxford there was no strong feeling against the repeal of the two statutes. An attempt by the Vice-Chancellor to raise a petition against repeal met with little enthusiasm from the heads of houses, and Lloyd advised Peel not to offer any further resistance. It had been necessary for his public position to oppose; now it would be wisest to let the question run its course.[1]

Peel himself thought it against the interests of the Church to carry on a rigid opposition in the Commons. It was true that the division of 26 February had not been a perfect trial of strength. Government whipping had been poor; Planta, the new Treasury Secretary, had not sent out his notes until the day before the debate; and there was

[1] 40343 fos. 183, 189, 214.

an impression that it would not be a government question. Nevertheless, it was clear that there was little encouragement in the Commons for an intransigent attitude. Many members with strong dissenting constituencies were pledged on the subject, and some who voted for the government did so reluctantly.[1] Certainly Peel had no illusions on the ability of the government to carry their view in the Commons. He had adopted what he believed to be the soundest tactics, and though they had failed, he did not think that a firmer line would have been more successful. There was little point, he wrote to Lloyd on 20 March, in arguing that the safety of the Establishment depended on the maintenance of the Test and Corporation Acts unless there was a certainty of winning a majority. In case of defeat the position would be all the worse because of the very arguments that had been put forward. The ministers could, of course, resign; but that would only enhance the completeness of the opposition victory.[2]

In fact he did what he could to mitigate the consequences of Russell's parliamentary success. The cabinet had some discussion on the subject the following day and Peel mentioned Acland's suggestion. But no decision was taken and meanwhile he had to improvise his own course of action in the Commons. Outwardly he affected indifference, though it is possible that his indifference covered a certain pique, for it was not his nature to stand idle or neutral in controversial issues. When on 28 February the House went into committee on Russell's motion he pleaded first for the acceptance of some alternative to an absolute repeal of the statutes, and then, when this was rejected, for a postponement of three or four days so that members could consider the question in all its bearings. But the whigs, conscious of their power, would make no concession; and Lord Milton, the son and heir of the great Earl Fitzwilliam, accused him of trying to recover the vantage ground he had lost under the pretence of delay. Peel warmly repudiated his remarks, and after saying that he would now decline any postponement, even if it were offered, left the House and was shortly after followed by other ministers. It seemed to those left behind that he had gone off in a fit of temper. Lord Milton offered an apology and said he had not wished to create any resentment; but a ministerial supporter, Sir

[1] *Ellenborough*, I, 42.     [2] 40343 f. 217.

George Warrender, affirmed testily that if anything could induce him to withdraw his confidence from the government, it was the scene he had just witnessed. Meanwhile, Peel, who had not eaten since breakfast that morning, was enjoying his dinner upstairs. When informed of Warrender's remarks, he returned—as he explained—to listen to the attacks made on him, though he feared he could not hope to secure the support of his gallant friend as he had no intention of voting on the question and would leave again as soon as it was put. It was not perhaps a line of conduct befitting the leader of the House; but Milton's unnecessary and unfounded insult had rankled, and the plain fact was that Peel could in no way control the proceedings.

When the cabinet resumed its deliberations, it was obvious that there was no more zeal for opposition among them than among the heads of the Oxford colleges. Ellenborough thought that Dudley, Lyndhurst, Aberdeen, Huskisson, Palmerston, and Melville all wanted to see the acts abolished; Peel was indifferent; and only Wellington and Bathurst were against. The real issue now was whether anything could be put in place of the old statutes; and while a bill founded on Russell's proposals received its first and second readings, Peel was in active consultation with the leaders of the Church. The archbishops, and most of those bishops available in London for discussion, were disinclined for any controversy. As churchmen they disliked the sacramental test, and as spiritual lords they feared a conflict on such an issue between the two Houses of Parliament. On 15 March Peel had a long conference at Lambeth with the two archbishops and the Bishops of Llandaff, Durham, London, and Chester. A form of declaration, binding the taker not to injure or subvert the Established church, was agreed upon as a substitute for the sacramental test for persons chosen for office in corporations, and at the discretion of the crown for holders of civil offices of trust, and commissions under the government. Peel's wish was that it should be proposed by some non-official member, such as Acland; but the bishops were anxious that Peel himself should bring it forward or at least prominently support, and he reluctantly consented. Van Mildert, the Bishop of Durham, who was thought to be considerably influenced by some of the ultra-tory peers, alone showed some resistance. But Peel told the assembled prelates that a stronger declaration would not pass the Commons, and he informed

Lloyd privately that even if Van Mildert carried an amendment in the Lords, he could not accept it.

This Lambeth agreement became the government policy. On 18 March, in a conciliatory speech when the Commons went into committee on the bill, Peel successfully proposed the insertion of the declaration. In the House of Lords, though formally moved by Lord Holland, the bill was for practical purposes a government measure and there was little resistance to its principle. The Bishop of Durham, who had a further reassuring talk with Peel at the end of March, spoke in favour of the bill, together with the Archbishop of York and the Bishops of Lincoln and Chester; and eighteen bishops voted with the government on the crucial issue of the declaration on 21 April. It was left to a layman, Lord Winchilsea, after vain efforts in private with Wellington and Peel, to propose unavailingly a substitute declaration of belief in the divinity of the Saviour. Some minor emendations to the wording of the declaration were made, notably the addition, at the instance of the Bishop of Llandaff, of the phrase 'upon the true faith of a Christian'. Peel himself did not think that the declaration had been thereby improved but no difficulty was raised by the opposition to this emendation and early in the beginning of May the Lords' amendments were finally accepted.[1] After the initial and decisive reverse, the government had conducted a neat rearguard action; and the compromise on the declaration had saved the credit both of the ministers and the Church. Nevertheless, as the *Annual Register* observed in its retrospective survey of the year, it was 'the first successful blow that had been aimed at the supremacy of the Established Church since the Revolution'; and the ease with which that success had been achieved was in itself a portent.

In the meantime tempers in the cabinet were strained on another issue. In the second week of March the cabinet took up the question of the Corn Bill. Wellington wished to incorporate his successful amendment of the previous session or else have a higher scale of duties. Huskisson wanted to retain Canning's original proposals though he was prepared to offer a modification whereby the duty would be increased by a quarter when in any period of twelve weeks

[1] *ibid.*, fos. 212, 248, 264; *Peel Memoirs*, I, 63-100; *W.N.D.*, IV, 409, 411; *Colchester*, III, 555-6.

more than 200,000 quarters of foreign corn entered the country, the increase to continue until the price reached 66s. He was supported by his immediate followers, Grant, Dudley, and Palmerston; but the Canningites were not alone. Melville, Goulburn, and more decisive still Peel, favoured the Canningite principle; and the Duke was left in a minority with Aberdeen, Ellenborough, and Bathurst. With Lyndhurst and Herries holding aloof, the Prime Minister faced the prospect of being out-voted in his own cabinet. There was room for compromise, however, and Peel for one was ready to accept an adjustment of the scale of duties to provide a greater degree of protection up to 65s. a quarter, in place of the pivot figure of 60s. proposed the previous year. Nevertheless, Huskisson adhered to his own plan and after hearing explanations of its administration the whole cabinet with the exception of the Duke were prepared to accept it. Peel urged the impolicy of the cabinet breaking up on the corn question at a time when war between Russia and Turkey seemed imminent; and Bathurst, Ellenborough, and Aberdeen were all ready to bow to the general feeling in favour of Huskisson's scheme. By 12 March there was a stalemate. Huskisson had made up his mind to resign if the pivot was changed; the Duke, even though he was alone in his opposition, would not give way. He felt that no one was prepared to make any concessions to him, and he was convinced that there was a personal opposition to him on the part of the Canningites. Next day Ellenborough went to take counsel with Peel, who advised him to talk with the Duke. He did so and succeeded in extracting concessions from both Wellington and Huskisson. The Duke gave up his warehousing proposal of the previous session, and Huskisson accepted a higher rate of duties than was provided by the 1827 bill. It was now Grant's turn to be obstinate. On 14 March he declared that he could not support the compromise in the House of Commons; Huskisson showed signs of retracting his earlier agreement; and the Duke consequently hardened his own attitude. For nearly a fortnight the cabinet was on the point of collapse. Huskisson was ready to compromise but he insisted that he could not go on without Grant's support. The difference in fact between Grant's wishes and the revised plan was very slight; but with the unreasonable obstinacy of a weak man Grant continued to cling to his position against the pleading of his colleagues, and from 18 March onward began to absent himself from cabinet meetings and dinners.

Theoretically Peel preferred Canning's original bill, which in fact was not so much Canning's as Liverpool's bill, but he attached greater importance to a firm and agreed settlement of the question. His efforts in and out of the cabinet were therefore directed towards concession and conciliation. He told Grant at the meeting on 15 March that he and Huskisson were as much responsible for last year's bill as Grant was; and made various proposals designed to narrow the gap between Grant's scale and the compromise agreed to by Huskisson and Wellington. These suggestions were well received and Grant promised to take them into consideration. Next day there was some confusion as to what had actually been decided but on 17 March the cabinet, with the exception of Grant, agreed to accept the modified scale that Peel had proposed. Grant, however, was still obdurate and though Huskisson remained in close consultation with Peel,[1] keeping him informed of all the details of the prolonged discussions with his reluctant colleague, by 25 March[2] matters were so far worse that a letter of resignation from the President of the Board of Trade was actually read out in the cabinet. The same evening, after dinner at the Duke's, there was some private discussion among those ministers present on the crisis. Grant with curious inconsistency had written to Huskisson that evening proposing an entirely new scale of duties, starting higher and falling more steeply than his original scale, and Huskisson at once forwarded this hopeful news to Peel. While still at Apsley House Peel wrote back a friendly letter of encouragement. After expressing his opinion that nothing would be more unfortunate for the credit of the government and the interests of the country than an irreconcilable difference on the corn question, he added:

> My opinion is that no chance of an amicable conclusion ought to be thrown away. For myself I do not hesitate to say that I am ready to give my decided support to any arrangement in which the

[1] 40396 fos. 83, 99-101.

[2] Palmerston in his *Journal* gave the date of the cabinet meeting at which Grant's resignation was read out as Monday, 24 March (Bulwer, *Palmerston*, I, 239). Peel's letter to Huskisson from Apsley House was 25 March.

Duke of Wellington and you can agree. I think a simple intelligible plan, founded on a permanent scale of duties, and affording the same degree of protection to agriculture, which is offered by the plan on which we all (with the exception of Grant) finally agreed, would be preferable to that plan, on account of its being free from complication. . . . Pray call on the Duke early tomorrow morning.[1]

Next day he saw Grant himself but could make little of him; and the other Canningites had no better success. Huskisson told Lyndhurst that his mind was in 'a hopeless state'. On 28 March Grant was still determined not to move the corn resolutions and in the afternoon Huskisson went to the king to proffer his own resignation. That same afternoon when Goulburn called to know his final decision, Grant at last agreed to the cabinet's proposals. Peel was at once informed, and at four o'clock sent off a hasty note to Huskisson, which actually reached him while he was still in audience. The king was delighted, and told Huskisson to kiss hands before he left as a token that he was to remain in office.

The crisis was over; but, like one of the Duke's other battles, it had been a near thing. He had been so irritated, in fact, by the behaviour of the Canningites that both he and Ellenborough were sorry that the affair had not ended with their resignations. But this was a minority view. Peel certainly had worked whole-heartedly for union, and in consequence he enjoyed greater confidence on the part of Huskisson and his followers than they were disposed to place in any other member of the cabinet. 'Peel is so rightheaded and liberal,' wrote Palmerston to his brother on 25 March, 'and so up to the opinions and feelings of the times, that he smooths difficulties which might otherwise be unsurmountable.'[2] As brought forward in the Commons on 31 March, the new scale of duties was approximately the same as in Canning's bill at two points: when the price of corn was 59s. a quarter, and 73s. a quarter. But between those points the new scale provided for a considerably heavier duty up to 67s. a quarter; and whereas by the earlier bill corn was admitted free at 70s., the bottom of the new scale was not reached until the price of domestic corn reached 74s. a quarter. It was in effect a concession

[1] 38755 f. 269, printed with some errors in *Huskisson Papers*, p. 300.
[2] Bulwer, *Palmerston*, I, 223.

to the agriculturalists, and Grant's manner when introducing the scheme showed his dislike of it. Inevitably it encountered the criticism of those who thought that the concessions were too great and of those who thought them too small. But it was a step, if not a long step, towards a freer trade in corn; and with the support of the liberal element in parliament, the government had little difficulty in resisting the various agriculturalist amendments put forward in both Houses. The bill was carried through parliament without any altera-tion; and Peel's own impression was that the moderate landowning members of the Commons were well satisfied.[1] When supporting Grant's resolution on 31 March he made his own views perfectly clear. He wanted a permanent law that might prevent heavy fluctuations in imports and prices; and he wanted a duty and not a prohibition. 'In consequence of the growing population of the country, there was a necessity for looking to other countries for a supply. . . . It was quite clear that Great Britain did not produce sufficient corn for her own consumption.'

Long before the Corn Bill reached the statute book, Wellington's uncomfortable cabinet was involved in yet another internal crisis. Early in the session bills were introduced to disfranchise two notor-iously rotten boroughs, Penryn in Cornwall and East Retford in Nottinghamshire, both of which had been previously declared by the House of Commons as corrupt and meriting disfranchisement. There were two principal methods of procedure in such cases: to enlarge the constituency by adding some of the neighbouring hundreds, or to transfer the representation outright to another town. Since the Commons had already pronounced on the general issue of disfranchisement, Peel was anxious to be prepared with the govern-ment's view of the question and brought the matter up in cabinet on 12 March. The Duke and Bathurst favoured the more conservative course of throwing the boroughs into the hundreds; the Canningites were anxious in principle to conciliate the advocates of parliamentary reform by enfranchising some of the new industrial towns; and Peel himself was inclined to be of that opinion. There was, however, a reluctance in his mind to a course of action which might seem a precedent for the regular transfer of the representation in all future

[1] For the Corn Bill crisis, see *Ellenborough*, I, 51-80; Bulwer, *Palmerston*, I, 231-46 (Palmerston's *Journal*).

cases. He proposed, therefore, that since there were two boroughs to be dealt with, Penryn should be transferred to Birmingham or Manchester, and Retford enlarged by the inclusion of the adjacent hundreds. Huskisson suggested the reverse procedure, though agreeing with Peel that it would be impolitic to establish a precedent by transferring both franchises to new constituencies. Dudley alone thought they should take the opportunity of satisfying the critics of the electoral system by enfranchising both the two great unrepresented industrial towns. If only one of the two corrupt boroughs was to lose its status, the case against Penryn was a strong one. Its record was even worse than that of Retford, and Cornwall was in any case so thickly studded with small corrupt or pocket boroughs that it would be difficult to find a sizeable area with which Penryn could be merged.

The final decision of the cabinet was therefore that Penryn should be transferred to an industrial town and East Retford extended to the hundreds. Peel accordingly put forward this arrangement to the House, on the explicit assumption that there would be two constituencies for disposal. Huskisson went further and on 21 March said in the Commons that if only one constituency was available, he would favour giving it to a town. On the strength of the government's views a motion was carried enabling the committee on the Retford bill to substitute the hundred of Bassetlaw for Birmingham. Further proceedings were then postponed until the Penryn bill passed into law. In May, however, the opposition in the House of Lords to the transfer of the Penryn franchise to Manchester was so strong that Lord Carnarvon who was in charge of the bill gave notice that he would withdraw that proposal. In these changed circumstances there was a move in the Commons to retain the original bill giving the Retford franchise to Birmingham. When the cabinet discussed the new situation a considerable confusion of view was revealed. It was not clear whether the ministry was committed to enfranchise at least one town, nor if so whether it should be Birmingham or Manchester. No decision was reached on 17 May, nor at another cabinet which Peel called the next day, Sunday. Finally, on Monday 19 May, the day of the renewed debate in the Commons on the Retford bill, it was settled in the cabinet that ministers would adhere to the arrangement proposed by Peel to the

House in March until a final decision was reached in the House of Lords over Penryn. There was a general feeling that if the Penryn transfer was thrown out in the Lords, ministers would have to reconsider the situation and it is probable that Peel's own view was that should the peers prove obstinate, it would be necessary to change the cabinet's policy over Retford. But he was primarily concerned with the immediate task—which had not proved easy—of securing an agreed government attitude for the debate in the Commons that night. Since Huskisson, who had headed the minority of critics in the cabinet, finally concurred in the general decision, Peel went down to the House with every assurance that he and his Canningite colleagues on the Treasury bench would present a common front.

In the course of the debate both Peel and Huskisson were charged with inconsistency in continuing to press for the substitution of Bassetlaw Hundred for Birmingham despite the fact that the bill transferring the Penryn franchise to Manchester had virtually been killed by the Lords. Peel was able to prove without difficulty that he had never pledged himself on what was to be done if only one borough were available. Huskisson, however, could offer no such defence and under pressure from the opposition began to exhibit considerable uneasiness. He asked Peel, sitting next to him, about the possibility of an adjournment but Peel said he must persevere with the line he had advocated. Up to the moment of the division Huskisson remained in great perplexity but in the end he followed Palmerston's suggestion to sit still and be counted with the supporters of the original clause of the bill. The new instruction to the committee was carried by fourteen votes but both Huskisson and Palmerston were numbered with the minority. Peel, who had no suspicion of his colleagues' impending defection until the division was taken, was not surprisingly discomposed; but he said nothing. Huskisson, however, went away with Planta, the government whip, who sharply reproached him for his desertion; and reaching home in a turmoil of spirits sat down at two o'clock in the morning to write a letter of resignation. There is little doubt that Huskisson intended, by placing his office at the Duke's disposal, to offer a complete apology and a means of making amends for his conduct. But the letter read like an unconditional resignation. Wellington took it as such; and Peel, to whom he immediately showed it, was of the same opinion. That afternoon the letter was laid before the king.

As soon as they heard what had happened, Dudley and Palmerston tried to convince the Duke that Huskisson did not mean to resign, but merely to express his readiness to resign if the Duke thought it necessary; and a stiff correspondence took place in the next few days between Huskisson and the Prime Minister. The breach, however, was irreparable. Wellington hinted to Dudley that as a man of sense Huskisson knew that the only way to end the matter was to withdraw his letter. Huskisson thought that this was an attempt to humiliate him and refused to withdraw it, though he insisted that he did not mean it as an unconditional resignation. Peel refused to intervene; he did not attach any special significance to the vote on the East Retford question in itself, but he was clear in his own mind that the cabinet had agreed as a body to support the line he had taken as leader of the House. Indeed, he quoted to Palmerston the last words of Huskisson on leaving the cabinet on 19 May—'Well, tonight at all events, we may stand upon the ground that the Lords have not disposed of Penryn.' Moreover, he was vexed at Huskisson's omission to give him the slightest hint during the debate that his earlier pledge on the subject would force him to depart from the agreed cabinet policy. Palmerston, who saw Peel the next day, found him 'evidently hurt and angry, though his manner to me was perfectly kind and conciliatory'. On 22 May, when Wellington had rebuffed Huskisson's first proffered explanation, Palmerston called on Peel at Whitehall Gardens to tell him that there seemed no possibility of accommodation and that the Canningites would have to resign. According to his own account of the discussion, Palmerston argued that it was unfair to take Huskisson up on a letter which had repeatedly been explained as not conveying the interpretation placed upon it; but Peel observed discouragingly that resignations given and not acted upon gave a minister making them a great advantage afterwards over his colleagues. However, the two men parted amicably with mutual expressions of regret. After waiting until 25 May, Wellington informed Huskisson that arrangements had been made to fill his office, and the resignation of the other Canningites—Palmerston, Grant, Dudley from the cabinet, together with Lamb, the Irish Secretary, Francis Leveson Gower, Howard de

Walden, and Frankland Lewis—followed in the next few days.[1]

In this crisis consistency and interest alike might have seemed to require from Peel a greater effort at mediation than he was apparently prepared to attempt. But patience with Peel was more the product of political training than temperament, and the point had been reached when he was perhaps weary of well-doing on behalf of the Canningites. He had been the chief advocate for their admittance into the cabinet in January; he had been on their side against the Prime Minister in the controversies over foreign policy and foreign corn. But his new allies scarcely made things easy for him. Grant's obstinacy over the Corn Bill had tried everybody's temper; and Huskisson's letter on 20 May was the third resignation emanating from the Canningite group in the first four months of the ministry. It is doubtful in any case whether Peel could have intervened with success. His influence with Huskisson would not have done more than that of Palmerston and Dudley; and though it is not known what conversations if any passed between Peel and the Duke on the subject, it is questionable whether he could have induced Wellington to hold out an olive-branch, even if he had thought that the Duke ought to do so. Peel's agreement with the Canningites on most of the controversial cabinet issues that had arisen—Greece, corn, parliamentary reform—had not strengthened his relations with the Prime Minister. Over the Greek question, for instance, Palmerston noted in April that the Duke was ill-pleased to find Peel advocating independence. If, after all that had taken place, Peel had come forward once more as the defender of the Canningites, his influence with the Duke might have been seriously strained. When, according to Palmerston's subsequent account of the crisis, Dudley was making eleventh-hour efforts to bridge the gap between the Duke and Huskisson, he was unable to elicit any helpful suggestion from Peel. If, he told Dudley, he proposed anything which he thought satisfactory and the Duke did not, he would be left himself in an unpleasant situation. To Leveson Gower, who attempted a similar mediation, Peel's reply was only a shade more sympathetic. He refused to intervene himself but he assented to Leveson Gower's

[1] F. Leveson Gower was Under-Secretary at War and Colonies; Frankland Lewis Vice-President of the Board of Trade; Howard de Walden Under-Secretary at the Foreign Office.

argument that the withdrawal of Huskisson's resignation was desirable on public grounds, and both advised and encouraged him to go in person to the Duke.[1]

Huskisson had in fact made it very difficult for any one to help him. He had made three mistakes in succession: in departing from the cabinet agreement when he could plausibly have argued—and indeed did argue—in the House that he could not be called upon to redeem his pledge until the Lords had finally rejected the Penryn bill; in writing his precipitate note of resignation without reflection or advice; and in refusing subsequently to withdraw the letter even though he said that he had not intended it as a resignation. If, like Palmerston, he had gone at once to Peel and Wellington to apologise and explain, the matter would have been over at once. But Huskisson's nature, as covert and awkward as his manner, made such an easy and friendly gesture impossible. Once the breach had become impassable, it was a human reaction for the Huskissonites to comfort themselves with the reflection that the Duke had intended all along either to humiliate them or force their resignation. But this was a retrospective interpretation. It was true, on the other hand, that the Duke's correct but politically rigid attitude was conditioned by the fact that his own stock of patience was exhausted. The Huskisson group had entered the government as a body; they resigned as a body; and, more irritating still, they had acted in the cabinet as a body. It was natural that they should have done so. The guarantees which were so much in Huskisson's mind when joining the ministry, consisted ultimately in his view of the physical presence there of his three companions. But though natural, it was politically disastrous. When the Duke felt frustrated at being continually placed in a minority in his own cabinet, it was equally natural if not entirely rational for him to attribute the blame to the existence within it of the independent Huskisson squad. The atmosphere of schism and imminent resignation, in which the cabinet seemed to have been living since March, he tended to regard as a systematic policy on their part to enforce their views; and in colleagues like Ellen-

---

[1] For the resignation of the Canningites see, Bulwer, *Palmerston*, I, 253ff.; *Ellenborough*, I, 106ff.; *W.N.D.*, IV, 449ff.; *Croker*, I, 409; Earl of Ellesmere, *Personal Reminiscences of . . . Wellington* (1903), p. 68; speeches of Huskisson and Peel, *Hansard*, N.S., XIX, 917ff.

borough he had counsellors who rejoiced in the prospect of getting rid of them. Difficult as it is for a professional soldier to adapt himself to politics, the Duke was not without certain civilian virtues. He had acquired considerable diplomatic experience; he was usually ready to take advice; and he had a strong sense of administrative expediency. But he was not skilled in human relationships. The framework of military discipline in which he had grown up and to which he owed his high position was designed to subordinate those relationships to other requirements; and he lacked the wide tolerance and comprehensiveness of an eminently political mind like that of Lord Liverpool.

Of all the members of his government, however, the loss of the Canningites was most acutely felt by Peel. This was not primarily on account of policy, for the liberal tendencies of the Wellington ministry had never depended solely on Huskisson and his three immediate followers; nor on account of the resultant decrease in sheer voting strength. Not all Canning's former followers recognised Huskisson as their leader, and not all of these ranged themselves in opposition after May 1828. The Canningite party had in fact broken up on the death of its first and only leader in 1827.[1] But the diminution of ministerial ability and debating talent in the House of Commons was a sensible loss, and one that directly affected Peel as leader of the House. On him rested the responsibilities of government in the lower House of the legislature; but he could not command an outright majority there and he felt that he was not adequately supported even by the nominal ministerial party. The extreme tories expected him to take a stronger line than he did, regardless of the fact that he had to deal with the House as a whole; and when they found him pursuing a middle course, they in turn grew dissatisfied and tended to absent themselves.[2] Now he was weakened still further by the defection of Huskisson and his followers: and the quality of their replacements sufficiently demonstrated the poverty of talent at the government's disposal. He pressed the Duke to take as many of the new ministers as possible from the Commons but the result was not impressive. Sir George Murray, Wellington's quartermaster general in the Peninsular War and more recently Commander-in-Chief in Ireland, became Secretary of

---

[1] Aspinall, 'Last of the Canningites' (E.H.R., L, 639).    [2] *Ellenborough*, I, 64, 66.

State for the Colonies; and another Peninsular veteran, Sir Henry Hardinge, took Palmerston's place as Secretary at War though not his seat in the cabinet. Vesey Fitzgerald became President of the Board of Trade and was succeeded as Paymaster-General by John Calcraft; Arbuthnot moved to the Duchy of Lancaster and was succeeded at Woods and Forests by Lord Lowther; and in the House of Lords Aberdeen was promoted to the Foreign Office. Francis Leveson Gower, who had resigned mainly in deference to his father's views, returned to the ministry as Chief Secretary for Ireland. Some lesser Canningites, like Planta, remained in the government and another, Spencer Perceval, took minor office in July.

Huskisson's resignation had in fact confounded rather than clarified the existing political differences, and though the ministry had no assured control of the House of Commons, the miscellaneous groups that confronted the government had even less. Indeed, it was doubtful whether Huskisson himself could command more than about a dozen votes in the Commons, and there was little prospect either of his joining the whigs or of a reunion of the old Canning party. But though the voting strength of the government was made little worse, if no better, by the events of May 1828, the quality of the front bench had decidedly deteriorated and a greater burden than ever was placed on Peel's shoulders.

# 14

# LAW AND POLICE

If cabinet quarrels seemed an inevitable accompaniment of office, Peel's return to the Home Office at least enabled him to resume his interrupted programme of legal reform. Much of his time in the 1828 session was wasted on a bill for the recovery of small debts. It was a subject to which Althorp had tried to draw the attention of parliament and even before the end of the Liverpool ministry Peel had undertaken to bring in a bill. But the measure ran into severe technical difficulties over the question of compensation to holders of patent offices in the higher courts if the jurisdiction of the county courts was extended and in the end the matter became merged in a wider movement of law reform in which the Home Office was only partially involved. Following an important speech by Brougham early in the session on the reform of the common law courts, two crown commissions were set up to enquire into the state of the common law and the law relating to real property. Peel eventually referred the small debts question to the first of these and after an interval of over a year a start was made on the preliminaries for a reform of the common law courts. On 18 February 1830, in a comprehensive speech indicating the various lines along which legal reform might develop, Peel moved for a specific bill regulating the fees of persons holding patent offices, as a first step towards the general reform of the courts which the commissioners had in view. A month later, when Brougham on his own account introduced a plan of reform for local courts, Peel referred to its agreement in principle with his own Small Debts Bill and offered him full support. 'He trusted he might be allowed to consider himself the associate of the hon. and learned gentleman in these reforms.'[1]

[1] For the Small Debts Bill see 40316 f. 25; speeches of 22 May, 23 June, 1828; 8 May 1829; 29 April 1830.

Long before that date, however, he had turned once more to his own chosen field of Criminal Law. In May 1828 he introduced two bills: one to alter the existing mode of receiving evidence in courts of law; the other to consolidate the existing statute law relating to offences against the person. Though the latter owed its inception to the general process begun by Peel of consolidating the Criminal Law, both these bills had been prepared in the Home Department under Lord Lansdowne. By the terms of the first, Quakers and Moravians were allowed to give evidence on affirmation in criminal as they were already allowed to do in civil cases; interested parties in forgery cases were admitted as witnesses; and convicted criminals who had served their sentences could give evidence in criminal causes or actions at law, except those previously convicted of perjury. By the terms of the second, the whole statute law of England relating to offences against the person was consolidated in one Act, and fifty-seven previous laws repealed. The principal object in condensing the obscure and intricate statutes on this subject was—as Peel told the House—'not so much to consolidate them as to simplify them and to make them clear'. Nevertheless, the opportunity was taken to make a number of changes. The distinction between murder and petty treason (the murder of husbands by wives, masters by servants, and ecclesiastical superiors by clergy) was abolished; the concealment of murderers was made a capital offence; and the procedure for trying cases of murder committed abroad was simplified. One major alteration to which he specifically drew the attention of the House was the simplification of proof in case of rape, sexual intercourse with children, and unnatural offences, where from the nature of the offence full and specific proof was not easy to obtain and on which there had been considerable variation of treatment by the courts in the previous century. Both bills passed with little discussion and were put on the statute book as 9 Geo. IV c. 31 (Offences against the Person) and c. 32 (Law of Evidence). The result of all his consolidating statutes, from 1825 to 1828, was that two hundred and seventy-eight Acts had now been repealed and those of their provisions that had been retained summarised in eight Acts.[1]

Nevertheless, Peel's appetite for reform was not yet sated and

[1] *Speeches*, II, 74 (18 February 1830).

when making his parliamentary survey of the whole field of legal reform in February 1830 he gave notice of his intention to bring in more consolidating bills, relating to laws affecting the office of justice of the peace, the coinage, and forgery offences, which if successful—he told the House—would mean that nine-tenths of the cases coming before the courts would have been brought within the scope of the reforms introduced since 1825. Of these topics, the question of forgery was the most controversial. The most common type of forgery was in connection with currency and bills of exchange; and partly because of its effect on public and commercial credit, and partly because of the difficulty of catching the skilled forger as distinct from the poorer and more ignorant men and boys employed to pass the false coins or notes, it had always been regarded as a particularly reprehensible crime. The 1819 committee had recommended the retention of the death penalty only for forgery of Bank of England notes and for uttering forged notes in the case of second offenders. But opinion was divided on the policy of weakening the deterrents for this offence and no legislation resulted. In the ensuing decade, however, the current of public opinion continued to flow in the direction of decreased severity for this as for other crimes; and it was noticeable that such middle-class organs as the *Edinburgh Review* and the *Westminster Review* advocated a relaxation of the forgery laws, although the middle classes were more liable than others to suffer from the activities of forgers.[1] The famous case of Hunton in 1828 exhibited the growing gap between the penalties prescribed by law and the attitude of public opinion. Hunton was a Quaker who as partner in a firm of London drapers had forged and uttered various bills of exchange. He was arrested when about to abscond to America and found guilty on a number of separate indictments; on his own statement his forgeries amounted to £5,000. The jury, however, recommended him to mercy on account of his wife and ten children. Massive petitions came in from the general body of Quakers and the king wrote to Peel asking for a reprieve. The Home Secretary, who had already consulted the Lord Chancellor and the Lord Chief Justice, was against any intervention. Of the three capital sentences for forgery in the last two Recorder's reports two had been commuted; in the third,

[1] cf. Radzinowicz, I, 599.

479

Hunton's case, renewed discussions with his legal advisers confirmed Peel's view that the law must be allowed to take its course. 'It appears to them, as it does to Mr. Peel,'. he replied to the king on 6 December, 'that it would be very difficult hereafter to enforce the capital sentence of the law in any case of forgery, if mercy be extended in this case.'[1] On the morning of 8 December, in the presence of an enormous crowd, Hunton was executed outside the Old Bailey. His guilt was clear and aggravated and, unless the punishment prescribed by law was to become a complete dead-letter, the administrative decision to enforce it in his case was justifiable. The fact remained, however, that increasingly the choice of life and death was being made less as an inevitable consequence of judicial sentence than as a result of executive policy on the part of the ministers; and their decisions were naturally framed, as in Hunton's case, with consideration not merely to the heinousness of the offence but also to the number and circumstances of similar crimes committed at the same time—'a very difficult and painful duty, executed, I believe, most conscientiously,' wrote Ellenborough, 'but I wish it did not fall to the King's ministers to execute it.'[2]

The remedy for this wide and painful discretion in the administration of the law was of course a change in the severity of the penalties it laid down; and in the course of the following year Peel began to make preparations for a reform of the forgery laws. The history of the Forgery Bill was an admirable illustration of his general methods of procedure in the matter of legal reform. Some time in the early summer of 1829 he had a discussion with Scarlett, who had succeeded Wetherell as Attorney-General, on the question of consolidating the forgery laws and making some adjustment in their penalties; and at the end of August Scarlett submitted to him the sketch of a bill embodying the principles which the Home Secretary had indicated he wished to follow. On the point of capital punishment the Attorney-General suggested a distinction between forgeries of such instruments as were immediately convertible into money, and those which needed time, preparation, and connivance to achieve their object. Peel, meanwhile, talked the problem over with Gregson and Hobhouse and the more closely they examined it, the

---

[1] *Peel*, II, 43-4; *Geo. IV Letters*, III, 449.
[2] *Ellenborough*, I, 268 (1 December 1828).

more complicated it appeared. One major difficulty was the existence side by side of general laws on forgery and a large number of particular acts (360 for the Customs alone) relating to forgeries connected with specified departments of state. In November Gregson sent Peel his comments on the sketch put forward by Scarlett. They were decidedly critical. In seeking a short cut through the difficulties, Scarlett had (in Gregson's opinion at least) merely multiplied them. His plan would have had the effect of converting all cases of forgery into felonies, whereas they were previously only misdemeanours unless specifically made felony by statute; and there were several kinds of forgery which Scarlett had omitted to consider at all.

Gregson's own suggestion was that a bill should be prepared dealing with all statutory forgeries except those affecting public departments. If the departments concerned could re-draft their own Acts, so much the better. If not, a short bill could be drawn up merely repealing the capital punishment prescribed by those Acts without altering the definition of the offence. By that simple expedient the whole body of the forgery laws could be amended and consolidated. The main issue would then be the selection of forgery offences for which the death sentence was to be retained. Peel adopted this plan in preference to that of Scarlett and by the end of the year a draft bill had been drawn up. Its principal effect was to reduce to one Act all capital forgeries, and to consolidate the remaining forgery provisions other than those affecting public departments. The proposal for the latter was that each department should prepare a bill embracing all capital forgeries relating to it and substituting in every case the penalty of transportation. In sending the bill to Lord Tenterden, soliciting once more 'the cheerful and most valuable aid which I have uniformly received from you throughout my labours on the consolidation of the criminal law', Peel indicated the conclusion to which he had come in the matter of the death sentence.

The principle followed in the selection of capital forgeries has been to give the highest protection to Government Securities which are immediately convertible into money, and to those commercial instruments which in the course of trade pass quickly from hand to hand as the representatives of money. The capital punishment is also retained for the forgery of wills as being an offence of easy commission and great enormity.

But he wished to keep the issue open and for the time being the circulation of the draft was confined to Lord Tenterden, the Lord Chancellor, the Attorney-General, the Solicitor-General, and Hobhouse.[1]

In January 1830 a fresh copy of the bill with comments and alterations was sent to Tenterden and a number of discussions took place between the two men in February and March. The Lord Chief Justice once more offered to take charge of the bill in the upper House, while Peel made himself responsible for it in the Commons. The Attorney-General was disposed to be more critical, probably (as Peel suggested to Lord Tenterden) because his own suggestions had not been adopted. Nevertheless, his comments were duly reported to Gregson for consideration. It was clearly on Gregson rather than on his more eminent legal colleague that Peel continued to rely, and before what was probably the last conclusive interview between Peel and the Lord Chief Justice on the bill, Gregson briefed the Home Secretary with a long memorandum on the subject.[2] When, therefore, on 1 April 1830 Peel rose in the Commons to introduce his Bill for the Consolidation of the Forgery Laws, it was after nine months of private discussion and examination of the issues involved. As it issued from the Home Department, the bill made no sweeping changes in the severity of the penalties imposed by the existing statutes. Disregarding the great number of forgery laws relating to public departments, which he proposed to refer to the offices concerned for revision, Peel concentrated on the hundred and twenty statutes dealing with public and personal forgeries— notes, bills, securities, documents relating to transfers of property, wills, marriage settlements, and public registers. Of those, sixty-one carried the death penalty. Peel's bill reduced this mass of legislation to four clauses, one of which enumerated the various categories of forgery whether public or departmental for which capital punishment was retained. The principle he followed was the retention of the death penalty for forgery of negotiable securities,

---

[1] 40399 fos. 312, 314, 375, 410.     [2] 40400 fos. 14, 30, 69-80, 89-91.

bank notes and all documents representing monetary value, wills involving personal property, and false entries relating to public stock, together with forgeries of the great seal, privy seal, and sign manual. He accepted the recommendation of the 1819 committee in removing the death penalty, in practice no longer enforced, for forgery of receipts, stamps, orders, other deeds and bonds, and for the fabrication of bank-note paper.

His bill, in fact, was similar to the amended bill of 1821 which even so had failed to pass into law, and he defended the extent to which he was still prepared to retain the death penalty not only on the general principle of cautious progress but also on account of the special temptations before men of ability and information to commit this particular type of crime. Nevertheless, a strong party in the Commons, headed by Mackintosh, Fowell Buxton, Brougham, and Russell, fought for a much greater relaxation of penalties on the ground that the public unwillingness to accept the punishment of death for forgery resulted in a general reluctance of injured parties to prosecute and of juries to convict. Peel was not so convinced and thought that fear of trouble and expense was a more powerful deterrent to prosecution than any inherent dislike of the death penalty.[1] The parliamentary controversy was spread over four months and aroused great interest in the country. Nearly two hundred petitions were sent in to the two Houses of parliament, and a significant number of those supporting relaxation were signed not merely by clergy and lawyers but by bankers and company directors, including the heads of the two great firms of Rothschild, and Overend, Gurney & Co. It was probable in fact that not only the bulk of the professional middle classes, but the majority of bankers were convinced that a more lenient system of penalties would result in more effective legal protection.

Though impressed by the weight of opinion against him, and ready to hold out the prospect of further mitigation of the criminal code once the great work of consolidation had been completed, Peel held to his initial position. 'It was after deliberate consideration,' he told the House in committee on 24 May, 'that he had attained to the honest conclusion, that it would be better to preserve the punishment of death for forgery than abandon it.' He reminded his

[1] cf. 40400 f. 164 (Peel to J. W. Freshfield, 1 May 1830).

audience once again that the recent limitations of the death penalty had been followed by an increase in capital offences, and pointed to the magnitude of the rewards to be obtained, the facility of committing and the difficulty-of detecting forgery, as special reasons for affixing to that crime particularly severe punishment. Other factors besides humanity, he argued, affected the decision of private persons not to prosecute; and as far as juries were concerned, in the last seven years, from 1823 to 1829, statistics showed that convictions for forgery were as high as the average for all offences, and higher than in the case of murder. If the death sentence were abandoned, what effect was to be expected from secondary punishments? During the last ten years various experiments with low diet, solitary confinement, and hard labour, had shown them to be dangerous and worthless; they would be still more inapplicable to the class of men from whom forgers were drawn; while transportation for such persons would be equally useless as a deterrent.

But all his debating skill was needed to maintain his slender majorities on that issue, and though Mackintosh was unable to carry his point in committee he won a notable victory a fortnight later. On the third reading of the bill on 7 June 1830, with less than half the House present, there was a majority of thirteen for his amendment substituting imprisonment or transportation up to fourteen years as the penalty for all cases of forgery with the exception of wills. Peel briefly expressed his dissent and said he would leave the future progress of the bill to Mackintosh, though in fact he moved the second reading of the new clause the following day and the bill thus passed. But he was piqued by his defeat, and thoroughly dissatisfied at the general weakness of the government in the House of Commons. Nevertheless the defeat was a fact, and whatever happened in the Lords, the verdict of the Commons would inevitably affect the course of public opinion. When the cabinet considered the issue on 13 June, the decision was taken to allow the bill to go through as amended, but it was agreed that Peel should sound the opinion of merchants and bankers. His own view was that it would now be impossible to secure a conviction for forgery under the death penalty.[1] In the Lords, however, the Mackintosh clause was struck out at the instance of the Lord

[1] *Ellenborough*, II, 264, 267.

Chancellor, Eldon, Wynford, and Lord Tenterden. When the bill
returned in July, the Commons were faced, as a result of the lateness
of the session, with the alternative of either accepting the amendment or dropping the bill entirely. They chose the former, and on
20 July, four days before prorogation, the bill passed into law (11
Geo. IV-1 Will. IV c. 66) in substantially the form in which Peel
originally introduced it.

The issue of the forgery laws in 1830 demonstrated more clearly
than any of Peel's previous legal reforms that moderate opinion was
becoming increasingly converted to the opinions of the Romilly-
Mackintosh school. To that extent Peel's cautious administrative
approach was being outpaced by public feeling. In 1830 he had his
way, but only with the help of the peers; and not for long. As soon
as the whigs came into power, they accelerated the process on which
Peel had tried to place a restraining influence while he was in office.
In 1832 Ewart carried a bill to abolish capital punishment for horse
and cattle-stealing, and stealing from dwelling-houses to the value
of £5. The same session Denman, the Attorney-General, introduced
a bill abolishing capital punishment for all cases of forgery, and
though the Lords retained the death sentence for the forgery of wills
and certain powers of attorney, the main clauses of Denman's bill
became law. In substance Mackintosh had already decided the issue
in 1830; for no one was executed for forgery in England after that
year. Finally in 1833 capital punishment for housebreaking with
larceny was abolished. In three years, therefore, substantial inroads
had been made on the barriers which Peel had wished to maintain.[1]

Yet it is doubtful if he himself took these changes as reflecting in
any way upon his own reforms. Over Ewart's bill he said he agreed
to a certain extent with the principle of the bill, though he offered
criticism of the details. He was still concerned with the problem of
secondary punishments, and he still thought that the work of reform
should proceed gradually. But 'he did not at all mean to say that the
time was not come for such an alteration to take place; he did not
mean to say that such an alteration ought not to take place at this
time'.[2] At the outset of his work in the Home Department he had
favoured a decreased severity in the criminal code; and despite

---

[1] Radzinowicz, I, 601-7 is misleading on Peel's attitude in 1832.
[2] *Speeches*, II, 524, 555 (27 March, 30 May 1832).

what had been accomplished since 1823, when he returned to the department in 1828 his mind continued to move in the direction of still further amelioration. When the cabinet in February 1830 was discussing legal reform, Ellenborough noted that Peel was in favour of a gradual diminution in the number of capital offences, despite the reluctance of the Prime Minister and his colleagues; and in private he told Buxton that he was on his side in the matter of capital punishments but 'you must give me time'.[1] His speech the following April, when introducing the forgery bill, was significant for a number of declarations on the general principle of reducing the severity of sentences.

> He thought it a most important object to diminish, as much as possible, the number of offences to which the punishment of death had been attached. He had indeed no hesitation in avowing that he was a strong advocate for the mitigation of capital punishments. He wished to remove, in all cases where it was practicable, the punishment of death; for it was impossible to conceal from ourselves, that capital punishments were more frequent, and the criminal code more severe, on the whole, in this country, than in any country in the world.

His own administration at the Home Office showed a notable continuation of the fall in the number of executions which had been a feature of the early nineteenth century. In the seven-year period that followed the close of the War of American Independence in 1783, the average number of executions in London and Middlesex was fifty-six a year; in the seven-year period from 1816 to 1822 they had fallen to twenty-seven a year; and from 1822 to 1829, to only seventeen a year.[2] In England and Wales as a whole, the number of executions in the seven years preceding 1822 had totalled 731; in the seven years since that date, 433.[3]

Peel's preference for a steady but cautious relaxation of the law rather than a sudden and sweeping change was based not on a desire to enforce the death penalty rigidly but on his view of the expediency of retaining discretionary powers in the hands of the judiciary

[1] *Ellenborough*, II, 195; *Memoirs of Sir Thomas Fowell Buxton* (Everyman edn.), p. 112.

[2] *Speeches*, II, 131 (1 April 1830).     [3] *ibid.*, 163 (24 May 1830).

to be used as circumstances required and until the effects of the various legal reforms were fully apparent. Moreover, he envisaged his own work of consolidation as a necessary forerunner to reforms in the temper of the law, and he did not wish to confound the two. What he had done in consolidating the law, he told the Commons in May 1830, was not to prevent the subject from being reviewed again; and when consolidation was complete, it might be expedient to mitigate still more the severity of its punishments. 'He looked forward to a time when the criminal law, after the consolidation of its different parts had been carried into effect, should be again brought under consideration.'[1] But by 1830 that work of consolidation was almost complete. Behind him lay an impressive range of major organising legislation: the Juries Act of 1825, the Criminal Justice Act of 1826, the Larceny and Malicious Injury to Property Acts of 1827, the Offences against the Person Act of 1828, and the Forgery Act of 1830. A mass of obsolete legislation, the debris of centuries of English legal history, had been reduced to the compass of a handful of intelligible statutes. In criminal law alone more than three-quarters of all offences had been covered by Peel's revision. Between the law-books of George III and those of William IV there was now a great divide.

## II

If in the matter of capital punishment Peel was not prepared to move as fast as public opinion, there was one sphere of administrative reform at the Home Department in which he had already shown that he took a bolder view than either the public or the majority of the politicians. It was to this that he now returned.

London in the third decade of the nineteenth century had a population rising to one and a half million, as great as that of the fifteen next largest towns in the British Isles; and outside its official boundaries, growing towns and villages like Brentford, Deptford, and Greenwich were already flowing together in an even wider coagulation of urban areas. Among the shops, offices, churches, warehouses, and mansions of the City, eastward round the great

[1] *Speeches*, II, 162.

docks where the ship-masts clustered against the skyline, in the teeming slums and rookeries of Holborn and St. Giles, in the trim new residential districts of Bloomsbury and Kensington, and in the endless rows of suburban streets, lived one-twelfth of the country's inhabitants. This vast conglomeration of people and buildings was still regulated and policed under the chaotic and inefficient system inherited from the eighteenth century. The City, with 125,000 people and one hundred and eight parishes crammed into six hundred acres, had its own police force of about a thousand watchmen, constables, and beadles, divided under twenty-six ward authorities, together with some fifty regular city police. Westminster, with a population larger than that of Dublin, and Southwark larger than Bristol, together with the outlying parishes and liberties, were controlled by the seven police offices set up by the Act of 1792, each staffed by three stipendiary magistrates aided by a couple of clerks and some eight to a dozen constables. In addition to these police offices, primarily responsible for their own districts and independent of each other, there were the Thames police set up under an Act of 1800, and the old Bow Street office, dating from the middle of the eighteenth century, with a general jurisdiction over the whole area outside the City. Early in the nineteenth century there had been some reinforcement of these sketchy organisations. In 1805 a horse patrol had been instituted to police the main roads leading into London up to a radius of twenty miles, while a foot patrol operated within a five-mile radius. While successful in clearing the environs of the capital, this patrolling had the effect of driving criminals into the centre; and in 1821 the foot patrol was confined to the metropolis while an additional force of dismounted patrolmen was used in their place on the outskirts of the urban area. Finally there were the ineffective constables and watchmen employed by the parishes and other local authorities, or by private individuals, firms, and associations, reinforced from time to time by special constables sworn in on particular occasions and paid 5s. a day by the Home Office. Though their numbers were much greater than the police of the magistrates' courts, the parochial police presented the familiar picture of inefficient, separate, and competing jurisdictions characteristic of the whole field of English local administration at the start of the century.

Just conceive [wrote Peel to the Duke of Wellington on one occasion] the state of one parish, in which there are eighteen different local boards for the management of the watch, each acting without concert with the others! . . . Think of the state of Brentford and Deptford, with no sort of police by night! I really think I need trouble you with no further proof of the necessity of putting an end to such a state of things.[1]

In this confusion the one co-ordinating element was the Home Office, and even before Peel came to the department in 1822 there had been an increasing assertion of control over the main body of the London police. Though acting separately, all nine police offices worked under the general supervision of the Home Secretary. From 1818 the Bow Street police were used as a force at his immediate disposal, and the horse patrol, though nominally attached to Bow Street, was under his direct orders. Even so, it was not a large concentration of strength. The eight land police offices had a total establishment in 1822 of one hundred and twenty-eight, of whom only sixty-eight were constables; the Thames police alone were almost as large a force with an establishment of a hundred of whom half were constables. The horse patrol with six inspectors, seventy ordinary patrol, one hundred and two dismounted patrol, and one hundred foot patrol, was not only as large as the whole of the magisterial force but constituted the most solid and homogeneous body of police in the metropolitan area. In their blue coats and trousers with red waistcoats, and armed with truncheons and cutlasses, they were the first uniformed police unit in the country and the first to come under immediate Home Office direction.[2] In all, leaving out of consideration the parochial officials, the Thames police, and the City police, Peel had under his control when he entered the Home Office in 1822 a total force of four hundred men, of whom the effective number of police was less than three hundred and fifty. With this he had to maintain order in a population (excluding the City) of over a million. The inadequacy of the force was aggravated by the defects of its personnel. The ordinary constables, who made up much of their earnings by special fees and presents, were subject

[1] 40308 f. 173, printed Peel, II, 111.
[2] H.O. 61/1/175 (Establishment of Police Offices, 1822); ibid., 101 (Brief Account of Police Horse Patrol).

to the constant temptation of conniving at offences for the sake of rewards. Their discipline was lax, and their associations with the criminal classes open to suspicion. Some kept public-houses or engaged in other businesses; many took bribes; and there was a disposition to treat the investigation of crime as a special matter over and above their ordinary duties, demanding appropriate payment. This was particularly marked with the Bow Street police, who usually worked singly or in couples on security duties with royalty or on special investigations in different parts of the country, and expected to be treated as though they were hired private detectives. Above all, as the continued connection between the magistrates and their separate police staffs indicated, the task of the police was still primarily regarded as a judicial function—the detection and capture of criminals, and the recovery of stolen property, rather than the prevention of crime.

The report of the committee of 1822 left little room for any fundamental improvement of this system. It had, however, recommended an extension of the foot and horse patrols at an initial cost of up to £2,000 per annum. This was of importance since only in an extension of the patrolling system was there any chance of developing effective policing of the streets as a standing deterrent to crime. Peel was prompt to take advantage of even this small opening by instituting the same summer a foot patrol to police the streets of Westminster and the boundaries of the City 'for the prevention of felonies and the apprehending of offenders in the daytime'. To make the men 'proud of their establishment' he ordered that they should wear the blue and red uniform of the old horse patrol. Distributed judiciously over their large area, the patrols were on duty from 9 a.m. to 7 p.m. when the night patrol took over. Another minor reform he brought in was the appointment of head or chief constables to each public office. Other possibilities seem to have occurred to his mind: the amalgamation of the horse and foot patrols with the Bow Street police, and the rebuilding of the cramped Bow Street office. None of this was accomplished, however, although in 1824 a new office for the horse patrol was procured at 8 Cannon Row. Meanwhile he endeavoured in a variety of ways to improve the efficiency of the whole force. In June 1825 the magistrates of the nine police offices had their salaries raised to the full rate of £800 per annum allowable by law; the wages of their clerks were improved at the same time; and those of the horse and foot patrol the following January. Simultaneously a sharp check was maintained on finance and discipline, and in July 1826 Peel laid down a general rule that no police officer was to be concerned, directly or indirectly, in any private business 'calculated to make him swerve from the exclusive, punctual, faithful, and honest discharge of his public duty; nor should he live in such a place, or in such a manner, as shall occasion a reasonable suspicion of his having any such bias upon his conduct'.[1]

Administrative probity, however, could not compensate for fundamental defects in organisation; and by 1826 Peel had determined on a fresh effort to bring about an organic reform of the London police. At the end of that year he invited the police magistrates to send him suggestions on the best method of preventing crime in the neighbourhood of the metropolis, and an enquiry was instituted into the state of the police in the townships in the immediate environs of London. He himself spared no time in examining carefully every means of improving police efficiency. A proposal was made by R. Hart Davies, M.P. to transform the old *Hue and Cry*, edited by Stafford at the Bow Street office, into a weekly police gazette, with the object of securing maximum publicity for the work of the police and the aid of the public in securing offenders. Peel did not accept his arguments but he went to the trouble of writing a ten-page letter in reply to Davies explaining all the difficulties and objections.[2] Meanwhile he was procuring statistics of crime and population from abroad, notably from Berlin, Vienna, Antwerp, Paris, Brussels, and Hamburg, to compare with the situation in London.[3] There was a general feeling in the Home Department and among its immediate correspondents in the winter of 1826-7 not only that Peel's legal reforms required a reform of the police to complement them, but that something was at last about to be done to bring about that reform. In December

---

[1] H.O. 60/1/225-9; see generally H.O. 60/1 and 61/1 (Police Correspondence 1820-30); P.P. 1822, IV (*Police of Metropolis*); P.P. 1828, VI (*Police of Metropolis*); cf. Radzinowicz, II, 171ff.; Hart, *British Police*, pp. 22ff.; Browne, *Scotland Yard*, pp. 28ff.

[2] H.O. 61/1/307ff. (December 1826-January 1827).     [3] *Speeches*, I, 556ff.

1826 Peel gave notice of his intention after the Christmas recess to move for an enquiry into the state of the police surrounding the metropolis. This in effect was to be an indirect way of bringing up once more the whole question of the policing of London. 'I can make a better arrangement,' he wrote to Hobhouse on 8 December, 'after a searching enquiry and a thorough exposure of the defects of the present system, in regard to the administration of justice by county magistrates, and the state of the police by night and day, than in any other mode'. His plan was to take the area within a radius of ten miles from St. Paul's, with the exception of the City ('with which I should be afraid to meddle'), and treat it as one administrative district, with stipendiary magistrates and police organised on a uniform basis. The area would be subdivided into six police divisions, based for convenience on the existing parochial boundaries but independent of the parochial authorities. In each division a police office would be established, partly but not exclusively controlled by the divisional magistrate; and all parishes in the area would be relieved of rates for the upkeep of parochial constables and watchmen in return for a general police rate. It was, as he realised, a bold scheme and one certain to arouse hostility. But he was convinced that only a radical reform would be successful, and he was confident of his ability at least to demonstrate the ineffectiveness of the existing system.

The illness of Lord Liverpool and Peel's final resignation brought his police plan to a halt; and after the Easter recess there was scarcely time for the new ministers, even if they had been so disposed, to carry on with his motion. Lord John Russell secured the appointment of a committee to enquire into the general causes of the increase in crime, but the only report which it had so far issued, in June 1827, ignored both the special problem of crime in London and the question of police reform.[1] No sooner was Peel back in office, however, than his mind turned once more to the police. His Under-Secretary was now Phillipps, since Hobhouse had taken his pension rather than work under Lansdowne. He declined a pressing invitation from Peel to return to his old post, but through the latter's influence was appointed Keeper of the State Paper Office and promised to aid Peel with his new legal and administrative proposals.

[1] Radzinowicz, III, 364.

Almost at once there was some discussion between the two men on the subject of the police. 'It has always appeared to me,' wrote Peel on 4 February, less than a week after he began work once more in the department, 'that the country has entirely outgrown its police institutions.' Though the task of reform on a national scale would clearly have to be approached piecemeal, he lost little time in taking up the immediate problem of the Metropolitan Police. On 28 February 1828 he rose in the Commons to propose once more an enquiry into the state of the police and the causes of the increased crime in the metropolis. The first part of his speech he devoted to a close statistical examination, designed to emphasise the increase in crime since 1824. It was a factual and unexciting analysis, perhaps deliberately intended to be dull, for he was careful throughout to handle the topic in a cautious and unemotional fashion. On the controversial subject of the police, he used the same oblique tactics he had employed in his general approach. 'I despair,' he said disarmingly, 'of being able to place our police upon a general footing of uniformity; I cannot hope to take St. Paul's as a centre, and have a radius of ten miles, in which our police could be able to act in unison'. With the negatives removed this was precisely the plan he had in mind; but it was perhaps the better part of valour to leave his ultimate policy enshrouded for the moment in modest deprecation. The rest of the speech was couched with the same deceptive mildness. If he wished for any changes, it was only with a view to improvement. If he adverted to the difficulties and expenses of criminal prosecutions, it was not because he thought that an effectual remedy could be devised. His immediate and limited objective was merely an enquiry into the increase of crime in the metropolis and its vicinity, and into the state of the Metropolitan Police; though he asked the members for rural constituencies to consider for themselves the general points he had raised. It was useless to disguise the fact that the country had outgrown its police institutions, and that the cheapest and safest course would be the introduction of some new mode of protection. And he ended, as he began, with more dampening statistics.

He had, in fact, said everything he had been saying in private to Hobhouse, but in such a way as to reassure the most timid of members. There seemed little to fear, therefore, if little to hope from

an enquiry entered upon in such a spirit, and he secured his committee without difficulty. It consisted of twenty-five members
representing a variety of classes and interests and under the chairmanship of Estcourt, the other member for Oxford University, it
began its task with exemplary despatch. Besides the reports of earlier
police committees, Peel provided a summary of the number of
persons charged with criminal offences committed to gaol in
London, Westminster, and Middlesex, from 1811 to 1827. The
remaining evidence was taken from a specialised body of witnesses:
metropolitan magistrates; police and prison officials; constables,
churchwardens, officers of charitable societies; and a newspaper
reporter from the staff of the *Morning Chronicle*. Seventeen days
between 10 March and 16 May were spent in hearing witnesses, and
on 11 July the finished report was presented to the House of
Commons.

It fell into two parts, corresponding to the double nature of the
enquiry. From the Home Office statistics it was shown that between
the two periods 1811-17 and 1821-7 there had been increases in all
offences except coining and forgery, the most notable being in
cattle- and horse-stealing. The annual average showed a gross
increase in convictions of 55 per cent. or, allowing for the growth
of population, a net increase of 36 per cent. The crux of the matter,
however, was the second half of the report dealing with the police
of the metropolis. Here, for the first time in the history of parliamentary police enquiries, the committee declared in favour of a
radical reform. It admitted the difficulties of effecting a change,
especially where ancient usages were involved.

> But these difficulties must be encountered if it be intended to in-
> stitute an efficient system of Police in this great Metropolis, for the
> adequate protection of property, and for the prevention and
> detection of crime. Your Committee earnestly intreat the attention
> of The House to the argument, to the evidence, and to the authority
> on which their proposition will be founded. If they can prove to the
> satisfaction of The House and the country that the present system is,
> and must continue to be defective; that its condemnation has been
> the almost uniform result of previous inquiries; and that a better
> system can be adopted, probably at less expense, and with no new
> restraint on the liberty of the subject—they will have made a most

material advance towards the important object for which they
were appointed.

After citing detailed evidence, the report went on to assert that
there was a strong presumption in favour of a material change in the
system of police in the metropolis and its neighbourhood, and
accordingly outlined a general plan of reform. The principal
recommendations were the establishment of a general police office
under the immediate direction of the Home Secretary, on which
should devolve the control of all the police establishments, including
the night-watch; the extension of its jurisdiction to the whole
built-up area of London and its environs; the exemption of the
magistrates in charge of the office from all the ordinary judicial
duties of police magistrates; and the defrayment of the cost of the
new establishment partly by public funds and partly by contributions
from the parishes within the new police area. On the delicate
question of the City of London, it was stated that there was no
intention of interfering with the existing powers of the City
authorities, especially in view of the recent improvements in the
City police, though it was hinted that it might be for the general
benefit if the City either relinquished its concurrent jurisdiction
over the borough of Southwark or assumed control of the whole of
its police.[1]

To have secured such a report was an achievement; it remained to
translate the recommendation into law. No more could be done in
the 1828 session, for parliament rose only a fortnight after the
report was presented. But before the end of the year preparations
were well under way for action in the new session. The invaluable
Gregson was employed in drafting a bill to put the committee's
recommendations into effect, and Hobhouse was also brought into
the discussion. On the main principle Peel was clear and decided. All
the night police of London, the existing magisterial forces, and the
horse, day and night patrols already under the direct supervision of
the Home Department, were to be amalgamated; a start was to be
made with the central district of London from the City boundaries
to Westminster and its area gradually extended; and a police rate
was to be levied on all parishes affected in lieu of the old watch-rate.

[1] P.P. 1828, VI (*Police of the Metropolis*).

The difficulties lay in the details: the assumption of authority over the out-parishes, and the exact proportion of expenses to be raised from the different parochial areas. By the spring of 1829 everything was ready and on 15 April 1829 Peel brought in his Metropolitan Police Improvement Bill for its first reading. Fresh statistics were read out to the House showing the steady increase of crime in London and Middlesex compared with the rest of the country; fresh emphasis was laid on the deficiencies of particular London parishes and particular districts within its borders. The main objects of the bill were briefly stated: to unite all the regular police under one authority, and to meet local expenses from local taxation. He assured the Commons that he would proceed cautiously; there would be no sudden abolition of parochial establishments. The details, however, were better left to a select committee; he proposed therefore to ask for the re-appointment of the police committee of the previous session to scrutinise the bill. It was true, he concluded, anticipating a familiar criticism, that the new police board would have powers of patronage, under the authority of the Secretary of State, but there could be no more solid objection to that than to similar powers with regard to the army and navy. What was certain was that there could be no hope for the progressive mitigation of the criminal code unless some such measures were adopted for the prevention of crime. A few questions were asked but there was no real opposition, or indeed much public interest; and the bill was launched smoothly on its way. The neat stratagem of securing the re-appointment of the old police committee ensured the essential continuity between the report and the bill; and the absorption of public and parliamentary interest in the Catholic emancipation crisis diverted what might otherwise have been vexatious opposition. With a remarkable absence of debate the bill was recommitted in May and before the end of the month it went up to the Lords with a long covering letter to Wellington from the Home Secretary. 'I hardly know what objections may be made to the bill,' wrote Peel confidently, 'as I have heard none in the Commons of the least force. There has only been one petition against the bill, from the parish of Hackney. . . . Pray pass the bill through this session, for you cannot think what trouble it has given me.'[1]

[1] *Speeches*, II, 2ff., 23; *Peel*, II, 39, 111.

As passed on 19 June 1829 the Metropolitan Police Act (10 Geo. IV c. 44) set up a new police organisation under the immediate supervision of two magistrates. The area under their jurisdiction included Westminster, Holborn, Finsbury, Tower Hamlets, Kensington, Hammersmith, Ealing, Acton, Brentford, Deptford, Greenwich; an area of Surrey extending to Barnes, Putney, Wandsworth, Tooting, Camberwell, and Bermondsey; and the borough of Southwark. The City was left to its own authorities; but for the rest, with a single police district stretching from Ealing to Poplar and from Hampstead to Tooting, Peel's conception of a ten mile radius from central London was virtually realised. The new magistrates, subject to the confirmation of the Home Secretary, were given wide powers of recruitment, training, and discipline; and were made responsible for the policing of the districts under their jurisdiction as the new force came into being. A special police rate, not exceeding 8d. in the pound on assessed rateable property, was to be levied by the Overseers of the Poor at the direction of the magistrates appointed by the Act. As a means of ensuring the financial efficiency and probity of the new organisation, the Act also provided for the appointment of a third official, the Receiver for the Metropolitan Police District, to control all receipts and expenditure for the police force, and to be responsible for all legal contracts and custody of property. His drafts were to be countersigned by one of the new magistrates; and his accounts were to be periodically audited in the usual manner of government departments. Such was the general framework erected by the Act; but the outstanding feature was the wide power left to the Secretary of State within that framework to constitute the new police force according to his own conception of what was required. The Act made the Metropolitan Police possible; it was left to the Home Secretary to establish its character.

Peel's first task, on which in a great measure the success of the whole scheme depended, was to find men to fill the three posts at the head of the organisation. His Metropolitan Police would be largely what they made it; but since the force itself was an innovation, there were no ready-made candidates for those cardinal appointments, particularly the posts of the two superintending magistrates. Although the nomenclature of the old London police system was carried into the 1829 Act, in fact Peel envisaged a very different function for his two chief magistrates under the new dispensation. Though commissioned as justices of the peace for Middlesex, Surrey, Hertfordshire, Essex, and Kent, they were forbidden to act as magistrates at general or quarter sessions, or out of sessions on any matter except the preservation of the peace, the prevention of crime, the detention or commitment of offenders, and the general execution of the statute under which they were appointed. Almost at once, in fact, the title by which they became known was that of commissioner and not magistrate. It was a significant change. The old police magistrates were primarily justices of the peace, aided by a handful of constables; the new police Commissioners were to be the executive heads of a force that would ultimately amount to two or three thousand men, the administration and direction of which would constitute their principal employment. In the context of previous police history, and still more of public prejudice against the whole notion of a police, this was not a light responsibility, and it was as well that it was to be shared. The object of having two men at the head of the organisation was to unite complementary qualities, rather than to balance identical offices. For one of the posts Peel hoped to find a practical and efficient lawyer; for the other a soldier accustomed to discipline and capable of enforcing it. For the third and lesser member of the triumvirate, he wanted a man with legal training and business experience.

His first thoughts not unnaturally turned to his Irish experiences, and in May 1829 he was enquiring from Gregory whether there was any military man, conversant with the details of the Irish constabulary, who might be suitable for appointment. He was not sanguine of finding what he wanted. 'He must be a very superior man to what I recollect of police magistrates in Ireland.' In his reply Gregory was equally dubious of getting anyone likely to fill Peel's requirements who would make the move from Ireland to London. However, some use was made of Irish police knowledge, and in July Captain Hunter, a Chief Constable recommended by Gregory, was given leave of absence to come to England for a short period to assist in the early stages of the Metropolitan Police.[1] By that time Peel had made his choice of men to take control of the

[1] 40334 fos. 292, 294, 302, 320; Peel, II, 114.

498

new force. His first offer, made within a week of the passing of the Act, was to Colonel James Shaw, a Peninsular veteran who had been appointed in 1826 to the Northern District, where his skill in dealing with problems of order during industrial disputes brought him to the favourable notice of the Home Department. On his refusal Peel turned to Colonel Charles Rowan, a retired officer of forty-six, who had been recommended to him by Sir George Murray. The salary offered was £800 per annum, with a house, but also the probability that his half-pay would be suspended during his period of office; and as Peel had warned Shaw, 'the experiment is a novel one and the undertaking arduous'. Nevertheless, it was an experiment that clearly attracted Rowan, since he had approached Murray about the appointment early in May; and the offer of the post was promptly accepted.

Rowan had been one of Sir John Moore's young officers of the 52nd (Oxfordshire) Foot, a light infantry regiment. He had served in the Corunna campaign, with the Light Brigade under Wellington throughout the Peninsular War, and at Waterloo. As second-in-command to Colborne he had led the attack by the 52nd on the head of the Imperial Guards column in the closing stages of the battle, and was wounded in the last attack. After the war he had commanded the regiment for several years and eventually sold his commission and retired from the army in 1822. As a subaltern he had seen Moore's enlightened training methods at close quarters, and as colonel of the 52nd he had brought his regiment—so Peel was told by competent military authorities—to the highest pitch of efficiency. As his civilian colleague Peel appointed Richard Mayne, a young Irish barrister, thirteen years junior to Rowan. The son of a judge of the King's Bench of Ireland, Mayne had been educated at Trinity College, Dublin, became a member of Lincoln's Inn, and subsequently practised on the northern circuit. He was a friend of Gregson, who brought his claims before the Home Secretary and cited Justice Park and Henry Brougham as additional sponsors. Both appointments were made in the first week of July 1829. On the 6th Mayne went for an interview with Peel at Whitehall Gardens, was offered the post, and the same day was introduced to Colonel Rowan at the Home Office. With his Police Act barely a fortnight on the statute-book, Peel was working with his accustomed rapidity and it was probably on the same day that he gave his general instructions to the two newly-appointed Commissioners to draw up a detailed plan for the organisation of the force.[1]

The third appointment, that of Receiver, caused as much difficulty as the other two together. At the beginning of June Lord Chandos, son and heir to the Duke of Buckingham, and a government supporter, pressed hard for the appointment of one of his friends, a Mr. Wyndham. Peel replied discouragingly; he had not considered any one for the post and would not do so until the bill passed.

> All that I can say with respect to these appointments is that I shall feel myself under a peculiar obligation and responsibility to make the very best that I can. The success of the bill mainly turns on the office of Receiver. The Receiver will have to fight the battle with all the parishes, to collect the rates from each of them. He will have the whole police property, watch-boxes, watch-houses, arms, etc., vested in him, and the making of all legal contracts for the purchase of land and buildings. He never can be absent a week from London and I much fear I have loaded him with too much duty. . . . You will see at once that I shall be absolutely bound to take the most efficient man I can find.

Chandos, however, remained importunate and brought in Planta, the government whip, to reinforce his efforts. In the end Peel was obliged to write specifically to Chandos, Planta, and Wyndham himself, to say that no one without legal training and knowledge of accountancy could satisfactorily fill the post. He found what he wanted eventually in the person of a solicitor named Wray, an active figure in the legal and commercial world, who proved to have a talent for property management, practical planning, and the production of clear memoranda.[2]

Peel's selection of men was singularly fortunate and the two Commissioners in particular combined admirably. Rowan's tact, patience, and imperturbability was the foundation of their success, but in Mayne he had not only a colleague of considerable intellectual powers and marked business skill, but one with whom he worked in

[1] For the appointment of Rowan and Mayne see Reith, *New Study*, pp. 126-33; 40399 fos. 262, 269.

[2] 40399 fos. 242, 276-8, 285; *Peel*, II, 114.

close harmony during the whole period of their collaboration. After Rowan's retirement in 1850 the higher command of the Metropolitan Police began to show certain defects; but for the first twenty years of its existence the force could scarcely have had better leadership. Within a fortnight Rowan and Mayne produced a draft establishment for a body of just over 1,000 men—8 superintendents, 20 inspectors, 88 sergeants, and 895 constables—together with a small clerical staff for the offices of the Commissioners and the Receiver. In a series of consultations with the Home Secretary during the summer months the details of the new organisation were worked out. The metropolitan area was divided into police divisions, subdivided again into sections and beats, with a company of police under a superintendent allotted to each division. It was decided to enforce the wearing of uniform, and a draft handbook of general instructions was drawn up by the Commissioners for Peel's scrutiny. Part one, dealing with organisation and rules of conduct, was probably written by Rowan; part two, on the legal powers of the constable, by Mayne. Colquhoun's principle of a preventive police was clearly enshrined in the first instructions: 'it should be understood, at the outset, that a principal object to be attained is the prevention of crime'. At the same time, emphasis was laid on the importance of good relations between the police and the public. Constables were enjoined to be 'civil and attentive' in all their dealings with the ordinary population. From the start, therefore, good public relations and the prevention of crime were made the tests of police efficiency. A circular from the Home Office on 21 July 1829 announced the appointment of Rowan and Mayne as Commissioners of the new force, and asked for the full co-operation of the old police magistrates in their work.[1]

The next major task was recruitment. One obvious source, with certain safeguards, was the existing London police; and in the autumn seventy men of the Bow Street foot patrol were transferred to the control of the Commissioners.[2] But external recruitment was also necessary, and from August onward a steady flow of recommendations from Rowan and Mayne for appointments and higher promotions reached the Home Secretary's desk. The initiative was clearly left to the Commissioners, and in December they were

[1] H.O. 60/1/477.    [2] ibid., 495.

formally given general authority for recruitment and promotion, subject to Home Office approval. But Peel had his own ideas on the principles to be followed. What he desired to see was a disciplined working force, and in his rates of pay, choice of men, and rules of promotion, he tried to ensure that the Metropolitan Police would not be regarded as a sanctuary for the incompetent and the genteel. In December he wrote to Leveson Gower, the Irish Secretary, that all his experience confirmed that subordinate positions in the police were better given to men who had not the rank, habits, or station of gentlemen. In the Metropolitan Police, for all posts below that of Commissioner, he had given preference to non-commissioned officers over all the scores of captains and reduced gentlemen who had volunteered their services with assurances of their readiness to waive the privileges and prejudices of their station in life.[1] After its initial formation the higher ranks in the force were filled from below. There was no caste system as in the navy or army; the Metropolitan Police was to be professional and homogeneous.[2] The rate of pay for a constable—a guinea a week—was also fixed with this principle in mind. Croker thought it too low to attract good men, and urged at least a rising scale according to service, irrespective of promotion. Peel was not easily shaken, however; he acknowledged that at the beginning he had thought it might prove necessary to increase the rates, but the flood of applications (over 2,000 by October 1829) showed that even 3s. a day was a fair inducement. In any case the real test was whether the wages offered would bring in the kind of men he wanted, and whether an increase of pay would add to the efficiency of the force. Just as he had preferred for the posts of superintendent and inspector ex-regular N.C.O.s, as being more fitted for the work than officers and gentlemen, so also he thought 'a three shilling a day man is better than a five shilling a day man' for the work the constables would have to do.[3] It is true that the wastage of recruits provided some justification for Croker and later critics[4] of Peel's salary scale. In its first two years the Metropolitan Police lost, by dismissals and resignations, more than its total establishment. But this heavy turnover was not caused

---

[1] 40337 f. 312.    [2] cf. Browne, *Scotland Yard*, p. 81.
[3] 40320 fos. 126, 133, printed *Croker*, II, 17-20.
[4] cf. Reith, *British Police*, pp. 38-9.

solely by low wages, nor was it peculiar to Peel's time. Many men joined with no intention of a permanency; many were found unsuitable; and many were dismissed on disciplinary grounds. Indeed, until a proper system of recruit-training at Peel House was introduced at the beginning of the twentieth century, the loss of men in their early years in the force continued to be one of the problems of the Metropolitan Police [1]

The headquarters of the new organisation was established at 4 Whitehall Place, with rear premises opening on Scotland Yard and accessible from the street. The general use of this back-entry by the police themselves soon provided the popular name for the entire building. Towards the end of September the men were on duty at headquarters and in the outlying police stations, undergoing instruction on their behaviour at court and in the streets. On the evening of 29 September 1829 the first new Metropolitan Police in their blue uniforms and iron-framed top-hats were seen on their beats by the London public. They were inevitably objects of curiosity, and with some sections of the London population outright hostility; but a month's experience of their conduct drew a gratifying compliment from that professional disciplinarian, the Duke of Wellington himself. 'I congratulate you,' he wrote to Peel on 3 November, 'upon the entire success of the police in London. It is impossible to see anything more respectable than they are.' But not all Londoners looked upon the new police with such approval. There was some early jealousy and obstruction on the part of the old police magistrates, who disliked and perhaps misunderstood the function of the new Commissioners at Scotland Yard. Many of the London parishes had difficulty in raising the police rate required from them and asked for an extension of time for payment or some method of payment by instalment. Select vestries were annoyed at the loss of their power and patronage, and in September the vestry of St. Luke's, Middlesex, wrote with portentous underlinings to say that 'the parochial authorities have determined to adopt every constitutional means within their reach to obtain their removal [i.e. of the new police] and to restore the ancient and more efficient, economical, and constitutional system of watch under the management of local authorities'. In St. Pancras a meeting was called in

[1] Browne, *Scotland Yard*, p. 171.

October 1830 to protest against the assumption by the Home Secretary of authority over nearly a hundred parishes, '*a truly formidable and dangerous power to be vested in the hands of* ONE SINGLE MAN and in open violation of the ancient and excellent laws of the realm'.[1]

Pamphlet and poster warfare, anonymous letters, even a peremptory demand for the dismissal of two constables by the Earl of Kinnoul, were met by firmness on the part of the Home Secretary. At the same time he kept a watchful eye on the behaviour of his new force. When in May 1830 the police authorities at Camberwell, without the knowledge of the Commissioners, intervened to stop cricket being played there, Peel at once wrote to Rowan drawing his attention to their officiousness.[2] The forcible resistance of the London mobs, encouraged by some of the extreme radicals, was a different matter. In the first few years of its existence the Metropolitan Police had to meet a series of direct challenges to its control of the London streets; and as late as 1833, at an inquest on a policeman killed in the Cold Bath Field riots, the jury returned a verdict of justifiable homicide. But the technique of crowd control was speedily learnt; the efficacy of a determined baton-charge demonstrated; and influential public opinion after 1830 turned decisively in favour of the new police. A committee of enquiry, set up by the whig ministry after the 1833 riots to enquire into the conduct of the police, produced a strongly favourable report and added an indirect tribute to the founder of the force. 'Much, in the opinion of your committee, is due to the judgement and discrimination which were exercised in the selection of the individuals, Colonel Rowan and Mr. Mayne, who were originally appointed, and still continue to fill, the arduous offices of Commissioners of Police.'[3]

Peel himself, in and out of office, continued to be the strong advocate of the new police. Indeed, there was a noticeable contrast in his utterances in the House of Commons after 1829. Before he had secured the passage of the Act, his remarks on police reform were deliberately moderate and judicious. After the force was established, his tone was stiffer and more uncompromising. In June 1830 he told the House that in the twelve months or less since the police were

---

[1] H.O. 61/2.     [2] 40400 f. 177-9.
[3] For the general history of the foundation of the Metropolitan Police see, Reith, *New Study*, and *British Police*; Hart, *British Police*; Browne, *Scotland Yard*.

formed, they had surpassed his expectations, and in another three or four years parliament would congratulate itself on having established the force. 'There was no other effectual way of checking crime than that of having a good police.' In November 1830, on a petition from St. John's parish, Southwark, he replied strongly to the 'gross misrepresentations which had been spread abroad by interested persons on this subject'; and on a number of other occasions in these early years he was prompt to defend the Metropolitan Police against any attempt to re-establish parochial authority or to impair its efficiency by financial economies. Indeed, his own thoughts were already turned to the possibility of extending the principle of the metropolitan organisation to the boroughs and counties. As early as April 1829 he told the Commons that he was contemplating a general police measure for the English counties, although it was clear that a prolonged period of preparation would be necessary before any such measure could be drafted. In May 1830 he publicly expressed the hope that all provincial towns would form their own police, and referred to the assistance his department had already given to such efforts; in June, while disclaiming any wish to enlarge further the police jurisdiction of the Home Secretary, 'he hoped every populous place would provide itself with a police'.

When the whigs came into power, he continued his efforts from the opposition benches. A sentence in the king's speech at the opening of parliament in December 1831, referring to the need to reform the municipal police, was at once taken up by Peel in subsequent debate. 'In the large towns he could see no security for property and the maintenance of order unless some change was effected. . . . Unless a stipendiary police was established in the large towns, there could be no security for good order.' When the government made no overt move to implement their recommendations, he tried to instil in them some of his own enthusiasm. There was no part of the king's speech of which he so much approved—he said in March 1832—as the suggestion to reform the municipal police; and he called upon Althorp to state the government's intentions on the matter. Althorp indicated a general intention to produce a measure; but still nothing was done and once more in June 1832 Peel asked whether the government had any measure to bring forward. Althorp's reply abandoned any hope of action during

that session and in the end it was not until the Municipal Corporations Act of 1835 that a clause was brought in requiring boroughs to
have watch committees empowered to appoint an adequate number
of constables.

If Peel was unable to carry out the wider plan of national police
reform which he had in view by 1829, the Metropolitan force he
created remained both the model and the recruiting-ground for the
various borough and county police forces that were gradually built
up in the next quarter of a century. The battle for the police idea of
Colquhoun and the early reformers was fought and won in 1828-9;
and the respect and trust which the London police rapidly obtained
from the public was as much an index of the value of the 'preventive'
principle as their nickname of 'Bobby' and 'Peeler' was a tribute to
the man who translated the idea and the principle into fact. By the
start of the Victorian era the half-affectionate, half-humorous position the policeman had achieved in the popular mythology marked a
revolution in the relationship between public liberty and public
security. It was not long before the street ballad-singers were
chanting with disrespectful familiarity,

> I'm waiting at the airey, cookey darling,
> Your fire burns brightly, I can see.
> Then hasten to your Peeler, cookey darling,
> For you know my love, I'm waiting for thee.[1]

It was a far cry from the Victorian ballad to the ferocious *gendarmerie*,
cutlass in hand and brace of pistols in the belt, depicted by the
London radicals of 1829.

But it was not only the London bobby that made his appearance
in cartoon and street-ballad. On 9 October 1829, on his way back
from discussing Canning's unfinished portrait with Sir Thomas
Lawrence, Peel stopped to look in a shop-window displaying
political caricatures, one of which by William Heath showed the
Home Secretary kicking an old watchman from behind and
dragging from his shoulders a patched and tattered coat. The little
incident was noticed in one of the newspapers.

[1] J. Ashton, *Modern Street Ballads* (1888), p. 63. Undated but the collection covers
the period 1798-1851.

## MINISTERIAL OCCUPATION

Yesterday afternoon, the Right Hon. Home Secretary amused himself for some time with viewing the caricatures at a shop in Henrietta Street, Covent Garden. At some of them he laughed heartily; but the one that attracted most attention was a picture entitled 'Spinning Bobby'. That represents the most illustrious Personage in the kingdom at one end of a table, and a person very like the Duke of Wellington at the other end of it. There is a top on the table spinning away right merrily, and seated on it, with legs in an extended and regularly fly-away condition, a Right Hon. Gentleman, very similar in appearance to the Home Secretary previously to the late Mr. Canning's Administration. The figure exclaims, 'At what a rate *I spin*'. Mr. Peel also laughed at this picture a little. The personages seated at the table appear to be most heartily enjoying the little Orange-looking gentleman's spinning.

Next day he wrote to Julia, enclosing the cutting.

I have been again busy all the morning about my Police. I think it is going on very well. The men look very smart and a strong contrast to the old Watchmen. We sometimes complain of our movements being noticed by the newspapers but the paragraph at the top of the next page shews a more than ordinary attention to them. It is all quite true. I did stop as I was coming from Sir T. Lawrence's and I did laugh, not at the caricature which it mentioned there but at one called 'Peeling a Charley' in which I am represented stripping one of the old watchmen of his great-coat, etc.[1]

By 1829, in fact, Peel had emerged in his own right as a popular and recognisable figure, the central character of numberless sketches and caricatures that reached a public indifferent to *Hansard* or the columns of *The Times*, and almost always portrayed as 'gay, handsome, and likeable'.[2]

[1] Letter and cutting in Peel MSS.; cf. Peel, *Letters*, p. 117.
[2] M. D. George, *Catalogue of Political and Personal Satires*, XI (1954), Intro. xxvii, and p. 190.

# THE CRISIS IN IRELAND

As in Peel's earlier period at the Home Department, the more political and infinitely the more controversial half of his work was Ireland and its related problems. Indeed, just as the situation in 1822 represented a deterioration since his resignation from the Chief Secretaryship in 1818, so on his return to office in 1828 he found the tide of agitation running even more strongly than a year before. The composition of the Irish executive had materially altered in the intervening period. Anglesey the Lord Lieutenant, William Lamb the Chief Secretary, Doherty the Solicitor-General, were not only new men but in effect the legacy of Canning's administration. Lord Anglesey, a professional soldier of sixty who lost a leg when commanding the cavalry at Waterloo, had held office as Master General of the Ordnance under Canning and Goderich. Once classed as a Protestant, he was beginning to be as sympathetic to Catholic claims as the previous Lord Lieutenant, though in politics he was impetuous and naïve where Wellesley had been cautious and irresolute. Of William Lamb, who besides being a 'Catholic' had both whig and Canningite affiliations, Peel was disposed to think well. Certainly if the mixed and moderate character of the Wellington ministry needed demonstration, it could scarcely be better done than by the appointment of such a liberal and well-connected politician to the crucial post of Chief Secretary. Nothing could be more damaging, on the other hand, to the reputation of the new administration than to begin its career with a complete remodelling of the Irish executive which it had inherited from its predecessors. With Ireland the touchstone of politics, it was from the composition of the Irish government that men would most decisively interpret the fundamental position of Wellington's cabinet.

On the same day that Peel formally took over the Home Department, he wrote to Anglesey expressing his hope that neither his own appointment nor the recent changes in the government would induce the Lord Lieutenant to relinquish his post; and since Anglesey had not yet taken up office, the two men were able to have a personal discussion before he left for Ireland.[1] The new régime started quietly. When he arrived in Dublin Anglesey found Gregory, against whom he had been warned, fair and candid enough as well as lively and agreeable. But in private the Lord Lieutenant regretted the change of ministry and was not inclined to share his Chief Secretary's optimistic view that the Catholics were more likely to be tranquil under the new cabinet than under the old. With Lamb in London for the parliamentary session and in constant touch with Peel, there was no need for much immediate correspondence between the Castle and the Home Office. Anglesey devoted himself instead to a policy of personal conciliation, carefully mixing the representatives of opposing Irish factions at his drawing-rooms and *levées*. At the end of March he wrote to Peel to enquire how often and in what detail he should write to the Home Secretary, and Peel stressed in his reply, as he had with Wellesley, the value of regular private correspondence outside routine matters or formal despatches. With this invitation Anglesey half-heartedly complied. He found it difficult to regard the ministry as a party to which he himself belonged, and politically if not personally he was conscious of an insuperable gap between their attitude to Irish affairs and his own. If Wellington acted by the Catholics as he had done by the dissenters, he wrote to Lamb towards the end of April, all would go well. 'If he does not, I wish he would come to govern Ireland himself.' And the following day, when informing the Chief Secretary of his intention to write to Peel on various Irish problems, he added that 'I fear he has so bad an opinion of *my subjects* that I must not expect much from him.'[2]

The immediate question before the government was the Act of 1825 for the suppression of unlawful societies in Ireland. It had been completely ineffectual in its principal aim of putting down the Catholic Association and it was due to expire at the end of the 1828 session. Peel had discussions in London on the subject with Lamb, who passed on to him a letter from Anglesey expressing the view that to attempt to renew or replace the Act would only create

[1] 40325 fos. 1, 3; *Peel Memoirs*, I, 20.  [2] Anglesey 1068/15 fos. 8, 13, 46–8.

trouble; that the Catholic lawyers of the Association would always find means of evading legislation; and that the only sensible course would be to let the Act expire without notice. Lamb himself, in a formal memorandum to Peel dated 29 March, advised against a renewal of the statute. He believed that there was no serious danger likely to arise from leaving either the Catholic Association or the Orange societies to the ordinary operation of the law; and if danger did arise it would be correspondingly easier to ask parliament for a remedy. Before Peel was prepared to accept a conclusion based on such general arguments, however, he was anxious to elicit more precise and detailed information. In a paper sent to Lamb on 31 March he posed a number of questions for the Irish executive to consider: the exact constitution of the Catholic Association, the mode of raising the 'Catholic Rent', the reasons for not enforcing the Act of 1825, the grounds for allowing it to expire in 1828. His purpose was not so much to argue against the views of the Irish government as to oblige them to give the whole question rather more examination than it seemed to him they had so far devoted to it. But, he added towards the end of his memorandum, 'it certainly does appear to me that the position of the government in abandoning the law without having made a trial of it, is a very embarrassing one. . . . I think the worst part of the case of the executive government is, that it has remained a quiet spectator of an increasing evil.'[1]

The authorities in Dublin bestirred themselves to answer his queries, and a number of documents arrived in London during April for his greater satisfaction. Joy, the Irish Attorney-General, delivered a long and intricate legal opinion, in which he drew attention to the loopholes in the 1825 Act which had been exploited by the Association, though he gave it as his view that the new Association formed in 1825 was in fact unlawful and the question of its suppression merely one of expediency. But he did not think that individual meetings of the Association were in themselves unlawful, or that either the Catholic Association or the Orange lodges were illegal by virtue of earlier statutes. Anglesey, in a more political memorandum of 12 April, argued that no bill could be framed capable of suppressing the Association that would not encroach so

---

[1] *Peel Memoirs*, I, 22-33.

arbitrarily on the ordinary civil rights of assembly and petition as to render its acceptance by parliament highly improbable. He did not believe, on the other hand, that the Association was likely to continue to flourish unless an ill-advised attempt was made to crush it by legal means; and he concluded with a recommendation that the Act should be silently allowed to expire. Supported as he was by the constabulary and the armed force—he assured the cabinet— 'no material mischief would arise during the short period of seven months when the parliament would probably reassemble'. The effect of these papers was decisive and on 2 May the cabinet decided to let the 1825 Act lapse.[1]

Anglesey, who was already showing a distinct proprietorial touch in his utterances on Ireland, now turned to a different subject. In the middle of May he wrote to Peel:

> Ireland is, I believe, now in a state of balance and a very little bad or a very little good management may turn it either way. Of this I feel convinced, that it will not remain as it is and if I were enabled to engage that it should not retrograde or deteriorate under my government, would you or would any friend to Ireland be satisfied with such a result? I feel that you would not and indeed that you ought not, and I must declare my conviction that unless I am furnished with some means of usefully setting to work the resources of this country, if things are allowed to remain as they are, without an effort to effect good, inevitable evil will result.

His proposal was the not unfamiliar remedy of an extensive programme of public works—barracks in Tipperary, cotton- and woollen-mills (capital to come from private enterprise but the government to indemnify against loss from violence), and road construction—and he supported his letter with various memoranda on the subject from the Attorney-General and the Society for the Improvement of Ireland.[2] Peel replied at once, assuring him that his suggestions would receive full attention even though there were real and solid objections to direct governmental interference in the establishment of manufactures either by subsidy or guarantee. 'Still,

[1] ibid., 39-58; Ellenborough, I, 96.
[2] Anglesey, 1068/1 f. 25, where the copy is dated 14 May, though Peel (Memoirs I, 165) gives the date as 16 May.

I am willing to admit that general principles must not be pushed too far in their application to a country wherein the necessity for an immediate remedy is so urgent as it is in Ireland.'[1]

Various causes prevented Peel from any considered reply until the end of the session, but on 26 July he sent a long letter to the Lord Lieutenant, taking up all the points covered by the documents that had been sent to him. To the suggestion that the government should encourage industry in remote parts of Ireland by offering an indemnification against loss by wilful damage, he returned a decided negative. But he promised to take into consideration the abolition of the duty on coal imports into Ireland, and authorised the Lord Lieutenant without delay to expend £10,000 on the construction of roads in Tipperary. At the same time he deprecated the tendency of the Society for the Improvement of Ireland to ignore the considerable sums granted by parliament in recent years for the encouragement of Irish commercial enterprise. When Peel was himself Chief Secretary, he pointed out, £300,000 had been voted to assist the construction of the Royal Canal and the Grand Canal, and in the five years ending January 1828 over two million pounds had been advanced from public funds for roads and other public works in Ireland, together with further non-repayable sums that brought the total to nearly two and a half million.

> While I admit the melancholy fact that there is a great want of employment for the poor in Ireland, and admit also that an increase in the demand for labour would be of the utmost advantage to society in that country, I must at the same time express a doubt whether ultimate advantage would arise from the creation of such a demand by the continual application of large sums of public money.[2]

Anglesey, however, returned to the charge and following a succession of letters at the end of July, Peel was once more obliged to express both his readiness to consider any measure calculated to provide employment and his conviction that any proposal that involved government intervention and the expenditure of public money would require strict and careful deliberation. In reply to a memorandum from the indefatigable Society for the Improvement

[1] 40325 f. 47.    [2] *Peel Memoirs*, I, 166ff.

of Ireland, he enclosed a long review of the progress in bog-drain-
age, road-construction, fisheries, and coal supplies, mainly designed
to place on record the considerable efforts already made by the
government to assist Irish economy: an average expenditure of
£43,500 per annum on road-building in the previous eight years as
compared with an average of £12,500 spent on roads and bridges
in the Highlands since the start of the century; £5,000 per annum
as a grant to the Irish Commissioners of Fisheries, as compared with
£3,000 to Scotland; £32,000 in bounties to Irish fisheries in 1827
as compared with £12,000 to British fisheries; 52 piers built or
building, and 20 more projected.[1] Anglesey, like some other
governors of Ireland, was inclined to assume that until his arrival no
one had seriously taken into consideration Ireland's multifarious
problems; and though Peel's long memorandum addressed itself
to the assertions of the Society for Improvement, there was a moral
in it for the Lord Lieutenant who had endorsed so many of their
proposals. Part at least of the Home Secretary's duty was to preserve
some kind of proportion in the handling of Irish affairs. England
might have done more for Ireland; it was patently untrue that she
had done nothing.

## II

In the interval between the beginning and end of this correspondence, political events had taken place which seriously affected the
position of both the Home Secretary and the Lord Lieutenant.
Early in May the House of Commons, which had already declared
itself in favour of the repeal of the Test and Corporation Acts, now
put on record its opinion that there should be a final and conciliatory
adjustment of the laws relating to Roman Catholics. The issue was
raised by a motion introduced by Sir Francis Burdett on 8 May;
and the succeeding debate extended over three days. Brougham,
Fitzgerald, Newport, Mackintosh, Charles Grant, William Lamb,
and Huskisson spoke in its favour; Wetherell, Inglis, George
Bankes, Leslie Foster, and Peel against. All arguments on the subject
could only be repetition; and the repetition itself a commonplace.
Peel himself began his speech by confessing that he could do no

[1] 40325 fos. 197, 202.

more than repeat 'to a reluctant audience topics and arguments which had been already urged almost to satiety', and said that the most welcome expectation he could hold out was that of being as brief as possible. For all that, he went over the bare-trodden ground yet again: the treaty of Limerick, the Union, Mr. Pitt, Mr. Fox; and emphasised once more the principal considerations which dictated his opposition. The admission of Roman Catholics to parliament would destroy every link that bound the constitution to the Protestant faith, except the link provided by the Crown; and he was persuaded that this implied a danger to Protestantism against which it was impossible to find a security equal to that provided by the existing Protestant constitution. Secondly, in Ireland, the result would be the transfer of power from the Protestant minority to the Catholic majority. If, however, that transfer would tranquillise Ireland, he would consent to it; but he could not believe it would do so, and the existing temper and attitude of the Irish Catholic Church held out no prospect of future reconciliation and union, should it gain preponderant power in that country. But the sands of Protestant strength were running out and at the division there was a majority of six (272-266) in favour of Burdett's motion. For the first time the House of Commons elected in 1826 had declared in favour of Catholic emancipation.

Following a conference with the Lords on 19 May, a debate was held in the upper House on a motion of Lord Lansdowne to concur in the Commons' resolution. The royal Dukes of Sussex and Gloucester, Goderich, Plunket (speaking for the first time in the Lords since his elevation as Lord Chief Justice of Ireland), Wellesley, Londonderry, and Haddington supported the motion; it was opposed by Wellington, Lyndhurst, and Bathurst among the ministers, Eldon and a phalanx of tory peers, the Archbishop of Canterbury and a handful of English and Irish bishops. The motion was lost by forty-four votes; but more significant than the voting was the speech made by Wellington. It was the first time he had spoken at length on the subject as Prime Minister, and his arguments in opposing the motion were grounded entirely on expediency. If the power of the Irish aristocracy had been destroyed, it was because of the alliance between the people and the Roman Catholic priests. If concessions were to be granted, he would wish first to see real securities. In other European countries governments had found it necessary to come to an agreement with the Pope in order to secure adequate control of the Roman Catholic Church in their domains. It was impossible for a British government to come to an arrangement of that kind, though perhaps other forms of security could be devised. The discussion of the question would, in his opinion, lead to no practical result and would only disturb the public mind. Nevertheless, he said finally, if the difficulties of the question were not aggravated by popular agitation, it might prove possible to do something. The division on the motion showed a Protestant victory; but it did not argue undue optimism on the part of the emancipationists, when studying the Prime Minister's speech, to believe it might be the last.

Wellington's speech was delivered in June. A fortnight earlier had taken place the retirement of Huskisson and his followers on the East Retford question. But these were not the only resignations meditated. When the House of Commons early in May carried Burdett's motion, Peel's first instinct had been, as in 1825, to abandon office. Now that he was leader of the House he had even more reason than on the previous occasion to regard his position as untenable. Not only numbers, but talent and most of the younger generation in the Commons were against him on the crucial domestic controversy of the day. In little over a week, however, the cabinet was unexpectedly plunged into the East Retford crisis, and to have insisted on his own immediate retirement when the body of the Canningites were withdrawing on a completely different issue, would have been an egotistic and irresponsible act. It might have brought about the fall of the government at a time when the wreckage of political connections left by the storms of 1827 made it an immensely difficult task to construct any government at all; and at best would have left Wellington's ministry crippled and ineffective. However, in the interval between the Catholic debates in the lower and upper Houses, he made it clear to the Prime Minister that his retirement could not be indefinitely delayed; and in those circumstances he urged Wellington, who was less committed than himself on the Catholic question, not to take a line in the House of Lords that would preclude him during the summer recess from taking into consideration the whole state of Ireland with a view to a final settlement. This advice was followed when Wellington came to take part in the debate on Lansdowne's motion. It was the first clear step on the path to Catholic emancipation, and it followed logically that Peel's tenure of office could thereafter only be regarded as provisional. For himself as a minister, if not as a private politician, he regarded the battle as already lost. With the waning of Protestant forces year by year both in the country and in the House of Commons, with a divided cabinet and Ireland a prey to agitators, Peel had come to the conclusion that it was no longer in the interests of the country for a stalemate of policy to continue.

Meanwhile, there was the short-term policy to consider; for not only the cabinet but in his own special sphere of responsibility the structure of the Irish executive had cracked under the shock of the Huskissonite secession. The first overt sign was the resignation of William Lamb. His loss was one which on personal and public grounds Peel regretted; but the Chief Secretary told Peel that he felt the character of the administration was so changed by Huskisson's retirement, that he could not consistently remain in office. There were perhaps other less political motives behind Lamb's departure. While in Ireland he had been foolish enough to have an affair with the wife of the Rev. William Crosbie, D.D., Lord Branden, who—if Creevey is to be believed—tried to use the relationship to obtain a bishopric for himself by pressure on the Chief Secretary. Anglesey wrote later to Lord Holland that 'he need not have gone, but as you *must* know, he was getting into a *scrape* here, which probably in some measure influenced his decision'; and Gregory had dropped a hint to Peel in the preceding February that Lamb had kept some very bad company in Ireland, though there was a hope that on his return he would shake them off.[1] There was no return to Ireland now for that pleasant if indiscreet individual, and somewhere a successor had to be found. It was agreed at the start that whoever he might be he must share his predecessor's views on the Catholic question; but that did not go very far to reassure Anglesey. The Lord Lieutenant pressed hard for the appointment of Sir George Clerk, a Scottish baronet who had served as junior Lord

---

[1] 40334 f. 199; Anglesey 1068/1 f. 59; *Creevey papers*, p. 502; cf. *Arbuthnot Journal*, II, 311. Lord Branden subsequently brought an action for *crim. con.* against Lamb.

of the Admiralty in the last years of Liverpool's administration and
had worked under Anglesey in the Canning and Goderich ministries
as Clerk to the Ordnance. Croker was known to be ready and
anxious for the post, but Anglesey wrote to both Wellington and
Peel discouraging that notion on the ground, familiar at least to Peel,
of the undesirability of appointing an Irishman. In the end the Prime
Minister chose Lord Francis Leveson Gower, the second son of the
Marquess of Stafford and the Countess of Sutherland. The Lord
Lieutenant fought hard against his appointment. What he wanted,
he told Wellington, was 'some steady and experienced person on
whom I can place the most explicit reliance' and to Peel he wrote
bluntly of the Prime Minister's nomination, that 'I cannot look
favourably upon the appointment and . . . I sincerely hope he may
not feel the necessity of pressing it.' When his objections were
overruled, he accepted the decision with a minimum of grace. 'If
Ld. Francis is fixed upon, I will make the best of what I feel to be an
unsatisfactory arrangement; and I will remain at my post as long as
I can do so with a fair prospect of rendering effectual service.'[1]

The Lord Lieutenant's dissatisfaction was not confined to his
disappointment over the Chief Secretary. The resignation of the
Huskisson party meant to him the departure from the government
of the men with whom he was politically allied, and he felt increasingly isolated from his political masters in London. It was inevitable
in the circumstances that he should entertain thoughts of his own
retirement. On 2 June he wrote candidly to Peel that 'you see I am
writing as if I was a fixture here, yet I fear I am holding on by a very
feeble tenure, and I will not disguise from you that the late transactions
distress and unsettle me very much'. His first reaction on hearing the
news was to conclude that both Huskisson and the Prime Minister
had behaved precipitately and with little judgement; but when the
full extent of the secession was revealed he began to suspect a plot
on Wellington's part to get rid of his unwelcome liberal colleagues.
Not unnaturally, but certainly unwisely, he turned to friends outside the government for comfort and advice. On 28 May he wrote
to Lord Holland, asking him to consult with Lamb, Sir John
Newport, and Doherty, whether Anglesey could remain at his post
with honour and satisfaction to himself and advantage to Ireland;

[1] Anglesey 1068/1 fos. 34, 44, 55, 61-5; 40325 fos. 52-6.

and in a following letter expressed the gloomy view that there must be 'a *dessous des cartes*' which the Huskisson group had discovered, 'or they would not all bolt'. He complained too of being kept in the dark by them. 'It is not fair to be left upon the rear-guard without support.' Holland replied with a friendly but indecisive letter, advising no action for the time being; and since Anglesey was assured by the cabinet that no change was envisaged in policy towards Ireland, he concluded that he had no tangible reason for throwing up his post. Moreover, he was tempted to believe that he had already achieved a creditable position in Ireland and was beginning to enjoy a degree of influence with the Catholic party which might ultimately be of value.

Nevertheless, the cabinet reconstruction of May 1828 had a profound if concealed effect on Anglesey's attitude. It destroyed his last remnants of confidence in the government, and drew him into a relationship with the political opposition to Wellington's ministry that was not only ethically indefensible in the head of the Irish executive, but steadily eroded his sense of duty to the cabinet of which he was the servant. On 5 June he sent Lord Holland a copy of his letter to Wellington on the subject of Huskisson's resignation. Then on 20 June, as an enclosure to a long letter on Irish affairs to the same correspondent, he provided him with copies of the exchanges that had passed between himself and the Prime Minister over the appointment of the new Chief Secretary. 'Perhaps it is not strictly correct,' he added with a twinge of conscience, 'to lay official correspondence before anyone unconnected with the government; but with you I know I am safe.' One confidential disclosure led to another. By July he was sending Lord Holland copies of his official memorandum on the Catholic Association dated 12 April, and his letter to Leveson Gower on the same subject dated 2 July. In August he offered to send Holland the minutes of an interview he had given to O'Connell, with the surprising comment that Holland must keep the information to himself as O'Connell had insisted on secrecy and Anglesey was convinced he would keep his word. From June 1828 onwards, in fact, Anglesey's real views were contained less in his despatches to his government than in this private correspondence with one of the most eminent members of the whig opposition. 'How I wish I could write thus confidentially to the Ministers,' he added on 24 August, at the close of a long letter to Holland on the Irish emancipation crisis. 'But how can I do so to Peel or to Wellington? They know the ground on which I act and the terms on which I stay here, but they are very distant, or rather silent upon the one great question.' Wellington and Peel had even more reason than they knew to distrust the discretion and fidelity of their Lord Lieutenant.[1]

If from folly rather than knavery Lord Anglesey was thus something less than a reliable agent of government, the new Chief Secretary himself was not among the more eminent holders of that office. Francis Leveson Gower was a well-connected, clever, and pleasant man of twenty-eight, with mild literary pretensions. He had spent six years in parliament and had some experience of office as Under-Secretary at War and Colonies. Anglesey's objections were therefore somewhat captious. The government's field of choice was not unlimited; and when writing to Anglesey on 12 June Peel assured him that he knew of no one likely to accept the post who was better calculated to act cordially with him, and from temper, manner, and coolness of judgement to give satisfaction in Ireland. He was at least a new man with no Irish connections; and as it proved, anxious to learn.[2] He had, however, a great deal to learn, and little time in which to do so. Appointed in the latter part of June, he had a month at the Irish Office in London under Peel's eye before going to Ireland in August. At the outset, though prudent and sensible in his observations, he obviously lacked confidence in his new post, and leaned heavily on Peel for guidance. Even with Goulburn, Peel had gone to great pains to give encouragement and support. With Leveson Gower he redoubled his care and consideration. In one of his first letters from the Home Office after the new Chief Secretary had arrived in Dublin, Peel observed tactfully that he would communicate with Leveson Gower from time to time on subjects that might escape the Chief Secretary's notice in the pressure of more urgent business. In August he reminded Leveson Gower that he would be grateful for regular reports not only on matters of importance but on any that made an impression on the public mind and on which he might be asked questions by his colleagues. The Chief

[1] Anglesey 1068/1 fos. 34, 38, 41, 45, 48, 52, 57, 61, 68, 75, 101-7.
[2] 40325 f. 54.

Secretary was at least a diligent correspondent and the two men remained in close contact all through the disturbed autumn of 1828. Even when Leveson Gower, with a year's experience in office, returned to Dublin after the 1829 session, a voluminous correspondence was carried on, letters passing almost daily between them. Peel himself was conscious of the unusual nature of the supervision he was giving to his junior colleague. In January 1829 he wrote half-apologetically that the intercourse between them had been more frequent and detailed than was customary between a Secretary of State and a Chief Secretary, but that he had been guided by a desire to help and not to dictate any views or judgements.[1]

Ellenborough in January 1830 made the unkind observation that Leveson Gower seemed only a clever little boy, had proposed nothing worth adopting, and had been saved from errors only by Peel's advice. This was perhaps unnecessarily harsh, though there was clearly some truth in the judgement.[2] It was evident at any rate in July 1828 that the cabinet could not lean with much assurance on the judgement and initiative of their Chief Secretary in Ireland, and the burden of responsibility on the ministers in London was consequently even greater than usual. The larger share of that burden fell on Peel; and though he, fortunately for the government, had wider experience of Irish administration than any other living politician, yet—as Wellington at least was aware—he himself held his office only on a temporary lease. It was not without some consequence that the administration had to face the critical summer of 1828 with an inexperienced Chief Secretary, an alienated Lord Lieutenant, and a Home Secretary who was anticipating his early retirement from office.

### III

After the resounding electoral successes of 1826, the movement of Catholic agitation in Ireland had momentarily slackened. With the end of the long Liverpool era and the friendly administration first of Canning, then of Goderich in office, the Irish leaders were content to lay on their oars and await events. The formation of the Wellington government, however, acted as an immediate signal for action.

[1] 40335 fos. 41, 43, 49; 40336 f. 199.　　[2] *Ellenborough*, II, 160.

January 1828 saw simultaneous meetings in two-thirds of all the Irish parishes, and O'Connell's claim to be the master of the Irish peasantry was demonstrated to be not far short of the truth. Behind that claim lay the implicit sanction of social warfare. Admittedly O'Connell was a constitutional and not a revolutionary leader; but he could not refrain from brandishing the threat of physical violence even if in private he was sometimes disturbed by the forces he had conjured up from the depths of Irish society. Endemic in that society was a social chaos and a brutal tradition of violence far removed from the verbal pyrotechnics of the Association's platform oratory; and though the 1826 general election had converted O'Connell to the view that the Irish peasantry represented an ally of vast political potentialities, their identification with the Catholic Association was only a degree less perilous for the lawyers, merchants, and journalists of that body than for the British government. To ride the tiger of popular discontent needed nerve and judgement; and without the assistance of the nationally organised Roman Church it is doubtful whether the Association would have been able to retain control of the savage energy it had set in motion.[1] But the known sympathies of the Lord Lieutenant, the success of Burdett's motion in the House of Commons, and the expiry of the 1825 Act, all encouraged the Catholic leaders to drive forward while the popular movement in the country was at its height.

As part of the reconstruction made necessary by the Huskisson resignations, Vesey Fitzgerald had been appointed President of the Board of Trade. He was thus obliged to stand for re-election in his constituency of Co. Clare. Since he was a 'Catholic', a good landlord, and on close terms with the Roman hierarchy, with whom he had negotiated a special grant for Maynooth College a few years earlier, there seemed little danger of his defeat. Certainly the election was likely to expose him to the violence and contumely of the Association; and knowing his sensitive temperament, Peel wrote from London urging him to despise all personalities. 'It really is quite unnecessary for a gentleman and a Minister of the Crown to notice the low slang of a county election.' But anxious as the Catholic leaders were to follow up the triumph of 1826, they did not find it easy to find any suitable candidate who would stand against him. Out of that

[1] cf. Reynolds, *Catholic Emancipation*, ch. 8.

difficulty came an improvisation of genius. In Fitzgerald the government had a master-card; to defeat it the Association played their
king of trumps. On 24 June O'Connell, after some genuine reluctance, announced his own candidature. In one stroke the situation
was completely transformed. Even Anglesey, while assuring the
government that O'Connell was losing ground and that his action
was deprecated by the Roman Church, was obliged to admit that he
would probably succeed; and all the subsequent reports that came
in from Ireland, including letters from Fitzgerald and Gregory,
convinced Peel that there was no hope. The only question was
whether his campaign would lead to an open outbreak of disorder.
The police and military in Co. Clare were accordingly strengthened,
and large reinforcements held in reserve.

Yet, as Anglesey and Peel realised, it was in the interest of the
agitators to prevent a breach of the peace; and the most intimidatory
aspect of the election was in fact the absence of riot and drunkenness,
and the discipline, order, and loyalty of the freeholders. The result
was a triumph for the Association: O'Connell 2,057 votes, Fitzgerald
982; and to the defeated candidate it seemed a wonder that he was
not beaten by an even greater margin. He polled the gentry and the
fifty-pound freeholders, a few tenants of his own, and virtually no
one else. 'All the great interests broke down, and the desertion has
been universal,' he wrote to Peel from Ennis on the evening of 5
July after the five-day poll was over. 'Such a scene as we have had!
Such a tremendous prospect as it opens to us. . . . The organisation
exhibited is so complete and so formidable that no man can contemplate without alarm what is to follow in this wretched country.'[1]
Defeated and harassed as he was, Fitzgerald even so was scarcely
exaggerating. Writing a few days later, Anglesey suggested that
unless the government had come to a firm decision on the Catholic
question, it would be wiser to regard the Clare election as an ordinary contest. In fact, he warned them, it was far otherwise. So
impressed was he by its extraordinary significance that he first
meditated the despatch to London of his A.D.C., Baron Tuyll, who
had been sent down to Ennis under colour of inspecting the constabulary force there; but since it was unlikely that his departure
for England would go unnoticed, Anglesey concluded that it

[1] *Peel Memoirs*, I, 114-15.

would be more prudent not to advertise so openly the concern of the executive. In his place Major Warburton, who had commanded the police in Co. Clare during the election, was shipped off to give a first-hand account to Peel of what had happened. Warburton, an intelligent and reliable officer in the Irish Constabulary, well known to Peel in the days of his Chief Secretaryship, arrived in London in the middle of July and confirmed all that Fitzgerald had reported.

What was significant in the Co. Clare election was not the nature but the degree of the transfer of power that it exhibited. The progressive loss of control by the Irish landowners and the growing political influence of the priests started a decade earlier and had been demonstrated to all observers in the 1826 election. Unless there was a startling change in the Irish situation, it was obvious then that the following general election would see a substantial number of emancipation supporters returned for the Irish counties. Now the second stage had been reached. The 1826 election had shown that the Irish representative system could be captured; Co. Clare in 1828 showed that it could be destroyed. It was not merely that the Anglo-Irish landowners had been defeated, in circumstances that could scarcely have been more favourable to them in any other Irish county outside Ulster, but that an aristocratic emancipationist candidate had been beaten by a Catholic lawyer who could not even take his place in parliament. The very strength of Fitzgerald's position in Co. Clare had stimulated the Association to carry out a feat which so far had hardly come within the range of its ambitions. From exploiting the electoral system in Ireland to return supporters of its policy to the House of Commons, it had passed almost without conscious design to an attack on the actual representative structure of Ireland itself. The legal form of Catholic disabilities did not preclude Roman Catholics from standing as candidates for parliamentary elections; it merely operated as a bar to taking their seats in the House of Commons. The absence of Catholic candidates before had merely been a practical consequence of this legal position, hardened by generations of usage. Now Co. Clare had dramatically broken the constitutional precedents; and the disciplined union of the Roman Church, the Association, and the Irish peasantry could repeat the action on an ever-widening scale. English laws forbade Roman Catholics to sit in parliament; Irish agitation could go some way to ensuring that only Roman Catholics would be elected. Even if the sphere of its effective operation was confined to the Irish counties, the results of such a breach in the Irish representative system was one which no British government could lightly contemplate. Within the legal structure of the constitution there would be a revolutionary clash of will; and it could not be assumed that the consequences would remain entirely legal. One of the most foreboding aspects of the crisis which Major Warburton reported to Peel on his arrival in London was that the split in Irish society was now visibly affecting even the police and constabulary, and that implicit reliance could not permanently be placed on their continued loyalty and discipline. For Peel at any rate the issue of the Clare election meant that the government had come to the cross-roads of decision. One road led to deepening disorder and repression, with little likelihood that a House of Commons could be found to sanction that policy; the other to concession.

In Ireland the Lord Lieutenant had already come to the same conclusion. Before the Clare election Anglesey had deluded himself that he had enough influence with the Catholic party to counteract O'Connell's excesses; but though he confided his hopes to Lord Holland, he felt unable to show the same degree of confidence to his government.

> It is most unfortunate that Lansdowne is not still Home Secretary [he wrote on 23 June] because I could have written to him upon the question and given him information that I cannot enter into with Peel. It is not that I am upon other than the best terms with Peel, but I cannot expect him to see things as I do and to take measures that I would advise, and therefore I am compelled to pursue a course upon my own opinion and judgment, on which it would have been most satisfactory to me to have advice.[1]

The events in Clare made him realise that he had overestimated, not necessarily his influence with the Roman hierarchy, but their influence with the political agitators and the parish priests. Nevertheless, he plucked comfort from the mere fact that matters had been brought to a head. 'I have made up my mind, or very nearly made

---

[1] Anglesey 1068/1 f. 75.

it up, to believe that this will be a very delightful termination of this odious question,' he wrote to Holland on 1 July; and again on 6 July 'nothing can be more clear than that Ireland cannot remain as it is. The Catholic question must be adjusted, or the Association and the Priests must be overruled.'[1]

It was in this mood of immediate concern and ultimate optimism that he proceeded to advise the government. On 2 July he wrote a long letter to Leveson Gower, dwelling on the enormous power in the hands of the agitators—'I am quite certain they could lead on the people to open rebellion at a moment's notice'—, the certainty of their ultimate success, the absence of any feasible means of suppressing the emancipation movement, and the impossibility of quietening the Irish situation except by allowing their leaders into parliament. Towards the end of the letter he allowed his inner feeling vent.

> It occurs to me that if O'Connell can force himself upon the House and thus establish the Catholics, it would probably be a most fortunate event. It would at once, and as it were, by accident, settle this accursed question and retire from great embarrassment many a man, who at this moment opposes the question from habit, and from having committed himself too deeply upon it to recede, but who also begins to be persuaded that the measure is inevitable.

He ended by saying that he felt it his duty to state his opinions thus, so that Leveson Gower could make them known at a convenient moment to Peel and so to the government.[2] In a following letter the next day he tabulated the possible courses of procedure, concluding that to go on as at present was impossible; that to attempt to suppress the Association would require a suspension of Habeas Corpus and the imposition of martial law, a policy which the House of Commons would almost certainly reject; and, finally, that to make a permanent settlement with suitable safeguards was the only practicable and advisable step.[3]

Suitable extracts from these letters were submitted, not without a degree of embarrassment, by Leveson Gower to Peel on 6 July.

---

[1] ibid., fos. 48, 61.
[2] ibid., 1068/15 f. 125, partly printed Peel Memoirs, I, 146 with exclusion of final quotation.
[3] Peel Memoirs, I, 148.

When Anglesey learned, however, that only extracts had gone to the cabinet, he wrote a sharp rebuke to his Chief Secretary. 'I really wish them to be acquainted with my whole thoughts regarding Ireland.' Guessing rightly that Leveson Gower had omitted the passage referring to O'Connell and the House of Commons, he went on, 'I conclude you suppressed it from the fear of outraging the feelings of the Ultras of the cabinet such for instance as my friend Bathurst', and ended by requesting him to show the cabinet the original letter. However, this was no more than a momentary ruffling of irascibility, and for the rest of July he continued to express to Leveson Gower his conviction that at a general election Ireland would return Roman Catholics in two-thirds of the constituencies; his curiosity to know the effects of his recent communication on Peel; and his confidence of being able to settle the Irish problem himself if only he were given a free hand. 'Why does not the Duke (for I know Mr. Peel is far too committed) set me to work to pave the way for an adjustment of every difficulty? . . . Alas, mine is a very uphill game and I get no help, and yet it is in my hands if I am allowed to play the game.' Fretful at being kept in the dark, he ended the month with the gloomy observation that 'if the first calm moment is not seized to declare an intention of adjustment . . . the Government must expect very serious disturbances and for aught I know, Rebellion'.[1]

Meanwhile, his letter of 2 July had been given by Leveson Gower to the Prime Minister. Conscious indeed that he had not chosen the best way of communicating with the cabinet, Anglesey wrote half-apologetically to Peel on 16 July to explain that he had wanted his letter to Leveson Gower to be seen by the Home Secretary and his colleagues so that 'they would judge of my fitness to carry into effect the measures they might decide upon adopting'.[2] The letter in question finally reached Peel through Wellington on 12 July and he read it to the cabinet the same day. It was decided that the king should see it; and Wellington, who had to go to Windsor on some other business the following day, took it with him. No immediate

---

[1] Anglesey 1068/15 fos. 140-55.

[2] *Peel Memoirs*, I, 152. The reference to the letter of 11 July must be a slip for 2 July. Most of the correspondence between Peel and Anglesey, and all that is important, at this date (40325 fos. 64-146) is printed in the *Memoirs*.

answer could, of course, be given on such a major point of policy, and in his reply Peel discussed instead the technical aspect of O'Connell's election. It was obvious that he could not take his seat as a member of parliament, and the cabinet had concluded that more public inconvenience would result from keeping parliament together for the issue to be settled than from allowing O'Connell to remain for the summer in his newly acquired status. The more urgent necessity seemed to be a decision whether to arm the Irish executive with fresh statutory powers to meet the crisis. Anglesey had indicated that he felt confident of preserving peace, but Peel expressed a willingness to introduce legislation even in the last weeks of the session, if the Lord Lieutenant thought there was any material advantage to be gained. Anglesey promptly answered that he had no such desire, and indeed would strongly object to being armed with any powers which he did not already possess. He explained in a subsequent letter that he did not think that more coercion, unaccompanied by concession, would have any beneficial effect; and that if rebellion should break out, he had enough force to meet it, at any rate in its early stages. There was some further discussion about the possibility of prosecuting some of the agitators for seditious speeches, but the Irish and English law officers gave their opinion against such a course; and though the Lord Lieutenant continued to write pessimistically about the chances of open rebellion and the growing unreliability of the Irish military units, he recurred persistently to the need for an early settlement of the Catholic question as the only means of ending the crisis.[1]

While conducting a correspondence on these executive matters with the Lord Lieutenant, Peel was already deeply involved in a consideration of the more fundamental issues. Even before the end of the Clare election he was taking legal opinion and making preparations for any action O'Connell might take. His Irish advisers —Fitzgerald, North, Leslie Foster, and Croker—were unanimous that the question of O'Connell's status should not be left undecided, and pressed for some expression of opinion from the House of Commons before the session ended. Peel was reluctant, however, to take any provocative step until it was seen what O'Connell would do, and the cabinet upheld this cautious policy. Prudence was all the

[1] *ibid.*, 141-65; 40325 f. 186.

more desirable at that juncture since Lord John Russell had put down a motion on Roman Catholic claims to be debated before the House of Commons dispersed for the summer. But in the end Russell did not persist with his intention and by the end of July the ministers were able to turn to a more deliberate consideration of the Irish problem, unencumbered by the presence of parliament. Immediately after the close of the session Peel and Wellington had a number of confidential discussions on the state of Ireland and the difficulties that would confront the government in attempting any solution of the Catholic question. Peel by this time had made up his mind not merely that he would resign from office—that decision had already been made—but that before he resigned he would formally place on record his conviction that the long-standing principle of government neutrality on the Catholic question should be abandoned and that the cabinet should during the summer consider the question and advise the crown as in the case of any other grave problem. He was also resolved to state firmly his view that there was less danger in attempting to solve that question by concession than in continuing to oppose a settlement; and he was ready to give assurances that out of office he would act on that conviction. When he went off to Brighton with Julia early in August, it was agreed that the Prime Minister should send him a copy of the formal memorandum he was preparing for the king on the subject, and that Peel should put his own views on paper in reply.[1]

Wellington's memorandum to the king, dated 1 August, was realistic to the point of brutality. After detailing the state of Ireland, he pointed out that the government was paralysed by the threat of a repetition of the Clare election in any matter that affected promotion, resignation, and dissolution, and concluded by saying that a rebellion was pending in Ireland and that in England the government was faced with a parliament it dare not dissolve with a majority in it of men who thought that the remedy was to be found in Catholic emancipation. He asked, therefore, for permission to consider the whole problem in confidence with Peel and the Lord Chancellor, and to report their deliberations to the king before opening the matter in the cabinet as a whole. The permission was granted, though a few days later George suggested the removal of Lord Anglesey.

[1] *Peel Memoirs,* I, 178-9; 40307 f. 179.

To this the Duke observed that though his presence in Ireland was inconvenient, his removal would be more so; and with that attitude Peel entirely agreed. Though he thought that in the event of an attempt to settle the Catholic question it might be desirable to have another Lord Lieutenant, the present need was for quietness and vigilance.[1]

On 9 August Wellington sent off to Peel copies of his correspondence with the king and the Lord Chancellor, together with a second memorandum outlining his own plan for the settlement of the Catholic question. It had been arranged that Wellington and Lyndhurst should see the king on 12 August and afterwards fix a time for a conference with Peel. Two days later Peel sent from Brighton a formal statement of his views, contained in two documents. The first, a letter to the Duke covering twenty-three sides of quarto, dealt with general principles. He prefaced his remarks by an expression of regret that his views on the broad question had not materially changed and that he could not believe either that full concession to the Roman Catholics could be made without the risk of the dangers he had always anticipated, or that concession would produce all the advantages which its advocates held out. But, he continued, it was a choice of evils, and it was impossible to escape from the fact that public opinion in England was narrowly divided on the issue, that its discussion could not be avoided, and that it could not be met without the government being in a minority in one branch of the legislature. There was, therefore, in view of the menacing state of Ireland, an advantage in a sincere attempt to end the problem. He personally was prepared to declare that there was less hazard in endeavouring to come to a decision than in continuing to leave it an open question. Though he was ready to assist as a private person, however, he was of the strong opinion that it would not be conducive to a satisfactory settlement for the conduct of the measure in the House of Commons to be entrusted to his hands. Out of office he would be more able to conciliate Protestant opinion, less likely to arouse Catholic distrust. Finally he turned to the practical question of securing a majority in parliament. Some of the best friends of the government would be in opposition, many would only give a reluctant assent. The great mass of support would come

[1] *W.N.D.*, IV, 564-82.

from those who, if not habitually opposed to the government, were under no special obligation to support it. Yet it was essential that a commanding majority should be obtained not merely for the principle but also for the details of the measure. If the question were to be taken up at all, therefore, there was clearly no safe alternative but the settlement of it. The final paragraph recapitulated his own personal attitude: he would retire at the most convenient time, he would assist out of office, but the measure must be entrusted to some person other than himself.[1]

The second document, a memorandum of equal length, dealt with the specific plan the Prime Minister had put forward for a settlement of Catholic claims. The three principal suggestions made by Wellington were that the laws excluding Roman Catholics from parliament should not be repealed but annually suspended; that the Irish county franchise should be limited; and that the Catholic clergy should be paid by the state and disabled from exercising any spiritual functions without royal licence. On this Peel's general comment was that if the government were to attempt a settlement, it must be a complete one. Partial concessions were useless; they would merely give to Roman Catholics power without satisfaction. The whole question must therefore be examined; and that, in his view, entailed consideration of three main points—the civil position of Catholics, the elective franchise in Ireland, and the relation of the Roman Catholic religion to the state. On the first his answer was brief and decided. There must be equality of political rights, though that did not necessarily exclude exceptions as regards particular offices, or conceivably a limitation on the number of Catholics sitting in parliament. He did not favour annual suspension of the disabling laws nor did he attach much significance to the imposition of oaths once the decision to admit Catholics had been made. On the second point he approved the principle of confining the vote to those who paid a minimum of £5 to the county rate, but he thought that the whole question of property qualification would need careful enquiry to discover the actual effect it would have on the Irish electorate, and he doubted the efficiency of contributions to the county rate as a test of actual property. The third point, in his view, constituted the major difficulty. There was no obligation to support

[1] *Peel Memoirs*, I, 181, partly printed *Peel*, II, 54, original 40307 f. 185.

as distinct from accepting the Roman Church; to do so might arouse jealousy both among the unestablished Protestant Churches and among the British taxpayers at large. Licensing of clergy might easily degenerate into a mere formality, providing sanction but no real control; and both payment of salaries and licensing would in effect be recognising the authority not merely of the Roman Church in Ireland but of the Papal See.[1]

These two long papers, the compilation of which must have occupied most of 10 and 11 August, were sent off to Wellington without copies being taken; since for greater secrecy Peel did not allow even his private secretary to see them. In a covering note he gave Wellington discretion to communicate them to the king, but asked him not to show them to anyone else except the Lord Chancellor and Goulburn, if he thought fit.[2] There for a time the matter rested. The Duke showed Peel's communications only to the Lord Chancellor. No mention was made of Peel's views to George IV, and Goulburn was excluded from the discussion by Wellington's promise to the king. The Lord Chancellor was busy with judicial duties till the end of August and in the meantime Wellington went off to Cheltenham after suggesting a meeting with his two colleagues early in September.[3] On 15 August Peel went up to London; but though he had some talk with Lyndhurst, he missed the Duke, who had gone to Cheltenham the same day, and he returned to Brighton with little accomplished. Ten days later he was in London again for a meeting of the Privy Council at Windsor from which the Prime Minister was absent; and early in September he and Julia joined Wellington after his Cheltenham cure at a Stratfield Saye house-party which included Lyndhurst, Arbuthnot, Greville the diarist, and several others. The three ministers took the opportunity to have further discussions on the subject, though not to any great purpose. The Duke had not given any maturer consideration to his views and the conversations mainly revolved round the personal position of Peel, who still maintained his determination to retire. Wellington was anxious for him to tell the king that he advised a settlement of the question even though he felt unable to take a part in it; Peel on the other hand extracted a promise from his colleagues not to let it be

---

[1] *Peel Memoirs*, I, 189, original 40307 f. 201.
[2] 40307 f. 198.     [3] *Peel Memoirs*, I, 201.

known that he would support the measure in parliament until the time came.[1]

The remainder of the month was passed between Drayton and Whitehall Gardens until he went off on a semi-public visit to Lancashire at the beginning of October from which he returned, as he told Gregory, 'satiated with good living and deaf with four times four and nine times nine'.[2] It was as the great Protestant minister that he was dined and fêted by the Lancashire gentry and manufacturers; and though he could say nothing to diminish that fame, he could hardly have been unconscious of a certain irony in the situation. Nor could he be any more outspoken with Gregory who came over from Ireland and had long talks with Peel on the Irish affairs. Nevertheless, even at this stage, besides the three ministers in the secret others had some knowledge of what was afoot. Herries, with whom Peel had discussed the Irish situation before going to Brighton, knew that he was convinced of the need for settling the question though unwilling to be a party to it. Wellington had gone even further. When visiting the Arbuthnots at Woodford on his way to Cheltenham, he had read them his memorandum to the king and showed them Peel's Brighton papers.[3]

All this time no progress was made in the great design. It was clear that the three ministers concerned had made up their minds that emancipation must be granted; but little further could be done until discussions could be opened in the cabinet, and that could not be attempted until the king's permission had been received. The task of securing that permission lay with Wellington, and in the autumn of 1828 the prospects of success were as discouraging as they could well be. In August the increasingly capricious behaviour of the Duke of Clarence in his post of Lord High Admiral had led to an appeal to George IV and Clarence's resignation; another of the king's brothers, the Duke of Cumberland, was writing stiff Protestant letters from Germany which probably further encouraged the king's temperamental reaction. When he talked to the king at the Privy Council meeting on 25 August Peel certainly thought he detected a deeper tinge of Protestantism than Wellington had encountered earlier, as well as signs of wavering on the matter of the Duke of Clarence's resignation. Wellington's tactical skill could

[1] *Arbuthnot Journal*, II, 206-7.     [2] 40334 f. 253.     [3] *Arbuthnot Journal*, II, 202.

make nothing of this situation. 'Between the King and his brothers the government of this country is become a most heart-breaking concern,' he wrote pessimistically from Cheltenham on 26 August. 'Nobody can ever know where he stands upon any subject.'[1] September brought no hope of an early decision. The king was extremely ill with gout and allied disorders, and to relieve the pain was taking up to a hundred drops of laudanum at a time. For weeks on end he was unable even to sign documents. On 10 October Wellington at last had an interview with him, but an interview in which the king did all the talking. Among other propositions he suggested recalling Anglesey, bringing Eldon back to the cabinet as Lord President, appointing Bathurst as Lord Privy Seal, dissolving parliament and going to the country on a tide of Protestant feeling. Unable to get a hearing for his own views, Wellington subsequently set them down on paper for the king's benefit, sending a copy for Peel's information. But apart from countering the royal proposals, he could do no more than emphasise the dangerous state into which Ireland had fallen and the need to take the whole Irish question into consideration. This was little more than he had already said in August.[2] The autumn months of 1828 that Peel had hoped would bring a final determination on the Catholic issue and his own position, thus ran to waste in the presence of a sick, uneasy, and querulous king.

The royal dukes were not the only relatives to muddy the waters. On 12 August, choosing with singular felicity the occasion of a public dinner at Londonderry to mark the erection of a monument to the resistance of the Derry garrison to James II, Dawson delivered a speech stressing the imperative need for a settlement of the Catholic question. In earlier years he had distinguished himself as a violent and unreasonable advocate of Protestant Supremacy; and in 1825 and 1826 Peel had endeavoured, without much avail, to persuade him to moderate his language and confine his partisan efforts to the House of Commons. That Dawson's convictions had undergone a change was known to his brother-in-law, and Peel had expected him to make his views public the following session. The time, place, and manner

[1] 40307 f. 241.
[2] *W.N.D.*, V, 133, 298; *Peel*, II, 70-1 where Wellington's letter of 14 October is misdated 19th, cf. 40308 f. 13.

which Dawson now chose for advertising his conversion could scarcely have been better calculated to defeat his professed object. As a near connection of the Home Secretary, as Secretary to the Treasury, and as a prominent Irish member, his words were bound to attract unusual interest; and there were many on both Protestant and Catholic sides who regarded his speech as a dexterous piece of kite-flying on the part of Wellington and Peel. To both of them Dawson sent letters explaining and defending his action; but annoyed as they were, the ministers thought there was no point in discussing the incident. Peel himself was unusually angry and refrained even from replying to Dawson's letter. To Gregory alone he commented hotly on the 'unfairness, the folly, and the indecency' of Dawson's exhibition. But there was no doubt in Peel's family circle of his exasperation. Dawson's wife, Mary Peel, was so conscience-stricken at her husband's blunder that she excused herself from dining at Whitehall Gardens a few days later in case the conversation turned on his speech.[1] The effects, however, could not be confined to a domestic circle. When Peel saw the king at Windsor on 25 August, George declared with royal freedom that Dawson must be mad; but it is not unlikely that the incident increased his growing tendency to revert to an uncompromising Protestantism. Certainly the Duke of Cumberland made much of it in his letters from Germany in the next few months and, indeed, used it as an argument for recalling Eldon so that doubts as to the government's intentions could be quieted.[2] But George knew more than Cumberland did. According to Vesey Fitzgerald the king's first impression was that the speech had been made in concert with Peel and Wellington, and it was almost impossible to persuade him that Dawson knew nothing of the ministers' intentions. Fitzgerald in fact went so far as to say that Dawson's speech 'very nearly overturned the whole design'.[3]

Even apart from Dawson, Ireland continued to be fertile in problems, large and small, for the Home Secretary's attention. His old Irish friend, James Daly, was recommended for a peerage but his election would have created a vacancy in the representation for Co. Galway. With the Clare election barely over, Gregory not

[1] 40334 f. 238; 40607 f. 105.    [2] *Geo. IV Letters*, III, 427-9, 438.
[3] *Greville*, 5 April 1829.

unnaturally pleaded for 'a little breathing space between the heats'. Nevertheless, secret information which at Peel's request he subsequently elicited on the balance of forces in Galway suggested that Martin, the likely government candidate, who was popular with the Catholic gentry and priests, might be returned in the face of all that the Association could do. By September Peel himself was half-inclined to try for the rich prize of defeating the Association with the aid of the Roman Catholic landowners of Galway. The Prime Minister, however, was doubtful of success and, even more significantly, unwilling to prejudice the chances of securing a change in the Irish franchise and some measure of control over the priesthood by a fortuitous victory in Galway arising from local circumstances not applicable to Ireland as a whole. 'In the existing state of the Roman Catholic question, and of our own discussion upon it,' he argued in a somewhat Machiavellian strain with Peel on 12 September, 'is it desirable that we should weaken the impression made upon men's minds of the strength of the combined factions of priests and demagogues?' If Peel, even at this late stage, was ready for a counter-attack, it was clear that the Duke was bent on preparing the ground for a strategic withdrawal.[1] In the end Wellington's decision prevailed and the unfortunate Daly had to wait (as it turned out another seventeen years) before his promotion to the Irish peerage as Baron Dunsandle.

Meanwhile much wider problems were calling for a solution. During the summer the Association had been active in holding special meetings of the peasantry for the ostensible purpose of settling private feuds; and by the autumn the peasants themselves were taking the initiative in coming together in great assemblages, organised in semi-military fashion, with banners, music, green sashes, and cockades. Though these meetings were for the most part peaceable and unarmed, there were inevitably some demonstrations against Protestants, clashes with the police, and minor outbreaks of rioting. Equally inevitably there was a growing sense of insecurity among the Protestant minorities in the districts where the meetings took place, and mounting anger in the north. In Ulster the response was to multiply the formation of Brunswick clubs, financed by small subscriptions in imitation of the Catholic Rent, and led by

[1] 40307 fos. 246-57, partly printed *Peel*, II, 62-4; 40334 fos. 228-32, 238, 243-5.

prominent members of the Protestant gentry and aristocracy. Jack Lawless, the radical Ulster ally of O'Connell, exacerbated public feeling in the north by a violent propaganda tour, raising money for the Association and inciting the Catholics to demand repeal of the Union, parliamentary reform, and disestablishment of the Church of Ireland. At one town, Ballybay, in Co. Monaghan near the border of Armagh, on 23 September a pitched battle between an armed Protestant crowd and Lawless's supporters was narrowly averted by the magistrates and a senior military officer, General Thornton. The continued maintenance of peace in Ireland seemed in fact to depend not on the normal instruments of law and order but on a tension of forces which it seemed impossible could be indefinitely prolonged. The passivity of the Irish executive in the face of these manifestations merely heightened the widespread feeling of crisis. The Protestant extremists, fearful of being deserted by the government, increasingly looked to their own organisation for salvation; the Catholic Association, springing into full activity with the expiry of Goulburn's Act, took on a new note of aggressive triumph; and O'Connell began to pose as the guarantor to the Lord Lieutenant of the safety of the dominion over which in the king's name he nominally presided.

In this critical atmosphere the Lord Lieutenant was caught between two impulses which a far more skilful politician would have found it difficult to reconcile. He wished to persuade the cabinet that the state of Ireland demanded an immediate settlement of the Catholic problem; but he also wanted to avoid any repressive action that would have the appearance of being directly aimed at the Catholic movement. In consequence his letters to London had an ambiguity which still further discredited his influence there. In a letter to Peel on 17 September, for example, while referring to 'frightful reports from the South' and discussing the strategic balance of forces in the event of a general insurrection, he still proclaimed his belief that there would be no formidable rising and his reliance on a policy of inaction. His Chief Secretary took a simpler view of the situation. Writing only the next day Leveson Gower told Peel that the popular meetings in Ireland formed the most urgent problem before the Irish government and that he could not say how long their abstention from violence would make it possible for their illegal and dangerous nature to be overlooked. In a long discussion he had with the Lord Lieutenant the same day, however, it was clear that Anglesey was indisposed to interfere and was hopeful that the disorders would die down of their own accord.

For the Home Secretary this policy of *laisser-aller* had little attraction. Writing from Drayton on 22 September he told the Lord Lieutenant that the system of public meetings being carried on in Ireland was one that called for immediate and serious attention, and asked point-blank whether the meetings were in fact legal, whether if illegal there was not danger in continued forbearance, and finally, if the law had no power, whether the executive government should not intervene. He announced his intention of consulting the English law officers on the subject, but clearly stated his own impression that it was the duty of the government to interfere, in the first instance by a warning proclamation. In the event of a sudden need for action before the whole question could be thoroughly considered, he assured Anglesey of the full support of the government. Two days earlier Anglesey had belatedly come to the same conclusion. Influenced by reports from the disturbed areas of Tipperary, Limerick, and Clare, he reluctantly made up his mind to suppress the meetings by proclamation. In anticipation of any outbreak of disorder that might follow, he asked the government to make available under his orders three battalions of infantry and a regiment of cavalry for immediate reinforcement if required.[1]

His letter reached Drayton on Tuesday 23 September and Peel took action at once. To Wellington he wrote off the same day enclosing the recent correspondence from Anglesey and Leveson Gower, and asked for a cabinet meeting on the following Friday or Saturday. At the same time he sent a letter to Lord Hill, the Commander-in-Chief, desiring him to hold in readiness the troops requested by the Lord Lieutenant and to give Anglesey the necessary authority to order them to Ireland without further reference to the Horse Guards. The cabinet was fixed for Friday afternoon and Peel waited at Drayton till six o'clock on Thursday evening when his Irish mail came in. Travelling all night he reached London early in the morning and before the cabinet meeting at 3 o'clock, he had

[1] 40326 fos. 3, 65-73; 40335 fos. 107, 118, 128, 133; *W.N.D.*, V, 76, 80-1; *Peel Memoirs*, I, 206-23.

conferences with the Attorney-General and Solicitor-General, to whom he had previously despatched all the relevant material he possessed on the character of the organised meetings in Ireland. At the cabinet it was agreed to sanction the issue of a proclamation declaring the meetings illegal and to give Anglesey authority to summon reinforcements from England on his own initiative. Minor alterations were made to the draft proclamation sent across by Leveson Gower, abbreviating and stiffening its terms; but a more awkward problem was the form in which it was to go out. With what seemed to Peel and Wellington culpable levity, the Lord Lieutenant had allowed both his Lord Chancellor and Attorney-General to go on holiday to the continent, and the ministers were doubtful whether he ought to issue it over his own name alone, and whether he would do so with the remnant of the Irish Privy Council left in Dublin. Any doubt as to the expediency of rapid decision was removed by the arrival on 27 September of a report from General Thornton on the affair at Ballybay, and a covering note from Leveson Gower stating his opinion that it would be wise for the government, in making its military preparations on the other side of the water, 'to consider Ireland as on the eve of rebellion or civil war, or both'.[1] Peel had already communicated to Anglesey the result of the cabinet's deliberations, and the following day, 27 September, he wrote twice more, once to inform him that six regiments of infantry and two of cavalry (the entire military force that was in fact at the disposal of the government) had been ordered to hold themselves in readiness for embarkation at the Lord Lieutenant's orders; and the second time to suggest the desirability of taking legal proceedings against Lawless's tour of agitation in the north. He ended his week of activity by sending to the king a full account of what had passed and copies of his correspondence with the Lord Lieutenant.[2]

The onus of responsibility now shifted to Dublin and on 30 September Anglesey took the decision to issue the proclamation, simultaneously calling over one regiment of infantry from Liverpool to Belfast and another from Bristol to Waterford. Alleging as his reason the absence of the Lord Chancellor and the inexpediency of

[1] 40326 f. 94; 40335 fos. 147, 149, 155.
[2] 40326 fos. 94, 98; *Peel Memoirs*, I, 230; *W.N.D.*, V, 87.

associating the two Irish Chief Justices with an executive action of that nature, he published the proclamation the next day, 1 October, on his sole authority. The ministers in England were annoyed at this mode of procedure and were unconvinced by his reason; but the thing was done, and Peel characteristically took the view that whatever their private feelings they must support the Irish executive to the utmost. To a certain extent the edge of Anglesey's proclamation was taken off by a series of resolutions passed at a meeting of the Catholic Association on 26 September calling for a cessation of the Tipperary meetings and invoking the intervention of O'Connell and the Catholic priests to put an end to the disturbances.[1] But Peel was not impressed by a policy of leaving the peace of Ireland in the hands of professed agitators and he continued to urge the Irish government to pursue a path of its own. Throughout October and November he continued in close correspondence with Leveson Gower, preaching the virtues of strong, impartial, and continuous action on the part of the executive rather than any reliance on extraordinary coercive measures, and emphasising the need for the strict discharge by magistrates of their duties. His pressure had some degree of effect. Lawless was arrested on 10 October, though he was eventually released without being brought to trial; and two magistrates who had been implicated in the disturbances, O'Gorman Mahon and Steele, whom Peel had suggested in October should be dismissed, were eventually removed from the Commission of Peace.

The Lord Lieutenant concurred only half-heartedly with the spirited policy forced on him. Indeed, he did what he could to minimise its effects. He had been aware of the uneasiness among the clerical leaders and some members of the Association at the growing strength of the peasant movement, and part of his delay in taking action against the meetings was to allow time for the Association to call them off of their own accord. 'I caused it to be whispered that I had come to this determination,' he wrote to Holland later, 'and that for the sake of the Catholic cause, it would be prudent and wise that my measure should not merely be acquiesced in, but approved.' He was conscious also of the unpopularity of his government with Protestants, and of the growing restiveness in the north. Writing to Holland on 2 October he asserted that 'my proclamation is

[1] *Ann. Reg.*, 1828, pp. [141-3.

directed at least as much to restrain them as the Catholics of the South and West'. It was only with reluctance that he agreed to the arrest of Lawless, and to his sympathetic whig correspondent he confessed that 'I find the Catholics mild, moderate, unaspiring. I confide even in the sincerity of the two great leaders. I am certain that O'Connell and Sheil may be depended upon.'[1]

In view of the delicate situation with the king, it was impossible for the ministers to take Anglesey into their confidence over their plans for emancipation, even if they had felt able to trust his discretion. The Lord Lieutenant knew that his views had been placed before the cabinet, and Peel had told him in August that the government would give their most serious attention to the 'whole state of Ireland' and decide some time before the commencement of the new session what advice should be offered to the crown.[2] But Anglesey did not regard this as a satisfying response, and while continuing during September to urge on Peel the need for a settlement, he complained in private to Holland that the ministers kept him in utter ignorance of their intentions and lacked the straightforwardness either to approve or disapprove his actions.[3] Despite this pressure, however, Peel was convinced that the most prudent course was to take as little notice as possible both of the manner and matter of Anglesey's correspondence. 'Under any circumstances,' he wrote to Wellington on 18 September, 'I should doubt the policy of communicating now to Lord Anglesey the resolution of the Government, supposing a resolution to have been formed.'[4]

Despairing of any satisfaction from the Home Secretary, Anglesey turned at the end of the month to the Prime Minister. To a letter of 24 September on the state of Ireland, he added a 'most private and *most confidential*' postscript in which, after adverting to his reluctance to embark on a discussion—'as you have never named the subject to me, I have had a delicacy in introducing it'—he expressed a conviction, based on private information, that the Catholic question could be adjusted on as good terms and with as little opposition as at any time. The Catholic bishops would be satisfied with fair terms as

[1] Anglesey 1068/1 fos. 161-2, 1068/21 (19 October 1828); cf. *Sheil Memoirs*, II, 24-30.
[2] *Peel Memoirs*, I, 203-4.  [3] Anglesey 1068/1 f. 101.
[4] *W.N.D.*, V, 61, partly printed *Peel*, II, 68.

regards crown nomination; they would offer only a feeble opposition to the payment of the clergy; and even on the matter of the 40s. freeholders there would only be a token resistance by the agitators.[1] Wellington replied on 28 September with a letter which, though non-committal, ought to have made Anglesey realise that the cabinet were hoping to make a settlement. The Prime Minister made three points: that he himself, as a private member of parliament, could only support a plan for emancipation that was brought forward by the government and offered guarantees for Church and State; that as a minister he was bound by the agreement maintained ever since 1811 not to bring forward the question officially; and that in consequence the first step must be to reconcile the king to an arrangement of that kind. Until that was done, it was useless for him to discuss the matter with anyone, least of all the Roman Catholic clergy or the Association.[2]

As the autumn of 1828 passed into winter, the relations between Anglesey and the ministers in London were increasingly strained. What they wished the Lord Lieutenant to do—indeed, all they wished him to do—was to maintain order in Ireland. But Anglesey, convinced of his ability to settle Irish troubles, could not refrain from actions which to the cabinet, and to many Irish Protestants, were incompatible with executive impartiality. Even such a moderate man as Fitzgerald wrote to Peel of the universal disgust, indignation, and alarm at the proceedings of the Lord Lieutenant. He gave interviews to O'Connell, visited Lord Cloncurry who had been in the Tower on a charge of high treason thirty years earlier, and declined to dismiss O'Gorman Mahon from the magistracy. Under constant pressure from the king to remove the Lord Lieutenant, Wellington wrote a stiff reprimand to Anglesey on 11 November to which he replied equally stiffly, defending his conduct and pointedly observing that 'up to this moment I have been left entirely in ignorance not only as to your intentions in regard to this country but also as to your sentiments in regard to my policy'. Wellington retorted on 19 November that the government had been in unreserved communication with him on questions of practical policy in Ireland, and that whatever the ultimate determination of the king's government, it was the duty of the Irish executive to enforce

[1] Anglesey 1068/1 fos. 140-4.    [2] *W.N.D.*, V, 92.

the existing law. This provoked another long exculpatory letter from Anglesey which Peel advised the Duke not to answer; but though in his first reply Anglesey had offered to resign his post should the king wish to make a change in the government of Ireland, the correspondence failed, much to George IV's disappointment, in bringing about his voluntary resignation.[1]

The November exchange of letters made it obvious, however, that the end had been reached; and as the king rightly pointed out, if Anglesey did not go himself, he would have to be dismissed. At a cabinet on 24 December the Prime Minister read out the correspondence between himself and the Lord Lieutenant, and there was general agreement that it was impossible to count any longer on cordial co-operation from the head of the Irish executive. On the 28th, having obtained the king's consent, Wellington wrote to Anglesey informing him of the decision to relieve him. The only question now was of a successor. Wellington thought of Lord Grantham or Lord Verulam; Peel of Lord Amherst. The king suggested Bathurst, but Wellington discouraged the notion and Bathurst said flatly that nothing would induce him to go. At the same time he also advised against the choice of Verulam. Lord Grantham was approached without success; Peel brought up the name of Lord Hill; Chandos canvassed on behalf of his father, the Duke of Buckingham; but in the end the post was offered to the Duke of Northumberland. In a letter of acceptance to Wellington on 18 January 1829, he made it clear that though he had previously opposed unofficial attempts at emancipation, he would welcome a final settlement at the hands of the government in the form of abolishing doctrinal oaths, except for certain high offices of state, but that he was opposed to any concordat, veto, or payment of Catholic clergy.[2]

By that date Anglesey had ceased to govern Ireland. The occasion of his premature departure was characteristically Irish. Curtis, the Roman Catholic Archbishop of Armagh, was an old acquaintance of Wellington from the time of the Peninsular War, when he had been rector of the Irish college at Salamanca; and he had been discreetly supported by the cabinet for the Irish primacy in 1819. He remained

[1] *ibid.*, 240ff., 270ff., 280, 290; Anglesey 1068/2 fos. 10 and letter of 23 November 1828.
[2] *W.N.D.*, V, 356-82, 428, 453.

in correspondence with the Duke on Irish clerical matters and on 4 December 1828 wrote to him, on the supposition that the government were about to propose a settlement of the Catholic question, suggesting a plan of obtaining government approval for Irish episcopal appointments. Wellington briefly replied, saying that though sincerely anxious for a settlement he saw no immediate prospect for it in the disturbed state of the public mind; but he added that if the question could be allowed to rest for a time, he did not despair of finding a remedy. Curtis passed this letter round his household circle and inevitably it found its way into the press. The sentiments were no more than the Prime Minister had already uttered in the House of Lords; the significance lay in the correspondent to whom it had been sent. Wellington had a right to complain of the betrayal of private correspondence; but only a very guileless politician would have assumed that such a letter to such a recipient would in Ireland remain secret. Another soldier then took a hand in this disastrous epistolary game with the Irish Catholic ecclesiastics.[1] Anglesey wrote to Curtis soon after, asking whether the version of Wellington's letter that had appeared in the press was in fact authentic. Curtis sent him the original and after a couple of days Anglesey returned it with a covering note. After observing, somewhat surprisingly, that he had not previously known the Duke's precise sentiments on the Catholic question, Anglesey went on to express his disappointment that the issue would not be settled in the forthcoming session; but he added that he derived consolation from the fact that the Prime Minister was not wholly averse to a solution, and advised the Catholics of Ireland to propitiate him by every means and throw no obstacle in his path.

This letter was written on 23 December, copied on the 24th, and reached the archbishop at Drogheda the same evening. Though marked private and confidential Curtis subsequently sent it to Murray, the Bishop of Dublin. A week later Anglesey received the news of his dismissal and by 31 December rumours were afloat in Dublin of his imminent departure—or so, at least, Anglesey affirmed. Conceiving that the publication of his letter would allay any uneasiness among the Catholics at his departure, he authorised Murray

[1] *ibid.*, 308, 326, 352; W. J. Fitzpatrick, *Life . . . of Dr. Doyle* (Dublin, 1861), II, 109.

to make its contents known, and on 2 January it appeared in the *Dublin Evening Post*. The evening before, for the first time, Anglesey showed the letter to his Chief Secretary with an explanation of the motives which had induced him to allow its publication. Leveson Gower wrote to Peel next day.

> I was surprised, I confess, by Lord A's letter to Dr. Curtis [replied the Home Secretary with pardonable dryness] but I should not be justly repaying the confidence with which you have written to me respecting it, if I did not add that I was almost as much surprised when I read for the first time in its printed form the Duke's letter to the same Reverend Divine.[1]

The effect on the cabinet was decisive. On 10 January Peel despatched a formal letter to the Lord Lieutenant instructing him to quit Ireland immediately, and enclosed a warrant for the appointment of Lords Justices to take over the government in his absence. On 19 January Anglesey left Dublin, arriving the same evening at Holyhead. To the last his self-confidence stayed with him.

> You are the older politician [he wrote to Huskisson on 3 January] but I am the older soldier. You was caught in a trap. I would not be *driven* to resign. Indeed, I have too much identified myself with this people to abandon them in a difficulty. I bore much and would have borne more for their sake, but I have been relieved from a distressing dilemma.[2]

It was not an unjust verdict on his administration; but identification between ruler and ruled can itself be a trap, both for politicians and for generals.

[1] 40336 fos. 196, 199, 209, cf. Anglesey 1068/21 (Anglesey to Curtis, 23 December 1828; to Holland, 6 January 1829); *W.N.D.*, V, 413.
[2] Anglesey 1068/21; 1068/2 (Anglesey to Peel and to the Lords Justices, 14, 22 January 1829); 40326 fos. 181, 183.

# CATHOLIC EMANCIPATION

In the middle of November 1828 Wellington sent to the king a long memorandum outlining a scheme for the settlement of the Catholic question and requested permission to lay it before some of the Church leaders, the Archbishop of Canterbury, and the Bishops of London, Durham, Winchester, Lincoln, Chester, and Oxford. George granted his request, directed him to lay the correspondence before Peel, but showed no sign of becoming converted on the main issue. The bishops when consulted were equally discouraging, only Chester and Durham being in favour of emancipation.[1] The year 1829 came, therefore, with the Catholic question still embedded in the quicksands of royal evasiveness, though a widening circle of persons were aware of Wellington's intentions and public speculation was growing. The margin of time was now very slender. Parliament was summoned for 5 February and if anything was going to be done, it would have to be announced at the opening of the session.

Early in January Wellington had discussions on the state of Ireland with the Archbishop of Canterbury and the Bishops of London and Durham. His object was not merely to persuade them that political considerations demanded the settlement of the Catholic question but even more perhaps to outflank the king's resistance by obtaining an expression of readiness on the part of the Church to make concessions. The manœuvre was fruitless; the interval for reflection and fears for the attitude of their lower clergy had merely strengthened the initial episcopal hesitation; and all three dignitaries declared their decided hostility to the removal of Catholic disabilities. The position was now worse than ever. Anglesey's dismissal would make it obvious that there had been a violent disagreement within

[1] *W.N.D.*, V, 252-68, 324-6.

the government on the Irish question. What Peel feared next was that the king, encouraged by the bishops' intransigence, would make some public utterance on the subject that would commit him to an attitude of resistance. Up to that point the Prime Minister, though he had argued against Peel's motives for resignation, had been reconciled to his departure from office on the understanding that he would assist the government on the question in his private capacity. Now even the Duke began to despair of success, and he was not a leader who was accustomed to defeat. In Peel's view, however, if the Catholic question was to be carried, only the Duke could do it. With Canning dead and Goderich discredited, the one conceivable opposition leader who might be able to form an administration was Lord Grey. Not only would it have taken a prolonged political crisis to force him into office against the king's will, but even so, in Peel's considered and not unjustifiable opinion, it would hardly be possible for him to prevail in circumstances where Wellington had tried and failed. The existing parliamentary system did not easily lend itself to the provision of alternative sets of ministers; nor was Catholic emancipation a cause for which an appeal to the electorate was likely to bring additional strength to any government. The situation resolved itself, therefore, into a question of Wellington or nothing; and as on the plains of Flanders fourteen years earlier, the Duke was in need of all the reinforcements that could be brought to the decisive field of battle.

Against the background of all these considerations Peel came to one of the crucial decisions of his life. On 12 January, immediately after the discussions with the bishops, he wrote to Wellington that if his resignation should prove in the Duke's opinion an insuperable obstacle to emancipation, he would be prepared to stay in office. With the letter he sent a long and carefully composed memorandum of his views on the Catholic question which could be laid before the king. The whole cabinet position was now unblocked. The Duke delivered Peel's memorandum to George IV on 14 January. The following day those members of the cabinet who had hitherto opposed Catholic emancipation—Wellington, Peel, Lyndhurst, Bathurst, Goulburn, and Herries—went to Windsor and each had separate interviews with the king. All expressed the view that the government must take the question into consideration. The last resistance in Peel's mind to his own continuance in office was destroyed unexpectedly and curiously by George himself. The king, pressed towards a decision from which he inwardly recoiled, turned the tables on his Home Secretary by demanding why, if he supported the measure, would he not make the same sacrifice of consistency which he asked the king to make, and remain in office to carry out the policy he advised. To this there could only be one answer and Peel made it.[1] Following this demonstration of solidarity George reluctantly gave his permission for the cabinet to consider the whole state of Ireland and submit their views to him, though he stipulated that he should not be regarded as pledged to accept their advice even if unanimous. There remained now the question of Peel's future and this was settled in an oddly formal interview on 17 January. On that day the Prime Minister came in person to Whitehall Gardens to hand Peel a letter in which he stated that he saw no chance of overcoming the difficulties which confronted him unless Peel continued in office. He entreated him therefore 'to give us and the country the benefit of your advice and assistance in this most difficult and important crisis'. Peel read the letter in his presence and told him at once that he would no longer press his retirement but would remain in office and bring forward, with the king's consent, the government's proposals for the settlement of the Catholic question. A cabinet meeting followed immediately at which Wellington described the negotiations with the king, the discussions with the bishops, and his own plan for the removal of Catholic disabilities. Peel then stated his own change of intention and his reasons for it; and the Prime Minister added emphatically that not only would the difficulties be increased tenfold by Peel's resignation but that the means of meeting those difficulties would be diminished to an equal extent.[2]

From none of this did his colleagues dissent. Peel's decision was

---

[1] *Speeches*, II, 427 (17 December 1831); *Portion of . . . Journal . . . by Thomas Raikes 1831-47* (1856), I, 127-8 (based on information from Sir Alex. Grant, Peel's neighbour in Whitehall Gardens). Though muddled, the version in Raikes both confirms that this conversation actually took place and helps to place it. The suggestion in G. Cornewall Lewis, *Administration of Great Britain* (1864), p. 459 n. 3, that Peel was describing an imaginary conversation was made in forgetfulness of the personal interview between Peel and the king at this date.

[2] *Ellenborough*, I, 297ff.

cordially welcomed and some at least of the cabinet were impressed by the courage it displayed. Two of them, Ellenborough and Bathurst, wrote to him afterwards to express their admiration of his conduct. Peel himself, mindful of his long-suffering Chief Secretary in Ireland, sat down at once after the cabinet meeting to convey the news to Leveson Gower. He enjoined him to strictest secrecy, and asked him to begin confidential discussions with the Irish law officers on the question that would probably be an indispensable preliminary to any Catholic measure, the suppression by law of the Catholic Association. The Chief Secretary replied immediately in a letter which even in its brevity betrayed the pleasure and relief with which he learnt the government's intentions. Peel could scarcely have shared his emotions. There was no division in the cabinet on the need to abandon the old principle of neutrality on the Catholic issue; but the real battle lay ahead—with the king, in parliament, and in the country—and by his own action he had placed himself in the forefront of what would inevitably be a bitter and painful encounter.

Yet Peel would have been false to his own temperament if his decision to participate in the government's action had not brought with it a corresponding access of vigour and resolution. For good or ill he had crossed his personal Rubicon and he would now be a protagonist in the struggle instead of a sympathetic onlooker. It was a role which he had always found more congenial and satisfying. Action and responsibility, especially when spiced with danger, brought out all his fundamental courage and high spirit. That did not detract from the sincerity of his previous offer to retire from office or from the considered nature of the reasons which prompted his offer to remain. For five months Peel's resignation had lain among the Prime Minister's papers, and at the very last, when he wrote his letter of 12 January, he had renewed his proposal to retire and reiterated his view that he was not the person to whom the conduct of the relief bill should be entrusted. But that long delay had in itself become an ingredient in the situation. He had been Wellington's closest associate; he had taken a leading part in all the difficulties arising from Lord Anglesey's administration; he knew better than anyone else in the cabinet the peculiar problems confronting the Prime Minister; and he had given prolonged thought to the technical legislation which emancipation would entail. At the start of the crisis he had shared Wellington's intellectual conviction that the Catholic question must at last be conceded; and during the autumn of 1828 when Wellington was working to obtain the king's co-operation, he had become more and more deeply implicated in the policy the Prime Minister was trying to put into effect. For nearly half a year, therefore, he had time to reflect on his own position and to watch the development of the situation both in Ireland and between the king and his chief minister. From being a consenting party to the Prime Minister's policy, he had become in fact almost a committed party.

Towards the end of November the Duke had reported to Mrs. Arbuthnot that he had had a very satisfactory conversation with Peel, and that though he was not sure that he would stay, he had better hopes of it than before. A fortnight later he was able to tell the Arbuthnots that from various small signs he had drawn the conclusion that Peel would not after all leave office.[1] At the very end of the year, on 31 December, Peel had written to Wellington to say that he wanted to have a long conversation with him and 'look thoroughly at our position and that of the government with respect to the Roman Catholic question and Ireland'. The final and decided refusal of the bishops to lend their support could only have been the occasion and not the cause of his decision to throw in his lot with Wellington if the Prime Minister really deemed it an indispensable condition of success. The decision itself must have been approached through a long process of reconsideration in which time and circumstance played a leading part. Much had happened to alter the situation between July 1828 and January 1829; and the accident that his resignation remained both secret and suspended throughout that period had enabled him to retain his freedom of action. He was able therefore at the last moment to alter his earlier resolution not to support emancipation as a minister, though up to that moment he had hoped and believed that he would not be required to do so. There were other considerations, too, less susceptible to precise analysis since they arose from the personal relationship in which Peel stood to his chief. Peel had always had a respect for Wellington, and the force of the Prime Minister's personal appeal for his support was peculiarly difficult for a man of his nature to resist. Loyalty for Peel

[1] *Arbuthnot Journal*, II, 224.

was among the cardinal virtues. Lack of it in others hurt and alienated him profoundly; in himself, whether with superiors, friends or subordinates, it was a quality that was almost an instinctive attribute of his character. In the hard game of politics that was not always perhaps an advantage. Nevertheless, the die was cast and there was little opportunity for retrospection. A great deal of work had to be done before parliament met in February; and they did not have much time.

To be exact, the cabinet had eighteen days. In this period they had to prepare the king's speech and decide, in principle at least, the various measures necessary for a settlement of the Catholic question. That in itself was a formidable programme, for so far it had been impossible to discuss in cabinet any of the vital points on which the precise character of the settlement would depend. There was, in addition, an even greater barrier to surmount. The king had merely given permission for the cabinet to discuss the problem. Before the main heads of the proposed legislation could be indicated in the speech from the throne, it would be necessary to secure his specific consent for the cabinet's plan to be laid before parliament. The principal burden of concerting the various measures fell naturally on Peel, since as leader of the Commons he would have to expound and carry them in the lower House. But the task of guiding the cabinet towards agreement in detail on these measures within the allotted time would have been difficult to the point of impossibility had it not been for the fact that Peel and Wellington had been reviewing all aspects of the question for the last twenty weeks. From that point of view alone there was justification for Wellington's declaration that without Peel's assistance the task could scarcely be accomplished. Of the extent to which the Prime Minister relied on the Home Secretary's intellectual preparedness there was immediate proof. On 17 January, the day of the cabinet meeting at which the Catholic question was first formally discussed, Peel drew up a memorandum for his colleagues, defining and analysing the issues involved.[1] Three main problems, he suggested, had to be solved: the removal of the civil restrictions, the regulation of the Irish franchise, and the future relationship between the state and the Roman Catholic Church. He confined the more discursive part of

[1] *Peel Memoirs*, I, 300ff.

the paper to a consideration of the first problem. There seemed no tenable line, he argued, between the position laid down by the Irish Act of 1793 and the general repeal, except for a few particular offices and functions which he proceeded to enumerate, of all civil disabilities. The mode of relief was largely decided by the form in which the disabilities were at present imposed. Admission to parliament and to high civil offices was barred by the Oath of Supremacy and the declaration against transubstantiation. The latter, he thought, should be repealed absolutely except for the monarch previous to coronation. The Oath of Supremacy offered greater difficulties since there was some difference of view on its precise significance. Though loth to abandon or alter the oath, Peel did not favour the device of legislative definition which Plunket had proposed in 1821 and preferred the institution of a fresh oath of civil allegiance for Roman Catholics, to be taken together with the oath of allegiance and possibly that of abjuration.

The cabinet began its real work on the Catholic measure on 18 January and from the 21st to the 26th there were daily meetings to work out both policy and details. It was decided as a preliminary that the king's speech should refer to the state of Ireland and recommend both the suppression of the Catholic Association and a consideration of the laws affecting Roman Catholics. Wellington, Peel, and Ellenborough all produced sketch paragraphs; and though obviously troubled and agitated the king agreed before the end of the month to the draft presented to him. The completed version was read in Council on 2 February. Lord Clive, the eldest son of Lord Powis and M.P. for Ludlow, was chosen as a suitable person to move the address, and though Peel first thought of Ward, the City member, as a seconder, in the end that honour was offered to Lord Corry, the son of the Earl of Belmore and member for Co. Fermanagh. Even here there was embarrassment. Sir Thomas Lethbridge, a high Protestant, taking for granted like many others that the recall of Lord Anglesey was a proof of the continued resistance of the government to emancipation, offered himself as a seconder to the speech. Corry himself, when first approached, expected the speech to be anti-Catholic, though he recovered sufficiently from his surprise to accept the invitation to second. The fact that the mover and seconder had to some extent to be admitted to the secret in itself caused the cabinet some concern. These, however, were incidentals. Of the main issues the easiest to settle was the suppression of the Association. After a discussion on 18 January, when Peel produced a draft bill empowering the Lord Lieutenant to declare any association unlawful by proclamation, the technicalities were referred to the law officers and it was not until three weeks later that the Attorney-General and Solicitor-General of England and the Irish Solicitor-General had progressed sufficiently to discuss their bill with the cabinet.

The question of disfranchisement offered more room for disagreement. Peel was anxious for the cabinet to be guided by the expert knowledge of some of their Irish supporters, and it was decided on 21 January that Lord Farnham, Leslie Foster, and Vesey Fitzgerald should form a small committee to consider the problem. George Dawson was later added to their number. The purpose of linking a disfranchisement bill with a Catholic relief bill was to diminish Catholic influence among the electors and remove the pernicious political motive for multiplying small tenant-holdings. Peel himself was not confident that the first would be achieved, and some members of the cabinet, including Ellenborough, disliked the principle of disfranchisement altogether. In writing to Fitzgerald on the matter Peel asked him to obtain full details of the relative proportion of 40s. freeholders in the different counties and to bear in mind that the object of the change was not merely to prevent a notorious abuse in the existing representative system but also to create an electorate that would not be a tool in the hands of either landlord or priest.[1] When the subject again came up for cabinet discussion in the middle of February there was still an evident reluctance on the part of Peel and most other members of the cabinet except Fitzgerald to adopt an open measure of disfranchisement. More informal talks were held in Peel's house where Goulburn, Leveson Gower, Doherty, and others joined the original committee of four. After much argument it was settled, with certain misgivings on the part of some present, to proceed by way of open disfranchisement. The Irishmen, with a more realistic knowledge of their own country, had no faith in any system of indirect tests that involved such fallible safeguards as affirmation on oath or the production of visible tests of value. On the other hand they abandoned under pressure their

[1] 40323 f. 31.

initial proposal to fix the new qualification at £20 and agreed to the lower level of £10 subject to previous investigation by an assistant barrister and jury. For the towns and cities, where the abuses of Catholic freeholders were balanced by the abuses of Protestant freemen, no change was proposed. There would be enough discontent engendered by the disfranchisement of the 40s. freeholders in the counties without trenching on the sanctity of corporate rights. What would be the ultimate effect on Protestant influence of the change in the county franchise could only be a matter for speculation; but there seemed a general agreement that the £10 voters would be more exempt from the influence of the priests than the old 40s. freeholders.

The next great practical issue was the question of the oaths. There was some discussion of the subject on 21 January and it was settled that Peel's memorandum on oaths should be placed on the cabinet table before the subject was resumed the following day. The new oath which he suggested was a compound of the existing oaths taken by Roman Catholics under the Acts of the 1781-93 period, amended in the light of experience. Both the principle of substituting a new civil oath for the declaration against transubstantiation and the formula for the new oath put forward by Peel were accepted by the cabinet. The offices to be excepted from the general rule of civil equality were based on the list suggested in the memorandum of 17 January, which in turn derived from earlier emancipation bills. They comprised offices in the Established Church, the universities, schools of ecclesiastical foundation, and ecclesiastical courts, together with the offices of Lord Chancellor in England and Ireland, and Lord Lieutenant in Ireland. The only real argument was over the offices of First Lord of the Treasury and Secretary of State. In view of the amount of Church patronage which they controlled, it was initially resolved to add them to the list. Had this decision been maintained, it would in effect have debarred Roman Catholics from the leading posts in government and would have formed not merely a large exception but a serious infringement on the principle of equality which was the professed aim of the bill. Peel had earlier suggested that the problem of presentation to benefices in the Established Church by political ministers might be overcome by the creation of Crown Commissioners to exercise the right of patronage when the office normally appointing was filled by a Roman Catholic. Ellenborough was one of those not happy at the additional exclusions and it was finally agreed in cabinet on 3 February merely to announce that a bill would be introduced to remove Catholic disabilities with such exceptions as seemed desirable on special grounds, but without entering into any more detail.

There remained the problem, more complex and more embarrassing, of relations between the state and the Roman Church. At the meeting of the cabinet on 17 January the Duke had expressed the view that there could be no formal concordat with the Pope in view of the special relationship between the monarch and the Established Church and the existence of statutory legislation prohibiting intercourse with Rome. But he was clearly anxious to consider the expediency of payment to the Catholic clergy and a system of clerical licensing, if only as a method of control. This attitude was essentially the same as that which he had elaborated in a memorandum of 7 August[1] originally drawn up for Peel and the Chancellor but shown to the king in November. In his reply from Brighton in the summer Peel had described the question of official relations with the Catholic Church as 'the great difficulty of the question' and his comments then indicated a considerable initial hesitation over Wellington's proposals. In the interval his feeling had hardened. It was significant that he put forward no draft on this aspect of the question. Instead he strongly advised his colleagues not to risk the failure of the two main measures of relief and disfranchisement by adding to them a legislative attempt to regulate relations with the Roman Church or Irish clergy. When the cabinet began its consideration of the problem on 21 January Wellington renewed his suggestion of a system of licensing for Catholic clergy. While agreeing to the principle, the Chancellor suggested instead the registration of clergy with power to strike off the register. Peel, on the other hand, said he did not value licensing and would rather be without it. He brought up a few minor points: the suppression of Jesuit colleges and giving power to the Crown to demand the disclosure of all communications with the Pope. The first of these found favour; the second was rejected. There was a general disinclination in the cabinet to attempt any supervision of the relations

[1] *W.N.D.*, V, 254.

between the Pope and the Catholic Church in Ireland, and the only securities that were seriously discussed were the questions of registration and stipend. The more closely these were examined, the greater the difficulties appeared. In a cabinet discussion on 23 January even the Lord Chancellor joined Peel and Fitzgerald in criticising the proposed method of registration, particularly the power of striking priests off the roll, which if seriously put into operation would invite a contest on the worst of all grounds for the government—the spiritual functions of the clergy. Their arguments finally prevailed. The Prime Minister and Ellenborough, who had been the chief supporters of the registration clause, reluctantly yielded to the majority, though Ellenborough regarded it as the best security and the Duke as the only one.

The case for granting financial support for the Catholic clergy received even less support. Peel, the Chancellor, and indeed the cabinet as a whole, concluded that even if desirable, the proposed state provision for the Irish clergy would arouse overwhelming opposition in the country, if not in parliament. The residuary question still remained, however, whether any securities or controls could be devised that would not encounter similar objections. Peel reviewed the possibility of licensing bishops, forbidding Jesuit and all monastic Orders, and controlling public ceremonies and processions; and read to the cabinet yet another memorandum he had prepared on the laws affecting English and Irish Catholic priests. On two successive days there was some inconclusive discussion of what Ellenborough called these 'little securities'. On 26 January Leslie Foster was smuggled into the cabinet room by way of St. James's Park and the Foreign Office, and was examined on the practicability of giving the Crown power within two months of ordination to prohibit the exercise of the spiritual functions of a priest. His evidence convinced the cabinet of the worthlessness of such a device; and there for nearly a month the question was left. It was clear that though the Duke and one or two of his colleagues wished to see securities written into the bill, the majority of the cabinet led by Peel could see none that were likely to be either technically effective or politically acceptable.[1]

---

[1] For the general course of cabinet deliberation see *Ellenborough*, I, 297ff.; *Peel Memoirs*, I, 298ff.

Meanwhile the last days of the great secret were rapidly running out. Early in February members of parliament were gathering in London from the distant shires and boroughs, ignorant of the 'thunder-clap' of the king's speech about to echo round their ears. With one or two of his close friends Peel anticipated that dramatic moment. His old mentor Lloyd, now Bishop of Oxford, had of course long been aware of the government's general intentions. In the middle of January Peel told him of his formal advice to the king that the Catholic question must be settled, and after visiting Peel in London immediately afterwards he could hardly have been unaware of his further intention to remain in office and introduce the bill. Though distressed and anxious, Lloyd's trust in the younger man remained unbroken; but it remained to be seen whether others at Oxford would share that confidence. On 31 January Peel wrote to Smith, the Dean of Christ Church, announcing his purpose of bringing in a bill for Catholic emancipation and offering, or at least suggesting his resignation if the feeling of the university desired it. The same day he saw Croker, told him the news, and showed him the correspondence on the subject between the king, the Duke, and himself. Croker for once found speech difficult, but two days later he told Peel bluntly (if his own account is to be trusted) that the greatest surprise would be not that the Catholic question was to be conceded at last but that Peel was to be its prime mover. He also asked him to see Lord Lowther, which Peel did though with little success in convincing him of the necessity of the measure.[1] On the first day of February Peel also found time to write a long letter to Gregory, explaining the course of events that had led up to his decision. 'I may be wrong,' he concluded, 'but at any rate I am prepared to make sacrifices which will prove that I think I am right.' He asked Gregory in strict confidence to communicate what he had written to Saurin. The answer that came back was a foretaste of the reception the 'thunder-clap' was to have even on some of his closest friends. 'Your letter has overwhelmed me with surprise and dismay,' wrote Gregory. 'It is an event for which I was not prepared, and I must have more time to collect my scattered senses. . . . Yet . . . I do not think this is the time you should yield to the demands of menacing rebels; they should first be subdued.'

[1] *Croker*, II, 7.

By that time the secret was scarcely so any longer. On 4 February Peel gave the usual eve of session dinner to the principal government supporters in the House of Commons at which the king's speech was read out. It was not, noted Croker, a lively occasion. Perhaps the guests, like himself, were deprived of speech by the shock, for he was told that some of them did not believe the current rumours of Peel's 'conversion' till they actually heard him read the speech.[1] A similar atmosphere was detectable the next day when parliament opened. Clive and Corry proposed and seconded the address, which was carried without a division. There was a full House which quickly thinned and the applause for Peel came mainly from the opposition. Yet even so he had to meet expressions of reproach from some of his former supporters. A few days earlier Ellenborough had advised him to speak as early as he could and take a high tone. Certainly there was nothing lacking in either firmness or frankness in his own contribution to the debate. He said at the outset that he pretended to no new lights on the Catholic claims. He retained the same opinions as before; he saw the dangers just as clearly. But the pressure of present evils was so great that he was willing to risk those contingent dangers rather than endure not merely a continuation but an aggravation of the existing system. He ended on a personal note. The conclusions to which he had come had been formed six months earlier and he had given his advice as minister of the crown accordingly. Though he would have preferred to be relieved of any share in the settlement of the problem, the Prime Minister had impressed on him the embarrassment that would be created by his resignation, and he had therefore consented to remain in office and uphold a measure which he had become convinced was necessary.

Next day the debate continued, and Peel intervened to clarify what had passed between himself and Wellington in August. The disclosure did little perhaps to strengthen his position, since the critics were enabled to enquire why he had subsequently changed his mind. But Peel, now that action had commenced, was in good spirits. At the Speaker's dinner on 7 February he even joked about a letter he had received from an Irish Protestant M.P. who, unaware of what was impending, had written to say that he was hastening up to support the good old cause. Not everyone was amused, and even

[1] *ibid.*, p. 8.

Peel perhaps felt the next moment that it was hardly the time or place to allow his sense of the ludicrous to find expression.[1] On the day of that dinner Peel also found a moment in which to write to his father at Drayton. The old baronet, in the evening of his life, could not be expected to abandon the principles on which he had acted ever since he entered public life, and he told his son that he feared the concession would only embolden resistance. In private perhaps his feelings ran deeper, for old age had not entirely extinguished the choleric side to his nature. But ties of affection were too strong for him to write in any but a friendly and sympathetic manner and in general conversation at Drayton his disapproval was soon confined to an occasional jest. His anxiety was chiefly directed to his son's public reputation, and the ultra-tory papers taken at the manor provided him with only too much ground for exasperation on the score.

Further north, in the tory industrial Lancashire from which the Peels had sprung, opinion was less restrained and the Home Secretary heard from his relative and fellow-sportsman Colonel Yates of the shock and indignation occasioned in Bolton and Manchester by the news. Meanwhile in press and public gossip the wits got to work. A story was circulated that the Pope had ordered a new festival to be inserted in the calendar, the conversion of St. Peel; it was said that the minister had become so distasteful to his former followers that instead of being Orange Peel he was now Lemon Peel; and the cartoonists showed Wellington and Peel with rosaries in their hands, kissing the Pope's toe. More ominous still, there were early signs of political defection. Bankes sent in his resignation at once; the Duke of Beaufort and the Earl of Westmorland both refused to accept the office of Privy Seal; Lord Lonsdale showed a reluctance to commit himself; and before the end of February Wetherell had yielded to the Protestant storm and announced that he could not vote for emancipation. From Lord Hotham, a friend and personal supporter, Peel received on the morrow of the king's speech a courteous but firm refusal to support the proposed measures. Even among the whigs, who were bound by consistency to lend their aid to the government's new policy, there were reservations on Peel's personal integrity. Lord John Russell and others were inclined to believe

[1] *Croker* II, 8.

that he must have had much the same views on the necessity of yielding the question when he made it the ostensible ground of separation from Canning in 1827.[1] All this had been foreseen by Peel as far back as the summer, but it did not make his task any easier.

In the middle of this gathering tension came the introduction of the first great measure foreshadowed in the king's speech. On 10 February Peel rose for leave to bring in a bill to terminate the existence of the Catholic Association. In an attempt to frustrate the legal subtlety of the Irish leaders, the government had framed a relatively simple bill giving power to the Lord Lieutenant to suppress any association or meeting which he thought dangerous to the public peace or incompatible with the proper administration of the law, and to interdict such assemblies from receiving or holding any financial contributions. In view of the arbitrary nature of the power thus bestowed on a single individual, it was proposed to limit the Act to one year. The bill, backed as it was by documentary proof of the disturbed state of Ireland, received little attention or opposition. The ultra-tories could not vote against such a measure; the emancipationists accepted it as a necessary preliminary to the main work of Catholic relief. But in the course of the discussions both on the bill and on various petitions for and against emancipation that were heard at the same time, Peel was made the object of further personal attacks. Sir Edward Knatchbull, the tory member for Kent, observed that he had allowed himself to be cheered through the countryside last summer when he must have been conscious of the policy he meant to pursue. To this Peel retorted that though he had certainly made up his mind then, he still had every reason at that stage to think that he would be allowed to take his course as a private individual unfettered by office. Henry Bankes then made an even more virulent onslaught on Peel's tergiversation and asked whose fault it was that the Association had grown to its present power and influence. This brought Peel to his feet with an explanation of the various reasons, not least the attitude of the House of Commons itself, which had made the 1825 Act inoperative. On the subject of inconsistency he made a crushing retort by quoting a speech of Bankes in 1812 when, in giving his support on Canning's motion

[1] Moore, *Memoirs*, VI, 15.

to consider Catholic claims, he had argued the right of politicians and governments to change their convictions with changing circumstances.

Two days later, on 12 February, Knatchbull again attacked Peel for inconsistency and added the pointed observation that he might more properly have taken his present course at a different time, when Canning was at the head of the government. Stung by the implications of the last charge, Peel declared that he would not condescend to offer any apology or explanation to Knatchbull. Instead he made a heated declaration of the duty of ministers to give their conscientious advice on matters of policy and of the evident impracticability of giving any advance notice of their intentions to the country before parliament met. As far as he himself was concerned, he said, he had no other duty and no other responsibility to any man or set of men. As for his Protestantism, he had for twenty years opposed any concession to the Catholics and what he did now was in defence of Protestant institutions at a time of danger, even at the expense of every kind of personal imputation and reproach. After a few more words from Knatchbull and Duncombe, he recovered his temper and rose once again to say in a more conciliatory tone that it was inconsistent with their deliberations to show any personal warmth. He would make no more reference to his personal share in the recent transactions but would carry on the discussions with the moderation that would best ensure their successful issue.

The bill passed both Houses without opposition and became law on 5 March. By that date Peel had ceased to be member for Oxford. The separation from his old university was not the least of the personal sacrifices which the crisis brought in its train.[1] His letter of 31 January to the Dean of Christ Church had produced nothing but discomfiture in the college. Smith consulted Lloyd and Gaisford, and they agreed at once that it was impossible for them to give any judgement on behalf of the university. They therefore returned his letter, and the explanatory memorandum that had accompanied it, with the advice to write direct to the Vice-Chancellor. Peel was hurt by the return of his correspondence but it did at least convince

[1] For the Oxford University election of 1829 see my article in *Oxoniensia* IV (1939), 162ff. on which the account here is largely based. Much of the correspondence is printed in *Peel Memoirs*, I, 310ff.

him that to ask individual members of the university whether he ought to resign was useless and embarrassing. He therefore altered his letter from a conditional to a formal and positive resignation and sent it to the Vice-Chancellor so that it reached him on 5 February, the day of the opening of parliament. All he requested was to be informed when it would be most convenient to the university for his resignation to take effect. By an unfortunate and ironical coincidence it was laid before Convocation the same day at a meeting called to discuss petitions to parliament against Catholic emancipation. Peel's letter was read out immediately after it had been decided by a large majority to approve the petitions, and the Vice-Chancellor's acknowledgement was accompanied by a request, in the absence of the other university member Estcourt, to present the petitions to the House of Commons. The following day a formal reply was sent by the board of heads of houses and proctors, begging him to use his own discretion as to the date of his resignation. This official courtesy was given more point by a private letter from the Dean of Christ Church, written with the approval of the Vice-Chancellor, earnestly advising him to delay his resignation until the measure for Catholic emancipation had been introduced and discussed in parliament, as until then no cool judgement on the issue could be expected in the university.

Opinion at Oxford was certainly divided; and in any case it was not known whether Peel wished or intended to stand for re-election. Much, of course, depended on the attitude of Christ Church. The Dean, though not enthusiastic, was prepared to re-nominate Peel, and he allowed the Senior Censor, T. V. Short, to write to Lloyd in order to discover what Peel's real feelings were. Short, a warm supporter of Peel, told Lloyd that he had no doubt it was the wish of the Common Room to put him forward again and that if they did, there would be no opposition to his return. Lloyd, who travelled to London on 5 February to see Peel, had fears as to the propriety of his standing again, and of aspersions on his character if he did so. But Marsham, the liberal-minded Warden of Merton, who talked with Lloyd on his return, dismissed these scruples as hyper-quixotism and said roundly that Peel's re-election was a duty which the university, if it were given the opportunity, would certainly fulfil. Lloyd thereupon decided to let the growing movement in Oxford for Peel's re-election have its way. This was decisive as far as his college was concerned. On 9 February the Common Room met and unanimously resolved to support Peel's candidature. A circular letter to the other colleges was drawn up but it was decided not to issue this before Wednesday 11 February. The delay may have been due to a desire on Lloyd's part to ensure that Peel would accept nomination. No decision on that point had been reached between them, and though the bishop had at once written off with the news of the college's decision, an answer could not be expected before the 10th. In fact the delay proved fatal. Peel's attitude was conveyed in two letters he sent to Lloyd on 10 and 11 February. He gave Lloyd a wide latitude in deciding, according to the chances of success, whether his name should go forward. For himself he expressed complete indifference. 'In very homely phrase I say to you (what I could not say to anyone else) I care very little about the matter.' He was not anxious to stand again, and considered that a protracted contest, even if successful, would be embarrassing and painful. But he did not wish to appear discourteous to the university or show any peevishness. Let the college, he concluded, take the course which would best ensure its continued influence in the university. Meanwhile, the day after the Christ Church resolution, Lloyd heard that a meeting of heads of houses was to be called for the express purpose of opposing Peel. Tired, nervous, and irresolute as he was already, Lloyd now fell into a fit of panic and determined to prevent the college from taking any further step in the matter of Peel's nomination. Interpreting Peel's letter in its broadest sense, he told the Censors that Peel had requested him to put a stop to the activities of the college on his behalf.

Even though they took some time to find—in the person of Sir Robert Inglis—a suitable opposition candidate, the anti-Peel party which now emerged formed a powerful body within the university; and once they had shown their strength, it was impossible to reunite Christ Church behind Peel's candidature. Other liberal members of the university, however, were determined not to see his cause go by default and on 12 February a committee was formed, under the chairmanship of the Warden of Merton, to secure his election. Within forty-eight hours a similar committee was set up in London with Granville Somerset, one of the government parliamentary managers at its head, and an active canvass started. But in all these activities Peel showed little interest. He had already written to the Vice-Chancellor to say that he would resign on 20 February. His parliamentary business made it essential for him to resume his place in the Commons as soon as possible, whereas in order to avoid a clash with the Oxford assizes at the beginning of March, Convocation had been anxious for the writ not to be moved immediately. Though apprised of his views, the committee at Oxford decided to persevere. In so doing they were possibly interpreting Peel's mind in a truer sense than his own words would convey. It is hard to doubt that he would have welcomed an honour which his pride and scrupulousness prevented him from soliciting. At any rate he agreed to remain out of parliament until 2 March and to do nothing to hinder his nomination provided the election would be held before that date. This proved possible to arrange and on 26 February polling began in scenes of clamour and confusion that rapidly degenerated into violence and insult. By the following afternoon the battle was seen to be lost. Peel was 126 votes behind with no hope of making up the deficiency; the final state of the poll was Inglis 755, Peel 609. It was not an ignoble defeat. Peel's minority included twice as many first-class men as Inglis's majority; fourteen out of twenty professors; twenty-four out of twenty-eight prizemen; thirty-eight out of forty members of parliament; and all the noblemen who voted. In Christ Church, Oriel, All Souls, Merton, New College, and Exeter, comprising some of the most distinguished colleges in the university, he had a majority. But a phalanx of lesser men, including what Greville described as an immense number of parsons, supplied the numbers where they could not provide the quality.[1]

Perhaps if Peel had delayed his retirement until the end of the session, when tempers had been given time to cool, the result would have been different. Some of his friends indeed thought he was at fault to offer his resignation at all. Croker, for example, told him that it was 'a democratical and unconstitutional proceeding and a precedent dangerous to the independence of the House of Commons'.[2] But on that point at least Peel had made up his mind from

[1] The several analyses of the poll printed at the time differ slightly but there is no substantial variance from what is given here.

[2] *Croker*, II, 7.

the start; to have done otherwise would have been contrary to his whole nature. The university was no ordinary constituency and Peel no ordinary politician. Even so, had the initial decision of Christ Church to nominate him at once been made public, the opposition might have been deterred and would certainly have been weaker. The seventy-nine votes from members of his college that went to Inglis (also a Christ Church man) alone would have turned the balance in Peel's favour. His opponents at least made capital out of the failure of Christ Church to agree on a candidate.

> Such is Peel—so much honoured,
> His college, d'ye see,
> Will not bring the man forward
> But leave him to me.

Greville thought, with much justice, that the whole election was mismanaged from start to finish. Yet whatever his private feelings, and they could not have been other than bitter, Peel took his defeat with outward calm. Men like Lord Bathurst had entreated him not to refuse nomination if he were asked; and to his supporters in Oxford afterwards he wrote without a shade of reproach. Asking Marsham on 28 February to convey his thanks to the Oxford committee, he assured him that 'I think they were entirely right in giving to such a minority as that which has voted for me the opportunity of recording their sentiments.'[1] The same day Lord Ellenborough, who was not an uncritical colleague in the cabinet though he had no love for parsons and college dons, wrote in his diary that 'Peel is himself perfectly indifferent, and really I must confess that he has shown himself *a great man* by his equanimity in all that has taken place.'

Meanwhile a constituency of some sort had to be found. This through the agency of the government managers was rapidly effected. Sir Manasseh Lopes, a wealthy Spanish Jew of doubtful electoral reputation, who was patron and member for the pocket borough of Westbury in Wiltshire, resigned his seat as soon as the Oxford result was known and an election was rushed through before

---

[1] *Peel Memoirs*, I, 339; cf. letters from Whateley and Marsham (40399 fos. 9, 13).

an opposing candidate could be found. Holmes, the Treasury Whip, went down to Westbury on 1 March and the next day the formalities of the return were completed. It was scarcely a dignified election, for even in this sleepy country town Protestant feeling was raised to a pitch of violence. Apart from Lopes and the mayor, who was his brother-in-law, the members of the corporation declined to take any share in the proceedings. Lopes was hit by one of the missiles showered on the town hall during the ceremony; the windows of his house were broken; and Holmes had to sit out a cold and draughty dinner with his host before leaving for London the same evening. An even narrower escape was the arrival of a Protestant candidate just too late to be nominated. But the deed was done, and in due course Lopes received his reward. It was not all he had hoped for, since his own estimate of a suitable recompense for his services was an English peerage. Peel, though he had little personal communication with Sir Manasseh, agreed however that he had in fact been of essential service to the government at some cost to his person and influence in vacating when he did, and he made three or four applications to Aberdeen on behalf of Lopes's nephew, a Mr. Cowper. In the inevitable waiting-period before a suitable vacancy occurred, he had to endure reminders from his uncongenial patron; but in October he was able to write with relief to Lopes announcing the appointment of his nephew as consul at Pernambuco at a salary of £1,000 per annum. Aberdeen had experienced some difficulty in satisfying himself that Cowper could properly be appointed at all, but decided in the end that for a place of no great business or difficulty he would be safe enough.[1]

While Oxford had been plunged into sectarian politics, the cabinet had proceeded with the business of the main bill. On 20 February there was a long, desultory, and unsatisfactory discussion, as Ellenborough described it, on the question of requiring an interval of two months during which the Crown would have the power of interdict before Roman Catholic bishops assumed their episcopal functions. The subject was renewed on the two following days with minor decisions on such points as the prohibition of territorial titles, the

[1] 40312 fos. 65, 73-4. For details of the Westbury election see W. G. Hoskins and H. P. R. Finberg, *Devonshire Studies* (1952), pp. 412ff.; cf. *Peel Memoirs*, I, 342.

Jesuit Order, and public ceremonies; while Peel suggested an alteration of the oath in order to bind M.P.s and other office-holders to
preserve the Union. But on the main issue it was increasingly realised
that no effective control over the Roman Catholic Church in
Ireland could be exercised without at the same time establishing a
relationship that would be more obnoxious to Protestants, and
ultimately perhaps more dangerous to Protestantism, than the
absence of any securities. Indeed, at the beginning of March, Peel,
Fitzgerald, and Murray were even opposed to the prohibition of
territorial titles and it was only maintained as cabinet policy to soothe
the susceptibilities of the king. Even on the matter of stipends it was
felt that neither the Protestants nor the Catholics in their existing
temper would accept it; and that being so, in Peel's view at least,
no attempt at any other ecclesiastical security could profitably be
considered. Political securities, such as the restrictions on the number
of Catholic M.P.s, seemed to him equally inadvisable as detracting
from the conciliatory value of the main principle of removing
Catholic civil disabilities. The more the question of securities was
examined, in fact, the less probability there seemed that they would
either be accepted by the Roman Church, or facilitate the passage
of the Relief Bill, or offer any prospect of safeguarding the Established Church for the future. In the result, therefore, the cabinet
abandoned the principle of basic securities which had been a feature
of Catholic relief bills ever since 1813. By the beginning of March
both remaining bills had been drafted under Peel's supervision with
the aid of Tindal the Solicitor-General, Doherty his Irish colleague,
and Leslie Foster, and received a final scrutiny by the cabinet.[1] On
3 March Peel resumed his place in the Commons as member for
Westbury and at once gave notice of his intention to raise in two
days' time the question of Catholic civil disabilities to which
reference had been made in the king's speech. With the bill for
suppressing the Association about to become law, the way at last
seemed clear for embarking on the most difficult part of the government's proposed legislation.

At this point opposition from another quarter suddenly threatened
to overturn the whole programme. So far the cabinet had acted
on the assumption that they had the king's sanction, however

[1] *Peel Memoirs*, I, 351ff.; *Ellenborough*, I, 353ff.

unwilling, for the general measures they had announced. In the middle of February, however, the Duke of Cumberland returned from Germany; and though he promised not to organise an opposition to the government's legislation, the effect of his strong uncompromising character on his volatile and irresolute brother was soon apparent. The king began to make difficulties over the voting of the members of the Royal Household, and it became clear that matters would have to be brought to a head. On 27 February Wellington, armed with the heads of the bills which the government proposed to introduce, had a long agitated interview with the king in the course of which George finally yielded on all points, even to the extent of agreeing to ask Cumberland to leave the country and allowing the Prime Minister to write in the king's name to the Household officers. Nevertheless, all was not yet over. On 1 March the Lord Chancellor was summoned to Windsor and found the king once more receding from the pitch of resolution to which Wellington had screwed him up a couple of days earlier. Lyndhurst went off at once to warn Wellington at Stratfield Saye, and then returned to London. The Cabinet met next day in the afternoon and about four o'clock the Duke arrived from Windsor. His report of the interview he had with George was gloomy; the king had refused to sanction his draft letter to the officers of the Household and was again talking of abdication. The cabinet had already agreed, in the light of what Lyndhurst had told them, that they could not proceed further without written authorisation from the king. A draft drawn up by Peel was now adopted, to the effect that the bill for suppressing the Catholic Association was only one of a series of related measures and that ministers could not advise the king to give his assent to that measure unless he continued to approve the general course of policy they were following with regard to Ireland, and unless the government were assisted by the royal influence and authority to which they were entitled as ministers of the crown.[1]

This letter was sent off the same day. The next evening, when the cabinet were immersed in the discussion of ecclesiastical titles, a note arrived from the king, desiring to see the Duke, the Lord Chancellor, and Peel at noon the following day, 4 March. When they arrived they found the king in a more serious mood, but still

[1] *Arbuthnot Journal*, II, 247; *Ellenborough*, I, 345-73, *W.N.D.*, V, 482-515.

labouring under great anxiety and uneasiness. He had taken some brandy and water before joining them, and sent for more which he continued to drink during the conference. At the outset of their talk he observed that it had caūsed him great pain to assent to the proposal that the cabinet should be at liberty to offer their collective advice on the Catholic question, and greater still to feel that he had no alternative but to act on that advice. He wished, therefore, to have a personal interview with those ministers whom he must regard as chiefly responsible. Peel, being most conversant with the details of the bill (which he was due to submit to the Commons the following day), explained the main heads of the measure. At the mention of the Oath of Supremacy and the modification of the section referring to the spiritual jurisdiction of the Pope, the king exclaimed in surprise and appealed to the other two ministers. He was assured that a measure of Catholic relief was futile without such a change and that a new oath against the civil and temporal jurisdiction of foreign princes and prelates would be required in its place from Roman Catholics. Seizing, however, at the one point on which he could make an intelligible stand, George said firmly that at no time had he understood that any change in the ancient Oath of Supremacy was intended, that he could not possibly sanction it, and that his consent to the general measure would therefore have to be withdrawn. The ministers agreed that he could not be bound by an assent given on a false apprehension, and there was a short pause in the conversation. The king then asked what action they intended to take in these circumstances. 'Now, Mr. Peel, tell me what course you propose to take tomorrow.' Peel replied that he could not have a moment's hesitation as to his course. He must entreat the king to accept at once his resignation and permit him to inform the Commons next day that the king's servants were prevented from bringing in the measure which had been announced and that he no longer held the seals of the Home Department. Wellington followed with a similar announcement, and the urbane Lord Chancellor indicated his agreement with the course his colleagues proposed to follow. With this the interview, which lasted five hours, virtually came to a close. The king expressed his understanding of their decision and parted with them in a kindly fashion, giving them his customary kiss on each cheek, and accepting their resignations. Before they left

Windsor the Duke had a word with Knighton, who was perturbed at the king's physical and political state, and wanted Wellington to see Lady Conyngham. This the Duke declined to do for fear of finding the king already there, it being his habit to go to her after any upsetting scene.

The three ministers returned to London, broke in shortly before ten o'clock on a cabinet dinner at Lord Bathurst's, and told their colleagues they were out. The cabinet were annoyed rather than distressed at the news. It was obvious to their minds that there was no alternative ministry and the Duke cheerfully expected to be called for again in a few days as soon as the king had realised the predicament in which he had placed himself. At the last moment, however, George recoiled from the final desperate remedy he had devised. Knighton and the Conynghams had gone to him as soon as the ministers had left. Together they persuaded him that no other ministry could be found and that to base his resistance on the issue of the oath would make it impossible for him to retract with any honour. About the same time as the three ministers reached London, the king was sitting down to write a letter to Wellington telling him that he had decided to yield his opinion to what the cabinet believed to be the immediate interests of the country. The ministers had his consent therefore to proceed with their measure. 'God knows,' he concluded, 'what pain it costs me to write these words.' This message was received by Wellington soon after he arrived home from the cabinet dinner and he at once sent it round to Whitehall Gardens. In returning the note Peel cautiously suggested, in view of its ambiguity, that in his own reply Wellington should say that the cabinet would proceed in the full confidence and understanding that they had the king's sanction and support, and that he was determined to go through with them. 'Do ask him to write approved upon your letter of yesterday',[1] he added. 'I still think that the King's letter is meant to reserve the power of a veto on the measure if he finds it practicable.'[2] These suggestions were incorporated almost verbatim in the reply to the king which Wellington

---

[1] This is clearly a reference to the Duke's letter of 2 March enclosing the cabinet memorandum.

[2] *W.N.D.*, V, 519, dated Thursday night (in fact the night of Wednesday-Thursday 4-5 March), cf. *Peel Memoirs*, I, 349-50.

sat down at midnight to compose. The king was awakened early
in the morning by this communication and wrote a hasty note from
his bed, assuring the Duke that he had put the right construction
on his letter of the previous evening. After three days and nights of
alarms and excursions, the way was clear at last.[1]

A few hours later Peel stood up in the House of Commons to
move for a committee of the whole to consider the laws imposing
disabilities on 'his Majesty's Roman Catholic subjects'. The moment
was a dramatic one, both in the history of the emancipation movement since 1801 and in Peel's personal career. Rumours had been
flying round London of dissensions between king and ministers, and
the little chamber of the House was packed to suffocation. The
lobbies were full and crowds gathered outside the building. It
was, as all realised, a great parliamentary occasion and Peel rose to it
superbly, making by common consent the greatest speech he had
ever delivered. He opened with an intentional emphasis: 'I rise as a
minister of the king, and sustained by the just authority which
belongs to that character, to vindicate the advice given to his
Majesty by a united cabinet.' In the early part of his speech he
touched briefly on his own peculiar position and the part he had
formerly played in maintaining the exclusion of Roman Catholics
from parliament and the high offices of state.

> I do not think it was an unnatural or unreasonable struggle. I
> resign it, in consequence of the conviction that it can be no longer
> advantageously maintained; from believing that there are not
> adequate materials or sufficient instruments for its effectual and
> permanent continuance. I yield, therefore, to a moral necessity
> which I cannot control, unwilling to push resistance to a point
> which might endanger the Establishments that I wish to defend.

With this preface he turned to the first part of his argument: that
the present position of the government with regard to the Catholic
question was untenable. Whatever was done, some change of policy
there must be. The divisions in the cabinet and in the legislature
which had twice caused him to proffer his own resignation—in

---

[1] *Peel Memoirs*, I, 343ff.; *W.N.D.*, V, 517-19; *Ellenborough*, I, 376-8, 384;
*Arbuthnot Journal*, II, 247-8.

1825 to Lord Liverpool and in 1828 to the Duke of Wellington—were only part of a long-standing schism in the government which had its origin as far back as 1794. Since that date every ministry had been divided and two had fallen on the issue. In 1812 it was settled that the question should be an open one, members of the government being free to take their own course upon it in parliament. The consequence had been unhappy jealousies and suspicions between public men, exacerbated by the efforts of partisans and the exaggerations of public comment; and in turn the frustration of any consistent and vigorous Irish policy. The same destructive situation was witnessed in the legislature. Four of the five Houses of Commons elected since 1807 had pronounced, in some form or other, in favour of a settlement of the Catholic question; the fifth voted against by the narrow margin of two votes. Both sides in effect were powerful enough to paralyse each other; and no effective legislation, whether for coercion or relief, could be carried. In this the House of Commons was merely reflecting the divided feelings of the country at large. The present House, elected shortly after the excitement of the emancipation struggle in 1825, gave no indication that a public opinion existed in the country capable of supporting a strong Protestant policy, and had itself 'after trembling in the nice balance of opinion, at length inclined on the side of concession and relief'. What, he asked, was to be the end of these interminable and fruitless contests? Should there be another general election, another attempt to rouse the people with the cry of *No Popery*? 'Never, Sir, under any circumstances. The parliament, and the parliament alone, will I ever acknowledge to be the fit judge of this important question.' But taking the feeling of the country as expressed through parliament, it was clear on examination of the fifteen most populous constituencies—the fifteen largest counties in England—that there was no overwhelming voice against concession. Of their thirty-two members, seventeen had voted in its favour. If a consistent Protestantism was not evident in the constituencies, still less was it evident in the rising generation of politicians. In the list of Protestant speakers in the last decade, the same names recurred with scarcely the addition of a single new advocate; but on the other side the youthful talent of the House was almost unanimously against them. Not only therefore was the government divided on the Catholic issue, but the Protestant element in it lacked the essential basis of a majority in parliament. The failure to sustain the Protestant cause was not personal but public; a failure on the part of parliament and public opinion. For ministers it was not a question of will but of ability to resist any longer.

Having demonstrated the purely domestic political reasons why resistance could no longer be maintained, he next analysed the conditions in Ireland which made concession necessary. His first point was that the Union had failed to bring about normal administrative conditions. In fact for scarcely a single year since that event had Ireland been governed by the ordinary process of law. Alongside the sequence of dates and parliamentary divisions on the Catholic issue, he placed the chronological catalogue of Ireland's endemic emergencies. In 1800 suspension of Habeas Corpus and an Act for suppressing rebellion, continued in 1801, renewed in 1803, continued in 1804. In 1807 the Insurrection Act, continued till 1810, renewed in 1814, and continued till 1817, renewed in 1822 and continued till 1825. In that year came a new Act for the suppression of dangerous associations which expired in 1828. Now it was 1829 and another Act was already being requested by the legislature. If this recital proved anything, it was that the principle of neutrality must be abandoned and a firm policy enforced by a united cabinet. Theoretically that unity could take the form either of resistance or concession. But was resistance practicable? Could an efficient administration be formed on the principle of resistance? Even conceding for the sake of argument that it could, there was the further and more difficult question. Could it hope to pacify Ireland? In particular, how could it meet the threat of the Catholic Association? This was not a new or temporary problem. Since the end of the eighteenth century successive governments had sought for legal methods of suppressing Irish agitation and had successively failed. Every legal device had been fruitless, and all legal opinion concurred in despairing of finding a legal remedy. The problem in fact was one which was not amenable to statutory regulation—'there exists a spirit too subtle for compression, a bond of union which penal statutes cannot dissolve'.

Even if a government of resistance could be formed and a new law passed, it would have to meet the further obstacle of the Irish

Catholic franchise, which would enable over twenty Irish counties to follow the example of Clare. The existing House of Commons, committed by its own resolution to extend the rights of Roman Catholics, would hardly vote for the disfranchisement of the Irish freeholders. A new House of Commons could only be obtained by a general election which would necessarily extend to Ireland. No conceivable Protestant majority that might be obtained in this way could possibly counterbalance the danger that would accrue from the inevitable return of a large body of Irish members elected in every circumstance of passion and resentment by the Irish freeholders. An Irish general election held in present circumstances would sever the last links between landlord and tenant, and make it impossible for the government of Ireland to be carried on with either energy or success. The fact was, he concluded, it was no longer practicable to impose fresh restrictions on the Roman Catholics.

> We have removed, with our hands, the seal from the vessel, in which a mighty spirit was enclosed—but it will not, like the genius in the fable, return within its narrow confines to gratify our curiosity, and enable us to cast it back into the obscurity from which we evoked it.

Coercion, therefore, was out of the question. To govern Ireland in the face of opposition from five out of the seven million of its inhabitants—and that two million minority largely concentrated in Ulster and itself divided on the expediency of concession— would be impossible in time of peace except through the unremitting use of the army and the police. In time of war it might be impossible by any methods and might even provoke foreign intervention and civil war. The sum of all his arguments was, then, that the government could not go on as it was, and that a united government based on the principle of resistance could not be formed in the present state of parties and public feeling, and could not govern Ireland with any prospect of satisfaction or efficiency. There remained, therefore, the one alternative—concession.

With that the purely argumentative part of his speech ended. As a piece of reasoning it was based entirely on factual considerations.

It was not a question of right but of expediency; not of what was desirable, but of what was possible. What he had demonstrated was that the government was in a situation which it could not master and from which there was no escape. Peel himself spoke not as a private individual exercising the luxury of private views on public issues, but as a minister who had to devise some solution, however imperfect and distasteful, to a problem which could not wait any longer. The rest of his speech was mainly devoted to an exposition of the details of the plan drawn up by the ministry: the admission of Roman Catholics to parliament without conditions or restrictions; the repeal of the oath against transubstantiation; the retention of the Oath of Supremacy; the prescription of a new oath incorporating the substance of the oaths of allegiance and abjuration, and disavowing the temporal jurisdiction of foreign authorities; the admission to corporate and municipal privileges, and offices in civil and criminal justice. Catholics would still be debarred, however, from the office of Regent, Lord Chancellor in England and Ireland, Lord Lieutenant of Ireland, and others connected with Church establishments, ecclesiastical courts, universities, public schools, and schools of ecclesiastical foundation. What was envisaged, he emphasised, was political and not religious concession. The scheme did not sanction, still less encourage, any religion other than that established by law. It rested indeed on the assumption that there was less danger to the Established Church in removing the civil disabilities of Catholics than in attempting to maintain them. There would be no compact with Roman Catholicism, and parliament would be free to exact any securities in future that might be deemed necessary. The one real security would be the alteration of the county franchise in Ireland from 40s. to £10 and the registration of such freeholds by judicial machinery. Otherwise the ministers had no veto to propose; no control over Roman Catholic Church appointments; no power of inspection or examination. Though there were powerful arguments in favour of ecclesiastical securities, there were even more powerful objections. The government could not negotiate with the court of Rome; even to propose a partial connection with the Roman Church would arouse great opposition in the country; and the Catholics themselves had resisted all previous proposals for establishing control over it. However, episcopal titles used by the Established Church would not be allowed to be assumed by bishops of the Roman Church; existing members of monastic communities would be registered; no fresh ones would be founded; and no new members of the Jesuit Order admitted to the country.

He ended with an eloquent appeal for charity and conciliation, and an expression of hope that the sanguine expectations of those who had so long advised the settlement would be fulfilled. For himself, if not so sanguine, at least he could say that he believed the settlement of the question in the mode the government proposed would give more security to the Protestant interest and establishment than any other that the present situation would admit. He knew he could have taken a more popular and more selfish line. He might have held language much more acceptable to the friends with whom he had long acted and to the constituents he had lately lost.

> His ego gratiora dictu alia esse scio; sed me vera pro gratis loqui, et-si meum ingenium non moneret, necessitas cogit. Vellem equidem vobis placere...; sed multo malo vos salvos esse, qualicunque erga me animo futuri estis.[1]

That was his defence; that was his consolation; that should be his revenge.

> Sir, I will hope for the best. . . . But if these expectations are to be disappointed, if unhappily civil strife and contention shall survive the restoration of political privilege; if there be something inherent in the spirit of the Roman Catholic religion which disdains equality and will be satisfied with nothing but ascendancy; still I am content to run the hazard of the change. The contest, if inevitable, will be fought for other objects and with other arms. The struggle will be, not for the abolition of civil distinctions, but for the predominance of an intolerant religion.

A few more sentences followed; the formal motion put to the chair; and he had done. The speech had taken over four hours to deliver,

[1] *Livy*, III, 68, 9. 'I know that there are other things that it would be more agreeable to say; but, even if my own character did not so prompt me, necessity compels me to speak the truth rather than what is agreeable. I would indeed like to give you pleasure; but I much prefer to secure your safety, whatever be the feelings which you will entertain towards me.'

and had been listened to with profound attention, punctuated only by bursts of applause. When he sat down a long roll of cheering went up that was heard as far away as Westminster Hall. He was followed by Bankes and several other Protestant members, including the new member for Oxford University, Sir Robert Inglis, who spoke poorly, and by Sir George Murray and Lord Milton in support of the government. But the House thinned rapidly at the conclusion of Peel's speech and after Milton had spoken the debate was adjourned to the following day.

It was a parliamentary triumph, and within forty-eight hours, when the provincial press had brought the text of his speech to towns and villages all over England, it was a national triumph as well. The cabinet shared in the glory and the gratification. 'He spoke very well indeed—better than he ever did before,' recorded Ellenborough. 'I never saw the world in better humour than it was tonight in the House. Even the protestants did not seem very ill-humoured. Such is the effect of a good speech.' The sardonic and worldly-wise Greville, while complaining that the speech was full of Peel's never-failing fault, egotism, admitted that it was certainly very able, clear, and statesmanlike, and the peroration very eloquent. 'The University of Oxford should have been there in a body to hear the member they have rejected and him whom they have chosen in his place.' A more impressionable member, J. C. Hobhouse, said much the same in more sympathetic language. 'Peel spoke for four hours and a quarter—admirably—indeed, a great deal better than I had ever heard him before; for although there was nothing new in his argument, yet he gave an ingenious turn to many points, and his concluding sentences were in the highest degree oratorical and affecting.'[1]

Up in Staffordshire the Birmingham newspapers containing the speech arrived at Drayton Manor on the afternoon of Friday 6 March, less than twenty-four hours after it had been uttered. Dean Cockburn, Peel's brother-in-law, read it aloud to Sir Robert after dinner and as the old man listened, he continually interrupted with ejaculations of a style familiar to friends and relations—'Robin's the lad after all'—'no administration can stand in this country without him'—'the Duke could do nothing without him'—'these

[1] Broughton, *Recollections*, III, 308-9.

gentlemen, the whigs, have no chance of getting in while Robert lives'. Everything else was drowned in his son's moment of fame and for the rest of the evening, while they played an interminable rubber of whist, he continued to pour out new commendations between every deal. But if Sir Robert could be carried away by the exultation of the hour, others could not; and beneath the shining surface of universal praise ran a darker current. As they listened to the lucid and powerful flow of his arguments in the House, or read his speech in the closely-printed press columns next day, men had almost forcibly to remind themselves that this was Peel, the Protestant champion, that was speaking. 'It was difficult to believe our senses,' wrote Hobhouse. 'Lord Sefton sitting next to me, said to me in his manner every now and then, "My God, did you ever hear anything like that? There he goes, bowling them down, one after another, Wilmot Horton and all!" '[1] The immediate impact of the speech was bound to be diminished by time; and as it diminished, the recollection of his past actions would recur with increasing force. Peel's triumph was achieved at a price, and the price remained to be paid.

Meanwhile the debate continued. Whigs and Canningites like Burdett, Sir John Newport, Charles Grant, and Huskisson, gave their vocal support to the government. Against them the old Protestant party, now shorn of all men of talent, found further undistinguished advocates in Estcourt, the other Oxford member, and Viscount Corry, who founded his change of attitude, after seconding the king's speech, on the absence of sufficient safeguards in the ministerial bill. Even Jonathan Peel made one of his rare excursions into debate to proclaim his opposition to the measure. The stormy feelings aroused by the crisis and the presentation of numerous petitions for and against the bill tended to slow down proceedings; but after a long debate on the night of 6 March the House decided by a majority of 188 to go into committee and accepted a resolution from Peel on the expediency of repealing the laws imposing civil disabilities on Roman Catholics. Over thirty members who had been expected to support voted against the government, including all Lord Lonsdale's followers. Even so, it was a two to one majority, ample for the immediate purpose of carrying the bill. Early the

[1] *ibid.*

following week leave was obtained to bring in the Relief and Disfranchisement Bills. They were introduced and read a first time on 10 March, and after a week's interval the debate proper began on 17 March.

For the government Goulburn, who was not a good speaker, made little impression on the opening night, but better support for the bill was forthcoming from Robert Grant and Palmerston. The main features of the opposition attack, though it included speeches by two prominent leaders of the country gentry, Knatchbull and George Bankes, were provided by Sadler and Wetherell. Sadler, who had been recently brought in for the Duke of Newcastle's borough of Newark expressly to oppose the bill, made a maiden speech full of emotion and with some eloquent touches, though he repeated the unpleasant innuendo that the ministers who had left Canning in 1827, and joined in hunting him down to his death, had been moved by anything but principle. Wetherell, though still in office, delivered a coarse and savage attack on his colleagues, particularly the Lord Chancellor, for their 'miserable, contemptible apostasy' and announced that Peel had only told him of the measure seven days before the start of the session. Some of the whigs had been urging Mackintosh to reply, but he went across to ask Peel what his wishes were and Peel said that he would answer Wetherell himself. Though in a passion of temper himself, he controlled his feelings admirably. Rising to a storm of cheering and counter-cheeering, he observed that about three-fourths of the Attorney-General's speech, ostensibly on the bill and in defence of the sacred cause of the Protestant constitution, had consisted of personal observation, personal imputation, and rancorous personal hostility; and he charged Wetherell with breach of confidence in disclosing matters only learned in his official capacity. As for the time when Wetherell had first learned of the bill, 'for a man who had that evening expressed such horror at what he now seemed to consider so atrocious a proceeding, he had never seen anyone who kept such complete control over his countenance as the hon. and learned gentleman did on that occasion'. Dropping Wetherell, he turned his offensive first against the arguments of Knatchbull, whose speech the previous night had been largely directed against Peel, and then to the criticisms of other opposition speakers. Once more he offered a forthright defence of expediency in government. To one speaker who apparently meant 'to class political emergencies with moral obligations, and to exclude the considerations of expediency from the management of public affairs, all that he would say was this —that he hoped the hon. gentleman and those who thought with him, might never have any influence in the direction of the affairs of this country'.

He ended on a generous note. Various speakers had given him credit for ending the Catholic controversy which he did not deserve. 'The credit belongs to others and not to me. It belongs to Mr. Fox, to Mr. Grattan, to Mr. Plunket, to the gentlemen opposite, and to an illustrious and right hon. friend of mine who is now no more. By their efforts, in spite of my opposition, it has proved victorious.' The reference to Canning led him to a brief mention of the charges that had been made in the debate.

> Whoever did join in the inhuman cry against him, I was not one. I was on terms of the most friendly intimacy with my right. hon. friend down even to the day of his death; and I say with as much sincerity of heart as man can speak, that I wish he were now alive to reap the harvest which he sowed and to enjoy the triumph which his exertions gained.

At the close of his speech Wetherell rose to deny any breach of official confidence, since he had not disclosed anything that Peel had stated to him on the occasion in question. 'Every gentleman will at once perceive,' retorted Peel coolly, 'that it may be extremely inconvenient for an officer of the government to take upon himself to state the precise moment at which a communication was officially made.' The House then divided and the bill passed by 180 votes after the two-day debate.

Next evening Peel was on his feet again with a short speech on the second reading of the Disfranchisement Bill. This had promised to be one of the most vulnerable parts of the government's programme, for many of the whigs who were lending their aid to the rest of the Catholic legislation were alienated by the penal aspect of the bill. Althorp and Spring Rice finally came to Arbuthnot in order to express in person their reluctance to disqualify existing franchises, and he took them to see Peel. They found him in no mood for compromise. He told them firmly that he could not give up the disfranchisement of the 40s. freeholders, for without it he could not hope to carry the bill; and for the same reason he refused to alter the main bill so as to allow O'Connell to take his seat for Co. Clare. The whig leaders returned to their followers and it was finally agreed by them that the settlement as a whole was so fair and satisfactory that they ought not to endanger it by opposing any part of it.[1] As a result of this whig party resolution the government obtained a majority of over 200 in a small House, the minority of seventeen including such incongruous bedfellows as Palmerston, Herries, and Bankes, with a few of their friends and followers. The succeeding week, 23-27 March, was largely taken up by a detailed consideration of the Relief Bill in committee. Various amendments were proposed and objections put forward. It was said that the bill conflicted with the terms of the Union with Scotland; it was proposed to add the First Lord of the Treasury and others to the list of excepted officeholders. Peel in turn brought up a few amendments of detail; one to allow the patronage of an office held by a Catholic to be vested in the Archbishop of Canterbury instead of a Crown Commissioner; and another to give power to the Secretary of State to license individual Jesuits to enter the country for a limited period. All the substantial opposition amendments were defeated, and on 30 March Peel was able to move the third reading of the bill.

Much of his speech he employed in answering Wetherell, now dismissed from office, who had delivered one last, furious, but disjointed onslaught; but he ended as on earlier occasions with a vindication of the right of politicians to alter their course according to changing needs. 'That has been the opinion of all former statesmen, at all times, and in all countries. My defence is the same, with that of all others under similar circumstances.' With a final apt Ciceronian quotation he sat down; Inglis and Sadler followed, and were answered by Fitzgerald. The House then divided for the last time, and the third reading of the bill passed by 320 votes to 142, a majority of 178, to the accompaniment of much cheering and throwing up of hats. The same night the Disfranchisement Bill was read a third time and passed by an even greater majority. It was the

[1] Broughton, *Recollections*, III, p. 309; *Arbuthnot Journal*, II, 250.

end of the great Catholic conflict in the House of Commons. Next day, in the incongruous company of Dawson, Fyshe Palmer, and Robert Wilson, and followed by nearly a hundred other members, Peel took the Catholic Relief Bill to the House of Lords where the Lord Chancellor with a smile on his handsome face received it from his hands. On 10 April the bill passed its third reading in the upper House by a two to one majority and on 13 April received the royal assent.

To the end the Protestant party fought desperately and bitterly for their lost cause; and the passionate denunciations of Wetherell and Knatchbull in the Commons were only a reflection of the violent feelings without. From the day of the king's speech it was clear that emancipation in some form was bound to come, but it was possible even then to hope for limitations on Catholics and securities for Protestants which would soften the shock. Peel's speech of 5 March, however, opened the floodgates of Protestant feeling, for it was revealed at last that what was intended was complete surrender, with no guarantees and no securities. The ultra-Protestants were justified in their worst anticipations; those who had trusted in Wellington and Peel not to leave them entirely defenceless were all the more alienated. Their mortification was expressed in every shade of emotion from saddened elegies on the destruction of the old constitution to gross personal attacks on the chief ministers—Wellington the soldier and Peel the weaver—who had ratted and betrayed them. At one point indeed the personal savagery evoked came near to shedding blood. Lord Winchilsea charged Wellington with having previously supported the foundation of the new Anglican college in London—King's College—as 'a blind to the Protestant and High Church party', so that under the cloak of outward zeal he could carry out his design for 'the infringement of our liberties, and the introduction of Popery in every department of the State'. Wellington promptly sent a challenge to Winchilsea and the two men fought a duel in Battersea Fields on 21 March. The Duke inevitably was criticised for deigning to notice his traducer; but equally so, Peel was criticised for refusing to challenge Wetherell. In the heated state of political society whatever the two ministers did was impugned; and even when the parliamentary contest was over, the ugly ground-swell of feeling persisted.

Vicious as were the passions raised by the crisis of 1829, however, the intensity of feeling on the Protestant side was not incomprehensible. If the liberals regarded emancipation as the long-delayed rectification of a social injustice, the Protestants saw in it the overthrow of the principle on which the constitution stood. Repeatedly a phrase used by Peel about 'breaking in upon the constitution' was cited as a complete condemnation of what he proposed; and here at least their instinct was right. The Act of 1829 was a sentence of death on the Anglican settlement made at the 1688 Revolution. By comparison the repeal of the Test and Corporation Acts the previous year was of secondary significance. Not only were those Acts for all practical purposes long obsolete, but the dissenters themselves could be regarded in some sense as members—if dissenting members—of the Established Church. The Emancipation Act, however, made a fundamental change and a deliberate revolution. Consciously and rightly the Protestant party felt that the country had come to the end of an historic period; and what the future would bring they could only speculate with foreboding. It was not just a question of liberal principle or passing factional conflict, but of a real alteration in the form and character of the constitution. A leading article in the *Courier*, after observing that the conflict 'has inflamed our public discussion, interfered with the relations of private life, checked the career of commercial enterprise, and diverted the attention of men of all classes', went on to emphasise 'that it should produce such effects cannot excite surprise, when we consider that a measure of greater importance has never occupied the attention of the Legislature for more than a century'.[1] This judgement was the more impressive since the *Courier*, though opposing the bill, had been unusually restrained and moderate in its language and had never indulged in personal vituperation against the ministers. In whatever form the final defeat of the Protestant party had come, therefore, it would have left its bitterness; but that it should have been inflicted on them by their own leaders was the last humiliation. The sense of helpless betrayal in the face of the government's decision to sponsor the bill engendered a fierce resentment that was slow to disappear.

There was one last minute alarm. A meeting was advertised for

[1] 30 March 1829.

10 April in London to organise a procession to Windsor and there deliver a petition against the bill to the Duke of Cumberland for presentation to the king. Wellington warned the king not to receive any petitions except through the Home Secretary; and Peel, having first taken precautions against riot, went down to Windsor to be in readiness. But the demonstration, organised by a certain John Halcomb, secretary of the London and Westminster Protestant Society, proved a fiasco. Halcomb and a handful of supporters drove to Windsor in carriages, were told by an equerry that their petition must be presented through a Secretary of State, and went quietly away.[1] On this note of anti-climax the Protestant storm died away. London itself was quiet, despite the placards, posters, and chalked *No Popery* signs that disfigured the streets. Though the cartoonists revelled in the crisis, the press and influential opinion in the capital were preponderantly behind the government.[2] During the Oxford election contest, the Lord Mayor had made a proposal to confer on Peel the Freedom of the City; and the Common Council voted accordingly at the end of February. Now, on 8 April, the ceremony took place. The Freedom was presented to Peel in a gold box; he made a speech in reply; and in the evening dined at the Guildhall in great state with the Lord Mayor and Corporation. Six weeks and sixty miles separated that festive scene in London from the angry hustings at Oxford. It was in its way a symbolic and perhaps an irrevocable transition.

But it was not only the confidence of Oxford that Peel had lost. He had once been the idolised champion of the Protestant party; that party now regarded him as an outcast. Even if they gave him credit—and some did—for honesty of motive and unselfishness of action, they could still only look upon what he had done as desertion. And desertion, on such an issue and after so many years of leadership, brought with it profound suspicions of Peel's own character that had never occurred to anyone before. Perhaps the hardest punishment for so proud a man to bear was not the bitter disappointment of friends and followers, but the damage to his own reputation which was the permanent legacy of that disappointment. It was a

[1] 40399 f. 134; *Ellenborough*, II, 9-11.
[2] cf. diary of Mr. Justice Day who was in London during the last stages of the bill.

change of feeling that he could not only hear in speeches and read in the press but witness among some of his closest friends. With Gregory in Ireland, for example, his relations were never the same again. What particularly hurt the Under-Secretary was the inescapable air of deception that surrounded the government's actions. In writing to Goulburn in February 1829 to express his sorrow and regret at 'the unexpected course adopted by you and Peel', he added with unmistakable bitterness,

> By both your statements, you both appear to have had the matter under consideration for some time, and it is only the avowal that is sudden. But I who was ignorant of such alterations in your opinions vainly thought I was continuing to act under the men on whom my reliance was so firmly placed as the most sincere supporters of our Protestant establishment, and in proportion to my Confidence, so is my disappointment.[1]

After Catholic emancipation he ceased to sign his letters to Peel 'affectionately yours' as before, but merely 'ever' or 'most truly yours'. Not until six years had passed did he acknowledge a kindly letter from Peel (about the successes of Gregory's grandson at Harrow) with a note written in a shaky hand but ending 'very affectionately yours'. Another friend, Lord Talbot, more commonplace and easy-going than Gregory, nevertheless reacted to Peel's 'conversion' in a manner typical of many men of his class and opinions. 'I hope,' he wrote to Gregory in April, 'I shall not be reproached with a wish to derogate from his character, if I say that in future I *cannot confide* in his stability.'[2] Many months were to pass before Peel's transformation of opinion over emancipation ceased to be a major topic of conversation; and even when other subjects drove it from men's minds, they never forgot. He had given a hostage to fortune; and it was irredeemable.

Meanwhile his father had written affectionately from Drayton.

> I am happy to learn that, having been exposed to every species of difficulty, you continue in pretty good health and spirits. Human nature cannot, however, long escape the effect of extreme irritation.

[1] 40334 f. 284.     [2] *Letter-Box*, p. 310.

Let me therefore persuade you to embrace the first opportunity of bringing dear Julia and the children to Drayton, and reposing as long as possible in the bosom of peace. . . . Planting has been in active progress at Tammoor, and your farm is in a visible state of improvement, aided by skill and industry.

## II

Catholic emancipation was achieved. The most controversial issue in British domestic politics had been settled, and the consequences were permanent both for the country and for Peel's own career. Statutes that merely remove outmoded restrictions are apt not to receive very close examination, and the greater part of the attention given to Catholic emancipation was directed to its principle rather than its detail. Yet as an act of fundamental legislation, apart from the principle it enshrined, the measure had great merit. Its supreme statesmanship was its simplicity. The few exceptions made to the admission of Roman Catholics to civil equality were too slight to create grievance, too firmly based to invite early revision. More important still, the refusal to enter into any organic relationship with the Roman Church precluded a host of prospective difficulties. Such a connection could only have been in the form of a lay and Protestant supervision of Catholic spiritual organisation, and it is hard not to believe that had it been established, it would have produced recurrent friction and conflict.

All that was deliberately avoided; there was to be no *Kulturkampf* in Victorian England. As it was, the storm that produced Russell's Ecclesiastical Titles Bill in 1851 was enough to indicate the kind of emotional and futile controversy that any well-intentioned religious safeguards passed in 1829 would inevitably have produced. Yet in abandoning the vain hope for securities, the 1829 Act turned aside from all previous solutions of the Catholic question. Any measure of emancipation that might have been forced through parliament before that year would almost certainly have been clogged by restrictions on the Catholic Church, if only as an inducement for the Protestants to accept the bill. Up to the last there were strong arguments, both of expediency and policy, for using the opportunity of emancipation to impose some measure of control over the

Roman ecclesiastic organisation in Britain. Wellington himself was a strong advocate of ecclesiastical securities and fought to the end for their retention. Substantially, however, they were all discarded and the bill that finally passed through parliament was a more clear-cut, radical solution than had ever been likely before. For this the responsibility lay primarily with Peel. Not the least consequence of his continued membership of the cabinet after 1828 was that he was able to put his own decisive stamp on the actual measures laid before parliament. Yet the long discussions in the cabinet in the early months of 1829 showed how closely the issue was balanced and how nearly the decision could have gone the other way. If the will to bring about Catholic emancipation was equally shared by Peel and Wellington, the form that emancipation took was due principally to the younger man. It was the Peelite and not the Wellingtonian formula that the cabinet adopted; and it is impossible to assume that the result would have been the same had Peel resigned office beforehand. When it was all over and the bill safe, Ellenborough wrote a handsome acknowledgement to the Home Secretary. 'I congratulate you on the passing of the bill. We owe its principle to you. We should all have gone wrong without you, and have attempted to introduce restrictions, securities, etc. We might have lost the bill and I am convinced it would not have produced tranquillity if we had carried it.'[1]

For the public at large, however, it was the mere fact that Peel did stay in office that aroused most interest and most controversy. Not Peel's effect on Catholic emancipation, but the effect of Catholic emancipation on Peel seemed the important aspect. Long afterwards, in a measured and intelligent review of the Catholic episode, Greville delivered an opinion that might stand as the considered verdict of many, perhaps most of his countrymen then and later. 'Historical justice demands that a large deduction should be made from Peel's reputation as a statesman and a patriot on account of his conduct through the last twelve years of the Catholic contest.'[2] At the time the main charges against Peel resolved themselves into two: that he changed his mind when he did; and that he had not changed it earlier. On the surface both are easy to refute. To argue, as Knatchbull did, that there was no new threat from Ireland in 1828 that did

---

[1] 40399 f. 148.     [2] *Greville*, 6 July 1850.

not exist in earlier years was to ignore the general election of 1826, the growth of the Catholic Association, its alliance with the priesthood and the peasantry, and the final challenge of the Clare election. Not Peel alone but the mass of informed and expert opinion in the Irish and English executives held that a potentially revolutionary situation had been created. To meet that situation by repression was to provoke the defection of most of the Irish county constituencies, a silent defiance of the constitution, a final breach between the Anglo-Irish landlords and their tenantry, and a paralysis of Irish local administration. Whether even that menacing prospect could have been met by firm resistance was perhaps a different matter; but to deny the existence of the crisis was foolish. It was also foolish to suggest that Peel should have allowed himself to be converted in 1827 and have assisted Canning in passing emancipation at that date. Then indeed it would have been pertinent to enquire what new lights had dawned upon him; and the inevitable conclusion would have been drawn that he had thrown over his convictions in order to remain in office. The obloquy that greeted him in 1829 would only have been anticipated, and with an appearance of greater justice, in 1827. The general approval and understanding for Peel's resignation on the formation of Canning's ministry among friends and opponents alike was a measure of the abuse and contempt he would have earned had he acted differently.

Yet behind and perhaps within the unreflecting personal rancour of dull men like Knatchbull and violent men like Wetherell, there was a real case which Greville later expressed in more rational and sober language. It was that for fourteen years Peel had led the Protestant party against a host of abler men, and by his personal efforts prolonged a hopeless contest which by reason of its prolongation brought the country at last to the brink of civil war. 'I do not see how he can be acquitted of insincerity,' wrote Greville, 'save at the expense of his sagacity and foresight.' If this was the charge, it was one that the accused himself with unwitting anticipation of the exact phrase had already acknowledged in his own private retrospect of the events of these years.

If it had been alleged against me that the sudden adoption of a different policy had proved the want of early sagacity and foresight on my part—if the charge had been that I had adhered with too much pertinacity to a hopeless cause—that I had permitted for too long a period the engagements of party or undue deference to the wishes of constituents to outweigh the accumulating evidence of an approaching necessity—if this had been the accusation against me, I might find it more difficult to give it a complete and decisive refutation.[1]

Not lack of prescience, perhaps, so much as delay in accepting the inevitable was the gravamen of the charge against Peel.

But politics is not merely an exercise in the art of prevision. The politician is also a creature of his time and a combatant in the struggle of forces which it is his duty to resolve. The cause for which Peel stood was lost in the end, but it would be cynicism to require men to abstain from conflict unless they are on the winning side. Peel himself was not without foresight on the outcome of the emancipation movement. He had been impressed early in his career by the passivity of Protestant feeling in the House of Commons and from 1819 onwards, if not 1817, he realised that the tide of opinion was on the side of emancipation and that it was only a question of time before it was carried to success. By 1826, if not earlier, he had arrived at a state in which he almost wished to be persuaded that the passing of Catholic Relief would end Irish discontents. Far more accurately than the parsons on their glebes or the squires in their provincial manor-houses he was able to gauge the swiftness with which the parliamentary basis of Anglican supremacy was crumbling away. But the consciousness that he was fighting a losing battle did not make him change his views. By temperament and upbringing he was a Church politician, and that position had been strengthened by the formal duty he owed to his university constituency. His task, as he envisaged it, was to fight to the end against emancipation; and when it came, to make as good terms as he could for the Anglican Church. What he did not foresee was that he would ever be placed in circumstances that would require him to be the author and parliamentary sponsor of a Catholic bill. But though in the end he yielded to that unexpected and brutal necessity, his judgement on the ultimate effects of emancipation remained unshaken; and on that

[1] *Peel Memoirs*, I, 364.

his pessimism was infinitely more prescient than the shallow optimism of those liberals who hailed emancipation as the dawn of a new era in Anglo-Irish relations. What was principally relevant in Peel's case, therefore, were other considerations: the reasons for his original opposition to Catholic claims, and the reasons for his conclusion in 1828 that the issue must be conceded.

The first must be sought both in his background and early environment, and in his initial political experiences. Born of a later generation than Canning or Castlereagh, he did not share the scepticism and cosmopolitan rationalism of the eighteenth-century aristocracy. He came from an old-fashioned family of plebeian stock and was nurtured in a traditional piety towards Church and State. He grew to manhood at a time when England, intellectually and physically, was isolated from the continent by a long and desperate war. At the same time his talents and character ensured him encouragement and success in the established institutions of society to which his father's wealth procured him access. It was natural therefore that his early views expanded easily into the orthodoxy of Harrow and Oxford. Yet that is not to deprive those views of any intellectual content. There was or at least there had been a case for Catholic disabilities, though it rested on assumptions increasingly unpalatable to prevailing modes of thought after 1815. The case for the Catholics scarcely needs recapitulation. Liberalism, equality, and expediency all spoke in their favour. What was the case against them? It was primarily historical. In 1689, as Eldon once reminded the House of Lords, it had been resolved 'that this country should have a Protestant King, a Protestant Parliament, and a Protestant Government'.[1] Under the constitution that had thus evolved, Britain had found domestic peace, imperial greatness, and material prosperity. By 1815 that constitution had stood the test of time as no other comparable European state had done. Religious toleration had been granted; but political equality was a different matter. To most educated men of Peel's generation the state was a structure of a special kind, raised upon specific principles. To grant Catholic emancipation, that is to say equality of rights, was to abandon those principles and so to weaken the whole structure. Eldon was one of the intellectual tories who opposed emancipation

[1] Twiss, *Eldon*, II, 330.

to the last and there was something not undignified in their stubborn adherence to a lost cause. They had a sense of the greatness and good fortune of England, and of the frailties and errors of human nature when deprived of the stability of historic institutions and an ordered tradition. Nor were some of them without a conviction that religion could not be separated from the state without damage to both. To admit Catholics to the constitution was to begin the process of dividing Church from State.

With all this Peel was fundamentally in sympathy. Not only did he feel the danger in any wilful tampering with a structure that alone among the great powers of Europe had stood the shock of the French Revolution and the Napoleonic dictatorship, but he had a particular reluctance to alter that structure in a way that affected the position of the Established Church. A believing and practising Christian, he looked upon the Anglican Church as the formal institution which bound state and society together in the exercise of religion. With Eldon he could have asserted that the reason for the Establishment was not that politics should be brought into religion, but that religion should be brought into politics. A Protestant as much as an Anglican, he also regarded the Established Church as the main bulwark in the British Isles against Roman Catholicism. Even in his Anglicanism he was disposed to take a lower and more Protestant line than his old High Church college tutor, Bishop Lloyd, always approved. There was an example of this in 1825 when to certain doubts expressed by Peel on the complete authority of every minister of the Church to absolve even repentant sinners, Lloyd half-jestingly replied 'I must needs tell you that in regard to the great doctrine of Christianity you are little better than a heretic.' It was this innate Protestant outlook in the first place, therefore, that bred in him a deep if rarely expressed distrust of Roman Catholicism as a Church claiming for its priests a spiritual authority to which he could not assent and exercising it in a manner which he regarded as intolerable. With his Lancastrian forebears he inherited a share of the profound English feeling against Catholicism whose roots ran back to the time of Mary Tudor; and when he went to Ireland he saw little to make him believe that the Roman Church had changed its nature. It was significant that even in 1825 he had argued against giving the Catholic priesthood any civil position in the state; and his

decisive opposition to ecclesiastical securities in the cabinet deliberations of 1829 owed as much perhaps to his essential hostility to the
character of the Catholic Church as to considerations of either
parliamentary tactics or administrative obstacles.

It is obvious in retrospect that the greater danger confronting the
Establishment was not the rise of a powerful intolerant Roman
Catholicism, taking its leadership from abroad and seeking to undermine the remaining institutions of the historic Protestant state, but
the slower more pervasive growth of secular liberalism, sceptical or
indifferent in matters of religion, and increasingly nourished by a
rational and semi-scientific attitude to the problems of society. But
these were influences of which the full force had not yet been
developed and which were alien to many of the protagonists on both
sides in the emancipation struggle. Toleration in British as in
European history came more as a product of exhaustion than conviction. But already there was a sufficient decline of fervent Protestantism in English society at large and a sufficient confidence in
the loyalty of English Roman Catholics to make their complete
legal rehabilitation a relatively easy process. Whatever his private
instincts and prejudices, Peel would have accepted emancipation for
the English Catholics as for English Protestant dissenters. But the
real stumbling-block was Ireland. It was this that transformed the
Catholic question from an academic controversy into an issue of
national politics.

In essence that problem was what it had always been: a question
of the unity and security of the British Isles. Since the battle of the
Boyne the Anglo-Irish connection had rested on a Protestant foundation and Pitt's Act of Union had been only a particular measure
to tighten the connection at a time of great danger. But though
Ireland had been conquered, it had never been assimilated. In the
nineteenth century it still offered the spectacle of an alien and discontented people, separated from the larger island by water and
history, and ruled by the executive power of the British government
based on a minority of the population which itself was detached by
race, rank, and religion from the mass of the Irish people. It was not
a situation created or desired by that government; it was the situation that confronted it. What haunted Peel, and many others, was
the fear that concessions on the matter of religion would lead to

other demands, and those in the end to disruption and independence. He found it impossible not to believe that the Catholic majority in Ireland would use every acquisition of political power to keep their interest distinct from that of the Protestant minority. If so, the outcome could only be first the undermining and destruction of the Protestant interest, and then the final separation of the two kingdoms. Of the artificial nature of the Union, and the abuses by Protestants to which it led, he had no need to be persuaded. It was, as he said in 1821, a choice of two evils and if he could be convinced that the concession of Catholic claims would lead to peace and concord, he would have abandoned his opposition. He was not so convinced, and he was forced back therefore on the lesser of the two evils: the continuation of the Union on its Protestant footing. Even so, he was not unhopeful that something could be done within that framework. Many of the evils of Ireland did not, in his opinion, come from the religious disabilities of the Catholics; and by patient continuous administration—education, poor relief, improved justice, better police, more constant attendance by landlords to their duties —much might be achieved. It was a limited and a long-term programme but at least it was not an acceptance of an unalterable condition of things.

What became increasingly questionable was whether time and opportunity would be provided for that programme. The divisions in parliament and the country brought the question of emancipation under almost yearly review; the divisions in the cabinet hampered the evolution of any coherent policy; and after Peel left Ireland in 1818 the principle of a divided administration was extended in a more serious form to the Irish executive itself. When he became Home Secretary in 1822 he might have hoped to restore some unity and direction by his own superintendence of Irish affairs; but by 1825 the essential basis of parliamentary support was beginning to give way. That year rather than 1827 was the first crucial time of decision. It was a crisis of Catholic affairs, not in Ireland but in the will and ability of the British governing class to maintain the policy of 1812. Three ministers saw the crisis clearly—Peel, Canning, and Liverpool. All in their different ways and according to the nature of their positions, made some attempt to resolve the crisis; and all three drew back under a common threat. But Peel, at least, went as far or farther than the other two. For him there was no question of conversion or of new lights on the subject; the problem, despite the rise of the Catholic Association, was not different from what it had been. Peel did not abandon belief in his own policy, but for a time he did give up hope that parliament would enable him to continue it and he offered his resignation accordingly. He was induced to withdraw his resignation by the most powerful and affecting plea that could have been made to a politician in his position. It was made clear to him that his retirement would cause the collapse of the government; and Bathurst warned him, in however friendly a tone, of the trouble and convulsions in the country for which he would be responsible if he persisted in his intention. To speak, as Greville did, of lack of patriotism in the course that he chose was to ignore the perennial truth that patriotism offers many roads and that often the difficulty is not to do one's duty but to know what one's duty is. The responsibility for maintaining a neutral policy on the Catholic issue after 1825, with only the frail guarantee of Liverpool's life and the House of Lords' veto to protect it, rested on the cabinet as a whole; and even Canning, though he raised, refrained from pressing the issue at that time.

So another year passed, with Peel envisaging the certain ultimate victory of emancipation and already considering what terms could best be made for the security of Protestants when the time came.[1] In one of the momentary eddies of opinion that marked if it did not conceal the slow recession of Protestant strength, the new parliament in 1827 reversed by a fragile majority of four votes the decision of 1825. But there was no security in this, and meanwhile the Irish election results the previous year offered a clear warning that the conflict over Catholic civil disabilities was becoming a conflict with the organised weight of the Roman Church. It was a development that confirmed Peel's innate conviction of the secular object of Catholic clerical power in Ireland; but if he still uttered a hope that the victory of the priests would be only temporary, it was a sign of his tenacity rather than of his judgement. When 1827 came, it was not so much a crisis for Peel as a deliverance. He could do then what he had wished to do in 1825, and without the ulterior consequences

[1] cf. letter to Leslie Foster, 3 November 1826, *Peel*, I, 422.

which Liverpool and Bathurst had presented to him two years earlier. It was the first and the only opportunity since 1812 to settle the Catholic question on natural lines, at the hands of a Prime Minister who was the leading advocate of a settlement and supported by a cabinet of preponderantly identical views. But even Canning was still enmeshed in the toils of a political system which made this of all questions painfully difficult to bring to a conclusion. What he could or would do was known only to Canning, and he carried the secret of his intentions to the grave. He left the Liverpool party in ruins and the problem of emancipation unsolved.

With the death of Canning and the collapse of the Goderich residuum of Canning's ministry, the last alternative disappeared. From that point events moved inexorably to the final act. It is barely conceivable that Peel might have made a settlement of the Catholic issue a condition of joining Wellington's ministry. There is no reason to suppose either that he had come to that necessity or that the condition would have been accepted. But whether before or after the Clare election, the result would have been the same. All that Clare did was to destroy any last hope that a six-year interval of suspense would separate 1826 from the next trial of electoral strength; and destroy it in a manner which brought to a head the powers and pretensions of the Catholic Association. With the House of Commons once more declaring in favour of emancipation, and a ministry still divided on the issue, Peel was at last driven to the conclusion that further resistance was useless. Five months experience of governing Ireland under the new conditions had been enough to convince him that the opportunity for an ameliorative administration had passed. 'It was not tolerable,' he wrote to his father afterwards, 'that men should remain in the position in which Lord Anglesey, Lord Francis Gower, and I were placed, pretending to govern a country in a state of distraction like Ireland, and yet differing as we differed on the cause and the cure of the agitation.' With the abandonment of the administrative solution, the only other course was to try the effects of religious conciliation. Only two issues remained: whether Wellington's government would deal with the crisis or make way for another that could; and whether, if it chose to act, Peel himself should remain in office.

On the first there could be little dispute; no visible alternative in fact existed to the ministry already in office. A government of resistance was out of the question; a liberal-whig government could have been formed with little less difficulty. It would have lacked command of the legislature and would have encountered at its inception the opposition of the king. To talk, indeed, in terms of parties is to falsify the situation. No organised opposition ready and able to take over the government existed. Moreover, the issue was literally not one of men but of measures, or at least of one specific measure. Wellington's ministry, in its corporate capacity, was not hostile to Catholic claims; like all its predecessors since 1812 it was neutral. What it required was permission to consider the question as it had considered other national questions. It would be time enough for the ministers to go out, when the king refused to allow them to go on. Their initial duty was to advise the king that the question would have to be dealt with by the government; but having advised the measure, they could hardly have resigned the task to another set of men. There was no question of reversing cabinet policy on Ireland; merely of insisting that a cabinet policy on Ireland must be formulated. Wellington himself had earlier shown that he had an open mind on the emancipation issue; and now that the crisis in Ireland had arrived, both he and Peel regarded it as their self-evident constitutional duty to act as responsible executive ministers. It was to the crown and the country and not to a party that their obligation lay. Indeed, it seemed to Peel that if the crisis was to be ended, it was indispensable that the government should stay in office. That conviction was also a sentence on himself; for as in 1825, and in language scarcely less compelling, he was made to feel that on his continuance in office depended the fate of the ministry and of the measure they prescribed. He made his final decision on grounds of national interest, and as he wrote himself afterward, through 'no fear except the fear of public calamity'. The long interval between July 1828 and January 1829 was an index of the struggle between his sense of public duty and his foreknowledge of the personal cost.

Yet it was not that Peel had changed his essential views. It was that when weighed against the situation of 1828 those views no longer tilted the balance. The choice of evils remained, but the lesser evils of 1825 had now become the greater. The process was one of political and not intellectual conversion: a not uncommon event in politics. He remained sceptical of the ultimate benefits claimed for emancipation by its more uncritical supporters, but he had become convinced of its immediate necessity. With no real change of belief, he had come to the conclusion that the government no longer had the power to act on his belief, and that only danger could come from such an attempt. He had in fact misjudged the situation. The power of the Catholic Association had spread faster and further than he had anticipated; and the evils of divided counsels in Dublin Castle had robbed his distant control from Whitehall of most of its efficacy. But he had not totally misjudged it; and in the course of the next hundred years all his ultimate fears for the Church of Ireland, the fate of the Anglo-Irish aristocracy, and the safety of the Union were successively realised. The more optimistic liberals thought that emancipation would heal the breach between England and Ireland; Peel was afraid it would merely provide a platform for fresh agitation. They thought concession would lead to equality and peace; he feared that the Protestant ascendancy would merely be replaced by a Catholic ascendancy. He was right; and they were wrong. It could of course be argued that it was precisely the delay caused by Peel's leadership of the Protestant party that made the difference; that the Irish would have received as a grateful boon from Canning what they took as an extorted concession from Peel and Wellington. The antithesis is a rhetorical one, since Canning was never able to offer emancipation; and it is futile to speculate whether by an earlier change of opinion Peel could have induced Liverpool and his cabinet colleagues to abandon the sacred principle of neutrality. He was not master either of the ministry or the crown; at most his individual influence was a marginal or incidental one in the situation that existed before 1827. It would be a travesty to make any one man responsible for the governmental evasion of the Catholic issue in the thirty years following the Union. Two successive monarchs, and a whole line of cabinet ministers, including Pitt, Castlereagh, and Canning, must take their share of that responsibility. Not even the Grenville ministry of 1806 nor Canning's ministry of 1827 could see their way to an immediate grant of emancipation. For that the causes lay deep in the structure of English political society: the power of the crown, the looseness of the cabinet system of government, the independence of the legislature; and deeper still, in the emotions and prejudices of the English nation. In such circumstances only determined leadership, aided by the progress of events, could hope to achieve a decision. It was the merit of Peel and Wellington that they were the first ministers since Pitt prepared to use their executive powers to force that decision. Whatever else might be said of them, they had strength of mind and political courage.

Yet Peel had misjudged the situation earlier as far as his own limited sphere of influence was concerned; and it was here perhaps that the intangible associations of family, education, political ties, and university connection conspired with his own stubborn temperament to make him delay to the last his acceptance of the need to settle the Catholic question by concession. It was a misjudgement that had unusually severe consequences. Had a more organised and symmetrical system of party politics allowed another set of men to propose and enforce the solution, Peel could have contented himself with a moderate and critical opposition, out of office and relieved of all responsibility as a minister of the crown. If so, he would have been free from the abuse and vilification that was heaped on him in 1829 and for long afterwards. What men disliked was not that he had erred in his calculations, but that he had confounded their expectations. Few could know and even fewer appreciate the chain of events whereby he had been caught in a situation from which in the end his finer instincts forbade him to withdraw. But because he disappointed so many who previously had followed him, he became, as Greville observed, the scapegoat for the government. He had been the acknowledged leader of the Protestant party; his change of attitude was more striking; he took the leading role in conducting the offending measure through the House of Commons. The Duke of Wellington, though he had initiated the measure, fought the battle of the royal closet, and induced Peel to remain in office, was more exempt from criticism. He had never been in the foreground of the Protestant leadership; in the upper House he was out of immediate contact with the mass of tory Protestant politicians; and his prestige as the victor of Waterloo imposed a respect and restraint on his former followers which they did not feel towards the professional politician who led them in the Commons.[1] From the

[1] *Greville*, 6 July 1850.

start of the crisis, therefore, first in the cabinet and later in parliament, the passing of Catholic emancipation hinged on the position of Peel. That, in itself, was a mark of his stature in politics. He had reached the summit, but he was more isolated than he had ever been since he entered parliament twenty years earlier. It was a lonely and dangerous eminence.

CHAPTER

# 17

# THE LAST OF THE OLD RÉGIME

The passing of Catholic emancipation left the king sulky and irritable. Had his ill-humour been confined to sarcasms, little harm would have been done, but in addition his behaviour became increasingly capricious. Part of the trouble was due to his growing burden of physical malady which made him more than ever inclined to shirk the routine of official duties. When the ministry took office Peel discovered a two-year arrears of commissions at the War Office waiting for the royal signature, and the accumulation was still there in the autumn of 1828.[1] But not all the difficulties were due to illness. In November 1829, when the Recorder was ill, the king obstinately refused to receive his report from Denman, the Common Serjeant, who had wounded him with an unhappy classical allusion when defending the queen in 1820. The Council had to be postponed after an angry interview between king and Prime Minister in which, Wellington told Peel, 'he manifested the very worst temper'.[2] On several occasions George tried to deal with ministers behind the Duke's back. In the autumn of 1829, for example, he recommended Lord Conyngham as Constable of Windsor Castle and Lord Combermere as Colonel of the 1st Life Guards to Peel and Hardinge, the respective departmental heads, without notifying the Prime Minister. Wellington decided in the end to make no protest, though Peel told him that he would be prepared on any repetition of this official impropriety to inform the king that Secretaries of State could not forward instruments conferring appointments to the crown for signature without the sanction of the First Lord of the Treasury.[3]

For the Home Secretary the main interest of the 1829 session

[1] 40307 fos. 40, 262.    [2] 40308 f. 274; cf. *Arbuthnot Journal*, II, 314.
[3] *W.N.D.*, VI, 162-6, 181; 40308 fos. 240-2.

after the conclusion of the emancipation debates was his Metropolitan Police Bill. Profiting from the concentration of attention on
the major measure, and perhaps a certain emotional exhaustion
among Commons members, he shepherded his bill through to the
statute-book with a surprising lack of opposition. But there had
been other more controversial if more ephemeral issues. In May
O'Connell had tried to take his place in parliament, rejecting the
usual oaths and relying on the Emancipation Act. Peel spoke in
favour of allowing him to state his case at the bar of the House, but
the subsequent argument was left largely to the lawyers. In fact
there could be little dispute on the legal issue. The Act entitled only
those Roman Catholics who were elected subsequent to its passing
to take their seats with the new form of oath. Short of retrospective
legislation, with its obvious drawbacks, it was impossible to admit
O'Connell. A new writ was issued for Co. Clare and O'Connell
was returned unopposed at the end of July, a month after the close
of the session.

Before the Commons completed their labours, however, there
was a small but significant demonstration of the lengths to which
ultra-tory discontent might go. At the beginning of June the Marquess of Blandford, the heir to the great ducal house of Marlborough, moved two resolutions of protest against rotten and
nomination boroughs on the grounds that Catholic emancipation
had proved the unrepresentative character of the House and that it
was now necessary to guard against the indiscriminate entry by
private influence of Catholic M.P.s. His motion was heavily
defeated in a thin House; yet if one effect of emancipation was to be
the emergence of an eccentric tory radicalism, the pattern of voting
in the Commons was likely to be more confused than ever. Already
the standing weakness of the government in the lower House was
causing concern to ministers. Hardinge reckoned at the end of the
session that they could count on fifty fewer supporters than in
Lord Liverpool's time; and a swing of fifty to the opposition meant
a difference of a hundred in a division.[1] However, these were cares
that for the moment could be put aside and on 14 June, in the
dying session, Peel was able to enjoy in his house the company of a
congenial and largely unpolitical dinner-party at which were

[1] *Ellenborough*, II, 60.

present Moore, Rogers, and Luttrell among the literary men, Smirke and Wyatville the architects, Wilkie and 'God knows how many artists besides', recorded Moore. 'The evening most lovely, and the effect of the water and St. Paul's, etc., etc., from Peel's balcony beautiful.'[1]

It had been a hard session, and the Home Secretary's attention had necessarily been spread over a wider field than the parliamentary scenes that monopolised the public mind. Few reports of industrial unrest had come in during 1828 other than evidence of the continuous activities of trade unions; but early in the following summer there was trouble again in Lancashire and Cheshire. Riots broke out at Manchester and Macclesfield; the yeomanry were called out at Wigan and Bolton; and at Stockport the Riot Act was read and the troops ordered to fire, though the mob dispersed without bloodshed. The government reinforced the troops under General Sir Henry Bouverie in the Northern District, and arms were made available to manufacturers for the protection of their property. Though the immediate disorders died down in May, there was continual friction throughout the summer between masters and men in Lancashire, and a number of strikes and lockouts in Manchester. From long experience in such matters, Peel followed a sparing and calculated policy. To Lord Stanley in May he wrote that while regretting the suffering and privation, 'to which alone any disposition to acts of insubordination and outrage appears to be ascribable', it was impossible for the government to devise any quick and effective solution for widespread distress.[2] At the end of June he utilised some of his new-found freedom from parliamentary distractions to write to a correspondent at Rochdale who had been making representations to the Home Office on the great and growing evils of combination among workmen. He promised to confer with the President of the Board of Trade on the subject, but emphasised at the same time the difficulty of contriving any legal control over the organisation and communication which naturally grew up among workpeople in all districts; and he threw doubts on the expediency of any fresh legislation designed to strengthen the existing statutes.[3] On the other hand, when in the autumn Doherty

---

[1] Moore, *Memoirs*, VI, 54.    [2] H.O. 41/7/463.
[3] *ibid.*, 478 (Peel to J. Roby, 24 June 1829).

the secretary of the cotton-spinners union tried to obtain a personal interview with the Home Secretary in order to discuss the Manchester wage dispute, he was desired to put his views in writing, as Peel not unreasonably feared the dangers of misrepresentation on such an issue and the effect of any such misrepresentation on the strained situation in Manchester.[1]

He was not, however, so passive as these official communications implied. Though it was no part of his duty to intervene in wage agreements, he took care to inform himself of the demands and counter-demands made by both sides in the textile dispute. In May, when there was a strike of silk-weavers at Manchester, he sent a request for detailed information on the rates of pay in force before the strike, the various classes of weavers and spinners, the difference between the earnings of a single man and a family, statistics of wages in previous years, and the extent to which machinery was used. A similar request was sent to Stockport; and in September Peel expressed the opinion in a private letter to Manchester that a settlement on the basis of a guaranteed wage to all spinners, varying from 25s. to 45s. a week according to ability, seemed a liberal offer, and a more rational one than the flat rate of 35s. for all demanded by the spinners.[2] He was averse, however, to any government enquiry into the dispute; it would be impossible to get an agreed opinion on the justice of the rival settlements advocated by the two sides, and any expression of opinion by government on such an issue would be 'the commencement of an interference in matters of private concern greatly to be deprecated'. What he was most concerned to ensure was the maintenance of peace during industrial disputes, and he hoped that the protracted struggle in the Manchester textile industry would result in a strengthening of the civil police in that district. 'It is not fit,' he wrote to General Bouverie in July, 'that so opulent a place should throw the chief burden of providing protection for the persons and property of its inhabitants upon the military and upon the public purse.'[3] The administrative problem of keeping order was much in his mind at this juncture—it was the summer that saw in London the creation of the Metropolitan Police—and when in

[1] H.O. 41/7/487 (Peel to J. F. Foster, 11 September 1829). The name in Peel's letter is spelled Docherty, but there can be little doubt of the identification.
[2] ibid., 468, 471, 487.    [3] ibid., 482.

October a report came that troops were frequently being called in to deal with disorders at Barnsley, Peel's first reaction was to call for information on the state of the civil police there.[1] But if a more efficient police could prevent disorder, it could not touch the sources from which disorder came; and for all his disavowals to Lord Stanley of the possibility of state relief, in private Peel used what resources he had to mitigate the hardships which the industrial disputes brought in their train. Agents were privately despatched to Burnley, Blackburn, and other districts in Lancashire to make enquiries, with authority from the Home Secretary to relieve distress where it was most severe. They were instructed, however, to say nothing of that authority, and indeed not to allow it to be known that they were agents of the government. If their mission had become publicly known, Peel believed that the object of their enquiry would have been defeated and the charitable exertions of local inhabitants greatly diminished.[2] In fact this exercise in doing good by stealth was not disclosed until four years later.

Across St. George's Channel lay the other great province of the Home Secretary's responsibilities, calculated as ever to produce an abundance of ministerial employment in and out of season. The announcement of the government's intentions on Catholic emancipation at the start of the 1829 session produced an expectant lull in Ireland, and making leisurely preparations, the Duke of Northumberland did not arrive in Dublin until the first week of March. It was the wish of the cabinet, after their unhappy experiences with his two predecessors, that he should rule in great state, deliberately holding himself aloof from politics and parties; and he carried out this role admirably. 'Splendidly did his Grace keep up the dignity of the office,' wrote the socially impressionable Colonel Blacker. 'In the general turnout and management of the Northumberland household there was a superiority to any thing I saw before or since.'[3] But the new Lord Lieutenant was something more than a magnificent aristocratic figurehead, and despite the somewhat fortuitous circumstances of his appointment his conduct of business soon began

[1] ibid., 493.
[2] Speech in House of Commons in answer to Cobbett, 16 May 1833 (Speeches, II, 701).
[3] Blacker, VI, 239.

to stamp him as perhaps the best Viceroy Ireland had seen since the Union. Sensible, calm, shrewd, with considerable insight into the real problems of the country, he was at the same time a most friendly and unassuming official colleague. The pomp and ceremony of his Viceregal court was for external purposes only. In his relations with the government he was singularly conscientious and hard-working, keeping up with Peel a full correspondence in his own hand; and some of his despatches were state-papers of the first order. The Chief Secretary, Leveson Gower, was no match for his superior in either intelligence or strength of character, and had in fact been virtually carried by Peel ever since his appointment. Nevertheless, his position had been both difficult and frustrating, and Peel was not unappreciative of this. Writing to Wellington at the end of July, he pointed out that the business of the session had been unfair to Leveson Gower personally, since the three bills which had constituted not only the Irish but the main work of the 1829 session had necessarily been taken out of his hands; and he suggested that the Duke should write a few encouraging lines to him. If not an ideal person for the post, it would be difficult to replace him; and the Duke complied with Peel's request.[1]

Ireland in the summer of 1829 certainly seemed as much in need of firm government as ever. To the Irish peasantry the only immediate effect of emancipation was the disfranchisement of the 40s. freeholders, while among Protestants the passage of the Act served only to excite their fears and stimulate the activities of the Orange and Brunswick clubs. The example and exhortation of the Duke of Cumberland as Grand Master of the Orange lodges did nothing to allay the apprehensions of the ministers in London; but though Peel enquired from Leveson Gower whether there was any evidence of Cumberland's activities in Ireland, and would have been prepared to take action if evidence was forthcoming, the Prime Minister was reluctant to touch so delicate a problem. Meanwhile the 12th of July celebrations resulted in many clashes between armed bodies of Catholic and Protestant partisans, and a number of deaths and woundings. Over a large part of the country only the presence of troops and yeomanry seemed to prevent the outbreak of civil war and the hostile temper on both sides continued into the autumn,

[1] *W.N.D.*, VI, 37-8; 40308 fos. 209, 211.

especially in Tipperary. The cabinet had already, at the close of session, begun to consider Irish legislation for the following year, especially in the fields of Poor Law, Education, and Legal Administration; but the growing disorder called for the application of more instant remedies. The one encouraging feature was the readiness of the Irish government under its new chief to take the lead in preserving order. On 18 July the Irish Privy Council of its own volition issued a proclamation against illegal meetings and processions. Peel sent prompt approval for this welcome show of initiative, and further strengthened the hands of the Irish executive by despatching the 4th Foot from Scotland. At his instance a special cabinet met on 2 August to discuss the Irish situation. Leveson Gower's recent letters had shown some signs of alarm, but while content to allow a wide latitude to the Irish officials, the cabinet was averse either to the use of the Catholic Association Act for suppressing political meetings in general or to any proclamation of martial law.[1]

Peel's own view, which he had urged on the Duke of Wellington a few days earlier, was that the only permanent solution for the disorders in Ireland was to enlarge the police force and place the financial burden for its upkeep on the land. It was unnecessary, in his view, to maintain any large body of regular troops in Ireland. There was no danger of foreign aggression; and the police could enforce any measures likely to be imposed by the government. 'For every purpose, excepting the resistance to physical force or the actual dispersion of organised assemblages, the police is much more efficient, I conceive, than the military.' But Ireland, he thought, should be given a material inducement to preserve the peace by being made to pay for suppressing its own disorders. To Leveson Gower he argued in the same strain. Little would have been achieved in getting rid of the Catholic question, he wrote on 30 July, unless it resulted in the assent of parliament for a 'vigorous unsparing enforcement and administration of the law, criminal and civil'. He recommended, therefore, that the Chief Secretary should review and extend the police force, consolidate it under one head and pay for it from one source; and combine with this a determined policy of criminal prosecution. 'Ten years experience of the advantage of obedience will induce a country to be obedient without much

[1] 40337 fos. 40, 49, 61, 92; *W.N.D.*, VI, 31, 60; *Ellenborough*, II, 63, 79.

extraordinary compulsion.' As to the principle of financing Irish administration from the land, 'why should an absentee Irish landlord draw ten thousand a year from Ireland, contributing nothing by personal exertion towards the maintenance of the peace in Ireland, and throw on the Army and therefore on the Treasury the charge of protecting his property and ensuring the receipt of his rent?' Only on a fundamental basis of law and order could any further measures be undertaken for the permanent civilisation of Ireland.[1]

This need for the continuous enforcement of the law by an efficient standing civil force was one to which he recurred in several long despatches in the late summer and winter of 1829. At the same time he was not blind to the policy of showing favour to those Catholics who seemed disposed to support the government. Sheil, in particular, who had taken a noticeably moderate course since emancipation and was probably glad to be relieved of connection with a turbulent mass movement, was one instance where a studied conciliation on the part of the government might prove valuable. Writing approvingly of one of Sheil's recent speeches, Peel encouraged Leveson Gower in September to show him marks of attention when opportunity occurred. But what Sheil wanted was promotion to the Inner Bar, both for himself and for other senior Catholic barristers; and this was a difficult matter. Peel broached the question to Wellington in October, pointing out the expedience of detaching Sheil and his friends from O'Connell and of giving Catholic barristers the advancement to which they were professionally entitled. The Duke, however, deprecated such excessive liberalism. He doubted whether the king could be brought to agree and was himself unconvinced that favour should be shown to agitators. Peel was consequently obliged to temporise and he asked Leveson Gower a few days later to avoid if possible giving any silk gowns in Ireland for the time being. Nevertheless, he expressed entire agreement with the Chief Secretary's desire to bury the past, and promised to keep the question of Sheil's promotion under review.[2]

Despite the known sympathies of Leveson Gower, therefore, the hopes of Sheil and his friends continued to be disappointed, and the

[1] 40308 f. 217; 40337 fos. 74, 123, partly printed *Peel*, II, 120-7; *W.N.D.*, VI, 52.

[2] 40337 fos. 181, 212; 40308 f. 250; *W.N.D.*, VI, 253-4.

opportunity that seemed momentarily to exist for diverting Irish interest into the more constructive channels of Education and Poor Relief appeared to be slipping away at the very time when O'Connell was meditating a new campaign for the repeal of the Union.[1] Yet behind the cover of official secrecy Peel was not altogether inactive in those matters. Before going off for three weeks shooting in Scotland during September, he sent a long letter to Leslie Foster on Irish education and the Maynooth grant. Referring to the first report of the Irish Education Commission of which Foster had been a member, he raised the possibility of creating an Education Board to preside over the whole system of Irish education financed by the state. The controversial issue of religious education he thought might be solved by avoiding any general system of regulations; leaving the appointment of individual schoolmasters to the board; prescribing a minimum of religious instruction, either from a common scriptural compilation or from separate Protestant and Catholic versions of the Testament; and allowing access to ministers of both Churches to teach children of their own denomination. Foster returned a discouraging answer. He did not think that the Roman Catholic clergy could be conciliated or would ever co-operate. 'The truth is, they fear every system of education, unless they are to be permitted to employ it as an instrument for the up-holding of their own dominion.' Moreover, any attempt to meet them halfway would rouse the suspicions of the Protestants and unite Anglicans, dissenters, and Brunswickers against the government. As for Maynooth, bad as its results had been and would continue to be, government interference would merely make bad worse. In the interlocking spheres of education and religion, the utter impossibility of finding common ground between Protestant and Catholic would always baffle attempts by government to bring about reforms in either. It was an old and hopeless story; but Peel knew Ireland too well not to realise the force of Foster's arguments. Nevertheless, he sent the correspondence to the Lord Lieutenant in the hope that with decreasing sectarian animosity there might yet be some opportunity of introducing constructive measures.[2] There was at least consolation in the fact that at the end of the year the general state of Ireland, except in Tipperary, had immeasurably

[1] cf. *Sheil Memoirs*, II, 68ff.    [2] 40327 f. 76; *Peel*, II, 127ff.

improved since 1828. To that extent emancipation had not been in vain.

## II

During the autumn of 1829 nothing happened to strengthen the position of the government. In October Arbuthnot had a conversation with Althorp, a leading whig in the House of Commons, and made it clear to him that though the ministry was not based on any exclusive principle, the Prime Minister would never sanction a formal alliance with a party. From Althorp's reply he gathered that the dilemma confronting the whigs was whether they should wait until the Duke was ultimately forced to take them into office, or themselves make a concerted effort to bring down the government. Althorp laid significant and unpleasing emphasis on the need for a strong and efficient ministry and as a corollary getting rid of one that was not able to carry its measures. The conclusion drawn by Arbuthnot and probably by Wellington, to whom he promptly reported the conversation, was that the whigs would only be content with office, and that if they joined the government would endeavour to obtain the lion's share of power.[1] In the existing state of the House of Commons, with radicals unalterably opposed to the ministry, the Huskisson group personally aggrieved, many of the country gentlemen dissatisfied, and a strong body of ultra-Protestant Brunswickers still alienated by the events of the previous session, the prospect for the coming year offered little encouragement for optimism in the cabinet. Indeed it might seem that all the whigs had to do was to sit neutral while the government was harried by its former supporters to the point at which a whig alliance offered the only means of salvation. Wellington's personal prestige and authority seemed one of the few elements of strength in the government, but even this was undermined by the strained relations with the king and the continued hostility of the Duke of Cumberland. Meanwhile in the country at large agriculture was going through a period of depression, rents were in arrears, and even Peel was apprehensive of what might happen if the government fell.[2]

When parliament reassembled in February 1830 these depressing

[1] *W.N.D.*, VI, 198.    [2] *Ellenborough*, II, 177.

anticipations had not long to wait for confirmation. In the Commons the king's speech was roughly handled, especially a phrase referring to the distress 'in some parts' of the kingdom. Knatchbull, who opened the attack, gathered evident strength from the general feeling of the House as he proceeded, and Huskisson put in an acute and damaging contribution. Althorp and Brougham for the whigs, speaking more cautiously, nevertheless leaned to the side of the critics; but the whig vote as a whole was prudently divided between their public attitude and their tactical policy. Peel, though he took Huskisson up sharply, was not at his best and it was a relief as well as something of a surprise to the ministerial party when the hostile amendment put forward by Knatchbull was defeated by 158 votes to 105.[1] Some thirty whig votes cast for the majority saved the government and there were many absentees among usual government supporters. It was not an auspicious beginning; and though, as the Duke was perhaps too fond of saying,[2] the opposition groups were so diverse in outlook that it was not easy for them to unite against the government, it seemed clear that the Treasury bench could at any time be outnumbered and outmanœuvred. In those circumstances their day-to-day business was likely to become increasingly obstructed and their authority perceptibly decline. All the signs pointed to a restive and indisciplined session; and when the cabinet discussed the situation on 7 February Ellenborough for one was already inclining to the belief that a coalition with the whigs was the one practicable remedy.

As soon as the real business of the session began, it became evident that the whigs and radicals were concentrating on two lines of attack, finance and parliamentary reform. On both issues it was possible to muster a numerous if disjointed opposition in the House; and on both the government had to endure a series of running encounters that lasted the greater part of the spring and early summer. If the aim of the whigs was to manœuvre the cabinet into surrender, the aim of the tory malcontents seemed to be to reduce the ministerial majorities and bring the government into general disrepute. It was a sterile policy but not less damaging for that. In February the indefatigable Marquess of Blandford, who had already unsuccessfully

[1] *The Taylor Papers,* ed. E. Taylor (1913), pp. 313-14.
[2] cf. letter to Duke of Northumberland (*W.N.D.,* VI, 532).

moved an amendment to the Address on the subject, put forward
a motion for the purification and enlargement of the electoral
system with the declared object of restoring the constitutional
influence of the House of Commons. There followed the East
Retford bill, crowded out of the 1829 session, over which an attempt
to transfer the franchise to Birmingham instead of the Hundred of
Bassetlaw was defeated by less than thirty votes. On 23 February
Lord John Russell introduced a bill to enfranchise Leeds, Manchester,
and Birmingham, which was supported by a composite group of
Huskissonites, radicals, whigs, and a few country gentry. Finally in
May came a set of extreme proposals from O'Connell formulated
according to the purest radical doctrine for triennial parliaments,
universal suffrage, and secret ballot, on which he only gathered
thirteen supporters. Both Blandford and O'Connell could, however,
be disregarded as irresponsible extremists. The important contests
came on Lord John Russell's carefully limited motion, and on the
protracted East Retford affair.

The debate on Russell's motion, though in general somewhat
confused, was notable for eliciting from Peel the first clear enunciation of his attitude to the general question of parliamentary reform.
It was true that in the earlier discussions on the Marquess of Blandford's motion to set up a parliamentary committee charged with
the scrutiny of all corrupt and decayed elements in the representative
system, Peel had said with some severity that he would never be a
party to 'that wholesale depreciation of the elective franchise' and
could never consent even to the first stages of a bill designed to place
such powers in the hands of a committee.[1] But this was in fact the
general feeling of the House, and otherwise he had largely been a
silent spectator in the previous parliamentary debates on the reform
question, listening (as he told the House) 'in the spirit of a witness of
the contest rather than in that of a partisan'. But if silent, he had not
been incurious; and he came to the debate on Russell's bill primed
with researches into the history of the question which included a
reading of Burke's speech to the Bristol electors in 1780 and an
analysis of the voting list on Fox's peace resolution of 1793. All his
reflection, all the arguments of such great masters as Burke and
Canning, persuaded him—as he began his speech by announcing—

[1] *Speeches*, II, 77.

of the danger 'in tampering on slight grounds with the Constitution'. The greater part of his speech was taken up, indeed, with a careful exposition of fundamental principle. He denied the assumption that the British system of constitutional representation was based either intellectually on the fine-spun philosophies of classical republics or historically on any literal theory of democratic representation. He distrusted the easy prophecies of the beneficial effects to be obtained by any radical change in the structure of the electoral system, and he could see nothing in the actual composition of the House of Commons or in its actual functioning to persuade him that such a change was necessary. He refused to believe that parliament had ever led an unwilling country into war; he refused to believe that a reform of the representative system was a necessary preliminary to reform in other branches of the state; he refused to believe that under any other system there could be a greater desire 'to promote the happiness and to secure the true glory of the country'.

Descending from this high plane of constitutional thought to the actual motion before the House, he argued on more conventional lines that the arbitrary addition of the six new English members proposed by the motion was incompatible with the Acts of Union with Scotland and Ireland; would lead to further demands for fresh enfranchisements; and would provoke a contest for additional representation between the industrial and landed interests. He professed a willingness to punish individual cases of corruption, but thought it inexpedient to commit the House to a rigid programme of allocation for such seats as might become available in future. Finally, in answer to a plea from Lushington that he should emancipate himself from his supporters and appeal to the educated and intelligent classes of the community, he said that he agreed entirely that it was not the duty of a minister of the crown to be the mere instrument of party; but there was an equal danger on the other side. 'He believed that the true course was the medium, that the ministers should not be the servants of a party nor, by consulting popular applause, lose sight of the interests of the country.'[1] It was a reasoned and not unimpressive statement of the classic theory of the constitution and of Peel's view of the primary duties of high political office. But it premised a degree of independence in the

[1] *Hansard*, N.S. XXII, 897-907 (not included in Peel's collected *Speeches*).

executive government which was already imperilled by the existing state of the House of Commons. The practical question in 1830 was whether any government could for long continue to be both independent of party and aloof from popular opinion. On the day the ministers gained a majority of nearly fifty. Yet it was not a satisfactory victory, for not much more than three hundred members voted in all and Sir Edward Knatchbull, together with a group of some two dozen who normally followed his lead, left the chamber before the division took place.[1]

The question of East Retford was an even more delicately balanced issue, for it was clear that a number of members not in favour of a comprehensive reform of the electoral system were nevertheless anxious to see the progressive elimination of small corrupt constituencies and the transfer of their seats to the larger industrial towns. It had been decided in the cabinet at the end of the 1829 session that the same course would be followed on the matter as in 1828. On 11 February, when speaking on the various solutions put before the House, Peel took the line that the case must be treated on its own merits, and that he saw no reason for departing from the previous arguments in favour of throwing the borough into the Hundred of Bassetlaw. He was not against giving representation to the large towns, as witness his previous vote for transferring the franchise from Penryn to Manchester, but he wished to see those seats which might fall to the disposal of parliament shared equally between the landed and the manufacturing interests. Of the motion brought forward by Lord Howick for a general reform of corrupt boroughs he completely disapproved. His tone was moderate; he said he would willingly accept whatever decision the House came to on the subject; and he made a joke against himself, when talking of Howick's motion, for being unable in the case of the borough of Westbury 'to involve its respectable electors in so sweeping a censure'. That raised a general laugh in which he joined. The high tories on this occasion voted with the government, and Calvert's original motion to deal with East Retford by enlargement and not disfranchisement was finally carried. A bill embodying this decision went up to the Lords, and though there was some prospect of obstruction there and a marked disinclination in the cabinet to press the issue, Peel insisted

[1] *Geo. IV Letters*, III, 472.

against the will of most of his colleagues on seeing the bill through
to a conclusion. Indeed Ellenborough, who disliked the whole
principle of interference with the franchise, thought he was very
obstinate and disagreeable on the matter. But Peel said that he could
not oppose reform in general unless the government showed a
readiness to punish particular cases of corruption; and in the last
days of the session the East Retford bill was pushed through the
almost deserted benches of the upper House.[1] It was obvious that the
departure of the Huskisson group had left the cabinet with little
disposition to respond to the growing pressure both in the country
and in the House of Commons for some positive approach to the
problem of parliamentary reform. In the Commons a conservative,
Peel in the cabinet appeared at times almost the only liberal. It was a
position that argued some discomfort for himself and a notable
degree of unrealism on the part of his colleagues.

The question of parliamentary reform was not, however, considered a strict governmental matter; and in any case the bulk of the
Commons were disinclined to any action which might appear to
sanction the principle of remodelling the representative system as
distinct from punishing cases of flagrant corruption. Finance was a
different and more vulnerable issue. It necessarily formed a large
part of the government's business in the House of Commons; it was
a field in which they could make few concessions. Yet economy was
a cry to which nearly all constituencies and a large number of M.P.s
were ready to respond with unreasoning alacrity. On 12 February
Sir James Graham, the whig member for Cumberland, moved for a
reduction in all official salaries. On the 15th Hume moved for an
address to the crown recommending the repeal or reduction of all
taxes required for the upkeep of naval and military establishments.
At the end of March Poulett Thomson, the whig member for
Dover, moved the appointment of a committee to revise the whole
system of taxation. Sir James Graham carried on the attack with
motions to abolish, or combine with other salaried posts, the offices
of Treasurer of the Navy and Lieutenant-General of the Ordnance;
and in May moved for a statement of all salaries and emoluments
paid to members of the Privy Council. The ministry met these
onslaughts with a variety of tactics. Graham's first motion was

[1] *Ellenborough*, II, 27, 194, 315-18.

parried by an amendment asking for a statement of what had already been achieved since 1821 in reducing offices and salaries. Hume's motion, brought on before the government's financial policy for the year was laid before the House, was generally considered extravagant and ill-timed. The Huskissonites and country gentry for the most part held aloof and the motion was lost by a substantial majority. Poulett Thomson's motion, after a sharp debate, was also lost by a considerable margin. Graham's attacks on individual offices, less damaging to the policy if not the prestige of the government, were beaten off by substantial majorities: ninety-eight on the Treasurership of the Navy and seventy-six on the Lieutenancy of the Ordnance. His motion relating to members of the Privy Council was conceded in the more general terms of a return of all official salaries exceeding £2,000 per annum.

By hard work and good tactics, therefore, aided by the absurdity of some of the opposition proposals and a residuary sense of responsibility among unattached members of the Commons, the ministers came through an exhausting session with their financial measures largely intact. Only once did they suffer defeat in this field and that on a minor issue. At the end of March the House sitting as a Committee of Supply struck out two items of pensions, amounting together to £900 per annum, granted in compensation to former holders of civil offices in the Navy Department. Though given in accordance with the general rules governing the reduction of civil offices, the fact that they concerned in this instance the sons of two members of the government, Lord Melville and Lord Bathurst, singled them out for attention. Peel was not disposed to argue the point. He said that it had been stipulated with the Admiralty that the two persons in question were to be removed from the superannuation list at the first opportunity; and he left it to the House to accept or reject the items as they thought proper. The committee rejected them by a majority of eighteen votes.

In the protracted warfare over finance the mainstay of the government was Peel's parliamentary experience and tactical skill. From the outset he had determined to reduce the estimates so low as to provide the smallest possible target to the opposition. He did not think he would be beaten on any fundamental question. The House would never yield a majority for stopping supplies, and he was prepared to ignore defeats on small items. If the opposition mustered enough unity to agree on abstract motions, he was ready to play Pitt's game of 1783 and carry on regardless of government minorities until better times should come.[1] If necessary, the ministry could use the ultimate weapon at its disposal, the threat of dissolution. In the debate on the reduction of public salaries, Peel stated firmly that the government would make no concessions for the sake of maintaining themselves in office; they would reform where reform seemed salutary, retrench where it could be done with advantage; and that whatever the results of a combination of parties in the House, there was a sufficient fund of good sense in the country that would confirm the rightness of their course. It was a clear hint that the ministers would not shrink in the last resort from an appeal to the electorate, and the lively manner in which Peel spoke was well received by the House. The cabinet was satisfied that it had produced a salutary effect, and the result of the debate—the withdrawal of Graham's motion—was a complete victory for the Front Bench.[2]

Nevertheless, the universal feeling in the House for some considerable alleviation of taxation could not be indefinitely staved off, and behind the façade of parliamentary warfare the cabinet engaged in earnest debate on the fundamentals of their financial policy. Reduction of taxes had already been brought to the point where the necessary services of the state were imperilled; the issue was whether the time had arrived for a revolutionary change in the principal sources of that revenue. The weakness of the opposition criticism was that it ignored the basic problem of raising revenue; and the palliatives it suggested—further reduction of government expenditure and currency manipulation—were equally unacceptable. Among many of the financial experts on both sides of the House, however, there was growing feeling in favour of restoring a tax on income. Arbuthnot corresponded with Peel on the subject in February, and in March assured him that the whigs, though not ready to propose an income tax as a matter of party policy, would support it if brought forward by the government. Peel's views had already travelled a long way down the same road. Before Arbuthnot wrote, he had already secured a postponement of the Irish

[1] *Ellenborough*, II, 198-9.    [2] *ibid.*, 195; *Speeches*, II, 61.

estimates and had held discussions with Goulburn and Herries on the central issue of taxation. There were three courses, he replied to Arbuthnot on 16 February, that would carry the ministry through against all opposition.

> 1st. The removal of all restrictions on the establishment by Charter of Banking companies with limited responsibility.
> 2ndly. A *bona fide* reduction of expenditure—to the lowest amount consistent with the *public safety*.
> 3dly. A commutation of taxes bearing on industry—and the comforts of the labouring poor—for other taxes reaching *Ireland— great capitalists* and absentees.[1]

His influence clearly had effect, for when at the beginning of March Goulburn put forward in the cabinet his budget proposals for the coming year, he included a proposal for a modified property tax (as the income tax was still generally called) on revenue from landed and fixed property, funds, and other offices, though not on profits from trade or occupation of land. Within the framework of the budget this would offset the reductions he intended on beer, hops, and sugar.

When the cabinet met to discuss taxation on 13 March, there was a strong movement on the part of the House of Commons members in favour of imposing an income tax of this nature, though Wellington and the peers were all against it. Next day the criticisms brought forward caused Goulburn to waver in his resolution. Herries remained favourable, chiefly to ensure a permanent surplus in accordance with the views of the finance committee of the Commons. The most outspoken support for the new tax came from Peel. He wished, he said vividly, to reach such people as Baring, the great banker, his own father, Rothschild, and others, as well as absentees and Irish landowners; and he argued the expediency of aiming at the wealthy in order to diminish the burden of taxation on the poor and so assist in reconciling the lower with the upper classes. Indeed, it was clear that over the issue of the income tax Peel headed the party of financial reformers. Wellington, who held with some justification that the tax would press most heavily on the landowning classes,

---

[1] *Arbuthnot Correspondence*, p. 124.

and more curiously that they were the classes most in need of relief, told Mrs. Arbuthnot on 12 March that he was disputing the issue with Peel; and both he and his *confidante* were agreed that Peel was merely actuated by a craven desire to appease the whigs.[1] However, with several members remaining neutral, the majority in the cabinet was against Peel and he finally stated his readiness to support the decision of his colleagues whatever it might be.[2] There seemed, on paper at least, a fair prospect of balancing the budget without an income tax, and apart from any technical criticisms of Goulburn's suggestion the general repugnance to any revival of Pitt's extra-ordinary war-tax among the more conservative-minded members of the government was too great to be overcome at the first attempt. The Duke indeed was so impressed by its impropriety that he told Ellenborough it would weaken the credit of the country in the eyes of foreign powers.

Nevertheless, the proposal had been formally made and the motion by Poulett Thomson for a general committee on taxation revision strengthened the hands of the financial reformers in the cabinet; for most of the advocates of the committee were known to be favourable to the tax. Both Peel and Herries continued to argue in the cabinet that the House of Commons would agree to such a measure, and that though the cabinet's decision had been reasonable enough for the current session, they would have to accept an income tax the following year. Peel himself favoured Poulett Thomson's motion and was only unwillingly brought to agree with the general cabinet view that it should be resisted. His colleagues, however, felt that it would only excite and disturb the commercial world, and that the government could not hand over its responsibility in this sphere to a parliamentary committee. Once more, therefore, he deferred to a majority in the cabinet and consented to support the agreed government view in the Commons.[3] In his public utterances, however, he went as far as he could to indicate the extent to which an income tax had received and would continue to receive the attention of the government. In a debate on the distress in the country on 19 March he spoke in strong terms of the need to raise the standard of living among the poorer classes. One means of doing

---

[1] *Arbuthnot Journal*, II, 343, 345.       [2] *Ellenborough*, II, 203, 206, 209-13.
[3] *ibid.*, 215-16.

so—he pointed out—was to decrease the burden of indirect taxation, and this in turn raised the question, hinted at by previous speakers, of finding some alternative. The government, he told the House frankly, had carefully considered the possibility of imposing a property tax, and though for the current year they had decided to limit their action to the repeal of £3,400,000 of existing taxation, they gave no pledge one way or another on the question of a property tax. Six days later, when Poulett Thomson's motion was debated, he reminded the House that it was they who had defeated the intention of the government after the war to continue the property tax; and without offering an opinion on its expediency, he advised his audience to leave the responsibility of proposing it to the government. So the decision was left; and as it proved, the failure in 1830 to revitalise the finances of the state by introducing the income tax was a momentous one. It was the last opportunity that was presented to the little knot of administrative experts— Peel, Herries, and Goulburn—who argued against their aristocratic colleagues in the spring of that year. Their defeat, temporary as it then seemed, in fact handed over the financial policy of the government to a decade of whig financial timidity and ineptitude. Peel was fifty-three before he was able to approach once more that fundamental problem.

### III

The distress in the country which was debated at length by both Houses in the course of the 1830 session had its customary impact on the administrative side of Peel's department. Trouble among the weavers of Norwich in the winter had been followed by a strike of colliers in Monmouthshire at the end of March and the despatch of troops to the disturbed area. In May there was a turnout of spinners at Manchester and Ashton-under-Lyne, and in August scattered minor troubles in the Midlands. Almost without exception the disorders reported to the Home Office arose from industrial distress and the activities of trade unions; and the problem confronting the authorities was not rioting but an explosive situation that might at any time lead to rioting. As always, it was the Home Office policy to pick a delicate path between condoning any illegal action by the unions and giving sanction to provocative action on the part of the employers. In May came reports of a conference held during the winter by delegates of cotton spinners from Manchester, Bolton, Oldham, Glasgow and Belfast, under the leadership of Doherty, on means of preventing a reduction of wages. This, in the view of the Home Department, amounted to conspiracy and an offence at Common Law not covered by the statute of 1825; but the law officers of the crown thought it would not be possible to convict any of the delegates on charges of conspiracy without evidence of overt acts.[1] The growing practice of 'picketing' was, however, an overt act which, whether traceable to the unions or not, was itself an offence when committed as a result of combination and for the purpose of intimidation; and it was to this problem that Peel gave considerable attention as the summer wore on. He told General Bouverie in September that if the men picketing mills should transgress the law or if the persons directing their activities could be indicted for conspiracy to obstruct the employment of labour, there would be great advantage in prosecution when instituted with reasonable prospect of success.[2] In private he expressed strong views on the irresponsibility of the unions in using their collective strength to force up wages even for the better paid section of the industrial workers. Writing with unofficial freedom to his brother Edmund in October he spoke roundly of the accounts he had received from Lancashire of 'an abominable tyranny . . . established by means of the union of trades and the colliers, who earn on an average five shillings, and five shillings and sixpence a day', and were nevertheless meditating a general turnout.[3] To General Bouverie he recommended a personal visit to Manchester and Ashton-under-Lyne, if his presence there would 'inculcate upon the masters and the magistrates the necessity of combining with firmness, great moderation, and discretion'.[4] Yet, as his careful phrasing indicated, he was at pains to withhold the employers and local authorities from any act which would exacerbate the workmen or alienate public opinion. While reinforcing the troops in the Northern District, he impressed on their commander that the twin evils to be guarded against were lack of temper and prudence in resisting the demands of the unions

[1] H.O. 41/7/515-20; Ramsay, *Peel*, p. 125.
[2] H.O. 41/7/533.　　[3] 40401 f. 253.　　[4] H.O. 41/7/525.

and lack of courage in allowing unjust concessions to be extorted by fear alone. Everything was to be done to prevent extremism and the use of force; and if force were used, it should only be when necessary and urgent, and its justice unquestionable.

Nevertheless, the point seemed reached in October when resistance would have to be envisaged. Reports came from Lancashire of renewed wage demands and threats of strikes among the cotton-workers, while lock-outs among the colliers menaced the supply of coal on which the whole industry depended. To Peel, able to compare the wages of the northern industrial worker, as reported to him by reliable informants, with the guinea a week he paid his new police, the men's demands seemed unreasonable and their tactics intolerable. On 25 October he brought the matter up in the cabinet, and read a number of letters he had received from Lancashire magistrates and manufacturers. Resistance on the part of the employers seemed not unreasonable; what appeared doubtful to the cabinet, however, was whether the available military forces would be adequate to preserve order if the employers were in fact encouraged to take a strong line. This double attitude was reflected in the letter which Peel sat down immediately in the cabinet room to write to J. F. Foster, the Manchester magistrate who was one of his chief correspondents in the troubled area. In ordinary circumstances, he began, no doubt could be entertained that the best policy would be for the manufacturers to resist exorbitant wage demands, and if necessary close the cotton-mills and collieries. It was clear that the wages received by the men were ample, that there was no real cause for complaint, and that nothing permanent would be gained by concession to unjust demands. But it was imperative, he emphasised, to consider what the consequences might be. The turn-out of several thousand men in the existing state of feeling would soon lead to breaches of the peace and the intervention of the troops; and the first conflict would be a signal to others. His counsel was, therefore, that the magistrates should confer with the local military commanders, General Bouverie and Colonel Shaw, on measures for preserving peace and protecting property. He was anxious to know whether Foster thought there would be a probability of a general disturbance in these circumstances, and whether anything could be done to organise a local force in aid of the military. Such a force should not be drawn exclusively from the upper classes since that would only accentuate the clash between 'property and physical force', but should include shopkeepers, household servants, and work-people. He also suggested the expediency of a public statement by the employers on the whole causes and development of the dispute, the wages paid to their workpeople, and the system of picketing.

It was the nearest that the Home Department came under his secretaryship to direct intervention in an industrial dispute; but the issue as presented to Peel and his colleagues was clearly the extent to which the government should stand neutral while employers were forced by illegal and violent methods into unreasonable concessions. It was not easy to define the exact point at which the executive authority should intervene, but defensible to believe that such a point existed somewhere. Foster, however, did not think that this stage had been reached in Manchester. The masters were divided in their will to resist; the press was on the side of the men; volunteers could not be raised. A collision seemed inevitable but only legislative enactment could protect the employers. Further than strengthening the forces of law and order, however, Peel was not prepared to go. In another letter to Foster at the end of October he once more emphasised that if a collision took place, it should be on an issue where not only the law but public opinion would be on the side of the authorities. Legislation against the activities of the union might perhaps be unavoidable, but 'I doubt whether Parliament would pass a law directed against unions of workmen without very clear proof not only of their mischievous tendency but of their unjustified acts'.[1] The innate caution of the Home Department, and the restraint of the military commanders and magistrates in the northern areas, had their effect. Though the industrial troubles continued into the autumn, the situation never degenerated into open violence.

Peel himself was not blind to the bitter root of poverty that lay beneath the social distress of his time. His financial views were increasingly influenced by a desire to reduce the indirect taxation that pressed on the working classes, and he knew too much about the

[1] H.O. 41/8/13, 18 (Peel to Foster, 25, 30 October 1830); *Ellenborough*, II, 400; Ramsay, *Peel*, pp. 130-3 puts a slightly different interpretation on this incident.

actual conditions in the industrial districts to accept the ironclad *laisser-faire* policy of the economic theorists. Speaking in the House in July, he had made a sharp comment on Hume's defence of the practice of giving part of industrial wages in truck. Interference by the legislature was justified, he said, when special reasons existed to override the general principles of non-intervention in economic matters.

> In his opinion the truck system had a direct tendency to undermine the independence of the workmen. . . . When one man was able to undersell another upon profits derived from extorting the comforts of the workmen, he accomplished it by a positive disadvantage. The great evil of the present day was a tendency to diminish the enjoyments of the poorer classes, to lower them in the scale of society, and widen their separation from the upper classes.

In the following December he supported Littleton's Truck Act on the grounds that the poor man's only commodity was his labour, and that it was right to enquire, when that commodity was exchanged, whether the bargain made with the poor man was free, just, and equitable. The science of economy applied to the production of wealth, but if he could be shown that the application of those rules tended to destroy the morals of the people, he would certainly throw aside the principle of political economy. Peel lived in a world in which *laisser-faire* was the rule, and intervention the exception; but he was not a doctrinaire, and both in England and Ireland he was prepared at need to sacrifice philosophy to humanity.

In Ireland, meanwhile, there had been a comparative lightening of the atmosphere. The basic problems of Irish society remained as deep and inveterate as ever, but there seemed some chance of being able to consider them in a more impartial context than existed in the decade preceding emancipation. In February 1830 the Irish Catholic bishops had sent a pastoral letter to their clergy, reminding them of their duty to the crown, the government, and parliament, and enjoining a withdrawal from political activities.[1] Sheil and some of the other agitators continued to be studiously moderate in their

[1] Broderick, *Holy See*, p. 45.

behaviour. Only the irrepressible O'Connell seemed bent on using the events of 1829 as an overture to an even more ambitious piece of political orchestration. Early in the new year he opened a parliamentary office in St. Stephen's Green, not far from the old site of Ireland's vanished parliament, as a centre for political agitation.[1] Shortly afterwards he formed a new association, the Friends of Ireland, to work for parliamentary reform and repeal of the Union. The Irish executive were anxious to suppress this new development under the Irish Associations Act of 1829 before its expiry, and at a special meeting called by Peel on 21 April the cabinet gave their support for this action. A proclamation was drawn up before the end of the month and the suppression of the Friends of Ireland was carried through without difficulty or disturbance. There was little, however, that O'Connell had to learn about evasive tactics. When he returned to Ireland after the parliamentary session, the powers of the Lord Lieutenant had again to be evoked against further associations he formed in quick succession and under various titles for the repeal of the Union. To suppress his activities completely was impossible; the real question was the degree of support he could obtain. The Belgian revolution in the autumn, offering the heartening spectacle of a Catholic community successfully throwing off an enforced union with Protestant Holland, caused considerable excitement in Ireland, on which O'Connell played with his accustomed skill. Even so, there was manifestly less popular enthusiasm for the repeal movement than there had been for the Catholic Association; and the Irish government did what it could to keep O'Connell and the extremists isolated.

On this, as on the necessity of offering a resolute resistance to the repeal association, there was general agreement between the cabinet and the Dublin executive. Both Northumberland and Leveson Gower wished to encourage Sheil and the Catholic moderates as a counterpoise to O'Connell, and their views found a sympathetic hearing in London. If Peel differed at all, it was on grounds of an even wider liberal policy. To give Sheil his coveted silk gown and pass over O'Connell, he thought, would be a piece of discrimination that could scarcely be justified on any principle, and would merely present the great Catholic agitator with a grievance

[1] McDowell, *Public Opinion*, p. 128.

in which public opinion would be on his side. The stumbling-block was, of course, the king. Wellington held that it would be difficult enough to get his consent to Sheil's promotion; but to carry both Sheil and O'Connell out of the question. When therefore the cabinet considered this thorny issue on 21 April, it was decided to give silk to Sheil and a few other Catholic barristers but not to O'Connell. Even this gesture of reconciliation was not easily accomplished. During April the king was too ill to transact any business of a disturbing nature and it was impossible to proceed without his sanction. However, the close of the Trinity Term saw Sheil and three other Catholic barristers called to the Inner Bar. As King's Counsel, friend of Leveson Gower, and guest at the Lord Lieutenant's table, Sheil provided some tangible proof of the government's conciliatory policy. But it was uncertain how much further that policy could be carried. Sheil's ambition was to enter parliament. In the summer of 1830 he had been defeated in a contest for Co. Louth and in the autumn he approached Hardinge, the new Chief Secretary, for government assistance in finding a seat. He promised in return to support the ministry on all subjects except parliamentary reform and minor matters connected with the Church of Ireland. Peel broached the matter with the Prime Minister; but though they were agreed on the desirability of giving encouragement to any Irish Catholic opposed to the repeal of the Union, they were reluctant to enter on the kind of connection which would ensue if Sheil were returned as a government candidate. They dreaded the recklessness of Irish oratory, they doubted Sheil's political honesty, and as for his reservations—wrote Peel to Hardinge—'this very question of reform may be the all-important, vital, question'. Civility and compliance with reasonable wishes was one thing; to sponsor his parliamentary appearance was another.[1]

In Irish society at large, however, the prospects were undoubtedly heartening. The winter of 1829-30 had produced the usual seasonal disorders; but the unrest in Tipperary, which continued into the new year and necessitated military reinforcements for that county, was a social rather than a political phenomenon. There was a disposition on the part of the resident gentry there, the Lord Lieutenant

[1] 40313 fos. 68, 100; 40327 fos. 145, 17, 1074; 40338 f. 98; *Sheil Memoirs*, II, 83-4.

wrote to Peel in January, to let their lands on grasping and impossible conditions, and a reckless willingness on the part of the peasantry to take out covenants with no hope of being able to keep them, with the inevitable consequences in evictions, processes, quarrels between outgoing and incoming tenants, and constant outbreaks of violence between classes and families. The Home Secretary showed his approval for this dispassionate diagnosis by reading the despatch to the cabinet and sending a copy to the king.[1] Peel himself was sick of constant recourse to Insurrection Acts. What he wanted was something new,[2] and one remedy at least to which the government could turn its hand was a reform and extension of the Irish police. His constant exhortations to Leveson Gower during 1829 at last bore fruit in a memorandum by the Chief Secretary on the Irish Constabulary which Peel brought before the cabinet early in January. The ministers in London had already given a preliminary discussion to the subject in November, and there was general agreement that what was needed was an enlargement of the force, the appointment of more stipendiary but non-resident magistrates, and a close control by the Lord Lieutenant over the selection and appointment of the whole constabulary.[3] But Leveson Gower was not destined to put his name to a new Irish Police Act. In May he expressed to the Prime Minister his disinclination, on grounds of private affairs, to return to Ireland, and though the appointment was delayed until the end of the session, in July Hardinge was formally announced as his successor.

Though Leveson Gower did not perhaps deserve all the strictures passed on him by Ellenborough (Northumberland at least was sorry to part with him), the change did not weaken the administration. Indeed, with Hardinge's arrival, it seemed as if a better team of officials was now at work in Dublin Castle than at any time since Peel took leave of Whitworth in 1817. Summer and autumn passed in the familiar round of meeting immediate exigencies and preparing for future policy. A shortage of provisions and partial distress in June was answered by an advance of £3,000 to the Lord Lieutenant for local committees or direct relief, with encouragement to ask for

---

[1] 40327 fos. 94, 106, partly printed *Peel*, II, 144.
[2] cf. letter to Leveson Gower, 20 November 1829 (40337 f. 275).
[3] 40338 f. 2; *Ellenborough*, II, 136, 160.

more if he needed it;[1] and to counter O'Connell's propaganda activities and the executive's lack of any journalistic support, Peel suggested to Hardinge the establishment of a government newspaper to ridicule the great agitator and convince Protestants that repeal of the Union would mean a repeal of the Act of Settlement.[2] Of more permanent importance were the three Irish problems which Peel warned the Chief Secretary would take up much of their time in the new session: Education, Estimates, and the Poor Law. For estimates it was only necessary to read economy and he urged Hardinge to cut down all useless and sinecure offices in the Lord Lieutenant's household.[3] The question of Poor Relief was less straightforward. In March a committee on the state of the poor in Ireland had been appointed at the instance of Spring Rice, the whig member for Limerick, with the support of the government. Though Peel was doubtful of the expediency of introducing the English Poor Law into Ireland, and still more of the practicability of establishing workhouses for Irish paupers, he agreed that a thorough examination of the whole problem ought to be undertaken before any attempt at legislation.[4] Irish poverty and Irish education were clearly the two fundamental social tasks to which the government would have to address itself now that the political issue of emancipation had been cleared from the surface of the Irish problem.

### III

By the spring of 1830 George IV was slowly dying. At the beginning of April he gave one last exhibition of his old waywardness in the Comyn case which involved both Peel and the Irish executive. Comyn was an Irish gentleman of Co. Clare who, having been ejected from a tenancy by his landlord, first used perjury and forged documents to secure a legal injunction against him, then burnt down the house that was in dispute, and finally gave sworn evidence against three innocent men accused of the crime. After he was convicted and condemned, his relatives approached Lady Conyngham; and the king, without consulting Peel, directed the Lord Lieutenant to commute the death sentence. Northumberland protested strongly to the Home Secretary. If the worst features of

[1] 40327 f. 176.    [2] 40313 f. 127.    [3] ibid., f. 43.    [4] Speeches, II, 105.

Whiteboyism, he wrote, were pardoned in a gentleman, merely as such, it would be useless to try to suppress it in the humbler tenantry. Peel sent a sharp note to the king about the irregular and objectionable procedure followed, and Wellington upheld his view that the sentence must stand.[1] Thereafter, in an atmosphere of pain, drugs, and acute physical prostration, the life of the king slowly ebbed. From the middle of April bulletins on his health were being regularly issued; and though to the last he fought with Hanoverian pertinacity against this final enemy, it was clear to the ministers that the end might come at any time.

At Drayton Manor another old man, twelve years senior to the king, in greater tranquillity was also drawing to his close. Sir Robert Peel had made a good recovery from a serious illness in 1824, and four years later, on 10 May 1828, he had the patriarchal pleasure of presiding over an assembly of fifty of his children and grandchildren. The gathering was held at his eldest son's house in Whitehall Gardens and a silver medal commemorating the occasion was presented to each of his descendants. But in the hard winter of 1829-30 his health began to break up and early in April came the first serious relapse. Peel, his sister Mary, and three of his brothers—William, Jonathan, and John—hastened down to Tamworth on 6 April to find him partially recovered, though thinner and weaker than in the previous autumn. 'He was a good deal affected when I went in to him,' Peel wrote to his wife the next day, 'cried, and kissed me two or three times. He was very feeble, and his voice very faint, but he was sitting in his dressing gown in his sitting-room upstairs.' He rallied again; and though Robert had to return to his parliamentary duties, Julia went to Drayton later in the month to keep him company. On 25 April he celebrated his eightieth birthday; and little Julia, his granddaughter, wrote on her own birthday, 30 April, to inform him that Mr. Tomlinson had presented her with a Greek and Latin Testament because she had finished reading the gospel of St. John in Greek and Latin before she was nine years old, and had given her leave to tell him that she was getting on very well indeed.[2] But the end was not far off, and Sir Robert Peel met it with his old independence. Not long before his death he invited

---

[1] 40327 fos. 121-34; cf. *Peel*, II, 146-51; *W.N.D.*, VI, 553-5.
[2] *Peel, Letters*, pp. 119-21.

three of his nephews to dine with him. At the meal he asked whether the champagne was good, drank a glass and seemed to recover some animation. After dinner they played his favourite whist but after a rubber or two his hands bègan to shake. One of the nephews, Mr. Willock, offered to deal for him but the old man refused. 'No, no, Robert. If I cannot deal my own cards, it is time to give up the game.' So, characteristically, the last rubber was left unfinished.[1]

At the beginning of May came news of another and more serious relapse. Taking his eldest son with him (the fourth Robert Peel in direct descent), Peel went down to Drayton on 3 May, hoping to be in time to make a last farewell. He arrived at midnight to find that his father had died some six hours previously. In the afternoon the old baronet had dozed in his armchair for three hours, and then about half-past five almost imperceptibly passed away from life. 'His death was so placid, so resembling sleep,' Peel wrote later to Fitzgerald, 'that perhaps I ought not to regret that he was not disturbed in his last moments by an interview which might have roused and affected him.'[2] While Goulburn and the leaderless Front Bench struggled on with the business of the Commons, Peel remained at Drayton to supervise the details of his father's funeral and the destruction of his private papers. Sir Robert was buried in the vault of the little parish church of Drayton Bassett beside his cherished Ellen. The funeral which took place on 11 May was attended by a great concourse of people; the whole corporation of Tamworth was present and sixty tenants on horseback in the traditional style. The will was read immediately afterwards at the manor, in the presence of the sons and sons-in-law. It contained no surprises, though it is apparent that Julia (recollecting perhaps the old man's displeasure over Catholic emancipation the year before) was apprehensive that he might have altered his will to his eldest son's disadvantage. A hurried note from her husband the same day set her mind at rest. After giving a brief summary of the contents Peel concluded:

All the lands in Staffordshire, Warwickshire, and Lancashire left to the eldest son and his descendants, and such an arrangement made with respect to money as gives upon the whole (land and

[1] Peel, *Life*, p. 55.    [2] 40323 f. 113.

money included) four times the amount to the eldest son of that sum which each younger son has. Do not, my dearest love, say a word on this subject to anyone. You may be quite at ease. In short the will is what I always told you I thought it would be.[1]

As executor with his brother William, it was necessary for him to embark immediately on various duties connected with the estate, and it was not until the end of the week that he was able to leave Drayton. On Monday 17 May Peel, now a baronet, resumed his place in the Commons.

The previous day he called at Windsor for an interview with the king. He found him huddled in a wheelchair, unshaven and unkempt, but still showing astonishing liveliness and intelligence. He talked kindly to Peel of his private affairs and old Sir Robert's arrangements with all his customary command of detail; and though Peel, to avoid wearying him, only stayed half an hour, the king was reluctant to let him go. In the minds of both men was the thought that it would be their final interview, and all past animosities were put away. After the recent scenes at Drayton, George's sympathetic references would have affected Peel in any circumstances; coming from a dying monarch they were singularly moving. Before Peel left, the king asked him to push his chair to the window. He glanced out for a while and observed it would be the last time he would look into the garden. Then he turned to Peel and said, 'You are just returned from your father's funeral; you will soon have to pay the like ceremony to me.'[2] But still he lived on, contesting—as Croker said—every inch with death. Before the end of the month a Royal Signature Bill was passed to enable his signature to be affixed by a stamp in his presence. Lord Farnborough was nominated by the king for that duty and Peel went down to Windsor to secure the necessary authority for the appointment. He saw the king on 30 May, and once more, for the last time, on 6 June when it was plain that a perceptible deterioration in his condition had taken place even in that short interval.[3]

It was now only a question of waiting for the end; it came at last

[1] Peel MSS., passages omitted in Peel, *Letters*, p. 121, where the letter of Tuesday is wrongly dated 12 instead of 11 May.
[2] 40323 f. 124; *Dyott*, II, 170; *Croker*, II, 61.
[3] *W.N.D.*, VII, 66-8; *Ellenborough*, II, 263-4.

in the early hours of Saturday 26 June. The event brought a sudden rush of work for the Home Secretary in settling the formal details consequent on the demise of one sovereign and the accession of another. He summoned a cabinet for half-past ten the same morning, which was followed by an audience with the new king. The Duke, Peel, Bathurst, Rosslyn, and the Lord Chancellor went in together to apprise William IV ceremonially of the late king's death, and he told them he would give his entire and determined support to his brother's ministers. The same day came a Privy Council, the taking of the royal oaths, the swearing-in of the councillors, and the arrangements for the disposal of the body of George IV. There followed a flow of loyal addresses to the new king for which Peel had to draw up the answers. The funeral took place at Windsor on the evening of 15 July; it was a fine day and many persons made it a public holiday. Peel, clad in the Windsor uniform, came about eight o'clock with a party that included the Archbishop of Canterbury, four other bishops and the Earl of Radnor; and in the procession took his place with the privy councillors. It was midnight before the service ended and the last of the Hanoverian Georges laid in his final resting-place.[1]

The new monarch, formerly Duke of Clarence, was a simple and unpolitical man, bred up in the navy, who carried the bluntness traditional to that service almost to the point of uncouthness. After many years of domestic if unsanctified happiness with the actress Mrs. Jordan, he had dutifully married Adelaide of Saxe-Meiningen in 1818, but no children had survived from that belated union. In this lay a problem for the ministers, since the heir-presumptive was the Princess Victoria, a girl of eleven, and next in line of succession was the Duke of Cumberland. Except for that unpleasant contingency, however, William IV promised to be a more comfortable sovereign than his predecessor. His impromptu reply to an address from the Dean and Canons of Windsor was a passable effort, though Peel advised the omission, for purposes of record, of his reference to Henry VIII as prime author of the Reformation—a doubtful moral if not historical ascription, thought the Home Secretary, quoting appositely if not quite accurately a stanza from Thomas Gray,

[1] *The Times*, 16 July 1830; *Ellenborough*, II, 308.

When love first taught a monarch to be wise
And gospel light had flashed from Boleyn's eyes.

Apart from a congenital lack of tact, and a royal eagerness to concern himself with the detail of military uniforms, William showed
himself obligingly ready to conform to his ministers' advice. When
almost at once Peel had to offer objections to an appointment to the
Lunacy Commission, his secretary, Sir Herbert Taylor, wrote back
to assure Peel that

> His Majesty is not only open to representations and objections upon
> any matter which suggests itself to Him, or upon which He may
> have stated a wish or opinion, but that He will give credit to and
> be pleased with those who offer their opinions on the objections
> which may occur frankly and without hesitation. He takes up
> matters *readily* and is disposed to act *eagerly* upon such fresh ideas
> or impressions, but He listens kindly and patiently to whatever
> may be submitted in opposition to what he may have proposed.[1]

This at least was a change, and despite his earlier clash with Wellington at the Admiralty Board, and a disposition on the part of the
popular press to endow him with strongly liberal views, William
IV did not appear likely to embarrass the government.

The same could scarcely be said of parliament. With the beginning
of the king's fatal illness, the cabinet lost the last sanction for their
control of the House of Commons. By the end of April it was clear
that the government could neither resign nor dissolve, and members
began to turn their gaze outward for signs by which to guide their
behaviour. 'The state of the king's health,' wrote Peel to Fitzgerald
on 9 May, 'has still more shattered the House of Commons, already
sufficiently distracted and dislocated. Everybody is looking out for
the vote or question on which he can stand a chance of recommending himself to his constituents.'[2] Peel's absence from the House in
April and May had further weakened the government. On 5 April,
when he was first summoned to Drayton, the front bench was
defeated by 115 votes to 97 on a motion to remove the political
disabilities of British Jews. Of those voting in the minority, Goulburn

[1] 40301 fos. 74ff.     [2] 40323 f. 113.

reported to Peel the next day, not more than sixty were usual supporters. Planta's efforts to whip up attendance were embarrassingly unsuccessful and even some official men left before the division. When the second reading of the bill came before the House on 17 May, Peel delivered a sharp attack on any attempt to 'unchristianise the legislature' for the sake of 27,000 natural-born Jews; and the Commons endorsed this attitude by a majority of over sixty. But during his second and longer absence in May, government business was persistently blocked or delayed; and on one particularly disastrous evening Goulburn was obliged to withdraw a vote for building expenses at Windsor with a promise to refer the whole matter to a Select Committee.

> If the country gentlemen who usually support us behave as they did last night [he wrote to Peel] (and I see no reason why they should behave less shabbily) we shall have to make a choice between submitting ourselves to a committee on every point on which any discretion is to be exercised or giving up the conduct of public business altogether.[1]

Even after Peel resumed normal attendance the situation did not greatly improve. At the beginning of June the government only carried their diplomatic expenses by eighteen votes, and to Peel's particular disgust were defeated on the Forgery Bill. At the end of the month Goulburn's sugar duties encountered opposition from a combination of whigs, tories, and the West India interests. Peel doubted whether he could hold a majority together on the issue; and in the end, indeed, the sugar duties were abandoned.

He himself as leader of the House worked harder perhaps than in any previous session. 'His single speech has, every night, supported the whole debate on our side,'[2] recorded Croker in May; and even against the growing pressure from all sides of the House, at the end of the session he was able still on occasions to dominate the assembly. On 30 June he rose to explain the intentions of the ministry, following the death of George IV, to dissolve parliament and postpone all major issues, including the question of a Regency and the Civil List,

---

[1] 40333, fos. 88, 101; 40309 f. 29, partly printed Peel, II, 145.
[2] Croker, II, 59; cf. Arbuthnot Correspondence, p. 126.

to the new session. Althorp and the whigs urged, with justification, the need for some immediate provision for a Regency in view of the king's age and the minority of the princess. Brougham, coming in half-drunk after supper, began a speech which became more wild and intemperate as he proceeded and finally accused the Front Bench of being 'mean, fawning parasites' of the Duke of Welling-ton. Hardinge and several others tried to rise to question him, but Peel stopped them, even pulling Hardinge back by his coat-tails. Instead he stood up himself and asked whether the allusion referred to him personally. Brougham tried to explain away the unhappy phrase, whereupon with great coolness Peel said he had no doubt that Brougham did not allude to him or to anyone else in person, but that it would have been better if he had said at once that he had been betrayed into an indiscretion by the heat of debate rather than attempt to make an unsatisfactory explanation. As he had not made that excuse, however, Peel would make it for him. There was a cheer from all round the benches, and Brougham rose to accept this interpretation.[1]

Yet Peel could not go on indefinitely sustaining the whole govern-ment in the lower House; and with the guarded courtesy of the whigs beginning to disintegrate into open impatience, the other ministers in the Commons were convinced that major alterations would have to be undertaken. It was made clear to the Duke that more speaking talent would have to be found for Peel in the Com-mons and Hardinge indeed wished to go further. He told Ellen-borough more than once that Peel's position was hampered by his subordination to the Duke, and that the ministry would be con-siderably strengthened if Peel became Prime Minister and Chancellor of the Exchequer, with Wellington as Secretary of State.[2] The Duke himself in some moods was more than half-disposed to meet these suggestions. Eighteen months as First Minister had almost brought him to the state in which Lord Liverpool had been in 1825 after thirteen years. With all the frustrations and annoyances of political life, and few of the qualities adapted to meet them, Welling-ton was sufficiently tired and angry at times to be ready to throw his burden on the shoulders of the younger man. He was depressed

[1] Broughton, *Recollections*, IV, 34-5; *Ellenborough*, II, 298; *Speeches*, II, 203-4.
[2] *Ellenborough*, II, 289, 297.

by the constant talk of the weakness of his government (which he did not think was weak); was opposed to a union with any of the various allies inconveniently suggested to him; and convinced that nobody in the cabinet paid him proper attention. In May he told the sympathetic Arbuthnots that he was determined to write to Peel and resign the government into his hands. Mrs. Arbuthnot used all her powers to dissuade him from such a step, and though unable to deter him completely by argument, won a promise from him not to send a letter to Peel without first showing it to her. A week later he had so far cooled in his original purpose as to tell her that he would only write a memorandum for Peel, pointing out the difficulties of a junction with another party.[1]

In fact, the surviving draft of a letter to Peel which he did draw up, apparently in anticipation of the king's death but before it took place, reflects his earlier attitude. He began by discussing at length the situation of parties; and the conclusion at which he arrived was not a hopeful one. He did not think that Lord Grey could be included in the government and said that he personally would rather see him at the head of a ministry than serve in one of which Grey was a member. Could the government continue against a united whig opposition? The Duke thought the present government had the confidence of the country and after the election would gain in numbers. He was sure of the House of Lords but what of the Commons? He did not think he could preside over a cabinet that once more included the Huskisson group. But he thought the powers of government should be concentrated in one person, and that person the leader of the House of Commons. He concluded, therefore, that the occasion of the king's death should be used for his own retirement and Peel's succession to the premiership with complete liberty to construct his ministry as he thought fit. The Duke would support or serve in any government which Peel formed.[2] The drift of Wellington's thoughts was obvious. He objected to a coalition with the whigs; he would accept a coalition with the Huskissonites

---

[1] *Arbuthnot Journal*, II, 355-6, 358.

[2] *W.N.D.*, VII, 106-8, dated 1830. No letter of this nature appears to exist in the Peel Papers and there is no trace of any reply. The original draft written by Wellington and printed in the *Civil Despatches* has been lost or destroyed but there is no record of such a letter in the outgoing letter-books of the Duke for this period. (I am indebted for this information to the Librarian at Apsley House.)

provided Peel took over the leadership. In any case he was prepared to step down from his high office.

This singularly unselfish proposal would have revolutionised the position of the government at one stroke. It is reasonably certain, however, that the document was never sent to Peel. As it stands it is merely the torso of a letter, undated and without beginning or end; and there is no evidence of its being either sent or received, or indeed of any further mention of such a drastic solution to the cabinet's difficulties. It is not impossible that the Duke had already written it when he first mentioned the subject to the Arbuthnots, and that all subsequent discussions tended to make him have second thoughts. When Peel returned to London after his father's funeral, he further alienated the Duke by a proposal to reform the Scottish burghs and to bring pressure on the king of Spain to recognise the independence of the South American colonies. These manifestations of liberalism were used by Mrs. Arbuthnot to strengthen her argument that it would be folly for the Duke to abdicate from his position. In the end another way out of the situation was tried. On 3 July Arbuthnot wrote to Peel, telling him how much the Duke admired his efforts in the House of Commons; and adverting to the obvious willingness of Althorp and Grey to join the ministry, said that Wellington would be gratified by knowing Peel's full and frank opinion on such an alliance.[1] It is unlikely that this letter was written without Wellington's knowledge; and it represented an entirely different line of development to that outlined in the Duke's draft. It proposed in effect an alliance with the whigs on the unspoken assumption that the Duke would continue in office. The conclusion is hard to resist that the influence of the Arbuthnots and perhaps misgivings of his own had made the Duke recoil at the last moment from his gesture of self-sacrifice.

Peel himself in the summer of 1830 was in a state of underlying weariness and ill-humour. The accumulated strain of the last two sessions, the death of his father, the increasing anarchy in the House of Commons, the lack of support from his ministerial colleagues, and the continued frustration in the cabinet, had all made inroads on his physical and nervous strength. He complained sharply of his intolerable position as leader of the House, and at various meetings

40340 f. 223.

of ministers after George IV's death he seemed noticeably flat and listless. The session had put a heavy burden on him. Day after day his administrative work of some seven or eight hours at the Home Office was followed by sometimes up to ten hours in the House of Commons, involving not only committee work and formal speeches but constant intervention in the business of the House. On a succession of points in the cabinet he had failed to carry his way, and the last—over the Regency Bill—had put the government at a serious disadvantage in the closing weeks of the session. When the cabinet discussed the question at the end of June he had been a strong advocate for an immediate Regency Bill and was highly dissatisfied at the decision to dissolve immediately and postpone all but indispensable legislation to the next parliament.[1] In both Houses the whigs moved amendments to the address on that issue and in the Commons the ministers gained a majority of only forty-six. The remainder of the government's business was got through the House, though the new sugar duties were abandoned; parliament was prorogued on 23 July and dissolved soon after.

The general election, when it came, brought little joy to Peel personally. His own return was safe enough, for the Duke of Northumberland had offered him a quiet seat without trouble or expense in one of his own boroughs;[2] but Peel, while appreciative of the offer, had already made arrangements to stand for Tamworth, of which he now owned a considerable portion under the terms of his father's will. Some of the local tories wanted to fight both seats; but since that would have upset the peaceful division of the borough between the Peel and Townshend interests, William Peel who had held one seat since 1818 retired in his brother's favour. Peel was decidedly averse to a repetition of the bitter personal contest of that year, and the election passed off quietly.[3] Not all his brothers were so fortunate. William who had been promoted to the Treasury at the end of the session, being succeeded at the Home Office as Under-Secretary by Sir George Clerk, came in for Yarmouth (Isle of Wight), a nomination borough. But Edmund, standing as a Canningite liberal at Newcastle-under-Lyme, was defeated after an expensive contest; and Jonathan Peel, an old-fashioned tory, in the equally

[1] *Ellenborough*, II, 280-4, 288-9.    [2] 40327 fos. 184-5.
[3] 40401 fos. 70-80; *Mitchell*, I.

corrupt and extravagant constituency of Norwich. In Ireland Dawson and Croker were both deprived of their seats. Conscious as he was of his own unpopularity, a feeling kept alive by the repeated jibes of opponents in the House of Commons at his tergiversation on the Catholic question, Peel was unable to resist the conviction that his brothers' defeats were due to their connection with himself, and the thought contributed still further to his depression of spirit.[1]

The elections as a whole did little to clarify the confused political situation. Only about a quarter of the constituencies in England and Wales were contested and both whigs and tories made the conventional claims to have improved their position. Government influence was weak, but that was no new phenomenon. The time had long gone by when government could return a praetorian guard of placemen and pensioners to the House of Commons. Yet it was not true that opposition was the only road to popular favour, and in many quarters there was probably a residuum of respect for Wellington and Peel as ministers of the crown. If traditional party divisions existed, there were no clear party policies, and candidates came to terms as best they could with the electorate. What was beyond all doubt was that many electors wanted reform of some sort or another—parliamentary reform, economies, abolition of slavery, cheap bread—and that irrespective of party affiliations many candidates expressed themselves willing to support those objects in the House of Commons. In Yorkshire, profiting by radical and dissenting zeal in the industrial West Riding and the divisions among the whig squires, Brougham was returned as one of the county members in the most spectacular election of the day; and at his victory dinner in September promised to bring in a grand plan of parliamentary reform.

It did not require much perspicacity to see that the new parliament would bring changes, and that if Wellington's government could not direct those changes it would have to give way to another. Much of the public attention, however, was diverted by the accounts of the July Revolution in Paris which reached the country early in August, followed in September by news of the outbreak of disturbances in Belgium. Ultra-radicals and ultra-tories both sought to

[1] *Ellenborough*, II, 360.

make capital out of these startling developments in the ensuing weeks. The radicals hailed the events on the continent as an example and an inspiration to the working-class movement at home; but they showed little disposition to risk their own lives on the streets. A police spy, whose communications were transmitted to the Home Office from Bow Street, reported on 7 August that despite the excitement caused by the French Revolution in the extreme radical circle of Carlile, Taylor, and Preston, there was nothing likely to lead to any mischief in London nor 'from all I can find will the conduct of the French have any other effect than that of talking of them'.[1] Of more political significance were the efforts of the ultra-tories, notably the eccentric Sir Richard Vyvyan of Cornwall, to identify Wellington with the foolish and discredited Polignac ministry in France, and Peel's Metropolitan Police with the French *gendarmerie*. But though the *Standard* exploited this accusation to the utmost, the bulk of the press and middle-class opinion in general were disinclined to see in the Duke an ally and accomplice of the reactionary Bourbons. They disliked the actions of the French monarchy, and welcomed the July Revolution; but it would have been an odd reversal of the traditional attitude of Englishmen to have looked across the Channel for their model in political conduct. The parallel which more flatteringly struck the insular British mind was that between the July Revolution and their own Revolution of 1688.[2]

Nevertheless, the events abroad brought their own cares for the British ministers. The first news of the July revolt reached the government through the Rothschilds, whose agent was able to elude the ban placed on diplomatic couriers. Their account was sent to Drayton by the Prime Minister and in his reply Peel commented sharply on the extravagance and folly of the Bourbon monarchy and its ministers, more resembling—he said—the actions of a foolish woman trying to revenge the Revolution of 1789 than those of a sane man accustomed to public affairs.[3] Most of August and September he spent at Drayton but his administrative sense of duty if

---

[1] H.O. 64/11.

[2] The account of the 1830 election is largely based on my article 'English Reform and French Revolution' in *Essays Presented to Sir Lewis Namier* (ed. R. Pares and A. J. P. Taylor).

[3] *W.N.D.*, VII, 136, 142; *Peel*, II, 156.

nothing else kept him actively engaged. Early in August, when in London, he called on Aberdeen to suggest the despatch of a special envoy to Paris to collect more precise information than the meagre details coming through the diplomatic bags; and there was much correspondence on the propriety of receiving the exiled king of France in the United Kingdom. Peel's opinion was that he should be given asylum as a political refugee, but not as a Pretender to the French throne; and that if he came to England, a clear written statement of conditions should be made to him which could if necessary be publicly produced. On 19 August he advocated the prompt recognition of Louis Philippe as the best means within their power of assisting the stability of the new French monarchy and averting the risk of war.

This danger became more real at the end of September when the disturbances in Belgium clearly pointed to the imminent disruption of the kingdom of the Netherlands set up at the Congress of Vienna by agreement among the European powers. Peel was summoned to London for a cabinet meeting on Belgium held on 2 October. The occasion was critical, for the king of the Netherlands had issued an appeal to his allies to assist in repressing the revolt. Aberdeen's draft letter to the British ambassador in Paris on the subject was criticised by Peel as resembling an invitation to put down the Belgian insurrection by force, and he indicated in a few words a more innocuous form of reply. It was agreed in the end that Peel should take the letter away for alteration. Next day he read in cabinet first Aberdeen's amended version and then a new draft despatch of his own. The second seemed far superior and it was decided to adopt it in preference to Aberdeen's.[1] The incident was a characteristic demonstration both of Peel's capabilities compared with those of most of his colleagues and of his fundamental attitude on foreign policy. In all earlier cabinet discussions on foreign affairs—Turkey, Greece, Russia—his influence had consistently been lent to the side of moderation and caution. He emphasised to Aberdeen over the French question that it was essential for the government not to become involved in any continental quarrel which was not demonstrably just and certain to have the backing of the country. In fact, with the Foreign Secretary in the upper House, a considerable burden

---

[1] *Ellenborough*, II, 376-80.

of representing the ministerial case in foreign affairs in the Commons fell on Peel, which added weight to his views in the cabinet. During the 1830 session alone he spoke at different times on Mexico, Cuba, Spain, the settlement of Greece, the affairs of Portugal, the general foreign relations of the country, and Rhine navigation, frequently in answer to attacks by Palmerston and Lord John Russell, and always exhibiting the same basic opinions that he expressed in the cabinet. The inconsequent attitude of the opposition, simultaneously urging reductions in establishments and a spirited foreign policy, made him more than ever contemptuous of the ways of political faction.

## IV

In the summer of 1830 the main tactical question for the government was how to strengthen itself without introducing fresh cause of dissension and rivalry. Early in July Stuart Wortley, who had joined the ministry as Secretary to the Board of Control on Bankes's resignation, told Arbuthnot that he had reason to believe that Palmerston and Grant were ready to join the cabinet and that Huskisson would acquiesce in his own exclusion. The overture was communicated both to Wellington and to Peel. The Prime Minister was at first dubious: Charles Grant, he thought, was out of the question, and for the rest he would have to talk it over with Peel. On 16 July Arbuthnot and Peel conferred with the Duke at Apsley House. Peel himself was inclined to be sceptical. He believed that Palmerston would not come in alone; and that if he did, he would be crippled by the reproaches of those he had left. Nevertheless, the subject was not dropped, for the Duke also asked Hardinge what he thought of taking in Palmerston and Huskisson. The difficulty was in the solidarity of the Huskisson group, for though Palmerston and Lamb were acceptable, many of the cabinet entertained different feelings about Grant and Huskisson. However, between Huskisson and the Duke the outward courtesies at least had been restored. Lord Hertford had brought them together at Sudbourne in the previous October, and they had shot and played whist together with apparent friendliness.[1]

[1] 40340 f. 226; Fay, *Huskisson*, p. 51: *Arbuthnot Journal*, II, 312, 372-3.

In the interval a preliminary scrutiny of the election results did little to remove the impression of the general weakness of the government. According to the Treasury lists sent to Peel by Planta in the middle of August there was a gain on balance of seventeen seats for the government, and the provisional estimate of the new House of Commons optimistically put the ministerialist party at 368 with the opposition at 234, a majority of 134. Whether this would prove a working majority, the leader of the House might have been justified in doubting. Equally significant, perhaps, was the size of the opposition. With absentees and waverers on the government side, a united and organised opposition of nearly 200 (excluding the ultra-tory malcontents) was a formidable threat to the Front Bench.[1] As important as arithmetic, moreover, was the continued absence of any reinforcement of the ministerial team in the Commons; and early the following month Wortley again raised with Arbuthnot the question of securing some of the Canningites. The Duke was shown his letter and Arbuthnot wrote to Peel once more about the need for the party leaders to confer together on 'the great question of additional strength and our means of obtaining it'. Since both Peel and the Duke were to attend the opening of the Liverpool-Manchester railway in the middle of the month, there would be some opportunity to speak to each other then; but Peel sensibly suggested that Wellington and Arbuthnot should come to Drayton after the festivities were over. Wortley's overture, as he had himself acknowledged, was not based on any real authority; but there was a general feeling among ministers in the House of Commons that something must be done during the vacation. Rumours from the whig camp suggested that the elections had emboldened them to adopt a policy of outright defiance. Even if this were a piece of calculated intimidation, it was reasonable to suppose that a whig alliance would only be obtained in return for large concessions.[2]

Everything pointed therefore to a reconciliation with the Canningites as the most prudent policy for the cabinet to follow; and since Huskisson himself was also to be present at the great railway celebrations, it seemed at last as though some tangible progress might be made. Out of this situation came the tragedy of

[1] 40401 fos. 127, 140. See Aspinall, *Diaries*, Intro. xx-xxiii for a detailed analysis.
[2] 40340 fos. 230-2.

Huskisson's death on 15 September. On the morning of that day the gathering of notabilities at Liverpool embarked in a procession of trains and proceeded at some sixteen miles an hour towards Manchester. At Parkside, where the engines halted for water, many passengers alighted and Holmes, the government Whip, brought Huskisson along to the Duke's carriage. They had scarcely exchanged a handshake and a few friendly words when the *Rocket* at the head of another train came up at speed, scattering the passengers standing on the line. Holmes flattened himself against the side of the carriage and escaped damage. Huskisson, clumsy and nervous to the last, made an attempt to scramble to the safety of Wellington's carriage, lost his nerve, and was knocked down beneath the oncoming locomotive. The terribly injured man was taken by train to Eccles where he died the same evening. For some time the shocked ducal party debated whether to continue with the procession. Peel suggested calling in the Directors of the line, and after discussion with them it was decided to carry on with the programme in view of the great crowds awaiting their arrival at Manchester. Peel himself had been a witness of the accident and as soon as he returned to Liverpool, he sent off a brief note to Julia telling her what had occurred and adding, in case exaggerated rumours should reach Drayton, a carefully underlined sentence—'*this was the single accident*'. The same evening he wrote another letter, in more detail, to inform the king of what had happened. Though he had not then heard the news of Huskisson's death, his report left little hope of his survival.[1]

In the circumstances the meeting at Drayton a few days later could scarcely have failed to be overclouded. In preparation for the event, however, Planta and Charles Ross had been analysing more minutely the composition of the new House of Commons, and sent the results to Peel on 21 September. It was not encouraging reading: 311 friends, 37 moderate ultras, 37 doubtful-favourable, 24 very doubtful, 188 foes, 25 violent ultras, 23 doubtful-unfavourable, and 11 Huskissonites.[2] Nevertheless, these figures emphasised once

---

[1] 40301 f. 175; Peel, *Letters*, pp. 123-4 where the dates of the two letters should be 15 and 16 September (originals in Peel MSS.). For a full account of the accident see Fay, *Huskisson*, pp. 4-15.

[2] 40401 fos. 179-81.

more that, without a clear majority in the House, an access of talent would be needed the following session to offset the deficiency of numbers. In one sense, perhaps, Huskisson's death had removed an obstacle to a junction with his followers; and Arbuthnot, who wrote again on 17 September, told Peel that he had impressed on the Duke the need for additional support in the Commons. The Duke was not—he admitted—so sensible of this lack as others; but he was ready to do what was thought best, and Arbuthnot urged Peel to have some proposition to lay before him. Otherwise, he added, the session would open with nothing done.[1] On 22 September, therefore, Wellington, the Arbuthnots, Aberdeen, Goulburn, and Holmes gathered at Drayton for a political conference. The Duke was not happy at the prospect, for any newcomers to the cabinet would mean the removal of some of the existing members; and the man marked down as first for sacrifice was the inarticulate Sir George Murray, one of the military politicians about whom he was particularly sensitive. After the recent shock of Huskisson's death Peel himself was probably not in any mood of enthusiasm. Nevertheless, it was decided that they should ask Palmerston to join them, and leave further possibilities unexplored until they had his reply.

The king's permission was duly secured, and at the end of the month Wellington sounded Lord Clive on the chances of Palmerston taking office. The reply to this overture was friendly enough, but Palmerston concluded by saying that he could not singly join the government as it was at present constituted. The clear meaning of this was that Palmerston would not come in alone; and to find further vacancies was not easy. Wellington suggested to Peel that Herries might be asked to vacate, but Peel said firmly that Herries was ten times more useful in his present post than any other man would be; and with this the Duke (perhaps with ulterior motives) was glad to agree. It left him at least in the agreeable position of having tried to do what his colleagues advised and retaining a cabinet that he did not fundamentally wish to alter.[2] The autumn thus passed away with the ministry no stronger than in June; and

[1] 40340 f. 236.
[2] *Arbuthnot Journal*, II, 385-90; *W.N.D.*, VII, 281, 328; Bulwer, *Palmerston*, I, 362.

by the first week of October Peel was back at Whitehall Gardens once more, working in his library under Aberdeen's portrait, while a steady flow of visitors knocked at his door. Office seemed less attractive than ever as he listened to importunate callers or ran the gauntlet of suitors for patronage on his way to the office.

If the lesser members of the government were alarmed for the prospects of the ministry, the Duke at least preserved his serenity. He wrote to the Duke of Northumberland on 10 October that though men's minds were unsettled on a variety of topics, he hoped that the meeting of parliament would tend to tranquillise them and that the government would get over its difficulties.[1] It was obvious that he did not share the urgency of his followers and that what he had done so far was more in response to reiterated pressure from men like Hardinge and Arbuthnot than from his own persuasion of its necessity. Moreover, he had the conviction that any reinforcement, to be acceptable, must come in the shape of individuals and not groups; coalition with a party would mean either sacrifice of principle or constant wrangling in the cabinet. That at least seemed to be the lesson of 1828; and he was not anxious to repeat the experiment. If the Front Bench in the House of Commons was thin, the government was not in any immediate danger of defeat. Their opponents were divided into many groups, and a proof of their weakness was that anyone of them would gladly join the ministry.[2] Even if the officers were few, the disciplined troops of the government—in the eyes of their commander at least—would defeat the numerically superior but scattered forces of the opposition.

Parliament met on 26 October for the swearing-in of new members, but the session did not formally open until 2 November. Despite the failure at the beginning of the month Arbuthnot had continued to urge on the Duke the necessity of coming to terms with the Canningites and offered to resign his own post to facilitate arrangements. Even without this painful sacrifice for the Duke, it was thought that Calcraft might be induced to vacate; and by despatching Lord Beresford to Spain as diplomatic representative, three vacancies might be available for bargaining purposes. Peel, not surprisingly, showed no enthusiasm for the return of Charles

[1] *W.N.D.*, VII, 295.
[2] cf. Wellington to Fitzgerald, 4 September 1830, *ibid.*, 240.

Grant but seemed interested in securing Wilmot Horton. At the eleventh hour, therefore, one more concerted effort was made to enlarge the government. On his return from Paris, where he had gone to avoid any further embarrassing overtures, Palmerston was summoned by Wellington and asked who were the friends by whom it would be necessary for him to be accompanied if he returned to office. Palmerston named Melbourne and Grant, but added that even with them he would be disinclined to join unless the cabinet were reconstructed. Wellington said he thought he could find places for Palmerston and his two friends but he was not prepared for a larger change in the ministry. Palmerston thanked him, repeated that he could not accept unless on the basis of a general reconstruction, and added that he had purposely refrained from mentioning the names of the other persons he had in mind. A month earlier, in the negotiations through Lord Clive, Palmerston (by his own account) had been thinking of Grey and Lansdowne—a completely unreasonable demand, Clive told him, and clearly an unacceptable one. If the leaders of the whig party were to come into the cabinet through the hole made by the returning Huskissonites, Wellington might as well abandon the struggle at once. He certainly understood Palmerston to be again referring to the whigs; that being so, the door seemed completely closed on further negotiations. The Duke went to Peel immediately afterwards and the two men were agreed that the interview had put the possibility of an alliance out of the question; they must fight it out as they stood.[1]

Yet it is probable that Palmerston was not so firmly attached to the whigs at this juncture as his autobiographical account makes it appear. For on 1 November Littleton approached Arbuthnot with the offer of an alliance with Palmerston, the two Grants, Sir James Graham, and Stanley, provided that satisfaction could be given on a number of points of policy, of which the only substantial one was parliamentary reform in the minimum shape represented by Russell's bill of the previous session. Both men knew of Palmerston's recent interview with the Duke, and when Arbuthnot observed that he had assumed that the other persons referred to by Palmerston were Brougham and the whigs, Littleton instantly contradicted that interpretation. But while protesting the friendly attitude to the

[1] *Arbuthnot Journal*, II, 392-5; Bulwer, *Palmerston*, I, 363-4.

Duke's government of himself and the others he had named, Littleton also made it clear that if this last overture failed they would go into immediate and determined opposition. Arbuthnot conveyed the news at once to Peel and Wellington.[1] The effect on the Prime Minister was curious and disastrous. Wholly averse to any tampering with the legislature, he made up his mind that the best way to check the drift towards parliamentary reform was to throw up an immovable opposition, a kind of political Torres Vedras before which the whig *sans-culottes* would come to a halt. Accordingly the next day, in the debate in the Lords on the king's speech, he replied to an observation of Lord Grey's on the need for temperate reform with his celebrated and unequivocal declaration that the legislature could not be improved by reform, that it was more nearly perfect than any other legislature had ever been, and that so far from bringing forward any measure of reform, he would resist all reform measures of any kind and at all times so long as he held any office in the government of the country. When he sat down he asked Aberdeen whether he had said too much. 'You'll hear of it', the Foreign Secretary replied dourly. In effect, having failed to get individual strength for the cabinet, the Duke had now united all parties against him.

In the Commons the debate on the address mainly turned on foreign policy. Althorp made a moderate speech; Lord Blandford, O'Connell, Hume, and Brougham—an incongruous galaxy of critics—made violent ones; but the opposition did not divide. Nevertheless, it was noted with amusement that Peel was the only one of the cabinet ministers to defend the king's speech, with the result that Brougham, speaking late in the debate, was answered only by the lighter armament of Fitzgerald and Hardinge. Peel was disgusted at his colleagues' inactivity and received indeed considerable sympathy from the cabinet peers on that score. But Wellington's declaration provided fresh combustible material and the ministers in the Commons were strongly pressed about it the following day. Murray, reluctantly impelled into speech, went further than he intended. He announced a willingness to consider the question and added, in an unfortunate phrase that drew ironical cheers from the whigs, that he was friendly to a reform of parliament

[1] 40340 f. 240, printed almost in full *Peel*, II, 163.

that would secure a good and efficient system of government. Peel, trying to correct the impression made by his inexperienced colleague, said that he could not go the length of some speakers who seemed to direct their arguments against aristocratic government altogether; nor did he see at present any prospect that a safe moderate reform, such as the government might be prepared to sanction, would satisfy the expectations of reformers. He wisely left his remarks at that and devoted the main part of his speech to the Belgian question. It was impossible, however, to counteract the effect of the Duke's declaration and the explanations in the Commons merely produced an impression that the cabinet was divided on the issue. On 4 November Littleton asked Arbuthnot whether he had anything to say to him, and receiving the expected negative, observed that the door was now shut against any alliance.[1] To several of the House of Commons ministers it seemed as if the days of the government were numbered. Brougham had already given notice of a motion on reform, and Stuart Wortley thought that the Duke's speech had not only killed all chances of securing fresh adherents but had ensured a majority against the ministry when the subject came up for debate. Hardinge told the Duke frankly that if he were put in a minority on reform, or merely had a small majority, he ought to resign; and Arbuthnot, even while dreading the consequences of an ultra-liberal government, was almost inclined to welcome the final *coup de grâce* that would put them out of their political misery. But still the Duke professed his unconquerable optimism and thought that things might yet go well.[2] In this tense and incalculable situation came a second bombshell, this time thrown by Peel and the Duke acting together.

In the late autumn of 1830 the country was sullen with unrest. Though the purely economic discontent of the industrial areas had died down, the use made by radical propaganda of the continental revolutions threatened, for the first time in over a decade, to reforge the links between industrial and political agitation. There were reports of plans to seize arms and as a precaution the government during October had reinforced the garrisons at the northern arms-depots. Meanwhile the depressed and forgotten agricultural labourers of the south, driven at last to demonstrate against the recurrent

---

[1] 40340 f. 244, partly printed *Peel*, II, 167.    [2] *Ellenborough*, II, 416.

misery of winter unemployment, broke out in open rioting. Following the failure of the hop harvest, disorders began in Kent at the end of August and continued unchecked all through September. By October the whole county was involved in the disturbances and the contagion spread to its neighbours. Sussex was affected in November, followed by Hampshire, Berkshire, Wiltshire, Dorset, and Oxfordshire. The movement took the form mainly of machine-breaking and demands for higher wages, but there was a good deal of incendiarism, mobbing, and threats against farmers and clergy; and many magistrates and local gentry not surprisingly inferred a close connection between the rural rioting and the inflammatory language of the political radicals. Peel himself, at the beginning of November, was clearly under the impression that the labourers were being directed from some hidden source, and while urging the magistrates in Kent to concert measures and resist forcible concessions, he did what he could with the slender forces at his disposal. All the police officers that could be spared were sent to Maidstone; the troops in Kent and Sussex were reinforced; and General Dalbiac was placed in command with injunctions to confer with local magistrates on the best methods to adopt. Meanwhile, in London the ultra-radicals held nightly meetings at the Rotunda, in Blackfriars, at which excited crowds listened to the outpourings of Cobbett, Carlile, and other demagogues, pinned up tricolour cockades, and demonstrated in the streets afterwards. Threatening letters and warnings of conspiracy began to arrive at the Home Office; the new police, their resources strained to the utmost, were the object of violent propaganda and physical attacks; and the riff-raff of the metropolis profited by the excitement to retaliate in person on their professional enemies. On the night of 2 November, after the royal procession to open parliament, there were sixty-six cases of assault on policemen. Attempts were made to rescue pickpockets arrested on the streets, and the authorities evinced a nervous disposition to call in the military, despite Rowan's pleas to let his men do their work alone.[2]

Lord Mayor's Day on 9 November, the first after the accession, when according to tradition the king and his ministers were to dine

[1] H.O. 41/8/29-65; *Speeches*, II, 240, 243.
[2] 40308 f. 268; *Ellenborough*, II, 412; *Croker*, II, 73; cf. Ramsay, *Peel*, pp. 137ff.

at the Guildhall, seemed likely to bring all these smouldering elements together in sudden explosion. There were warnings of riot and of an attack on Wellington's house at Hyde Park Gate as soon as the police were drawn off to the other end of London; and thousands of printed handbills were circulated, calling Londoners to arms on that day and announcing that the 'damned police'—'Peel's bloody gang'—were to be provided with cutlasses supplied from the Tower of London. Hume, the cautious radical, came in person to the Home Office to show Peel an invitation he had received as M.P. for Middlesex to head an attack on St. James's Palace during the king's absence in the City—'our friends at Manchester will furnish pikes, and we expect assistance from Kent to the amount of 8 or 10 thousand'.[1] Both Peel and Wellington had received threats of assassination, and it was arranged that Hardinge and Arbuthnot, with a supply of pistols, should go down to the Guildhall in the Duke's carriage. Even to a cool soldier like Hardinge it seemed probable that an attempt would be made to turn 9 November into a day of barricades on the model of Paris and Brussels; and the Lord Mayor-elect wrote to Wellington that there was an intention among the disaffected elements in the City to attack him and that the City civil force would not be strong enough to ensure his protection. On Saturday 6 November two aldermen—Key the Lord Mayor-elect and Hunter who said he was deputed to act for the outgoing Lord Mayor—came to Peel. Both stated that the City Police would not be adequate to preserve order on the following Tuesday and asked for military aid.

Next day, in the afternoon, Peel and Wellington met at the Home Office to consider the situation. The Duke, in the face of the information that was before them, concluded that his presence in the City on the 9th would provoke disorder and probably bloodshed. His own courage was unquestionable; but he had seen too much of death to risk other and innocent lives in a tumult caused by the government's own action. Peel, for his own part, looking to the administrative question of preserving order, felt unable to guarantee the safety of all London on that night. It was clear that a deliberate campaign of incitement against his new police was being waged, and though the police and military could control the streets along

[1] Printed Ramsay, *Peel*, p. 138, in full.

which the procession would pass to the Guildhall, it would require a concentration of forces that would expose the rest of the metropolis to outbreaks of disorder. Whatever happened, their credit would be injured. If they took a calculated risk and blood was spilt, the consequences would be politically disastrous. If they chose the course of prudence, they would be accused of moral cowardice and dragging the king down to the level of their own unpopularity. In that dilemma Peel and the Duke preferred the claims of humanity and common sense to considerations of prestige. A cabinet had been called for that day, Sunday 7 November, at three o'clock and when an hour late the two ministers joined their colleagues, it was to tell them that they had decided to cancel the king's visit. Lyndhurst expostulated but the documents and arguments put before them brought the rest of the cabinet round to an unhappy consent. A letter was prepared for the king and Peel and Wellington went off to deliver it in person shortly before seven.[1] Later in the evening the cabinet discussed the measures still to be taken for 9 November. Phillipps, Colonel Rowan, and other magistrates and military commanders came to the cabinet room, and it was settled that the precautions already planned were to remain in force.

Having resolved on a policy of combined prudence and firmness, the Home Office carried it through with spirit and efficiency. It was decided to take strong measures against the mobs outside the Rotunda, and when on the night of 8 November a crowd of some hundreds came running into Westminster, they received some brusque handling from the police. Next evening, the day of the cancelled visit, the crowds were out in force; disorderly bands of up to a hundred roamed the town; and there was much scattered rioting. But the Home Office arrangements and the new police stood fast and Peel, who stayed on duty in the Home Office till midnight, was able to send a series of reassuring notes to Wellington and the king. At Temple Bar, the boundary between the City and the metropolitan area, which had long been a favourite no-man's-land for criminals and rioters, the mob overpowered the City Police and proceeded on their way. Rowan's men were made of stiffer material and gave the rioters what Ellenborough described as a 'terrible licking' near Southampton Street and again in Piccadilly. Large

[1] *Ellenborough*, II, 416ff.; *Speeches*, II, 234.

military reinforcements were in readiness but the civil police were completely effective in clearing the streets. There was no bloodshed and though some of the constables were severely hurt by stones, the authorities remained in control of the situation throughout the night of 9 November.[1] Yet the greater the success of the Metropolitan Police, the easier it was for the opposition to claim that the danger had been exaggerated. When Peel made his explanations in the Commons on 8 November, the reading of Alderman Key's letter, giving warning of an attack on Wellington, produced cheering and laughter from the other side of the House. 'Good God, a sarcastic cheer,' Peel observed bitterly, singling out Colonel Davies, one of the loudest cheerers, '—and from an officer in the army, too'. His vigorous exposition of the motives that had led to the government's decision was not without effect; but Brougham and some of the radical City members argued, nevertheless, that the government had acted in panic and on insufficient evidence, and were able to produce a resolution of the Court of Aldermen passed that day to the effect that there was no cause for alarm. Even Hume, with a remarkable effrontery that Peel disdained to expose, joined in the attack and expressed his surprise that the House did not move for the dismissal from the king's service of evil councillors whose conduct had excited so much alarm and irritation. There were probably many in the succeeding days who found it easy to believe that the ministers had merely contrived to make themselves look foolish and unpopular.

All this, however, was but preliminary skirmishing, though not without its damaging effect. The real trial of strength would come on the Civil List and on Brougham's reform motion, which was due for discussion on 16 November. On both issues Peel had made up his mind not to surrender. The government's new Civil List showed a saving of £85,000 on that of the previous reign and had it not been for the necessary provision for the queen, would have shown a reduction of £135,000.[2] If the ministers were beaten, it would not be on the merits of the case. The Civil List was introduced on 12 November and when Brougham launched an attack on its

---

[1] 40301 fos. 288, 290–3; 40309 f. 213, partly printed *Peel*, II, 168–9; *Ellenborough*, II, 425–8; *Ann. Reg.*, 1830, pp. 190–3.

[2] 40401 f. 290.

details as exhibiting stupidity and ignorance on the part of the government, he was answered sharply by Peel and Scarlett. The cabinet discussed the opening debate the following day in a mood of mild optimism, and Peel received the sanction of his colleagues for taking a strong line and refusing either to submit the Civil List to a special committee or to separate the diplomatic expenditure. A committee had never been conceded before and he thought that it would only exhibit weakness to concede it now. The question of parliamentary reform aroused more divided feelings. It was obvious that many of the government's usual supporters would vote for some measure of reform, if only in deference to public opinion. In a preliminary talk in the cabinet on 9 November Ellenborough was inclined to yield a committee with the object of defeating later any specific proposals. But Peel, with most of the other cabinet members, was against any tactical devices. In the rigid frame of mind with which he had started the session, he argued that it was a question simply of reform or no reform; and he personally could never undertake such a measure. To his brother William he wrote on 12 November that 'whatever may be the result of Tuesday next, I think it is better for the country and better for ourselves that *we* should not undertake the question'.[1]

When the cabinet returned to the subject two days later, he went further and said that whatever the figures in the division, the question was virtually carried. If the county members voted for it— and he clearly expected them to do so—it would be impossible to block the issue by the vote of the Scottish and English boroughs. To the king, who expressed some concern on the issue and was prepared himself to concede something to the popular demand, Peel argued that by opposing reform at the outset the government would be able to make better terms afterwards. This attitude seemed to Ellenborough obstinate and inexplicable. If the government objected in principle to reform, they would probably be turned out of office and have no subsequent power to influence the question; and he was tempted to attribute Peel's behaviour to an irrational reluctance to expose himself once more to a charge of ratting.[2]

In a few days, however, all argument was put at rest. On 15 November Parnell formally moved for a select committee to

[1] 40401 f. 267.    [2] *Ellenborough*, II, 425-8, 432-3.

examine the Civil List. There was a brief debate, and on a division the government was left in a minority of twenty-nine, the voting being 233-204. Hobhouse at once asked whether the ministers intended to remain in office. Peel refused to reply but immediately after the House rose Goulburn, Arbuthnot, and himself went to the Duke. They were convinced that even in a full House the majority would have been against them. Seventeen of their usual supporters had voted against them or paired off, and the majority of those regarded as generally favourable had on this occasion supported the whigs. The Huskisson group and twenty-three ultra-tories had voted against the government; and, most damaging of all, forty-nine of the sixty-six English county members who were present.[1]

They found the Duke dining at Apsley House with the Prince of Orange and a large party. A note was privately sent up to him and Wellington went downstairs alone to see his colleagues. When he heard the news he summoned Lyndhurst who at once declared that the game was up. The only question was whether to resign at once or stay to be defeated on Brougham's reform motion next day. It seemed incomparably wiser to go out at once, leaving the question of parliamentary reform to be met by the new ministry. The following morning, therefore, the Duke laid his resignation before the king, followed by Peel and the other ministers. Peel and Wellington announced the news in parliament the same day. Peel's speech in the Commons was brief, and though he rose later to correct a possible misinterpretation in the country of Althorp's phrase that there was now no administration in existence, he did it with complete calm and courtesy. Campbell, the whig lawyer, who afterwards went to hear Wellington in the Lords, recorded that 'Peel spoke with much more life, and what he said in answer to Lord Althorp was very dignified and was amazingly well received'. So moved was he that he bowed to Peel as he passed in the House of Lords—'which I never did while he was in office, and he seemed pleased with the salutation'.[2] The result of the division on the Civil List had taken both sides by surprise, and the whigs for the moment seemed as stunned as the ministerialists; but for Peel resignation had come as a welcome release. Mrs. Arbuthnot, who remained behind after the company at the Duke's had dispersed on the fatal evening,

[1] Aspinall, *Diaries*, Intro. xxi-xxii.    [2] *Campbell*, I, 487-8.

came down later to hear all about it. 'I never saw a man so delighted as Peel,' she wrote a few days afterwards. 'He said when the opposition cheered at the division, that he did not join in it but that it was with difficulty he refrained, he was so delighted at having so good an opportunity for resigning.'[1]

For another week, while a new ministry was being constructed, he continued to direct the Home Department. The chief object of his attention was the continued unrest in the south of England; and up to 22 November he was active in advising local authorities and despatching fresh military reinforcements. The ministerial resignation included inevitably the Irish executive, and judging with quick sympathy that the Duke of Northumberland would prefer to quit office before the arrival of his successor, Peel made arrangements for him to leave Ireland as soon as possible, leaving Lords Justices to govern in the intervening period. He added to his final letter a striking compliment to the outgoing Lord Lieutenant. 'I deeply regret for the sake of Ireland,' he wrote on 21 November, 'that any circumstances should have occurred to deprive that country of the services of the best chief Governor who ever presided over her affairs.'[2] Early on the afternoon of the following day he went with Wellington and the rest of the ministers to St. James's to hand over his seals. They each saw the king separately in his closet and then held a brief Privy Council to swear in George Dawson as privy councillor. Meanwhile the whigs had been arriving; and immediately after their departure the business of installing the new ministry began. That same afternoon Peel, with Goulburn, Herries, Hardinge, Scarlett, Calcraft, Croker, and others, took his seat on the opposition benches.

[1] *Arbuthnot Journal*, II, 402.     [2] 40327 f. 198.

# ENVOI

The fall of the Wellington government in 1830 was the first time since 1804 that a ministry had been driven to resign by a hostile House of Commons; and it resulted in the first complete change of ministers since the end of the Grenville administration in 1807. In the history of cabinet government it was the end of an era largely shaped by the characteristics of Lord Liverpool's long premiership. But it was scarcely the end of the Liverpool system, for that had vanished three years earlier. Whether in any case that system could have survived much longer is doubtful, but the fact remained that the Wellington ministry had completely failed in its professed object of reviving it. Liverpool's system had depended on the support of the country gentry, neutrality on the Catholic question, and a broad moderate policy in the cabinet. In less than three years Wellington had shed all those attributes. The Catholic question had been carried by the government itself; the ultra-tories were alienated; and all hope of reconciling moderate liberal opinion, faint enough after the Huskisson secession of 1828, had been killed by the Duke's declaration against parliamentary reform. It followed that Peel, who more than any other politician after Canning's death represented the Liverpool principle, was increasingly placed in a false position. For that his own attitude on emancipation was partly responsible. From Canning, the other great heir to Liverpool, he had been divided only by the Catholic question. With Wellington his only real political coincidence was their agreement in 1828 that the Catholic question must be settled. Once emancipation had been passed, there was a widening gap between himself and the Prime Minister, and an ever narrowing basis for his own position. Catholic emancipation cut him off from the extreme tory Protestant element in the country; the Duke's policy in the cabinet deprived him of the moderate liberal support which alone would compensate for that loss. Not the least momentous result of the separation from Canning in 1827 was Peel's gradual realisation that in accepting the Duke's leadership he had entered a political blind alley.

Wellington's prestige and his outstanding qualities as a public servant had brought him into politics; but he was no politician. That did not imply, however, that he had no political views. Catholic emancipation he had dealt with as an administrative problem, yet fundamentally all his instincts were with the tory side in politics. Bathurst and Ellenborough were his most congenial colleagues in the cabinet and the restraint with which he handled the tory malcontents of 1829 was in significant contrast to his stiff attitude towards the Canningites in 1828. Despite all the tory abuse, he was slow to relinquish, even if he ever did, the hope that their animosity would eventually subside and solidarity once more be established. The experiment of the Huskisson alliance, undertaken largely under Peel's influence at the start of his ministry, had ended in disaster and he determined never again to expose himself to the trials of a divided command. But politics were not war, and the Duke's refusal to share power meant that the government's policy was increasingly Wellingtonian and negative. It was a feature of the 1828-30 ministry that the longer it continued, the greater was the influence exerted over it by the Prime Minister and the greater the frustration to which Peel was condemned. In this there was at first nothing personal. The Duke respected Peel's abilities, was anxious to assist, and was open to representations. But Wellington's position in the Lords and his own imposing reputation insulated him against the daily pressures of the House of Commons, the real engine of power, and his own circle of admirers, both male and female, contributed to the unreality of his situation. As a soldier he was accustomed both to command and to success; he found it difficult to believe that politics was any different. The compromises and adjustments that made up half of Liverpool's preoccupations as Prime Minister were alien to the hard simplicity of the Duke's nature; and the inadequacy of his attempts to recruit individual talent for the Front Bench sprang from his unwillingness to admit any alteration in his outlook. In the end, therefore, Peel found himself a prisoner in a cabinet to whose composition and policy he was increasingly averse; and the political intransigence whereby the Duke brought his government to self-imposed defeat was welcome to Peel as the only means of escape from an intolerable captivity.

It is to this that is attributable Peel's final attitude on the test question of parliamentary reform which Ellenborough found so inexplicable. All his earlier utterances, even his speech of 3 November, had indicated at least a readiness to entertain some consideration of the question even if he was against any radical or continuous principle of reform. In December, out of office, he told the Commons that he had never said anything to preclude him on any fit occasion from transferring the franchise from any corrupt borough to Birmingham or another large unrepresented town.[1] In November, however, his acute consciousness of the weakness of the government in the Commons made him dread the dangers of taking up a question of such significance when there was no guarantee that the ministers would in the end have their way. Rather than precipitate a landslide, he preferred to leave the problem in the hands of a stronger and more united government than Wellington's could pretend to be. Under the responsibilities of office, Lord Grey and his colleagues were likely to loosen rather than draw tighter the political ties with their radical supporters; and if they needed support in that attitude, Peel for one was prepared to give it to them. The charge against the ministry to which he himself belonged was that it was too weak to control events; if so, it was time that it gave way to a more effective political combination. His unyielding attitude, over the Civil List as well as parliamentary reform, was designed as a decisive trial of the government's strength in the new parliament. If it failed, he could quit office with a clear conscience. The consequences of a whig administration were not all calculable, and the immediate promotion of Brougham as Lord Chancellor hardly promised well for the future of aristocratic government. However, 'it was much better that even this should happen,' he wrote to his old friend Hobhouse on 24 November, 'than that we should continue to administer the government in difficult times without the requisite support.'[2]

There were, of course, personal and emotional factors underlying this rationalisation. He was immensely tired and overworked. With only one substantial break of three and a half years after his Irish secretaryship, he had been in office for two decades; and the strain of combining a major department of state with the leadership of the Commons that killed Castlereagh, had brought Peel almost

[1] *Speeches*, II, 257.     [2] 40401 f. 290.

to the end even of his great physical and mental resources. With his weariness went an increasing irritability. He had a passion for efficiency and effectiveness, and the conditions in which he was placed in parliament allowed him neither. His colleagues on the Front Bench seemed content to let him bear the brunt of his work and their work, too. Fitzgerald was, when in the mood, a lively and telling speaker, but ill-health or the persuasion of it had made him relinquish office in January 1830 and he declined an invitation from Wellington to return the following September. Goulburn was a poor speaker and was already showing the limitations of his talents; Herries and Murray were almost mutes; Calcraft and Stuart Wortley insignificant. On the benches behind him were ostensible supporters who showed an indifference to the daily needs of the government in the business of the House; and whatever Planta's merits or demerits as Chief Whip, he could rarely enforce the steady discipline of attendance and voting which the slender forces of the government required. Not merely, perhaps not most culpably, the country gentry but also the minor office-holders and connections of the ministry showed little sense of loyalty. In his letter to Hobhouse of 24 November, Peel instanced four cabinet ministers—the Duke, Bathurst, Melville, and Rosslyn—with sons in the House of Commons who never spoke and, only able to serve by a silent vote, were absent from the division which brought about the fall of the government in which their fathers held office. 'Can I personally,' he ended bitterly, 'regret the end of such a government?' Under the strain some of his old liveliness and confidence had disappeared. The defection of the ultra-tories on his own side was a peculiarly damaging weakness, and after 1829 he was continually exposed to taunts from all parts of the House of his personal inconsistency over Catholic emancipation. Certainly the wounds of 1829 were still raw a year later. On Huskisson's death he was invited to stand for Liverpool; when adverting in his letter of refusal to the difficulties inherent in the double responsibility of official duties and constituency obligations, he could not refrain from a reference to 'the penalty which I have paid for the discharge of what appeared to me an imperative public duty. I allude of course to the withdrawal of its confidence by the University of Oxford'.[1]

---

[1] *Peel*, II, 163.

Beneath these surface strains was a deeper rift that had opened up between Peel and the Duke. With all their respect for each other—and Peel at least could never forget the debt owed to Wellington by his country—they were never intimate. In character and temperament they differed widely, and as early as the Huskissonite secession Peel had probably realised the limits of his powers over the Prime Minister. Indeed, there were few men of his generation who could claim to influence the Duke. His authoritarian masculine nature was amenable only to pleasant young men like Francis Leveson Gower or to the subtler sexual persuasions of adoring women. Peel had no such arts at his disposal and in proportion as he realised the impossibility of affecting the Duke through political arguments, he tended to withdraw into a position of deliberate isolation. Many months afterwards, in July 1831, Arbuthnot complained to Greville that at the Drayton conference following Huskisson's death it had been impossible to elicit anything from Peel. Not much importance should be attached to a secondhand account so long after the event; but it is clear at any rate that there was a noticeable lack of communication between the two leaders. In September 1830 when discussing with his brother-in-law Greville the weakness of the Duke in having no one about him who would speak frankly, Leveson Gower remarked that though Peel was the man who might be expected to be the spokesman in such circumstances, he never would and often got Leveson Gower to write or speak to the Duke rather than go himself. Himself too singly attached to one woman to be easily influenced by others, Peel disliked the atmosphere of the Duke's private circle and his moral sense was affronted by the sight of Mrs. Arbuthnot as the Duke's constant companion. At a house-party at Sudbourne in 1828 at which Mrs. Arbuthnot, Lady Strachan, and Lady Beckett were present, he wrote slightingly to Julia that the only decent woman there was Mrs. Huskisson. In this he was unjust, but he was not alone among contemporaries in his opinion of the relationship. The growing political tension and the optimistic carelessness of the Duke—or what seemed to be such, despite the protestations of the faithful Arbuthnot—about the straits to which his government was reduced in the House of Commons, steadily brought all these feelings to a head.

The anger and irritation, moreover, were not only on Peel's side.

At the end of February 1830 Mrs. Arbuthnot noted how ill-tempered the Duke had become. 'The truth is, he is worried by everybody; he is tormented by people asking for places which he has not got to give, and by complaints of the weakness of the Govt. and the bad management of Mr. Peel.' His colleagues had to bear a fuller share of this irritability than Harriet Arbuthnot; and it was not long after this that Peel told her husband that the Duke seemed altered in his manner towards him and always dissatisfied, as though something were on his mind. Peel was not mistaken in his sense of growing estrangement between himself and the Prime Minister. In July, when the Arbuthnots were talking with the Duke on the perennial theme of strengthening the government in the Commons, they were treated to an alarming exhibition of ill-temper, principally directed at the absent figure of his chief colleague.

> The Duke was very violent about it, put himself into a furious passion, said he would not meet Mr. Peel about it for that it was all his fault and his own bad management, and that if he turned those people out and took whoever Mr. Peel chose, he should have him coming in a fortnight's time with exactly the same complaints. . . . He was violent to the greatest degree, stormed and raved in a furious manner.

When Mrs. Arbuthnot renewed the question again at Walmer in August, the Duke again flew into a rage and abused Peel, and she was obliged to beat a retreat. Even to the Arbuthnots, in fact, Wellington seemed at times unreasonably incensed and obstinate.[1] This increasing coolness between himself and the Duke had been peculiarly painful to Peel, and it is difficult not to believe that it materially contributed to his own anxiety to end as soon as was decent his connection with Wellington's government. At the same time he was resentful at the manner in which that connection was breaking up. Much of the discomfort of his own situation he could with some justice ascribe to his loyalty to the Duke over emancipation. By the end of 1830 it seemed as if that loyalty was scarcely being repaid.

All these thoughts and emotions broke out on the fall of the ministry in a conversation with Princess Lieven, the wife of the

[1] *Arbuthnot Journal*, II, 340-2, 372, 381.

Russian ambassador; and that the outburst was an uncharacteristic revelation of Peel's inner feelings to such a notoriously indiscreet person was only a proof of their intensity. On 20 November, two days before the formal resignation of the government, Princess Lieven dined with the Peels. At dinner she questioned her host on the reasons for the fall of the ministry and received a startling reply. For the last year, said Peel, the government had been tottering and not progressing. They had alienated the tories without conciliating the whigs. The collapse of the ministry was imminent and had been hastened by the Duke's declaration against reform. The head of a government should never allow his secrets to be penetrated; one might do everything, but one should not say everything. The Duke had the misfortune to be surrounded by women of the most mediocre ability. No men had any influence with him; he was led by women. The foolish ones enveloped him in incense, and he had fallen victim to his own weakness and vanity. As for himself, his own plan was settled. He was an enemy only of the radicals; and the new government was equally so. In that respect he would loyally support it. For the rest, he would await the new ministers' profession of faith to know whether he should oppose or not.[1] It is hard to doubt that the account of this conversation given by the princess was not substantially true. Certainly the following month Lord Lyndhurst told Greville that he knew that Peel would never again serve under Wellington, that all the 'Duke's little cabinet (the women and the toad-eaters)' hated Peel, and that there was never any real cordiality between them. If these were in effect Peel's opinions, he was not alone. Greville himself at the time wrote an acid criticism of the Duke's obstinacy and egotism which had brought his government to a calamitous and unnecessary end.[2]

The recriminations were mutual, however, and Peel himself on other grounds was exposed to bitter comment from his own party. Even in October Arbuthnot had complained to Greville of Peel's

---

[1] *Letters of Dorothea, Princess Lieven*, ed. L. G. Robinson (1902), pp. 277-8. Though the princess was not always a reliable witness, there are several reasons for accepting the substance of this account. Writing to her brother in Russia, the princess had no motive for misrepresentation; the circumstantial details suggest veracity; and it accords with what is known of Peel's attitude at the time (cf. *Greville*, 16 December 1830).

[2] *Greville*, 5, 15 December 1830.

reserve, his indisposition to encourage other men in the House of Commons or delegate business to other hands. Other people had the same impression, or at least repeated each other's language. Hardinge in April had spoken of Peel's cold unencouraging manner. Stuart Wortley told J. C. Hobhouse in May that it was not a very pleasant task acting under Peel; his manners were cold, and very little assistance was required by him from anybody.[1] Much of this was probably true, and for various reasons: partly Peel's growing reserve; partly his perfectionist instinct which to the end of his life made him take too much on himself rather than trust to inferior hands; partly too, in the summer of 1830, his underlying tiredness and nervous strain. A working day of fifteen to eighteen hours during the session hardly conduced to affability or small-talk. It was in May of that year that Rickman, the caustic Clerk-Assistant of the House, had trenchantly remarked that 'at present the bodily and mental fatigue of all efficient members of the Administration destroys them as rational beings'.[2] To outsiders Peel frequently gave the impression of aloofness. In his own sphere he was himself becoming isolated by office and reputation. To those who penetrated the outer manner, and it was not difficult to penetrate, there was a modesty and kindliness which was all the more winning for being unexpected. Campbell, the whig lawyer whom Peel had put on the Real Property Commission, dined with Peel for the first time in December 1828, expecting to find his host dull and formal. 'But I must own,' he confessed afterwards to his brother, 'he was lively and unaffected, and very civil without being condescending.'[3] Ellenborough had made a similar discovery a few months before. Himself a proud and unpopular figure, ambitious but frustrated in his comparatively minor post as Lord Privy Seal, Ellenborough had run foul of Peel early in the ministry. In June he was noting that his criticisms annoyed the Home Secretary, who answered captiously. Since in the previous month, over the reconstruction of the ministry after the Huskissonite resignations, he had told Peel in the presence of Dawson and William Peel that he had managed ill, united the opposition, and made a weak government, some frigidity on Peel's part was perhaps not surprising. But when in July, at a cabinet

---

[1] Broughton, *Recollections*, IV, 25; *Ellenborough*, II, 221.
[2] Williams, *Rickman*, p. 263.      [3] *Campbell*, I, 462.

dinner given by Ellenborough at Roehampton, he asked Peel to drink a glass of wine with him, and showed him a few pictures, Peel responded at once with a marked warmth of manner. 'I really believe,' Ellenborough recorded afterwards, 'he is only rather a proud touchy man, and that the least attempt at management would make him very cordial.'[1]

Yet not everyone could take wine with Peel or discuss paintings, and to the ordinary country gentleman on the back benches there was much that was alien and objectionable in his public manner. 'Peel, tho' able, honest, and high-minded, is too selfish, too proud and haughty in his manner to have a personal following', wrote William Holmes (admittedly to Mrs. Arbuthnot) in September 1827. 'He lost himself very much in the last session by his constantly talking about himself and his criminal laws.'[2] Holmes, a coarse third-rate party politician, who passed his life between aristocratic house-parties and the lobbies of the House of Commons, was himself little equipped to understand Peel; but he understood the country squires whose whipper-in he was, and was undoubtedly voicing a general feeling. The charge of egotism was a common one, and Peel lent himself to it more than he realised. There was a tendency in his speeches to dwell on his own personal attitudes and convictions, and after Catholic emancipation the constant sneers at his recantation strengthened still more his trick of self-explanation and exculpation. Egotist in that sense he was; egoist in the sense of a fundamentally selfish and self-centred man he was not. In many respects Peel was singularly free from self-centredness. He kept no diary to embalm his daily doings in the written page; on his father's death when he burnt, apparently without a qualm, all his father's private correspondence, he must have destroyed many of his own early letters that would have filled an irreparable gap for later biographers. After 1827, when out of office, he rarely if ever kept copies of letters which he wrote. A phrase by the editor of the Peel Papers[3] referring to his practice as

___

[1] *Ellenborough*, I, 130, 153, 175.     [2] *Arbuthnot Correspondence*, p. 93.
[3] *Peel*, II, Preface, p. 6; taken up by E. L. Woodward, *The Age of Reform*, p. 104 n. 3 who refers to 'the care which he took, as early as 1812, to bind copies of his official letters in volumes of red morocco with gilt edges'. The letters were copied, not bound; they consisted of his private and confidential correspondence (40280-40295); and the fact that no other copies existed in the office is shown by his loan of them to Grant when the latter succeeded as Chief Secretary in 1818.

Irish Secretary of having his letters 'copied into quarto volumes in all the pomp of red morocco with gilt edges' is misleading if it is taken to denote any special degree of self-interest. The practice for official men to keep official letter-books in durable bindings was so common in the period as scarcely to deserve attention; and there is no discernible psychological difference between the not very imposing red morocco of Peel's letter-books and the soft brown calf of, for example, those of Lord Anglesey when Lord Lieutenant. For the rest there was not much suggestion of egoism in his literary remains. His *Memoirs* were state papers, not autobiographical fragments. Indeed, for a man who left such a large quantity of correspondence for his executors, there is astonishingly little material dealing with his private life. It was Julia, not her husband, who seems to have kept what was preserved of their personal letters.

For natural egoism, on the other hand, it would have been difficult to match, as a class, the English country gentlemen of the period whose representatives were so apt to criticise Peel in the Commons. Invulnerable in their independence, their rank, their property, they moved through life with a hard assurance that bespoke their restricted outlook and fixed prejudices. They concerned themselves for little in politics except rents, corn, and taxes: and if they deferred to anyone it was more likely to be a master of fox-hounds than a minister of state. For three parts of Peel's work they cared little, and they loved him less for hearing about it so much. The egotism of which they complained in Peel, however, was primarily the compulsion of a highly self-conscious mind, endeavouring to explain a personal relationship that was better left unexplained. This almost painful scrupulousness was evident, for example, in his reference over currency reform in 1819 to the superior sagacity of Horner and in his ascription of all the credit for Catholic emancipation in 1829 to Fox, Plunket, and Canning. Of this self-conscious trait in Peel's nature there were several early indications; but it was not until he had moved to the higher levels of political life that comments began to be made on his coldness of manner. In the intimate community of Dublin Castle or in the small circle of Irish government M.P.s he had seemed a friendly and popular figure. But from 1827 onwards, after the breach with

Canning and still more after Catholic emancipation, he was in the centre of bitter personal feuds and under the hostile observation of men with whom he was little acquainted. With the House of Commons as an audience he was completely at ease; dealing with them as individuals he was less happy. His integrity prevented him from any calculated bidding for popularity; his reserve with strangers limited the growth of his own circle of friends; his increasing experience of the difficulties of securing constant support and attendance from the country gentry engendered impatience. For the fox-hunters, gamblers, and men of fashion he had the contempt of the professional for the amateur; and it did not help him to know that partly at least he was dependent on such men. When after 1827 he began to encounter the rough handling inseparable from any major career in politics, his nature contracted into a cold and repellent manner which offended many and of which he was partly unaware.

Yet the appearance was there and it could hardly have attracted the adverse comment it did unless one side of Peel's character had justified it. It is significant that conceit and egotism were the qualities that his enemies ascribed to him quite early in his career. In the political squibs published by the whig *Morning Chronicle* between 1815 and 1819, for instance, this is the stock characterisation. In a satiric list of ministers as performers in a musical programme the item allotted to Peel was ' "Ladies and Gentlemen, I'm a Beau", with a solo on the Trumpet (his own)'. In another skit in which the members of the government appeared as inhabitants of a menagerie he figured as *Psittacus Pullarius* or Redheaded Parrakeet— 'this is one of the Parrot species. The bird is in no way remarkable, but as being the most vain and conceited of little birds.'[1] This type of criticism extended to—indeed perhaps originally sprang from— his outward appearance in the House of Commons.

> I do not like his physiognomy as an orator [wrote Sheil, referring to the period about 1825]. He has a handsome face, but it is suffused with a smile of sleek self-complacency, which it is impossible to witness without distaste. He has also a trick of closing his eyes, which may arise from their weakness, but which has something

---

[1] *The New Tory Guide* (1819), reprints of extracts from the *Morning Chronicle*.

mental in its expression; and however innocent he may be of all offensive purpose, is indicative of superciliousness and contempt.[1]

In ordinary conversation the outward manner that to his friends seemed smooth and gentle, to his critics appeared priggish and frigid; and his habit of looking away from interlocutors and listening rather than talking increased the impression of aloofness and disdain. The truth was that Peel had no natural manner; and it was the sensed artificiality of his behaviour that alienated so many casual observers. The excessive politeness which Lady Shelley noticed, the unhappy intrusion of self into many of his public utterances, the iciness which displayed itself to enemies and strangers, his reputation for unsociability, all sprang from this central characteristic. Lawrence Peel, though he never experienced the coldness and conceit of which others complained, remarked on the contrast between Peel's outer suavity and the nervous, almost feminine qualities within.[2] It was as though for all his talent and success there was an element of unsureness in his character. External circumstances may have accentuated even if they did not create this psychological deficiency. He was a plebeian making his way by wealth and brains in an aristocratic society; and the constant stimulus of his father from earliest years had left perhaps a certain strain. Old Sir Robert had projected his still unconsumed will and ambition into his first and brilliant son's career, sparing neither money nor influence on his behalf. He had his reward when he read Robert's speeches in the press or invited his Staffordshire neighbours to dine with the Home Secretary at Drayton. But for the son this silent and subconscious pressure had its reverse side. The perpetual knowledge of the expectations formed of him could scarcely have failed to lay a burden on Peel which was made even more onerous by his own pride and ambition. For an imaginative man these were heavy responsibilities to carry. Masterful as Peel was in action, he was often curiously nervous beforehand. It showed in small ways: in his fit of depression before his degree examination, and in the characteristic expressions of apprehension when accepting the Irish Secretaryship in 1812 and the Home Office in 1821. Hardinge noted that Peel as leader of the

[1] R. L. Sheil, *Sketches Legal and Political*, ed. M. W. Savage (1855), II, 39ff.
[2] Peel, *Life*, pp. 49, 65-7.

House of Commons 'had a sad want of moral courage before the debate, but once in for it his physical courage carried him on'.[1] This contrast between the mental anticipation and the actual event was a reflection of the contradictory forces within.

In Peel's nature there was in fact a discordancy between the inner person and the person he presented to the world. He had created, perhaps had always had to create, an artificial self with which to deal with others. It was this dualism which explains the widely different views about him held by his friends and his critics. But though Peel had perhaps created this secondary personality as a form of protection for himself, use and habit had made it a second nature; and it is not surprising that observers often failed to distinguish between the two. Moreover, vulnerability has its own methods of retaliation. The need for self-protection easily enlists less amiable qualities on its side; and of these Peel had his full share. His humour tended to be secretive and sometimes malicious; his detachment from others bred contempt; his integrity could degenerate into self-righteousness; the unnecessary emphasis on the purity of his motives made him on occasion sanctimonious. Ingrowing virtues have a trick of developing ingrowing vices; and though Peel saw much of the world, he held himself too consciously apart from it. The very success and ease of his career distilled their own subtle poisons. He never had to struggle; and he had too much scorn for politicians who could less afford to be nice in the methods they used in making their careers. He was above temptation; and had too little sympathy for the human motives behind the petty political dishonesty he constantly witnessed. He never had to court the patronage of powerful ministers; and he let himself too readily despise the flattery and supplication which were the weapons of lesser men. These, in the political world of the early nineteenth century, were no doubt faults on the right side and it could be argued that what the world needed was more Robert Peels and fewer ordinary politicians. But politics, like the world itself, is made up of ordinary men. Only a person of great humility could have held Peel's standards and retained complete humanity; and Peel was not humble. He lacked therefore the natural touch which is one of the most endearing traits of human beings. There was nothing in Peel comparable

[1] *Ellenborough*, I, 177.

to the earthiness of Walpole, the simplicity of Fox, the cynicism of Melbourne, or the insouciance of Palmerston. To speak of him as though he were above all a great House of Commons man is misleading; he commanded their respect but rarely their devotion.

For Peel, also, there was the standing contrast between the asperities of politics and the peacefulness of his private life. When he spoke, as he did increasingly after his marriage, of the sacrifices he made to public life and his indifference to office, he was speaking at least a part-truth; it was not an affectation reserved for a public audience. 'Oh, believe me, my own dearest life,' he wrote to his wife after he had been summoned to London by Wellington in January 1828, 'that my heart is set upon home and not upon ambition.'[1] Unlike many he had private wealth, domestic happiness, and personal tastes and pursuits that made continuance in politics only necessary if seen as a pleasure or a duty. Sessions such as those of 1828-30 robbed him of leisure, deprived him of the company of his wife and children, and transformed him for long periods into a mere drudge of the state. When tired, angry or depressed, it was natural for him to wonder whether a voluntary submission to the discipline of ministerial life was worth the toil, the abuse, the accusations of sordid ambition, the need to suffer, if not gladly, the fools and the bores, and to take part, however distastefully, in the petty traffic of political favours. Moreover, he was conscious, though in a half-disdainful way, of his own disqualifications for the rough and tumble of politics.

> I feel a want of many essential qualifications [he wrote some time after his resignation to Goulburn] which are requisite in party leaders, among the rest personal gratification in the game of politics and patience to listen to the sentiments of individuals whom it is equally imprudent to neglect and an intolerable bore to consult.

It was in this mood that his followers found him on the eve of quitting office in 1830 while the world waited to see what the whig ministry would bring forth. On 17 November, just before they

---

[1] Peel, *Letters*, p. 103.

went out, there was a meeting at Peel's house of some forty official members of the House of Commons. Granville Somerset asked Peel whether he would lead them in the House and received a discouraging answer. He said he wished to retire to private life, undertake no opposition, and not lead a party—in effect, he would leave them to their own devices. This, for the professionals who looked to office as a career, was both depressing and irritating. But there were others who knew Peel better than that. Ellenborough, to whom Hardinge complained of this attitude, comforted him with the assurance that within a fortnight, as soon as Peel had recovered his health and spirits, he would be in opposition again. In fact Peel told Croker a few days later that he had spoken with excessive caution because he feared the discretion and loyalty of some present. William Peel was assuring people by 20 November that though his brother would not be violent or factious, he thought an attentive opposition desirable and would not desert those who looked to and supported him; and by 30 November Croker, finding Peel more cordial and zealous, was able to write cheerfully to Lord Hertford that 'the Conservative party of observation under General the Duke of Wellington and Lieut. Gen. Sir Robert Peel have taken their position, and will act if, and when, necessary'.[1] Ellenborough was right in his diagnosis. The crash of November 1830 had exposed all the flaws and strains that had been accumulating for several years. The weaknesses were still there, and perhaps would occur again under similar stress; but when the dust and smoke had subsided, the central features of both men and parties would be visible once more. If there was a game, there was also a business of politics to which Peel could never be indifferent; and after two decades of office it was unlikely that he could ever bring himself to retire from the career that had occupied all his public time and energies since he left Oxford. At the age of forty-two, with a record of administration unmatched by any contemporary and a reputation which no transient unpopularity or momentary lassitude could destroy, it was unthinkable that the future should hold nothing for him.

It was true that the Wellington ministry had seen the culmination of his work as Home Secretary. He had virtually ended the massive task of consolidating the criminal law, and he had achieved what had

[1] *Croker*, II, 77-9; *Ellenborough*, II, 441.

previously seemed impossible, the creation of the Metropolitan Police on Colquhoun's preventive principle. But if the years 1828-30 had enabled him to complete one instalment of administrative reform, it had also produced the first sketch of another. Education and Poor Law in Ireland; raising the standard of living for the working classes in England; tariff reform and retrenchment; the fundamental revolution contained in the proposal to revive the income tax as an essential feature of peacetime finance; all these issues to which he had devoted his attention in the last years of office represented an even more far-reaching social and economic programme. Even the Wellington ministry had not been an entirely uneducative experience. As leader of the House of Commons Peel had markedly expanded his political horizon; and even outside the wide field of authority given to him by the Home Department, the attitude of the Wellington cabinet to problems of finance and foreign policy bore the imprint of his influence. There were still large reserves of creative statesmanship in the Home Secretary, and it was unlikely that he would ever again be satisfied with the limitations of one department.

It was the fashion among the radicals to decry Peel as a timid, unimaginative reformer. This was not the view of his colleagues. Once, when discussing with Hardinge the prospects of Peel's early succession to Wellington as head of the government, Ellenborough commented that he feared he would be 'a very Radical minister'.[1] In fact much of Peel's weariness and irritation in the last phase of Wellington's ministry came from his sense of having responsibility without power. Not lack of policy, but inability to make the Duke's cabinet the instrument of policy, was the root cause of his dissatisfaction. The typical radical sneer at Peel as 'a very tiny statesman'[2] was founded partly on ignorance of what went on behind the scenes in Wellington's government, and partly on Peel's opposition to such publicised matters as Catholic emancipation and parliamentary reform. The radical movement looked primarily to constitutional reform and a transfer of political power, and tended to assume that legislative benefits would automatically result from those changes. Peel, looking primarily to administrative reform, had no reason to think that organic changes in the constitution must necessarily

[1] *Ellenborough*, II, 220.    [2] *The People's Book*, ed. W. Carpenter (1831), p. 342.

precede, or indeed would necessarily assist, the new social and financial conceptions to which he was moving. One of the difficulties of government was lack of control over the House of Commons, and it was not easy to see that the admission of new populous constituencies and their members would make the task of the executive any lighter. What the country needed, in his view, was more efficient government; the whole attitude of the radical opposition seemed to point towards less and more ineffective government.

The difference was one of completely contrasting outlook and experience. The most unreasonable critics of a system are those who are outside it; the most indulgent supporters those whom it has served well. By 1830 a large part of public opinion was persuaded that many if not all of the ills from which society suffered were caused by misgovernment and that the remedy lay in a reform of parliament. To men like Peel neither the limitations nor the potentialities of executive policy had much to do with the structure of representation. Given a free hand he was confident of his ability to meet his critics. But to depart from the paths of good government and sound administration to play on the political passions of the people seemed to him a dangerous negation of leadership. By temperament, upbringing, and the mentality engendered by nearly twenty years in office, he was cautiously conservative on all questions that affected the historic institutions of the country. Revolutionary France had demonstrated in an unforgettable fashion to his generation of Englishmen the perils of an abrupt change in the political habits of society, and he conceived the task of statesmanship to be the reconciliation of the institutions of government with social needs rather than a wanton dismantling of those institutions to satisfy ephemeral discontents. Whether England, any more than Ireland, would be content with—or would make even possible—the slow solid advantages of practical improvements in place of a sudden dramatic shift in political power, was another matter.

Yet to be conservative by instinct did not mean that Peel had evolved an explicit conservative policy on all public issues. Indeed, the short but eventful Wellington ministry showed clearly that Peel had given relatively little consideration to more than one issue on which he had to act. He was a busy man, and it was not easy for him to devote much time to problems which did not actually confront him either at the Home Office or in parliament. Moreover, the obsessive influence of Catholic emancipation had the effect of obscuring to many politicians besides himself other issues of significance. Russell's motion for the repeal of the Test and Corporation Acts, backed as it was by a sudden intensive propaganda effort by the organised body of English dissenters, had caught the ministers unawares, and Peel's attitude had as it were to be improvised almost overnight. It was natural, therefore, that he fell back on the argument of inexpediency, and for all his Church connections was unwilling to take up a stand on High Church but tactically dangerous principles. His handling of the question was conditioned largely by what could be done in the House of Commons. Similarly the emergence of parliamentary reform as a major issue in the 1830 session found him with little more than instinct to guide him. To reproduce the arguments of Burke and Canning was a respectable but unoriginal contribution; it did not prove either that he had thought the question out *de novo* or that he had evolved a specific answer to the demands being voiced in parliament and in the public press. He was certainly against any large reconstruction of the representative system; equally clearly he was against the dead negation of Wellington and Ellenborough. He opposed the whig and radical demands not only because they went too far but also because he wished to keep his hands free. But what he stood for, and what he would do if his hands were free, was not obvious to others and possibly not to himself.

The truth was perhaps that personally and politically he had come to the cross-roads of his career. What he required was not so much a change of direction as an opportunity to halt and take stock of his surroundings. He had been in office too long and he needed time to rest and think. Nevertheless, there was no likelihood of any abrupt change when he resumed his progress. Two attributes above all—an imaginative and flexible readiness for administrative reform and a fundamental aversion to any organic constitutional change—marked out Peel's position in a disordered and expectant world at the end of 1830. It was a situation that contained sources of weakness and contradiction; but it was not a sterile or negative position. Indeed, one of the most acute political onlookers of the day could see in it seeds of promise for a not too distant future. 'Peel will be the leader of a party,' wrote Greville in November 1830, 'to which all the conservative interest of the country will repair; and it is my firm belief that in a very short time (two or three years or less) he will be Prime Minister and will hold power long.'

*Finis*

# BIBLIOGRAPHICAL NOTE

Except where otherwise indicated, quotations from Peel's speeches are taken from the collected *Speeches* (*v. infra*). Quotations from the standard collection of correspondence in Parker, *Peel*, (*v. infra*) are occasionally given without references where the passage can easily be located under date and subject. Other references are given in the footnotes either in full or in abbreviated form. The following lists comprise only manuscript sources and those printed sources for which a shortened title has been used in the footnotes.

## A. MANUSCRIPT COLLECTIONS, ETC.

1. *British Museum Additional Manuscripts*

   Peel Papers 40181-40617

   A full and important selection of papers from this large collection is in the three volumes of C. S. Parker's *Sir Robert Peel* (*v. infra*). Parker was an industrious, honest, but careless editor. His habit of altering words and phrases, failing to indicate omissions, and conflating letters of different dates, is one that no longer accords with conventional editorial practice. Better edited selections on specific topics (Catholic Emancipation, the 1834-5 Ministry, and the Repeal of the Corn Laws), together with Peel's own subsequent commentary, are in the two volumes of the *Peel Memoirs* (*v. infra*).

   Liverpool Papers 38190-38489

   Bentham Papers 33537-33564

   Huskisson Papers 38734-38770

2. *Public Record Office, London*

   i. Colonial Office

   C.O. 324/132 Correspondence 1810-11

        /134     do.     1811-12

   ii. War Office

   W.O. 6/29-30 Correspondence with Wellington 1810-12

        /50   Peninsula 1810-12

        /122-23 General Correspondence 1810-13

iii. Home Office

H.O.  41/7-8 Disturbances 1822-30
43/31-39 Domestic Correspondence 1821-30
44/14-16 Misc. Correspondence
60/1 Police Entry Books 1821-30
61/1-2 Metropolitan Police 1820-30
64/11 Police and Secret Service 1827-31
100/211 Ireland (misc. letters).

iv. Close Rolls
C 54/7308

3. *State Paper Office, Dublin*

i. Private Official Letters 1811-1823

ii. General Private Correspondence 1804-14, and 1814-21.

iii. Official Papers 1790-1831 Second Series
a. Military
b. Privy Council
c. Finance
d. Trade and Industries

iv. State of Country Series I 1796-1831
a. MS Calendar
b. Correspondence

v. Irish Privy Council Minute Books 1812-18

4. *Public Record Office, Belfast*

i. Marquess of Anglesey Papers (T 1068)
1068/1-2 letters to ministers, etc., 1828-9
/15    do.  to Chief Secretary 1828-9
/20-21 misc. letters 1827-9

ii. Foster Papers 1812-22
Correspondence of the Hon. John Foster,
cr. Baron Oriel 1821.

5. *Surrey Record Office*

Goulburn Papers

a. Correspondence with Sir Robert Peel II /13-20
b. Misc. documents relating to Sir Robert and Lady Peel and the Peel
estate.

6. *Christ Church, Oxford*

Muniments: Siga 1806–1823
Collections Book 1789–1814
Battels 1805–9
Misc. Pamphlets etc.

7. *National Library, Dublin*

Richmond Papers (Letters and Papers of the 4th Duke of Richmond).
Numbered references are to individual letters and documents
(1–1930) which are numbered consecutively throughout the successive volumes though they are not in strict chronological or
topical sequence.

8. *The Royal Irish Academy*

MS. Diary of Mr. Justice Day

9. *County Museum, Armagh*

Blacker Autobiography
Seven MS. volumes of personal recollections mixed with other
topics written *c.* 1840 by Lt. Col. William Blacker (1777–1855),
High Sheriff for Co. Armagh and Vice-Treasurer of Ireland
1817–29.

10. *Tamworth Public Library*

Mitchell Collection
Several volumes of news-cuttings, etc., relating to the history of
Tamworth and its neighbourhood.

11. *Private MSS.*

Peel MSS.    Mr. G. F. Peel
Personal letters, etc., relating to Sir Robert Peel and his wife,
which did not form part of the political papers now in the
British Museum. The original collection was used very fully by
the late Hon. George Peel in *The Private Letters of Sir Robert
Peel* (*v. infra*) and the larger part of it was later destroyed by
enemy action in London in 1941.

Canning Papers (transcripts)

## B. PARLIAMENTARY REPORTS AND PROCEEDINGS

1. *Parliamentary Papers*

   House of Commons, Reports of Committees, etc.

   | | | |
   |---|---|---|
   | 1816 | III | *Children in Manufactories* |
   | 1816 | V | *Police of the Metropolis* |
   | 1819 | III | *Cash Payments* |
   | 1822 | IV | *Police of the Metropolis* |
   | 1828 | VI | *Police of the Metropolis* |
   | 1839 | XIX | *County Constabulary* |

2. *Parliamentary Debates*

   Cobbett's *Parliamentary Debates*

   Hansard's *Parliamentary History of England* (to 1803)

   do.      *Parliamentary Debates 1803-1820*

   do.    do.    do.   New Series 1820-30

   A full but not completely exhaustive collection of Peel's parliamentary speeches is to be found in *The Speeches of Sir Robert Peel* (*v. infra*) with a useful index and chronological summary.

## C. LIST OF TITLES ABBREVIATED IN FOOTNOTES

For unspecified five-figure numerals see above A (1).

Abram, W. A., *History of Blackburn* (Blackburn, 1877).

Anglesey: see A (4) i.

*Ann. Reg.: Annual Register.*

Arbuthnot, *Correspondence of Charles*, ed. A. Aspinall (Camden 3rd series, LXV, 1941).

Arbuthnot, *Journal of Mrs.*, ed. F. Bamford & the Duke of Wellington, two vols. (1950).

Aspinall, A., *Formation of Canning's Ministry* (Camden 3rd series, LIX, 1937).

—— *Three Early Nineteenth Century Diaries* (1952).

—— *Early English Trade Unions* (1949).

Bagot, Josceline, *George Canning and his Friends*, two vols. (1909).

*Bathurst, Report on Manuscripts of Earl* (Hist. MSS. Commission, 1923).

Blacker: see A (9).

Broderick, J. F., *The Holy See and the Irish Movement for the Repeal of the Union* (Rome, 1951).

Broughton, Lord: *Recollections of a Long Life*, ed. Lady Dorchester, four vols. (1910).

Browne, D. G., *Rise of Scotland Yard* (1956).

Buckingham, Duke of, *Memoirs of the Court of George IV*, two vols. (1859).

Bulwer, Sir Henry Lytton, *Life of Viscount Palmerston*, two vols. (1871).

*Campbell, Life of Lord*, ed. Mrs. Hardcastle, two vols. (1881).

Chart, D. A., *Ireland from the Union to Catholic Emancipation* (1910).

Clapham, J. H., *The Early Railway Age* (1926).

—— *The Bank of England*, two vols. (1944).

*Cloncurry, Recollections of Lord* (Dublin, 1849).

Close Rolls, see A (2) iv.

C.O., see A (2) i.

Cobbett, *Debates*, see B (2).

*Colchester, Diary and Correspondence of Charles Abbot, Lord*, ed. Lord Colchester, three vols. (1861).

Connell, K. H., *Population of Ireland, 1750–1845* (1950).

*Creevey's Life and Times*, ed. John Gore (1934).

*Creevey Papers, The*, ed. Sir H. Maxwell (1923).

Croker, *Correspondence and Diaries of J. W.*, ed. L. J. Jennings, three vols. (1884).

Curtis, R., *History of the Royal Irish Constabulary* (Dublin, 1869).

Davies, Rev. Richard, *Memoirs of Sir Robert Peel* (pub. anon. N.D.). The authorship of this panegyric on the 1st Bt. is given in the copy in the Hawarden Library; date of publication is *c.* 1803-4.

Day, Diary of Mr. Justice, see A (8).

*Dudley, Letters of 1st Earl of, to the Bishop of Llandaff* (1841).

*Dyott's Diary*, ed. R. W. Jeffery, two vols. (1907).

E.H.R.: *English Historical Review*.

Ellenborough, *Political Diary of Edward Law, Lord*, ed. Lord Colchester, two vols. (1881).

Fay, C. R., *Huskisson and His Age* (1951).

Foster, see A (4) ii.

*George IV, The Letters of King*, ed. A. Aspinall, three vols. (1938).

G.M.: *The Gentleman's Magazine.*

*Greville Memoirs, The.* The definitive edition is that ed. by L. Strachey and R. Fulford, seven vols. (1938).

Goulburn, see A (5).

*Hansard*, see B (2).

*Harrow School Register, 1571-1800* (1934), and *1800-1911* (1911).

Hart, J. M., *The British Police* (1951).

H.O., see A (2) iii.

*Hobhouse, Diary of Henry*, ed. A. Aspinall (1947).

*Huskisson Papers, The*, ed. Lewis Melville (1931).

*Letter-Box, Mr. Gregory's*, ed. Lady Gregory (1898).

Lewis, Sir G. Cornewall: *Local Disturbances in Ireland* (1836).

Lockhart, J. G., *Memoirs of the Life of Sir Walter Scott*, ten vols. (Edinburgh, 1839).

McDowell, R. B., *Public Opinion and Government Policy in Ireland, 1801-1846* (1952).

*Mitchell*, see A (10).

Moore, T., *Life and Letters of Byron* (1908).

—— *Memoirs, Journals and Correspondence*, ed. Lord John Russell, eight vols. (1853-6).

N & Q: *Notes and Queries.*

*O.U.C. Rep. 1852: Oxford University Commission, Report of H.M. Commissioners* (1852).

*Parl. Hist.*, see B (2).

*Peel: Sir Robert Peel from his Private Papers*, ed. C. S. Parker, three vols. (1891-9).

Peel, Jonathan, *The Peels, A Family Sketch* (1877).

*Peel, Letters: The Private Letters of Sir Robert Peel*, ed. George Peel (1920).

*Peel, Life*: Sir Lawrence Peel, *Sketch of the Life and Character of Sir Robert Peel* (1860).

*Peel Memoirs: Memoirs by the Rt. Hon. Sir Robert Peel*, ed. Lord Mahon and E. Cardwell, two vols. (1856-67).

*Peel MSS.*, see A (11).

Pellew, Hon. George, *Life and Correspondence of Henry Addington, Viscount Sidmouth*, three vols. (1847).

Plunket, D., *Life, Letters and Speeches of Lord Plunket*, two vols. (1867).

P.P., see B (1).

Radzinowicz, L., *History of English Criminal Law*, three vols. (1948).

Ramsay, A. A. W., *Sir Robert Peel* (1928).

Reith, C., *British Police and the Democratic Ideal* (1943).

—— *New Study of Police History* (1956).

Reynolds, J. A., *Catholic Emancipation Crisis in Ireland* (Yale, 1954).

Richmond, see A (7).

Sheil, *Memoirs of the Rt. Hon. R. L.*, by W. Torrens McCullagh, two vols. (1855).

Shelley, *Diary of Frances Lady*, ed. R. Edgcumbe, two vols. (1912-13).

*Speeches of the late Rt. Hon. Sir Robert Peel delivered in the House of Commons*, four vols. (1853).

S.P.O., see A (3).

Stapleton, A. G., *George Canning and His Times* (1859).

*State of Ireland, Digest of Evidence on the* (taken before the Select Committees of the two Houses of Parliament, *1824-25*), ed. W. Phelan and M. O'Sullivan, two vols. (1826).

Twiss, H., *Life of Lord Chancellor Eldon*, three vols. (1844).

Walpole, Spencer, *Life of the Rt. Hon. Spencer Perceval*, two vols. (1874).

*Ward, Memoirs of R. Plumer*, ed. E. Phipps, two vols. (1850).

W.N.D.: *Despatches, Correspondence and Memoranda of the Duke of Wellington* (in continuation of former series), *1819-32*, ed. Duke of Wellington, eight vols. (1867-80).

W.S.D.: *Supplementary Despatches, Correspondence and Memoranda of the Duke of Wellington*, ed. Duke of Wellington, fifteen vols. (1858-72).

Williams O., *Life and Letters of John Rickman* (1912).

W.O., see A (2) ii.

Wyse, T., *Historical Sketch of the Late Catholic Association*, two vols. (1829).

Yonge, C. D., *Life and Administration of the 2nd Earl of Liverpool*, three vols. (1868).

# BIBLIOGRAPHICAL NOTE TO NEW EDITION

Of publications since 1960 the following may be mentioned as having a particular bearing on Peel's career, or on aspects of his policy and administration, in the period up to 1830. Place of publication is London unless otherwise stated.

### A. GENERAL

J. E. Cookson, *Lord Liverpool's Administration 1815–1822* (Edinburgh 1975).

Boyd Hilton, *Corn, Cash, Commerce: The Economic Policies of the Tory Governments 1815–1830* (1977).

G. I. T. Machin, *The Catholic Question in English Politics 1820–1830* (Oxford 1964).

### B. IRELAND

R. B. McDowell, *The Irish Administration 1801–1914* (1964).

A. P. W. Malcolmson: *John Foster: The Politics of the Anglo-Irish Ascendancy* (Oxford 1978).

G. O'Tuathaigh: *Ireland before the Famine 1798–1848* (Dublin 1972).

### C. BIOGRAPHIES

Anglesey, Marquess of, *One-Leg, Life and Letters of . . . First Marquess of Anglesey 1768–1854* (1961).

Baker, William J., *Beyond Port and Prejudice, Charles Lloyd of Oxford 1784–1829* (University of Maine 1981).

Bartlett, C. J., *Castlereagh* (1966).

Bourne, Kenneth, *Palmerston, The Early Years 1784–1841* (1982).

Gash, Norman, *Lord Liverpool* (1984).

Hinde, Wendy, *George Canning* (1973).

—— *Castlereagh* (1981).

681

Jones, W. D., *Prosperity Robinson, The Life of Viscount Goderich 1782–1859* (New York 1967).

Oman, Carola, *The Gascoyne Heiress, The Life and Diaries of Frances Mary Gascoyne-Cecil 1802–1839* (1968). Useful for uninhibited comments by Wellington on events and personalities of his time.

Ziegler, Philip, *Addington* (1965).

—— *Melbourne* (1976).


### D. ARTICLES

J. C. D. Clark, 'A general theory of party, opposition and government 1688–1832', *Historical Journal*, 23, 2 (1980).

Fraser, Peter, 'Party voting in the House of Commons 1812–1827', *Eng. Hist. Review* XCVIII (Oct. 1983).

Jones, D. J. V., 'The new police, crime and people in England and Wales 1829–1888', *Trans. R.Hist. Soc.*, 5th Series, vol. 33.

Davis, R. W., 'The Tories, the Whigs, and Catholic emancipation 1827–1829', *Eng. Hist. Review*, XCVII (Jan. 1982).
A discussion of the cabinet 'neutrality' principle but with insufficient attention to the precedents of Lord Liverpool's administration. A more balanced account is given in:

Machin, G. I. T., 'Canning, Wellington and the Catholic question 1827–29', *Eng. Hist. Review*, XCIX (Jan. 1984).

—— 'The Catholic emancipation crisis of 1825', *Eng. Hist. Review*, LXXVIII (July 1963).

——'Resistance to repeal of the Test and Corporation Acts 1828', *Historical Journal*, 22, 1 (1979).

# INDEX